D0580351

CORE
Web Programming

ISBN 0-13-625666-X

PRENTICE HALL PTR
CORE SERIES

CORE

Web Programming

To join a Prentice Hall PTR Internet mailing list, point to
http://www.prenhall.com/mail_lists/

Marty Hall

Prentice Hall PTR, Upper Saddle River, NJ   07458

Library of Congress Cataloging-in-Publication Date
Hall, Marty, 1962–
    Core Web Programming / Marty Hall
        p. cm.
    Includes index.
    ISBN 0-13-625666-X
    1. Internet programming. 2. HTML: (Document markup language) 3. Java (Computer programming
language) 4. CGI (Computer network protocol) 5. World Wide Web (Information retrieval system). I. Title.
QA76.625.H35   1997   76-45522
005.2'76--DC21   CIP

Editorial/Production Supervision: Joanne Anzalone
Acquisitions Editor: Greg Doench
Editorial Assistant: Mary Treacy
Development Editor: Ralph E. Moore
Marketing Manager: Stephen Solomon
Manufacturing Manager: Alexis Heydt
Cover Design: Talar Agasyan
Cover Design Direction: Jerry Votta
Art Director: Gail Cocker-Bogusz
Series Design: Meg VanArsdale
Technical Review: Paul Schmidt

© 1998 Prentice Hall PTR
Prentice-Hall, Inc.
A Simon & Schuster Company
Upper Saddle River, NJ 07458

Prentice Hall books are widely used by corporations and government agencies for training, marketing, and
resale. The publisher offers discounts on this book when ordered in bulk quantities.
For more information, contact
Corporate Sales Department,
Prentice Hall PTR
One Lake Street
Upper Saddle River, NJ 07458
Phone: 800-382-3419; FAX: 201-236-714
E-mail (Internet): corpsales@prenhall.com

The clip art used in this product is a copyright of Masterclips 101,000 Premium Image Collection. Masterclips is copyrighted and a registered trademark of IMSI 1895 Francisco Blvd. East, San Rafael, CA
94901 (415) 257-3000 X209.

Printed in the United States of America

10 9 8 7 6 5 4 3 2

ISBN 0-13-625666-X

Prentice-Hall International (UK) Limited, London
Prentice-Hall of Australia Pty. Limited, Sydney
Prentice-Hall Canada Inc., Toronto
Prentice-Hall Hispanoamericana, S.A., Mexico
Prentice-Hall of India Private Limited, New Delhi
Prentice-Hall of Japan, Inc., Tokyo
Simon & Schuster Asia Pte. Ltd., Singapore
Editora Prentice-Hall do Brasil, Ltda., Rio de Janeiro

Contents

CHAPTER 5
CASCADING STYLE SHEETS,   146

CHAPTER 8
BASIC JAVA SYNTAX, 298

CHAPTER 9

APPLETS, GRAPHICAL APPLICATIONS, AND BASIC DRAWING,   356

CHAPTER 10

HANDLING MOUSE AND KEYBOARD EVENTS,   448

CHAPTER 11
WINDOWS, 498

CHAPTER 12

ARRANGING WINDOWS USING LAYOUT MANAGERS,   592

CHAPTER 13

GRAPHICAL USER INTERFACE CONTROLS,   640

CHAPTER 14
CONCURRENT PROGRAMMING USING JAVA THREADS,   748

CHAPTER 15
CLIENT-SERVER PROGRAMMING IN JAVA,   794

CHAPTER 18
CGI PROGRAMMING AND BEYOND—THE SERVER SIDE,   972

Figures

Introduction

In late 1995, I proposed a new course for the Johns Hopkins University's part-time graduate program in Computer Science, for which I had been teaching part-time for a number of years. My idea was to bring together the major Web-related topics in a single course dubbed "Distributed Development on the World Wide Web," with Java as a unifying theme. We would look at HTML, Java, HTTP, CGI Programming, and JavaScript, with lots of hands-on projects and no exams. Little did I know what I was getting myself into. By the time I taught the first section in the summer of 1996, the Java tidal wave had swept through the university and the employers that the students represented. Shortly after enrollment opened, the class was filled. There were more students on the waiting list than in the course. I got frantic phone calls from students insisting that they absolutely *had* to be in the course. Several local companies called asking for on-site courses. What fun! I even found myself switching to Java for the majority of the software development in my "real" job.

However, when I went shopping for texts over the next semester or two, I got a rude surprise. Despite the availability of good books in most of the areas I wanted to cover, I found that I needed three, four, or even five *separate* books to get good coverage of the material I wanted for the course. Similarly, for my day job, I was constantly switching back and forth among the best of the huge stack of books I had accumulated and the various on-line references. Surely there was a better way. Shouldn't it be possible to fit 95 percent of what professional programmers use in about 35 percent of the space, and get it all in one book? Well, about that time I struck up an acquaintance with Gary Cornell, author of *Core Java*, and he suggested that I use my class notes as the outline for a World Wide Web developer's reference, and that I entitle it *Core Web Programming*. Well, after a new version of Java, two new versions of JavaScript, several new browser releases, and a year or two of full-time Web development and Java hacking, here it is. I hope you find it useful.

Real Code for Real Programmers

This book is aimed at serious software developers. If you are looking for a book that shows you how to use a browser, lists the current hottest Web sites, and pontificates about how Java will break the Microsoft monopoly, you've come to the wrong place. If you're already a programmer of some sort and want to get started with HTML, Java, CGI, and JavaScript as quickly as possible, this is the book for you. I will illustrate the most important approaches and warn you of the most common pitfalls. In order to do so, I will include plenty of working code: over 250 complete Java classes, for instance. I've tried to give detailed examples of the most important and frequently used features, summarize the lesser used ones, and refer you to the API (available on-line) for a few of the rarely used ones.

DILBERT © United Features Sundicate. Reprinted by permission

A word of caution, however. Nobody becomes a great developer just by reading. *You* have to write some real code too. The more, the better. In each chapter, I suggest that you start by making a simple program or a small variation of one of the examples given, then strike off on your own with a more significant project. Skim the sections you don't plan on using right away, then come back when you are ready to try them out.

If you do this, you should quickly develop the confidence to handle the real-world problems that brought you here in the first place. You should be able to balance the demand for the latest features in Web pages with the need for multiplatform support. You should be comfortable with frames, style sheets, and layered HTML. You should have no qualms about developing Web interfaces to your corporate database, either via CGI or through JDBC. You should be able to make portable stand-alone graphical applications in Java 1.0 or 1.1. You should be able to connect these applications to remote systems over the network. You should be able to easily distribute computation among multiple threads, or even spin it off to separate systems using RMI. You should be able to use JavaScript to validate CGI forms or to animate Web pages, while still supporting older browsers. You should get a raise.

How This Book Is Organized

This book is divided into four parts, as follows:

Part I: The HyperText Markup Language

Web pages are created using HTML, the HyperText Markup Language. HTML lets you mix regular text with special tags that describe the content, layout, or appearance of the text. These tags are then used by Web browsers like Netscape Navigator or Microsoft Internet Explorer to format the page. This first part of the book will cover the following topics in HTML.

- *HTML 3.2.* Full coverage of all the elements in the latest official HTML standard. Hypertext links, fonts, images, tables, client-side image maps, and more.
- *Major Netscape and Internet Explorer extensions.* Forwarding pages, using custom colors and font faces, embedding audio, video, and ActiveX components. Knowing when extensions make your pages nonportable.
- *Frames.* Dividing the screen into rectangular regions, each associated with a separate HTML document. Borderless frames. Floating frames. Targeting frame cells from hypertext links. Solving common frame problems.
- *Cascading Style Sheets.* Level one style sheets for customizing fonts, colors, images, text formatting, indentation, lists, and more.
- *Layers.* Using extended style sheets or the LAYER and ILAYER elements for dynamic, layered HTML.

Part II: Java

Java is a powerful general-purpose programming language that can be used to create stand-alone programs as well as ones that are embedded in Web pages. Java topics that are covered include

- *Unique features of Java.* What's different about Java? The truth about Java myths and hype.
- *Object-oriented programming in Java.* Variables, methods, constructors, overloading, and interfaces. Modifiers in class declarations. Packages and the CLASSPATH.
- *Java syntax.* Primitive types, operators, strings, vectors, arrays, input/output and the Math class.
- *Graphics.* Applets. Applications. Drawing, color, font, and clipping area operations. Loading and drawing images.
- *Mouse and keyboard events.* Processing events in Java 1.02. Handling them in Java 1.1. Event types, event listeners, and low-level event handlers. Inner classes.
- *Windows.* Canvas, Panel, Applet, ScrollPane, Frame, Dialog, FileDialog, and Window. Component and Container. Lightweight components and containers in Java 1.1. Saving and loading windows using object serialization.
- *Layout Managers.* FlowLayout, BorderLayout, GridLayout, CardLayout, and GridBagLayout. Positioning components by hand. Strategies for using layout managers effectively. Writing your own layout manager.
- *GUI Controls.* Buttons, checkboxes, radio buttons, combo boxes, list boxes, textfields, text areas, labels, scrollbars, and pop-up menus. Creating slider and image button classes.
- *Threads.* Threads in separate or existing objects. Synchronizing access to shared resources. Grouping threads. Multithreaded graphics and double buffering.
- *Client-server programming.* Clients and servers using sockets. The URL class. An HTTP client and server. Remote Method Invocation (RMI). Java DataBase Connectivity (JDBC).

Part III: CGI Programming

Web pages can be connected to databases and other programs on the server by means of the Common Gateway Interface (CGI). Part III covers the following CGI areas.

- *HTTP.* Request types. Request headers. Response headers. Cookies. Public-key cryptography.
- *The client side.* HTML forms and form elements. Using applets to talk to CGI programs. Sending via GET and POST. Bypassing the HTTP server and talking directly to programs from applets.
- *The server side.* Reading GET and POST data. CGI environment variables. Manipulating cookies. Java classes to decode and parse CGI data. Server-side Java and the servlet API. CGI alternatives.

Part IV: JavaScript

JavaScript is a scripting language that can be embedded in Web pages and interpreted as the pages are loaded. The final part will cover the following topics in JavaScript.

- *JavaScript syntax.* Fields, methods, functions, strings, objects, arrays, and regular expressions.
- *Customizing Web pages.* Adapting to different browsers, JavaScript releases, and screen sizes.
- *Making pages dynamic.* Animating images. Manipulating layers. Responding to user events.
- *Validating CGI forms.* Checking form entries as they are changed. Checking data when form is submitted.
- *Handling cookies.* Reading and setting values. The Cookie object.
- *Controlling frames.* Sending results to specific frames. Preventing documents from being framed. Updating multiple frame cells. Giving frame cells the focus automatically.
- *Integrating Java and JavaScript.* LiveConnect and the JSObject class.
- *JavaScript quick reference.* Major classes in JavaScript 1.0, 1.1, and 1.2. All fields, methods, and event handlers. Document, Window, Form, Element, String, Math, RegExp, and so forth.

Conventions

Throughout the book, concrete programming constructs or program output will be presented in a monospaced font. For example, when abstractly describing Java programs that can be embedded in Web pages, I will refer to "applets," but when I say `Applet` I am talking about the specific Java class from which all applets are derived.

User input will be indicated in boldface, and command-line prompts will either be generic ("`Prompt>`") or indicate the operating system to which they apply ("`Unix>`"). For instance, the following indicates that "`Some Output`" is the result when "`java SomeProgram`" is executed.

```
Prompt> java SomeProgram
Some Output
```

Important standard techniques are indicated using specially marked entries, as in the following example.

Core Approach

Pay particular attention to items in "Core Approach" sections. They indicate techniques that should always or almost always be used.

Notes and warnings will be called out in a similar manner.

About the CD-ROM

To get you started quickly, the CD-ROM contains the following elements formatted for Windows 95/NT and Macintosh platforms. For other operating systems, please see the on-line archive at http://www.apl.jhu.edu/~hall/CWP-Sources/.

- An HTML guide to all resources given in this book, organized by chapter. This includes
  - More than 200 HTML and JavaScript documents used throughout the text. You can view them on-line, examine their source code, and adapt them for your projects.
  - Complete source code for more than 250 Java classes listed or used in various chapters. You can freely use or adapt these classes.
  - On-line versions of all Java applets.
  - Hypertext links to all URLs listed in this book.
- The Java Development Kit, version 1.02.
- The Java Development Kit, version 1.1.(Windows 95/NT only)
- The WinEdit text editor, customized for Java programming (Windows 95/NT only).
- Microsoft Internet Explorer version 3.

Acknowledgments

Many people have helped me out with this book. Without their assistance, I would still be on the fourth chapter. Paul McNamee, multilingual hacker extraordinaire, provided valuable technical feedback on virtually every chapter. Hopefully I learned from his advice. Ralph Moore kept the book organized, coherent, and on schedule. He improved the situation immensely. Joanne Anzalone produced the final version; she did a great job despite my many last-minute changes. Bob Grossman and Ralph Semmel encouraged me to teach the first Hopkins course, defended it against critics, and got it into the curriculum. By doing so, they provided me with a steady supply of people to try out my ideas and approaches and to give me perspective on what professional programmers most need when learning Web programming. Ralph also provided a supportive work environment and a flexible schedule; I never would have made any progress otherwise. Randy Pack and Elsie Hardwick let me try out courses on slightly different audiences at RWD Technologies, Inc. and JHU/APL. Michael Whitehead got me started with JDBC. Lis Immer and Bob Evans gave useful suggestions and pointed out cross-platform compatibility issues. Greg Doench and Gary Cornell gave the book a chance at Prentice Hall. Thanks to all.

Most of all, thanks to B.J., Lindsay, and Nathan for their patience with long hours and disrupted schedules. I've been blessed with a great family.

About the Author

Marty Hall is a Senior Computer Scientist in the Research and Technology Development Center at the Johns Hopkins Applied Physics Lab, where he helps develop software and software technology for a variety of sponsors. For the last ten years, he has also been on the adjunct faculty of the Hopkins part-time Masters program in Computer Science. His interests include Web technology, Java, distributed applications, Artificial Intelligence, automated optimization techniques, and simulation systems. He can be reached at the following address

Research and Technology Development Center
The Johns Hopkins University Applied Physics Laboratory
Johns Hopkins Road
Laurel, MD 20723
hall@apl.jhu.edu

CORE

Web Programming

THE HYPERTEXT MARKUP LANGUAGE

DESIGNING WEB PAGES WITH HTML 3.2

Topics in This Chapter

- An overview of the HyperText Markup Language, and how HTML 3.2 differs from other HTML specifications

- The process of creating and publishing a Web page

- The fundamental structure of HTML documents

- Elements in the header of an HTML document

- Using the BODY tag to set up the basic look of the page

Chapter 1

This chapter gets you started in the process of creating Web pages. It introduces the HyperText Markup Language, and gives a summary of the steps involved in creating and publishing a WWW page. It then gives an overview of the general structure of Web pages, describes which HTML elements are required in all documents, and explains how to specify settings that affect the document as a whole.

1.1 The HyperText Markup Language

Web pages are created using the HyperText Markup Language (HTML), which lets you mix regular text with "markup" tags describing the text. These tag elements can describe the *appearance* ("display this in red") or *layout* ("arrange the following in a 3-row, 4-column table") of the text, but the majority simply describe the *content* ("this is a main heading") and leave many of the appearance and layout decisions to the browser. For example, Listing 1.1 shows the HTML document used to create the Web page shown in Figure 1–1. For now, don't worry about the details of each of the HTML elements; they will be discussed in detail in the rest of Part I of this book. However, even at first glance you can pick out some basic features, such as the mix of regular text and elements enclosed in angle brackets, and that some but not all the elements come in pairs of the form <NAME> and </NAME>.

Listing 1.1   An HTML Document for a Simple Home Page

```
<!DOCTYPE HTML PUBLIC "-//W3C//DTD HTML 3.2//EN">
<HTML>
<HEAD>
  <TITLE>Home Page for Marty Hall</TITLE>
</HEAD>

<BODY BGCOLOR="WHITE">
<H1 ALIGN="CENTER">Home Page for Marty Hall</H1>
<HR>
<IMG SRC="images/JHUAPL.gif" WIDTH=432 HEIGHT=182
     ALIGN="RIGHT" ALT="JHU/APL Logo">
<B>Marty Hall</B><BR>
Senior Computer Scientist<BR>
Research and Technology Development Center<BR>
The Johns Hopkins University<BR>
<A HREF="http://www.jhuapl.edu/">
Applied Physics Laboratory</A><BR>
Johns Hopkins Rd.<BR>
Laurel, MD 20723-6099<BR>
<I>email:</I> <A HREF="mailto:hall@apl.jhu.edu">
hall@apl.jhu.edu</A><BR>
<I>Phone:</I> (410) 792-6221 / (301) 953-6221<BR>
<I>Fax:</I> (410) 792-6904 / (301) 953-6904
<BR CLEAR="ALL">
<P>
This is my personal homepage. For more specific
programming-related resources pages, please see:
<!-- Rest of Sample Page Deleted -->
</BODY>
</HTML>
```

Now, the Web page shown in Figure 1–1 is the result for a particular browser (Netscape 3.01) on a particular operating system (Windows 95) with particular user settings (choice of default font face, size, and color). In addition to user customizations, browsers usually have wide latitude in how they implement the various types of elements, and authors who try to enforce an

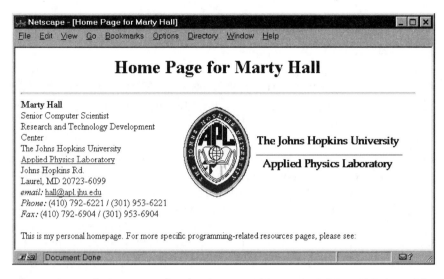

Figure 1–1   This page, rendered in Netscape Navigator 3.01 on Windows 95, is the result of the document in Listing 1.1.

exact appearance for pages that will be viewed by multiple browsers often end up frustrated. In Chapter 5 (Cascading Style Sheets), you will see an emerging standard that gives authors a high degree of control over the final look of their pages. Even without style sheets, in some intranet applications authors may know what types of browsers will access their pages, and can design accordingly. But until support for style sheets becomes more widespread, authors of general Web pages should realize that they cannot control all aspects of the final appearance of their page.

Core Note

Trying to enforce an exact look for pages that will be viewed by people using a variety of browsers will only lead to frustration.

In fact, Web browsers are not the only type of programs that use HTML documents. They can be used by a variety of applications that display, print, index, or even synthesize speech based on them. For the purposes of this book, however, we will concentrate on how HTML documents are used by WWW browsers.

1.2 HTML 3.2 and Other HTML Standards

Until January 1997, HTML 2.0 was the most up-to-date HTML standard available. The HTML 2.0 specification describes the capabilities supported by most browsers as of mid-1994. Even before the HTML 2.0 spec was published, work was underway to define the next generation specification, known first as HTML+ and later as HTML 3.0. Unfortunately, however, the vendors that emerged as the dominant players in the Web browser world could not agree on supporting HTML 3.0, and the effort was dropped. Instead, HTML 3.2 (originally code-named "Wilbur"), an intermediate specification, was drafted. Perhaps it should have been called "HTML 2.3," because it supports less features than HTML 3.0 would have, not more. At any rate, HTML 3.2, like HTML 2.0, is intended to describe standard practice as of a given date. HTML 3.2 reflects consensus among the major vendors on what features could be expected to be widely supported as of mid-1996, and is the specification that most closely matches the versions of HTML used by Netscape Navigator 2.02, 3.0, and 3.01, and Microsoft Internet Explorer 3.0, 3.01, and 3.02. This text provides a complete reference to *all* of HTML 3.2, with the most important Netscape and Internet Explorer extensions described as well. Compared to HTML 2.0, HTML 3.2 provides:

- Text flow around images
- More alignment options for paragraphs
- Tables
- Clickable hot spots in images (client-side image maps)
- The ability to embed Java programs into pages
- More explicit control over font sizes and colors

Since the HTML 3.2 standard was accepted, work has begun on the HTML 4.0 specification, intended to represent the next generation of standard practice after HTML 3.2. If accepted, HTML 4.0 will probably be official near the beginning of 1998.

HTML Specifications

The official HTML on-line specifications are available from the following sites:

HTML 3.2

```
http://www.w3.org/pub/WWW/TR/REC-html32.html
```

HTML 4.0 (drafts and proposals)

> `http://www.w3.org/TR/WD-html40/`

HTML 2.0 (Obsolete)

> `http://ds.internic.net/rfc/rfc1866.txt`

HTML 3.0 (Abandoned)

> `http://www.w3.org/pub/WWW/MarkUp/html3/`

Cascading Style Sheets (Level 1)

> `http://www.w3.org/pub/WWW/TR/REC-CSS1`

Frames

> `http://www.w3.org/pub/WWW/TR/WD-frames`

Other accepted or proposed industrywide HTML-related specifications

> `http://www.w3.org/pub/WWW/MarkUp/`

HTML supported by Netscape Navigator

> `http://developer.netscape.com/library/documentation/`
> `htmlguid/index.htm`

HTML supported by Internet Explorer

> `http://www.microsoft.com/workshop/author/newhtml/`

HTML Scripting and Dynamic HTML

Many authors would like to define their own HTML elements as an abbreviation for a series of HTML elements they use frequently, or to include common elements in a wide range of documents without repeating the text multiple places. Although there is no standard HTML construct that supports this, there are a variety of widely supported options that permit it. One such option is to use an HTML scripting language that is evaluated by the client browser when the page is loaded to build part of the page. Java-Script (Chapter 19) is the most popular choice in that category, but Internet Explorer also supports VBScript, which has many of the same capabilities but uses syntax more familiar to Visual Basic programmers. There are also a variety of scripting languages that are executed by the HTTP server before the page is delivered. Netscape's LiveWire allows JavaScript on the server to be used to build pages dynamically, while Sun's Java Web Server supports a similar capability in Java. Microsoft's Internet Information Server supports "Active Server Pages" for building documents dynamically, and many Unix HTTP servers support "Server-Side Includes" that let you include static files or the output of arbitrary programs into the HTML document when it is transmitted by the server. Some C programmers even use `#define` and `#include` in their HTML documents, then run the C preprocessor on them before putting them on the Web. Finally, cascading style sheets (Chapter 5) lets you define many characteristics of built-in and custom HTML elements, and permits you to supply definitions by an external set of rules that can be used in multiple HTML documents. For details on these topics, see the following locations:

VBScript

```
http://www.microsoft.com/vbscript/
```

LiveWire

```
http://developer.netscape.com/library/documentation/
livewire/
```

Java Web Server

```
http://jserv.javasoft.com/
```

Active Server Pages

```
http://www.microsoft.com/iis/usingiis/resources/
aspdocs/
```

Server-Side Includes

```
http://hoohoo.ncsa.uiuc.edu/docs/tutorials/
includes.html
```

1.3 Publishing Your Document on the Web

There are three main steps involved in posting a document to the WWW, as follows:

1. Create an HTML document.
2. Place it in a Web-accessible location.

3. Verify that the HTML is legal and results in the presentation you had in mind.

These steps are explained more thoroughly in the following sections.

Create the Document

Because HTML is a markup language where ASCII tags are inserted in ordinary text, you can create an HTML document using a text editor, an HTML editor, or by using a utility that converts an existing word processor document to HTML. Because HTML is primarily a logical markup language, not a page layout language, automatically converting a word processor document to HTML often results in HTML documents that differ somewhat from the original and require some hand tuning. Similarly, because browsers are allowed significant flexibility in how they display many HTML elements, and because users can select their preferred fonts and colors, a "WYSIWYG" (What You See Is What You Get) HTML editor is not strictly possible, at least in the absence of cascading style sheets (Chapter 5). Of course, however, an editor could tailor the display to the default look of a particular browser. Nevertheless, HTML editors can be a big time saver: many let you visually lay out tables and frames; some even support style sheets. If you do use an HTML editor, you will want one that allows you to directly edit the HTML if desired, because you will inevitably want to use some capability not supported by your HTML editor. For more information on HTML editors and converters, see the following sites:

Reviews of HTML Editors
```
http://www.yahoo.com/Computers_and_Internet/Software/
Reviews/Titles/Internet/Web_Authoring_Tools/
HTML_Editors/
```

Converters to (and from) HTML
```
http://union.ncsa.uiuc.edu/HyperNews/get/www/html/
converters.html
```

Put the Document on the Web

To be accessible to the Web, your document needs to be on a computer that is on the Internet and running an HTTP server. If you don't already have Internet access through a work or school system or via a commercial Internet Service Provider (ISP), "The List" (`http://thelist.internet.com`)

gives information on thousands of ISPs throughout the world. Some authors create their Web pages on the same machine from which they will be accessed. This is common for work and university computers. Frequently, however, authors create the pages on a home or office PC and then upload the page to the server machine. In this latter case, they need to be sure that they upload to an accessible location. This process is discussed in the following subsections. The initial creation of the directory and establishment of access permissions typically only needs to be done once.

Create a Directory for the File

The computer hosting your Web page will be running an HTTP server. HTTP, the HyperText Transfer Protocol, is discussed in more detail in Chapter 16, but for now, all you need to know is that it is the protocol by which WWW *clients* (browsers) talk to systems that are hosting Web pages. The program that answers the client's request for files is the HTTP *server*. This server takes the URL (Uniform Resource Locator, which is the Web "address") specified by the client and translates it into a specific filename on the server's system. Typically, when a client requests a file from a user's directory, the server looks in an intervening subdirectory such as "public_html" or "www" that is not listed in the URL but is part of the real location of the file. The webmaster or system administrator on the machine or Internet Service Provider you are using can give the definitive name. For many users, the system hosting their Web page is their only exposure to the Unix operating system. If you are in that category, note that "mkdir" is the Unix command for creating a directory.

For instance, suppose that user janedoe wants to publish a page named test.html on the system www.some-isp.com. In such a case, she would put the document in /home/janedoe/public_html/test.html, assuming that her home directory is /home/janedoe and that public_html is the "hidden" directory name on that system. Outsiders could access the page by designating a URL of http://www.some-isp.com/~janedoe/test.html.

Note that "~" is generally interpreted as "the home directory of." Some programs encode characters using their ASCII or ISO Latin-1 numbers, so you sometimes see "%7E" instead of "~". In fact, Internet Explorer changes "~" to "%7E" when storing an entry in the favorites list. So don't be confused if you see http://some.host/%7Euser/path/.

Put File in That Directory

If you are working on the same system that is running the HTTP server, you will probably create your HTML documents directly in the target directory (e.g., `public_html`). If you create the document on a remote system that is on the Internet (e.g., via PPP or a direct connection), you can upload the file using an FTP client such as `Fetch` on a Mac, `ftp.exe` from the main `Windows` directory on a Windows 95 system, or `/usr/bin/ftp` on a Unix system. Remember that filenames are case sensitive on many operating systems.

In addition to a default "hidden" directory name, most HTTP servers also have a default filename that will be used if the URL specifies a directory but no filename. Some common defaults are `index.html`, `Welcome.html`, `default.html`, and variations ending in ".htm" instead of ".html". For instance, Jane's home page might be in `/home/janedoe/public_html/index.html`, but could be accessed remotely simply via `http://www.some-isp.com/~janedoe/`. The URL listing the filename explicitly (`http://www.some-isp.com/~janedoe/index.html`) would be legal also.

Set File and Directory Permissions

In order for the file to be accessible on the Web, the file and directory must be readable by the process running the HTTP server. This often means that they must be world readable, because the HTTP server is typically run in an unprivileged mode. Many ISPs that use Unix set the proper permissions by default, so this step may not be necessary if you use a commercial service provider. Unix users can look at their `umask` to determine this. If it *is* necessary, the Unix incantation would be:

```
Unix> cd
Unix> chmod a+x .
Unix> cd public_html
Unix> chmod a+x .
Unix> chmod a+r file
```

Because Web browsers can display plain-text documents as well as HTML documents, a good first step is to create a simple file called `test.txt` that contains a single line like "`Hello`," put it in the Web subdirectory of your account, and try to access it via `http://your.isp.com/~your-account/test.txt`. If that works, you don't have to mess around with the cryptic file permission settings. Also, note that many HTTP servers allow you to restrict who has access to your documents, either based on the host making the request, or on an individual basis using passwords. CGI programs (Chapter 18) can be used to implement password checking, and many HTTP servers have a standard mechanism as well. One commonly supported method is the `.htaccess` file, which lets individual users set up passwords for various directories without requiring any changes to the global server configuration files. For details, see `http://hoohoo.ncsa.uiuc.edu/docs/setup/access/Overview.html`.

Validate the Document

Once you place a document on the Web, you want to check that it does not have any syntax errors. Checking how the page looks in your Web browser is a good first step, but is not sufficient. This is because browsers try to "guess" what to do when they see incorrect HTML, but different browsers may guess differently. So if your HTML document contains errors, your browser might guess well and the page might still look fine in it. But it might look completely differently or have portions not display *at all* on other browsers. Because HTML 3.2 is defined using the Standard Generalized Markup Language (SGML), a program can use the official SGML specification for HTML 3.2 to verify that your document is conforming. Some HTML editors do this automatically, or you can submit the URL to one of the free on-line validators. Two of the most popular ones are the WebTechs validator and Gerald Oskoboiny's "Kinder, Gentler" validator. In addition, there are several free or commercial validators that can be installed on your local machine. See the following URLs for details:

The WebTechs Validator
`http://www.webtechs.com/html-val-svc/`

The Kinder, Gentler Validator
`http://ugweb.cs.ualberta.ca/~gerald/validate/`

Other Validators
`http://www.yahoo.com/Computers_and_Internet/`
`Information_and_Documentation/Data_Formats/HTML/`
`Validation_Checkers/`

Core Approach

Trust, but verify: Check the syntax of your Web pages using a formal HTML validator.

1.4 The Basic Structure of HTML Documents

HTML *elements* are indicated by markup *tags*, which are written using angle brackets. For instance, `<TITLE>` is the starting tag for the title element. The tags are not displayed in the resultant Web page, but rather provide descriptive information to the browser. HTML elements can also have *attributes,* which are used to supply information via attribute *values* after an equals sign. For instance, with `<IMG SRC="images/sample.gif">`, "`images/sample.gif`" is the *value* of the `SRC` *attribute* of the `IMG` *element*. Most nonalphanumeric characters in attribute values require you to have double quotes around the value, so a wise convention is to always enclose values in double quotes unless the value is a simple integer. Some attributes can be minimized, so that just the attribute is listed. For instance, with the `<HR NOSHADE>` tag, `HR` is the element name and `NOSHADE` is the element attribute (an optional one in this case). All HTML element and attribute names are case insensitive, but the attribute values can be case sensitive. Extra white space is ignored inside most parts of the document and around element names and attributes, but may be significant inside attribute values.

Some elements are *containers* which have a start tag (e.g., `<BODY>`) and a corresponding end tag that starts with a "`</`" (e.g., `</BODY>`). Other elements are stand-alone (e.g., `<HR>`). If a browser does not recognize a given HTML element or attribute, it simply ignores it. It does not ignore the regular text between unrecognized start and end tags; it only ignores the tags themselves.

HTML Document Template

HTML 3.2 documents start with a `DOCTYPE` declaration followed by an `HTML` element. This `HTML` element contains a `HEAD` element followed by a `BODY` element. The `HEAD` element must contain a `TITLE` element. The `BODY` element normally starts with the largest heading (`H1`) followed by the body of the Web page. Listing 1.2 gives a good starting point for all HTML 3.2 documents except for those that use frames (Chapter 4).

Listing 1.2   `HTML3.2-Template.html`

```
<!DOCTYPE HTML PUBLIC "-//W3C//DTD HTML 3.2//EN">
<HTML>
<HEAD>
  <TITLE>Title</TITLE>
</HEAD>

<BODY>
<H1>Main Heading</H1>

<!-- Rest of page goes here -->

</BODY>
</HTML>
```

This might look like Figure 1–2.

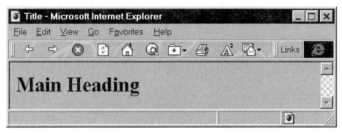

Figure 1–2   A standard HTML 3.2 template, as rendered in Internet Explorer 3.01 on Windows 95.

Strictly speaking, only the DOCTYPE and TITLE are required, because HTML, HEAD, and BODY can be inferred by the parser. But in practice, the template shown is a recommended starting point for HTML documents, and it is a good idea to keep a copy around to insert into new HTML documents if your text editor or HTML editor cannot be configured to do so automatically. HTML comments, shown in Listing 1.2, are normally enclosed between <!-- and -->, can span multiple lines, and should not contain a double hyphen (i.e., "--") in the body of the comment.

Frames

Some browsers such as Netscape Navigator (version 2.0 and later) and Microsoft Internet Explorer (3.0 and later) implement an extension to HTML 3.2 that allows the author to divide the window into rectangular regions, each associated with a separate HTML document. In such a case, the top-level document replaces the BODY section with a FRAMESET element describing the layout of the various frame cells. The FRAMESET element contains FRAME entries, possibly inside nested FRAMESETs, which reference the URLs of the documents that go into each of the cells. These files can be normal HTML documents or another frame specification. Frames are discussed in Chapter 4.

1.5 HEAD Elements

HTML Element: `<HEAD>` ... `</HEAD>`
Attributes: None

The HEAD section is the first main section of an HTML document, coming immediately after the DOCTYPE declaration and the `<HTML>` start tag, and just before the BODY section, as shown in Listing 1.3. The TITLE tag is required and is often the only element inside the HEAD. The HEAD element itself has no attributes.

Listing 1.3   Where the header fits in the overall HTML document

```
<!DOCTYPE HTML PUBLIC "-//W3C//DTD HTML 3.2//EN">
<HTML>
<HEAD>
  <TITLE>Title</TITLE>
</HEAD>
<BODY>
<!-- Remainder of Document -->
</BODY>
</HTML>
```

Required HEAD Element

HTML Element: `<TITLE>` ... `</TITLE>`
Attributes: None

The TITLE element is required in all HTML 3.2 documents, and consists of plain text with no other HTML tags. It can, however, contain character or entity references such as "`&copy;`" to get "©" (see Table 2.1). This title normally appears on the browser window and is typically used in the bookmarks (favorites) and browsing history lists. However, it does not necessarily appear when printed or in the main document itself, so should not be confused with the first main heading of the document, often informally viewed by readers as the "title."

Optional HEAD Elements

In addition to the required TITLE element, there are a number of optional elements occasionally employed by advanced HTML authors. If you're just starting with HTML, you're probably better off skipping this part until you have a handle on the more important and more frequently used options (discussed in the following chapters) for embedding images, creating hypertext links, inserting Java programs, making tables, changing fonts, and so forth.

HTML Element: <BASE HREF="..." ...> (No End Tag)
Attributes: HREF (required), TARGET (nonstandard)

The BASE tag is used to indicate the starting location for *relative URLs*, i.e., incompletely specified URLs that give the filename without hostname or protocol. The default location is the directory from which the current document was loaded. If a document is copied to a different site but its supporting documents are not, the BASE entry can be used to make sure that relative URLs will still refer to correct locations. For example, suppose that http://www.microsoft.com/PR/Buy-Win95.html is a document that the authors know will be mirrored at www.apple.com and www.sun.com. In such a case, a HEAD such as the following could be used:

```
<HEAD>
   <TITLE>Why You Should Buy Windows 95</TITLE>
   <BASE HREF="http://www.microsoft.com/PR/">
</HEAD>
```

An extension for browsers that support frames allows a TARGET attribute specifying the default frame cell in which to display selected links. See the discussion of frames in Chapter 4 for an explanation of TARGET.

HTML Element: <META ...> (No End Tag)
Attributes: NAME, CONTENT, HTTP-EQUIV

META elements can be used to record document info, forward and refresh pages, and include sound files. The exact way in which META tags are used to record document info varies from system to system. Common entries used with NAME are author (person who wrote the document), description (brief summary), `keywords` (search keywords to be used by search engines), and `generator` (program that generated the document). Search engines such as Alta Vista and Infoseek use the `keywords` entry for their internal indexing (but ignore the entire entry if a word appears more than seven times) and use the `description` entry in lieu of the first part of the document itself when describing the document to the search engine user. This is illustrated in Listing 1.4.

Listing 1.4   A sample HEAD section using META

```
<HEAD>
  <TITLE>Why You Should Buy Windows 95</TITLE>
  <BASE HREF="http://www.microsoft.com/PR/">
  <META NAME="author" CONTENT="Bill Gates">
  <META NAME="keywords"
        CONTENT="Windows Advocacy OS Operating Systems">
  <META NAME="description"
        CONTENT="A summary of the advantages of Windows 95">
</HEAD>
```

If `HTTP-EQUIV` is used instead of `NAME`, then if the document is retrieved via HTTP, the HTTP server is supposed to use the `CONTENT` to generate HTTP headers. HTTP headers are discussed in Chapter 16, "The HyperText Transfer Protocol," but as a quick example:

```
<META HTTP-EQUIV="Expires"
      CONTENT="Tue, 31 Dec 1997 23:59:59 GMT">
```

should result in the HTTP server including the following response header:

```
Expires: Tue, 31 Dec 1997 23:59:59 GMT
```

Another use of `HTTP-EQUIV` is to set automatic refreshing or forwarding of pages for browsers such as Netscape that support this nonstandard feature. For instance, an on-line newspaper or magazine might have headlines that change periodically, and should automatically update every 30 minutes (1800 seconds). Listing 1.5 gives an example of a fictional page located at `http://www.microsoft.com/PR/Buy-Win95.html` that shows how `META` could be used to do this by specifying `HTTP-EQUIV="refresh"` and a `CONTENT` attribute that gives a time in seconds and URL that is the same as the one from which the page was loaded.

Listing 1.5   A Web page with automatic reloading every 30 minutes

```
<HEAD>
  <TITLE>Why You Should Buy Windows 95</TITLE>
  <META HTTP-EQUIV="refresh"
        CONTENT="1800;
        URL=http://www.microsoft.com/PR/Buy-Win95.html">
</HEAD>
...
```

Note that if the specified URL is a sound file in a format supported by the browser, this method will play it on some browsers. There are also several browser-specific methods of playing sound files. For instance, Internet Explorer supports the BGSOUND element (discussed next) and both Netscape and Internet Explorer support EMBED (Section 3.6, Embedding Other Objects in Documents) for some types of sound files. But be cautious; many users consider it to be a bug, not a feature, when sound files begin playing automatically when they visit a site.

Core Approach

Rather than playing sound files automatically, inform the user if a given link will play a sound file, or give users a choice of using or not using sound.

Instead of reloading the same page, an author might want a document to automatically send readers to a new location (see Listing 1.6). This could happen when the URL of a page has changed and the author wants to leave a forwarding address so that people connecting to the old URL get the new page after five seconds. To do this, use the refresh value but specify a different URL than that of the current page. Be aware however, that on some browsers this breaks the "Back" button; clicking "Back" returns to the original page containing the META tag, which reforwards the user back to where they were before clicking "Back."

Whether refreshing the current page or forwarding to a new page, the document author should be aware that using the HTTP-EQUIV attribute in this way is an extension that will not work on all browsers, so should explicitly supply the new location inside an <A HREF...> link (see Section 3.3, "Specifying Hypertext Links") in the BODY section. In older browsers, people sometimes used this to implement "client pull" animations where you had a circular series of pages, each forwarding to the next in the chain and differing

Listing 1.6   Forwarding users to a new destination

```
<HEAD>
  <TITLE>Why You Should Buy Windows 95 (New Address)</TITLE>
  <META HTTP-EQUIV="refresh"
        CONTENT="5;
        URL=http://www.apple.com/PR/Buy-Win95.html">
</HEAD>
...
```

only in certain image files. However, animated GIFs, Java-based animations, or using JavaScript to cycle through image files are all better options.

HTML Element: `<BGSOUND SRC="..." ...>` (No End Tag)
Attributes: SRC (required), LOOP

This is a nonstandard element supported by Internet Explorer for playing sound files. The BGSOUND element can appear in the BODY as well as the HEAD.

SRC

SRC specifies the URL of the sound file, which should be in .wav, .au, or MIDI format.

LOOP

LOOP specifies how many times the sound file will be repeated. The default is 1. Specifying a value of –1 or INFINITE will result in the sound file playing continuously while the page is open.

HTML Element: `<ISINDEX ...>` (No End Tag)
Attributes: PROMPT, ACTION (nonstandard)

ISINDEX is used in simple CGI forms. Note that it can also appear in the BODY of the document. See Chapter 18, "CGI Programming and Beyond—The Server Side," for details on using ISINDEX.

HTML Element: `<SCRIPT ...> ... </SCRIPT>`
Attributes: LANGUAGE, SRC

SCRIPT is used for embedded programs, usually in JavaScript. See Chapter 19 (JavaScript: Adding Dynamic Content to Web Pages) for details.

HTML Element: `<NOSCRIPT>` ... `</NOSCRIPT>`

Attributes: None

The intention of NOSCRIPT is that its contents be ignored by browsers that support JavaScript and thus can be used for alternate text for browsers that do not support JavaScript. However, because it was introduced by Netscape only in version 3.0, neither Netscape 2.0 or Internet Explorer 3.0 ignore its contents. Thus, in practice, it can be used as a way either to provide alternate text for non-JavaScript 1.1 browsers or (if embedded inside SCRIPT) to provide JavaScript code that is only processed in JavaScript 1.0. See Chapter 19 (JavaScript: Adding Dynamic Content to Web Pages) for details.

HTML Element: `<STYLE ...>` ... `</STYLE>`

Attributes: TYPE

STYLE is used to specify cascading style sheets, an extremely useful and flexible capability that allows you to specify details about the fonts, colors, backgrounds, margins, and other features used for various elements in the document. Although style sheets are not part of HTML 3.2, full support is expected in version 4.0 of Netscape and Internet Explorer, and version 3.0 of Internet Explorer already supports a useful subset of the style sheet standard. See Chapter 5 for a discussion of style sheets.

HTML Element: `<LINK ...>` (No End Tag)

Attributes: HREF, REL, REV, TITLE

Finally, the LINK element is not widely supported, but is intended to provide information on how the current document fits into a larger set of documents by specifying a table of contents location, the previous and next document in the series, an advisory title, and so forth. The idea is that REL gives the relationship of the specified document to the current one; REV gives the reverse relationship, that of the current document to the specified one. The most common types of relationships are CONTENTS, INDEX, GLOSSARY, HELP, NEXT, and PREVIOUS for navigation, MADE for the document author, and STYLESHEET for links to cascading style sheets. For example:

```
<LINK REL=CONTENTS
      HREF="Table-of-Contents.html">
<LINK REV=MADE
      HREF="mailto:document.author@some.host.com">
```

1.6 BODY—Creating the Main Document

HTML documents should have exactly one BODY section defining the main contents of the page. The only exception is a document that uses frames. In such a case, the top-level document will simply define the general layout and specify which documents go in which frames, omitting the BODY altogether. See Chapter 4 (Frames) for more details. In nonframes documents, the BODY element contains the text and HTML markup comprising the main document. Because the TITLE portion of the HEAD element appears on the title bar of the window, not in the page itself, and because that title does not always appear on printouts of the document, the BODY normally starts with a "title," often using the largest heading size (H1) and frequently with the exact same text as in the TITLE element. Thus, many HTML documents look like Listing 1.7.

Listing 1.7   HTML 3.2 template with first heading matching title

```
<!DOCTYPE HTML PUBLIC "-//W3C//DTD HTML 3.2//EN">
<HTML>
<HEAD>
  <TITLE>My First Web Page</TITLE>
</HEAD>
<BODY>
<H1>My First Web Page</H1>
<!-- Remainder of HTML Document Here -->
</BODY>
</HTML>
```

The BODY section uses two major classes of HTML elements. The so-called "block-level" elements normally cause paragraph breaks, can contain text-level elements almost anywhere and nested block-level elements in many places (e.g., list elements and table cells), and are discussed in Chapter 2. These elements include headings, basic text sections, lists, tables, horizontal lines used as dividers, and input forms. The so-called "text-level" elements don't cause paragraph breaks. They can be embedded inside block-level elements and often nested in other text-level elements, but cannot contain block-level elements. They are discussed in Chapter 3, and include tags for fonts, hypertext links, embedded images, Java applets, plugins, ActiveX components, image maps, and more.

HTML Element: `<BODY ...> ... </BODY>`

Attributes: BACKGROUND, BGCOLOR, TEXT, LINK, VLINK, ALINK, BGPROPERTIES (nonstandard), ONLOAD (nonstandard), ONUNLOAD (nonstandard), ONFOCUS (nonstandard), ONBLUR (nonstandard), ONERROR (nonstandard), ONMOVE, (nonstandard), ONRESIZE, (nonstandard), ONDRAGDROP (nonstandard),

The BODY tag is often used without attributes, (e.g., simply <BODY> as the start tag), but can optionally contain attributes designating the background image; the background color; and the foreground colors of normal text, unvisited hypertext links, visited hypertext links, and links that are being selected. JavaScript-enabled browsers also support attributes that specify code to be executed under various conditions. Finally, the cascading style sheet specification adds CLASS, ID, and STYLE attributes to *all* HTML elements, but these attributes will not be discussed separately for each HTML element. See Chapter 5 for details.

BACKGROUND

This attribute gives the URL of an image file that will be tiled across the background of the page. The fact that the image is repeated (tiled) can be used to minimize download time when creating a repetitive background pattern. For instance, a page with colors that fade left to right across the page can be created by specifying a BACKGROUND image with fading colors that is very wide but only one pixel high. It is a good idea to supply a background color (BGCOLOR) as a backup when specifying a background image (BACKGROUND) in case the reader has image loading disabled.

BGCOLOR, TEXT, LINK, VLINK, and ALINK

These specify the foreground color of normal text, of unvisited hypertext links (based on the browser's current history), of visited links, and of links currently being selected. This last category is a temporary color to show when the user has pressed the mouse down over a link, but not yet released it. However, some browsers (e.g., Internet Explorer) don't make use of it. Colors can be specified either by a symbolic name taken from the original Windows VGA palette (see Table 1.1) or by specifying color component levels via a "#" followed by two hexadecimal digits each for red, green, and blue. In addition to the standard HTML 3.2 colors, both Netscape and Internet Explorer allow the use of the X11 window system color names (yes, even lavendarblush, oldlace, and my personal favorite, papayawhip). An example of each of the X11 colors is provided at http://developer.netscape.com/

`library/documentation/htmlguid/colortab.htm`, with
the specific RGB values (taken from the X11 `rgb.txt` file) given at
`http://search.netscape.com/comprod/products/`
`navigator/version_2.0/script/script_info/`
`colors.html`. Although browsing the X11 color chart may be useful
for choosing a color, rather than using these non-standard names, you
are better off using the equivalent RGB values. This will give you the
same results as the color name on Netscape and Internet Explorer, plus
will give correct results on other HTML 3.2 browsers.

Table 1.1   Predefined color names in HTML 3.2

Color Name	Hex Equivalent	Color Name	Hex Equivalent
AQUA	#00FFFF	NAVY	#000080
BLACK	#000000	OLIVE	#808000
BLUE	#0000FF	PURPLE	#800080
FUCHSIA	#FF00FF	RED	#FF0000
GRAY	#808080	SILVER	#C0C0C0
GREEN	#008000	TEAL	#008080
LIME	#00FF00	WHITE	#FFFFFF
MAROON	#800000	YELLOW	#FFFF00

If *any* colors are specified, it is a good idea to supply *all* of the colors to
avoid conflicts with defaults set by the user. For instance, suppose you
set the background color (BGCOLOR) to blue, while leaving the foreground color (TEXT) unspecified, thinking that this would result in
black text. Then, your page is loaded by a user who has set the default
background and foreground colors to yellow and blue, respectively.
Since you have set an explicit background color, your blue color will
override the yellow default. But since you haven't supplied a foreground
color, the default blue specified by the reader will be used. This results
in blue text on a blue background: invisible text!

Core Approach

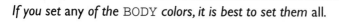

If you set any of the BODY *colors, it is best to set them all.*

Most browsers use white (WHITE or #FFFFFF) or light gray
(#C0C0C0) as the default BGCOLOR, black (BLACK or #000000) as
the default TEXT color, blue (BLUE or, in the case of Netscape, a very
slightly darker #0000EE) as the default LINK color, dark purple/blue
(#551A8B in Netscape) as the default VLINK color, and red (RED or
#FF0000) as the default color for ALINK. For instance, if you were
using Netscape and wanted to change the BGCOLOR to a light grayish
tan but also wanted to maintain the ordinary foreground colors, you
would specify

```
<BODY BGCOLOR="#F0F0DC" TEXT="#000000"
      LINK="#0000EE" VLINK="#551A8B"
      ALINK="#FF0000">
```

BGPROPERTIES

In Internet Explorer, supplying BGPROPERTIES="FIXED" indicates
that the background image specified via the BACKGROUND attribute
should not scroll with the rest of the page. This is sometimes described
as a "watermark."

ONLOAD, ONUNLOAD, ONFOCUS, ONBLUR, ONERROR, ONMOVE, ONRESIZE, and ONDRAGDROP

These attributes are not part of HTML 3.2, but are used by browsers
that support JavaScript to specify JavaScript code that should be executed when the page is first loaded, when the user leaves the page,
when the page gets the input focus, and when the page loses the input
focus, respectively.

1.7 Summary

HTML 3.2 is the specification that most closely matches the capabilities supported by today's browsers. HTML 3.2 documents should contain a DOC-TYPE declaration followed by an HTML element containing a HEAD and a BODY. The HEAD should always contain a TITLE, and can also contain STYLE, META, or other high-level information that specifies the author, gives a forwarding location, or otherwise describes the overall document. The BODY tag itself can be used to set up the foreground colors and background color or image for the document.

Now that you have the outline of the HTML document in place, you will want to actually put something in it. The following chapters describe how to do this. Chapter 2 describes the major text blocks that make up your documents, while Chapter 3 covers the smaller elements that can go inside the various text sections. Next, Chapter 4 discusses a common extension to HTML 3.2 that lets you divide your Web page into cells and place a different HTML document in each cell. Finally, for those who want to customize the way certain browsers display various HTML elements, cascading style sheets can be used. They are described in Chapter 5.

BLOCK-LEVEL ELEMENTS IN HTML 3.2

Topics in This Chapter

- Section headings
- Basic paragraph types
- Bulleted and numbered lists
- Tables
- Data-entry forms
- Horizontal separator lines
- Options for setting default paragraph alignment

Chapter 2

This chapter describes how to specify the major paragraph types or text "blocks" that appear in the BODY portion of an HTML document. These block-level elements are in contrast to "text-level" elements that describe the content or appearance of items that are already inside a paragraph. Most block-level elements can contain other block-level elements as well as text-level elements, while text-level elements define in-paragraph formatting and thus can generally only contain other text-level elements.

2.1 Headings

HTML Element: `<H1 ...> ... </H1>`
`<H2 ...> ... </H2>`
`<H3 ...> ... </H3>`
`<H4 ...> ... </H4>`
`<H5 ...> ... </H5>`
`<H6 ...> ... </H6>`

Attributes: ALIGN

H1 through H6 are used for document headings, with H1 indicating the top-level section headings, H2 first-level subheadings, H3 second-level subheadings, and so forth. However, a common style is to start the BODY with a level-one heading containing the same text as the TITLE element, treating H1 as a document title. In the remainder of the document, level-two headings (H2) are used for the major section headings, H3 for section subheadings, and so forth.

Most browsers render headings in boldface, with H1 the largest and H6 the smallest. The smaller headings should be used with caution because, depending on the browser being used and the user's selection of font sizes, the minor headings may be rendered smaller than the default paragraph text. Unlike many other block-level elements, headings cannot contain or be contained in most other block-level items except for table cells and input forms. They can, however, contain text-level elements. Thus, the two headings of Listing 2.1 are legal, because the text-level elements that change the color and create an anchor for a hypertext link are completely contained within the heading element.

Listing 2.1   Properly formatted headings containing text-level elements

```
<H2><FONT COLOR="RED">
   A Red Heading</FONT></H2>
<H2><A NAME="Section5">
   Section Five</A></H2>
```

On the other hand, the two headings of Listing 2.2 are illegal, because they are embedded in text-level elements.

Listing 2.2   Illegally formatted headings contained inside text-level elements

```
<FONT COLOR="RED">
  <H2>A Red Heading</H2></FONT>
<A NAME="Section5">
  <H2>Section Five<</H2>/A>
```

This example also illustrates the benefits of a formal HTML validator. Because most but not all browsers will display both sets of headings identically, authors who use a browser that permits it could conclude that either format is fine, leaving a resulting head that could display poorly on other browsers.

ALIGN

Headings are left aligned by default, but centered or right-aligned headings can be created by using the ALIGN attribute (legal values LEFT, RIGHT, CENTER). The default alignment can be changed with the CENTER or DIV tag (Section 2.6). In systems that support style sheets, headings have CLASS, ID, and STYLE attributes as well, because the cascading style sheet specification adds these attributes to *all* HTML elements. However, these attributes will not be discussed separately for each HTML element. See Chapter 5 for details.

A sample of the six heading types with various alignment options and an embedded font change are shown in Listing 2.3. Figure 2–1 shows a typical result in Internet Explorer 3.01 on Windows 95.

Listing 2.3   `Document-Headings.html`

```
<!DOCTYPE HTML PUBLIC "-//W3C//DTD HTML 3.2//EN">
<HTML>
<HEAD>
  <TITLE>Document Headings</TITLE>
</HEAD>

<BODY>
Samples of the six heading types:
<H1>Level-1 (H1)</H1>
<H2 ALIGN="CENTER">Level-2 (H2)</H2>
<H3><FONT COLOR="WHITE">Level-3 (H3)</FONT></H3>
<H4 ALIGN="RIGHT">Level-4 (H4)</H4>
<H5>Level-5 (H5)</H5>
<H6>Level-6 (H6)</H6>
</BODY>

</HTML>
```

2.2 Basic Text Sections

The basic text section elements include P (basic paragraph), PRE (preformatted text where white space is preserved), XMP (text with interpretation of HTML markup suppressed), ADDRESS (for listing addresses), and BLOCK-QUOTE (for large quotations, or, controversially, for regular paragraphs with indented left and right margins).

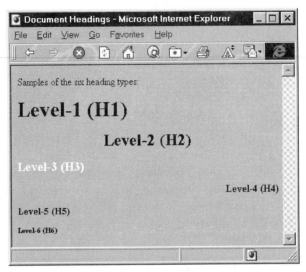

Figure 2–1 Typical rendering of `Document-Headings.html`

Basic Paragraphs

HTML Element: `<P ...> ... </P>` (End Tag Optional)

Attributes: `ALIGN`

The `P` element designates basic paragraphs, resulting in a section of text with blank space above and below. Although `P` is a container, the end tag is optional and most other block-level elements imply an end to the previous paragraph. Furthermore, body text not appearing inside any other block-level element is assumed to be inside a `P` element. So Listings 2.4 and 2.5 are equivalent.

Listing 2.4   Fully-specified paragraph tags

```
<BODY>
<P>
Paragraph 1
</P>
<P>
Paragraph 2
</P>
<P>
Paragraph 3
</P>
</BODY>
```

Listing 2.5   Implied paragraph tags

```
<BODY>
Paragraph 1
<P>
Paragraph 2
<P>
Paragraph 3
</BODY>
```

Extra white space inside a basic paragraph is ignored, with the text filled to fit the space currently available. Multiple consecutive P tags do not necessarily result in extra blank space. Cascading style sheets (Chapter 5) let you specify the size of the top and bottom paragraph margins. But in the absence of style sheets, the BR tag (see Section 3.7, "Controlling Line Breaks") or a PRE element (discussed next) can be used to put blank lines in a Web page.

Core Alert

Multiple consecutive <P> entries generally do not result in multiple blank lines.

ALIGN

The ALIGN attribute of P is used just like ALIGN in headings. Like headings, basic paragraphs are aligned flush left with a ragged right margin by default, but can be centered or right aligned by use of the ALIGN attribute (legal values LEFT, RIGHT, CENTER). The default alignment can be changed with the CENTER or DIV tag (Section 2.6).

Paragraphs with Whitespace Preserved

HTML Element: <PRE> ... </PRE>
Attributes: WIDTH

The PRE element indicates a "preformatted" paragraph that maintains the white space from the source document and uses a fixed-width font. It is often used to display sections of code from sample programs. Images and elements that change the font size are not allowed inside a PRE element. Although the indentation, blank lines, and extra spaces are maintained, special characters such as "<" or "&" can still be interpreted as HTML markup. So, sample code like "if (a < b && c < d)" will likely cause formatting errors, and such text needs to be modified to replace "<" with "<" and so forth, according to the defined character entities in HTML 3.2 (see Table 2.1). The XMP element simplifies this somewhat, but in any case the insertion of code samples containing these characters is tedious and error prone, and is a prime example of where an HTML editor, converter, or preprocessor is valuable. In general, any ISO 8859-1 ("Latin-1") character can be inserted by using "&#xxx;", where xxx is the decimal value of the character in the ISO Latin-1 character set. Values 0–127 represent the normal ASCII character set, but most browsers support the other printable Latin-1 characters. For instance, "©" results in "©". In addition, most characters also have a mnemonic entity reference, such as "©" in the case of the copyright symbol. A full list of the Latin-1 character set, with mnemonic character entities, can be found at http://www.w3.org/pub/WWW/TR/REC-html32.html#latin1. Samples of all the printable characters in this set can be found at http://www.w3.org/pub/WWW/TR/REC-html32.html#charset. Entity references supported by all HTML 3.2 browsers that are of particular import are given in the following table. These characters are considered plain text, and as a result can be used in the TITLE element, as labels of SUBMIT buttons, and other places that prohibit HTML markup.

Table 2.1   Special characters in HTML

Desired Character	HTML Required
<	&lt;
>	&gt;
&	&amp;
"	&quot;
Non-breaking Space	

WIDTH

The WIDTH attribute is not widely supported, but is intended to indicate the expected width *in characters* so that the browser can choose an appropriate font and/or indentation.

Paragraphs with Interpretation of HTML Turned Off

HTML Element: `<XMP>` ... `</XMP>`
Attributes: None

The `PRE` element renders text in a fixed-width font and preserves whitespace. However, HTML tags are still interpreted, so you can't paste sample HTML (or Java or C++ or anything else that has "<", "&", and so forth) directly into it without replacing special characters first. The `XMP` element lets you do this; the interpretation of HTML elements is suppressed until the closing `</XMP>` tag is reached. The HTML 3.2 specification states that this tag is obsolete and should be replaced by `PRE` for future documents. However, it is more convenient in some instances and is supported by most if not all major browsers. For instance, suppose that an instructor wants to prepare a Web page for students illustrating how certain HTML constructs work. This would be very inconvenient using `PRE`, because the instructor would have to replace all the special characters, but very simple using `XMP`. The sample code would be included twice: once inside an `XMP` element to show the reader the code, and once outside the element to show the reader the result as their browser renders it. For instance, Listing 2.6 presents a document that illustrates the use of the `TABLE` element by using an `XMP` element in this way. Figure 2–2 shows the resultant Web page in NCSA Mosaic 3.0.

Listing 2.6 `XMP.html`

```
<!DOCTYPE HTML PUBLIC "-//W3C//DTD HTML 3.2//EN">
<HTML>
<HEAD>
  <TITLE>A Simple Table</TITLE>
</HEAD>

<BODY>
<H1>A Simple Table</H1>

<HR>
<H2>Code:</H2>
<XMP>
<TABLE BORDER=1>
  <CAPTION>Table Caption</CAPTION>
  <TR><TH>Heading1</TH>        <TH>Heading2</TH></TR>
  <TR><TD>Row1 Col1 Data</TD><TD>Row1 Col2 Data</TD></TR>
  <TR><TD>Row2 Col1 Data</TD><TD>Row2 Col2 Data</TD></TR>
  <TR><TD>Row3 Col1 Data</TD><TD>Row3 Col2 Data</TD></TR>
</TABLE>
</XMP>
```

continued

Listing 2.6 `XMP.html` **(continued)**

```
<HR>
<H2>Result:</H2>
<TABLE BORDER=1>
  <CAPTION>Table Caption</CAPTION>
  <TR><TH>Heading1</TH>        <TH>Heading2</TH></TR>
  <TR><TD>Row1 Col1 Data</TD><TD>Row1 Col2 Data</TD></TR>
  <TR><TD>Row2 Col1 Data</TD><TD>Row2 Col2 Data</TD></TR>
  <TR><TD>Row3 Col1 Data</TD><TD>Row3 Col2 Data</TD></TR>
</TABLE>
<HR>

</BODY>
</HTML>
```

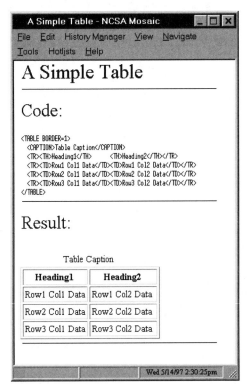

Figure 2–2 Using XMP makes cut-and-paste of code samples simple and convenient.

HTML Element: `<SAMP> ... </SAMP>`

Attributes: None

This nonstandard synonym for `XMP` is supported by Netscape and Internet Explorer.

Indented Quotations

HTML Element: `<BLOCKQUOTE> ... </BLOCKQUOTE>`

Attributes: None

The `BLOCKQUOTE` element is intended for large quotations. The vast majority of browsers display `BLOCKQUOTE` sections with indented left and right margins. However, because this is technically not required, authors should be wary of using `BLOCKQUOTE` purely for indentation unless it is for an internal application where they can be confident of the browsers readers will be using. Furthermore, some HTML advocates object to using conceptual elements for purposes other than their originally intended ones, partly based on the principle that HTML should describe content and browsers/readers (not authors) should decide on details of appearance, and partly because it prevents the effective use of indexing programs that analyze HTML documents. A one-column, centered, borderless table with a width of around 90 percent might be a better alternative. On the other hand, tables (Section 2.4) can take longer to load than regular text, so should be avoided for very large text sections. The best option would be cascading style sheets (Chapter 5), but unfortunately they are not supported in Netscape Navigator 3.01 or earlier. For options for implementing paragraphs with left indentation but normal right margins, see definition lists in Section 2.3.

Core Approach

> HTML 3.2 does not define an element to give indented left and right margins. Many people use *BLOCKQUOTE* or a centered, borderless table as a way to implement this. Both approaches have some drawbacks, but are the best available options in the absence of cascading style sheets.

Addresses

HTML Element: `<ADDRESS>` ... `</ADDRESS>`
Attributes: None

The `ADDRESS` element is used to supply author and contact information for the current document, and usually appears at the top or bottom of the document. Most browsers display it in italics. With `ADDRESS`, just as with most section types other than `PRE`, the browser wraps the resulting text. So if you want line breaks in specific places, `BR` should be inserted explicitly.

2.3 Numbered, Bulleted, and Indented Lists

HTML 3.2 allows you to create numbered or "ordered" lists (`OL`), bulleted or "unordered" lists (`UL`), and "definition" lists with left-indented sections but no number or bullet (`DL`). Lists can be nested or appear inside table cells. The older `MENU` and `DIR` lists are still officially supported, but have been superseded by newer constructs, and will not be discussed here.

Numbered Lists

HTML Element: `<OL ...>` ... `</OL>`
Attributes: `TYPE`, `START`, `COMPACT`

The `OL` element is used to create numbered lists. The `LI` ("list item") tag specifies individual entries within a list, and can contain most other block-level elements (including tables and other lists) except for headings and address elements. For instance, Listing 2.7 shows a simple ordered list, with the result in Netscape 3.0 on Sun/Solaris shown in Figure 2–3.

Listing 2.7   A simple numbered list

```
A sample list:
<OL>
  <LI>List Item One
  <LI>List Item Two
  <LI>List Item Three
</OL>
```

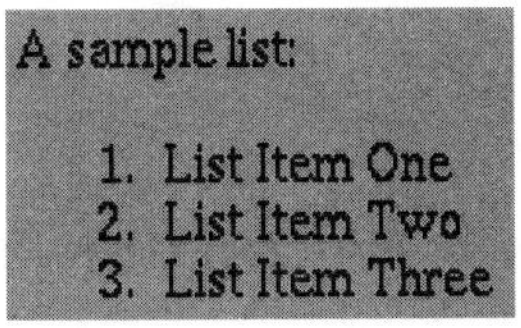

A sample list:

1. List Item One
2. List Item Two
3. List Item Three

Figure 2–3 Numbers in OL lists, like this one from Listing 2.7, are generated automatically.

The OL tag has 3 optional attributes: TYPE, START, and COMPACT.

TYPE

The TYPE attribute specifies the style of numbering to use. Legal values for TYPE are summarized in Table 2.2.

Table 2.2   Values for the TYPE attribute of numbered lists

Value	Meaning
1	Arabic: 1,2,3, etc. Default.
A	Alphabetic uppercase: A, B, C, etc.
a	Alphabetic lowercase: a,b,c, etc.
I	Roman numeral uppercase: I, II, III, IV, etc.
i	Roman numeral lowercase: i, ii, iii, iv, etc.

START

START is an integer specifying where numbering should start. It can be used with any value of TYPE. There is no option to specify a prefix to appear before each number.

COMPACT

<OL COMPACT> is intended to indicate that the list should be rendered more compactly (i.e., in less space) than usual, but it is not widely supported.

Listing 2.8 gives a more complex use of numbered lists. Note that nested lists are indented and have numbering that starts at 1, not at the value of the outer list.

Listing 2.8   Nested ordered lists

```
<OL TYPE="I">
<LI>Headings
  <LI>Basic Text Sections
  <LI>Lists
      <OL TYPE="A">
        <LI>Ordered
            <OL TYPE="1">
              <LI>The OL tag
                  <OL TYPE="a">
                    <LI>TYPE
                    <LI>START
                    <LI>COMPACT
                  </OL>
              <LI>The LI tag
            </OL>
        <LI>Unordered
            <OL TYPE="1">
              <LI>The UL tag
              <LI>The LI tag
            </OL>
        <LI>Definition
            <OL TYPE="1">
              <LI>The DL tag
              <LI>The DT tag
              <LI>The DD tag
            </OL>
      </OL>
  <LI>Miscellaneous
</OL>
```

Figure 2–4 shows a typical result.

HTML Element: `<LI ...> ... </LI>` (End Tag Optional)
Attributes: (When inside OL) VALUE, TYPE

LI entries support different attributes depending on what type of list they are in. Numbered lists support VALUE and TYPE attributes in list items. Strictly speaking, LI is a container element, but in most cases the end tag is omitted.

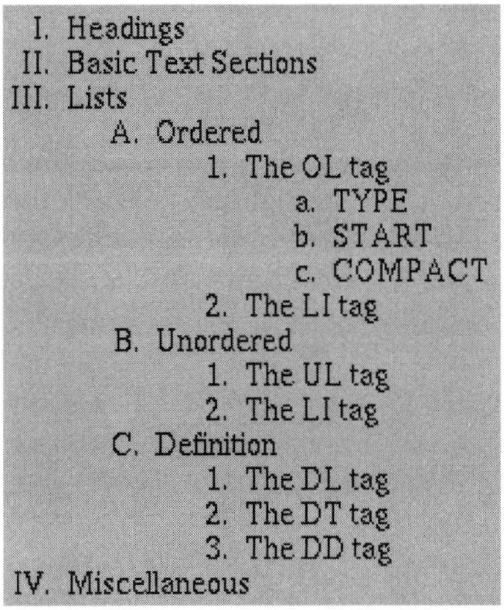

```
    I. Headings
   II. Basic Text Sections
  III. Lists
          A. Ordered
                1. The OL tag
                      a. TYPE
                      b. START
                      c. COMPACT
                2. The LI tag
          B. Unordered
                1. The UL tag
                2. The LI tag
          C. Definition
                1. The DL tag
                2. The DT tag
                3. The DD tag
   IV. Miscellaneous
```

Figure 2–4 Nested lists, like this one from Listing 2.8, are automatically indented.

VALUE

The VALUE attribute can be used to specify a specific number for an entry in a list. It can be used instead of the START attribute on OL itself to get noncontinuous numbering.

TYPE

List items can also have a TYPE attribute with the same potential values as in the OL element, used in the rare case when you would switch numbering styles within a list.

Bulleted Lists

HTML Element: `<UL ...> ... </UL>`
Attributes: TYPE, COMPACT

The UL element is used to create bulleted (*unordered*) lists. The LI (*list item*) tag specifies individual entries within a list. For instance, Listing 2.9 shows a simple bulleted list, with the result in Netscape 3.0 on Sun/Solaris shown in Figure 2–5.

Listing 2.9   A simple bulleted list

```
A sample list:
<UL>
  <LI>List Item One
  <LI>List Item Two
  <LI>List Item Three
</UL>
```

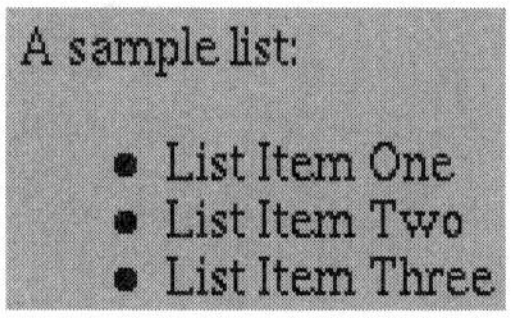

A sample list:

- List Item One
- List Item Two
- List Item Three

Figure 2-5   The UL element generates bullets for each LI item.

The UL tag has 2 optional attributes: TYPE and COMPACT.

TYPE

The TYPE attribute specifies the style of bullet to use. Legal values for TYPE are summarized in Table 2.3.

Table 2.3   Values for the TYPE attribute of bulleted lists

Value	Meaning
DISC	A solid circle. Often the default for nonnested lists.
CIRCLE	A hollow circle. Often the default for nested lists.
SQUARE	A solid or hollow square, depending on the browser.

COMPACT

COMPACT is intended to indicate that the list should take up less space than usual, but it is not widely supported.

Listing 2.10 gives a more complex bulleted list.

Listing 2.10 Nested bulleted lists

```
<H2>Unordered Lists</H2>
<UL TYPE="DISC">
  <LI>The UL tag
      <UL TYPE="CIRCLE">
        <LI>TYPE
          <UL TYPE="SQUARE">
            <LI>DISC
            <LI>CIRCLE
            <LI>SQUARE
          </UL>
        <LI>COMPACT
      </UL>
  <LI>The LI tag
      <UL TYPE="CIRCLE">
        <LI>TYPE
          <UL TYPE="SQUARE">
            <LI>DISC
            <LI>CIRCLE
            <LI>SQUARE
          </UL>
        <LI>VALUE
      </UL>
</UL>
```

Figure 2–6 gives a typical result.

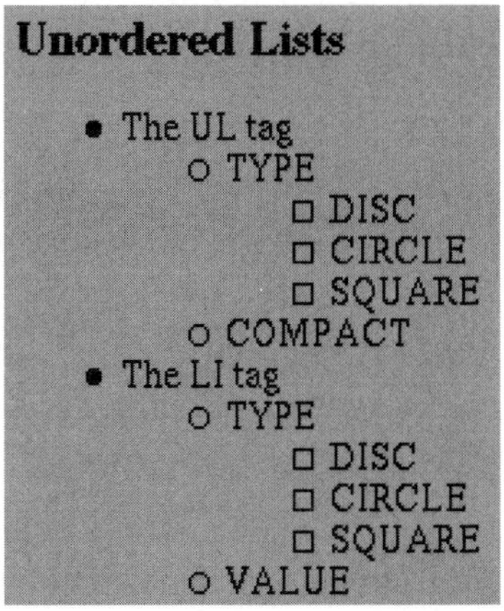

Figure 2–6   Like nested numbered lists, nested bulleted lists are indented automatically.

HTML Element: `<LI ...> ... </LI>` (End Tag Optional)
Attributes: (When inside `UL`) `TYPE`

`LI` entries support different attributes depending on what type of list they are in. Bulleted lists support only the `TYPE` attribute in list elements. Strictly speaking, `LI` is a container element, but in most cases the end tag is omitted.

TYPE

The `TYPE` attribute specifies the bullet type of the particular list element. It has the same allowable values as the `TYPE` attribute for `UL` itself (`DISC`, `CIRCLE`, `SQUARE`).

Definition Lists

HTML Element: `<DL ...> ... </DL>`
Attributes: `COMPACT`

HTML Element: `<DT> ... </DT>` (End Tag Optional)
Attributes: None

HTML Element: `<DD> ... </DD>` (End Tag Optional)
Attributes: None

The `DL` element creates lists containing both indented and nonindented items. Items do not get numbers or bullets. The standard usage is for definition terms (`DT`) to have normal margins and the definition descriptions (`DD`) to have indented left margins. For instance, Listing 2.11 gives a simple definition list. `DL` has an optional `COMPACT` attribute, but it is rarely used and not widely supported. Strictly, `DT` and `DD` are container elements, but the end tags are commonly omitted.

Listing 2.11 A simple definition list

```
<DL>
  <DT>Term One
  <DD>The definition of term number one.
  <DT>Term Two
  <DD>The definition of term number two.
</DL>
```

Figure 2–7 shows a typical result.

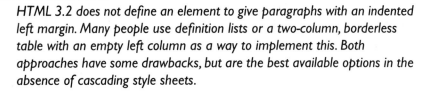

Figure 2-7 This typical rendering of Listing 2.11 illustrates the typical indent of the <DD> tag.

DD elements are allowed to contain other block-level elements except for headings and addresses. A DD element can appear in DL lists without an associated DT, and is the only HTML block-level element that is normally rendered with an indented left margin but a standard right margin. Consequently, DL lists with DD elements are sometimes used to create left-indented paragraphs. However, there is no *requirement* that a browser render definition lists indented in this manner, and because the author typically cannot control which browsers are used to access their document, this is not absolutely safe for nonintranet applications. However, it is much safer than the common but misguided trick of using an "invisible" transparent GIF as a spacer, because text-oriented browsers (e.g., lynx) and graphical browsers with image loading disabled are quite common. Style sheets (Chapter 5) are the ideal solution to this problem, but in their absence left-aligned borderless table with an empty fixed-width first column is probably the best bet, although it should be noted this can be significantly slower to load than the DL version. For options for creating paragraphs with indented left *and* right margins, see the section on BLOCKQUOTE in Section 2.2.

Core Approach

HTML 3.2 does not define an element to give paragraphs with an indented left margin. Many people use definition lists or a two-column, borderless table with an empty left column as a way to implement this. Both approaches have some drawbacks, but are the best available options in the absence of cascading style sheets.

2.4 Tables

Tables are one of the major features of HTML 3.2 that do not appear in HTML 2.0. They are widely used not only for traditional "tables" (data presented in tabular format) but also to group related items together. This latter use of tables to control layout includes applications such as a section of two-column text, a picture with a label always above or below it, and similar types of layouts. To achieve this effect, it should be noted that table entries can contain images, multiple paragraph types including lists, and even other tables. Furthermore, the border around the table and between cells can be suppressed so that the reader may be unaware that a table is being used. Note that creating complex tables by hand can be tedious and error prone, especially if there are nested tables or multiple entries that span rows and columns. HTML editors that let you lay tables out visually can be a big help, especially if they let you go back to the "raw" HTML to add features (such as BGCOLOR) that they might not support.

The Basic Table Structure

An HTML table consists of the TABLE element containing an optional CAP-TION element and then table rows specified via TR. The rows can contain either TH (table heading) elements or TD (table data) elements. TH uses centered, bold text by default, while TD uses normal left-aligned text. This is illustrated in Listing 2.12, with a typical result shown in Figure 2–8. Note that the </TR>, </TH>, and </TD> end tags are optional.

Listing 2.12 A simple HTML table

```
<TABLE BORDER=1>
<CAPTION>Table Caption</CAPTION>
  <TR><TH>Heading1</TH>       <TH>Heading2</TH></TR>
  <TR><TD>Row1 Col1 Data</TD><TD>Row1 Col2 Data</TD></TR>
  <TR><TD>Row2 Col1 Data</TD><TD>Row2 Col2 Data</TD></TR>
  <TR><TD>Row3 Col1 Data</TD><TD>Row3 Col2 Data</TD></TR>
</TABLE>
```

Table Caption	
Heading1	**Heading2**
Row1 Col1 Data	Row1 Col2 Data
Row2 Col1 Data	Row2 Col2 Data
Row3 Col1 Data	Row3 Col2 Data

Figure 2–8 This is a typical rendering of the simple table given in Listing 2.12.

HTML Element: `<TABLE...>` ... `</TABLE>`

Attributes: `BORDER, ALIGN, WIDTH, CELLSPACING,`
`CELLPADDING, BGCOLOR` (nonstandard), `BORDERCOLOR`
(nonstandard), `BORDERCOLORDARK` (nonstandard),
`BORDERCOLORLIGHT` (nonstandard), `BACKGROUND`
(nonstandard), `RULES` (nonstandard), `FRAME` (nonstandard)

The `<TABLE>` tag can be used with no attributes, yielding a borderless left-aligned table. For more control, the following attributes can be specified:

ALIGN

The `ALIGN` attribute gives the horizontal alignment of the table as a whole. Legal values are `LEFT`, `RIGHT`, and `CENTER`, with `LEFT` being the default. However, because few browsers support `ALIGN=`
`"CENTER"`, centered tables should be implemented by placing the table between `<CENTER>` and `</CENTER>` tags. Furthermore, note that right-aligned tables allow text that follows it in the HTML document to appear on the left side of the table in the resulting Web page, at least in Netscape and Internet Explorer. Use `<BR CLEAR="ALL">` after the table to prevent this. See Section 2.6, "Miscellaneous Block-Level Elements," for the `CENTER` and `BR` elements.

Core Approach

For centered tables, use the following structure:
`<CENTER>`
`<TABLE ...>`
`...`
`</TABLE>`
`</CENTER>`

BORDER

This specifies the width in pixels of the border around the table. This is in *addition* to the border around each cell (the `CELLSPACING`). The default is zero, which also results in the visible 3D divider between cells being turned off. Some browsers allow `<TABLE BORDER>` to mean the same as `<TABLE BORDER=1>`, but this should be avoided because it prevents validation by the formal HTML validators.

Core Note

The thickness of the outside border is the <u>sum</u> of BORDER *and* CELLSPACING, *assuming* BORDER *is not zero.*

CELLSPACING

This gives the space in pixels between adjacent cells. Drawn as a 3D line if BORDER is nonzero, otherwise empty space in the background color is used. The default is usually about 3.

CELLPADDING

CELLPADDING determines the empty space, in pixels, between the cell's border and the table element. The default is usually about 1.

WIDTH

This specifies the width of the table, either in pixels (<TABLE WIDTH=250>) or as a percentage of the current browser window width (<TABLE WIDTH="75%">). Specify absolute sizes with caution, because in most cases you know little about the window sizes used by visitors to your page. If you specify a percentage, be sure to enclose the value in double quotes. The default size is derived from the size of table elements.

BGCOLOR

Although not part of HTML 3.2, the BGCOLOR attribute of TABLE (and TR, TD, and TH) is relatively widely supported, including by Netscape and Internet Explorer in version 3.0 and later. Apart from frames or style sheets (which only work on some browsers) or a background image (which depends on knowing the window and font sizes), this is the only way to have different background colors for different parts of a WWW page, so it is quite useful for such elements as colored sidebars and headings that are set in blocks of different colors (perhaps using border-less tables) as well as for traditional shaded tables. The color for the overall table can be overridden by specifying a color for an individual row or table cell.

BORDERCOLOR, BORDERCOLORDARK, BORDERCOLORLIGHT

Supported only by Internet Explorer, these attributes specify the colors to use for the borders of the table. BORDERCOLOR defines the main color while BORDERCOLORDARK and BORDERCOLORLIGHT define the colors to use for the 3D shading. They are only applicable when the BORDER attribute is nonzero.

BACKGROUND

This is an Internet Explorer-specific method to specify an image file that will be tiled as the background of the table. With borders turned off, this provides a way to overlay images with text, but is not portable to other browsers. Furthermore, because Internet Explorer version 3.0 supports style sheets, and style sheets provide the same capability in a manner that will be supported by many new browsers, the BACK-GROUND attribute should be avoided even for internal applications that will be accessed primarily with Internet Explorer.

RULES

This Internet Explorer-specific attribute specifies which inner dividing lines are drawn. All are drawn if this attribute is omitted. Legal values are NONE, ROWS, COLS, and ALL.

FRAME

This is an Internet-Explorer extension which specifies which outer borders are drawn. All four are drawn if this attribute is omitted. Legal values are BORDER or BOX (all), VOID (none), ABOVE (top), BELOW (bottom), HSIDES (top and bottom, despite the somewhat confusing name), VSIDES (left and right), LHS (left), and RHS (right). Listing 2.13 gives a simple example, with the result shown in Figure 2–9.

Listing 2.13 `TTT.html`

```
<!DOCTYPE HTML PUBLIC "-//W3C//DTD HTML 3.2//EN">
<HTML>
<HEAD>
  <TITLE>1997 World Championship</TITLE>
</HEAD>

<BODY>
<H2 ALIGN="CENTER">1997 World Championship</H2>
Final result in the 1997 world tic-tac-toe championship.
Deep Green is "X", Barry Kasparov is "O".
<CENTER>
<TABLE BORDER=1 FRAME="VOID">
  <TR><TH>X<TH>O<TH>X
  <TR><TH>X<TH>O<TH>X
  <TR><TH>O<TH>X<TH>O
</TABLE>
</CENTER>
</BODY>
</HTML>
```

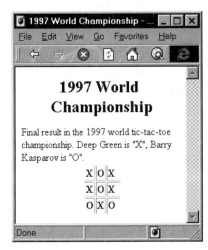

Figure 2-9   A table with the outside borders turned off

HTML Element: `<CAPTION ...>` ... `</CAPTION>`
Attributes: `ALIGN`

The CAPTION element places a title above (ALIGN="TOP") or below (ALIGN="BOTTOM") the table.

Defining Table Rows

HTML Element: `<TR ...> ... </TR>` (End Tag Optional)
Attributes: `ALIGN`, `VALIGN`, `BGCOLOR` (nonstandard), `BORDERCOLOR`
(nonstandard), `BORDERCOLORDARK` (nonstandard),
`BORDERCOLORLIGHT` (nonstandard)

`TR` is used to define each row in the table. Each row will then contain `TH`
and/or `TD` entries.

ALIGN

`ALIGN` (legal values `LEFT`, `RIGHT`, or `CENTER`) is used to set the
default horizontal alignment for table cells.

VALIGN

`VALIGN` (legal values `TOP`, `MIDDLE`, or `BOTTOM`) is used to set the
default vertical alignment for table cells.

BGCOLOR

This is a nonstandard attribute supported by Netscape and Internet
Explorer in version 3.0 and later. It sets the color for the table row, overriding any values set for the table as a whole via the `BGCOLOR` attribute
of `TABLE`. It, in turn, can be overridden by a `BGCOLOR` attribute in a `TD`
or `TH` entry in the row. This is useful for making tables where the header
row is shaded differently than the remaining rows. For instance, Listing
2.14 shows a table with the headers presented with white text on a black
background, and the remainder of the table presented with black text on
a light gray background. The result is shown in Figure 2–10, and is a
common table format that is preferred by a number of users. However,
this reliance on nonstandard features to achieve a particular appearance
in some browsers comes at a cost. If a browser supports the `FONT` tag
but not the `BGCOLOR` attribute of tables, the heading text will be invisible. This is illustrated in Figure 2–11, shown in Netscape 2.02, which
does indeed support `FONT` but not `BGCOLOR`. So, for Internet applications where a variety of browsers will be accessing your page, choose
foreground colors with enough contrast to show up even if the `BGCOLOR`
is ignored. This reinforces the basic rule of thumb when using extensions
that are not part of HTML 3.2: Use extensions that *add* value to your
page, but make sure that the fundamental look of your page doesn't
depend on them. On the other hand, style sheets (Chapter 5) provide a

safe alternative for building tables with colored cells. The foreground and background colors for TH cells can be specified together, and a browser will either support both (yielding white text on a black background) or neither (yielding black text on a white background).

Listing 2.14 BG-Colors.html

```
<!DOCTYPE HTML PUBLIC "-//W3C//DTD HTML 3.2//EN">
<HTML>
<HEAD>
  <TITLE>WWW Standards</TITLE>
</HEAD>

<BODY BGCOLOR="WHITE">
<H1 ALIGN="CENTER">WWW Standards</H1>

<TABLE BORDER=1 BGCOLOR="#EEEEEE">
  <TR BGCOLOR="BLACK">
    <TH><FONT COLOR="WHITE">Standard</FONT>
    <TH><FONT COLOR="WHITE">
        Obsolete Version</FONT>
    <TH><FONT COLOR="WHITE">
        Most Widely Supported Version</FONT>
    <TH><FONT COLOR="WHITE">
        Upcoming Version</FONT>
  <TR><TD>HTML
      <TD>2.0
      <TD>Wilbur (3.2)
      <TD>Cougar
  <TR><TD>HTTP
      <TD>0.9
      <TD>1.0
      <TD>1.1
</TABLE>

</BODY>
</HTML>
```

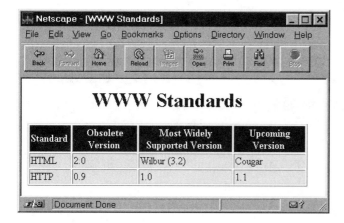

Figure 2-10 The BGCOLOR attribute makes some tables look nicer.

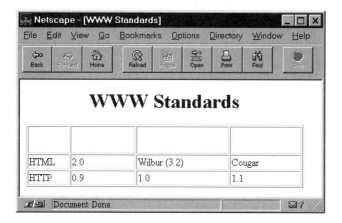

Figure 2-11 Forgetting that BGCOLOR is nonstandard can lead to bad results in some browsers.

BORDERCOLOR, BORDERCOLORDARK, BORDERCOLORLIGHT

Supported only by Internet Explorer, this specifies the color to use for the borders of the row. BORDERCOLOR define the main color while BORDERCOLORDARK and BORDERCOLORLIGHT defines the colors to use for the 3D shading. They are only applicable when the BORDER attribute of the TABLE is nonzero.

Table Headings and Data Cells

HTML Element: `<TH ...>` ... `</TH>` **(End Tag Optional)**
`<TD ...>` ... `</TD>` **(End Tag Optional)**

Attributes: COLSPAN, ROWSPAN, ALIGN, VALIGN, WIDTH, HEIGHT, NOWRAP, BGCOLOR (nonstandard), BORDERCOLOR (nonstandard), BORDERCOLORDARK (nonstandard), BORDERCOLORLIGHT (nonstandard), BACKGROUND (nonstandard)

COLSPAN

COLSPAN defines a heading or cell data entry that spans multiple columns. Listing 2.15 gives a simple example.

Listing 2.15 A heading that spans two columns

```
<TABLE BORDER=1>
<TR><TH COLSPAN=2>Col 1&2 Heading
      <TH>Col3 Heading
  <TR><TD>Col1 Data
      <TD>Col2 Data
      <TD>Col3 Data
</TABLE>
```

Figure 2–12 shows a typical result.

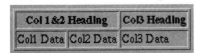

Figure 2–12   This is a typical result from the column spanning example of Listing 2.15.

ROWSPAN

ROWSPAN defines a heading or cell data entry that spans multiple rows. Listing 2.16 gives a simple example.

Listing 2.16 A data cell that spans two rows

```
<TABLE BORDER=1>
<TR><TH>Heading1<TH>Heading2
  <TR><TD ROWSPAN=2>Data for Row 1&2, Col1
      <TD>Row1 Col2 Data
  <TR><TD>Row2 Col2 Data
</TABLE>
```

Figure 2–13 shows a typical result.

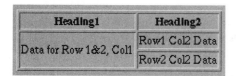

Figure 2–13 This is a typical result from the row spanning example of Listing 2.16.

ALIGN and VALIGN

The ALIGN attribute (LEFT, RIGHT, CENTER) specifies the horizontal alignment of items in a table cell. The default is LEFT for TD and CENTER for TH, unless overridden by the ALIGN option of TR. The VALIGN attribute (TOP, MIDDLE, BOTTOM) specifies the vertical alignment. The default is MIDDLE.

WIDTH and HEIGHT

In the absence of WIDTH and HEIGHT attributes, cell sizes are set by the browser, based on the window size and the data contained in the cell. The WIDTH and HEIGHT attributes allow the specification of an exact size in pixels. Absolute sizes should be used with caution, because they may prevent reasonable formatting if the browser window is not the size the document author expected. According to the HTML 3.2 specification, percent values are not allowed, although both Netscape and Internet Explorer allow this, using the value as a percentage of the table width or height (not of the browser window width or height).

NOWRAP

The NOWRAP attribute suppresses word wrapping within a cell. Similar effects can be achieved by using nonbreaking spaces ( ) between words, or using a PRE paragraph inside a cell (this also results in a fixed-width font). NOWRAP should be used with caution as it can result in text being offscreen if the browser window is not sized appropriately.

BGCOLOR

The BGCOLOR attribute, although not part of HTML 3.2, is supported by Netscape and Internet Explorer in version 3.0 and later. It sets a background color for the particular table cell.

BORDERCOLOR, BORDERCOLORDARK, BORDERCOLORLIGHT

Supported only by Internet Explorer, this specifies the color to use for the borders of the cell. BORDERCOLOR defines the main color while BORDERCOLORDARK and BORDERCOLORLIGHT define the colors to use for the 3D shading. Only applicable when the BORDER attribute of the TABLE is nonzero.

BACKGROUND

This is an Internet Explorer-specific method to specify an image file that will be tiled as the background of the cell.

2.5 Fill-Out Forms

These elements let you create data-entry forms that can be filled out by the reader, to be used with CGI programming. They are summarized briefly as follows, and discussed in detail in Chapter 17 (CGI Programming and Beyond—The Client Side).

HTML Element: `<FORM ...> ... </FORM>`
Attributes: ACTION, METHOD, ENCTYPE, TARGET (nonstandard), NAME (nonstandard), ONSUBMIT (nonstandard), ONRESET (nonstandard)

This element sets up an area for data input forms. Forms are usually used to send data to CGI programs, and this use of forms and examples of each element type is presented in Chapter 17 (CGI Programming and Beyond—The Client Side). Forms can also be used to initiate JavaScript actions. This is described in Chapter 19 (JavaScript: Adding Dynamic Content to Web Pages).

ACTION

ACTION gives the URL of the CGI program to which data will be sent. HTML forms can be set up as follows

```
<FORM ACTION="SomeURL">
  <INPUT ...> Other HTML
  <INPUT ...> Other HTML
  <INPUT ...> Other HTML
  <SELECT ...> ... </SELECT>
  <TEXTAREA ...> ... </TEXTAREA>
  <INPUT TYPE="SUBMIT" VALUE="Submit the Data">
</FORM>
```

When the form is submitted, a data string containing the names and values of all active input elements is sent to the URL specified in the ACTION attribute. See Chapter 17 for details.

METHOD

This determines the HTTP request method; GET (default) or POST.

ENCTYPE

ENCTYPE determines the way in which data being sent to a CGI program is encoded. The default is application/x-www-form-urlencoded.

TARGET

TARGET is used only by browsers that support frames (Chapter 4), and designates the frame in which the result will be displayed.

NAME

NAME is used only by browsers that support JavaScript (Chapter 2), and gives the form a name that can be used instead of using the appropriate index in the forms array of the document object.

ONSUBMIT, ONRESET

These attributes are also used only by JavaScript browsers, and specify code to be executed when the form is submitted and when the user resets the form (e.g. with a reset button).

HTML Element: `<INPUT ...>` (No End Tag)

Attributes: TYPE, NAME, VALUE, ALIGN, CHECKED, MAXLENGTH, SIZE, SRC, ONCLICK (nonstandard), ONDBLCLICK (nonstandard), ONSELECT (nonstandard), ONCHANGE (nonstandard), ONFOCUS (nonstandard), ONBLUR (nonstandard)

TYPE

The TYPE attribute specifies the variety of input form to use: TEXT (default), PASSWORD, CHECKBOX, RADIO, SUBMIT, RESET, FILE, HIDDEN, IMAGE, or BUTTON (JavaScript only). All of these are explained in Chapter 17, "CGI Programming and Beyond—The Client Side," because they are almost exclusively used for CGI programming. However, a SUBMIT button can be used as a graphical hypertext link to non-CGI locations. For instance, in Listing 2.17, multiple forms are created with hypertext links to Web search engines. Each contains a single input element of the form `<INPUT TYPE="SUBMIT" VALUE="SearchEngineName">`. Figure 2–14 and Figure 2–15 show the results of Listing 2.17

Listing 2.17 `SearchEngines.html`

```html
<!DOCTYPE HTML PUBLIC "-//W3C//DTD HTML 3.2//EN">
<HTML>
<HEAD>
  <TITLE>Search Engines</TITLE>
</HEAD>

<BODY>
<H1>Search Engines</H1>

Can't find what you were looking for?
Try one of the search engines below.
<P>
<TABLE BORDER=1>
  <TR><TD><FORM ACTION="http://www.yahoo.com/">
          <INPUT TYPE="SUBMIT" VALUE="Yahoo">
          </FORM>
      <TD><FORM ACTION="http://www.excite.com/">
          <INPUT TYPE="SUBMIT" VALUE="eXcite">
          </FORM>
      <TD><FORM ACTION="http://www.altavista.com/">
          <INPUT TYPE="SUBMIT" VALUE="AltaVista">
          </FORM>
  <TR><TD><FORM ACTION="http://www.lycos.com/">
          <INPUT TYPE="SUBMIT" VALUE="Lycos">
          </FORM>
      <TD><FORM ACTION="http://www.hotbot.com/">
          <INPUT TYPE="SUBMIT" VALUE="HotBot">
          </FORM>
      <TD><FORM ACTION="http://www.infoseek.com/">
          <INPUT TYPE="SUBMIT" VALUE="InfoSeek">
          </FORM>
</TABLE>

</BODY>
</HTML>
```

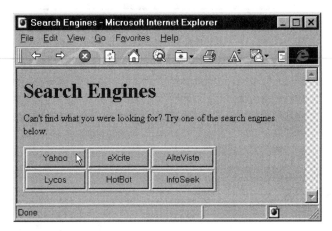

Figure 2-14 SUBMIT buttons can be used as hypertext links.

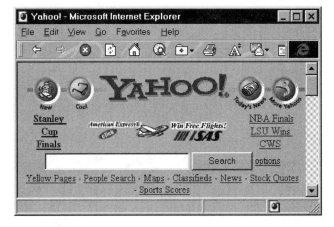

Figure 2-15 Clicking the Yahoo SUBMIT button takes you to Yahoo's site.

NAME
NAME identifies the form to the target CGI program and is required in all cases except for SUBMIT, RESET, and BUTTON.

VALUE
This is used to initialize the field or to provide labels for buttons. It is required for radio buttons and checkboxes.

ALIGN
Used only for the IMAGE type, ALIGN gives an alignment of TOP, MIDDLE, BOTTOM, LEFT, or RIGHT. The default is BOTTOM.

CHECKED
CHECKED sets the initial state of radio buttons and checkboxes.

MAXLENGTH
MAXLENGTH specifies the *maximum* number of characters permitted in a textfield. This is in contrast to the *visible* number of characters, which is specified via SIZE.

SIZE
SIZE sets the *visible* number of characters permitted in a textfield. This is in contrast to the *maximum* number of characters, which is specified via MAXLENGTH. Value is in terms of the average width of characters in the current font.

SRC
SRC applies only to the IMAGE type, and gives the URL of the image source.

ONCLICK, ONDBLCLICK, ONSELECT, ONCHANGE, ONFOCUS, and ONBLUR
These attributes apply only to browsers that support JavaScript, and specify code to be executed when certain conditions arise. ONCLICK and ONDBLCLICK describe what to do when a button or checkbox is clicked; ONSELECT describes what to do when text in a textfield or password field is selected by the user; ONCHANGE refers to the situation when the user leaves a textfield that has changed; ONFOCUS and ONBLUR specify what to do when an element gets or loses the input focus.

HTML Element: `<TEXTAREA NAME="..." ROWS=xxx`
`COLS=yyy>`
`... </TEXTAREA>`

Attributes: NAME (required), ROWS (required), COLS (required), WRAP (nonstandard), ONSELECT (non-standard), ONCHANGE (nonstandard), ONFOCUS (non-standard), ONBLUR (nonstandard), ONKEYDOWN (nonstandard), ONKEYPRESS (nonstandard), ONKEYUP (nonstandard)

This creates a multiline textfield. Text between the start and end tags is used as the initial contents of the text area.

NAME

This specifies the name that will be sent to the CGI program.

ROWS and COLS

These attributes specify the visible size of the text area. If more lines of text than can fit are entered, scrollbars will be added.

WRAP

The nonstandard WRAP attribute specifies what to do with lines that are longer than the size specified by COLS. It is supported by Netscape in version 2.0 and later. A value of OFF disables word wrap, and is the default. The user can still enter explicit line breaks in such a case. A value of HARD causes words to wrap and the associated line breaks to be transmitted when the form is submitted. Finally, a value of SOFT causes the words to wrap on screen, but no extra line breaks to be transmitted when the form is submitted.

ONSELECT, ONCHANGE, ONFOCUS, ONBLUR, ONKEYDOWN, ONKEYPRESS, and ONKEYUP

These attributes apply only to browsers that support JavaScript, and specify code to be executed when certain conditions arise. ONSELECT describes what to do when text in the text area is selected by the user; ONCHANGE refers to the situation when the user leaves the text area after it has changed; ONFOCUS and ONBLUR specify what to do when the text area acquires or loses the input focus; ONKEYDOWN, ONKEY-PRESS, and ONKEYUP designate action to take for each keystroke.

HTML Element: `<SELECT NAME="..." ...> ... </SELECT>`

Attributes: NAME (required), SIZE, MULTIPLE, ONCLICK (nonstandard), ONFOCUS (nonstandard), ONBLUR (nonstandard), ONCHANGE (nonstandard)

The SELECT element creates a combobox or listbox to let the user select among predefined options.

NAME

NAME identifies the form to the target CGI program.

SIZE

SIZE gives the number of visible rows. If it is used, the SELECT menu is usually represented as a listbox instead of a combobox (the normal representation when neither SIZE nor MULTIPLE is supplied).

MULTIPLE

The MULTIPLE attribute specifies whether multiple entries can be selected simultaneously. The default allows only one selection.

ONCLICK, ONFOCUS, ONBLUR, ONCHANGE

These nonstandard attributes are supported by browsers that understand JavaScript, and indicate code to be executed when the entry is clicked on, gains the input focus, loses the input focus, and loses the focus after having been changed, respectively.

HTML Element: `<OPTION ...>` **(No End Tag)**

Attributes: SELECTED, VALUE

Only valid inside a SELECT element, this specifies the menu options.

SELECTED

If present, SELECTED specifies that the particular menu item is shown selected when the page is first loaded.

VALUE

VALUE gives the value to be associated with the NAME of the SELECT menu if the current option is selected.

2.6 Miscellaneous Block-Level Elements

The remaining block-level elements include HR for a horizontal "rule" used as a divider, DIV for setting up default alignments for other block-level elements, and CENTER for centering a section of text.

HTML Element: <HR ...> (No End Tag)

Attributes: ALIGN, WIDTH, SIZE, NOSHADE, COLOR (non-standard)

Horizontal rules, indicated by the HR element, divide sections by drawing a horizontal "etched" line all or partway across the browser window. Frequently, HR is used without attributes (i.e., simply <HR>), but it has four optional attributes, summarized in the following paragraphs.

ALIGN

ALIGN specifies the horizontal alignment. Legal options are LEFT, RIGHT, and CENTER, with CENTER being the default.

WIDTH

This attribute gives the width in pixels (<HR WIDTH=75>) or as a percentage of current window width (<HR WIDTH="50%">). The default is 100%.

SIZE

SIZE is the thickness of the main line in pixels. This is in addition to any shadowing used to make it look etched. The default is about 1.

NOSHADE

If present, NOSHADE tells browser to use solid color instead of the default etched line.

COLOR

COLOR is a nonstandard attribute supported by Internet Explorer that changes the color of the line. Either color names or RGB values (see Table 1.1) are legal.

HTML Element: `<DIV ALIGN="...">` ... `</DIV>`
Attributes: `ALIGN`

The `DIV` element sets the default horizontal alignment for block-level elements it contains. The `ALIGN` attribute can be one of `LEFT`, `RIGHT`, or `CENTER`.

HTML Element: `<CENTER>` ... `</CENTER>`
Attributes: None

`<CENTER>` is shorthand for `<DIV ALIGN="CENTER">`, and is widely used because it was supported by Netscape prior to the introduction of the `DIV` element.

HTML Element: `<MULTICOL COLS=xxx ...>` ... `</MULTICOL>`
Attributes: `COLS` (required), `GUTTER`, `WIDTH`

`MULTICOL` is a Netscape extension introduced in Navigator 3.0 to support multicolumn text. Creating multicolumn text using `MULTICOL` differs from standard HTML tables (Section 2.4) in that `MULTICOL` lets text flow from one column to another, but requires that all the columns be the same width. Tables, on the other hand, require you to assign sections of text to table cells in advance, but lets the columns be of varying sizes. Tables in Netscape and Internet Explorer also let you assign different background colors to different cells, something that `MULTICOL` does not support.

COLS
This required attribute specifies the number of columns of text, and should be two or greater.

GUTTER
This optional attribute specifies the number of pixels between the columns. The default is 10.

WIDTH
This optional attribute specifies the width in pixels of each of the columns. If `WIDTH` is omitted, then Netscape divides the space available, after the gutters, evenly among all the columns.

Listing 2.18 gives an example of `MULTICOL` and several of the other miscellaneous block-level elements, with the result shown in Figure 2–16. In the particular case of Listing 2.17, it is probably a bit easier to use

`<H1 ALIGN="CENTER">` instead of wrapping the header inside a CENTER element, but CENTER would be more convenient when aligning several consecutive paragraphs.

Listing 2.18 `Multicol.html`

```
<!DOCTYPE HTML PUBLIC "-//W3C//DTD HTML 3.2//EN">
<HTML>
<HEAD>
  <TITLE>The MULTICOL Tag</TITLE>
</HEAD>

<BODY>
<CENTER>
  <H1>
  The <CODE>MULTICOL</CODE> Tag
  </H1>
</CENTER>
<HR>
<MULTICOL COLS=2>
<CODE>MULTICOL</CODE> is an extension present only in
Netscape 3.0 and later that supports multicolumn text.
It differs from standard HTML tables in that
<CODE>MULTICOL</CODE> lets text flow from one column to
another, but requires that all the columns be the same
width. Tables, on the other hand, require you to assign
sections of text to table cells in advance, but let
the columns be of varying sizes. Tables in Netscape
and Internet Explorer also let you assign different
background colors to different cells, something that
<CODE>MULTICOL</CODE> does not support.
</MULTICOL>
</BODY>
</HTML>
```

Figure 2–16 Netscape adjusts text in columns to keep each column about the same length.

2.7 Summary

Block-level elements let you define the major sections of your Web page. You can define headings, several different paragraph types, lists, tables, data-input forms, and a few miscellaneous elements. However, you will also want to embed elements or specify formatting changes within a larger text section. That is the role played by the text-level elements discussed in the following chapter.

TEXT-LEVEL ELEMENTS IN HTML 3.2

Topics in This Chapter

- Using explicit character styles
- Using logical character styles
- Specifying hypertext links
- Embedding images
- Setting clickable regions in images
- Embedding Java programs, audio, video, and ActiveX controls
- Controlling line breaks

Chapter 3

This chapter describes how to change font settings, specify hypertext links, set line breaks, and embed objects in paragraphs. The "text-level" elements used to accomplish this specify the appearance of text within existing text blocks, and do not cause paragraph breaks as do block-level elements. Text-level elements can contain other text-level elements, but not block-level elements.

3.1 Physical Character Styles

These elements specify the type of font or character style that should be applied to the text they enclose. They can be used almost anywhere, with a few exceptions such as the TITLE, labels of SUBMIT buttons, and (for elements that change the font size) within a PRE paragraph. Character styles can be nested to compose styles for bold-italic, an underlined fixed-width font, a large, green, bold, italic, strike-through font, and so forth.

HTML Element: <B> ... </B>
Attributes: None

This element instructs the browser to use a bold version of the current font for the enclosed text. This rendering can be overridden by the use of style sheets, plus style sheets add CLASS, ID, and STYLE attributes to *all* HTML elements including the physical character styles. See Chapter 5 for details.

HTML Element: `<I>` ... `</I>`
Attributes: None

This element instructs the browser to use italics for the enclosed text.

HTML Element: `<TT>` ... `</TT>`
Attributes: None

TT instructs the browser to use a monospaced (fixed-width or "teletype") font for the enclosed text.

HTML Element: `<U>` ... `</U>`
Attributes: None

The U element specifies that the enclosed text be underlined.

HTML Element: `<SUB>` ... `</SUB>`
Attributes: None

This element instructs the browser to use subscripts for the enclosed text.

HTML Element: `<SUP>` ... `</SUP>`
Attributes: None

This element instructs the browser to use superscripts for the enclosed text.

HTML Element: `<BIG>` ... `</BIG>`
Attributes: None

This element instructs the browser to use text one size bigger than the current size, on a scale of seven possible sizes. The actual point sizes that these correspond to are determined by the browser. For more details, see the FONT tag later in this section.

HTML Element: `<SMALL>` ... `</SMALL>`
Attributes: None

This element instructs the browser to use text one size smaller than the current size, on a scale of seven possible sizes. The actual point sizes that these correspond to are determined by the browser. For details, see the FONT tag later in this section.

HTML Element: `<STRIKE>` ... `</STRIKE>`
Attributes: None

The STRIKE element tells the browser to draw a horizontal line through the enclosed text.

HTML Element: `<S>` ... `</S>`
Attributes: None

S tells the browser to draw a horizontal line through the enclosed text. This shorter version of STRIKE is not in HTML 3.2, but is supported by Netscape and Internet Explorer in version 3.0 and later and is expected to be part of upcoming HTML standards such as HTML 4.0. Future revisions of HTML may replace STRIKE with S altogether.

HTML Element: `<BLINK>` ... `</BLINK>`
Attributes: None

This tag, supported only by Netscape, causes the enclosed text to blink on and off. Many users find it annoying, so it should be used sparingly (if at all) for high-priority warnings and notes.

Listing 3.1 gives a sampling of various character styles, with Figure 3–1 showing a typical result.

Listing 3.1   A sample of physical character styles

```
<!DOCTYPE HTML PUBLIC "-//W3C//DTD HTML 3.2//EN">
<HTML>
<HEAD>
  <TITLE>Physical Character Styles</TITLE>
</HEAD>

<BODY BGCOLOR="WHITE">
<H1>Physical Character Styles</H1>

<B>Bold</B><BR>
<I>Italic</I><BR>
<TT>Teletype (Monospaced)</TT><BR>
<U>Underlined</U><BR>
Subscripts: f<SUB>0</SUB> + f<SUB>1</SUB><BR>
Superscripts: x<SUP>2</SUP> + y<SUP>2</SUP><BR>
<SMALL>Smaller</SMALL><BR>
<BIG>Bigger</BIG><BR>
<STRIKE>Strike Through</STRIKE><BR>
<B><I>Bold Italic</I></B><BR>
<BIG><TT>Big Monospaced</TT></BIG><BR>
<SMALL><I>Small Italic</I></SMALL><BR>
<FONT COLOR="GRAY">Gray</FONT><BR>

</BODY>
</HTML>
```

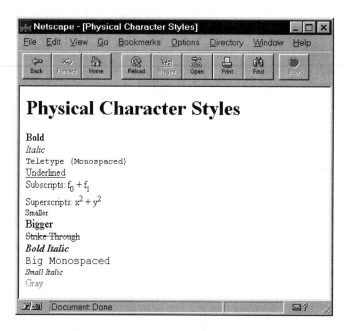

Figure 3–1   Rendering of physical character styles in Netscape Navigator 3.01 on Windows 95.

HTML Element: `<FONT ...> ... </FONT>`

Attributes: SIZE, COLOR, FACE (nonstandard)

The FONT tag specifies the size and/or color to use for the enclosed text. The SIZE attribute gives the author control over font size and the COLOR attribute is the *only* HTML 3.2 construct that lets the user assign text colors on other than a global document basis. Remember that text-level elements cannot enclose paragraphs. This means that if you have several consecutive paragraphs, lists, or tables that you want to be in a particular color or size, you need to repeat the FONT entry in each. However, global colors can be set in the BODY element (Section 1.6), and global sizes can be set using BASEFONT (discussed later in this section). For browsers that support the new cascading style sheet standard, style sheets provide a very flexible way of specifying font size, color, and face information for paragraphs or sections of text. See Chapter 5 for details.

SIZE

The SIZE attribute can be an absolute value from 1 (smallest) to 7 (largest), or a relative value (SIZE="+1", SIZE="-1", SIZE="+2", and so forth) indicating the change with respect to the current font. The actual point sizes that these correspond to are determined by the browser. Be careful with absolute sizes; they can be annoying to users who have customized their browser to use a particular sized font.

Core Approach

Whenever possible, use relative font sizes, not absolute ones.

COLOR

As with the colors in the BODY element, these colors can be a logical color name (Table 1.1) or an explicit RGB value, and care should be taken to avoid the likelihood of text in the same color as the background, which would appear to be blank to the reader. This can be difficult to guarantee, however, because many browsers permit the user to override the colors the author supplied for the foreground and background of the main text, but not for FONT. So if the user selected a green background, stipulating that it should override the settings in the BODY, and <FONT COLOR="green"> is used, the text will appear invisible. On the other hand, users rarely set bold/bright background colors to override defaults, so if you use bold/bright FONT colors, it is unlikely (but still possible) that your text would be invisible to some readers.

FACE

Although not officially part of HTML 3.2, some browsers (including Netscape and Internet Explorer in version 3.0 and later) allow a FACE attribute containing a list of preferred font names, separated by commas. The first font in the list should be used if available on the client machine, otherwise the second should be used, and so on. If no font in the list is available, a default should be used, just as if the FACE attribute was omitted. For instance, a user could request that certain headings be in Arial or another sans-serif font. Be careful about choosing unusual fonts for graphic characters or foreign-language text, however. Doing this can easily result in unreadable text on browsers that don't have that particular font.

Some examples of working with the FONT element include:

```
<FONT COLOR="RED">Red Text</FONT>
<FONT SIZE=5>Large Text</FONT>
<FONT SIZE="+1" COLOR="BLUE">Larger Blue Text</FONT>
```

HTML Element: `<BASEFONT SIZE=xxx>` (No End Tag)

Attributes: `SIZE` (required)

BASEFONT sets the default font size for nonheading text for the remainder of document, using absolute values from 1 (smallest) to 7 (largest). The default is 3. As with FONT, BIG, and SMALL, the mapping from these 7 values to actual pixel sizes is determined by the browser. For instance:

```
<BASEFONT SIZE=5>
```

BASEFONT doesn't affect colors; to set the default color, use the TEXT attribute of BODY for global values or FONT for local color changes. Use BASEFONT with caution because many users set the default text size for their browser to suit their own tastes.

3.2 Text-Level Elements: Logical Character Styles

Rather than specifying the specific font to be used, some authors prefer to describe the type of text being rendered, and let the browser decide the details of the resultant look. This may also provide additional information to automatic document indexers, but in the absence of style sheets gives the author less explicit control over the look of the document. All of these elements require start and end tags, can be nested to compose styles, and can be combined with the physical character style tags.

HTML Element: `<EM>` ... `</EM>`

Attributes: None

EM specifies that the browser emphasize the enclosed text. It is rendered in italics by most browsers.

HTML Element: `<STRONG>` ... `</STRONG>`

Attributes: None

This tells the browser to strongly emphasize the enclosed text. It is usually rendered in boldface.

HTML Element: `<CODE> ... </CODE>`

Attributes: None

The CODE element is used for excerpts from computer code. It is rendered in a fixed-width font. Don't forget that certain characters such as "<" and "&" get interpreted as HTML markup and need to be replaced with "<", "&", and so forth. See Table 2.1 for a list of these characters.

Core Alert

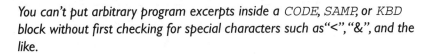

You can't put arbitrary program excerpts inside a CODE, SAMP, or KBD block without first checking for special characters such as "<", "&", and the like.

HTML Element: `<SAMP> ... </SAMP>`

Attributes: None

SAMP is used for sample program output. It is typically rendered in fixed-width font just like CODE.

HTML Element: `<KBD> ... </KBD>`

Attributes: None

This element is used for keyboard input to be entered by the user. It is typically rendered in fixed-width font just like CODE. Internet Explorer also uses boldface; Netscape doesn't.

HTML Element: `<DFN> ... </DFN>`

Attributes: None

The DFN element is used for the defining occurrence of a term. There is no consensus on how this should be rendered. For instance, Internet Explorer uses italics and Netscape Navigator uses the current character style unchanged.

HTML Element: `<VAR> ... </VAR>`

Attributes: None

VAR represents a variable or argument to a function or procedure. It is rendered in italics by Netscape and in the default font by Internet Explorer.

HTML Element: `<CITE>` ... `</CITE>`
Attributes: None.

CITE indicates that the enclosed text is a citation or reference. It is usually rendered in italics.

Listing 3.2 gives a sample of each of these character styles, with a typical result shown in Figure 3–2.

Listing 3.2   A sample of logical character styles

```
<!DOCTYPE HTML PUBLIC "-//W3C//DTD HTML 3.2//EN">
<HTML>
<HEAD>
   <TITLE>Logical Character Styles</TITLE>
</HEAD>

<BODY BGCOLOR="WHITE">
<H1>Logical Character Styles</H1>

<EM>Emphasized</EM><BR>
<STRONG>Strongly Emphasized</STRONG><BR>
<CODE>Code</CODE><BR>
<SAMP>Sample Output</SAMP><BR>
<KBD>Keyboard Text</KBD><BR>
<DFN>Definition</DFN><BR>
<VAR>Variable</VAR><BR>
<CITE>Citation</CITE><BR>
<EM><CODE>Emphasized Code</CODE></EM><BR>
<FONT COLOR="GRAY">
   <CITE>Gray Citation</CITE>
</FONT><BR>

</BODY>
</HTML>
```

HTML Element: `<SPAN ...>` ... `</SPAN>`
Attributes: CLASS, ID, STYLE

SPAN is a text-level element added to support cascading style sheets. The default behavior is to leave the enclosed text unchanged, but it is intended as a delimiter for user-defined character styles. It is discussed in Chapter 5 (Cascading Style Sheets).

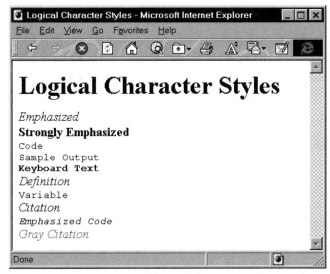

Figure 3–2 Rendering of logical character styles in Internet Explorer 3.01 on Windows 95.

3.3 Specifying Hypertext Links

One of the central ideas of HTML is that documents do not have to be read from top to bottom in a linear fashion. Instead, authors can create documents or sets of documents with links to other sections or documents, thus allowing readers to proceed in various orders based on their interests. The anchor element A allows the author to specify sections of text or images that, when selected by the reader, will transfer the browser to a specific section of a designated document. It also allows the author to name a section of the document so that other links can reference it.

HTML Element: <A ...> ... </A>
Attributes: HREF, NAME, TARGET (nonstandard), REL, REV, TITLE, ONCLICK (nonstandard), ONDBLCLICK (nonstandard), ONMOUSEOUT (nonstandard), ONMOUSEOVER (nonstandard)

The anchor element is a container with a required end tag. With HREF, the section enclosed becomes the clickable region in the resultant page. This region is often underlined and highlighted in the default link color (often blue) or the color specified by the LINK attribute of the BODY element. Links that have been visited in the current session are generally underlined and highlighted in the VLINK color. Depending how the browser's history mechanism is configured, links visited in previous sessions may be indicated this way as well.

HREF

The HREF attribute specifies the address that the browser should visit when the user clicks upon the designated region. The value can be an absolute URL, a relative URL, a pound sign followed by a section name (see the NAME attribute), or a URL followed by a pound sign followed by a section name. If a specific section is supplied, the browser transfers to that section of the designated document when the active region is selected. Otherwise the browser transfers to the top of the given document. The region enclosed by hypertext links can be inside table cells, in list elements, in various character styles, can include images, and so forth. However, Netscape Navigator has a minor bug when displaying images inside hypertext links. In most cases, when an image is part of a link, a narrow border is drawn around it (see the BORDER attribute of IMG in Section 3.4). In HTML in general, whitespace at the end of a line is collapsed to a single space, except when the following line closes the current HTML element. In such a case, the line break at the end of the previous line should be ignored. Thus,

```
<A HREF="c++-anonymous.html">
<IMG SRC="12-step.gif">
</A>
```

and

```
<A HREF="c++-anonymous.html">
<IMG SRC="12-step.gif"></A>
```

should be equivalent. In practice, however, Netscape leaves a single space in the former case, which, in conjunction with the usual convention of presenting hyperlinked text underlined, results in a single underscore appearing after the image. So the latter method should be used.

Core Approach

If an image is used as a hypertext link, be sure to put the </A> *on the same line as the* IMG *element.*

As will be explained in more detail in Chapter 16 (The HyperText Transfer Protocol), URLs that specify directories but omit the trailing slash result in the browser making two connections to the HTTP server; the first to request the original URL and the second to request the one with the trailing slash included, based on a `Location` response header from the HTTP server. This can waste time if the network connection to the referenced site is slow. So use "`http://some.host.com/ some/directory/`", not "`http://some.host.com/some/ directory`".

Core Performance Tip

If a URL specifies a directory, be sure to include the trailing slash.

For instance, Listing 3.3 shows four types of hypertext links: to an absolute URL, to a relative URL, to a section within the current document, and to a section within a specific URL. In addition to `http:` links, most browsers also support `mailto:` links (to specify an e-mail address), `file:` links (to a local file on the client machine, usually used for testing), `ftp:` links (to FTP sites), and `gopher:` links (to sites still supporting the "gopher" protocol, a predecessor to HTTP). Netscape also allows a variety of special-purpose `about:` links:

Browsing cached files

```
about:cache
about:disk-cache
about:image-cache
```

Browser Info

```
about:global
about:document
about:plug-ins
about:license
```

Logos

```
about:logo
about:javalogo
about:rsalogo
about:security?banner-secure
```

Silliness

```
about:mozilla
```

Check out the "N" logo next time you visit a page after doing
about:mozilla.

```
about:hype
about:jwz
about:marca
```

Listing 3.3   Hypertext links

```
The official HTML specifications are available from
<A HREF="http://www.w3.org/pub/WWW/MarkUp/">
the World Wide Web Consortium (W3C)</A>, with some examples
given in
<A HREF="HTML-Examples.html">my example page</A>.

The Java programming language is discussed in
<A HREF="#Section-3">Section 3</A>. For a discussion of COBOL,
see <A HREF="johndoe.html#COBOL">my husband's home page</A>.
```

Finally, a stylistic note on the use of hypertext links: It generally makes
for more readable text to have the linked text itself to be descriptive,
rather than putting the description before or after the link and having
the linked text simply be a filler such as "click here." For instance, it is
generally better to say

```
Recent Dilbert strips are available on-line at
<A HREF="http://www.unitedmedia.com/comics/dilbert/
">
The Dilbert Zone</A>.
```

than to say

```
<A HREF="http://www.unitedmedia.com/comics/dilbert/
">
Click here</A> to see recent Dilbert strips that are
available on-line at The Dilbert Zone.
```

Core Approach

*Avoid "click here" links. Instead, make the linked text descriptive enough so
users know where it goes.*

NAME

The NAME attribute gives a section a name so that other links can reference it via HREFs containing "#". For instance:

```
<A NAME="COBOL">COBOL: A Programming Language for the
Future</A>
```

Note that this name is case sensitive. Deciding when to combine sections in a single document and when to break them out into separate documents is a difficult problem. On the one hand, if the readers will want to access one section but not another, separate files can save download time. On the other hand, if the user is likely to want hardcopy, a large logical document composed of many different files is tedious for the reader to print.

TARGET

The TARGET attribute is not officially part of HTML 3.2, but allows browsers that support frames to specify that the referenced document be placed in a particular frame, or even in a new browser window. It is discussed in Chapter 4 (Frames).

TITLE

This can be used to supply a title for documents that wouldn't already have one (e.g., an FTP directory or a Gopher menu). Is used by some browsers to suggest an e-mail subject line in mailto: links, and could be used by indexing programs to build a menu of links.

REL and REV

The REL and REV attributes are used much less frequently than the other attributes. They are intended to be used to describe the relationship of the current document to the linked document (REL) or the linked document to the current one (REV) so that the browser can create a site navigation map, customize printouts, and the like.

ONCLICK, ONDBLCLICK, ONMOUSEOVER, and ONMOUSEOUT

These nonstandard attributes are used only by JavaScript-capable browsers, and are used to designate JavaScript code to be executed when the user clicks on the link, moves the mouse over a link, and moves the mouse out from over a link, respectively. See Chapter 19 (JavaScript: Adding Dynamic Content to Web Pages) for more details.

3.4 Embedded Images

DILBERT © United Feature Syndicate. Reprinted by Permission

The IMG element enables you to insert images into the document. Most browsers support GIF (Graphics Interchange Format) and JPEG (Joint Photographic Experts Group) graphics formats, but some browsers support others such as xbm, xpm, or bmp either directly or via plug-ins. In most cases, GIF images are more compact than JPEGs for images that have few color changes, such as drawings generated by graphics packages. JPEGs tend to be smaller for images with many changes, such as scanned photographs. Because image loading time can dominate the total Web page loading time, it is worth trying images both ways and checking the resulting sizes and quality if you have a graphics package that supports this. Figure 3–3 gives a typical example, where the JPEG image is less than one-third the size of the corresponding GIF.

Animated GIFs

Many browsers include support for the GIF89A standard, which allows multiple frames to be incorporated into an image file. The frames are overlaid on top of each other in a predefined cycle, resulting in a simple animation. Browsers that only support the GIF87 format but that are given an animated GIF in GIF89A format will still correctly display the first frame. An animated GIF is a good alternative to Java-based animations when the requirements are simple. Many commercial packages support the creation of animated GIFs from multiple GIF, TIFF, or other single-image formats, or by converting AVI or QuickTime movies. In addition, there are shareware and free tools available on the Web that perform many of the same tasks. Some starting places:

Figure 3–3   JPEG format is usually more compact for images derived from photographs.

Shareware: GIF Construction Set for Windows

```
http://www.mindworkshop.com/alchemy/gifcon.html
```

Freeware: GifBuilder for Macs

```
http://iawww.epfl.ch/Staff/Yves.Piguet/clip2gif-
home/GifBuilder.html
```

More tools and animated GIF collections

```
http://www.yahoo.com/Computers_and_Internet/Graph-
ics/Computer_Animation/Animated_GIFs/
```

The IMG Element

HTML Element: `<IMG SRC="..." ...>` (No End Tag)

Attributes: SRC (required), ALT, ALIGN, WIDTH, HEIGHT, HSPACE, VSPACE, BORDER, USEMAP, ISMAP, LOWSRC (nonstandard), NAME (nonstandard), ONLOAD (nonstandard), ONERROR (nonstandard), ONABORT (nonstandard)

IMG inserts an image at the current location. Note that IMG is a text-level element, and thus does not cause a paragraph break. IMG is not a container and has no end tag.

SRC

This required attribute specifies the location of the image file to be inserted. The URL can be either an absolute or a relative one. For instance:

```
<IMG SRC="http://www.some-isp.com/~jane/portrait.jpg"
    ALT="Jane Doe">
<IMG SRC="images/biff.gif"
    ALT="My dog Biff">
```

ALT

ALT designates a string to display to text-only browsers, browsers with graphics temporarily disabled, or temporarily in regular browsers if text is loaded before images. Although not formally required, it is a good idea to always include alternate text.

ALIGN

The ALIGN attribute specifies the position of the image with respect to the line of text in which it occurs. Possible values are LEFT, RIGHT, TOP, BOTTOM, and MIDDLE, with BOTTOM being the default. The LEFT and RIGHT values allow the text to flow around the image, and are generally used when the image is being used as an "illustration." If you use LEFT or RIGHT alignment and do not want text to appear beside the image, use `<BR CLEAR="ALL">`. See Section 3.7 (Contolling Line Breaks). Using MIDDLE is useful when a small image is being used as a "bullet." Listing 3.4 gives an example of each of the alignment options, with the result shown in Figure 3–4.

Listing 3.4   Image-Alignment.html

```
<!DOCTYPE HTML PUBLIC "-//W3C//DTD HTML 3.2//EN">
<HTML>
<HEAD>
  <TITLE>Image Alignment</TITLE>
</HEAD>

<BODY>
<H1 ALIGN="CENTER">Image Alignment</H1>

<TABLE BORDER=1>
  <TR><TH>Alignment
      <TH>Result
  <TR><TH><CODE>LEFT</CODE>
      <TD><IMG SRC="rude-pc.gif" ALIGN="LEFT"
              ALT="Rude PC" WIDTH=54 HEIGHT=77>
          This positions the image at the left side,
          with text flowing around it on the right.
          This option was not available in HTML 2.0.
  <TR><TH><CODE>RIGHT</CODE>
      <TD><IMG SRC="rude-pc.gif" ALIGN="RIGHT"
              ALT="Rude PC" WIDTH=54 HEIGHT=77>
          This positions the image at the right side,
          with text flowing around it on the left.
          This option was not available in HTML 2.0.
<TR><TH><CODE>TOP</CODE>
      <TD><IMG SRC="rude-pc.gif" ALIGN="TOP"
              ALT="Rude PC" WIDTH=54 HEIGHT=77>
          Here, the image runs into the paragraph
          and the line containing the image is
          aligned with the image top.
<TR><TH><CODE>BOTTOM</CODE>
      <TD><IMG SRC="rude-pc.gif" ALIGN="BOTTOM"
              ALT="Rude PC" WIDTH=54 HEIGHT=77>
          Here, the image runs into the paragraph
          and the line containing the image is aligned
          with the image bottom.
  <TR><TH><CODE>MIDDLE</CODE>
      <TD><IMG SRC="rude-pc.gif" ALIGN="MIDDLE"
              ALT="Rude PC" WIDTH=54 HEIGHT=77>
          Here, the image runs into the paragraph
          and the line containing the image is aligned
          with the image bottom.
</TABLE>

</BODY>
</HTML>
```

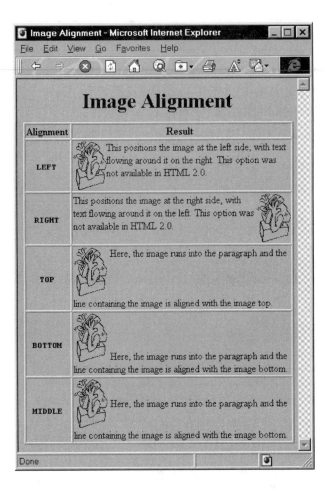

Figure 3–4   There are five ways to align images.

WIDTH and HEIGHT

These attributes specify the intended size of the image in pixels. Providing a WIDTH and HEIGHT allows many browsers to load the text first then come back and insert the image without rearranging any of the rest of the page, giving a much more pleasing result to the reader. This can also significantly speed up the loading of tables that contain images. If you load an image file directly in Netscape, choosing "Document Info" from the "View" menu will tell you the dimensions of the image. Unfortunately, there is no similar option in Internet Explorer, but any image processing or paint package will give this information. Note that if you

supply dimensions different than the original image dimensions, the
image will be stretched or shrunk to fit.

Core Approach

Always supply *ALT, WIDTH,* and *HEIGHT* attributes for images.

HSPACE and VSPACE

These attributes stipulate the number of empty pixels to leave on the
left and right (HSPACE) or top and bottom (VSPACE) of the image. The
default is usually about two. HTML 3.2 does not support methods for
overlapping images or overlaying them with text, but this can be done
by using negative margins with cascading style sheets. See Chapter 5 for
details.

BORDER

BORDER designates the width of the border to draw around the image
when it is part of a hypertext link. The default is usually about two.

USEMAP

USEMAP supplies the name of a MAP entry, specified as "#name" or
"URL#name". See Section 3.5 for explanation and an example.

ISMAP

ISMAP causes the image to be used as a server-side image map connected to a CGI program. Only legal when the image is part of a hypertext link. See Chapter 17, "CGI Programming and Beyond—The Client
Side."

LOWSRC

LOWSRC is a Netscape extension that allows the user to give the URL of
a low-resolution image to be loaded before the main image (specified
via SRC), so that the user can get the preliminary look of the page
before the slower, high-resolution images are done loading. Although
this attribute is not supported by Internet Explorer or most other
browsers, it is worth remembering that nonstandard attributes are simply ignored by browsers that do not support them.

NAME

The NAME attribute is not part of HTML 3.2, and is used by browsers that support JavaScript to give a name that can be used by JavaScript to refer to the image.

ONLOAD, ONERROR, and ONABORT

These attributes are extensions for JavaScript-enabled browsers. They are used to specify code to be executed when the image is loaded, when an error occurs in loading the image, and when the user terminates image loading before completion, respectively.

3.5 Client-Side Image Maps: Creating Clickable Regions in Embedded Images

HTML Element: `<MAP NAME="...">` ... `</MAP>`
Attributes: NAME (required)

The MAP element enables the author to designate client-side image maps and is new in HTML 3.2. This enables the author to associate URLs with different regions of an image, a useful capability for creating toolbars and navigation images as well as for more traditional maps. These image maps are processed entirely in the user's browser, as opposed to the server-side image maps provided by ISMAP or the image INPUT type (both described in Chapter 17, "CGI Programming and Beyond—The Client Side"), which require communication with the server to determine the action to take. The NAME attribute is required, and provides a target for the USEMAP attribute of the IMG element. Each of the clickable regions is described by an AREA element appearing inside between the start and end MAP tags. Listing 3.5 gives an example that divides an image into four quadrants with an HTML document associated with each. Results in Mosaic before and after clicking in the southeast corner are shown in Figures 3–5 and 3–6.

Listing 3.5 An image map

```
<!DOCTYPE HTML PUBLIC "-//W3C//DTD HTML 3.2//EN">
<HTML>
<HEAD>
  <TITLE>Kansas Topography</TITLE>
</HEAD>

<BODY>
<H1 ALIGN="CENTER">Kansas Topography</H1>
Click on a region of Kansas to get information on
the terrain in that area.
<P>
<IMG SRC="kansas.gif" ALT="Kansas" WIDTH=385 HEIGHT=170
     USEMAP="#Kansas" BORDER=0>
<MAP NAME="Kansas">
  <AREA HREF="nw.html"
        SHAPE="RECT"
        COORDS="0,0,192,85"
        ALT="North West">
  <AREA HREF="ne.html"
        SHAPE="RECT"
        COORDS="193,0,385,85"
        ALT="North East">
  <AREA HREF="sw.html"
        SHAPE="RECT"
        COORDS="0,86,192,170"
        ALT="South West">
  <AREA HREF="se.html"
        SHAPE="RECT"
        COORDS="193,86,385,170"
        ALT="South East">
</MAP>
</BODY>
</HTML>
```

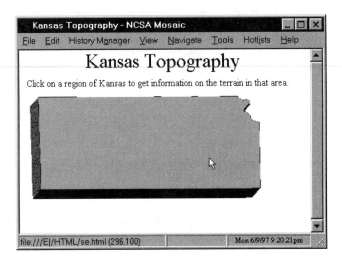

Figure 3–5   Client-side image maps allow you to associate Web pages with various parts of an image.

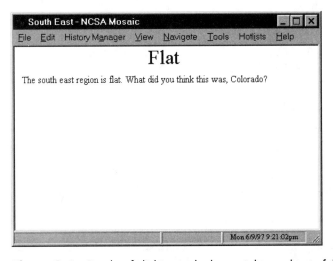

Figure 3–6   Results of clicking in the lower-right quadrant of the map of Figure 3–5.

HTML Element: `<AREA ALT="..." ...>` (No End Tag)

Attributes: HREF, SHAPE, COORDS, ALT (required), NOHREF, TARGET (nonstandard), ONMOUSEOVER (nonstandard), ONMOUSEOUT (nonstandard)

The AREA element can only appear inside a MAP element, and describes a clickable region in an image map. One AREA entry is used for each region and describes the location of the hot zone, the destination URL, and a textual description normally displayed by the browser in the status line when the mouse or cursor moves over the designated region. If regions overlap, the first region specified takes precedence.

HREF

The HREF attribute specifies the target document, and as is typical with URLs, it can be absolute or relative and can include a section name following a "#".

COORDS

COORDS is used to supply a comma-separated list of the coordinates of the particular region. The number and interpretation of coordinates expected depends on the SHAPE attribute (see examples in following section). The coordinates should be integers and are interpreted as pixels relative to the top left corner of the image. The HTML 3.2 specification indicates that values can also be represented as percentages of the image size, but this is not supported in Netscape or Internet Explorer.

SHAPE

The SHAPE attribute should be one of RECT (the default shape), CIRCLE, POLY, or DEFAULT (Netscape only). Except for the DEFAULT value, it should be followed by a COORDS entry supplying coordinates appropriate to that type of region. The RECT entry should have associated coordinates in a comma-separated string of the form "left, top, right, bottom." For instance, the following associates region3.html with a 200x200 area whose top-left corner is at (20,40).

```
<AREA HREF="region3.html"
      SHAPE="RECT"
      COORDS="20,40,220,240">
```

The CIRCLE entry takes a COORDS string of the form "x, y, radius," and the POLY entry takes a string of the form "$x_1, y_1, x_2, y_2, ... , x_n, y_n$" giving the vertices of the bounding polygon. The DEFAULT entry has no associated COORDS, and indicates the entire image. Since DEFAULT is specific to Netscape, if a default entry is desired a better alternative is to simply include an AREA element that encloses the entire map. The URL belonging to overlapping regions is determined by the first AREA element enclosing it. Thus, the default entry should always come last, whether or not it explicitly uses DEFAULT.

ALT

The ALT attribute supplies a string describing the destination URL. It is often shown by the browser in the status line when the mouse moves over the associated hot zone.

NOHREF

The NOHREF attribute designates a region with no associated URL. It is only needed if you want to turn off part of a region that would otherwise be active based on some other AREA entry. Because the action associated with more than one AREA is determined by the first AREA entry, NOHREF entries should always come first.

Core Approach

Because the URL of areas in multiple regions is determined by the first applicable AREA element, NOHREF entries should come first in a MAP element, and the entry for the default URL should come last.

TARGET

The TARGET attribute, used by frame-enabled browsers, designates the target frame in which to show the results. Frames are particularly prevalent for documents that use image maps; see the discussion of frames in Chapter 4 for details.

ONMOUSEOVER and ONMOUSEOUT

This attribute, supported only by JavaScript-enabled browsers, designates JavaScript code to be executed when the user moves the mouse cursor on and off the area, respectively.

3.6 Embedding Other Objects in Documents

Although there are a few text-only browsers, most current browsers support embedding image files. But these are not the only kind of objects that can be placed in Web pages. Java applets are supported by most major browsers, although they are still not as pervasively supported as images. Other audio, video, VRML, and ActiveX objects typically depend on the user having a specific plug in or are browser specific.

Embedded Java Programs

HTML Element: `<APPLET CODE="..." WIDTH=xxx`
                                         `HEIGHT=xxx ...>`
                  `... </APPLET>`

Attributes: CODE (required), WIDTH (required), HEIGHT (required), CODEBASE, ALT, ALIGN, HSPACE, VSPACE, NAME, OBJECT (nonstandard), ARCHIVE (nonstandard), MAYSCRIPT (nonstandard)

The APPLET tag enables you to embed a Java program into a page. It is discussed in Chapter 17 (CGI Programming and Beyond—The Client Side).

CODE

CODE designates the filename of the Java class file to load. This is not an absolute URL; it is interpreted with respect to the current document's default directory unless CODEBASE is supplied. It is required in JDK 1.02 and in JDK 1.1.1 unless OBJECT is present.

Core Note

CODE cannot be used to give an absolute URL. Use CODEBASE *if you want to load applets from someplace other than the current document's location.*

WIDTH, HEIGHT

These attributes specify the size of the area the applet will occupy. They can be specified in pixels or as a percentage of the browser window width. However, Sun's "appletviewer" (a lightweight pseudobrowser that ignores all the HTML except for the APPLET part) cannot handle percentages because there is no preexisting window for the percentage to refer to. WIDTH and HEIGHT are required in all applets.

Core Alert

Sun's appletviewer cannot handle WIDTH *and* HEIGHT *attributes as percentages.*

CODEBASE

The base URL. The entry in CODE is taken with respect to this directory.

ALT

Java-enabled browsers ignore markup between <APPLET ...> and </APPLET>, so alternative text for these browsers is normally placed there. The ALT attribute was intended for browsers that support Java but have it disabled, but is not widely supported. I recommend avoiding it.

ALIGN

This specifies alignment options, and has the same possible values and interpretation of values as the IMG element (Section 3.4).

HSPACE

HSPACE specifies the empty space at the left and right of the applet in pixels.

VSPACE

VSPACE specifies the empty space at the top and bottom of the applet in pixels.

NAME

NAME gives a name to the applet. Used in Java for inter-applet communication and by JavaScript to reference an applet by name instead of using an index in the applet's array.

OBJECT

The OBJECT attribute can be used to supply a serialized applet that was saved using JDK 1.1.1's object serialization facility.

ARCHIVE

ARCHIVE is used in JDK 1.1.1 and by some 1.02 browsers to specify an archive of class files to be preloaded. The archive eventually will be in Java Archive (.jar) format, but Netscape 3.01 allows *uncompressed* Zip (.zip) archives.

MAYSCRIPT

This attribute is used by Netscape 2 and 4 to indicate that the applet can be controlled from JavaScript. For details see Chapter 19, "Java-Script: Adding Dynamic Content to Web Pages."

HTML Element: `<PARAM NAME="..." VALUE="...">` (No End Tag)

Attributes: NAME (required), VALUE (required).

This supplies customization values to the Java applet, which can read them by using `getParameter`. Note that a PARAM name of WIDTH or HEIGHT overrides the WIDTH and HEIGHT values in the APPLET tag. So you should avoid `<PARAM NAME="WIDTH" ...>` and `<PARAM NAME="HEIGHT" ...>`.

Core Alert

Never use WIDTH or HEIGHT as PARAM names.

Embedding Video, Audio, and Other Formats via Plug Ins

HTML Element: `<EMBED SRC="..." ...> ... </EMBED>`
Attributes: SRC, WIDTH, HEIGHT, *Plugin-Specific-Attributes*

The EMBED element can be used to create in-line objects of types supported by plug ins for a particular browser. Text inside the element is ignored by browsers that support plug ins. In addition to the standard SRC, WIDTH, and HEIGHT attributes, there can be additional attributes particular to a specific plug in. For instance, both Netscape and Internet Explorer have standard plug ins such as LiveVideo that support the playing of video clips in AVI format. These plug ins support an additional attribute of AUTOSTART with values of TRUE or FALSE that determines if the movie should begin playing automatically when the page is loaded or wait until the user clicks on it (the default). For instance, the following would embed a video file in browsers with an appropriate plug in that would begin playing only when the user clicks on it:

```
<EMBED SRC="martian-invasion.avi"
       WIDTH=120 HEIGHT=90>
```

A large list of free and for-fee plug ins, along with usage descriptions and EMBED attributes supported, can be found at:

```
http://home.netscape.com/comprod/products/navigator/
version_2.0/plugins/index.html.
```

Highlights include support for VRML, QuickTime, streaming audio, Adobe Acrobat files, PNG images, and more.

Embedding ActiveX Controls

HTML Element: `<OBJECT CLASSID="..." ...> ...`
                        `</OBJECT>`
Attributes: CLASSID, CODEBASE, ALIGN, BORDER, WIDTH, HEIGHT,
                HSPACE, VSPACE, STANDBY, TITLE

Internet Explorer allows authors to embed any ActiveX control in a Web page. Customization parameters are supplied via PARAM elements, just as with Java applets. Due to security concerns, readers shouldn't allow arbitrary controls to be downloaded, but certain controls are bundled with Internet Explorer, and third-party controls can be digitally signed to verify their source. Of course, just because a component comes from an official source doesn't guarantee that it won't (perhaps accidentally) do damage to the local system. Consequently, many users are reluctant to allow any ActiveX controls to be downloaded to their machine, and Web pages with such controls shouldn't be considered portable even to readers using Internet Explorer. However, third-party ActiveX controls can be *very* useful for trusted intranet environments. The most important attributes are as follows.

CLASSID
This specifies the URL. For registered controls, it is of the form "clsid:*class-identifier*".

CODEBASE
This specifies the directory from which to load, just like the CODEBASE attribute of APPLET.

ALIGN, BORDER, WIDTH, HEIGHT, HSPACE, VSPACE

These attributes are used exactly the same way as they are for the IMG element. See Section 3.4 (Embedded Images).

STANDBY

This supplies a string to be displayed while the object is loading.

A wide variety of third-party ActiveX controls can be found at Microsoft's ActiveX Component Gallery at `http://www.microsoft.com/activex/gallery/`. The controls bundled with Internet Explorer release 3.0 include:

- **Label**. Displays text in an arbitrary font at a specified angle or along a curve.

- **Marquee**. Creates scrolling, sliding, or bouncing text. See the MARQUEE element in the following section.

- **Menu**. Displays a menu button or pull-down menu.

- **Popup Menu**. Displays a popup menu whenever the PopUp method is called (e.g., from a script).

- **Popup Window**. Displays HTML in lightweight popup windows.

- **Preloader**. Loads a URL in advance and places it in the browser cache for fast display at a later time.

- **Stock Ticker**. Displays changing data in a scrolling format.

- **Timer**. Invokes an event at predefined intervals.

The customization parameters each of these accepts is described in the Microsoft ActiveX programming reference, available at

```
http://www.microsoft.com/workshop/prog/
default.asp#activex
```

As an example, Listing 3.6 uses the Caption, Angle, Alignment, BackStyle, FontName, FontBold, and FontSize PARAM values to control various aspects of the appearance of a Label control. The result is shown in Figure 3–7.

Listing 3.6 `ActiveX.html`

```html
<!DOCTYPE HTML PUBLIC "-//W3C//DTD HTML 3.2//EN">
<HTML>
<HEAD>
  <TITLE>Embedding ActiveX Controls</TITLE>
</HEAD>

<BODY>
<H1 ALIGN="CENTER">Embedding ActiveX Controls</H1>

<OBJECT
  CLASSID="clsid:99B42120-6EC7-11CF-A6C7-00AA00A47DD2"
  WIDTH=275
  HEIGHT=275
  VSPACE=0
  ALIGN="LEFT"
>
  <PARAM NAME="Caption" VALUE="ActiveX">
  <PARAM NAME="Angle" VALUE="45">
  <PARAM NAME="Alignment" VALUE="2">
  <PARAM NAME="BackStyle" VALUE="0">
  <PARAM NAME="FontName" VALUE="Arial">
  <PARAM NAME="FontBold" VALUE="1">
  <PARAM NAME="FontSize" VALUE="50">
</OBJECT>

Microsoft Internet Explorer lets authors embed
ActiveX controls in Web pages. The following
controls are bundled with I.E. release 3:
<UL>
  <LI><B>Label.</B> Display text at any angle.
  <LI><B>Marquee.</B> Slide, scroll, or bounce text.
  <LI><B>Menu.</B> Menu button or pull-down menu.
  <LI><B>Popup Menu.</B> Triggered by PopUp method.
  <LI><B>Popup Window.</B> Displays HTML docs.
  <LI><B>Preloader.</B> Preload docs into browser cache.
  <LI><B>Stock Ticker.</B> Display changing data.
  <LI><B>Timer.</B> Invoke events periodically.
</UL>

</BODY>
</HTML>
```

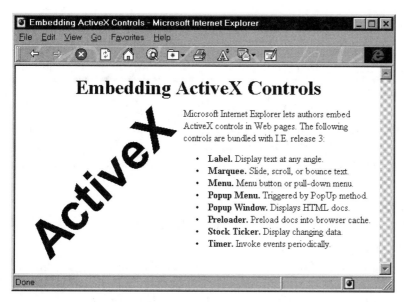

Figure 3–7 Using the bundled Label control.

Scrolling Text Banners

HTML Element: `<MARQUEE ...> ... </MARQUEE>`

Attributes: WIDTH, HEIGHT, ALIGN, BEHAVIOR, BGCOLOR, DIRECTION, HSPACE, VSPACE, LOOP, SCROLLAMOUNT, SCROLLDELAY

This is an Internet Explorer extension that displays the text enclosed between the start (`<MARQUEE ...>`) and end (`</MARQUEE>`) tags in a scrolling banner, or "marquee." Text-level markup is not allowed inside MARQUEE, but a MARQUEE element can be embedded inside markup such as a FONT element to give, for instance, large, scrolling, blue text. Browsers other than Internet Explorer will ignore the MARQUEE tags and treat the enclosed text as part of the current paragraph. It should be used with caution not only because it is unsupported in Netscape and other browsers, but because scrolling text can be distracting to readers. However, it certainly serves to catch the reader's attention. You can simply use `<MARQUEE>` as the start tag, or can supply one of the following attributes to customize the behavior.

WIDTH, HEIGHT

These attributes define the width and height for the marquee region, either in pixels or as a percentage of the Internet Explorer window's size. The default width is 100% and the default height is based on the current font.

ALIGN

This specifies how the marquee should be aligned with respect to the surrounding text. Legal values are LEFT, RIGHT, CENTER, TOP, BOTTOM, MIDDLE, and they are used in exactly the same way as in the IMG element.

BEHAVIOR

This attribute describes how the text should move. SCROLL, the default, means that the text should scroll in one direction until off the screen, then repeat. SLIDE means that the text should scroll until it reaches one side, then stop. BOUNCE means that it should alternate back and forth within the defined region.

BGCOLOR

BGCOLOR defines the background color of the region.

DIRECTION

This attribute specifies the direction in which the text scrolls (or first scrolls, in the case of BEHAVIOR="BOUNCE"). Legal values are LEFT (from right to left) and RIGHT (from left to right). LEFT is the default.

HSPACE, VSPACE

These attributes give the amount of horizontal and vertical space (in pixels) around the region.

LOOP

This specifies how many times the scrolling will repeat. A value of –1 or INFINITE means that it will repeat indefinitely, and is the default.

SCROLLAMOUNT

SCROLLAMOUNT specifies the number of pixels between each successive drawing of the text.

SCROLLDELAY

SCROLLDELAY specifies the number of milliseconds between each successive drawing.

3.7 Controlling Line Breaks

When displaying most types of text, line breaks are inserted by the browser to fit the available space. In Section 2.2 (Basic Text Sections), you saw the PRE tag that set a fixed-width font and turned off word wrapping for an entire paragraph. In addition to this, HTML lets you insert explicit line breaks via the BR tag and prevent line breaks by the use of either non-breaking spaces or the non-standard but widely supported NOBR tag.

HTML Element: `<BR ...>` (No End Tag)
Attributes: CLEAR

BR inserts a line break without ending the current paragraph. Because carriage returns in the HTML source are ignored except within a few special elements such as PRE or TEXTAREA, BR is necessary to guarantee a line break in the resultant page. The CLEAR attribute, with possible values LEFT, RIGHT, and ALL, allows you to skip down past floating images at the left or right margins. On most browsers, including Netscape Navigator and Microsoft Internet Explorer, multiple consecutive <BR> tags result in extra blank lines (unlike consecutive empty <P> tags). However, this is not true of all browsers. For instance, Mosaic 3.0 generates only a single line break in such a case.

HTML Element: `<NOBR> ... </NOBR>`
Attributes: None

This element is not part of HTML 3.2, but is supported by Netscape version 2.0 and later and Internet Explorer version 3.0 and later. It suppresses word wrapping for the enclosed text, except possibly at places indicated by WBR. The same effect can be obtained in standard HTML 3.2 by using non-breaking spaces ( ) between each word in the region of interest.

HTML Element: `<WBR>` (No End Tag)
Attributes: None

This element, which should be used only inside a NOBR element, indicates that a line break can be placed there if necessary. It is not part of HTML 3.2, but is typically supported by browsers that support NOBR.

3.8 Summary

Text-level elements let you specify character styles, line breaks, and hypertext links in paragraphs in a Web page. You can also embed images, either purely as static graphics, as a hypertext link, or with multiple hypertext links associated with different regions of the image. Finally, depending on your browser, you can embed Java applets, audio, video, Adobe Acrobat files, VRML, or ActiveX components. The following two chapters cover extensions to HTML 3.2 that let you go further. In Chapter 4 we will look at frames, a capability that allows you to divide the Web page into rectangular regions and load a separate HTML document in each region. Finally, in Chapter 5 we discuss cascading style sheets, which give you much more control over the fonts, indentation, and style used for the various block-level and text-level elements.

FRAMES

Topics in This Chapter

- The basic structure of framed documents
- Specifying how the main browser window is divided
- Supplying the content of each of the frame cells
- Specifying that certain hypertext links be displayed in particular frames
- Using the pre-assigned frame names
- Solving common frame problems
- Using inline (floating) frames

Chapter 4

Frames let you divide the current window into various rectangular cells, each associated with a separate HTML document. They were first developed by Netscape Corporation for use in Navigator 2.0, and although they are not part of HTML 3.2, they are now supported by Internet Explorer (version 3.0 and later) and several other browsers in addition to Netscape. However, they remain somewhat controversial because they provide significant capabilities not obtainable with other HTML constructs but have some significant drawbacks as well. There are quite a few advantages:

- The author can guarantee that certain parts of the interface (e.g., a table of contents) are always on the screen.
- The author can avoid retyping common sections of multiple Web pages. Instead, the same document can be included in a frame in each of the Web pages.
- Consistent use across a large site sometimes simplifies user navigation.
- They are a convenient way to mix text-oriented HTML with Java applets.
- Image maps are more convenient if the map image remains on screen and only the results section changes.

As a result, some users *love* frames, and prefer pages that use them. However, frames have quite a few disadvantages:

- The meaning of the "Back" and "Forward" buttons can be confusing to users.

- Poorly designed frames can get the user lost.

- Because the address bar at the top of the document shows the URL of the *top-level document*, it can be hard to find the URL of a particular *frame cell* when they want to remember or bookmark it.

- Because a bookmark (favorite) can only specify a particular URL, users cannot save a particular frame *configuration* (i.e., the way the document looks after several selections).

- Some browsers do not support frames, and it is difficult to create framed documents that are usable by nonframes-capable browsers.

- Framed documents cannot yet be validated by SGML-based validators due to inconsistent syntax.

As a result, some users *hate* frames and strongly prefer pages that do not use them. Although this chapter will help you avoid many of the disadvantages of frames, a good rule of thumb is to reserve frames for situations where:

- All users will be using a frames-capable browser (e.g., in an intranet application), or

- The advantages provided by frames are significant enough that you are willing to risk losing the readers that are using non-frames-capable browsers or dislike frames.

Although no official standard for frames existed at the time this book was published, a working draft of a proposed specification similar to what Netscape and Internet Explorer support in versions 3 and 4 can be found at `http://www.w3.org/pub/WWW/TR/WD-frames`.

4.1 Frame Document Template

In a normal HTML document, the BODY section immediately follows the HEAD and contains the body of the Web page that the user sees. In a frames document, the BODY is omitted or relegated to a NOFRAMES section only seen by nonframes browsers. In lieu of BODY, a FRAMESET element is used to define the basic row and column structure of the document. Listing 4.1 gives a basic template illustrating this structure. This FRAMESET can contain nested FRAMESETs that further subdivide the window, or FRAME elements that reference the URLs of the actual documents that will be displayed in the frame cells. Because frames are not part of the HTML 3.2 specification, the HTML 3.2 DOCTYPE declaration should be omitted. An alternate declaration for the Netscape or Internet Explorer specification could be substituted, but is often omitted because top-level frame documents cannot be validated by most validators due to inconsistent syntax. However, the HTML documents that appear *inside* the frame cells can be standard HTML 3.2 documents, and can be validated in the usual way except that they may contain some non-HTML-3.2 TARGET attributes.

Listing 4.1   Template for frame documents

```
<HTML>
<HEAD>
  <TITLE>Document Title</TITLE>
</HEAD>

<FRAMESET ...>
  <!-- FRAME and Nested FRAMESET Entries -->
  <NOFRAMES>
    <BODY>
      <!-- Stuff for non-frames browsers -->
    </BODY>
  </NOFRAMES>
</FRAMESET>

</HTML>
```

4.2 Specifying Frame Layout

The FRAMESET element defines the number and size of frame cells in a page.

HTML Element: <FRAMESET ...> ... </FRAMESET>
Attributes: ROWS, COLS, FRAMEBORDER, BORDER, FRAMESPACING, BORDERCOLOR, ONFOCUS, ONBLUR, ONLOAD, ONUNLOAD

FRAMESET divides the current window or frame cell into rows or columns. Entries can be nested, letting you divide the window into complex rectangular regions. Because frames are not yet part of any official standard, the attributes supported vary even among vendors that purport to support frames. ROWS and COLS are basic to frames, and are supported wherever frames are. FRAMEBORDER is supported by both Netscape and Internet Explorer in versions 3.0 and later. The other attributes are supported either by Netscape or Internet Explorer, but not both. So for applications where the user's browser is not known in advance, the other attributes should be used with caution.

ROWS

The ROWS attribute is used to divide the browser window (or current cell, in the case of nested frames) horizontally, as used below.

```
<FRAMESET ROWS="Row1-Size, ... , RowN-Size">
   ...
</FRAMESET>
```

This divides the current window or frame cell into *N* rows. Each size entry can be an integer (representing absolute pixels), an integer followed by "%" (indicating percentage of total available space), or an entry containing "*". The "*" indicates "whatever space is left," and can be weighted by placing an integer in front if there is more than one such entry. For instance:

```
<FRAMESET ROWS="50,10%,*,2*">
   ...
</FRAMESET>
```

This indicates that there will be four rows. The first will be 50 pixels high, the second will be 10% of the total height, and the remaining space will be allocated to the last two rows, with the third row getting one third of it and the fourth getting two thirds (see Figure 4–1).

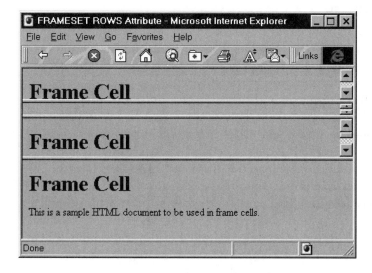

Figure 4-1   A frame document with a row specification of "50,10%,*,2*".

As can be seen in Figure 4–1, small frame cells can result in sections that are hard or impossible to read, and you should keep in mind the possibility that the reader might use different sized windows or fonts than the ones you normally use. One of either ROWS or COLS is required. Finally, note that ROWS values should always have at least two entries or it will not display properly in Netscape. See Section 4.6 for more details.

Core Alert

FRAMESET entries should always specify at least two rows or columns.

COLS

This attribute divides the current window or frame cell vertically; the syntax is the same as for the ROWS attribute. Like the ROWS attribute, it can appear at the top level or within another cell that was specified via FRAMESET. COL values should always have at least two entries; there is no need to wrap FRAMESET around a single FRAME entry, and in fact doing so can cause incorrect results (see Section 4.6). One of either ROWS or COLS is required.

FRAMEBORDER

This attribute indicates whether borders will be drawn between frame
cells. The default is to use borders. FRAMEBORDER=0 is often used in
conjuction with BORDER=0 and FRAMESPACING=0. The FRAME-
BORDER setting for the overall FRAMESET can be overridden by
FRAMEBORDER settings in individual FRAME entries or in nested
FRAMESETs. Netscape 3.0 and later accepts YES or 1 to indicate that
borders should be shown, and NO or 0 to indicate that no borders
should be used. Internet Explorer version 3 accepts only 1 and 0 to
indicate to turn borders on and off. Netscape 2 supports frames
(unlike Internet Explorer 2) but not the FRAMEBORDER attribute. So,
while there is no option that works across all frame-capable platforms,
the most portable option is to use 1 to turn on borders, and 0 to turn
them off. As an example, Listings 4.2 and 4.3 show the source for two
framed documents that are identical except for the FRAMEBORDER
value. Figures 4–2 and 4–3 show the results.

Listing 4.2   Frame-Borders.html

```
<HTML>
<HEAD>
  <TITLE>Frames with Borders</TITLE>
</HEAD>

<FRAMESET ROWS="40%,60%">
  <FRAME SRC="Frame-Cell.html">

  <FRAMESET COLS="*,*">
    <FRAME SRC="Frame-Cell.html">
    <FRAME SRC="Frame-Cell.html">
  </FRAMESET>

  <NOFRAMES>
    <BODY>
      Your browser does not support frames. Please see
      <A HREF="Frame-Cell.html">non-frames version</A>.
    </BODY>
  </NOFRAMES>
</FRAMESET>

</HTML>
```

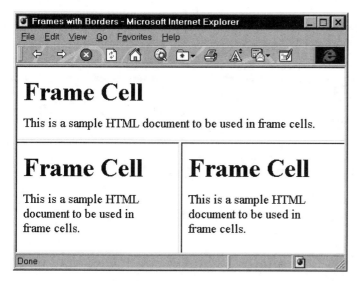

Figure 4–2   By default, 3D borders are drawn between frame cells.

Listing 4.3   `Frame-Borderless.html`

```
<HTML>
<HEAD>
  <TITLE>Borderless Frames</TITLE>
</HEAD>

<FRAMESET ROWS="40%,60%" FRAMEBORDER=0
                         BORDER=0 FRAMESPACING=0>
  <FRAME SRC="Frame-Cell.html">

  <FRAMESET COLS="*,*">
    <FRAME SRC="Frame-Cell.html">
    <FRAME SRC="Frame-Cell.html">
  </FRAMESET>

  <NOFRAMES>
    <BODY>
      Your browser does not support frames. Please see
      <A HREF="Frame-Cell.html">non-frames version</A>.
    </BODY>
  </NOFRAMES>
</FRAMESET>

</HTML>
```

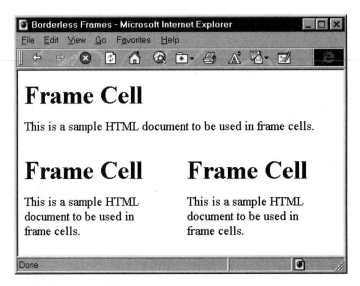

Figure 4–3   The 3D border between frame cells can be suppressed by using the FRAMEBORDER attribute.

BORDER (Netscape 3), FRAMESPACING (Internet Explorer)
These attributes specify the thickness of the border between cells. They apply to the outermost FRAMESET only. The default is 5.

BORDERCOLOR
BORDERCOLOR sets the color of the border between cells. The default is to use a 3D shadowed version of the background color. They can be overridden by BORDERCOLOR in FRAME entries or in a nested FRAMESET. BORDERCOLOR is available only in Netscape 3.0 and later.

ONFOCUS, ONBLUR
These attributes designate JavaScript code to be executed when the frame gains/loses the input focus. They are supported only in Netscape 3.0 and later. Although attribute names are always case insensitive in HTML, it is traditional in JavaScript to call them onFocus and onBlur rather than ONFOCUS and ONBLUR.

ONLOAD, ONUNLOAD
These specify JavaScript code to be executed when the frameset is loaded and unloaded (i.e., when the user enters and exits the page). They are supported by most JavaScript-capable browsers (e.g. Netscape 2.0x and 3.0x, Internet Explorer 3.0x), not just Netscape 3.0. These attributes are usually called onLoad and onUnload in JavaScript.

4.3 Specifying the Content of Frame Cells

HTML Element: `<FRAME SRC="..." ...>` **(No End Tag)**
Attributes: SRC, NAME, FRAMEBORDER, BORDERCOLOR,
              MARGINWIDTH, MARGINHEIGHT, SCROLLING, NORESIZE

The FRAME element designates the HTML document that will be placed in a particular frame cell. FRAME entries are legal only inside FRAMESET containers.

SRC

SRC specifies the URL of the document to be placed in the current cell. It is not strictly required, as you are permitted empty frames. However, to avoid unexpected results, SRC should be treated as required in Netscape Navigator versions 2 and 3. See Section 4.6 for more details.

Core Alert

FRAME entries with NAME but no SRC give unexpected results in Netscape.

NAME

This attribute gives a name to the current cell. The TARGET attribute of A, BASE, AREA, and FORM can then be used to display new documents in the cell. See Section 4.4 for details. Similarly, a showDocument call in Java can supply a second argument with the cell name. The name must be begin with an alphanumeric character, but there are four predefined cell names that begin with an underscore. More details on these predefined names can be found in Section 4.5.

FRAMEBORDER

FRAMEBORDER specifies whether or not the 3D border between cells is drawn. A FRAMEBORDER entry in an individual FRAME overrides that of the enclosing FRAMESET, with the proviso that a border is omitted only if adjacent cells also have FRAMEBORDER turned off. Netscape 3.0 and later accepts YES or 1 to indicate that borders should be shown, and NO or 0 to indicate that no borders should be used. Internet Explorer version 3 accepts only 1 and 0 to indicate to turn borders on and off. Netscape 2 supports frames (unlike Internet Explorer 2) but not the FRAMEBORDER attribute.

BORDERCOLOR

This attribute, supported only by Netscape in Navigator 3.0 and later, determines the color of the frame's borders, and can be a color name or a hex RGB value (see Table 1.1). When colors conflict at shared borders, the innermost definition wins, with Netscape resolving ties in an unspecified fashion.

MARGINWIDTH

MARGINWIDTH specifies the left and right cell margins.

MARGINHEIGHT

MARGINHEIGHT specifies the top and bottom cell margins.

SCROLLING

This attribute specifies whether cells should have scrollbars. In Netscape, YES results in cell always having scrollbars, and AUTO (the default) means that a cell should have scrollbars only if the associated HTML document doesn't fit in the allocated space. In Internet Explorer, YES (the default) means the same as AUTO in Netscape. NO disables scrollbars in both cases.

NORESIZE

By default, the user can resize frame cells by dragging the border between cells. NORESIZE disables this.

HTML Element: `<NOFRAMES>` ... `</NOFRAMES>`
Attributes: None

A browser that supports frames will ignore text inside the NOFRAMES container. However, the text will be shown by other browsers, which simply ignore the `<NOFRAMES>` and `</NOFRAMES>` tags, just like all other unrecognized tags. The text and markup inside a NOFRAMES element can be used to give a nonframes version of the page, or to supply links to a separate nonframe version or the "main" cell of the document. Inflammatory alternate text like

```
<NOFRAMES>
Your browser doesn't support frames.
Get a <B>real</B> browser.
</NOFRAMES>
```

y be amusing (we hackers are easily amused), but not particularly helpful. Despite the presence of NOFRAMES, maintaining equivalent nonframes versions can be quite time consuming, so many authors don't bother. Even if you do, be aware that it is not completely transparent to users with nonframes browsers, because the reader will still have to take some action (e.g., click on a link) to get the nonframes version.

Examples

Listing 4.4 divides the top-level window into two rows, the first with three columns, and the second with two columns. The result is shown in Figure 4–4.

Listing 4.4   `Frame-Example1.html`

```
<HTML>
<HEAD>
  <TITLE>Frame Example 1</TITLE>
</HEAD>

<FRAMESET ROWS="55%,45%">
  <FRAMESET COLS="*,*,*">
    <FRAME SRC="Frame-Cell.html">
    <FRAME SRC="Frame-Cell.html">
    <FRAME SRC="Frame-Cell.html">
  </FRAMESET>

  <FRAMESET COLS="*,*">
    <FRAME SRC="Frame-Cell.html">
    <FRAME SRC="Frame-Cell.html">
  </FRAMESET>

  <NOFRAMES>
    <BODY>
      Your browser does not support frames. Please see
      <A HREF="Frame-Cell.html">non-frames version</A>.
    </BODY>
  </NOFRAMES>
</FRAMESET>

</HTML>
```

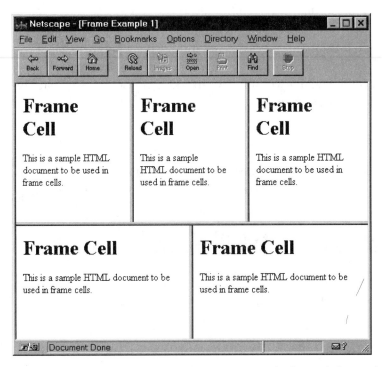

Figure 4–4   A document divided into two rows; the first with three columns, the second with two.

Listing 4.5 divides the top-level window into two columns, the first with three rows, and the second with two rows. The result is shown in Figure 4–5.

Listing 4.5 `Frame-Example2.html`

```
<HTML>
<HEAD>
  <TITLE>Frame Example 2</TITLE>
</HEAD>

<FRAMESET COLS="55%,45%">
  <FRAMESET ROWS="*,*,*">
    <FRAME SRC="Frame-Cell.html">
    <FRAME SRC="Frame-Cell.html">
    <FRAME SRC="Frame-Cell.html">
  </FRAMESET>

  <FRAMESET ROWS="*,*">
    <FRAME SRC="Frame-Cell.html">
    <FRAME SRC="Frame-Cell.html">
  </FRAMESET>

  <NOFRAMES>
    <BODY>
      Your browser does not support frames. Please see
      <A HREF="Frame-Cell.html">non-frames version</A>.
    </BODY>
  </NOFRAMES>
</FRAMESET>

</HTML>
```

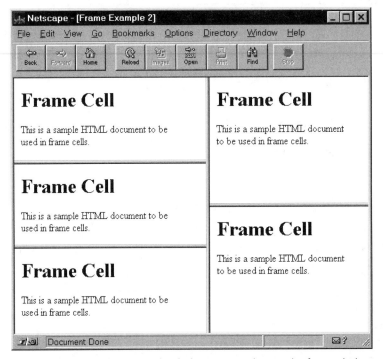

Figure 4–5   A document divided into two columns; the first with three rows, the second with two.

4.4 Targeting Frame Cells

A document can specify that pages referenced by hypertext links be placed in certain frames when selected. To do this, the frame cell is named via the NAME attribute of FRAME, then the hypertext reference gives a TARGET using that name. In the absence of a TARGET attribute, the new document will appear in whatever cell the selected cross reference is in. If you supply a TARGET that does not yet exist, the designated document is placed in a new browser window and assigned the given name for future reference. Elements that allow a TARGET attribute include A, BASE (for giving a default target), AREA, and FORM. Java applets can target named frame cells by supplying a second argument to getAppletContext().showDocument.

One common use of frames is to supply a small toolbar or table of contents frame at the top or left of the document, with a larger region reserved for the main document. Clicking on entries in the table of contents displays the designated link in the main document area. For instance, consider the example layout shown in Figure 4–6.

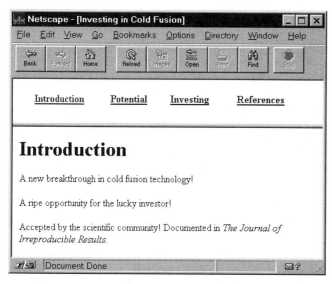

Figure 4–6   A document containing two frames: a table of contents frame and a second frame displaying one of the content sections.

The overall page is laid out giving the table of contents a fixed amount of space, with the remaining space devoted to the main document (named Main). Listing 4.6 gives the HTML used for the top-level layout.

Listing 4.6   Cold-Fusion.html

```
<HTML>
<HEAD>
  <TITLE>Investing in Cold Fusion</TITLE>
</HEAD>

<FRAMESET ROWS="50,*">
  <FRAME SRC="TOC.html" NAME="TOC">
  <FRAME SRC="Introduction.html" NAME="Main">
  <NOFRAMES>
    <BODY>
      This page requires Frames. For a non-Frames version,
      <A HREF="Introduction.html">the introduction</A>.
    </BODY>
  </NOFRAMES>
</FRAMESET>

</HTML>
```

Next, links in the `TOC.html` document supply a `TARGET` attribute of `Main`, so that links selected in the upper frame get displayed in the lower frame. The table of contents document would have targeted anchor links, as shown in Listing 4.7.

Listing 4.7   `TOC.html`

```
<!DOCTYPE HTML PUBLIC "-//W3C//DTD HTML 3.2//EN">
<HTML>
<HEAD>
  <TITLE>Table of Contents</TITLE>
</HEAD>

<BODY>
<TABLE WIDTH="100%">
  <TR><TH><A HREF="Introduction.html" TARGET="Main">
        Introduction</A></TH>
      <TH><A HREF="Potential.html" TARGET="Main">
        Potential</A></TH>
      <TH><A HREF="Investing.html" TARGET="Main">
        Investing</A></TH>
      <TH><A HREF="References.html" TARGET="Main">
        References</A></TH></TR>
</TABLE>
</BODY>

</HTML>
```

The idea is that if one of the entries in the table of contents is selected, the designated page gets shown in the lower frame, with the table of contents remaining unchanged. Note that the same effect could have been achieved by omitting the `TARGET` attributes in the links, and supplying `<BASE TARGET="Main">` in the `HEAD`. Figure 4–7 shows the result after the "Investing" link was selected. Note that, despite the `DOCTYPE`, `TOC.html` is not a completely standard HTML 3.2 document because of the `TARGET` attribute. However, validating such a page (see Section 1.3, "Publishing Your Document on the Web") against an HTML 3.2 specification should result only in "Unknown Attribute TARGET" warnings, and other constructs will still be checked appropriately. Given the use of tables, omitting the DOCTYPE (thus implying it is HTML 2.0) is a worse option, and specifying a nonstandard specification via a DOCTYPE specific to some browser would open the door to other nonportable extensions. Note that the four documents referenced by TOC.html can be standard HTML 3.2 with no TARGET attributes because untargeted links automatically display in the current frame cell.

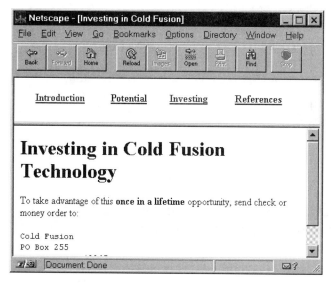

Figure 4-7   A table of contents frame simplifies navigation.

4.5 Predefined Frame Names

There are four built-in frame names that can be used when specifying TAR-GET attributes: _blank, _top, _parent, and _self. Since user-defined frame names cannot begin with an underscore, these names have the same interpretation in all framed documents. To illustrate their use, consider the frame layout given in Figure 4–8 (with source in Listings 4.8 and 4.9). Each of the four bottom cells contains a hypertext link to Cell-Example.html, targeted using each of the four standard names.

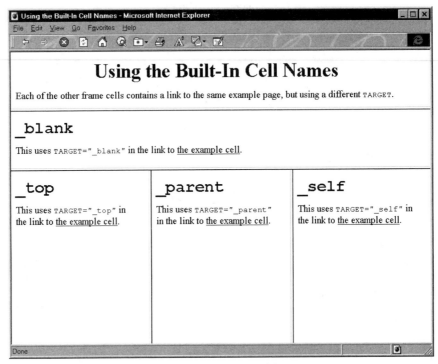

Figure 4-8   A page to illustrate the pre-assigned frame names.

Listing 4.8   Top-level layout of frame-name demo page

```
<HTML>
<HEAD>
  <TITLE>Using the Built-In Cell Names</TITLE>
</HEAD>

<FRAMESET ROWS="20%,20%,60%">
  <FRAME SRC="Cell-Name-Intro.html">
  <FRAME SRC="Cell-Blank.html">
  <FRAME SRC="Cell-Group.html">

  <NOFRAMES>
    <BODY>
      Your browser does not support frames. Please see
      <A HREF="Cell-Example.html">non-frames version</A>.
    </BODY>
  </NOFRAMES>
</FRAMESET>

</BODY>
</HTML>
```

Listing 4.9   Layout of the bottom three cells of frame-name demo
               page

```
<HTML>
<HEAD>
  <TITLE>Cell Grouping</TITLE>
</HEAD>

<FRAMESET COLS="*,*,*">
  <FRAME SRC="Cell-Top.html">
  <FRAME SRC="Cell-Parent.html">
  <FRAME SRC="Cell-Self.html">

  <NOFRAMES>
    <BODY>
      Your browser does not support frames. Please see
      <A HREF="Cell-Example.html">non-frames version</A>.
    </BODY>
  </NOFRAMES>
</FRAMESET>

</BODY>
</HTML>
```

_blank

Using a link target of "_blank" causes the linked document to be loaded into a new unnamed window. For example, Figure 4–9 shows the result of clicking on the link in the middle row of the frame-name demo page shown in Figure 4–8. Listing 4.10 gives the HTML source for the cell containing this link.

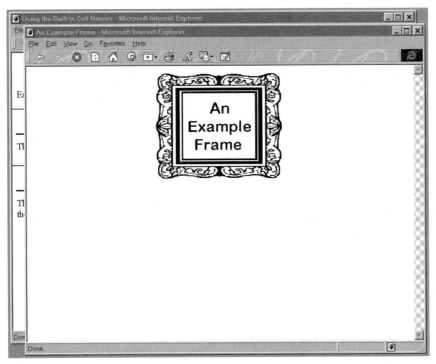

Figure 4-9   Using TARGET="_blank" places the document in a new browser window.

_top

Using "_top" as a link target causes the linked document to take up the whole browser window. That is, the document referenced by the link will not be contained *in* a frame cell, although the document can still *contain* frames. For example, Figure 4–10 shows the result of clicking on the link in the bottom left cell of the frame-name demo page shown in Figure 4–8. Listing 4.11 gives the HTML source for the cell containing this link.

Listing 4.10 Targeting a blank frame

```
<!DOCTYPE HTML PUBLIC "-//W3C//DTD HTML 3.2//EN">
<HTML>
<HEAD>
  <TITLE>_blank</TITLE>
</HEAD>

<BODY>
<H1><CODE>_blank</CODE></H1>

This uses <CODE>TARGET="_blank"</CODE> in the link to
<A HREF="Cell-Example.html" TARGET="_blank">
the example cell</A>.

</BODY>
</HTML>
```

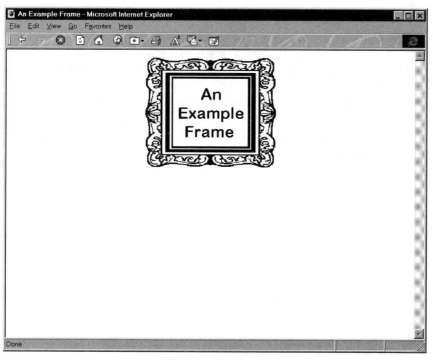

Figure 4-10 Using TARGET="_top" places the document in the outermost cell of the current window.

Listing 4.11 Targeting the top-level frame

```
<!DOCTYPE HTML PUBLIC "-//W3C//DTD HTML 3.2//EN">
<HTML>
<HEAD>
  <TITLE>_top</TITLE>
</HEAD>

<BODY>
<H1><CODE>_top</CODE></H1>

This uses <CODE>TARGET="_top"</CODE> in the link to
<A HREF="Cell-Example.html" TARGET="_top">
the example cell</A>.

</BODY>

</HTML>
```

_parent

Using a target of "_parent" causes the linked document to be placed in the cell occupied by the immediate FRAMESET parent of the document. This gives the same result as _top if there are no nested frames. For example, Figure 4–11 shows the result of clicking on the link in the bottom center cell of the frame-name demo page shown in Figure 4–8. Listing 4.12 gives the HTML source for the cell containing this link.

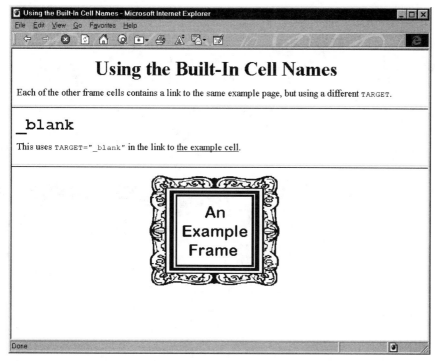

Figure 4–11 Using `TARGET="_parent"` places the document in the cell occupied by the parent frame.

Listing 4.12 Targeting the parent frame

```
<!DOCTYPE HTML PUBLIC "-//W3C//DTD HTML 3.2//EN">
<HTML>
<HEAD>
  <TITLE>_parent</TITLE>
</HEAD>

<BODY>
<H1><CODE>_parent</CODE></H1>

This uses <CODE>TARGET="_parent"</CODE> in the link to
<A HREF="Cell-Example.html" TARGET="_parent">
the example cell</A>.

</BODY>
</HTML>
```

_self

Finally, "_self" causes the linked document to go in the current cell. Explicitly specifying _self is only necessary to override a BASE entry. In the absence of <BASE TARGET="*frameName*">, the default behavior is to place the linked document in the cell containing the link. For example, Figure 4–12 shows the result of clicking on the link in the bottom right cell of the frame-name demo page shown in Figure 4–8. Listing 4.13 gives the HTML source for the cell containing this link.

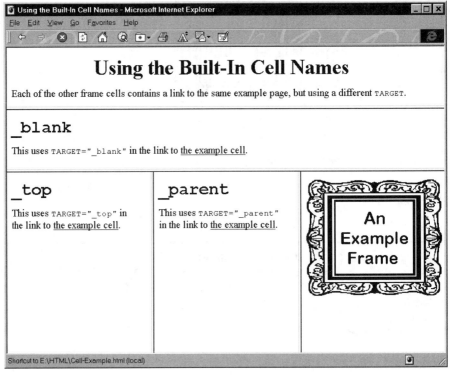

Figure 4–12 Using TARGET="_self" places the document in the current cell.

> **Listing 4.13 Targeting the current cell**

```
<!DOCTYPE HTML PUBLIC "-//W3C//DTD HTML 3.2//EN">
<HTML>
<HEAD>
  <TITLE>_self</TITLE>
</HEAD>

<BODY>
<H1><CODE>_self</CODE></H1>

This uses <CODE>TARGET="_self"</CODE> in the link to
<A HREF="Cell-Example.html" TARGET="_self">
the example cell</A>.

</BODY>
</HTML>
```

4.6 Solving Common Frame Problems

Frames can cause difficulties for users and developers. Some of these problems are due to misconceptions that people have about the page stemming from a single HTML document, and others are the result of bugs in current implementations. This section describes the most common difficulties, and provides suggestions for avoiding them or minimizing their impact.

Bookmarking Frames

Suppose you are visiting a page that uses frames. Call this page Url1. You browse around for a while and find a document that is of particular interest to you. Call this Url2. So you try to save a reference to Url2 by adding it to your bookmarks list (also called "favorites" or "hotlist," depending on the browser). Later, you select that bookmark, but it brings you to the *original* frames-based page (Url1), not the *second* page you found (Url2). What's going on? The problem is that selecting "Add" from the Bookmarks or Favorites menu saves the URL of the top-level document (as shown on the address/location field at the top of the browser), not the one displayed in the frame cell you were interested in. This problem can be particularly unexpected if visiting a page that has frame borders turned off, because if you are not watching the address bar, you might not even realize that frames are being used. For instance, Figures 4–13 and 4–14 show the Microsoft HTML authoring page before and after the link to the Reference Guide was selected. Although there is no obvious indication that frames are in use when the original page is visited, the URL displayed at the top is unchanged after the selection. This original URL is the one that would be saved if "Add to Favorites" was chosen from the "Favorites" menu, as is the usual practice.

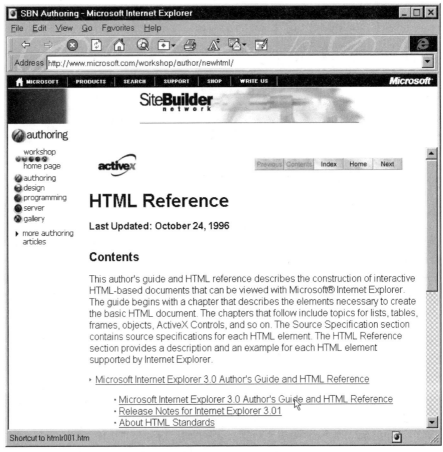

Figure 4–13 A frame with borders disabled via
```
<FRAMESET FRAMEBORDER=0 ...>.
```

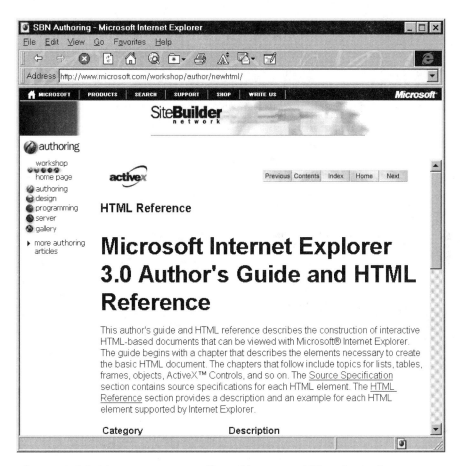

Figure 4–14 Navigating to a new "page" leaves top URL unchanged.

In Netscape and Internet Explorer on Windows, clicking with the secondary (right) mouse button in a frame cell will bring up a menu that allows you to save a bookmark to the URL of that particular cell. This is illustrated in Figure 4–15, which saves an entry to the actual URL of interest. Now, selecting that entry later doesn't return you to the page shown in Figure 4–15, but rather to a page with the Reference Guide shown by itself without frames. This is because there is no option in current browsers that lets a user save a reference to a particular frame *configuration*.

Knowing how to save bookmarks to individual frame cells is important to Web users, but a realization that many users have trouble with this is also important to developers of frame-based sites. First of all, you should provide navigation aids so that users who bookmark your top-level page can quickly find the sub-page of interest. Secondly, pages that are likely to be commonly referenced should contain their URL in plain text in the body of the document. Thirdly, you should consider maintaining a nonframes version of the site that contains links to all the documents in your main site. Although a full nonframes version can be difficult to maintain for sites that change frequently, a simple option that also satisfies the goal of putting the URL in the document is to make the reference to the current URL be part of a link that places the document in an unframed window, as below:

```
The original of this page can be found at
<A HREF="http://some-site.com/some-page.html
    TARGET="_top">
http://some-site.com/some-page.html</A>.
```

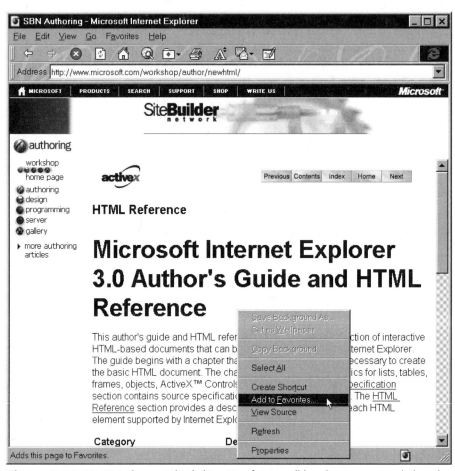

Figure 4–15 On Windows, right-clicking in a frame cell lets the user save a link to that cell's location.

Printing Frames

Because each part of a frame is a separate HTML document, current browsers do not have the ability to print an entire framed document formatted in the same general layout as on-screen. Instead, they print a single frame cell. The question is: Which cell do they print? Many users assume that the answer is the cell that was most recently updated, but in fact it is the cell with the current input focus. Selecting a hypertext link that displays a document in a particular frame cell does *not* change the input focus to the new frame. It can be extremely annoying to click on a link in the table of contents frame, get the result you want, select "Print," and get a printout of the table of contents instead of the newly displayed frame! The solution is to explicitly click on the frame cell of interest before printing.

Core Tip

Before attempting to print part of a framed document, always click on the frame cell you want printed.

As a developer, you can minimize the difficulties users will have in printing your pages. First, you can attach JavaScript code to the `OnClick` attribute of targeted hypertext links, specifying that the designated frame automatically gets the input focus whenever the link is selected. For details, see Chapter 19, "JavaScript: Adding Dynamic Content to Web Pages." Second, you can provide the users with a composite document to use for printing. This is particularly convenient when making a reference page that is broken down into many separate documents, which would otherwise be tedious for users to print.

Updating Multiple Frame Cells Simultaneously

HTML does not have a method that allows a single hypertext link to update the contents of more than one frame cell. However, there are two potential solutions:

- Combine the cells into a single `FRAME`
- Use JavaScript

Each of these will be detailed in the following sections.

Combine the Cells into a Single Frame

Suppose that the initial FRAMESET looked like this:

```
<FRAMESET ROWS="*,*,*">
  <FRAME SRC="Top.html">
  <FRAME SRC="Middle.html" NAME="MIDDLE">
  <FRAME SRC="Bottom.html" NAME="BOTTOM">
</FRAMESET>
```

In a case like this, there is no pure-HTML method for a link in the Top.html document to replace the contents of *both* Middle.html and Bottom.html. However, the initial design could be replaced by:

```
<FRAMESET ROWS="*,2*">
  <FRAME SRC="Top.html">
  <FRAME SRC="Middle+Bottom.html" NAME="LOWER">
</FRAMESET>
```

Then, Middle+Bottom.html can itself contain a FRAMESET entry:

```
<FRAMESET ROWS="*,*">
  <FRAME SRC="Middle.html" NAME="MIDDLE">
  <FRAME SRC="Bottom.html" NAME="BOTTOM">
</FRAMESET>
```

Now, links can target the frame named LOWER, supplying the URL of a file that also contains two FRAME entries. This solution is not completely satisfactory, because it requires that the cells of interest be next to each other, and that all of the HTML documents in question are under the control of the author of the main layout and can be modified to fit the new design. On the other hand, this approach works even for users who have disabled JavaScript or whose browsers do not support it, unlike the JavaScript alternative described next.

Using JavaScript

JavaScript allows authors to attach code to the `OnClick` attribute of a hypertext link. This code can call any number of JavaScript statements, including `top.`*`frameName`*`.location  =  `*`someURL`*, which assigns new documents to particular frame cells. Any number of cells can be updated, and there is no requirement that the top-level framed document change structure, nor that the updated cells be next to each other. Of course, this solution only works for browsers that support JavaScript. JavaScript is described in more detail in Chapter 19, but we'll look at a quick example here. Consider Listing 4.14, which creates one cell in the top row and three named cells in the bottom row.

Listing 4.14 `Multiple-Updates.html`

```
<HTML>
<HEAD>
  <TITLE>Updating Multiple Frames Simultaneously</TITLE>
</HEAD>

<FRAMESET ROWS="75,*">
  <FRAME SRC="Top-Frame.html">
  <FRAMESET COLS="*,*,*">
    <FRAME SRC="Bottom1.html" NAME="Bottom1">
    <FRAME SRC="Bottom2.html" NAME="Bottom2">
    <FRAME SRC="Bottom3.html" NAME="Bottom3">
  </FRAMESET>
</FRAMESET>
</HTML>
```

Now, to have a link in the top frame send results to bottom cell 1 and 3, the top frame can contain JavaScript code that references the names `Bottom1` and `Bottom3`. This is shown in Listing 4.15, which defines the `UpdateCells` function and then attaches it to the hypertext link's `OnClick` attribute. Figures 4–16 and 4–17 show the results before and after the link is selected.

Listing 4.15 Top-Frame.html

```
<!DOCTYPE HTML PUBLIC "-//W3C//DTD HTML 3.2//EN">
<HTML>
<HEAD>
  <TITLE>Table of Contents</TITLE>

<SCRIPT LANGUAGE="JavaScript">
<!--
function UpdateCells() {
  top.Bottom1.location = "Result1.html";
  top.Bottom3.location = "Result3.html";
}
// -->
</SCRIPT>
</HEAD>

<BODY BGCOLOR="WHITE" TEXT="BLACK">
When selected on JavaScript-capable browsers,
<A HREF="Result1.html" TARGET="Bottom1"
   OnClick="UpdateCells()">
this link</A> will update cell one and
three below.

</BODY>
</HTML>
```

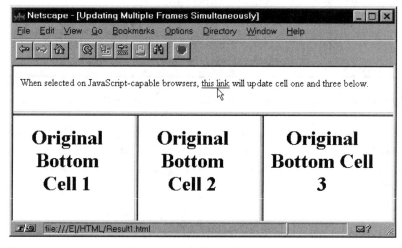

Figure 4–16   Framed document before selecting hypertext link.

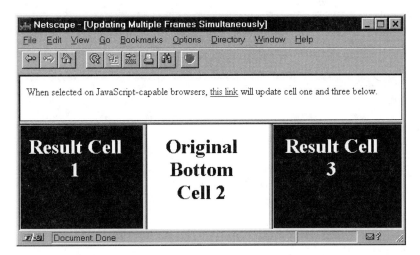

Figure 4–17 Framed document after selecting hypertext link, showing two updated cells.

Preventing Your Documents From Being Framed

Some authors don't want their pages to appear as frames in other people's documents. One solution is to specify `<BASE TARGET="_top">` in the HEAD of your document. Although this doesn't prevent the initial appearance of your page, it prevents the page from remaining part of a frame after a link has been selected. JavaScript can also be used to prevent a page from appearing in a frame at all. Simply insert the following in the HEAD of the document:

```
<SCRIPT LANGUAGE="JavaScript">
<!--
if (top.frames.length > 0)
  top.location = document.location;
// -->
</SCRIPT>
```

See Chapter 19 for more details on JavaScript. Since some users may have JavaScript disabled, you might want to use *both* techniques if you really want to prevent framing.

Specifying FRAMESETs with Only a Single Entry

In Netscape (but not Internet Explorer), FRAMESET entries must have at least two entries or they will not display properly. For instance, consider the simple layout of Listing 4.16, with the result shown in Figure 4–13.

Listing 4.16 A three-frame document

```
<HTML>
<HEAD>
  <TITLE>FRAMESET Must Have Multiple Entries</TITLE>
</HEAD>

<FRAMESET ROWS="*,*">
  <FRAME SRC="Frame-Cell.html">

  <FRAMESET COLS="*,*">
    <FRAME SRC="Frame-Cell.html">
    <FRAME SRC="Frame-Cell.html">
  </FRAMESET>

  <NOFRAMES>
    <BODY>
      Your browser does not support frames. Please see
      <A HREF="Frame-Cell.html">non-frames version</A>.
    </BODY>
  </NOFRAMES>
</FRAMESET>

</HTML>
```

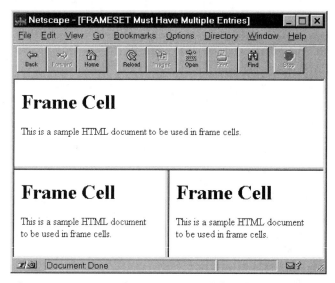

Figure 4–18 Nested FRAMESETs work fine if they contain two or more entries.

Now, suppose that for the sake of symmetry the author enclosed the first FRAME entry inside a FRAMESET entry, assuming that the redundancy would do no harm. The resultant HTML is shown in Listing 4.17.

Listing 4.17 A FRAMESET with a single entry

```
<HTML>
<HEAD>
  <TITLE>FRAMESET Must Have Multiple Entries</TITLE>
</HEAD>

<FRAMESET ROWS="*,*">
  <FRAMESET COLS="*">
    <FRAME SRC="Frame-Cell.html">
  </FRAMESET>

  <FRAMESET COLS="*,*">
    <FRAME SRC="Frame-Cell.html">
    <FRAME SRC="Frame-Cell.html">
  </FRAMESET>

  <NOFRAMES>
    <BODY>
      Your browser does not support frames. Please see
      <A HREF="Frame-Cell.html">non-frames version</A>.
    </BODY>
  </NOFRAMES>
</FRAMESET>

</HTML>
```

On Internet Explorer, the result is exactly the same as before. However, on Netscape, the result is unexpected, as shown in Figure 4–19.

The same result occurs with FRAMESET entries with only a single row, and is consistent across operating systems and Netscape releases from 2.0 to 4.01.

Creating Empty Frame Cells

In Internet Explorer version 3.0, a FRAME can have a NAME but no SRC. In such a case, space is allocated for that cell as specified in the enclosing FRAMESET. Hypertext links that have a TARGET that designates the empty cell will behave as expected, with the associated file appearing in that cell. In Netscape Navigator version 3.0 and earlier, space is also allocated for frame cells based on the enclosing FRAMESET. However, hypertext links that have a TARGET designating the initially empty cell behave as though no such frame exists. That is, they appear in an entirely new browser window. This behavior

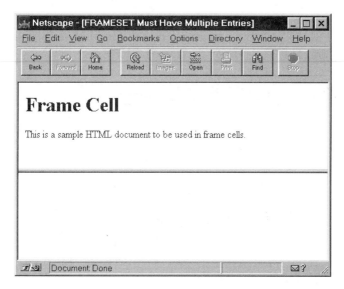

Figure 4-19 Netscape does not accept FRAMESETs with only a single entry.

is a bit inconvenient, because it is quite reasonable to want to populate certain frame cells in advance but fill in others only when the author makes a selection. For instance, consider the test case shown in Listing 4.18.

Listing 4.18 No-SRC.html

```
<HTML>
<HEAD>
  <TITLE>A Frame with No SRC</TITLE>
</HEAD>

<FRAMESET ROWS="*,*">
  <FRAME SRC="Top.html">
  <FRAME NAME="BOTTOM">
</FRAMESET>

</HTML>
```

Now, suppose that the `Top.html` file has a hypertext link targeted for the bottom cell, as shown in Listing 4.19.

Listing 4.19 `Top.html`

```
<!DOCTYPE HTML PUBLIC "-//W3C//DTD HTML 3.2//EN">
<HTML>
<HEAD>
  <TITLE>Top Frame</TITLE>
</HEAD>

<BODY>
<H1>Top Frame</H1>
In Internet Explorer, a Frame with no SRC is allowed.
Empty space is reserved, and the frame's name is
associated with that cell.
<A HREF="Frame-Cell.html" TARGET="BOTTOM">
Links that are targeted to that name</A>
will be displayed there. In Netscape Navigator,
space is reserved, but future targeted links create
a new window.
</BODY>
</HTML>
```

The incompatibility arises when this hypertext link is selected. In Internet Explorer, the result appears in the bottom half of the page, as most people would expect. This is illustrated in Figures 4–20 and 4–21, which show the resultant page in Internet Explorer 3.01 before and after the targeted link is selected. In Netscape, however, the result appears in a whole new browser window. This is illustrated in Figures 4–22 and 4–23, which show the resultant page in Netscape Navigator 3.01 before and after the targeted link is selected. Netscape Communicator 4.01 has the same behavior. The solution is to treat SRC as a required attribute, supplying the URL of an HTML document that has an empty BODY in situations where you want an "empty" cell.

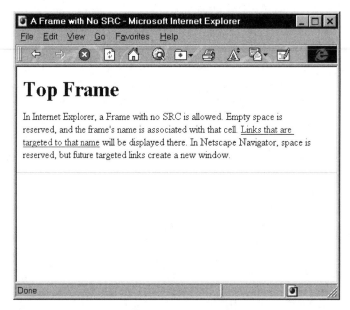

Figure 4–20 `No-SRC.html` in Internet Explorer, before the link is selected.

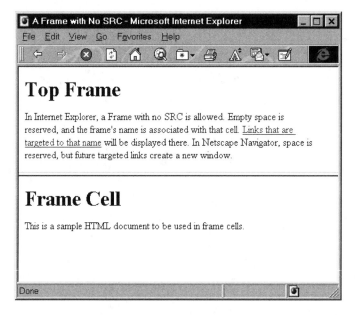

Figure 4–21 `No-SRC.html` in Internet Explorer, after the link has been selected.

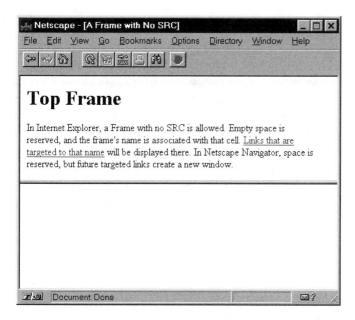

Figure 4–22 No-SRC.html in Netscape Navigator, before the link is selected.

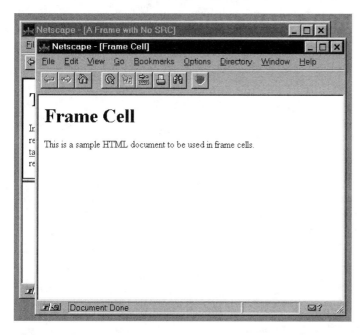

Figure 4–23 No-SRC.html in Netscape Navigator, after the link has been selected.

4.7 Inline Frames

Internet Explorer has a nice feature whereby a frame can be defined in a manner very similar to an image. You specify a width, height, source URL, and alignment, and it occupies a fixed position *in the HTML document*. This is in contrast to normal frames, which occupy a fixed position *in the browser window*. This is very convenient for sidebars, contact information, and other things that you want to include in multiple documents. Unfortunately, however, although floating frames are part of the proposed frame specification, they are unsupported by most current frame-capable browsers (including Netscape Communicator 4.01) other than Internet Explorer. On the other hand, Netscape Communicator supports *layers*, and inline layers provide a more general mechanism for this type of application. See Section 5.12 for a discussion of layers.

To illustrate floating frames, suppose that Professor Ithim teaches a variety of Computer Science courses. Being at a modern University, he naturally publishes the syllabus and other class information on Web pages. He wants to put his name, campus mailing address, and e-mail address on every page, but like all good programmers, hates to repeat himself and risk inconsistent versions. To avoid this, he can create a simple contact information file first, as in Listing 4.20.

Listing 4.20   `Contact-Info.html`

```
<!DOCTYPE HTML PUBLIC "-//W3C//DTD HTML 3.2//EN">
<HTML>
<HEAD>
  <TITLE>Prof. Al Gore Ithim</TITLE>
</HEAD>

<BODY>
Prof. Al Gore Ithim<BR>
Computer Science Department<BR>
Podunk University<BR>
<A HREF="mailto:algy@podunk.edu">
algy@podunk.edu</A>
</BODY>
</HTML>
```

Once he has the contact file, he can include it at the bottom of each Web page that he creates via an IFRAME element. For instance, Listing 4.21 shows a simplified version of a page for Computer Science 401.

Listing 4.21 `CS-401.html`

```
<!DOCTYPE HTML PUBLIC "-//W3C//DTD HTML 3.2//EN">
<HTML>
<HEAD>
  <TITLE>Design and Analysis of Algorithms</TITLE>
</HEAD>

<BODY>
<H1>Design and Analysis of Algorithms</H1>

This course covers the techniques required to design
and analyze computer algorithms. The textbook is
<I>Introduction to Algorithms</I> by Cormen, Leiserson,
and Rivest (McGraw Hill, 1990, ISBN 0-07-013143-0).
<P>
Blah, blah, blah, algorithms. Yada, yada, yada,
time. Blah, blah, blah, space. Yada, yada, yada,
iterative. Blah, blah, blah, recurrences.
Yada, yada, yard, data structures. Blah, blah,
blah, sorting. Yada, yada, yada, dynamic programming.
Blah, blah, blah, graph algorithms.
Yada, yada, yada, NP-Completeness.
<P>
<IFRAME SRC="Contact-Info.html" FRAMEBORDER=0></IFRAME>
</BODY>
</HTML>
```

Now, when this page is displayed in Internet Explorer, the contact information is placed at the bottom of the Web page, as illustrated in Figures 4–24 and 4–25.

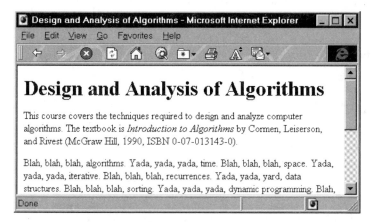

Figure 4–24 Top part of `CS-401.html`; floating frame does not appear.

As can be seen, floating frames, unlike normal frames, do not occupy a fixed part of the Web browser window, but rather scroll with the rest of the document.

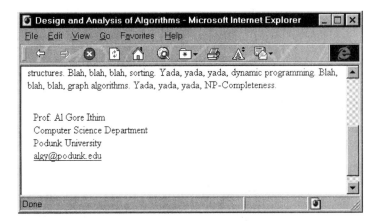

Figure 4–25   Bottom part of `CS-401.html`; floating frame scrolls into view.

HTML Element: `<IFRAME SRC="..." ...> ... </IFRAME>`

Attributes: SRC, WIDTH, HEIGHT, ALIGN, NAME, FRAMEBORDER, MARGINWIDTH, MARGINHEIGHT, SCROLLING

IFRAME specifies a floating or "inline" frame. It is available only in Internet Explorer in version 3.0 and later. Text for incompatible browsers can be placed between the start and end tags, and will be ignored by compatible browsers.

SRC

SRC specifies the URL of the document to be displayed in the floating frame.

WIDTH, HEIGHT

These attributes give the size of the floating frame in pixels. A percentage value is not permitted. An author can omit these and let the browser size the frame appropriately.

ALIGN

ALIGN specifies the alignment of the frame with respect to the surrounding text, in a manner similar to embedded images. Legal values are LEFT, RIGHT, CENTER, TOP, BOTTOM, and MIDDLE.

NAME

Floating frames can be the end points of targeted links, just like normal frames. The NAME attribute gives the name for this purpose.

FRAMEBORDER

This attribute determines whether (FRAMEBORDER=1) or not (FRAMEBORDER=0) borders should be drawn around the floating frame. The default is to use borders.

MARGINWIDTH

MARGINWIDTH gives the width of the left and right margins, in pixels.

MARGINHEIGHT

MARGINHEIGHT gives height of the top and bottom margins, in pixels.

SCROLLING

The SCROLLING attribute determines if scrollbars should be used (SCROLLING="YES") or not (SCROLLING="NO").

4.8 Summary

Frames are one of the two most important extensions to HTML 3.2, and are widely supported by current browsers. The FRAMESET element is used to divide window or current cell into rectangular regions, and HTML documents are associated with the regions via the FRAME element. Hypertext links, forms, and Java applets can target user-defined or standard frame names, specifying that certain documents be displayed in particular frames. The most common frame problems can be avoided by careful design and/or use of JavaScript. Finally, floating frames provide a logical next step from fixed frames.

Cascading style sheets are the second most important extension to HTML 3.2. They allow you to customize the appearance and layout of standard and custom HTML elements, providing you with much more control over the final layout and look of Web pages you create. An extension to cascading style sheets let you define "layers" which allow Web pages to define separate markup for various absolute or relative regions of the page. Layers go two steps byond frames, since these regions can be overlapping and since their size and position can be dynamically changed through the use of JavaScript functions. Style sheets are discussed in the next chapter.

CASCADING STYLE SHEETS

Topics in This Chapter

- How style rules are defined
- How sets of style rules are associated with an HTML document
- The types of elements that rules can be applied to
- The precedence rules that arbitrate among conflicting rules
- Properties that define font characteristics
- Properties that describe color and image characteristics
- Properties that describe text formatting characteristics
- Properties that describe the bounding box around HTML elements
- Properties that define images and floating text elements
- Properties that describe lists
- The units used to specify size and color properties
- Extended style sheets for dynamic, layered HTML

Chapter 5

C ascading style sheets are a powerful and flexible way of specifying formatting information for Web pages. They let you define the font, size, background and foreground color, background image, margin, and other characteristics for each of the standard HTML elements. In addition to specifying how standard elements should be displayed, style sheets let you define your own classes, effectively letting authors define new HTML elements, albeit with some constraints on the characteristics these new elements can have. Formatting rules are applied in a hierarchical or "cascading" manner, letting default rules from the browser combine with explicit rules from both the reader and the author. Style sheets can be loaded from external sites, permitting sharing of style sheets and letting authors change the look and feel of entire Web sites by changing only a single file. The current standard for style sheets is "Cascading Style Sheets, level 1," known as "CSS1." This is supported by Netscape Communicator (i.e., Netscape 4.0) and Internet Explorer 4.0. In addition, Internet Explorer version 3 supports a subset of CSS1 capabilities.

Core Note

Capabilities supported by Internet Explorer 3.0x are indicated by "†" throughout this chapter.

147

Some lesser-known browsers such as Arena and Emacs-w3 support a subset as well, and style sheets are expected to be a component of most future browsers. In addition to CSS1, there is a proposed standard that lets style sheets designate HTML "layers," which let you position HTML elements at absolute locations and create overlapping regions that can be moved dynamically. Netscape Communicator supports layers, and Internet Explorer 4.0 is expected to support at least a subset as well. The full style sheet specifications can be found at the World Wide Web Consortium's site:

Cascading Style Sheets, Level 1
```
http://www.w3.org/pub/WWW/TR/REC-CSS1
```

Layers
```
http://www.w3.org/pub/WWW/TR/WD-positioning
```

Style Sheet News and Proposed Extensions
```
http://www.w3.org/pub/WWW/Style/
```

5.1 Specifying Style Rules

HTML elements are customized by the use of *style rules*. Style rules normally go inside a STYLE element in the HEAD of an HTML document, and consist of a set of rules of the form

```
selector { property: value }
```
or
```
selector { property1: value1;
           property2: value2;
           ...
           propertyN: valueN }
```

The types of selectors that can be used are discussed in Section 5.3, but the most basic type is simply the name of an HTML element, signifying that the properties listed inside the braces should apply to all occurrences of that element in the document. The available properties and their possible values are described in Sections 5.5 through 5.10. For instance, consider the small HTML document shown in Listing 5.1.

Listing 5.1 `Fizzics1.html`

```
<!DOCTYPE HTML PUBLIC "-//W3C//DTD HTML 3.2//EN">
<HTML>
<HEAD>
  <TITLE>New Advances in Physics</TITLE>
</HEAD>

<BODY>
<H1>New Advances in Physics</H1>

<H2>Turning Gold into Lead</H2>
In a startling breakthrough, scientist B.O. "Gus"
Fizzics has invented a <STRONG>practical</STRONG>
technique for transmutation! For more details, please
see <A HREF="give-us-your-gold.html">our
transmutation thesis</A>.

<H2>Perpetual Inactivity Machine</H2>
In a radical approach that turned traditional
attempts to develop perpetual motion machines on
their heads, Prof. Fizzics has developed a
verified bona-fide perpetual <STRONG>inaction</STRONG>
machine. To purchase your own for only $99.00 (plus
$43.29 shipping and handling), please see
<A HREF="rock.html">our order form</A>.

</BODY>
</HTML>
```

When displayed in Internet Explorer 3.01 on Windows 95, the result looks like Figure 5–1.

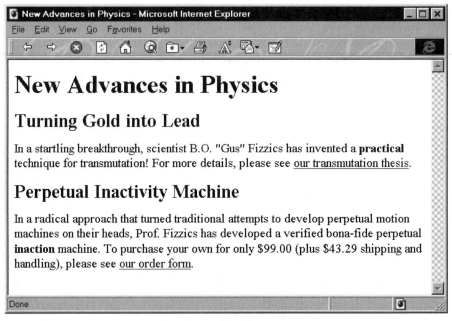

Figure 5–1   `Fizzics1.html` without style information.

However, when the style information shown in the following snippet is added to the document HEAD, the result changes to that of Figure 5–2. Note the use of HTML comments to prevent non-CSS-capable browsers from seeing the text between <STYLE> and </STYLE>.

```
<STYLE>
<!--
BODY { background: URL(images/confetti-background.jpg) }
H1 { text-align: center;
     font-family: Blackout }
H2 { font-family: MeppDisplayShadow }
STRONG { text-decoration: underline }
-->
</STYLE>
```

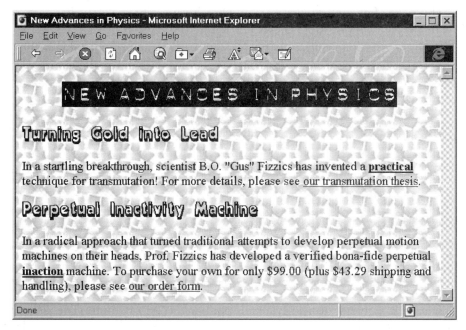

Figure 5-2   `Fizzics1.html` after adding style information.

5.2 Using Local and External Style Sheets

Style rules are commonly specified inside a STYLE element in the head of the document, but documents can also link to external style sheets, import remote style rules into local style sheets, and even specify style information directly in the body of the document. Capabilities supported by release 3.0 of Microsoft Internet Explorer are indicated by "†".

The STYLE Element† and JavaScript Style Sheets

The STYLE element lets you define formatting rules inside the HEAD section of the HTML document. The standard syntax is:

```
<STYLE>
Style Rules
</STYLE>
```

This works fine on browsers that understand style sheets. However, browsers that do not support style sheets will ignore the `<STYLE>` and `</STYLE>` tags, but see the style rules in between. This can cause unpredictable results. Consequently, unless you are creating pages only for an internal network with a standard browser, it is wise to enclose the style rules in HTML comments, as follows:

```
<STYLE>
<!--
Style Rules
-->
</STYLE>
```

Core Approach

Enclose your STYLE rules in HTML comments.

The `STYLE` element also takes an optional `TYPE` attribute. The default value is `"text/css"`, but Netscape Communicator (Netscape 4.0) also supports a value of `"text/javascript"`. JavaScript style sheets use the `tags` object, normal JavaScript syntax, and change property names of the form `property-name` to `propertyName`. For instance,

```
<STYLE>
<!--
H1 { text-align: center;
     font-family: Arial }
-->
</STYLE>
```

is equivalent to

```
<STYLE TYPE="text/javascript">
<!--
tags.H1.textAlign="center";
tags.H1.fontFamily="Arial";
-->
</STYLE>
```

The standard syntax is more portable, but for Netscape-specific applications, JavaScript allows you to *calculate* values, rather than just specify them statically. JavaScript is discussed in more detail in Chapter 19.

External Style Sheets[†]

If you plan to use the same formatting styles in several documents, you can create a separate style sheet in a WWW-accessible file. You could then link this file to HTML documents by using a LINK element in the document HEAD with a REL value of STYLESHEET, an HREF giving the location, and a TYPE of text/css. For instance, if the external style sheet is called site-style.css and is located in the css directory, it could be associated with the current document via a LINK element that looked like:

```
<LINK REL=STYLESHEET
      HREF="http://www.oursite.com/css/site-style.css"
      TYPE="text/css">
```

Importing Style Sheets Using "@import"

The "@import" construct lets you break style sheets up into logical sections, then import each piece separately. You can import into either external style sheets or ones defined via STYLE, but the @import statements must come first in the style sheet. For example:

```
<STYLE>
<!--
@import URL(http://www.oursite.com/css/margins.css);
@import URL(http://www.oursite.com/css/fonts.css);
...
-->
</STYLE>
```

Inline Style Specification[†]

The CSS1 specification allows you to specify formatting information directly in an HTML element by use of the new STYLE attribute that was added to all HTML elements. Inline rules look just like normal rules except that the braces and HTML element name are omitted. For instance:

```
<H1>New Advances in Physics</H1>
<P STYLE="margin-left: 0.5in;
          margin-right: 0.5in;
          font-style: italic">
This paper gives the solution to three
previously unsolved problems: turning lead into gold,
antigravity, and a practical perpetual motion machine.
```

Separate style rules are easier to extend and maintain than inline styles, and should generally be used when defining complex rules.

5.3 Selectors

Style rules are normally defined by placing an entry of the following form in the STYLE element in the HEAD of the document:

```
selector { property1: value1; ... ; propertyN: valueN }
```

Up to this point, we have only given examples where the selector was an HTML element name, indicating that the rule should be applied to all elements of that type unless overridden in the element declaration itself. For instance, to specify that strongly emphasized text be rendered in bold with a 50% increased font size, you could use:

```
STRONG { font-weight: bold; font-size: 150% }
```

Although HTML elements are a common selector type, they are not the only option. The cascading style sheet standard allows a variety of selector types to define formatting rules that only apply in certain situations. The six legal categories of selectors are:

- HTML Elements
- HTML Elements in Certain Contexts
- User-Defined Classes
- User-Defined IDs
- Pseudo Classes
- Pseudo Elements

To support style rules that only apply in certain conditions, the attributes CLASS, ID, and STYLE have been added as legal attributes of *all* HTML elements, and a new text-level element SPAN has been created as a way of applying formatting rules to sections that are not part of existing HTML elements. Selector types supported by version 3.0x of Internet Explorer are indicated with "†".

HTML Elements†

Any HTML element can be used as a selector, although BR has no associated text, so rules would be meaningless. Property settings are inherited; background colors for BODY apply to paragraphs within the body by default, font sizes for P apply to CODE sections within the paragraph unless overridden, and so forth. For instance, to make blue the default color for all text except first-level headings, with top-level headings in red, you could use:

```
BODY { color: blue }
H1 { color: red }
```

Elements can be grouped in comma-separated lists to allow common styles to be set for multiple HTML elements. For instance,

```
H1, H2, H3, H4, H5, H6 { text-align: center;
                         font-family: sans-serif }
```

could be used rather than setting each of H1 through H6 separately.

HTML Elements in Certain Contexts[†]

Property settings are inherited. Elements contained within stylized elements receive the styles of the outer elements. In general, this is a convenient time-saving feature. However, sometimes you want to list exceptions to a general rule. For instance, suppose that colors were set as in the preceding section, with the main body being blue and top-level headings being red. Suppose further that you want emphasized text to be rendered red. This could be done by the following:

```
BODY { color: blue }
H1 { color: red }
EM { color: red }
```

This leaves the problem that emphasized text inside a level-one heading would not be distinguishable from the rest of the heading. So, you could add a rule specifying that emphasized text be green *only* when inside a main heading, as follows:

```
H1 EM { color: green }
```

Contexts can be arbitrarily nested.

User-Defined Classes[†]

You can also define your own classes of selectors, separated by a period from the associated HTML element. For instance, to define an "abstract" paragraph type with indented left and right margins and italic text, you could use the following:

```
P.abstract { margin-left: 0.5in;
             margin-right: 0.5in;
             font-style: italic }
```

To use this class, you would supply the name of the class inside the CLASS attribute of the HTML element in the body of the document. For example, given the preceding abstract class, you could use it as follows:

```
<H1>New Advances in Physics</H1>
<P CLASS="abstract">
This paper gives the solution to three
previously unsolved problems: turning lead into gold,
antigravity, and a practical perpetual motion machine.
```

You can also define classes that apply to any HTML element, by omitting the HTML element that normally precedes the class name in the definition. For instance, the following defines a class that sets the foreground color to blue and uses a bold font:

```
.blue { color: blue; font-weight: bold }
```

This could be used in an existing paragraph:

```
This text is in the default color, but
<SPAN CLASS="blue">this text is blue.</SPAN>
```

or could be applied to an entire block:

```
<H2 CLASS="blue">A Blue Heading</H2>
```

User-Defined IDs[†]

An ID is like a class, but can be applied only once in a document. It is defined by preceding the name with a # and referenced with the ID attribute, as follows:

```
<HEAD>
<TITLE>...</TITLE>
<STYLE>
<!--
#foo { color: red }
-->
</STYLE>
</HEAD>
<BODY>
...
<P ID="foo">
...
</BODY>
```

In most cases, classes are better choices than IDs. However, HTML "layers" (Netscape Communicator, Internet Explorer 4.0) can be applied only once each, and are referenced using ID, not CLASS. Layers are discussed in Sections 5.12 and following.

Anchor Pseudo Classes[†]

Although HTML has a single element to indicate a hypertext link (the anchor element A), browsers typically treat links in one of three different ways, depending on whether the links are new, visited, or active. The CSS1 standard lets you specify separate properties for each link type. You do this by specifying one of the following selectors:

A:link or :link
This selector matches anchor elements only if they have *not* been visited, based on the browser's history log.

A:visited or :visited
This selector matches anchor elements only if they *have* been visited, based on the browser's history log.

A:active or :active
This selector indicates how links should be displayed as the user clicks on them (but before releasing the mouse).

These pseudo classes can be combined with other selectors. For instance, the first style rule that follows applies only to visited links inside text sections in a particular class, while the second applies only to images that are inside hypertext links that have not been visited.

```
.bizarre :active { font-size: 300% }
A:link IMG { border: solid green }
```

Typographical Pseudo Elements

CSS1 specifies two selectors that are supposed to let you create two common typographical effects: having the leading character or leading line of a paragraph displayed differently than the remainder of the text. These selectors are named first-letter and first-line respectively, and can only be applied to block-level elements. However, these two elements are described as "noncore" in the CSS1 specification, and are not supported by either Netscape Communicator 4.01 or Internet Explorer 3.01.

Core Warning

Most browsers ignore the first-letter and first-line pseudo elements.

Element:first-letter

This property allows the user to display the first character of a line in a different font, to use drop caps, and similar conventions. For instance, the drop cap example shown later in Listing 5.7 and Figure 5–10 could have been implemented by using a selector of P:first-letter instead of SPAN, then omitting the SPAN element in the main text.

Element:first-line

This property allows the user to change the characteristics of the first line of a paragraph. Note that the definition of "the first line" is based on the actual display in the user's browser; it can change if the user resizes the browser window.

Both pseudo elements can be applied to the same paragraph, and they can be combined with other types of selectors, as in the following examples:

```
P:first-letter { float: left; font-size: 400% }
P:first-line { color: blue }
P.funkyType { ... }
P.funkyType:first-letter { font-family: Algerian }
```

5.4 Cascading: Style Sheet Precedence Rules

There often are multiple style rules that can apply to a particular section of text, and the system needs to know the order in which to apply them. The rules with the highest precedence are applied last so that they replace conflicting values from lower-priority rules. The rules for determining the precedence (or "cascading") order are as outlined in the following sections.

Rules marked "important" have the highest priority

A style rule can have the tag "!important" appended. For instance, in the following example, the foreground color property is marked as important.

```
H1 { color: black !important;
     font-family: sans-serif }
```

These declarations are normally used sparingly, if at all.

Author's rules have precedence over reader's rules

Browsers may permit readers to create style sheets to override the system defaults. In such a case, explicit settings by the author have higher priority.

More specific rules have precedence over less specific rules

In determining specificity, ID attributes in the selector have the highest priority. Ties based on ID selectors are broken by counting the number of class attributes in the selector. Finally, if a rule is still tied, the number of HTML element (tag) names is used to determine specificity. For instance, the following rules are sorted in order of specificity. The first is most specific because it has an ID selector. The other three are tied based on this measure, but the second rule has a class selector (big), so has precedence over rules three and four, which don't. Finally, rule three is more specific than rule four because it contains two tags rather than one.

```
#foo { ... }
P.big H1 { ... }
P STRONG { ... }
STRONG { ... }
```

In case of a tie, the last rule specified has priority

If two or more rules have the same priority after applying the previous three rules, later rules are given priority over earlier rules.

5.5 Font Properties

CSS1 gives the author control over several aspects of the font: whether it is bold, italic, or normal, what size to use, what font families are preferred, and whether a small-cap variation should be used. Netscape Communicator also supports *dynamic fonts*, which let you attach a font definition file to a document rather than depending on certain fonts already being on the client system. Underlined text, subscripts, and superscripts are not set using these font properties, but rather by the text-decoration and vertical-align properties covered in Section 5.7 (Text Properties). Properties already supported by Internet Explorer in versions 3.0, 3.01, and 3.02 are indicated with "†".

font-weight†

This specifies the weight of the font. Internet Explorer version 3 permits values of extra-light, light, demi-light, medium, demi-bold, bold, and extra-bold. However, in the CSS1 specification, these names were deemed too confusing, and replaced with options of 100 (lightest) through 900 (heaviest) in units of 100, plus the relative values normal, bold, bolder, and lighter.

font-style†

This property specifies italic text, and has legal values of normal, italic, and oblique. Internet Explorer 3.0x supports normal and italic only.

font-size†

This specifies the font size. Values can be in standard length units (Section 5.11), a symbolic value, or a percentage. Symbolic values can be absolute (xx-small, x-small, small, medium, large, x-large, and xx-large) or relative (smaller or larger). A percentage will be interpreted with respect to whatever font size would have otherwise been used. Internet Explorer 3.0x supports normal size units but not symbolic size names. It also supports percentages, but interprets them with respect to the paragraph's *default* style, not the *current* size as inherited from outer elements. For instance,

```
STRONG { font-size: 150% }
```

should mean that text in a STRONG element should be 50% larger than the current font size. However, suppose STRONG was used in Internet Explorer version 3.01 in a paragraph whose font-size had been set to 50pt, but where the default was 12pt. Given the rule for STRONG, STRONG text would then be rendered in 18pt type, not 75pt.

font-family[†]

This specifies the typeface. For instance, Listing 5.2 shows a rather dry page describing "Camp Bear Claw" with the standard look in Internet Explorer 3.01 shown in Figure 5–3.

Listing 5.2   A boring summer camp

```
<!DOCTYPE HTML PUBLIC "-//W3C//DTD HTML 3.2//EN">
<HTML>
<HEAD>
  <TITLE>Camp Bear Claw</TITLE>
</HEAD>

<BODY>
<H1>Camp Bear Claw</H1>
We have the following activities:
<H2>Archery</H2>
<H2>Arts and Crafts</H2>
<H2>Horseback Riding</H2>
<H2>Hiking</H2>
<H2>Campfire Song Times</H2>
<H2>C++ Programming</H2>

</BODY>
</HTML>
```

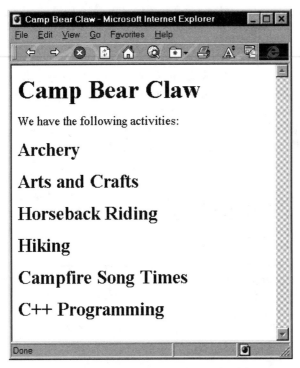

Figure 5–3   Bear Claw page with standard fonts.

However, by adding `font-family` entries (Listing 5.3), we obtain a much more pleasing result (Figure 5–4).

Listing 5.3   An exciting summer camp

```
<!DOCTYPE HTML PUBLIC "-//W3C//DTD HTML 3.2//EN">
<HTML>
<HEAD>
  <TITLE>Camp Bear Claw</TITLE>

<STYLE>
<!--
H1 { text-align: center;
     font-family: Funstuff }
H2.archery { font-family: ArcheryDisplay }
H2.arts { font-family: ClampettsDisplay }
H2.horseback { font-family: Rodeo }
H2.hiking { font-family: SnowtopCaps }
H2.campfire { font-family: Music Hall }
H2.java { font-family: Digiface }
-->
</STYLE>
</HEAD>

<BODY>
<H1>Camp Bear Claw</H1>
We have the following activities:
<H2 CLASS="archery">Archery</H2>
<H2 CLASS="arts">Arts and Crafts</H2>
<H2 CLASS="horseback">Horseback Riding</H2>
<H2 CLASS="hiking">Hiking</H2>
<H2 CLASS="campfire">Campfire Song Times</H2>
<H2 CLASS="java">Java Programming</H2>

</BODY>
</HTML>
```

Note that if font-family is used inside a STYLE attribute enclosed in double quotes (e.g., <P STYLE="font-family: Some Font">), the CSS1 specification says that multiword font names can be enclosed in single quotes. This works as expected in Netscape 4.01, but is not supported by Internet Explorer 3.01. Instead of a single font name, you can use a comma-separated list indicating the preferred order. The system will choose the first one it has available. You can put a generic typeface name such as "sans-serif" at the end, or let the system choose a default font if none of the preferred choices is available. Inter-

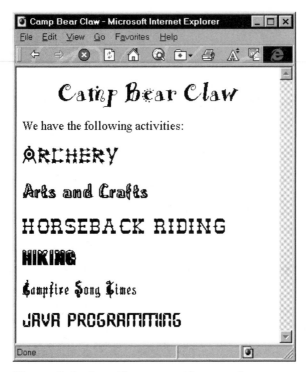

Figure 5–4   Bear Claw page with custom fonts.

net Explorer 3.0x requires that if you use such a list, you make `font-family` the last property in the specification.

Choosing font faces appropriately can make pages significantly more attractive, especially for intranet applications where a standard set of fonts can be assumed. On the Web, however, it is hard to choose fonts that are likely to be installed on all of the different systems that access your page. As a result, you should exercise care not to have your page *depend* on the font being used. For instance, if you use a graphical or foreign-language font to present icons or cyrillic text and your page is accessed by a user with a non-CSS-capable browser, or with style sheets disabled, or without that particular font installed on their machine, your page will appear as a jumbled mess. Your best bet is to create GIF files in such a case, but this can result in much longer download times, and prevents users and Web indexing robots from correctly searching your page. When the page doesn't fundamentally depend on the font being available, or when all your readers will be using Netscape 4, Netscape

Communicator offers an extremely useful extension: dynamic fonts. See `fontdef` later in this section for more information.

font-variant

This property is intended to be applied to text to make a variation in small caps. Legal values are `normal` and `small-caps`.

font[†]

The font property lets you group `font-weight`, `font-variant`, `font-style`, `font-size`, `line-height`, and `font-family` in a single entry. Items can be omitted, but if included should appear in that order, with spaces in between all except `font-size` and `line-height`, which should be separated by a slash (/). For instance,

```
P { font-weight: demi-bold;
    font-style: italic;
    font-size: 14pt;
    line-height: 150%;
    font-family: Times, serif }
```

could be replaced by

```
P { font: demi-bold italic 14pt/150% Times, serif }
```

fontdef

Netscape Communicator supports *dynamic fonts*: an extension to CSS1 that lets you supply a font definition file with a document, then use that font in various style rules throughout the document. Tools that support BitStream's TrueDoc standard even let you create downloadable fonts from local system fonts. To associate a font definition file with a document, use

```
<STYLE>
<!--
@fontdef URL(http://.../font-file.pfr);
...
-->
</STYLE>
```

or

```
<LINK REL="fontdef"
      SRC="http://.../font-file.pfr">
```

After this, you simply use the font normally. To accommodate browsers that support style sheets but not dynamic fonts (e.g., Internet Explorer), you can specify both dynamic fonts and system fonts in the same `font-family` list. For more information on dynamic fonts, and for several free font-definition files, see the following sites:

```
http://home.netscape.com/comprod/products/communicator/
fonts/
http://www.bitstream.com/world/
```

5.6 Foreground and Background Properties

Style sheets support a powerful and convenient way of changing foreground colors, background colors, and background images for regions of text. If user's rules are allowed to override author's rules, they are allowed to override *all* the colors. This is in contrast to the most pre-CSS browsers, where the user could set the default text color and background, but couldn't override FONT colors. So style sheets don't suffer from the problems of the FONT element whereby a foreground color might become invisible if the user overrides the author's settings on the BODY's BGCOLOR. Properties supported by Internet Explorer in version 3 are indicated with "†".

color†

This specifies the text or foreground color of the associated section, using any of the standard color designators (see Section 5.11).

background-color

This specifies the background color of the associated section using any of the standard color designators. Alternatively, the keyword `transparent` can be used to let an inherited color show through.

background-image

This specifies an image to be used as the background of the specified region only. Authors should supply a background color to use if the image is unavailable or the user has disabled image loading.

background-repeat

This property takes values of repeat, repeat-x, repeat-y, or no-repeat, and indicates that the image should be tiled in both directions, just in the x direction, just in the y direction, or displayed once in the background but not tiled, respectively.

background-attachment

This property determines if the background image scrolls with the content (value: scroll) or is fixed (value: fixed). Scrolling is the default.

background-position

The background-position property specifies the position of the background image with respect to the upper-left corner of the region it is associated with. You normally specify a pair of values (separated by a space), specified using the keywords left/center/right, top/middle/bottom, percentages, or distances in the standard units (see Section 5.11). For instance, a value of 50% means to put the center of the image at the center of the region. Similarly, a horizontal value of 25px means to position the left side of the image 25 pixels from the left side of the region. If you supply a single value instead of a pair, it applies just to the horizontal position; the vertical position is set to 50%. Negative positions are permitted, allowing images to hang into margins or previous text sections.

background[†]

The background property lets you combine background-color, background-image, background-repeat, background-attachment, and background-position in a single entry. Note that in Internet Explorer 3.01, you *must* use background in lieu of the individual properties.

As an example, consider Listing 5.4, which defines a page for Joe's Carpenter Shop, using wooden boards repeated horizontally as the background image of the title banner. Figure 5–5 shows the result in Netscape 4.01. The result is substantially the same in Internet Explorer 3.01.

Listing 5.4 Cabinets.html

```
<!DOCTYPE HTML PUBLIC "-//W3C//DTD HTML 3.2//EN">
<HTML>
<HEAD>
  <TITLE>Joe's Cabinets</TITLE>
<STYLE>
<!--
.banner { background: url(images/boards.jpg) repeat-x;
          font-size: 50pt;
          font-family: Arial Rounded MT Bold }
-->
</STYLE>
</HEAD>

<BODY>
<CENTER>
<TABLE WIDTH=360 HEIGHT=199>
  <TR><TD ALIGN="CENTER" CLASS="banner">Joe's Cabinets
</TABLE>
</CENTER>
<P>
Welcome to Joe's Cabinets. We specialize in
<UL>
  <LI>Custom Cabinets
  <LI>Kitchen Remodeling
  <!-- Etc -->
</UL>
<!-- Etc -->
</BODY>
</HTML>
```

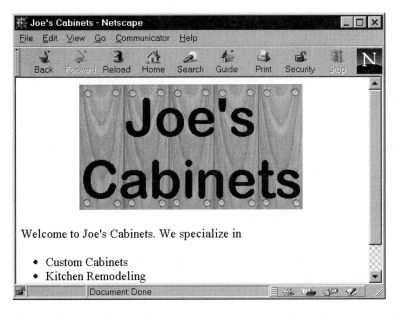

Figure 5–5   Background images can be used for individual text sections.

5.7 Text Properties

The text properties control the way text in a paragraph is laid out. Options let the user customize characteristics like inter-word spacing, paragraph justification, and indentation of leading lines in paragraphs. The `text-decoration`, `text-align`, `text-indent`, and `line-height` properties are supported by Internet Explorer 3.0, as indicated by "†".

word-spacing, letter spacing

These properties specify a change to the default spacing between words or characters. Values are expressed using the standard length units (see Section 5.11) or by the keyword `normal`. Numeric values can be positive (add the space to the default word spacing) or negative (subtract the space from the default).

text-decoration†

The `text-decoration` property describes text additions, or "decorations" that are added to the text of an element. Legal values are `none`, `underline`, `overline`, `line-through`, and `blink`. For instance, to make hypertext links be blue but not underlined, use:

```
A:link { color:blue; text-decoration: none }
```

Note that Internet Explorer version 3 does not support the `overline` or `blink` values.

vertical-align

This property determines how elements are positioned vertically. The value can be a percentage (positive or negative) indicating how far to raise the baseline of the element above the baseline of the parent element, or a symbolic value. Legal symbolic values are `top` (align the top with the tallest element in the line), `bottom` (align the bottom with the lowest element in the line), `baseline` (align the baseline of the element with the baseline of the parent element), `middle` (align the middle of the element with a point halfway up from the parent element's baseline), `sub` (make the element a subscript), `super` (make the element a superscript), `text-top` (align the top with the top of the parent element's font), and `text-bottom` (align the bottom of the element with the bottom of the parent element's font).

text-transform

This property determines if the text should be changed to all uppercase (`uppercase`), all lowercase (`lowercase`), have the first letter of each word uppercase (`capitalize`) or have inherited text transformations suppressed (`none`).

text-align[†]

Prior to style sheets, HTML 3.2 supported left-aligned paragraphs and paragraphs with centered lines, but not paragraphs that were right-aligned or aligned on both sides (i.e., justified). The `text-align` property adds these capabilities. Legal values are `left`, `right`, `center`, or `justify`. Note that Internet Explorer 3.0x supports `left`, `right`, and `center`, but not `justify`.

text-indent[†]

This specifies the indentation of the *first* line of the paragraph and is calculated with respect to the existing left margin as specified by `margin-left`. Values can be in normal length units or can be a percentage interpreted with respect to the width of the parent element.

Negative values can be used to indicate that the first line should hang out into the left margin.

line-height[†]

This specifies the height of each line. This is the distance between two consecutive baselines in a paragraph, and is sometimes known as *leading* (rhymes with "wedding," not "weeding"). In addition to the standard length units (see Section 5.11), a percent value can be supplied, interpreted with respect to the font size. For instance, the following would create a `double` class that could be applied to paragraphs to make them double spaced:

```
.double { line-height: 200% }
```

white-space

The `white-space` property specifies how spaces, tabs, carriage returns, and newlines should be treated within the element. Legal values are `normal` (collapse whitespace to a single space), `pre` (maintain whitespace as in the `PRE` element), and `nowrap` (only wrap at `BR` elements).

By way of example, consider a Web page that is intended to look like a business letter. Listing 5.5 gives the HTML source. First, the default spacing between all paragraphs is reduced using

```
P { margin-top: 5px }
```

Next, right-aligned (`rhead`) and left-aligned (`lhead`) paragraph classes are created for the date, return address, and receiver's address. The main body of the letter (`body`) uses indented lines and justified text, and the footer used for the signature (`foot`) is indented 60% and has a large interline spacing. Figure 5–6 shows the result in Netscape Communicator. The look is similar in Internet Explorer 3.01, with the main difference being that the body text is left-aligned instead of justified. Note that for Netscape Communicator (but not Internet Explorer 3.01), the headings could have specified a `white-space` style of `pre` and then omitted the explicit `BR`s.

Listing 5.5 Bates.html

```html
<!DOCTYPE HTML PUBLIC "-//W3C//DTD HTML 3.2//EN">
<HTML>
<HEAD>
  <TITLE>An Open Letter to the IRS</TITLE>
<STYLE>
<!--
P { margin-top: 5px }
P.rhead { text-align: right;
          margin-right: 0.5in;
          font-family: sans-serif }
P.lhead { font-family: sans-serif }
P.body { text-align: justify;
         text-indent: 0.5in }
P.foot { margin-left: 60%;
         line-height: 300% }

-->
</STYLE>
</HEAD>

<BODY BACKGROUND="images/bond-paper.jpg">
<P CLASS="rhead">
April 1, 1998
<HR>
<P CLASS="rhead">
William A. Bates<BR>
Macrosoft Corporation<BR>
Blumond, WA 12345
<P CLASS="lhead">
Internal Revenue Service<BR>
Philadelphia, PA 67890
<P>
<BR>
Dear Sirs,
<P CLASS="body">
I am writing to inform you that, due to financial
difficulties, I will be unable to pay my taxes this
year.
<P CLASS="body">
You see, my company has had reduced profits this year.
In fact gross revenues have now dropped below the
GDP of <B>twelve</B> foreign countries! Given this
intolerable situation, I am sure you will understand.
<P CLASS="foot">
Sincerely,<BR>
William A. Bates
</BODY>
</HTML>
```

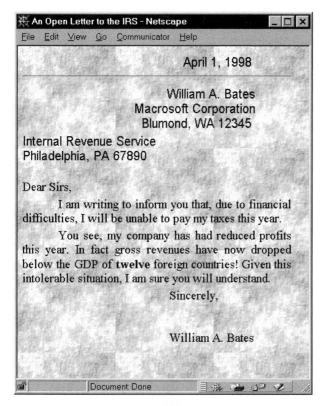

Figure 5-6   Using text properties enables customized text formatting.

5.8 Properties of the Bounding Box

Cascading style sheets assume that all elements will result in one or more *rectangular* regions. This region is known as the "bounding box" (or simply "box") and contains a margin, border, padding area, and main element, each nested within the other. The width and height of the total box is the sum of the width and heights of the main element, the padding area that surrounds it, the border surrounding the padding, and the margins surrounding the border. Margins are always transparent, letting the color and/or image underneath show through. The padding always takes on the background color or image of the main element. The border, which is in between, can have its own background. For instance, you could set margins, border, and padding to a quarter of an inch each (but using different colors/patterns) via the following:

```
P { margin: 0.25in;
    border: 0.25in solid black;
    padding: 0.25in;
    background: URL(images/bond-paper.jpg) }
BODY { background: URL(images/bricks.jpg) }
```

Figure 5–7 shows a page created using these settings. The details of the property specifications will be explained later, but for now the important point is that the margin is outside the border, which is outside the padding, which is outside the main element area.

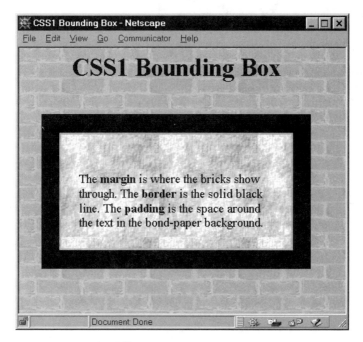

Figure 5–7   The differences between margin, border, and padding

Internet Explorer 3.0x supports most of the margin properties (indicated with "†"), but not the border or padding area properties.

Margins

An element's margins are the reserved areas around the element where the background colors or images show through. Margins can be negative to allow paragraphs to overlap.

margin-left[†], margin-right[†], margin-top[†], margin-bottom
These properties set the left, right, top, and bottom margins, using normal length units (Section 5.11), percentages, or the keyword `auto`. Internet Explorer 3.0x supports `margin-left`, `margin-right`, `margin-top`, but not `margin-bottom`. Negative values are permitted; this allows text or graphics to hang into the left margin or overlap previous paragraphs.

margin[†]
This property lets you set the top, right, bottom, and left margins (in that order) in one property. If only one value is supplied, it applies to all four margins. If two or three values are supplied, values for any unspecified margin are taken from the margin directly across from it. Negative values are permitted, and are sometimes used to implement layered text effects. For instance, Listing 5.6 sets two paragraph classes `layer1` and `layer2` where `layer1` uses gray text and is set 20 pixels below (assuming that Internet Explorer ignores `margin-bottom` settings) and to the right of `layer2` which uses black text. When used in consecutive single-line paragraphs, the result is striking, as shown in Figure 5–8. However, using style sheets in this manner shifts their role from a supporting to a leading role, with the page now *depending* on style sheets being available rather than using them to *augment* the appearance of an already accessible page. When displayed in a browser that doesn't support style sheets, the "Drop Shadows" heading is displayed twice, as illustrated in Figure 5–9, which uses Netscape Navigator 3.01. So authors should think twice about using such tricks except on internal networks that use a particular browser consistently.

Listing 5.6   Drop-Shadows.html

```
<!DOCTYPE HTML PUBLIC "-//W3C//DTD HTML 3.2//EN">
<HTML>
<HEAD>
  <TITLE>Drop Shadows</TITLE>
<STYLE>
<!--
.layer1 { font-size: 100px;
          color: gray;
          text-align: center;
          margin: 20px 0px 0px 20px;
          font-family: Impact, Arial, sans-serif }
.layer2 { font-size: 100px;
          color: black;
          text-align: center;
          margin-top: -160px;
          font-family: Impact, Arial, sans-serif }
-->
</STYLE>
</HEAD>


<BODY BGCOLOR="WHITE">
<P CLASS="layer1">Drop Shadows
<P CLASS="layer2">Drop Shadows
<P>
Support for negative margins tempts authors to use
style sheets to implement drop shadows and other
layered-text effects. Although the result can be
dramatic when it works, the page will appear jumbled
on browsers that do not support style sheets or
where the user has disabled them. Tricks of this type
can also make the pages dependent on assumptions about
the user's window size.
</BODY>
</HTML>
```

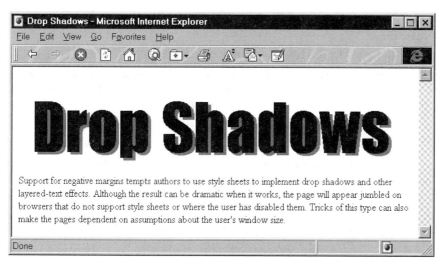

Figure 5-8 Negative margins can be used to implement drop shadows.

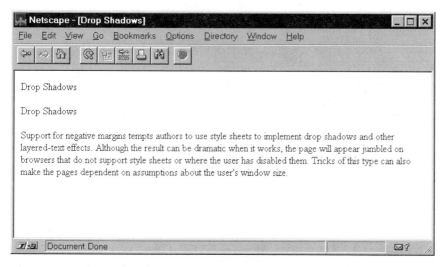

Figure 5-9 Pages that *depend* on style sheets can look poor on browsers that don't support style sheets.

Borders

An element's borders are the reserved areas around the element where a specific color or background image is displayed. The borders are inside the margins. Borders can have zero thicknesses, but cannot be negative.

border-left-width, border-right-width, border-top-width, border-bottom-width

These properties set the left, right, top, and bottom border sizes, using normal length units (Section 5.11) or the symbolic names `thin`, `medium`, `thick`, or `none`. Negative values are prohibited.

border-width

This property is a shorthand method for setting `border-width-top`, `border-width-right`, `border-width-bottom`, and `border-width-left` (in that order) in one fell swoop. If only one value is supplied it applies to all four borders. If two or three values are supplied, values for any missing border are taken from the border directly across from it.

border-color

This sets the border colors. One to four values can be supplied, specifying characteristics for the top, right, bottom, and left borders in the same manner as with `border-width`. Each value can be a color specified in the normal way (Section 5.11).

border-style

This property specifies the way in which the borders will be drawn. One to four values can be supplied, specifying characteristics for the top, right, bottom, and left borders in the same manner as with `border-width`. Each value can be one of `none`, `dotted`, `dashed`, `solid`, `double`, `groove`, `ridge`, `inset`, or `outset`. The main element's background shows through for nonforeground parts of `dotted`, `dashed`, and `double`.

border-left, border-right, border-top, border-bottom

This lets you set the width, style, and color for each of the four borders. For instance, to display major headings in red with a solid blue line above and below, you could use:

```
H1 { color: red;
     border-top: 10px solid blue;
     border-bottom: 10px solid blue }
```

border

This sets the width, style, and color for all four borders at once. For instance, the quarter inch solid black border of Figure 5–7 was specified via:

```
border: 0.25in solid black
```

Padding

An element's padding area is the reserved space around an element and inside its borders where the background color or image of the element itself shows through. Padding area sizes cannot be negative.

padding-left, padding-right, padding-top, padding-bottom

These properties let you set the left, right, top and bottom sizes of the padding area. Recall that the padding area is inside the margin and the border. The margin lets the background of the parent element (often the BODY) show through, the border can have an independent background, and the padding area has the same background as the main element it is associated with. Values can be lengths (Section 5.11) or percentages, where percentages are interpreted with respect to the parent element's width and height. Negative values are not allowed.

padding

This property lets you set the sizes of the top, right, bottom, and left sides of the padding area in one location. If only one value is supplied it applies to all four. Otherwise, if less than four values are supplied, the value for any missing side is taken from the side directly across from it. For instance, the quarter inch padding area used in Figure 5–7 was specified with:

```
padding: 0.25in
```

Bounding Box Display Types

Most HTML elements can have margins, borders, and padding areas. However, the way this is interpreted depends on whether an element is embedded in another paragraph (i.e., an inline, text-level element), is a separate block-level element, or is part of a list. The display property can be used to determine this.

display

This property determines if the element should be considered to have a separate bounding box as a paragraph such as P or PRE would, or have inline bounding boxes on each line inside an existing box, as the various character-style elements (B, I, CODE, and so forth) would. Legal values are block, inline, list-item, and none. The list-item value is treated just like block except that a list item marker is added (see Section 5.10).

5.9 Images and Floating Elements

Most style rules apply to elements at fixed locations. Images and text items that "float" to the margins are in a special category, however.

width, height

These properties specify a fixed size for the element, and are usually applied to images. Values can be in normal length units (Section 5.11) or be the keyword auto. For instance, a "bullet" type might be created as follows:

```
IMG.bullet { width: 50px; height: 50px }
```

The auto keyword applies to images where only one of width or height is specified as a length, and indicates that the image should be scaled maintaining its original aspect ratio.

float

This property lets elements float into the left or right margins with text wrapping around. The legal values are left, right, and none. This can be used to implement drop caps, floating images, and the like. For instance, Listing 5.7 implements a 75 point drop capital to lead off

Psalm 23. The result is shown in Figure 5–10. In principle, instead of a
SPAN element, the `first-letter` pseudoelement could have been
used. In practice, however, neither Internet Explorer 3.01 nor Netscape
Communicator 4.01 support `first-letter`.

Listing 5.7   `Psalm23.html`

```html
<!DOCTYPE HTML PUBLIC "-//W3C//DTD HTML 3.2//EN">
<HTML>
<HEAD>
  <TITLE>The 23rd Psalm</TITLE>
<STYLE>
<!--
SPAN { float: left;
       font-family: Algerian;
       font-size: 75pt }
-->
</STYLE>
</HEAD>

<BODY>
<H2 ALIGN="CENTER">
The 23rd Psalm (King James Version)</H2>
<SPAN>T</SPAN>he LORD is my shepherd; I shall not want.
He maketh me to lie down in green pastures:
he leadeth me beside the still waters. He restoreth
my soul: he leadeth me in the paths of righteousness
for his name's sake. Yea, though I walk through the
valley of the shadow of death, I will fear no evil:
for thou art with me; thy rod and thy staff they
comfort me. Thou preparest a table before me in the
presence of mine enemies: thou anointest my head
with oil; my cup runneth over. Surely goodness and
mercy shall follow me all the days of my life: and I
will dwell in the house of the LORD for ever.
</BODY>
</HTML>
```

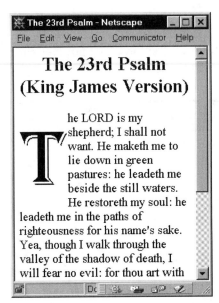

Figure 5-10 The `float` property can be used to implement "drop caps."

clear

This property specifies whether the element permits floating elements on its sides. Legal values are `left` (skip below any floating elements on the left), `right` (skip past floating elements on the right), `both` (skip past all floating elements), and `none` (permit floating elements). The default is `none`. For instance, in the 23rd Psalm shown in Listing 5.7 and Figure 5–10, suppose a new paragraph was inserted after the first sentence. If the paragraph break were simply <P>, the result would be as shown in Figure 5–11, with the second sentence beginning before the bottom of the drop cap T.

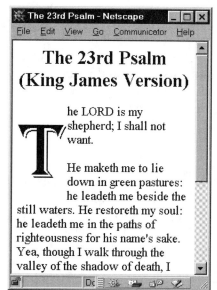

Figure 5–11 The default behavior is to permit floating elements from previous paragraphs

However, if the paragraph was `<P STYLE="clear: left">`, then the result would be as shown in Figure 5–12, with the second sentence beginning below the bottom of the initial T.

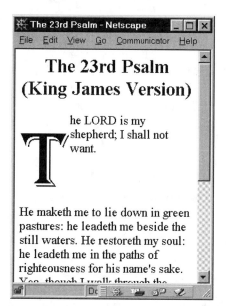

Figure 5–12 Paragraphs can skip past floating elements from previous paragraphs.

5.10 Properties of Lists

Cascading style sheets allow the user to customize the way list items are formatted in ordered lists (OL), unordered lists (UL), and definition lists (DL). These properties are not supported by Internet Explorer version 3, and Netscape Communicator 4.01 supports only the list-style-type property.

list-style-image

This property is intended to allow authors to set their own "bullets" for lists. However, it is not supported by either Internet Explorer or Netscape Communicator. The value should be a URL or the keyword none. For instance, the following would set the default bullet for unordered lists to be a diamond, plus set up a "star" class that can be used in unordered lists to get a star as a bullet.

```
UL { list-style-image: URL(diamond.gif) }
UL.star { list-style-image: URL(star.gif) }
```

If a browser supports animated GIFs, they should be permitted as bullets.

list-style-type

This property sets the list item marker in the cases when the list-style image is none (the default for OL and DL). Legal values are disc (solid circle), circle (hollow circle), square, decimal (1, 2, 3, and so forth), upper-alpha (A, B, C, and so forth), lower-alpha (a, b, c, and so forth), upper-roman (I, II, III, and so forth), lower-roman (i, ii, iii, and so forth), and none.

list-style-position

This property, with legal values of outside (default) and inside, determines whether the list item marker runs into the paragraph (inside) or hangs out to the left (outside). Neither Netscape Communicator nor Internet Explorer release 3 support list-style-position.

list-style

The list-style property permits you to set the list's image, style type, and position in a single property.

5.11 Standard Property Units

Cascading style sheets allow authors to specify sizes and colors in a variety of different formats. Lengths can be specified in either absolute or relative units, using either integers or decimal floating point numbers. Some properties allow negative lengths, and are indicated by a leading minus sign ("–") before a length otherwise specified in the normal manner. Units supported by Internet Explorer in version 3 are indicated with "†".

Lengths

Cascading style sheets permit you to use any of the following formats for properties that describe lengths (sizes).

Relative Units

em
The height of the current font.

ex
The height of the letter "x" in the current font.

px[†]
Pixels.

Absolute Units

pt[†]
Points; 72 points per inch.

pc
Picas; 6 picas per inch (12 points per pica).

in[†]
Inches.

cm[†]
Centimeters.

mm
Millimeters.

Colors

Cascading style sheets allow the user to specify colors in any of the following ways:

color-name†
This should be one of the standard HTML colors listed in Table 1.1. Netscape and Internet Explorer also support the X11 window system color names.

#RRGGBB†
Each of RR, GG, and BB should be hexadecimal numbers ranging from 00 to FF, as with standard HTML colors.

#RGB
This is a shorthand notation for #RRGGBB. For instance, #0AF is equivalent to #00AAFF.

rgb(rrr, ggg, bbb)
In this format, each of rrr, ggg, and bbb should be decimal numbers ranging from 0 to 255.

rgb(rrr%, ggg%, bbb%)
In this format, each of rrr, ggg, and bbb should be decimal numbers ranging from 0 to 100.

5.12 Layers

Netscape Communicator supports a new capability known as *layers*. Internet Explorer 4.0 is expected to support this as well. Layers allow you to place HTML markup in separate rectangular regions, then to position the regions at particular absolute or relative positions on the page. Regions can overlap, and upper regions can be transparent to let lower regions show through. This lets you create overlapping banners and sidebars, make multi-column text, annotate diagrams and other pictures, and to create composite images by placing transparent GIFs over top of other images. Furthermore, JavaScript can be used to dynamically make regions visible or invisible, to change the stacking order, or to shrink, expand, or move regions on the screen. The specifics of how to change layers dynamically will be covered in Chapter 19, "JavaScript:

Adding Dynamic Content to Web Pages," but it is worthwhile to keep this capability in mind when evaluating the benefits of layers. Layers can be defined in the BODY of the document using the LAYER and ILAYER elements (Section 5.13), or in the HEAD using cascading style sheets (Section 5.14).

To illustrate the capabilities offered by layers, consider the example shown in Figure 5–13. This layout was created by making a top-level region containing the computer image, and three nested regions, as shown in Figures 5–14 through 5–19. The HTML markup used in this example is given in Section 5.13, "Specifying Layers Using the LAYER and ILAYER Elements."

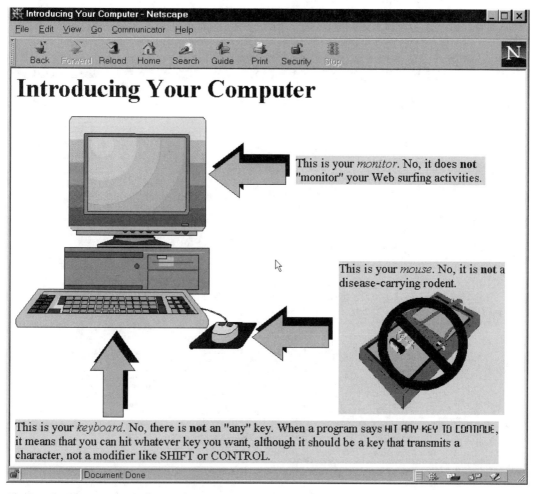

Figure 5–13 Layers can be used to create overlapping regions.

To create this effect, we first define a region that starts below the "Introducing Your Computer" heading, then insert three nested regions used to make the three textual boxes shown in Figure 5–13. Creating a region to contain these other regions is preferable to laying the regions down over the main Web page, because the location of the three description regions will be independent of the size or margins of the introductory heading. This main region is highlighted in Figure 5–14.

After defining the main region (Figure 5–14), we then create a region used to describe the monitor (Figure 5–15). This region is broken into two subregions. The first contains the left-pointing arrow, and is transparent. The second contains the descriptive text. Nesting these two regions in their own

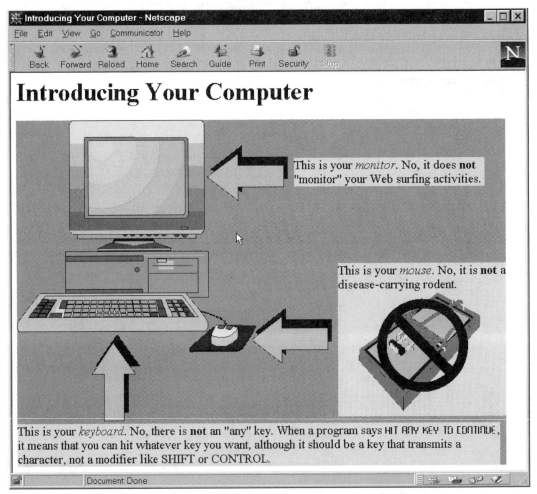

Figure 5–14 Except for the initial heading, the entire page is contained in one large region.

region is preferable to making them independent, because the text region can supply coordinates relative to the size of the arrow, rather than having to calculate absolute positions in the main region.

The approach to creating the mouse region (Figure 5–16) is similar to that for the monitor region, except that the region holding the descriptive text also contains a region for the bottom illustration. This illustration region contains two more regions: the first for the mousetrap image and the second for the circle and slash picture that goes over top of the mousetrap. The regions for these two pieces of the illustration are shown in Figures 5–17 and 5–18.

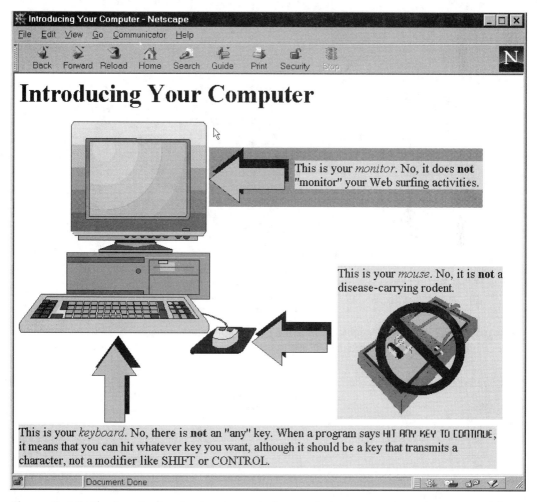

Figure 5–15 The "monitor" region is composed of two regions, one containing the arrow and the other containing the text.

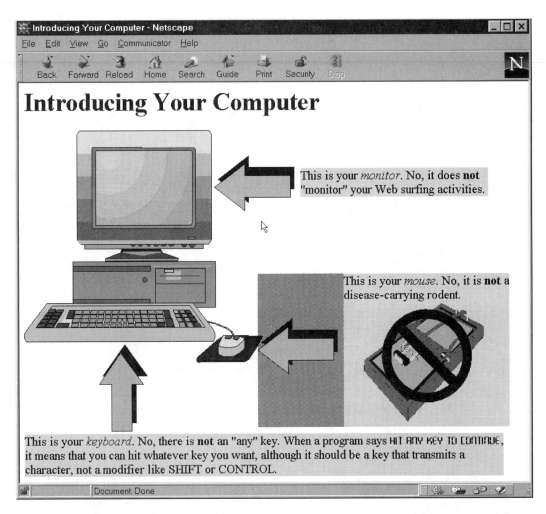

Figure 5-16 The "mouse" region is composed of two regions, one containing the arrow and the other containing the composite text/mousetrap region.

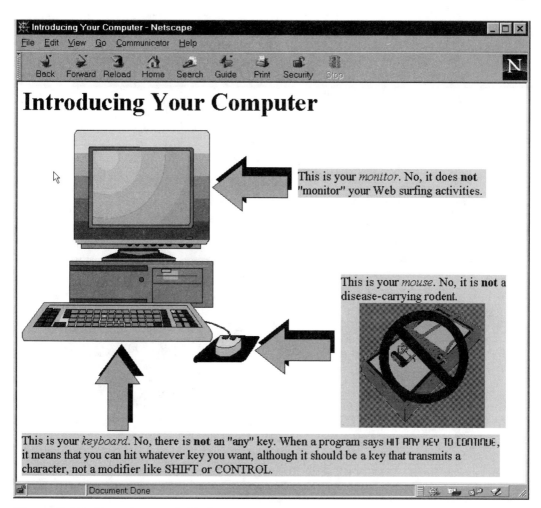

Figure 5-17 One sub-region holds the mousetrap image.

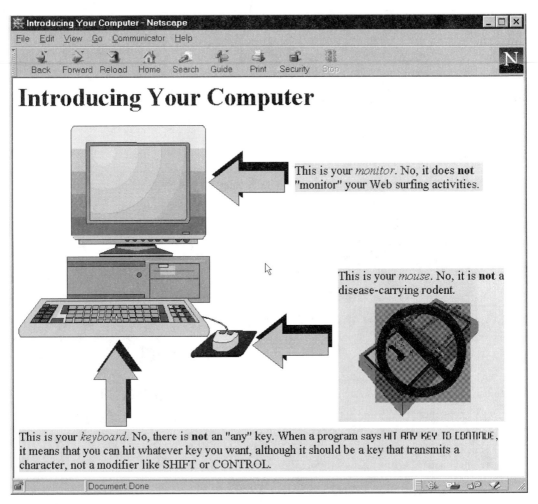

Figure 5–18 The other sub-region holds the image of the circle and slash.

Finally, Figure 5–19 shows the region used to create the keyboard description. This region is similar to the monitor region, except that the nested regions are under each other, rather than side by side.

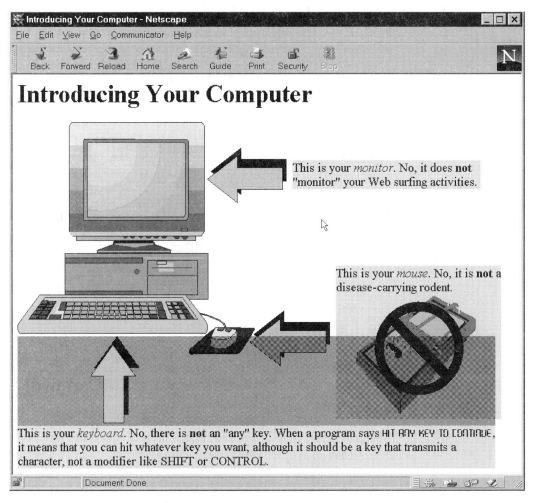

Figure 5–19 The "keyboard" region is composed of two regions, one containing the arrow and the other containing the text.

5.13 Specifying Layers Using the LAYER and ILAYER Elements

There are two different ways to create layers. The first, described in this section, is to use the LAYER and ILAYER elements. The second, described in the next section, is to create style sheet elements that use the position attribute. Netscape Communicator supports both methods, while Internet

Explorer 4.0 is expected to support only the style sheet approach. Layers are not supported in release 3 of Netscape or Internet Explorer.

HTML Element: `<LAYER ...> ... </LAYER>`
`<ILAYER ...> ... </ILAYER>`

Attributes: `ABOVE , BACKGROUND, BELOW, BGCOLOR, CLIP, HEIGHT, ID, LEFT, ONBLUR, ONFOCUS, ONLOAD, ONMOUSEOVER, ONMOUSEOUT, PAGEX, PAGEY, SRC, TOP, VISIBILITY, WIDTH, Z-INDEX`

The `LAYER` element is used to create regions that have an absolute position with respect to the window or parent layer. `ILAYER` is used to create "inline" layers: regions that are embedded in the flow of the text. Alternate text for browsers that do not support layers can be placed in a `NOLAYER` element. Contents of `NOLAYER` will be ignored by browsers that support `LAYER`.

ABOVE, BELOW, Z-INDEX

Normally, layers are stacked in the order they appear in the document, with the first being on the bottom and later ones stacking above. You can use these attributes to override this behavior. Only one of `ABOVE`, `BELOW,` or `Z-INDEX` should be used for a given layer. `Z-INDEX` takes a positive integer, where layers with higher numbers are stacked on lower-numbered layers. `ABOVE` and `BELOW` are used to give the `ID` of a layer that should be immediately above or below the current layer. This is a bit counter intuitive to some people; `<LAYER ID="Foo" ABOVE="Bar">` means that `Bar` is above `Foo`, not that `Foo` is above `Bar`.

Core Warning

ABOVE and *BELOW* specify whether the referenced layer is above or below the current layer, not whether the current layer is above or below the referenced one. Thus, `<LAYER ID="currentLayer" ABOVE="referencedLayer">` means that `currentLayer` is **below** `referencedLayer`.

Listing 5.8 gives a simple example, with the result shown in Figure 5–20.

Listing 5.8   Using ABOVE and BELOW

```
<!DOCTYPE HTML PUBLIC "-//W3C//DTD HTML 3.2//EN">
<HTML>
<HEAD>
  <TITLE>Using ABOVE and BELOW</TITLE>
</HEAD>

<BODY>
<H1>Using <CODE>ABOVE</CODE> and <CODE>BELOW</CODE></H1>

<LAYER ID="Top" LEFT=60 TOP=120
       WIDTH=500 HEIGHT=300 BGCOLOR="#F5DEB3">
This layer is on top, even though it appears
first in the HTML document.
</LAYER>

<LAYER ID="Bottom" ABOVE="Top" LEFT=10 TOP=70
       WIDTH=500 HEIGHT=300 BGCOLOR="gray">
This layer is on the bottom, even though it appears
second in the HTML document.
</LAYER>

</BODY>
</HTML>
```

BACKGROUND, BGCOLOR

By default, layers are transparent. However, a background image or color can be used to make the layer opaque. BACKGROUND and BGCOLOR are used for these purposes. For instance, the two layers shown in the ABOVE and BELOW example (Listing 5.8, Figure 5–20) use BGCOLOR to assign colors to each layer. Although BGCOLOR always creates an opaque background, BACKGROUND can make a partially transparent background if a transparent GIF is specified. For instance, the gray boxes used to highlight various layers in Figures 5–14 through 5–19 were created by specifying a background image containing a 2x2 GIF where the top-left and bottom-right quadrants were black and the other two quadrants were transparent.

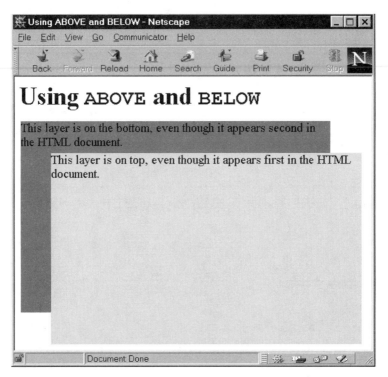

Figure 5–20   ABOVE, BELOW, and Z-INDEX can override layer stacking order.

CLIP

This attribute takes comma-separated integers as a value, specifying the boundaries of the visible area of the layer. The HTML is rendered in the full size of the region, but part of it may be chopped off when displayed. Boundaries are specified either by `"left, top, right, bottom"` or `"right, bottom"`. The latter form is equivalent to `"0, 0, right, bottom"`. For example, Listing 5.9 creates two frames with the same size and content. The second one uses CLIP to obscure part of the layer. The result is shown in Figure 5–21.

Listing 5.9   Using the CLIP attribute

```
<!DOCTYPE HTML PUBLIC "-//W3C//DTD HTML 3.2//EN">
<HTML>
<HEAD>
  <TITLE>Using CLIP</TITLE>
</HEAD>

<BODY>
<H1>Using <CODE>CLIP</CODE></H1>

<LAYER BGCOLOR="#F5DEB3" LEFT=10 TOP=75
       WIDTH=500 HEIGHT=200>
<H2>No Clipping:</H2>
The <CODE>CLIP</CODE> attribute can change
the clipping region of a layer.
The <CODE>CLIP</CODE> attribute can change
the clipping region of a layer.
The <CODE>CLIP</CODE> attribute can change
the clipping region of a layer.
The <CODE>CLIP</CODE> attribute can change
the clipping region of a layer.
</LAYER>


<LAYER BGCOLOR="#F5DEB3" LEFT=10 TOP=300
       WIDTH=500 HEIGHT=200
       CLIP="50, 10, 405, 190">
<H2>Clipping:</H2>
The <CODE>CLIP</CODE> attribute can change
the clipping region of a layer.
The <CODE>CLIP</CODE> attribute can change
the clipping region of a layer.
The <CODE>CLIP</CODE> attribute can change
the clipping region of a layer.
The <CODE>CLIP</CODE> attribute can change
the clipping region of a layer.
</LAYER>

</BODY>
</HTML>
```

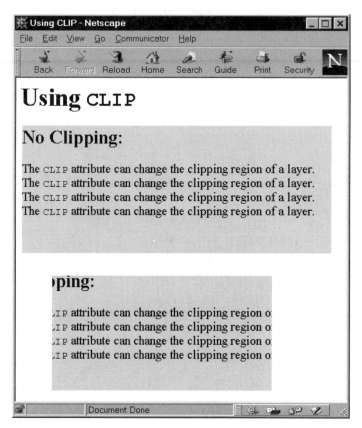

Figure 5–21   CLIP changes the visible area, not the area in which the HTML is rendered.

WIDTH, HEIGHT

These attributes specify a minimum width and height for the layer. Otherwise, the browser uses the smallest possible width and height that encloses the layer's content. These values give minimums, not maximums; the width and height will be expanded if necessary to fit the content of layer. For example, the two layers shown in the ABOVE and BELOW example (Listing 5.8, Figure 5–20) use WIDTH and HEIGHT to specify sizes for the layers.

ID

This gives a name to the layer. The name can be used by the ABOVE or BELOW attributes, or by JavaScript code.

LEFT, TOP, PAGEX, PAGEY

For positioned layers (LAYER), these attributes specify the position of the layer in pixels relative to the position of the enclosing layer (LEFT, TOP), or with respect to the entire page (PAGEX, PAGEY). In the absence of these attributes, the layer starts at the current location in the Web page. For instance, the two layers shown in the ABOVE and BELOW example (Listing 5.8, Figure 5–20) use LEFT and TOP to specify locations for the layers.

For inline layers (ILAYER), the LEFT and TOP attributes are interpreted with respect to the current location in the Web page. For instance, Listing 5.10 uses TOP to move each of the words in the line "Gently down the stream" 10 pixels down from the previous word. The result is shown in Figure 5–22.

Listing 5.10 Using TOP in ILAYER

```
<!DOCTYPE HTML PUBLIC "-//W3C//DTD HTML 3.2//EN">
<HTML>
<HEAD>
  <TITLE>Row, Row, Row Your Boat</TITLE>
</HEAD>

<BODY>
<IMG SRC="images/Rowboat.gif" ALIGN="RIGHT">
<HR>
<B>Row, Row, Row Your Boat</B><BR>
Row, row, row your boat<BR>
Gently
<ILAYER TOP=10>down</ILAYER>
<ILAYER TOP=20>the</ILAYER>
<ILAYER TOP=30>stream<BR>
Merrily, merrily, merrily, merrily<BR>
Life is but a dream<BR>
<HR>
</ILAYER>
</BODY>
</HTML>
```

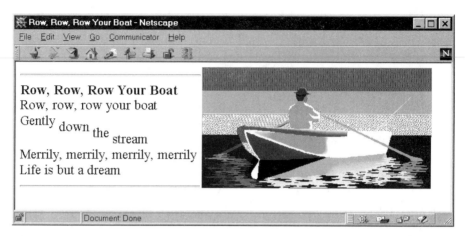

Figure 5–22   Using TOP in ILAYER can move text up or down in the current paragraph.

SRC

This attribute gives the URL of an HTML document to be placed inside the specified layer. Any layers in the designated file will be treated as child layers of the current layer. This is particularly useful for including components that you want to put in multiple documents, or for a frequently changing part of an otherwise static page. For instance, you could include contact information at the bottom of every Web page in a site by specifying `<LAYER SRC="Contact-Info.html"></LAYER>` just before the `</BODY>` tag of each document. Alternatively, you could specify a dynamic piece of an otherwise fixed document as follows:

```
<H1>Menu for Joe's Diner</H1>
<ILAYER SRC="Blue-Plate-Special.html"></ILAYER>
<H2>Appetizers</H2> ...
<H2>Main Dishes</H2> ...
<H2>Vegetables</H2> ...
```

VISIBILITY

This attribute determines if the layer will be displayed or not. Legal values are SHOW, INHERIT, and HIDDEN, indicating that the layer should be shown, should inherit the parent layer's visibility, or be hidden, respectively. Hidden frames are not particularly useful for static pages, but can be used with JavaScript to hide and display regions interactively. See Listing 5.12 (Dynamically changing a layer's visibility) for an example.

ONBLUR, ONFOCUS, ONLOAD, ONMOUSEOVER, ONMOUSEOUT

These attributes can be used to supply JavaScript code to be executed in various situations. For details, see Chapter 19, "JavaScript: Adding Dynamic Content to Web Pages."

An Example

The "Introducing Your Computer" example shown in Figure 5–13 uses many of the attributes discussed in this section. The HTML source is given in Listing 5.11.

Listing 5.11   Introducing Your Computer (Using Layers)

```
<!DOCTYPE HTML PUBLIC "-//W3C//DTD HTML 3.2//EN">
<HTML>
<HEAD>
  <TITLE>Introducing Your Computer</TITLE>

<STYLE>
<!--
CODE { font-family: digiface }
-->
</STYLE>
</HEAD>


<BODY>
<H1>Introducing Your Computer</H1>
<LAYER ID="Computer">
  <IMG SRC="images/Computer.gif" WIDTH=390 HEIGHT=366>
  <LAYER ID="Monitor" LEFT=310 TOP=40>
    <LAYER ID="Monitor-Arrow">
      <IMG SRC="images/Arrow-Left.gif">
    </LAYER>
    <LAYER ID="Monitor-Text"
           LEFT=140 TOP=20 BGCOLOR="#F5DEB3">
    This is your <I>monitor</I>. No, it does
    <B>not</B> "monitor" your Web surfing activities.
    </LAYER>
  </LAYER>
</LAYER>
```

continued

**Listing 5.11 Introducing Your Computer
          (Using Layers) (cont'd)**

```
<LAYER ID="Mouse" LEFT=380 TOP=225>
    <LAYER ID="Mouse-Arrow" LEFT=0 TOP=70>
      <IMG SRC="images/Arrow-Left.gif">
    </LAYER>
    <LAYER ID="Mouse-Text"
          LEFT=140 TOP=0 BGCOLOR="#F5DEB3">
      This is your <I>mouse</I>. No, it is
      <B>not</B> a disease-carrying rodent.<BR>
      <LAYER ID="Trap" LEFT=30>
        <LAYER ID="Trap-Picture">
          <IMG SRC="images/Mousetrap.gif"
              WIDTH=200 HEIGHT=190>
        </LAYER>
        <LAYER ID="Trap-No" LEFT=30 TOP=10>
          <IMG SRC="images/No.gif"
              WIDTH=150 HEIGHT=150>
        </LAYER>
      </LAYER>
    </LAYER>
  </LAYER>


<LAYER ID="Keyboard" LEFT=0 TOP=335>
    <LAYER ID="Keyboard-Arrow" LEFT=120 TOP=0>
      <IMG SRC="images/Arrow-Up.gif">
    </LAYER>
    <LAYER ID="Keyboard-Text"
          LEFT=0 TOP=140 BGCOLOR="#F5DEB3">
      This is your <I>keyboard</I>. No, there is
      <B>not</B> an "any" key. When a program says
      <CODE><B>Hit any key to continue</B></CODE>, it
      means that you can hit whatever key you want,
      although it should be a key that transmits a
      character, not a modifier like SHIFT or CONTROL.
    </LAYER>
  </LAYER>
</LAYER>

</BODY>
</HTML>
```

5.14 Specifying Layers Using Style Sheets

Using style sheets to create layers is described in the draft specification, "Positioning HTML Elements with Cascading Style Sheets," available at http://www.w3.org/pub/WWW/TR/WD-positioning. Netscape Communicator (i.e., Netscape 4.0) supports this specification, and Internet Explorer 4.0 will probably support it as well. This is not guaranteed, however. On the one hand, Microsoft helped develop this draft specification, but on the other hand the very early "platform preview" release of Internet Explorer 4.0 did not support it. This was the latest version of Internet Explorer available at the time of publication.

Style sheets let you do most, but not all, of the things that can be done with the LAYER and ILAYER elements. Style sheets don't let you specify an external file for the content of a layer ala the SRC attribute, and there are no attributes equivalent to PAGEX and PAGEY for positioning nested layers independently of the parent layer's location. Furthermore, Netscape's support for layers is more complete and reliable when the LAYER or ILAYER element is used. For instance, you have to hit RELOAD after resizing a window that has style sheet layers, but not after resizing one containing LAYER. And when style sheets are used to specify a background color for a layer, the background of the underlying layer or page shows through in the margins between paragraphs. Background images work as expected, however. Nevertheless, using style sheets for layers fits more cleanly with the general way style sheets are used, supports positions using standard CSS length units (rather than just pixels), and is expected to work in Internet Explorer 4.0 as well as in Netscape 4.0. So it is a good potential option for creating layers that run on both platforms. By way of example, consider the page shown in Figure 5–23. This is a variation of the example of Figure 5–13 and Listing 5.11, created using style sheet syntax instead of the LAYER and ILAYER elements. The illustrations in the left margin are created using layers with negative left value and an unspecified top value. This positions the illustration to the left of the main layer's left side, with the top of the illustration aligned with whatever location in the document contained the reference to the layer. As before, the mousetrap illustration was created by overlaying a transparent circle and slash image on top of the main image. The HTML source for this example is given at the end of this section in Listing 5.13.

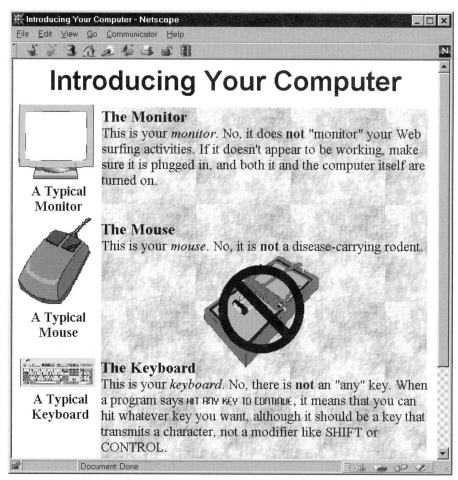

Figure 5-23   Layers can be created using style sheet syntax instead of LAYER and ILAYER.

Layer Properties

Layer declarations should use either the ID tag format (#tag) in the header, or be declared inline via <DIV STYLE="..."> (block-level) or <SPAN STYLE="..."> (text-level). Layer declarations should contain a position property. For instance, combining the style rule

```
#layer1 { position: absolute;
        left: 50px; top: 75px;
        ... }
```

with

```
<SPAN ID="layer1">
...
</SPAN>
```

is roughly equivalent to

```
<LAYER ID="layer1" LEFT=50 TOP=75 ...>
...
</LAYER>
```

Similarly, combining

```
#layer2 { position: relative;
          top: 10px;
          ... }
```

with

```
<SPAN ID="layer2">
...
</SPAN>
```

is roughly equivalent to

```
<ILAYER ID="layer2" TOP=10 ...>
...
</ILAYER>
```

In addition to the standard attributes available in CSS1, layers support the following attributes:

clip

Clipping is specified via `rect(top right bottom left)` or by the keyword `auto` (the default). The `clip` property is equivalent to the CLIP attribute of LAYER and ILAYER. Note that the clipping region, like each of the other layer positions, can be specified using normal CSS length units (Section 5.11). These included pixels, points, inches, and centimeters, not just pixels like LAYER and ILAYER.

left, top

These properties specify the left and top sides of the layer, in normal CSS length units. They are equivalent to the LEFT and TOP attributes of LAYER and ILAYER.

overflow

This property determines what happens when an element's contents exceed its height or width. A value of none (the default) indicates that it should be drawn normally, obscuring any underlying layers. A value of clip indicates that clipping should occur, while scroll indicates that the browser should scroll to accommodate it.

position

This property can have the value absolute, relative, or static. These correspond to LAYER elements, ILAYER elements, and normal, unlayered CSS elements, respectively. The default is static.

visibility

This property determines whether a layer is visible or hidden. Legal values are show (or visible), hidden, or inherit, signifying that the layer should be shown normally, hidden, or that the parent layer's visibility be used, respectively. It is useful when using JavaScript to change visibility values dynamically. JavaScript is discussed at more length in Chapter 5, but Listing 5.12 gives a simple example. A two button input form is created with two invisible layers sharing the same region below it. This is shown in Figure 5–24. Clicking on the first button displays the first hidden layer (Figure 5–25), hiding the second if necessary. Clicking on the second button reverses the process: the second layer is shown and the first is hidden (Figure 5–26).

Listing 5.12 Dynamically changing a layer's visibility

```html
<!DOCTYPE HTML PUBLIC "-//W3C//DTD HTML 3.2//EN">
<HTML>
<HEAD>
  <TITLE>Changing Visibility Dynamically</TITLE>

<STYLE>
<!--
#layer1 { position: absolute; left: 0.25in; top: 1.5in;
        color: black; background-color: #F5DEB3;
        visibility: hidden }
#layer2 { position: absolute; left: 0.25in; top: 1.5in;
        color: #F5DEB3; background-color: black;
        visibility: hidden }
H1 { text-align: center;
    font-family: Arial }
FORM { text-align: center }
-->
</STYLE>
</HEAD>


<BODY BGCOLOR="WHITE">
<H1>Changing Visibility Dynamically</H1>

<FORM>
  <INPUT TYPE="BUTTON" VALUE="Show Layer1"
        onClick="layer1.visibility='show';
                layer2.visibility='hidden'">
 <INPUT TYPE="BUTTON" VALUE="Show Layer2"
        onClick="layer2.visibility='show';
                layer1.visibility='hidden'">
</FORM>

<DIV ID="layer1">
<H1>This is layer1.</H1>
</DIV>

<DIV ID="layer2">
<H1>This is layer2.</H1>
</DIV>

</BODY>
</HTML>
```

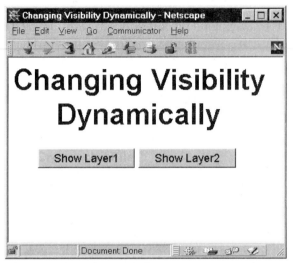

Figure 5-24 This page shows two JavaScript buttons and has two hidden layers.

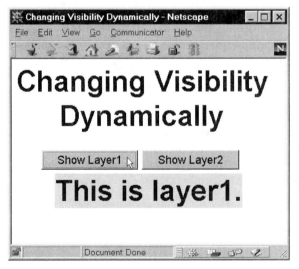

Figure 5-25 Clicking the first button displays the first hidden layer.

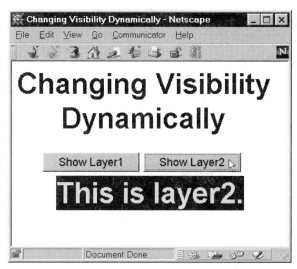

Figure 5–26 Clicking the second button replaces the first layer with the second.

width, height
These properties specify the size of the layer, and are equivalent to the WIDTH and HEIGHT attributes of LAYER and ILAYER.

z-index
Normally, layers are stacked from the bottom to the top in the order they appear in the HTML source. The z-index property can be used to override this behavior. Values are integers; lower numbers are stacked below higher numbers. This is equivalent to the Z-INDEX attribute of LAYER and ILAYER.

An Example

Listing 5.13 gives the HTML used to create the "Introducing Your Computer" example shown at the beginning of the section in Figure 5–23.

Listing 5.13 Introducing Your Computer (Using Style Sheets)

```
<!DOCTYPE HTML PUBLIC "-//W3C//DTD HTML 3.2//EN">
<HTML>
<HEAD>
  <TITLE>Introducing Your Computer</TITLE>

<STYLE>
<!--
#main-body { position: absolute;
             left: 150px; top: 75px;
             background: url(images/bond-paper.jpg) }
H1 { text-align: center;
     font-family: Arial }
-->
</STYLE>
</HEAD>


<BODY BACKGROUND="WHITE">
<H1>Introducing Your Computer</H1>

<DIV ID="main-body">

<SPAN
  STYLE="position: absolute; left: -140px; width: 140px">
  <IMG SRC="images/Monitor.gif" WIDTH=130 HEIGHT=124>
  <CENTER><B>A Typical Monitor</B></CENTER>
</SPAN>
<BIG><B>The Monitor</B></BIG><BR>
This is your <I>monitor</I>. No, it does
<B>not</B> "monitor" your Web surfing activities.
If it doesn't appear to be working, make sure
it is plugged in, and both it and the computer itself
are turned on.
<BR><BR><BR>

<SPAN
  STYLE="position: absolute; left: -140px; width: 140px">
  <IMG SRC="images/Mouse.gif" WIDTH=130 HEIGHT=146>
  <CENTER><B>A Typical Mouse</B></CENTER>
</SPAN>
<BIG><B>The Mouse</B></BIG><BR>
This is your <I>mouse</I>. No, it is
<B>not</B> a disease-carrying rodent.
<CENTER>
<IMG SRC="images/Mousetrap.gif" WIDTH=200 HEIGHT=190>
<BR>
<SPAN STYLE="position: relative; top: -180px">
  <IMG SRC="images/No.gif" WIDTH=150 HEIGHT=150>
</SPAN>
</CENTER>
```

Listing 5.13 Introducing Your Computer (Using Style Sheets) (cont'd)

```
<SPAN STYLE="position: relative; top: -180px">
<SPAN
  STYLE="position: absolute; left: -140px; width: 140px">
  <IMG SRC="images/Keyboard.gif" WIDTH=130 HEIGHT=49>
  <CENTER><B>A Typical Keyboard</B></CENTER>
</SPAN>
<BIG><B>The Keyboard</B></BIG><BR>
This is your <I>keyboard</I>. No, there is
<B>not</B> an "any" key. When a program says
<CODE STYLE="font-family: digiface"><B>
Hit any key to continue</B></CODE>, it
means that you can hit whatever key you want,
although it should be a key that transmits a
character, not a modifier like SHIFT or CONTROL.
</SPAN>

</DIV>
</BODY>
</HTML>
```

5.15 Summary

Cascading style sheets provide a powerful capability for customizing the look of Web pages. They let you specify fonts, background colors, and images for individual sections of text, floating elements, margins and indentation, and list styles. In addition to the new effects that style sheets enable, they also allow you to give pages a much more consistent look across browsers--at least browsers that support style sheets. An extension to style sheets lets you create layered HTML regions that can overlap and can be changed dynamically when the user performs various actions. Even with this capability, however, HTML is still a markup language, not a programming language. So the types of applications you can create are limited. Java, however, lets you create general programs that can be attached to Web pages and run in the browser when the page is loaded. Java is also widely used as a general purpose programming language, independent of any association with an HTML document or Web browser. Onward! Java is the topic of Part II.

Part 2

JAVA
PROGRAMMING

GETTING STARTED WITH JAVA

Topics in This Chapter

- Unique features of Java: What's so unusual, and why is everyone so excited about it?

- Separating hype from reality: Debunking Java myths

- The evolution of Java: Current and upcoming Java versions

- Getting ready: The software and documentation you'll need

- Getting started: How to compile and run a Java program

- Whetting the appetite: Some simple Java programs

- Java in the real world: Some sample applications

Chapter 6

J ava is a new programming language that looks a lot like C++ and can be used for general-purpose applications and for embedding programs in WWW pages. Programmers think it's cool; software managers think it's hot. Why? Here are a few reasons I'll elaborate upon in this chapter:

- Java is Web-Enabled and Network Savvy
- Java Is Cross-Platform
- Java Is Simple
- Java Is Object Oriented
- Java Has Lots of Powerful Standard Libraries

These features are described in Section 6.1. However, the hype about Java is sometimes overblown. Although Java can do Windows and take out the garbage, some Java advocates would have us believe that it is the One True Programming Language to which all unenlightened programmers will convert for all applications. On the other hand, some of the supposed drawbacks to Java are imagined or exaggerated as well. Some common myths I'll debunk in Section 6.2 are:

- Java Is Only for the Web
- Java Is Cross-Platform
- Java Is Simple

- Object-Oriented Programming Is the One True Way
- All Software Should Be Developed in Java

If you're not sure which version of Java is for you, Section 6.3 summarizes the differences among the current and upcoming releases. Now, I have heard rumors of some programmers that were cut off by an earthquake and don't already have Java on their machines. If you're in this category, Section 6.4 will show you where to get all the software and documentation you need. Finally, Section 6.5 shows some simple ready-to-run programs to let you get your feet wet.

Origin of a Name

If you are wondering what Java stands for, it is not an acronym at all; it was chosen because of the use of "java" as American slang for "coffee." This came about after Sun had to change the original name (Oak) due to a conflict with an existing name. The name is meant to imply something exciting and hip. Coffee became known as "java" because of coffee imports from Indonesia, where the main population lives on the island of Java. But where did the island get its name? When I first wondered this, I sent e-mail to a friend who lives in West Java, and got a reply saying that he didn't know, but that he would be happy to answer more practical questions such as:

1. *What is the cost of a baycuk ride from pasar Seder-hana to Jalan Gegerkalong?*
2. *How many trips are required for the second renewal of a six-month renewal sosial budaya visa?*
3. *What is the worst pothole in north Bandung?*
4. *How do you explain cat litter to someone who has never heard of cat food?*
5. *At what stage is a papaya most likely to be eaten by a fruit bat?*

Eventually, however, I was able to determine that "Java" came from "Yava," which meant "rice" in an eighth-century dialect where Java was known as "Yava Dwipa," or "Rice Island." There, doesn't that make you feel better?

6.1 Unique Features of Java

Actually, many of the capabilities described here are *not* truly one of a kind, just unique in the experience of most developers. Java is an excellent language, but not, as some proponents claim, a brilliant new breakthrough packed with ideas that have never been seen before. The vast majority of Java language features have already been seen in other languages. So why all the excitement about Java? What Java has done that few other languages have been able to do is to combine standard capabilities (C/C++ syntax), powerful features of niche-market languages (automatic memory management, byte code interpreters), and some key new features (Web execution) into a coherent package that has gained widespread acceptance in the mainstream programming community. The following sections highlight some of the most important characteristics.

Java is Web-Enabled and Network Savvy

It is the Web that helped catapult Java to its current prominent position. If you're writing applications that need to run on the Web, access Web resources, or simply talk to other programs on the network, Java has many facilities that will make your life easier.

Safety in Java Programs Can Be Enforced

Because Java checks array bounds, forbids direct manipulation of memory addresses, and enforces types, Java programs cannot access arbitrary memory locations. This allows Java programs to be reliably analyzed to see what operations they perform. This analysis permits a restricted class of Java programs known as "applets" to be run in your Web browser without fear of them introducing viruses, finding and reporting on private information about your system, erasing your disk, snooping behind your corporate firewall, or starting up programs like Doom just when your boss is entering your office.

DILBERT © United Feature Syndicates. Reprinted with permission

The Web Can Be Used for Software Delivery

Because Java applets run in Netscape Navigator, Microsoft Internet Explorer, Sun's HotJava, and Lotus Notes 4.5, they can be run in the vast majority of Web browsers on the vast majority of operating systems. This opens up a whole new way of viewing the WWW and a browser: as a medium for software delivery and execution, not just as a medium for document delivery and display. If you have an application that you update frequently, you no longer need your users to reinstall the latest version every time you make a change. In fact, your users don't need to install anything at all; all they have to do is keep a bookmark to your applet in the Web browser they already have on their system. This shifts the burden of software installation and maintenance from the user to the developer, who can control versions at a single centralized location. For example, the Hubble Control Center System, shown in Figure 6–1, is accessed in a variety of locations over the Web, providing up-to-the-minute status on the Hubble Space Telescope.

Java's Client/Server Library Is Easy to Use

Java's networking library is used exactly the same way on all operating systems. And ordinary mortals can actually use it, a welcome change from other languages where you leave such magic to the local wizards who are probably on another project just when you need them the most.

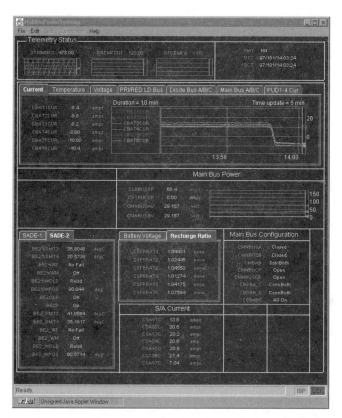

Figure 6–1 Control Center System applet for Hubble Space Telescope, developed at NASA.

Compared to, for instance, Berkeley sockets or the POSIX Transport Layer Interface, creating clients or servers is positively a joy in Java. Furthermore, Java already understands the HTTP protocol, letting you retrieve files on the Web and communicate with HTTP servers without even dealing directly with sockets. For example, Applix Anyware (Figure 6–2) uses a "thin client" to minimize disk and memory requirements on the client machine.

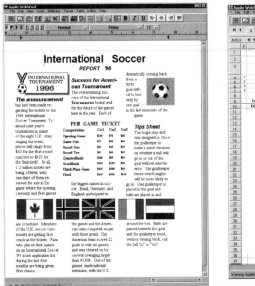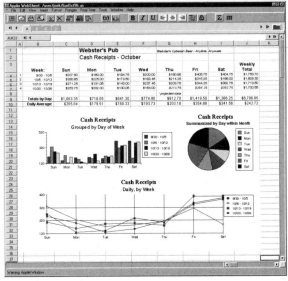

Figure 6-2   Applix Anyware, a server-based office automation suite.

Java 1.1 Includes a Distributed Object Protocol and an API for Network Database Access

Java 1.1 includes RMI, The Remote Method Invocation package and JDBC, the Java DataBase Connectivity package. RMI lets you invoke methods in objects on remote platforms, allowing you to pass arbitrary Java objects back and forth. Think of this as an object-oriented version of remote procedure calls. This provides an easy to use built-in alternative to CORBA for applications that only need to talk to other Java programs and don't need to make use of transaction processing or other advanced CORBA capabilities. JDBC lets your applications interface with multiple database vendors in a standard manner and lets your applets bypass the CGI interface and talk directly to a database.

Java Is Cross-Platform

Java is designed to be portable, and Java programs developed on one platform can often run unchanged on many other computer systems (see Figure 6-3). Why? Well, there are a number of reasons, but the three most important characteristics that make Java so portable are outlined here.

Figure 6–3 JavaSoft advertisement trumpeting Java's cross-platform nature.

Java Compiles to Machine-Independent Bytecode

Java is typically compiled and executed in a two-step process, as illustrated in Figure 6–4. In the first step, Java source code is compiled to "bytecode"—assembly language for an idealized Java virtual machine (JVM). In the second step, this bytecode is executed by a run-time system. This run-time system can either be an interpreter (an emulator for the Java VM) or a "Just In Time" (JIT) compiler that first compiles the bytecode to native code, then executes the result. The beauty of this process is that the two steps can be performed on totally separate platforms. The source can be compiled on a Windows 95 machine using Symantec's compiler, then the result executed on a Mac via Apple's runtime system, on a Sun using Sun's software, or on a Windows NT system using Microsoft's virtual machine. Most modern Web browsers include a Java VM, letting Web page developers compile applets and attach the resultant bytecode to Web pages for execution on a variety of platforms.

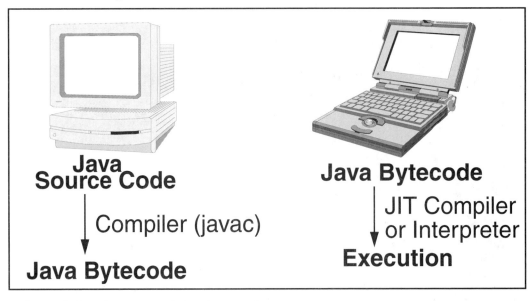

Figure 6–4   Java is compiled and executed in two steps.

Java Has a Portable Graphics Library

In many software systems, the biggest hindrance to portability is the user interface. Interfaces have typically been developed using the native windowing system rather than a cross-platform graphics toolkit because until now this was the most convenient and widely available option. However, this often meant that distribution on a different operating system required a complete rewrite of the GUI. The Java developers realized that a truly portable language would need a standard graphics library, and put one in at the beginning. Figure 6–5 illustrates several of the standard GUI elements in a network interface I developed for testing a routing system for spacecraft telemetry data. Unfortunately, this library is a bit weak compared to the rest of Java, but it is improving as new Java versions are released.

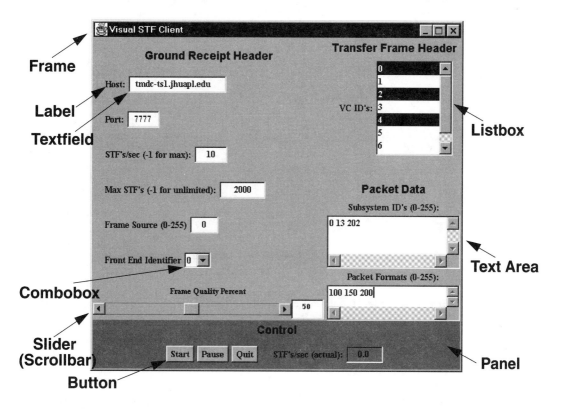

Figure 6–5   Spacecraft telemetry simulator developed at the Johns Hopkins University Applied Physics Laboratory.

Java Avoids Hard-to-Port Constructs

The Java specification defines the size of primitive-data structures such as ints, booleans, and doubles, unlike some languages that allow this to vary among implementations. For objects, Java programs can't inadvertently depend on implementation-specific details such as the amount of memory an object consumes (Java has no need for the equivalent to the C/C++ sizeof operator), the internals of how fields or functions are laid out within an object, or the like. Java even avoids reference to the local file system when specifying which classes your program needs, using operating-system-neutral class and package names instead.

Figure 6–6 shows the applet created when NASA was faced with the problem of making Pathfinder data available to a huge number of users on different platforms.

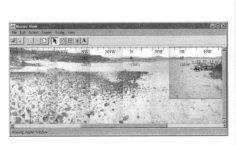
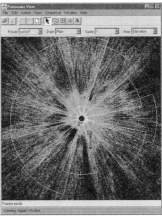

Figure 6–6   Jet Propulsion Lab's Web Interface for Telescience, used for worldwide viewing of Mars Pathfinder data.

Java Is Simple

Java started with familiar C++ syntax but cleaned up many of the most complicated syntactic features. In addition, header files are never needed, makefiles are usually not necessary, the networking process is easier, and there are several other improvements. In addition to a long list of similar relatively minor features, Java has two major features that simplify life for the programmer: automatic memory management and simplified pointer handling.

Java Has Automatic Memory Management

The Java programmer is freed from the time-consuming and error-prone process of manually allocating and deallocating memory for objects. Instead, an automatic system, known as a *garbage collector*, doles out memory when it is needed and reclaims memory from objects that can no longer be accessed. Poof! In one fell swoop, Java has eliminated dangling pointers (references to memory that has been recycled) and memory leaks (inaccessible memory that is never reclaimed), two problems that often account for half of the development time in large systems built in languages with manual memory management.

Java Simplifies Pointer Handling

When you pass an object (i.e., any nonprimitive data type) to a function in Java, the system actually passes a pointer or "reference" to the object. That is, the entire object is not copied onto the run-time stack, just the reference is. However, all the details of this are hidden from the user, who can simply view "the object" as being passed. You do not need to explicitly reference or dereference the pointer, pointer arithmetic is unnecessary (banned, in fact), and the whole process is considerably simpler. This lets the programmer avoid thinking in terms of pointers altogether if desired, while still making it easy to implement data structures that depend on pointers, such as linked lists and trees. Although at first this seems strange to the C or C++ programmer, it is the way things have worked for decades in languages like Smalltalk and Lisp.

Java Is Object Oriented

Java is pervasively and consistently object oriented. "Object obsessed," some people would say.

All Functions Are Associated with Objects

In many other object-oriented languages, there are "normal" functions that are independent of objects as well as "methods" or "member functions" that are associated with objects. Java, however, is like Smalltalk in this regard, with methods being the *only* type of allowable function.

Almost All Datatypes Are Objects

In some object-oriented languages, there is a distinction between regular datatypes and classes. Strings, arrays, structures, files, sockets, and other types might not be objects that can be processed in the same way as user-defined objects. In contrast, in Java all complex types are true objects, and there is a common ancestor for all objects (`Object`), simplifying the creation of arrays or other collections of heterogeneous object types. Although there are a few "primitive" datatypes (`int`, `double`, `boolean`, `char`, among others) that are kept distinct from objects for efficiency reasons, there is a corresponding object for each of them (`Integer`, `Double`, `Boolean`, `Character`, and so forth). This object can be obtained from the primitive type by simple conversion methods.

Java Has Lots of Powerful Standard Libraries

In addition to the graphics and client/server libraries already mentioned, Java has standard libraries for, to name a few:

- Building and using hash tables
- Manipulating and parsing strings and streams
- Saving objects (even graphical ones) to disk and reassembling them later
- Using arbitrary-precision fixed-point numbers
- Accessing files on the WWW
- Granting security privileges based on digital signatures
- Invoking remote Java objects
- Interfacing with relational databases
- Distributing computation among multiple threads of execution

As a result, even large applications can be written completely in Java without recourse to libraries specific to a particular operating system. Figure 6–7 illustrates one such system.

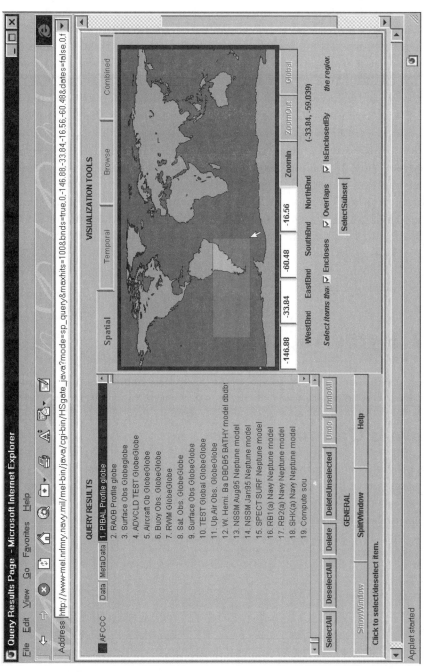

Figure 6–7 Master Environmental Library interface, used for international access to oceanic data. From Naim Alper and the MEL project.

Now, such a wide array of built-in capabilities is a mixed blessing. On the one hand, it provides a large set of standard, portable tools that you can pick through for your particular application. On the other hand, Java as a whole is so large that learning it seems intimidating. Fortunately, you don't have to learn it all at once. Everyone will need to know how to construct and use objects (Chapter 7) and understand the core syntax (Chapter 8). Other than that, the pieces are pretty independent. Because Java loads classes dynamically, the size of the Java run-time environment and compiled classes is independent of the total language size. And you don't have to get a handle on everything before making good progress. If you're going to be writing a server that doesn't require a user interface, you can skip learning about the Abstract Window Toolkit (AWT) until you actually need it. Similarly, there is no need to know anything about the networking library when writing a typical applet. Even so, no doubt you'll occasionally write some utility only to discover it is already built-in. Okay, I admit that seems frustrating. But it's still better than using a bare-bones language where you *always* have to write every utility you need.

6.2 Myths About Java

Java burst on the software scene so suddenly that many misconceptions still remain. I'll try to refute some of the most prevalent ones here.

Java Is Only for the Web

Java programs can easily use the World Wide Web. Certain Java programs can even run in Web pages. But this does not mean that all Java programs have to use the Web or be embedded in WWW pages. In fact, the long-term impact of Java is likely to be larger as a general-purpose programming language than as a method for putting programs into Web pages.

Java Is Cross-Platform

Yes, Java was designed with portability in mind. It succeeded in many ways. Many Java programs run unchanged on multiple operating systems. Nevertheless, there are things than can make some Java programs difficult or even impossible to port to other platforms. I will describe the three most important ones here.

Java Programs Can Execute Local, Nonportable Programs

The exec method of the Runtime class lets Java applications call local programs. The "native method" interface supports linking Java and C programs together. The first can make Java programs completely nonportable, while the second makes them only as portable as the associated C code. Now, it is hardly fair to say that Java is nonportable just because it connects to something that is. After all, that is not "pure" Java (Figure 6–8). That is very true, but it is still worth remembering that not all "Java" programs are completely in Java, and that many do indeed connect to other components. Many programs, of course, can avoid this. But some programs need to format a disk, get a list of users currently logged in, or link with legacy C or C++ code, even if the programs need to sacrifice portability to do so. This is not necessarily a bad thing; accessing local applications is sometimes more important than portability. And if your Java program starts JASC's Paint Shop Pro when the user double clicks on an image, you don't *expect* the call to work on systems that don't have Paint Shop installed. The important thing is not to sacrifice portability *without knowing it*, and Java has done a good job of avoiding nasty surprises in this regard. Be wary of third-party libraries that don't make it clear which part is pure Java and which part is nonportable.

Figure 6-8   JavaSoft ad touting "100% Pure" Java.

The Graphics Library Behaves Differently on Different Systems

When designing the graphics library, the Java team decided to have the graphic elements adopt the look and feel of the local windowing system, rather than trying to have a consistent look and feel across platforms. This was wise; experience has shown that some Macintosh users would rather die than use an application that looks like Windows

95, no matter how much you preach that they should. Similarly, Unix users want nothing but Motif widgets, Windows users will rebel against "foreign" looking GUI controls, and so forth. Trying to reason with them is useless; if you can't give them the look they are accustomed to, they simply won't use your application. But supporting a native look and feel comes at a price; scrollbars, buttons, textfields, and the like can be slightly different sizes and behave slightly differently on different platforms. I will discuss techniques for mitigating this problem later, and with the help of layout managers and a little experience, you will be able to write simple interfaces on one platform and run them on multiple platforms the first try. However, complicated interfaces *must* be tested on every major platform on which they are to be delivered, and getting the GUI working on multiple platforms often requires several iterations.

DILBERT © United Feature Syndicate. Reprinted by permission

The Behavior of the Thread Scheduler Is Only Loosely Defined

Java has one of the best threading libraries around. It lets you execute independent parts of your program in separate processes. However, in order to allow a compiler to use efficient mechanisms on a particular OS, some of the interactions among threads are only loosely specified. For instance, how long a given thread will run before being replaced by another is almost certain to vary from machine to machine and even from run to run on the same machine. In some sense, this nondeterminism is an advantage of using threads, but it can lead beginning programmers to inadvertently depend on certain behavior by the scheduler in order to operate correctly. For example, suppose you develop a program that uses two threads. Imagine that the first takes 50 units of time to complete while the second takes 35. If the application was developed using an implementation that gave each thread 30 units before switching to the next, the first thread would always finish first. If you came to depend on this, the code would not work properly on a system where each thread gets 10 units, where the second thread would always finish first. So multithreaded programs should be carefully tested on a variety of platforms and configurations until you gain experience.

Java Is Simple

Simple? Ha. Who said it was simple? Oh, I did? Hmm.

The problem is that simplicity is a relative concept. Compared to some of the intricacies of C and C++, Java syntax seems positively streamlined. People who have fought with memory leaks and dangling pointers will be relieved to let the Java garbage collector take over the battle. But Java is a full-blown programming language, and programming is anything but simple. So, for instance, the HTML developer will find Java programming a huge leap up in complexity. And given the ever-increasing number of standard and third-party libraries, it is becoming harder and harder to be knowledgeable in all of them.

Not only is programming hard, but programmers tend to continually push the envelope of what can reasonably be done. In many other languages, only the guru would attempt client-server or multithreaded applications, but Java makes these techniques accessible to "ordinary" programmers. This is a two-edged sword. On the one hand, developers can do useful things they couldn't before. On the other hand, programs using these techniques can be very tricky to develop and debug.

So Java programming is certainly not simple. Far from it. But Java is designed so that the various libraries and approaches can be learned in bite-sized pieces, and the relatively clean syntax and design makes the learning process more palatable than in most other languages.

DILBERT © United Feature Syndicate. Reprinted by permission

Object-Oriented Programming Is the One True Way

"It's not?" you say, "Blasphemy!" There are various ways to view programming. Some take the religious view, where technical evangelists argue fervently to convert disciples of one software dogma to another. In some arenas, there *is* a single right answer. But I think the carpenter's model fits the software world better. Using this analogy, the various technical approaches are tools in the software developer's toolbox. Clearly some tools are more broadly applicable than others, and certain tools are well suited to certain jobs. OOP is a useful and broadly applicable tool, and it should be in a central place in the developer's toolkit. But functional programming, structured programming, rule-based programming, divide-and-conquer approaches, greedy algorithms, and the like are also useful tools, and the expert craftsman should be skilled with them as well. OOP is complementary to some of them, independent of others, and occasionally in conflict with some. Choosing OOP as the underlying structure for Java was a wise choice, but once in a while the object-oriented viewpoint will get in the way. Rejecting a useful technique in Java simply because it "doesn't fit with the object-oriented philosophy" is, well, heresy.

All Software Should Be Developed in Java

Java is a good general-purpose programming language. It is an excellent tool, perhaps even the best, for a number of jobs. But it's not the best tool for *every* job. Sometimes it will be more convenient to write a Unix utility in C, a Windows utility in Visual Basic, or a quick Web application in JavaScript or VBScript. To return to the carpenter analogy, the expert practitioner will be more successful knowing the strengths and weaknesses of various tools instead of using the same tool in all circumstances. On the other hand, portability and interoperability are important considerations, and heterogeneous systems tend to be less portable and interoperable than homogeneous ones. So sticking to Java even when a small piece of the system is easier in another language is sometimes preferable. Knowing where the balance lies requires experience.

6.3 Java Versions

Java was first released by Sun Microsystems in 1995. It really started to take off in early 1996, when Netscape released Navigator version 2.0, the first widely used browser that supported Java. After a couple of bug fixes, Java version 1.02 was released, which is what most people mean when they say "Java 1.0." Java 1.1 was released in early 1997, and contains a variety of enhancements and new features. Chief among these are:

- Improvements to the Abstract Window Toolkit. Lightweight components, scrolling windows, popup menus, and a much improved event-handling model are the highlights.

- Remote method invocation and object serialization. Java 1.1 contains a nice distributed-object protocol and a system for writing the state of an object to the disk or a socket and putting it back together at the other end.

- Inner classes. You can now create nested and/or anonymous classes.

- Arbitrary precision integers and floating point numbers.

- A standard relational database interface. The Java DataBase Connectivity API is now directly supported by most major database vendors, plus there are bridges to connect JDBC to ODBC.

- JavaBeans. This is Java's answer to ActiveX: a component architecture for Java.

- Digitally signed applets. This offers the promise of applets with extended security privileges without resorting to the "all or nothing" model of browser plug ins or ActiveX.

- A large variety of small changes to improve naming consistency, performance, and to fix bugs.

Version 1.2, which will probably be released in early 1998, will contain the Java Foundation Classes, a huge improvement over the AWT. The JFC provides a more robust drawing model, a wider selection of GUI controls, and a look and feel that can be changed at run-time and kept consistent across platforms.

Which Version Should You Use?

If you are going to be writing stand-alone applications, you almost certainly want to use Java 1.1. However, for Java programs on the Web, you probably need to stick with version 1.02 for some time to come. For one thing, neither Netscape Navigator nor Internet Explorer support Java 1.1 in release 3 of their browsers. Netscape Communicator has only limited support for 1.1 in release 4.01. In particular, the new AWT is not supported at all. Netscape 4.02 and the first release of Internet Explorer 4 are expected to fully support Java 1.1. But even when the browsers *do* fully support Java 1.1, applets designed for the WWW (as opposed to intranets) will need to stick with 1.0 at least until the majority of users migrate to the new browsers.

6.4 Getting Started: Nuts and Bolts

Okay, okay, enough talk. Let's get on with it.

If you're wise, you won't sit down and read these Java chapters straight through, engrossing though they may be. <SARCASTIC>No doubt it will be difficult to tear yourself away, but you've got to do it.</SARCASTIC> Seriously though, I suggest installing Java as soon as possible, reading a little, practicing a little, reading a bit more, trying a more complex application, and so on. Write some real programs as *soon* as possible, and experiment with as many techniques as possible. There's no substitute for practice. Here's how to start:

- Install Java
- Install a Java-Enabled Browser
- Bookmark or Install the On-Line Java API
- Optional: Get an Integrated Development Environment
- Create and Run a Java Program

Install Java

Java is already bundled with some operating systems (e.g. OS/2, MacOS 8, Solaris 2.6), and most OSvendors have announced it will be included with their next release. So you may have Java on your system already. If not, there are *free* versions of Java for Windows 3.1, Windows NT, Windows 95, MacOS, OS/2, Novell IntranetWare, Solaris, Irix, HP-UX, AIX, SCO Unixware, Linux, Amiga, BeOS, and most other major operating systems. Following is a list of a few of the most important download sites and the versions available there as of the book publication date. For other operating systems and for-fee systems, check out Sun's list of Java ports at

```
http://java.sun.com/products/jdk/jdk-ports.html
```

Note that each of these URLs, like every URL listed in the book, is accessible on-line via the CD-ROM Web pages.

Windows 95/NT

Java 1.02 from Sun

```
http://java.sun.com/products/jdk/1.0.2/
```

Java 1.02 from Microsoft

```
http://www.microsoft.com/java/download/dl_sdk-f.htm
```

Java 1.1 from Sun

```
http://java.sun.com/products/jdk/1.1/
```

Java 1.1 from Microsoft

```
http://www.microsoft.com/java/download/dl_sdk2-f.htm
```

Windows 3.1

Java 1.02 from IBM

```
http://www.ibm.com/Java/tools/jdk.html
```

MacOS

Java 1.02 from Apple

```
http://applejava.apple.com/
```

Java 1.02 from Sun

```
http://java.sun.com/products/jdk/1.0.2/
```

OS/2 Warp

Java 1.02 from IBM

```
http://www.ibm.com/Java/tools/jdk.html
```

Novell Netware 4.1/IntranetWare

Java 1.02 and Java 1.1 from Novell

http://developer.novell.com/java/

Solaris

Java 1.02 from Sun

http://java.sun.com/products/jdk/1.0.2/

Java 1.1 from Sun

http://java.sun.com/products/jdk/1.1/

Irix

Java 1.1 from SGI

http://www.sgi.com/Fun/Free_webtools.html

Linux

Java 1.02 and 1.1 for Linux

http://www.blackdown.org/java-linux.html

HP-UX

Java 1.02 and 1.1 from HP

http://www.hp.com/gsyinternet/hpjdk/software.html

AIX

Java 1.02 from IBM

http://www.ibm.com/Java/tools/jdk.html

SCO Unixware and Open Server

Java 1.1 from SCO

http://www2.sco.com/cgi-bin/php.cgi/download/
free.html

Install a Java-Enabled Browser

This will let you run Java programs embedded in Web pages (applets). Many IDE's and free versions of Java include "appletviewer," a mini-browser that ignores all of the HTML except for the applets. This is a quick way to test applets. For a fuller test, you'll want Netscape Navigator or Communicator, Microsoft Internet Explorer, Sun's HotJava, Lotus Notes 4.5, IBM WebExplorer (OS/2), or another Java-enabled browser. This is a bit of a chicken and egg problem, since many of the download sites are accessible only by HTTP, which won't help you much if you don't have a browser already. The CD-ROM includes Internet Explorer for Windows 95/NT and MacOS. For other platforms, hopefully you have *some* browser that came with your system or was provided by your ISP. If not, try using Netscape's anonymous FTP site.

Netscape Navigator

```
http://home.netscape.com/download/
```

Netscape Navigator (FTP)

```
ftp.netscape.com in /pub/
```

Microsoft Internet Explorer

```
http://www.microsoft.com/ie/download/
```

Sun's HotJava

```
http://java.sun.com/products/hotjava/
```

IBM WebExplorer

```
http://www.networking.ibm.com/WebExplorer/
```

Bookmark or Install the On-Line Java API

The official Application Programmer's Interface (API) describes *every* non-private variable and method in *every* standard library, something neither this nor any other single book can do. HTML versions for both JDK 1.02 and 1.1 are available at Sun and are bundled with many IDE's. The API can be browsed directly from Sun's site, but the serious developer with plenty (5-10 MB) of extra disk space will want to install a local version for faster access.

Java 1.02

Top-Level Package Hierarchy
```
http://java.sun.com/products/jdk/1.0.2/api/pack-
ages.html
```

Index of All Fields and Methods
```
http://java.sun.com/products/jdk/1.0.2/api/
AllNames.html
```

Class Hierarchy
```
http://java.sun.com/products/jdk/1.0.2/api/
tree.html
```

Downloading API to Your Machine
```
http://java.sun.com/products/jdk/1.0.2/
ftp_docs.html
```

Java 1.1

Top-Level Package Hierarchy
```
http://java.sun.com/products/jdk/1.1/docs/api/pack-
ages.html
```

Index of All Fields and Methods
```
http://java.sun.com/products/jdk/1.1/docs/api/a-
names.html
```

Class Hierarchy
```
http://java.sun.com/products/jdk/1.1/docs/api/
tree.html
```

Downloading API to Your Machine
```
http://java.sun.com/products/jdk/1.1/#docs
```

Optional: Get an Integrated Development Environment

In addition to a Java compiler and run-time system, you may want an integrated environment with a graphical debugger, class browser, drag-and-drop GUI builder, templates/wizards for database connectivity, and so on. There are a wide variety of these available from Symantec, Microsoft, Sun, Borland, IBM, Metrowerks, Roaster Technologies, SGI, PowerSoft and others. You might want to pick up a trade magazine that reviews the alternatives for your operating system, or take a look at John Zukowski's collection of IDE reviews and download sites at `http://java.miningco.com/msub9.htm`.

Create and Run a Java Program

Create the File

Write and save a file (say `Test.java`) that defines the public class `Test`. Note that the filename and classname are case sensitive, and must match exactly. If you are not using a Java development environment, use the text editor of your choice. Section 6.5 gives some simple examples.

Compile it

If you are using the standard "javac" compiler from the Sun JDK on Windows or Unix, compile `Test.java` via "`javac Test.java`". On a Mac, drag the source file onto the Java compiler. If you are using an Integrated Development Environment, refer to the vendor's instructions. This creates a file called `Test.class`.

Run it

For a stand-alone Java application with a command-line interface, run it via "`java Test`". Note that this is `java`, not `javac`, and that you refer to `Test`, not `Test.class`. On a Mac, drag the class file onto the Java runner. For an applet that will run in a browser, run it by loading the Web page that refers to it. For example, if you want the file `Test.html` to run the applet, then `Test.html` needs to refer to the URL of `Test.class` in an `<APPLET>` tag. I will give details of this later.

6.5 Some Simple Java Programs

Following are some very basic programs to give a flavor of the language. Don't worry about understanding every detail; I'll go over things step by step later on. But it *is* a good idea to run these programs. Try making a few changes after successfully executing the original versions.

The Basic Hello World Application

"Application" is Java lingo for a stand-alone Java program. An application *must* contain a class whose name exactly matches the filename (including case) and that contains a `main` method declared `public static void` with an a single string array as an argument. A string array can be declared "`String[] argName`", or "`String argName[]`". Listing 6.1 presents a simple application that prints "Hello, world." when run. Lots more application examples will be given in Chapter 7, "Object-Oriented Programming in Java." Also, Java applications frequently use a graphical user interface. Section 9.8 (Graphical Applications) gives an overview of this, with more details given in Section 11.9 (Frame).

Core Approach

A public class named `SomeClass` must be defined in SomeClass.java. Case matters even on Windows 95; SOMECLASS.java or someclass.java will not work.

Listing 6.1   `HelloWorld.java`

```java
public class HelloWorld {
  public static void main(String[] args) {
    System.out.println("Hello, world.");
  }
}
```

Compiling:
```
javac HelloWorld.java
```

Running:
```
java HelloWorld
```

Output:
```
Hello, world.
```

Command-Line Arguments

Listing 6.2 shows a program that reports on user input. This example looks a lot like C but illustrates a couple of important differences: `String` is a real type in Java, Java arrays have `length` associated with them, and the file-name is not part of the command-line arguments. If you've never seen C or C++ before, you'll want to read the description of basic loops and conditionals given in Chapter 8, "Basic Java Syntax." Note that you *can* read command-line input on Macintosh systems, even though there is no "command line"; in most implementations a small window pops up when the program starts to collect that input.

Listing 6.2   `ShowArgs.java`

```
public class ShowArgs {
  public static void main(String[] args) {
    for(int i=0; i<args.length; i++)
      System.out.println("Arg " + i + " is " + args[i]);
  }
}
```

Compiling:

```
javac ShowArgs.java
```

Running:

```
java ShowArgs fee fie foe fum
```

Output:

```
Arg 0 is fee
Arg 1 is fie
Arg 2 is foe
Arg 3 is fum
```

The Basic Hello World (Wide Web) Applet

"Applet" is Java lingo for a Java program that runs as part of a WWW page in a browser. Like an application, an applet must contain a class matching the file-name, but applets don't use the `main` method. Instead, initialization is typically performed in the `init` method and drawing in `paint`. Listing 6.3 shows a simple Java applet that draws "Hello, World Wide Web." in a small window. Listing 6.4 shows the HTML document that loads it. Note that the name of the HTML file need not match the name of the Java file, but it is sometimes a useful convention. For more information on creating applets and drawing in windows, see Chapter 9, "Applets, Graphical Applications, and Basic Drawing."

Listing 6.3   `HelloWWW.java`

```java
import java.applet.Applet;
import java.awt.*;

public class HelloWWW extends Applet {
  private int fontSize = 40;

  public void init() {
    setBackground(Color.black);
    setForeground(Color.white);
    setFont(new Font("Helvetica", Font.BOLD, fontSize));
  }

  public void paint(Graphics g) {
    g.drawString("Hello, World Wide Web.",
                 5, fontSize+5);
  }
}
```

Listing 6.4   `HelloWWW.html`

```html
<!DOCTYPE HTML PUBLIC "-//W3C//DTD HTML 3.2//EN">
<HTML>
<HEAD>
  <TITLE>HelloWWW: Simple Applet Test.</TITLE>
</HEAD>

<BODY BGCOLOR="WHITE">
<H1>HelloWWW: Simple Applet Test.</H1>
<P>
<APPLET CODE="HelloWWW.class" WIDTH=460 HEIGHT=50>
  <B>Error! You must use a Java enabled browser.</B>
</APPLET>

</BODY>
</HTML>
```

Compiling:
```
javac HelloWWW.java
```

Running:
Load `HelloWWW.html` in a Java-enabled browser.

Output:
Figure 6–9 shows a typical result.

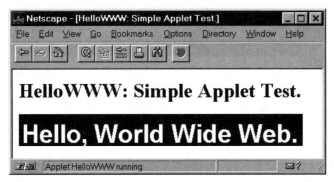

Figure 6–9   A simple applet, shown in Netscape Navigator 3.01 on Windows 95.

Applet Customization Parameters

Applets don't get command-line arguments because they are started by the browser. However, parameters can be supplied to the applet by putting them inside PARAM elements between the <APPLET ...> and </APPLET> tags. The applet reads the values by calling getParameter. Listing 6.5 shows a variation of the HelloWWW applet that bases message text on PARAM values supplied. Listing 6.6 shows an HTML document that loads this applet

four times with various messages. The use of PARAM is explained in detail in
Section 9.7 (Reading Applet Parameters).

Listing 6.5   Message.java

```java
import java.applet.Applet;
import java.awt.*;

public class Message extends Applet {
  private int fontSize;
  private String message;

  public void init() {
    setBackground(Color.black);
    setForeground(Color.white);

    // Base font size on window height:
    fontSize = size().height - 10;

    setFont(new Font("Helvetica", Font.BOLD, fontSize));

    // Read heading message from PARAM entry in HTML.
    message = getParameter("MESSAGE");
  }

  public void paint(Graphics g) {
    if (message != null)
      g.drawString(message, 5, fontSize+5);
  }
}
```

Listing 6.6	Message.html

```html
<!DOCTYPE HTML PUBLIC "-//W3C//DTD HTML 3.2//EN">
<HTML>
<HEAD>
  <TITLE>The Message Applet</TITLE>
</HEAD>

<BODY BGCOLOR="WHITE">
<H1>The <CODE>Message</CODE> Applet</H1>
<P>
<APPLET CODE="Message.class" WIDTH=325 HEIGHT=25>
  <PARAM NAME="MESSAGE" VALUE="Tiny">
  <B>Sorry, these examples require Java</B>
</APPLET>
<P>
<APPLET CODE="Message.class" WIDTH=325 HEIGHT=50>
  <PARAM NAME="MESSAGE" VALUE="Small">
  <B>Sorry, these examples require Java</B>
</APPLET>
<P>
<APPLET CODE="Message.class" WIDTH=325 HEIGHT=75>
  <PARAM NAME="MESSAGE" VALUE="Medium">
  <B>Sorry, these examples require Java</B>
</APPLET>
<P>
<APPLET CODE="Message.class" WIDTH=325 HEIGHT=100>
  <PARAM NAME="MESSAGE" VALUE="Giant">
  <B>Sorry, these examples require Java</B>
</APPLET>

</BODY>
</HTML>
```

Compiling:

```
javac Message.java
```

Running:

Load Message.html in a browser that supports Java.

Output:

Figure 6–10 shows the result of a Web page that loads the same applet four different times, supplying various PARAM values and differing HEIGHTs.

Figure 6–10   Four versions of the same applet, shown in Internet Explorer 3.01 on Windows 95.

6.6 Summary

Java burst on the scene a couple of years ago, and has been growing rapidly ever since. There are a number of features of Java that will be new to most developers, even though many of the ideas were taken from existing languages, not invented just for Java. Hopefully this chapter helped you understand these, and you now recognize the common misconceptions about Java as well. After installing Java, a Java-capable browser, and the Java API, you're ready to really get hacking. Where you go next depends on your experience. If you've never used an object-oriented language before, you should carefully read Chapter 7, "Object-Oriented Programming in Java." If you're an OOP expert already, you can just skim the chapter to pick up on Java differences. Similarly, if you've never seen C or C++, you'll need to read through Chapter 8, "Basic Java Syntax," and try writing a number of programs. The experienced C/C++ hacker can quickly browse that chapter and move on. After that, the subsequent chapters will cover graphics, windows, event-handling, GUI controls, threading, client-server programming, and similar advanced Java topics.

OBJECT-ORIENTED PROGRAMMING IN JAVA

Topics in This Chapter

- Instance variables: Creating classes with named fields

- Methods: Adding functions to classes

- Constructors: Defining functions that help build classes

- Destructors: Why Java does not need functions to destroy objects

- Overloading: Creating more than one method with the same name

- Javadoc: Making hypertext documentation for your classes

- Inheritance: Reusing and augmenting capabilities from other classes

- Interfaces: Describing the behavior of multiple different classes

- Packages: Organizing classes

- The Classpath: Telling Java where to look for classes

- Visibility modifiers: Specifying who can see which parts of your class

- Other modifiers: Giving special characteristics to classes, fields, and methods

Chapter 7

Objects are central to Java. Understanding how they are created and used is the first task for a beginning Java programmer. It is even more fundamental than the basic syntax summarized in Chapter 8. If you've never seen object-oriented programming, you'll want to take your time with this chapter. As usual, trying things out is more important than reading; be sure to write several of your own classes along the way. The time spent will more than pay for itself in increased productivity later. If you have worked with objects in other languages, you can skim most of these sections. But pay close attention to Sections 7.7 (Javadoc), 7.9 (Interfaces and Abstract Classes), and 7.10 (Packages and the Classpath); they are specific to Java.

7.1 Instance Variables

In the simplest case, a class is like a structure or record. An object (an instance of a class) is normally created by using new before a call to a class constructor. The constructor looks like a method with the same name as the class being created. For example:

```
Point p1 = new Point(2, 4);
Scrollbar bar = new Scrollbar();
```

Sometimes, however, the call to new may be hidden. For instance, it is common to have objects returned from method calls; the methods may call new internally or might return an object that already exists. For instance:

```
OutputStream out = someSocket.getOutputStream();
Point p1 = someWindow.location();
```

In a very few cases such as for strings and arrays, Java has shorthand syntax for creating an object. For instance, the following are equivalent ways of creating a String object:

```
String string1 = new String("A String");
String string2 = "Another String";
```

The "fields" or "data members" of a class are often called "instance variables" in Java nomenclature. They are accessed via objectReference.variableName; that is, by supplying the name of the instance variable separated by a dot from the reference to the actual object.

To illustrate, Listing 7.1 shows a class named Ship1 used to represent a boat, perhaps for a simple simulation system. The test routine creates two Ship1 instances using new Ship1(), then initializes the various instance variables. These fields are then updated to represent one "move" of the ship, and the new values printed out.

Listing 7.1   Test1.java

```
// Create a class with five instance variables (fields):
// x, y, speed, direction, and name.
// Note that Ship1 is not declared "public", so that it
// can be in the same file as Test1.

class Ship1 {
  public double x, y, speed, direction;
  public String name;
}

// The "driver" class containing "main".

public class Test1 {
  public static void main(String[] args) {
    Ship1 s1 = new Ship1();
    s1.x = 0.0;
    s1.y = 0.0;
```

Listing 7.1	`Test1.java` (continued)

```
    s1.speed = 1.0;
    s1.direction = 0.0;    // East
    s1.name = "Ship1";
    Ship1 s2 = new Ship1();
    s2.x = 0.0;
    s2.y = 0.0;
    s2.speed = 2.0;
    s2.direction = 135.0; // Northwest
    s2.name = "Ship2";
    s1.x = s1.x + s1.speed
            * Math.cos(s1.direction * Math.PI / 180.0);
    s1.y = s1.y + s1.speed
            * Math.sin(s1.direction * Math.PI / 180.0);
    s2.x = s2.x + s2.speed
            * Math.cos(s2.direction * Math.PI / 180.0);
    s2.y = s2.y + s2.speed
            * Math.sin(s2.direction * Math.PI / 180.0);
    System.out.println(s1.name + " is at ("
                + s1.x + "," + s1.y + ").");
    System.out.println(s2.name + " is at ("
                + s2.x + "," + s2.y + ").");
  }
}
```

Compiling and Running:
```
    javac Test1.java
    java Test1
```

Output:
```
    Ship1 is at (1,0).
    Ship2 is at (-1.41421,1.41421).
```

You may have noticed a pattern in the variable and class names used in this example. There is a convention in Java to name local variables and instance variables with the initial letter in lowercase (e.g., someString, window, outputStream1) and to name classes with a leading uppercase letter (e.g., String, Window, OutputStream). Subsequent "words" in the variable or class name typically have leading uppercase letters (e.g., someInstance-Variable, SomeClass), although that is not quite as universal a convention since some people prefer underscores (some_instance_variable, Some_Class). Constants typically are all uppercase (PI). These conventions help people reading your code, and I suggest that you adopt them.

Core Approach

*Name variables with an initial lowercase letter (*myVar*). For class names, use an initial uppercase letter (*MyClass*).*

Now, the astute reader may observe that the example of Listing 7.1 appears to violate this naming convention. For instance, if Math is some global variable containing an object with a PI constant, why does Java name it Math instead of math? It turns out that this is not a global variable (Java has no such thing, in fact!), but is indeed the name of a class. In addition to instance variables, Java allows class variables; variables that are shared by all members of the class. These variables are indicated by the static keyword in their declaration, and can be accessed either through an object reference or via the class name. So the naming convention actually makes things clearer here; a reader who has never seen the Math class can tell that PI is a static final (constant) variable in the Math class simply by seeing the reference to Math.PI.

7.2 Methods

In the previous example, virtually identical code was repeated several times to update the x and y instance variables of the two ships. This is bad not only because the initial repetition takes time, but more importantly because updates require changing code in multiple places. To solve this problem, classes can have functions associated with them, not just data. Java calls them "methods" as in Lisp/CLOS rather than "member functions" as in C++. Notice that, unlike in C++, instance variables can be directly initialized, as with

```
public double x=0.0;
```

Note also the use of public and private. These modifiers are discussed in more detail in Section 7.11, but the basic point is that you use public for functionality that you are deliberately making available to users of your class. Any changes to public entries would require changes by the users of your class. You use private for functionality you use internally to implement the class but that you could change without affecting users of your class.

Listing 7.2   Test2.java

```java
// Give the ship public move and printLocation methods.

class Ship2 {
  public double x=0.0, y=0.0, speed=1.0, direction=0.0;
  public String name = "UnnamedShip";

  private double degreesToRadians(double degrees) {
    return(degrees * Math.PI / 180.0);
  }

  public void move() {
    double angle = degreesToRadians(direction);
    x = x + speed * Math.cos(angle);
    y = y + speed * Math.sin(angle);
  }

  public void printLocation() {
    System.out.println(name + " is at ("
                      + x + "," + y + ").");
  }
}

public class Test2 {
  public static void main(String[] args) {
    Ship2 s1 = new Ship2();
    s1.name = "Ship1";
    Ship2 s2 = new Ship2();
    s2.direction = 135.0; // Northwest
    s2.speed = 2.0;
    s2.name = "Ship2";
    s1.move();
    s2.move();
    s1.printLocation();
    s2.printLocation();
  }
}
```

Compiling and Running:

```
javac Test2.java
java Test2
```

Output:

```
Ship1 is at (1,0).
Ship2 is at (-1.41421,1.41421).
```

7.3 Constructors and the "this" Reference

A class constructor is a special routine used to build an object. One is called when you use new ClassName(...) to build an instance of a class. It is defined similarly to an ordinary public method, except that the name must match the class name, and no return type is given. Note that if you include a return type (e.g. public **void** Ship2(...) {...}), it will compile without warning on most Java systems, but not get called when you try to invoke a constructor. For instance, Listing 7.3 shows a class with an x variable with a default value of 0. The supposed "constructor" changes the default to 1, but as the output shows, it never gets invoked. So if it looks like the body of your constructor is being ignored, make sure you didn't declare a return type.

Listing 7.3   NoConstructor.java

```java
public class NoConstructor {
  public static void main(String[] args) {
    NoConstructor test = new NoConstructor();
    System.out.println("X is " + test.x + ".");
  }

  private int x = 0;

  // Oops! Not a constructor since it has return type.

  public void NoConstructor() {
    x = 1;
  }
}
```

Compiling and Running:
```
javac NoConstructor.java
java NoConstructor
```

Output:
```
X is 0.
```

Core Warning

Be sure your constructor does not specify a return type.

If you fail to define a constructor yourself, you automatically get an empty zero-argument constructor. If you define any constructors yourself, they replace this default version. You can define your constructors with any number of arguments to let the user supply parameters at the time the instance is created.

For instance, a drawback to `Ship2` is that changing multiple fields takes multiple steps. It would be more convenient to specify all of the fields when the ship is created. Furthermore, some people feel that relying on default values makes the code more difficult to read, since someone looking only at the code that creates the ship wouldn't know what values the various fields take. So I could make an improved `Ship3` with a constructor like the following:

```
public Ship3(double x, double y, ...) {
   // Initialize fields
}
```

However, this presents a problem: the local variable named x "shadows" (hides) the instance variable of the same name. So doing

```
public Ship3(double x, double y, ...) {
  x = x;
  y = y;
   ...
}
```

would be perfectly legal, but not too useful. All you'd be doing is reassigning the local variables back to their current values. One alternative is to simply use different names, as follows:

```
public Ship3(double inputX, double inputY, ...) {
  x = inputX;
  y = inputY;
   ...
}
```

A second alternative is to use the `this` reference, as in Listing 7.4. Inside any class you can always refer to `this` to get a variable that refers to the current instance. This will be useful later on when you want windows to pass a reference to themselves to external routines, so you might as well get used to the syntax now. It is legal to use `this` whenever you refer to internal fields or methods, so that the `move` method could be implemented as:

```
public void move() {
   double angle = this.degreesToRadians(this.direction);
   this.x = this.x + this.speed * Math.cos(this.angle);
   this.y = this.y + this.speed * Math.sin(this.angle);
}
```

instead of the much simpler:

```
public void move() {
   double angle = degreesToRadians(direction);
   x = x + speed * Math.cos(angle);
   y = y + speed * Math.sin(angle);
}
```

However, the former is quite cumbersome and tedious, so I recommend that you save this for situations that require it: namely passing references to the current object to external routines, and differentiating local variables from fields with the same names.

Listing 7.4   Test3.java

```
// Give Ship3 a constructor to let the instance variables
// be specified when the object is created.

class Ship3 {
  public double x, y, speed, direction;
  public String name;

  public Ship3(double x, double y,
               double speed, double direction,
               String name) {
    this.x = x; // "this" differentiates instance vars
    this.y = y; //  from local vars.
    this.speed = speed;
    this.direction = direction;
    this.name = name;
  }

  private double degreesToRadians(double degrees) {
    return(degrees * Math.PI / 180.0);
  }

  public void move() {
    double angle = degreesToRadians(direction);
    x = x + speed * Math.cos(angle);
    y = y + speed * Math.sin(angle);
  }
```

Listing 7.4   `Test3.java` (continued)

```java
public void printLocation() {
    System.out.println(name + " is at ("
                        + x + "," + y + ").");
  }
}

public class Test3 {
  public static void main(String[] args) {
    Ship3 s1 = new Ship3(0.0, 0.0, 1.0,   0.0, "Ship1");
    Ship3 s2 = new Ship3(0.0, 0.0, 2.0, 135.0, "Ship2");
    s1.move();
    s2.move();
    s1.printLocation();
    s2.printLocation();
  }
}
```

Compiling and Running:
```
javac Test3.java
java Test3
```

Output:
```
Ship1 is at (1,0).
Ship2 is at (-1.41421,1.41421).
```

Static Initialization Blocks

If you need something a little more complex than default variable values but a little less complicated than constructors, you can use a static initialization block, such as:

```java
public class SomeClass {
  int[] values = new int[12];

  static {
    for(int i=0; i<values.length; i++)
      values[i] = 2 * i + 5;
  }

  int lastValue = values[11];

  ...
}
```

In most cases, I put such behavior in the constructor instead. You probably won't want static initializers very often either.

7.4 Destructors

This section intentionally left blank.

Just kidding, but destructors (functions to destroy objects) aren't needed in Java. If no reference to an object exists, the garbage collector frees up the memory for you automatically. If the only reference to an object is a local variable, the object will be available for collection when the method exits, earlier if the variable is reassigned. If an instance variable has the only reference to an object, the object can be collected whenever the variable is reassigned. It seems amazing to C++ programmers, but it really works. No dangling pointers: Java will *not* collect an object if there is a forgotten reference to it hanging around somewhere. No memory leaks: Java *will* collect any object that can't be reached from a live object, even if it has nonzero references (as with objects in a circularly linked structure disconnected from everything else). You still have to worry about "leaklets" (stashing a reference in an array or variable and forgetting to reassign it to `null` or some other value), but that is a relatively minor problem.

Although Java will collect all unused objects automatically, you sometimes want to do some bookkeeping when an object is destroyed. For instance, you might want to decrement a count, write a log to disk, or some such. For this kind of situation, you can use the `finalize` method of an object:

```
protected void finalize() throws Throwable {
   doSomeBookkeeping();
   super.finalize(); // Use parent's finalizer
}
```

Don't worry about the `throws` business or how Java knows which methods have `finalize` methods; that will become clear later. For now, just declare the method exactly as written but do whatever you want for the `doSomeBookkeeping` part.

7.5 Overloading

As in C++ and other object-oriented languages, Java allows more than one method with the same name, but with different behaviors depending on the type or number of its arguments. For instance, you could define two `isBig` methods: one that determines if a `String` is "big" (by some arbitrary measure) and another that determines if an `int` is, as follows:

```
public boolean isBig(String s) {
  return(s.length() > 10);
}

public boolean isBig(int n) {
  return(n > 1000);
}
```

Note that

```
return(n > 1000);
```

is a more compact way of accomplishing the same thing as:

```
if (n > 1000)
  return(true);
else
  return(false);
```

In Listing 7.5, the `Ship4` constructor and the `move` method are overloaded. One constructor can call another by using `this(args)`, but the call has to be the first line of the constructor. Also, don't confuse the `this` constructor call with the `this` reference. For example:

```
public class SomeClass {
  public SomeClass() {
    this(12); // Invoke other constructor
    doSomething();
  }

  public SomeClass(int num) {
    doSomethingWith(num);
    doSomeOtherStuff();
  }

  ...
}
```

We also want to define a new version of move that lets you specify the number of "steps" the ship should move. If you assume that you will create a new method but leave the original one unchanged, the question is whether the new move should use the old version, as follows:

```java
public void move() {
   double angle = degreesToRadians(direction);
   x = x + speed * Math.cos(angle);
   y = y + speed * Math.sin(angle);
}

public void move(int steps) {
   for(int i=0; i<steps; i++)
      move();
}
```

or if it should repeat the code, as in the following version:

```java
public void move() {
   double angle = degreesToRadians(direction);
   x = x + speed * Math.cos(angle);
   y = y + speed * Math.sin(angle);
}

public void move2(int steps) {
   double angle = degreesToRadians(direction);
   x = x + (double)steps * speed * Math.cos(angle);
   y = y + (double)steps * speed * Math.sin(angle);
}
```

The first approach has the advantage that changes to the way movement is calculated only have to be implemented in one location, but has the disadvantage that significant extra calculations are being performed. This illustrates a common dilemma; the tension between reusability and efficiency. In some instances, reuse can be achieved with no performance reduction. In others, performance has to be traded off against extensibility and reuse, and the appropriate balance depends on the situation. In this particular case, it is possible to get the best of both worlds by modifying the original move method, as follows:

```java
public void move() {
   move(1);
}

public void move(int steps) {
   double angle = degreesToRadians(direction);
   x = x + (double)steps * speed * Math.cos(angle);
   y = y + (double)steps * speed * Math.sin(angle);
}
```

You can find this type of solution more often than you might think, so you should look for such an approach whenever you are faced with a similar problem. However, this would not have been possible if the original move was in a class that we could not modify.

Listing 7.5 gives the full class definition.

Listing 7.5   Test4.java

```java
class Ship4 {
public double x=0.0, y=0.0, speed=1.0, direction=0.0;
  public String name;

  // This constructor takes the parameters explicitly.

  public Ship4(double x, double y,
              double speed, double direction,
              String name) {
    this.x = x;
    this.y = y;
    this.speed = speed;
    this.direction = direction;
    this.name = name;
  }

  // This constructor requires a name, but lets you
  // accept the default values for x, y, speed, and
  // direction.

  public Ship4(String name) {
    this.name = name;
  }

  private double degreesToRadians(double degrees) {
    return(degrees * Math.PI / 180.0);
  }

  // Move one step.

  public void move() {
    move(1);
  }
```

continued

Listing 7.5   `Test4.java` **(continued)**

```
// Move N steps

public void move(int steps) {
  double angle = degreesToRadians(direction);
  x = x + (double)steps * speed * Math.cos(angle);
  y = y + (double)steps * speed * Math.sin(angle);
}

public void printLocation() {
  System.out.println(name + " is at ("
                     + x + "," + y + ").");
}
}

public class Test4 {
  public static void main(String[] args) {
    Ship4 s1 = new Ship4("Ship1");
    Ship4 s2 = new Ship4(0.0, 0.0, 2.0, 135.0, "Ship2");
    s1.move();
    s2.move(3);
    s1.printLocation();
    s2.printLocation();
  }
}
```

Compiling and Running:
```
javac Test4.java
java Test4
```

Output:
```
Ship1 is at (1,0).
Ship2 is at (-4.24264,4.24264).
```

7.6 Public Version in Separate File

Classes that are used in a single place are often combined in the same file as in the previous examples. Often, however, classes are designed to be reused, and are placed in separate files where multiple other classes can use them. For instance, Listing 7.6 defines the `Ship` class while Listing 7.7 defines a driver routine that tests it. When building reusable classes, there is a much greater burden on the developer to be sure the code is documented and extensible. Two particular strategies help in this regard:

Replace public instance variables with accessor methods

Instead of allowing the variables to be directly accessed, it is common practice to create a pair of helping methods to set and retrieve the values. For instance, in the ship example, instead of the x and y fields being `public`, they are made `private` and `getX`, `getY`, `setX`, and `setY` methods are created to provide users the ability to look up and modify them. Although this appears to be considerable extra work, it is time well invested for classes that will be widely used. First of all, it provides a place holder for later functionality. For instance, suppose that the developer decides to provide error checking to ensure that directions are nonnegative or that the ship's maximum speed wasn't exceeded. If users explicitly manipulated the variables, there would be no mechanism for doing this check without having all the users change their code. But if `setX` and `setY` methods were already in place, checking could be performed there without any changes in user code. Similarly, suppose that the ship becomes part of a simulation, and a graphical representation needs to be updated every time the x and y locations change. The `setX` and `setY` methods provide a perfect place for doing this. Secondly, using accessor methods shields users of the class from implementation changes. Suppose that the developer decides to use a `Point` data structure to store x and y instead of storing them individually. If the x and y variables were being directly referenced, users of the class would have to change their code. But if the accessor methods were being used, the definitions of `getX` and `getY` could be updated with no required changes by users of the class.

Use javadoc to create on-line documentation

Documentation enclosed between `/**` and `*/` can be used by the `javadoc` program to create hypertext documentation for all the non-private methods and variables (if any). Javadoc is described in Section 7.7. Again, this is likely to require considerable extra effort, but is well worth it for classes that will get a lot of use by multiple developers. For instance, Figure 7–1 was generated directly from the documentation of `Ship.java` (Listing 7.6).

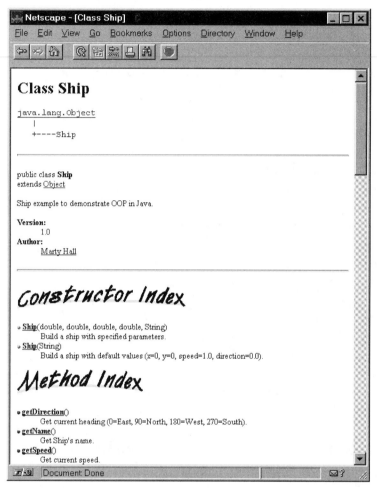

Figure 7–1 Javadoc will generate hypertext documentation from Java source code.

Listing 7.6 `Ship.java`

```java
//----------------------------------------------------
/**
 * Ship example to demonstrate OOP in Java.
 *
 * @author <A HREF="mailto:hall@apl.jhu.edu">
 *         Marty Hall</A>
 * @version 1.0
 */

public class Ship {
  //----------------------------------------------------
  // Instance variables

  private double x=0.0, y=0.0, speed=1.0, direction=0.0;
  private String name;

  //----------------------------------------------------
  // Constructors

  /** Build a ship with specified parameters. */
  public Ship(double x, double y,
              double speed, double direction,
              String name) {
    setX(x);
    setY(y);
    setSpeed(speed);
    setDirection(direction);
    setName(name);
  }

  /** Build a ship with default values
   *  (x=0, y=0, speed=1.0, direction=0.0).
   */
  public Ship(String name) {
    setName(name);
  }

  //----------------------------------------------------
  /** Move ship one step at current speed/direction. */

  public void move() {
    moveInternal(1);
  }

/** Move N steps. */

  public void move(int steps) {
    moveInternal(steps);
  }
```

continued

Listing 7.6   `Ship.java` (continued)

```java
private void moveInternal(int steps) {
  double angle = degreesToRadians(direction);
  x = x + (double)steps * speed * Math.cos(angle);
  y = y + (double)steps * speed * Math.sin(angle);
}

private double degreesToRadians(double degrees) {
  return(degrees * Math.PI / 180.0);
}

//------------------------------------------------------
/** Report location to standard output. */


public void printLocation() {
  System.out.println(getName() + " is at (" + getX()
                     + "," + getY() + ").");
}

//------------------------------------------------------
/** Get current X location. */

public double getX() {
  return(x);
}

/** Set current X location. */

public void setX(double x) {
  this.x = x;
}

//------------------------------------------------------
/** Get current Y location. */

public double getY() {
  return(y);
}

/** Set current Y location. */

public void setY(double y) {
  this.y = y;
}

//------------------------------------------------------
/** Get current speed. */
```

Listing 7.6 `Ship.java` **(continued)**

```java
  public double getSpeed() {
    return(speed);
  }

/** Set current speed. */

  public void setSpeed(double speed) {
    this.speed = speed;
  }

  //----------------------------------------------------
  /** Get current heading (0=East, 90=North, 180=West,
   *  270=South). Ie uses standard math angles,
   *  <B>not</B> nautical system where 0=North,
   *  90=East, etc.
   */
  public double getDirection() {
    return(direction);
  }

  /** Set current direction (0=East, 90=North, 180=West,
   *  270=South). Ie uses standard math angles,
   *  <B>not</B> nautical system where 0=North,
   *  90=East, etc.
   */
  public void setDirection(double direction) {
    this.direction = direction;
  }

  //----------------------------------------------------
  /** Get Ship's name. Can't be modified by user. */

  public String getName() {
    return(name);
  }

  private void setName(String name) {
    this.name = name;
  }

  //----------------------------------------------------
}
```

Listing 7.7 `ShipTest.java`

```java
public class ShipTest {
  public static void main(String[] args) {
    Ship s1 = new Ship("Ship1");
    Ship s2 = new Ship(0.0, 0.0, 2.0, 135.0, "Ship2");
    s1.move();
    s2.move(3);
    s1.printLocation();
    s2.printLocation();
  }
}
```

Compiling and Running:

```
javac ShipTest.java
java ShipTest
```

The first line calls `javac` on `Ship.java` automatically. The Java compiler will automatically check the file creation date of each .class file used by the class it compiles, compare it to the creation date of the source file (if available), and recompile if necessary. If you use "`javac -depend`" this process will be repeated for third-level classes and so on, virtually eliminating the need for C/C++-style makefiles. If you want to keep a given .class file in use even while you are updating the .java source, simply keep the source in a separate directory.

Core Note

*You don't need "makefiles" in Java. Use "`javac file`" to compile a class and recompile any out-of-date classes it **directly** uses. Use "`javac -depend file`" to compile a class and recompile all out-of-date classes it **directly or indirectly** uses.*

Output:

```
Ship1 is at (1,0).
Ship2 is at (-4.24264,4.24264).
```

7.7 Javadoc

The javadoc program is distributed with Sun's JDK and by most third-party vendors. It uses comments enclosed between /** and */ to generate on-line documentation that includes hypertext links to other user-defined and system classes. You generally place javadoc comments above the class definition and before every nonprivate method and class. The first sentence of the variable/method description will be placed in the alphabetized index at the top of the resultant page, with the full description available in the detailed sections at the bottom. To create the documentation, supply one or more file or package names to javadoc, as follows:

```
javadoc Foo.java
javadoc Foo.java Bar.java
javadoc graphics.newWidgets
javadoc graphics.newWidgets math.geometry
```

You can also supply various options to javadoc. These are described later in this section, but here are some simple examples:

```
javadoc -author -version SomeClass.java
javadoc -noindex -notree somePackage
```

Packages will be described in Section 7.10.

The text inside the comments can include HTML markup, not just standard text. Thus, you can use <A HREF="..."> to create hypertext links to your organization's home page, use the IMG element to include a screen dump of your program in action, and even use the APPLET element to load an interactive demonstration that illustrates some of the most important uses of your class. You probably want to avoid headings, however, since they are likely to break up the outline Javadoc generates. Extra whitespace is ignored inside these comments unless they occur inside a space-preserving element such as PRE.

Surprisingly, the Java 1.0 version of javadoc generates HTML that is not strictly legal in HTML 2.0 or 3.2, since it has an <A NAME=...> entry in the HEAD. This was moved to the top of the BODY in Java 1.1.

Tagged Paragraphs

In addition to HTML markup and text, there are some special tags that can be inserted in the documentation to get certain effects. For instance, you can use @param to describe individual parameters that a method expects,

@return to describe the return value, and @see to reference related classes or methods. Here's an example:

```
/** Converts an angle in degrees to one in radians.
 *
 * @param degrees The input angle in degrees.
 * @return The equivalent of the input, in radians.
 * @see #radiansToDegrees.
 */

public double degreesToRadians(double degrees) {
   return(degrees * Math.PI / 180.0);
}
```

These special tags must occur at the beginning of a line, and all text following the tag and before the next tag or the end of the comment is considered part of the tagged paragraph. In most Java 1.0 implementations there must be *exactly* one space between the "*" and the "@". If you don't use the "*" on intermediate lines, the "@" should be the first character in the line. In Java 1.1, the parser was improved, and these restrictions no longer apply.

Core Approach

Leave exactly one space between the "" and the "@" in javadoc comments.*

The legal tags are described below; Table 7.1 gives a summary.

@author
This is used in the class documentation to specify the author. You must use "javadoc -author ..." for this to take effect. HTML markup is allowed here; for example:

```
/** Description for SomeClass
 *   ...
 * @author <A HREF="mailto:ellison@microsoft.com">
 *         Larry Ellison</A>
 */
```

@deprecated [Java 1.1]
This tag, available only in Java 1.1, is used to indicate classes, fields, or methods that should no longer be used. That is, ones that are currently

supported for backward compatibility but that might be dropped in future releases.

@exception

This tag is used to document methods and constructors, and should be followed by an exception classname, a space, and a description.

@param

The `@param` tag is used to document the arguments that a method (or constructor) takes. It should be followed by the parameter name, a space, and the description of the parameter.

@return

This tag documents the return value of a method.

@see

This can be used to create hypertext links to the javadoc documentation for other methods or classes. Methods should normally be prefaced by the classname and a "#", but the classname can be omitted for methods in the current class. For instance:

```
/**
 * ...
 * @see #getWidget
 * @see Widget
 * @see Frob#setWidget
 */

public void setWidget(Widget w) { ... }
```

@since [Java 1.1]

This tag creates a "Since" section used to document when the class, field, or method was added. It is typically used for classes or packages undergoing revisions to distinguish new features from preexisting ones.

@version

This is used in the class documentation to list a version number. You must use "`javadoc -version ...`" for this to take effect.

Table 7.1	Summary of Javadoc Tags		

Tag	Applicable Sections	Java Versions	Javadoc Command-Line Args Required
@author	Classes	1.0, 1.1	-author
@deprecated	Classes, fields, methods	1.1	None, but -nodeprecated suppresses entries with this flag
@exception	Methods	1.0, 1.1	None
@param	Methods	1.0, 1.1	None
@return	Methods	1.0, 1.1	None
@see	Classes, fields, methods	1.0, 1.1	None
@since	Classes, fields, methods	1.1	None
@version	Classes	1.0, 1.1	-version

Javadoc Command-Line Arguments

Javadoc lets you supply a number of options to customize its behavior. For instance, I normally use

```
javadoc -author -version -noindex -notree Class.java
```

to honor the @author and @version tags and to suppress generation of the index and class hierarchy. The available options are described in this section.

-author
This tells javadoc to include the author information, which is omitted by default.

-classpath
-sourcepath
This tells javadoc where to look for the specified .java files. Directories should be separated by colons. Directories specified in the CLASSPATH variable are searched automatically.

-d
This is used to supply a destination directory for the HTML files. An absolute or relative directory can be used. If omitted, the HTML files are placed in the same directory as the source file. You often use -d to specify a directory that already contains the images subdirectory holding the GIF files used by documentation files.

-doctype [Java 1.0]
In Java 1.02 and earlier, you could specify -doctype=mif to produce documentation in Maker Interchange Format, used by the FrameMaker desktop publishing system (the same software used to produce this book, by the way). This option was dropped in Java 1.1.

-encoding [Java 1.1]
-docencoding [Java 1.1]
These Java 1.1 options allow you to specify the character encoding used for the source file (-encoding) or that should be used for the documentation (-docencoding).

-J [Java 1.1]
Javadoc is itself a Java program. The -J flag lets you pass parameters directly to the Java run-time. For instance, if the documentation set will be very large, you might want to specify a large (24 megabyte) start-up size via

```
javadoc -J-ms24m ...
```

-nodeprecated [Java 1.1]
This tells javadoc to omit deprecated entries.

-noindex
This tells javadoc not to generate the AllNames.html index. The index is useful for packages, but you often want to omit it when building documentation for a single class.

-notree

This tells javadoc not to generate the `tree.html` class hierarchy.

-public [Java 1.1]
-protected [Java 1.1]
-package [Java 1.1]
-private [Java 1.1]

These Java 1.1 options let you specify which classes and members get documented. They are ordered here from the most restrictive to the most inclusive, and each option automatically includes all of the ones above it in the list. The default is `protected`, which generates documentation only for `public` and `protected` members. This is what users of your class normally want, but developers that are changing the class might want to know about `private` data as well.

-verbose

This tells javadoc to print information about the time taken to parse each file.

-version

The `-version` option tells javadoc to include version numbers (as specified via `@version`). They are omitted by default.

Fixing Hypertext Links: The Images Subdirectory and the Standard API

Javadoc generates HTML files containing `IMG` elements with relative URL references to GIF files in the `images` subdirectory. This directory comes in the `/apibook` (Java 1.0) or `docs/api` (Java 1.1) subdirectory of the installation directory. Consequently, you have to make sure this directory is available to the documents you generate. On Unix, you can include a symbolic link to this directory in each directory containing documentation. On Windows, you might want to use the `-d` option to put documentation in an appropriate directory.

In Java 1.0, javadoc also creates relative references to each of the built-in classes that your class extends or that is used by your methods. Unfortunately, it assumes you have integrated your class documentation into the overall Java API, something few people do. So all of the hypertext links to the built-in classes are broken. In Java 1.0, you can fix them in one fell swoop in a text editor by replacing all occurrences of

```
<a href="java.
```

with

```
<a href="http://java.sun.com/products/jdk/1.0.2/
api/java.
```

In JDK 1.1, fewer links to the built-in classes are created, but the links are still used for methods and fields that override standard methods. So you need to replace all occurrences of

```
<a href="java.
```

with

```
<a href="http://java.sun.com/products/jdk/1.1/docs/
api/java.
```

7.8 Inheritance

Inheritance is the process by which a new class is built on top of a previously written class without having to rewrite the existing class's functionality. The extends keyword is used to indicate that one class inherits from another. The original class is usually referred to as the "parent class" or "superclass" (called "base class" in C++ lingo). The new class is known as the "child class" or "subclass" (called "derived class" in C++ lingo). The new child class gets the nonprivate instance variables and methods but *not* the constructors of the parent class. However, a constructor in a child class can explicitly call the constructor in the parent class by using super on the first line of the new constructor. Here is a simplified example:

```
// ParentClass.java: original parent/base/super class.
// Has fields a and b and methods foo and bar.
// Has two constructors.

public class ParentClass {
    public int a;
    private int b;

    public ParentClass() { ... }
    public ParentClass(double z) { ... }

    public String foo(int x, String s) { ... }

    private void bar() { ... }
}
```

```
// ChildClass.java: the new child/derived/sub class.
// Has fields a (by inheritance) and c, and methods
// foo (by inheritance) and baz. Has one constructor
// which uses ParentClass's constructor.

public class ChildClass extends ParentClass {
  public int c;

  public ChildClass(double z) {
    super(z); // call ParentClass's constructor
    ...
  }

  public void baz(boolean isReady) { ... }
}
```

In addition to adding new variables and methods, a child class might want to replace (or "override") versions from the parent class.

For methods, the child class simply redefines the method. The new method can access the previous version by calling super.methodName. The super *method call* is used in constructors only to invoke superclass constructors. The super *variable* can be used in any method to access superclass fields and methods.

For variables, the new constructor can change the default value; you should *not* repeat the variable declaration in the child class.

For example, Listing 7.8 presents a Speedboat class that adds color methods and variables plus overrides the printLocation method.

Listing 7.8   Speedboat.java

```java
/** A fast Ship. Red and going 20 knots by default. */

public class Speedboat extends Ship {
  private String color = "red";

  /** Builds a red Speedboat going N at 20 knots. */

  public Speedboat(String name) {
    super(name);
    setSpeed(20);
  }

  /** Builds a speedboat with specified parameters. */

  public Speedboat(double x, double y,
                   double speed, double direction,
                   String name, String color) {
    super(x, y, speed, direction, name);
    setColor(color);
  }

  /** Report location. Override version from Ship. */

  public void printLocation() {
    System.out.print(getColor().toUpperCase() + " ");
    super.printLocation();
  }

  /** Gets the Speedboat's color. */

  public String getColor() {
    return(color);
  }

  /** Sets the Speedboat's color. */

  public void setColor(String colorName) {
    color = colorName;
  }
}
```

Listing 7.9   `SpeedboatTest.java`

```
/** Try a couple of Speedboats and a regular Ship. */

public class SpeedboatTest {
  public static void main(String[] args) {
    Speedboat s1 = new Speedboat("Speedboat1");
    Speedboat s2 = new Speedboat(0.0, 0.0, 2.0, 135.0,
                                 "Speedboat2", "blue");
    Ship s3 = new Ship(0.0, 0.0, 2.0, 135.0, "Ship1");
    s1.move();
    s2.move();
    s3.move();
    s1.printLocation();
    s2.printLocation();
    s3.printLocation();
  }
}
```

Compiling and Running:

```
javac -depend SpeedboatTest.java
java SpeedboatTest
```

The first line above calls `javac` on `Speedboat.java` and `Ship.java` automatically.

Output:

```
RED Speedboat1 is at (20,0).
BLUE Speedboat2 is at (-1.41421,1.41421).
Ship1 is at (-1.41421,1.41421).
```

Java, unlike C++ and Lisp/CLOS, but like Smalltalk, supports single inheritance only. This means that although your class can have many ancestor classes, it can have only one *immediate* parent. This is normally what you want, but in some situations a *mixin* style of programming is very useful, something Java doesn't support. However, many of the other benefits of multiple inheritance can be attained with less complexity by the use of *interfaces*, which is discussed in the next section (Section 7.9).

7.9 Interfaces and Abstract Classes

Suppose that you want to define a class to act as a parent of other classes, but don't want to let people directly instantiate the class. For instance, you might want to provide some common behavior in the class, but the class will not have enough information to be used by itself. In this case, Java lets you declare a class abstract, and the compiler will not let you build an instance of it. For instance, Listing 7.10 shows an abstract Shape class. It says that all Shape subclasses will have methods to look up and set locations (getX, getY, and so forth), but that you are prohibited from directly building a Shape object.

Listing 7.10   Shape.java

```java
/** The parent class for all closed, open, curved,
 *  and straight-edged shapes.
 */

public abstract class Shape {
  protected int x, y;

  public int getX() {
    return(x);
  }

  public void setX(int x) {
    this.x = x;
  }

  public int getY() {
    return(y);
  }

  public void setY(int y) {
    this.y = y;
  }
}
```

Java also lets you define abstract methods; methods that define the return type and parameters, but don't provide a method body, as follows:

```java
public ReturnType methodName(Type1 arg1, Type2 arg2);
```

Classes that contain an abstract method *must* be declared abstract. Their subclasses must also be abstract *unless* they implement all of the abstract methods. Abstract methods are useful when you want to require all members of a class to have certain general categories of behavior, but where each member of the class will implement the behavior slightly differently.

Since the Shape class did not have abstract methods, its subclasses could be abstract or concrete. In this particular case, I will create two further abstract subclasses for curved shapes and for those with straight edges. See Listings 7.11 and 7.12.

Listing 7.11   `Curve.java`

```
/** A curved shape (open or closed). Subclasses will
 *  include arcs and circles.
 */

public abstract class Curve extends Shape {}
```

Listing 7.12   `StraightEdgedShape.java`

```
/** A Shape with straight edges (open or closed).
 *  Subclasses will include Line, LineSegment,
 *  LinkedLineSegments, and Polygon.
 */

public abstract class StraightEdgedShape extends Shape {}
```

Now, suppose that I want to extend the Curve class to create a Circle, and want the Circle to have a method to calculate its area. I could simply have Circle extend Curve (*without* including the abstract declaration) and include a getArea method. This works fine if circles are the only shapes whose area can be measured. But if I planned ahead for a Rectangle class descended from StraightEdgedShape, I might be dissatisfied with this approach, since the areas of rectangles can be measured as well. Creating general routines that deal with areas will now be difficult, because Rectangle and Circle have no common ancestor containing getArea.

For instance, how would I easily make an array of shapes whose areas can be summed? A `Circle[]` wouldn't allow rectangles, and a `Rectangle[]` would be too restrictive also, since it would exclude circles. But a `Shape[]` would not be restrictive enough, since it would permit shapes that didn't have a `getArea` method. Similarly, if I wanted to return the larger area from two shapes, what argument types should such a `maxArea` method take? Not `Shape`, since some shapes lack `getArea`. Putting an abstract `getArea` method into `Shape` doesn't make sense since some shapes (line segments, arcs, and such) won't have measurable areas. In fact, there *is* no clean approach using regular classes.

Fortunately, Java has a solution for just this type of dilemma: interfaces. Interfaces look like abstract classes where all of the methods are abstract. The big difference is that a class can directly implement multiple interfaces, while it can only directly extend a single class. A class that implements an interface must either provide definitions for all methods or declare itself abstract. To illustrate, Listing 7.13 shows a simple interface:

Listing 7.13 `Interface1.java`

```java
public interface Interface1 {
  ReturnType1 method1(ArgType1 arg);
  ReturnType2 method2(ArgType2 arg);
}
```

Note the use of the `interface` keyword instead of `class`, and that the method declarations end in a semicolon with no method body (just like abstract methods). Also note that the `public` declarations before methods in an interface are optional; the methods are implicitly public so the explicit declarations are normally omitted. Listing 7.14 shows a class that uses the interface.

Listing 7.14   `Class1.java`

```
// This class is not abstract, so it must
// provide implementations of method1 and method2.

public class Class1 extends SomeClass
                    implements Interface1 {
  public ReturnType1 method1(ArgType1 arg) {
    someCodeHere();
    ...
  }

  public ReturnType2 method2(ArgType2 arg) {
    someCodeHere();
    ...
  }

  ...
}
```

Listing 7.15 presents another interface.

Listing 7.15   `Interface2.java`

```
public interface Interface2 {
  ReturnType3 method3(ArgType3 arg);
}
```

Next, Listing 7.16 outlines a class that uses *both* interfaces. It is abstract, so does not have to provide implementations of the methods of the interfaces.

Listing 7.16   `Class2.java`

```
// This class is abstract, so does not have to provide
// implementations of the methods of Interface 1 and 2.

public abstract class Class2 extends SomeOtherClass
                      implements Interface1,
                                 Interface2 {
  ...
}
```

Finally, Listing 7.17 shows a concrete subclass of `Class2`.

Listing 7.17 `Class3.java`

```
// This class is not abstract, so it must provide
// implementations of method1, method2, and method3.

public class Class3 extends Class2 {
  public ReturnType1 method1(ArgType1 arg) {
    someCodeHere();
    ...
  }

  public ReturnType2 method2(ArgType2 arg) {
    someCodeHere();
    ...
  }

  public ReturnType3 method3(ArgType3 arg) {
    someCodeHere();
    ...
  }

  ...
}
```

Since interfaces do not contain method definitions, they cannot be directly instantiated. However, an interface can `extend` (not `implement`) one or more other interfaces (use commas if you extend more than one), so that interface definitions can be built-up hierarchically just like class definitions can. Interfaces cannot include normal instance variables, but can include constants. The `public`, `static`, and `final` declarations for the constants are implicit, so are normally omitted. Listing 7.18 gives an example.

Listing 7.18 `Interface3.java`

```
// This interface has three methods (by inheritance)
// and two constants.

public interface Interface3 extends Interface1,
                                     Interface2 {
  int MIN_VALUE = 0;
  int MAX_VALUE = 1000;
}
```

Now, how does all this help us with the Shape class hierarchy? Well, the key point is that methods can refer to an interface as though it were a regular class. So we first define a Measurable interface, as shown in Listing 7.19. Note that it is pretty common to name interfaces ending in "-able" (Runnable, Serializable, Sortable, Drawable, and so on).

Listing 7.19   Measurable.java

```
/** Used in classes with measurable areas. */

public interface Measurable {
  double getArea();
}
```

Next, we define a Circle class that implements this interface, as shown in Listing 7.20.

Listing 7.20   Circle.java

```
/** A circle. Since you can calculate the area of
 * circles, class implements the Measurable interface.
 */
public class Circle extends Curve implements Measurable {
  private double radius;

  public Circle(int x, int y, double radius) {
    setX(x);
    setY(y);
    setRadius(radius);
  }

  public double getRadius() {
    return(radius);
  }

  public void setRadius(double radius) {
    this.radius = radius;
  }

  /** Required for Measurable interface. */

  public double getArea() {
    return(Math.PI * radius * radius);
  }
}
```

Having `Measurable` as an interface lets us define a class that uses it without having to know which specific classes actually implement it. Listing 7.21 gives an example.

Listing 7.21 `MeasureUtil.java`

```
/** Some operations on Measurable's. */

public class MeasureUtil {
  public static double maxArea(Measurable m1,
                              Measurable m2) {
    return(Math.max(m1.getArea(), m2.getArea()));
  }

  public static double totalArea(Measurable[] mArray) {
    double total = 0;
    for(int i=0; i<mArray.length; i++)
      total = total + mArray[i].getArea();
    return(total);
  }
}
```

Because of this design, other classes can implement the `Measurable` interface and automatically become available to the `MeasureUtil` methods. For instance, Listings 7.22 and 7.23 show an abstract `Polygon` class and one of its concrete subclasses. All polygons should have measurable areas, but will be calculated differently.

Listing 7.22 `Polygon.java`

```
/** A closed Shape with straight edges. */

public abstract class Polygon extends StraightEdgedShape
                              implements Measurable {
  private int numSides;

  public int getNumSides() {
    return(numSides);
  }

  protected void setNumSides(int numSides) {
    this.numSides = numSides;
  }
}
```

Listing 7.23   `Rectangle.java`

```java
/** A rectangle implements the getArea method.
 *  This satisfies the Measurable interface, so
 *  rectangles can be instantiated.
 */

public class Rectangle extends Polygon {
  private double width, height;

  public Rectangle(int x, int y,
                   double width, double height) {
    setNumSides(2);
    setX(x);
    setY(y);
    setWidth(width);
    setHeight(height);
  }

  public double getWidth() {
    return(width);
  }

  public void setWidth(double width) {
    this.width = width;
  }

  public double getHeight() {
    return(height);
  }

  public void setHeight(double height) {
    this.height = height;
  }

  /** Required to implement Measurable interface. */

  public double getArea() {
    return(width * height);
  }
}
```

Although *I* took a long time explaining what was going on, using interfaces did not substantially increase the *code* required in the Shape hierarchy. The

Measurable interface took three lines, and the only other thing needed was the "implements Measurable" declaration. However, it saved a large amount of work in the `MeasureUtil` class, and made it immune to changes in which classes actually have `getArea` methods. Listing 7.24 shows a simple test of the `MeasureUtil` class.

Listing 7.24 `MeasureTest.java`

```
/** Test of MeasureUtil. Note that we could change
 *  the actual classes of elements in the measurables
 *  array (as long as they implemented Measurable)
 *  without changing the rest of the code.
 */

public class MeasureTest {
  public static void main(String[] args) {
    Measurable[] measurables =
      { new Rectangle(0, 0, 5.0, 10.0),
        new Rectangle(0, 0, 4.0, 9.0),
        new Circle(0, 0, 4.0),
        new Circle(0, 0, 5.0) };
    System.out.print("Areas:");
    for(int i=0; i<measurables.length; i++)
      System.out.print(" " + measurables[i].getArea());
    System.out.println();
    System.out.println
      ("Larger of 1st, 3rd: " +
       MeasureUtil.maxArea(measurables[0],
                           measurables[2]) +
       "\nTotal area: " +
       MeasureUtil.totalArea(measurables));
  }
}
```

It has been widely claimed in the Java community that interfaces provide all of the good features of *multiple inheritance* (the ability of a class to have more than one immediate parent class) with little of the complexity. I suspect that these claims are mostly made by people without significant experience with multiple inheritance. It is absolutely true that interfaces are a convenient and useful construct, and you'll see them used in several places in the rest of the book. However, if you come from a language that supports multiple inheritance (e.g., C++, Eiffel, Lisp/CLOS, among others), you will find that they do not provide everything that you are used to. From the viewpoint of someone who will be *using* a class (e.g., the person writing `MeasureUtil`), interfaces are better; they let you treat classes in different hierarchies as though they were part of a common class, but without all the confusion multiple inheritance can cause. However, from the viewpoint of the person *writing* the classes themselves (e.g., the person writing the `Shape` hierarchy), they may save little. In particular, interfaces do not let you inherit the implementation of methods, which can sometimes be a time saver. For example, suppose that you have a variety of custom buttons, windows, and textfields, each of which have a private `name` field used for debugging, and each of which should have a `debug` method that prints out the location, parent window, and name of the graphical component. In Java, you would have to repeat this code in each subclass, while multiple inheritance would have let you place it in a single parent class (`Debuggable`) and have each graphical object simply extend this class. The use of multiple inheritance to provide characteristics shared by classes at varying locations in the class hierarchy is sometimes known as a "mixin" style, and Java provides nothing equivalent. Whether the simplicity benefit gained by leaving out this capability is worth the cost in the relatively small number of cases where mixins would have been valuable is open to debate.

7.10 Packages and the Classpath

Java lets you group class libraries into separate modules or "packages" to avoid naming conflicts and to simplify their handling. For instance, in a real project, the `Ship` and `Shape` class hierarchies would have been easier to make and use if placed in separate packages. To create a package called `packagename`, first make a subdirectory with the same name and place all source files there. Each of these files should contain

```
package packagename;
```

as the first non-comment line. Files that lack a package declaration are automatically placed in an unnamed package. Files in the main directory that want to use the package should include

```
import packagename.ClassName;
```

or

```
import packagename.*;
```

before the class definitions (but after the package declaration, if any). This tells the compiler that the specified classes ("*" means "all") should be available for use if they are needed. Otherwise the compiler only looks for classes it needs in the current directory, or, as we will see shortly, in directories specified via the CLASSPATH variable. Package names can contain dots ("."); these correspond to subdirectories. For example, assume that your application is being developed on Windows 95 or NT in C:\Java\classes. Now suppose that the classes shown in Listings 7.25 through 7.28 are created. They include the package1 package (in C:\Java\classes\package1) containing Class1, the package2 package (in C:\Java\classes\package2) containing Class2, the package2.package3 package (in C:\Java\classes\package2\package3) containing Class3, and the package4 package (in C:\Java\classes\package4) containing Class1.

Note that there is a name conflict between package1 and package4; they both contain a class named Class1. If a single program needs to use both, it simply omits the import statement for one of them, using packagename.Class1 instead. This is known as the "fully qualified classname," and can be used in lieu of import any time. For instance, an applet could explicitly extend java.applet.Applet and not import java.applet.Applet or java.applet.*.

Also notice that the printInfo methods of the test classes are declared static. Static methods can be invoked by using the name of the class (like Math.cos) without creating an object instance.

Listing 7.25   C:\Java\classes\package1\Class1.java

```java
package package1;

public class Class1 {
  public static void printInfo() {
    System.out.println("This is Class1 in package1.");
  }
}
```

Listing 7.26   `C:\Java\classes\package2\Class2.java`

```
package package2;

public class Class2 {
  public static void printInfo() {
    System.out.println("This is Class2 in package2.");
  }
}
```

Listing 7.27   `C:\Java\classes\package2\package3\`
`Class3.java`

```
package package2.package3;

public class Class3 {
  public static void printInfo() {
    System.out.println("This is Class3 in " +
                        "package2.package3.");
  }
}
```

Listing 7.28   `C:\Java\classes\package4\Class1.java`

```
package package4;

public class Class1 {
  public static void printInfo() {
    System.out.println("This is Class1 in package4.");
  }
}
```

Now, let's make a test program that uses these classes (Listing 7.29). This file will be placed back in the root directory, not in the package-specific subclasses.

Listing 7.29   `C:\Java\classes\PackageExample.java`

```
import package1.*;
import package2.Class2;
import package2.package3.*;

public class PackageExample {
  public static void main(String[] args) {
    Class1.printInfo();
    Class2.printInfo();
    Class3.printInfo();
    package4.Class1.printInfo();
  }
}
```

Compiling and Running:

```
javac PackageExample.java
java PackageExample
```

The first line above compiles all four other classes automatically.

Output:

```
This is Class1 in package1.
This is Class2 in package2.
This is Class3 in package2.package3.
This is Class1 in package4.
```

The Classpath

Up to now, we've been acting as though you have to have a single root directory for all your Java files. This would be pretty inconvenient if you develop a large number of applications. Rather than just looking in the current directory, Java lets you supply a list of directories in which it should look for classes. This mechanism complements packages; it doesn't replace them. In particular, the directory list should contain the *roots* of package hierarchies, not the subdirectories corresponding to the individual packages. The classpath defines the starting points for the search; the import statements specify which subdirectories should be examined. Most Java systems also allow entries in the classpath to be uncompressed zip files; this is a convenient mechanism for moving large package hierarchies around.

There are two ways to specify the classpath. The first is to supply a -classpath argument to javac and java. The second, and more common, approach is to use the CLASSPATH environment variable. If this variable is not set, Java looks for class files and package subdirectories relative to the current directory. This is usually what you want, so if you set the CLASS-PATH variable, be sure to include "." if you want the current directory to be examined. Directories are separated by semicolons. For instance, on Unix (csh, tcsh), you could do:

```
setenv CLASSPATH .:~/classes:/home/mcnealy/classes
```

On Windows 95/NT, you could do

```
set CLASSPATH=.;C:\BillGates\classes;D:\Java\classes
```

MacOS doesn't have the concept of environment variables, but you can set the classpath on an application-by-application basis by changing the 'STR ' (0) resource. Fortunately, most Mac-based Java IDE's have easier ways of doing this. It is not necessary to include the location of the standard Java classes in the CLASSPATH; it is included automatically. Furthermore, java.lang.* is automatically imported, so there is no need to do this yourself.

Many browsers, including Netscape, HotJava, and appletviewer, look for classes in the CLASSPATH before trying to load them from the network. These classes are then granted special privileges. If someone knew your CLASSPATH and could look at the classes in it (e.g. on a multi-user system), they could make an applet that uses these classes to perform privileged or destructive operations from your account. As a result, you want to make sure CLASSPATH is not set when you start the browser.

Core Security Warning

Unset *CLASSPATH* before starting your Web browser.

7.11 Modifiers in Declarations

We've used a variety of class, method, and instance variable modifiers in this chapter: public, private, protected, and static. These were relatively obvious from context or from the brief explanation provided when they were used, but it is worth reviewing all the possible modifiers and explicitly stating their purpose.

Visibility Modifiers

These modifiers designate who can see the data inside an object you write. Table 7.2 summarizes them, with more details given below. If you are not familiar with object-oriented programming already, just look at `public` and `private` and forget the other options for now. For people with a C++ background, consider classes within the same package to be friendly to each other.

Table 7.2 Summary of Visibility Modifiers				
Variables or Methods with this Modifier Can Be Accessed By Methods In:	*Variable or Method Modifier*			
	public	*private*	*protected*	*No Modifier (default)*
Same Class	Y	Y	Y	Y
Classes in Same Package	Y	N	Y	Y
Subclasses	Y	N	Y	N
Classes in Different Packages	Y	N	N	N

public

This indicates that the variable or method can be accessed by anyone who can access an instance of the class. This is what you normally use for the functionality you are deliberately providing to the outside world, and should generally be documented with `javadoc`. Many people feel that instance variables should *never* be public and should be accessed *only* via methods. See Section 7.6 for some of the reasons. This is the approach used in the `Ship` example (Listing 7.6) and a convention necessary for JavaBeans, Java's component architecture. However, some practitioners feel that "never" is too strong, and that public fields are acceptable for small classes that act simply as records (C-style structs). They feel that for such classes, if the get/set methods only set and read the variables without any modification, side-effects, or error checking, then the methods are a unnecessary level of abstraction and the variables should be public instead. For instance, the `java.awt.Point` class contains public x and y variables, since the whole idea of a `Point` is to wrap up two integers into a single object. At the very least, I recommend that you avoid public instance variables for all complex classes.

Core Approach

Avoid public instance variables.

A *class* can also have the designation `public`, which means that any other class can load and use the class definition. The name of a public class must match the filename.

private

This indicates that the variable or method can only be accessed by methods within the same class. This is what you normally use for internal data and methods that are needed to implement your public interface but which users need not or should not (due to potential changes) access.

protected

This indicates that the variable or method can be accessed by methods within the class, within classes in the same package, and is inherited by subclasses. This is what you use for data that is normally considered private but might be of interest to people extending your class.

No Modifier (default)

Omitting a visibility modifier indicates that the variable or method can be accessed by methods within the class, within classes in the same package, but is not inherited by subclasses. Although this is the default, the other modifiers represent more common intentions.

private protected [Java 0.9]

This designation was in beta releases of Java, but has been removed from the language. Several early textbooks used it, and discussion of it has refused to die, perhaps because of similarities between it and C++ protection mechanisms. It is gone. Dead. Kaput. It is *not* coming back.

Other Modifiers

static

This indicates that the variable or method is shared by the entire class.
It can be accessed via the classname instead of just by an instance. So if
a class Foo had a static variable bar, and there were two instances,
foo1 and foo2, bar could be accessed by foo1.bar, foo2.bar, or
Foo.bar. All three would access the same, shared, data. A similar
example is Math.cos: cos is a static method of the class Math.

Static methods can only refer to static variables or other static methods
unless they create an instance. For instance, in Listing 7.30, code in
main can refer directly to staticMethod, but requires an instance of
the class to refer to regularMethod.

Listing 7.30   Statics.java

```java
public class Statics {
  public static void main(String[] args) {
    staticMethod();
    Statics s1 = new Statics();
    s1.regularMethod();
  }

  public static void staticMethod() {
    System.out.println("This is a static method.");
  }

  public void regularMethod() {
    System.out.println("This is a regular method.");
  }
}
```

final

For a class, final indicates that it cannot be subclassed. This declaration may let the compiler make optimizations to method calls on variables of this type. For a variable or method, final indicates that it
cannot be changed at run-time or overridden in subclasses. Think of
"final" as "constant."

abstract

This declaration can apply to classes or methods, and indicates that the class cannot be directly instantiated. See Section 7.9 (Interfaces and Abstract Classes) for some examples.

synchronized

The synchronized declaration is used to set locks for methods in multi-threaded programming. Only one thread can access a synchronized method at any given time. For more details, see Chapter 14, "Concurrent Programming Using Java Threads."

volatile

For multithreaded efficiency, Java permits methods to keep local copies of instance variables, reconciling changes only at lock and unlock points. For some data types (e.g. longs), multithreaded code that does not use locking, risks having one thread partially update a field before another accesses it. The `volatile` declaration prevents this.

transient

Variables can be marked `transient` to indicate that they should not be saved by the object serialization system when writing an object to disk or network.

native

This modifier indicates that a method is implemented using C or C++ code that is linked to the Java image.

7.12 Summary

Java is pervasively and consistently object-oriented. You cannot go anywhere in Java without a good grasp of how to use objects. This chapter summarized how to create objects, give them state (instance variables), and assign them behavior (methods). Using inheritance, you can build hierarchies of classes without repeating code that is shared by subclasses. Although Java lacks multiple inheritance, interfaces are a convenient mechanism for letting one method handle objects from different hierarchies in a uniform manner. Class hierarchies that are intended to be reused should be documented with javadoc and can be organized into packages for convenience.

Getting comfortable with objects takes a bit of a conceptual leap, and may take a while if you've never seen them before. Chapter 8 requires no such leap; it is a laundry list of basic constructs supported by Java. It should be quick going. In fact, if you know C or C++ you can just skim through looking for the differences.

BASIC JAVA SYNTAX

Topics in This Chapter

- Primitive Types
- Operators
- Mathematical Methods
- Input and Output
- Executing Local Non-Java Programs
- Reference (Object) Types
- Strings
- Vectors
- Building a Binary Tree
- Arrays
- Exceptions

Chapter 8

Once you have a handle on object-oriented programming (Chapter 7), you're ready for a whirlwind tour of the basic structure of Java. If you are a C++ programmer, you can skim much of the material: Primitive types, operators, arrays, and exceptions are pretty similar to the C++ versions. However, you'll want to look more closely at Sections 8.4 through 8.8; they will be new to you.

8.1 Primitive Types

Java has two fundamental kinds of data types: primitives and references. Primitive types are those simple types that are not "objects" (described in the previous chapter)—integers, characters, floating-point numbers, and the like. There are eight of these types: `boolean`, `char`, `byte`, `short`, `int`, `long`, `float`, and `double`.

boolean
This is a type with two possible values: `true` and `false`. It is a real type; *not* a disguised `int`. For example:

```
boolean flag1 = false;
boolean flag2 = (6 < 7); // true
boolean flag3 = !true;   // false
```

char

This is a 16-bit unsigned integer representing a Unicode character. You specify values numerically or with characters in single quotes. These characters can be keyboard chars, unicode escape chars (\u*xxxx* with *x* in hex), or one of the special escape sequences \b (backspace), \t (tab), \n (newline), \f (form feed), \r (carriage return), \" (double quote), \' (single quote), or \\ (backslash). For instance:

```
char c0= 3;
char c1 = 'Q';
char c2 = '\u0000'; // Smallest
char c3 = '\uFFFF'; // Biggest
char c4 = '\b';     // Backspace
```

byte

This is an 8-bit signed two's-complement integer. See the description of int for ways to represent integer values.

short

This is a 16-bit signed two's-complement integer. See the description int for ways to represent integer values.

int

This is a 32-bit signed two's-complement integer. You can enter ints in base 10 (1, 10, and 100 for 1, 10, and 100, respectively), octal (01, 012, 0144 for 1, 10, 100), or hex (0x1, 0xA, 0x64 for 1, 10, 100). For hexadecimal numbers, you can use uppercase or lowercase for x, A, B, C, D, E, and F. Ints range from Integer.MIN_VALUE (-2^{31}) to Integer.MAX_VALUE ($2^{31}-1$). For example:

```
int i0 = 0;
int i1 = -12345;
int i2 = 0xCafeBabe; // Magic number of .class files
int i3 = 0777;
```

long

This is a 64-bit signed two's-complement integer. Use a trailing "1" or "L" for literals. You can use base 10, 8, or 16 for values. Longs range from Long.MIN_VALUE (-2^{63}) to Long.MAX_VALUE ($2^{63}-1$). Some examples:

```
long l0 = 0L;
long l1 = -123451;
long l2 = 0xBabeL; // Tower of Babel?
long l3 = -067671;
```

float

This is a 32-bit IEEE 754 floating-point number. Use a trailing "f" or "F" for floating-point literals. For instance:

```
float f0 = -1.23f;
```

You can use an "e" or "E" to indicate an exponent (power of 10). For instance, the first expression below assigns the value 6.02×10^{23} to the variable f1 while the second gives the value 4.5×10^{-17} to f2.

```
float f1 = 6.02E23F;
float f2 = 4.5e-17f;
```

Floats range from Float.MIN_VALUE to Float.MAX_VALUE. Floating-point arithmetic never generates an exception, even in divide-by-zero cases. The Float class has POSITIVE_INFINITY, NEGATIVE_INFINITY, and NaN (not-a-number) fields to use for some of these special cases. Use Float.isNaN to compare to NaN, because (Float.NaN == Float.NaN) returns false, in conformance with the IEEE spec, which says all comparisons to NaNs should fail.

double

This is a 64-bit IEEE 754 floating-point number. You are allowed to append a trailing "d" or "D", but this is normally omitted. Some examples:

```
double d0 = 1.23;
double d2 = -4.56d;
double d3 = 6.02214E+23;
double d4 = 1e-99;
```

Doubles range from Double.MIN_VALUE to Double.MAX_VALUE. Again, floating-point arithmetic never generates an exception, even in divide-by-zero cases. The Double class has POSITIVE_INFINITY, NEGATIVE_INFINITY, and NaN (not-a-number) fields to use for some of these special cases. Use Double.isNaN to compare to Double.NaN.

Primitive-Type Conversion

Unlike C and C++, Java requires explicit *typecasts* to convert among the various types. For example:

```
Type2 type2Var = (Type2)type1Var;
```

Truncation or loss of some significant digits may result from these casts, but even so an exception will not be thrown. For instance:

```
int i = 3;
byte b = (byte)i; // Cast i to a byte
long l = 123456L;
short s = (short)l; // Cast l to a short
```

You can also use some of the rounding methods in the `Math` class. See Section 8.3 for more information.

8.2 Operators

This section describes the basic arithmetic operators (`+`, `-`, `*`, and so forth), conditionals (`if`, `switch`, and so forth), and looping constructs (`while`, `do`, `for`).

Arithmetic Operators

Table 8.1 summarizes the basic numerical operators. You might notice the lack of an exponentiation operator. Don't panic; that's in the `Math` class (Section 8.3). Also, note that "`+`" can also be used for `String` concatenation; see Section 8.7 for details.

Table 8.1	Numerical Operators	

Operators	*Meaning*	*Example*
`+`, `-`	addition, subtraction	`x = y + 5;`
`*`, `/`, `%`	multiplication, integer-division, remainder	`int x = 3, y = 2;` `int z = x / y; // 1`

`++`, `--`	prefix/postfix increment/decrement	`int i = 1, j = 1;`
		`int x = i++; // x=1, i=2`
		`int y = ++j; // y=2, j=2`

`<<`, `>>`, `>>>`	signed and unsigned shift	`int x = 3;` `int y = x << 2; // 12`
`~`	bitwise complement	`int x = ~127; // -128`
`&`, `|`, `^`	bitwise and, or, xor	`int x = 127 & 2; // 2` `int y = 127	2; // 127` `int z = 127 ^ 2; // 125`

Java, like C and C++, lets you write

```
var op= val;
```

as a shorthand for

```
var = var op val;
```

That is, instead of

```
i = i + 5;
x = x * 3;
```

you could write

```
i += 5;
x *= 3;
```

Conditionals

Java has three basic conditional operators: if, switch, and "? :". They are summarized in Table 8.2, with more details given in the following section. If you are familiar with C or C++, you can skip this section because these operators are virtually identical to their C/C++ counterparts except that conditions must be boolean valued. Table 8.3 summarizes the boolean operators that are frequently used in conjunction with these three conditionals.

Table 8.2   Conditionals

Operator	*Standard Forms*

if	`if (expression) statement`
	`if (expression)`
	`  statement1`
	`else`
	`  statement2`

?:	`expression ? val1 : val2;`

switch	`switch(someInt) {`
	`  case val1: statement1;`
	`            break;`
	`  case val2: statement2;`
	`            break;`
	`  ...`
	`  default: statementN;`
	`}`

Table 8.3	Boolean Operators

Operator	*Meaning*
==, !=	Numeric equality, inequality. In general, == tests if two objects are identical (the same object), not just if they appear equal (have the same fields). This is the same as in C and C++.
<, <=, >, >=	Numeric less than, less than or equal to, greater than, greater than or equals to.
&&, ||	Logical and, or.
!	Logical negation.

if (expression) statement
if (expression) statement1 else statement2

The if construct expects a boolean expression in parentheses. If the expression evaluates to true, the subsequent statement is executed. If the expression is false, the else statement (if present) is executed. Supplying a non-boolean expression results in a compile-time error, unlike C and C++, which treat anything not equal to zero as false. Here's an example that returns the larger of two integers:

```
public static int max2(int n1, int n2) {// See Math.max
  if (n1 >= n2)
    return(n1);
  else
    return(n2);
}
```

Multiple statements can be combined into a single statement by enclosing them in brackets, as elsewhere in Java. For instance:

```
public static int max2Verbose(int n1, int n2) {
  if (n1 >= n2) {
    System.out.println(n1 + " is larger.");
    return(n1);
  } else {
    System.out.println(n2 + " is larger.");
    return(n2);
  }
}
```

Next, note that an `else` always goes with the most recent previous `if` that doesn't already have an `else`, as below:

```
public static int max3(int n1, int n2, int n3) {
  if (n1 >= n2)
    if (n1 >= n3)
      return(n1);
    else
      return(n3);
  else
    if (n2 >= n3)
      return(n2);
    else
      return(n3);
}
```

Notice that the indentation makes the association of the `else` clauses clear. This brings up a very important stylistic rule:

Core Approach

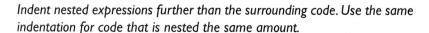

Indent nested expressions further than the surrounding code. Use the same indentation for code that is nested the same amount.

There are several different styles consistent with this approach. Following are a few of the most popular; I will use the first throughout most of the book.

```
// Indentation Style 1
public SomeType someMethod(...) {
  if {
    statement1;
    ....
    statementN
  } else {
    statementA;
    ...
    statementZ;
  }
}
```

```
// Indentation Style 2

public SomeType someMethod(...)
{ if
  { statement1;
    ...
    statementN;
  } else
  { statementA;
    ...
    statementZ;
  }
}

// Indentation Style 3

public SomeType someMethod(...)
{
  if
  {
    statement1;
    ...
    statementN;
  }
  else
  {
    statementA;
    ...
    statementZ;
  }
}
```

To simplify comparisons, you can use the logical and (&&) or logical or (||) operators. As in C and C++, these operators perform "short-circuit" evaluation in that they return an answer as soon as they have enough information to do so, even if not all expressions have been evaluated. In particular, && returns false if the left side is false without evaluating the right side; || immediately returns true if the left side is true. Here's an example:

```
public static int max3Simpler(int n1, int n2, int n3) {
  if ((n1 >= n2) && (n1 >= n3))
    return(n1);
  else if ((n2 >= n1) && (n2 >= n3))
    return(n2);
  else
    return(n3);
}
```

expression ? thenValue : elseValue

The `if` operator does not have a return value. If the purpose of the `if` is to assign to a single variable, Java provides a shortcut. Instead of

```
if (someCondition)
   someVar = value1;
else
   someVar = value2;
```

you can use

```
someVar = (someCondition ? value1 : value2);
```

In fact, you can use this form whenever you need to return a value, although overuse can make code difficult to read. Here is a variation of `max2` that uses it:

```
public static int max2Short(int n1, int n2) {
   return((n1 >= n2) ? n1 : n2);
}
```

switch(integralExpression) { switchBody }

The `switch` construct provides a compact way to compare an expression to a variety of integer types (`char`, `byte`, `short`, or `int`, but *not* `long`). The idea is to supply an integer expression and then provide one or more `case` statements inside the `switch` body that designate different possible values of the expression. When one matches, it *and all subsequent cases* are executed. Here's an example that uses `switch` to generate the string representation of single-digit integers:

```
public static String number(int digit) {
   switch(digit) {
      case 0: return("zero");
      case 1: return("one");
      case 2: return("two");
      case 3: return("three");
      case 4: return("four");
      case 5: return("five");
      case 6: return("six");
      case 7: return("seven");
      case 8: return("eight");
      case 9: return("nine");
      default: return("Not a single digit");
   }
}
```

The most confusing thing about `switch` statements is that code "falls through" cases; *all* statements after the first matching `case` are executed. This is handy in some situations, because it lets you combine cases as follows:

```
switch(val) {
  case test1:
  case test2:
    actionForTest1and2();
  ...
}
```

However, it can catch you by surprise if the `case` statements do not contain an explicit `return` or `break`. For example, consider the following verbose variation of the `number` method:

```
// Incorrect version that forgets about case
// fall through. Children should not try this at home.

public static String numberVerbose(int digit) {
  String result;
  switch(digit) {
    case 0: System.out.println("zero");
            result = "zero";
    case 1: System.out.println("one");
            result = "one";
    case 2: System.out.println("two");
            result = "two";
    case 3: System.out.println("three");
            result = "three";
    case 4: System.out.println("four");
            result = "four";
    case 5: System.out.println("five");
            result = "five";
    case 6: System.out.println("six");
            result = "six";
    case 7: System.out.println("seven");
            result = "seven";
    case 8: System.out.println("eight");
            result = "eight";
    case 9: System.out.println("nine");
            result = "nine";
    default: System.out.println("Not a single digit");
            result = "Not a single digit";
  }
  return(result);
}
```

Because there is no explicit construct that exits the switch after the first match, multiple cases get executed. For instance, here is the output when numberVerbose(5) is called:

```
five
six
seven
eight
nine
Not a single digit
```

The standard solution is to use the break statement to exit the switch after the first match, as in the following corrected version:

```java
public static String numberVerboseFixed(int digit) {
    String result;
    switch(digit) {
      case 0: System.out.println("zero");
              result = "zero";
              break;
      case 1: System.out.println("one");
              result = "one";
              break;
      ...
      default: System.out.println("Not a single digit");
               result = "Not a single digit";
    }
    return(result);
}
```

Listing 8.1 shows the complete method.

Listing 8.1   Switch.java

```java
/** Some examples of the switch statement. */

public class Switch {
  public static void main(String[] args) {
    System.out.println(number(9));
    System.out.println(number(5));
    numberVerbose(5);
    numberVerboseFixed(5);
  }
```

continued

Listing 8.1   `Switch.java`   (continued)

```java
public static String number(int digit) {
  switch(digit) {
    case 0: return("zero");
    case 1: return("one");
    case 2: return("two");
    case 3: return("three");
    case 4: return("four");
    case 5: return("five");
    case 6: return("six");
    case 7: return("seven");
    case 8: return("eight");
    case 9: return("nine");
    default: return("Not a single digit");
  }
}

// Incorrect version that forgets about case
// fall through. Children should not try this at home.

public static String numberVerbose(int digit) {
  String result;
  switch(digit) {
    case 0: System.out.println("zero");
            result = "zero";
    case 1: System.out.println("one");
            result = "one";
    case 2: System.out.println("two");
            result = "two";
    case 3: System.out.println("three");
            result = "three";
    case 4: System.out.println("four");
            result = "four";
    case 5: System.out.println("five");
            result = "five";
    case 6: System.out.println("six");
            result = "six";
    case 7: System.out.println("seven");
            result = "seven";
    case 8: System.out.println("eight");
            result = "eight";
    case 9: System.out.println("nine");
            result = "nine";
    default: System.out.println("Not a single digit");
             result = "Not a single digit";
  }
  return(result);
}
```

| Listing 8.1   `Switch.java` (continued) |

```java
// Correct version: uses the break statement
// to get jump out of the switch.

public static String numberVerboseFixed(int digit) {
  String result;
  switch(digit) {
    case 0: System.out.println("zero");
            result = "zero";
            break;
    case 1: System.out.println("one");
            result = "one";
            break;
    case 2: System.out.println("two");
            result = "two";
            break;
    case 3: System.out.println("three");
            result = "three";
            break;
    case 4: System.out.println("four");
            result = "four";
            break;
    case 5: System.out.println("five");
            result = "five";
            break;
    case 6: System.out.println("six");
            result = "six";
            break;
    case 7: System.out.println("seven");
            result = "seven";
            break;
    case 8: System.out.println("eight");
            result = "eight";
            break;
    case 9: System.out.println("nine");
            result = "nine";
            break;
    default: System.out.println("Not a single digit");
             result = "Not a single digit";
  }
  return(result);
}
}
```

Loops

Java supports the same basic looping constructs as C: while, do, and for. They are summarized in Table 8.4 and described in more detail following. In addition, Java supports the C/C++ break and continue statements to exit the loop or to interrupt the statement and restart at the beginning, respectively.

Table 8.4   Looping Constructs

Construct	Standard Form
while	while (continueTest) statement
do	do statement while (continueTest);
for	for(init; continueTest; updateOp) statement

while (continueTest) statement

The while construct tests the supplied boolean continuation test, executing the statement as long as the test returns true. For example, the following method uses the number method shown in the previous section to print out the numbers from 0 to some small value.

```java
public static void listNums1(int bound) {
  int i = 0;
  while (i < bound) {
    System.out.println(i + ": " + Switch.number(i));
    i++;
  }
}
```

Executing listNums1(5) results in

```
0: zero
1: one
2: two
3: three
4: four
```

do statement while (continueTest)

The do construct differs from while in that the test is evaluated after the statement rather than before. This means that the statement will always be executed at least once, regardless of the test's value. Following is a variation of the listNums method using do. The results of listNums2(5) is identical to that shown for listNums1.

```java
public static void listNums2(int bound) {
    int i = 0;
    do {
        System.out.println(i + ": " + Switch.number(i));
        i++;
    } while (i < bound);
}
```

for(init; continueTest; updateOp) statement

The for construct is the most common way to create loops with numbered counters. First, the init part is executed once. Then, as long as the continuation test evaluates to true, the statement is executed and the update operation performed. Here's an example that gives the same result for an argument of 5 as the previous two versions:

```java
public static void listNums3(int bound) {
    for(int i=0; i<bound; i++)
        System.out.println(i + ": " + Switch.number(i));
}
```

It is also legal to omit any of the three for clauses. A missing continueTest is treated as true. Thus,

```java
for(;;) { body }
```

and

```java
while(true) { body }
```

are equivalent. These forms are occasionally used when the termination test cannot be easily placed in the initial for or while clause. Instead the body contains a conditional return or break.

8.3 The Math Class

Math provides a range of arithmetic methods not available as built-in operators. All methods are static, so there is never any need to make an instance of the Math class.

Constants

public static final double E
This is e, the base for natural logarithms, 2.7182818284590452354.

public static final double PI
This is π, 3.14159265358979323846.

General-Purpose Methods

public static int abs(int num)
public static long abs(long num)
public static float abs(float num)
public static double abs(double num)
These methods return the absolute value of the specified number.

public static native double ceil(double num)
public static native double floor(double num)
The `ceil` method returns a `double` corresponding to the smallest integer greater than or equal to the specified number; `floor` returns the smallest integer less than or equal to the number.

public static native exp(double num)
This returns e^{num}.

public static native double IEEEremainder(double f1, double f2)
This returns the remainder of `f1` divided by `f2` as specified in the IEEE 754 standard.

public static native double log(double num)
This returns the natural logarithm of the specified number. Java does not provide a method to calculate logs using other common bases (e.g. 10 or 2), but following is a method that does this using the relationship:

$$\log_{b1}(n) = \frac{\log_{b2}(n)}{\log_{b2}(b1)}$$

```
public static double log(double num, double base) {
    return(Math.log(num) / Math.log(base));
}
```

public static int max(int num1, int num2)
public static long max(long num1, long num2)
public static float max(float num1, float num2)
public static double max(double num1, double num2)
public static int min(int num1, int num2)
public static long min(long num1, long num2)
public static float min(float num1, float num2)
public static double min(double num1, double num2)

These return the bigger (`max`) or smaller (`min`) of the two numbers.

public static native double pow(double base, double exponent)

This returns $base^{exponent}$.

public static double random()

This returns a random number from 0.0 (inclusive) to 1.0 (exclusive). For more control over random numbers, use the `Random` class.

public static native double rint(double num)
public static int round(double num)
public static long round(double num)

These methods round toward the nearest number. They differ in their return types and what they do for a number of the form `xxx.5`. The `round` methods round up in such a case; `rint` rounds to the nearest even number, as specified in the IEEE 754 standard. Although less intuitive, the behavior of `rint` avoids skewing sums of rounded numbers upwards.

public static native double sqrt(double num)

This returns $\sqrt{num}$.

Trigonometric Methods

public static native double sin(double radians)
public static native double cos(double radians)
public static native double tan(double radians)

These methods return the sine, cosine, and tangent of the specified number, interpreted as an angle *in radians*. Convert degrees to radians using

```
public static double degreesToRadians(double degrees) {
    return(degrees * Math.PI / 180.0);
}
```

public static native double acos(double val)
public static native double asin(double val)
public static native double atan(double val)
These methods return the arc cosine, arc sine, and arc tangent of the specified value. The result is expressed *in radians*.

public static native double atan2(double x, double y)
This returns the θ part of the polar coordinate (r, θ) that corresponds to the cartesian coordinate (x, y). This is the atan of y/x that is in the range $-\pi$ to π.

BigInteger and BigDecimal

In Java 1.1, there are two arbitrary-precision number formats: java.math.BigInteger and java.math.BigDecimal. These classes contain methods for addition, multiplication, division, exponentiation, primality testing, greatest common divisors, and more. See the API for details, but the key point is that they can be used to obtain any desired level of accuracy. For instance, *every* digit in a BigInteger is significant, and it cannot overflow. To illustrate this, Listing 8.2 uses BigInteger to represent the exact value of N! (the factorial of N, i.e. (N)(N–1)(N–2)...(1)) for large values of N. Listing 8.3 shows the result.

Listing 8.2 `Factorial.java`

```java
import java.math.BigInteger;

/** Computes an exact factorial using a BigInteger.
 *  Java 1.1 only.
 */

public class Factorial {
  public static void main(String[] args) {
    for(int i=1; i<=512; i*=2)
      System.out.println(i + "!=" + factorial(i));
  }

  public static BigInteger factorial(int n) {
    if (n <= 1)
      return(new BigInteger("1"));
    else {
      BigInteger bigN =
        new BigInteger(String.valueOf(n));
      return(bigN.multiply(factorial(n - 1)));
    }
  }
}
```

Listing 8.3   Factorial Output

```
1!=1
2!=2
4!=24
8!=40320
16!=20922789888000
32!=263130836933693530167218012160000000
64!=12688693218588416410343388933516148080286551617454519219880
18943752147042304000000000000000
128!=38562048236258042173567706592346364061749310959022359
0278828403276373402575165543560686168588507361534030051833
0589163475921729322624988577766114955245039357760034644709Z
79247692495585280000000000000000000000000000000000000000
```

continued

Listing 8.3   Factorial Output (continued)

```
256!=8578177753428426541190822716812326251577815202794856198596
5565037726945255314758937744029136045140845037588534233658430 61
5719683469369647532228928849742602567963733256336878644267520 76
2679456018796886797152114330770207752664645146470918732610083 28
7632570281898077367178145417025052301860849531906813825748107 02
5281755945947698703466571273813928620523475680821886070120361 10
8315209350194743710910172696826286160626366243502284094419140 84
2461593600000000000000000000000000000000000000000000000000000 00
0000000000000
512!=3477289793132605363283045917545604711992250655643514 5
7034247483155161041206635254347320985033950225364432243 311
0213945454529500170207006901326415311326093794135871186404 47
1618686104089955749736142758828235625496842501248039685 523
9725120562512065555822121708786443620799246550959187232 026
8380814151785881725352800207863134700768597399809657208 738
4990429137382684158471279861843038733804232977180172476 769
1095019545758986942732515033551529595009876999279553931 070
3785929170990023970619071471434241132521175859508178508 966
1843399414023282331643218741035634126238633249695431997 313
0407342567282027398579382543048456876800862349928140411 905
4312761974356746032818425307441775273658857216295122538 723
8661311882154084789749310739838195608176369523642279588 029
6204301770808809477147632428639299038833046264585834888 158
8473877378418434136648928335862091963669797757488958218 269
2404005784514028752223867508213757031595452672743709490 491
4796782641000740777897919134093393530422760955140211387 173
6500473583473533792343876092613066737732814128930269419 274
2400000000000000000000000000000000000000000000000000000 000
0000000000000000000000000000000000000000000000000000000 000
000000000000
```

8.4 Input and Output

The simplest forms of I/O are discussed in this section: printing to standard output and reading from standard input. Input and output will be discussed in much more detail in later chapters. The most detail will be given in Chapter 15, "Client-Server Programming in Java"; Section 15.1 (Implementing a Client) discusses how to attach various types of input and output streams to sockets, and the following sections give many concrete examples of the process. You can also attach these streams to files; Section 11.12 (FileDialog) gives an example. In addition, Section 11.10 (Serializing Windows) explains `ObjectOutputStream` and `ObjectInputStream`, classes that let you read and write complex Java objects rather than bytes, strings, and primitive types. These streams are attached to `FileOutputStream` and `FileIn-putStream` objects in the examples of Section 11.10, but they can be attached to network sockets as well. It should be mentioned here that Java includes a `RandomAccessFile` class not illustrated explicitly, but that using it is only slightly different than the examples provided. For instance, instead of writing a new file, you could append to an existing one by using a `RandomAccessFile`, seeking to the end, then writing there.

Printing to Standard Output

You've already seen examples of printing using `System.out.println`. As you probably guessed from the Java naming conventions, `out` is a `static` (class) variable in the `System` class, and `println` is a method in the class `out` belongs to. That class is `PrintStream`; it also contains a `print` method that works just like `println` except that it omits the trailing newline. Both `println` and `print` take a single argument of any type. Primitive types are converted to strings using the `String.valueOf` method, and non-`String` objects are converted to strings using their `toString` method. Multiple arguments can be combined into a single `String` using the "+" concatenation operator. In addition to `println` and `print`, the `PrintStream` class also contains a `flush` method. This is useful when you want to be sure that output has not been cached (e.g., when reading from standard input just after writing a prompt). For full details, see the on-line API for `java.io.PrintStream`.

Surprisingly, Java does not have a method equivalent to C's `printf` or `sprintf` that controls the spacing and formatting of numbers. In Java 1.1, the `java.text.MessageFormat` class provides some of this functionality, but it is really intended for internationalized code. A better alternative is to obtain one of the public domain `printf` substitutes. One of the best ones is from Jef Poskanzer; see `http://www.acme.com/java/software/Acme.Fmt.html`.

`System.out` can be reassigned in Java 1.0; it is `final` in Java 1.1.

Printing to Standard Error

In addition to the `System.out` variable, there is a `System.err` variable for use on operating systems that maintain a distinction between normal output and error output. It is also a `PrintStream` and can be used in exactly the same way as `System.out`.

`System.err` can be reassigned in Java 1.0; it is `final` in Java 1.1.

Reading from Standard Input

It is relatively uncommon to read from standard input in Java. Nongraphical applications typically use the command-line arguments for the data they need. Graphical programs use a `TextField`, `TextArea`, or other GUI control. However, if you need to read input this way, the standard approach is first to turn `System.in` into a `DataInputStream` as follows:

```
DataInputStream in =
    new DataInputStream(System.in);
```

Then, you can use `in.readLine` and `in.readChar` to read a string or a character. See Listing 8.21 (`URLTest.java`) for an example.

8.5 Executing Non-Java Programs

Although applets (Java programs embedded in Web pages) cannot execute system programs due to security restrictions, applications (stand-alone Java programs) are permitted to. Starting a local program involves the following four steps:

1. *Get a Runtime object.* Use the static `getRuntime` method of the `Runtime` class for this, as follows:

   ```
   Runtime rt = Runtime.getRuntime();
   ```

2. *Execute the program.* Use the `exec` method for this, which returns a `Process` object, as illustrated below:

   ```
   Process proc = rt.exec("someProgram");
   ```

   This starts the program, but does *not* wait for the program to terminate or print the program results. Note that the `exec` method does not make use of your `PATH` environment variable (used on Windows 95/NT and Unix to identify where to look for programs), so you need to specify the full pathname. Also, `exec` does not start a shell, so special shell characters (such as ">" or "|" in Unix) will not be recognized. Finally, note that there are variations of exec that take an array of strings and use that to pass command-line arguments to a program.

3. *Optional: wait for the program to exit.* The exec method returns immediately, regardless of how long it takes the program to run. This is so that you can start long-running programs such as Netscape and still continue processing, but it catches many users off guard. If you want the program to wait until the program exits before returning, use the waitFor method, as in the following example:

```
proc.waitFor();
```

While you might simply use exec to start Netscape, you would add waitFor if one program needs to terminate before another can begin. For example, you might call javac on a source file than use java to execute the result, but need to wait until the compilation finishes before starting the program execution. Note that waitFor does not print the program results, it simply waits for the program to finish before returning.

4. *Optional: print the results.* Rather than simply waiting for the program to terminate, you might want to print its output. For example, telling the system to do a directory listing is not too useful unless you print the results. Printing the results can be accomplished by attaching a DataInputStream to the process, then reading from it, as in the following example:

```
BufferedInputStream buffer =
  new BufferedInputStream(proc.getInputStream());
DataInputStream commandResult =
  new DataInputStream(buffer);
String s = null;
try {
  while ((s = commandResult.readLine()) != null)
    System.out.println("Output: " + s);
  commandResult.close();
} catch(Exception e) { /* ignore read errors */ }
```

The fourth step is somewhat oversimplified since opening the streams potentially generate an IOException which you are required to catch. Listing 8.4 shows this process, wrapping all four steps up into an easy to use Exec class containing exec, execPrint, and execWait methods. Listing 8.5 illustrates its use.

Listing 8.4   `Exec.java`

```
import java.io.*;

/** A class that eases the pain of running external
 *  processes from applications.
 *  Lets you run a program three ways:
 *  <OL>
 *    <LI><B>exec</B>: Execute the command, returning
 *        immediately even if the command is still
 *        running. This would be appropriate
 *        for printing a file.
 *    <LI><B>execWait</B>: Execute the command, but
 *        don't return until the command finishes.
 *        This would be appropriate for
 *        sequential commands where the first depends
 *        on the second having finished (e.g.
 *        <CODE>javac</CODE> followed by
 *        <CODE>java</CODE>).
 *    <LI><B>execPrint</B>: Execute the command and
 *        print the output. This would be appropriate
 *        for the UNIX command <CODE>ls</CODE>.
 *  </OL>
 *  Note that the PATH is not taken into account,
 *  so  you must specify the <B>full</B> pathname to
 *  the command, and shell built-in commands
 *  will not work. For instance, on Unix the above
 *  three examples might look like:
 *  <OL>
 *    <LI><PRE>Exec.exec("/usr/ucb/lpr Some-File");</PRE>
 *    <LI><PRE>
 *        Exec.execWait("/usr/local/bin/javac Foo.java");
 *        Exec.execWait("/usr/local/bin/java Foo");
 *        </PRE>
 *    <LI><PRE>Exec.execPrint("/usr/bin/ls -al");</PRE>
 *  </OL>
 *
 * @author Marty Hall
 *  (<A HREF="mailto:hall@apl.jhu.edu">
 *   hall@apl.jhu.edu</A>)
 * @version 1.0 1997
 */
```

| Listing 8.4   `Exec.java`   (continued) |

```java
public class Exec {
  //--------------------------------------------------

  private static boolean verbose = true;

  /** Determines if the Exec class should print which
   *  commands are being executed, and print error
   *  messages if a problem is found. Default is true.
   *
   *  @param verboseFlag true: print messages.
   *           false: don't.
   */

  public static void setVerbose(boolean verboseFlag) {
    verbose = verboseFlag;
  }

  /** Will Exec print status messages? */

  public static boolean getVerbose() {
    return(verbose);
  }

  //--------------------------------------------------
  /** Starts a process to execute the command. Returns
   *  immediately, even if the new process is still
   *  running.
   *
   *  @param command The <B>full</B> pathname of the
   *           command to be executed. No shell built-ins
   *           (e.g. "cd") or shell meta-chars (e.g. ">")
   *           allowed.
   *  @return false if a problem is known to occur, but
   *           since this returns immediately, problems
   *           aren't usually found in time.
   *           Returns true otherwise.
   */

  public static boolean exec(String command) {
    return(exec(command, false, false));
  }

  //--------------------------------------------------
```

continued

Listing 8.4 `Exec.java` (continued)

```java
/** Starts a process to execute the command. Waits
 *   for the process to finish before returning.
 *
 * @param command The <B>full</B> pathname of the
 *        command to be executed. No shell built-ins
 *        or shell meta-chars allowed.
 * @return false if a problem is known to occur,
 *         either due to an exception or from the
 *         subprocess returning a non-zero value.
 *         Returns true otherwise.
 */

public static boolean execWait(String command) {
  return(exec(command, false, true));
}

//-----------------------------------------------------
/** Starts a process to execute the command. Prints
 *   all output the command gives.
 *
 * @param command The <B>full</B> pathname of the
 *        command to be executed. No shell built-ins
 *        or shell meta-chars allowed.
 * @return false if a problem is known to occur,
 *         either due to an exception or from the
 *         subprocess returning a non-zero value.
 *         Returns true otherwise.
 */

public static boolean execPrint(String command) {
  return(exec(command, true, false));
}

//-----------------------------------------------------
// This creates a Process object via
// Runtime.getRuntime.exec(). Depending on the
// flags, it may call waitFor on the process
// to avoid continuing until the process terminates,
// or open an input stream from the process to read
// the results.
```

Listing 8.4   `Exec.java` (continued)

```
private static boolean exec(String command,
                           boolean printResults,
                           boolean wait) {
  if (verbose) {
    printSeparator();
    System.out.println("Executing '" + command + "'.");
  }
  try {
    // Start running command, returning immediately.
    Process p = Runtime.getRuntime().exec(command);

    // Print the output. Since we read until
    // there is no more input, this causes us
    // to wait until the process is completed
    if(printResults) {
      BufferedInputStream buffer =
        new BufferedInputStream(p.getInputStream());
      DataInputStream commandResult =
        new DataInputStream(buffer);
      String s = null;
      try {
        while ((s = commandResult.readLine()) != null)
          System.out.println("Output: " + s);
        commandResult.close();
        if (p.exitValue() != 0) {
          if (verbose)
            printError(command +
                       " -- p.exitValue() != 0");
          return(false);
        }
      // Ignore read errors; they mean process is done
      } catch (Exception e) {}

    // If you don't print the results, then you
    // need to call waitFor to stop until the process
    // is completed
    } else if (wait) {
      try {
        System.out.println(" ");
        int returnVal = p.waitFor();
        if (returnVal != 0) {
```

continued

Listing 8.4   `Exec.java` (continued)

```java
        if (verbose)
          printError(command);
        return(false);
      }
    } catch (Exception e) {
      if (verbose)
        printError(command, e);
      return(false);
    }
  }
} catch (Exception e) {
  if (verbose)
    printError(command, e);
  return(false);
}
return(true);
}

//-----------------------------------------------------

private static void printError(String command,
                               Exception e) {
  System.out.println("Error doing exec(" +
                     command + "): " + e.getMessage());
  System.out.println("Did you specify the full " +
                     "pathname?");
}

private static void printError(String command) {
  System.out.println("Error executing '" +
                     command + "'.");
}

//-----------------------------------------------------

private static void printSeparator() {
  System.out.println
    ("=============================================");
}

//-----------------------------------------------------
}
```

Listing 8.5 illustrates the Exec class in action on a Unix system, with the result shown in Listing 8.6.

Listing 8.5   `ExecTest.java`

```
/** A test of the Exec class. */

public class ExecTest {
  public static void main(String[] args) {
    // Note: no trailing "&" -- special shell chars
    // not understood, since no shell started.
    // Besides, exec doesn't wait, so the program
    // continues along even before Netscape pops up.
    Exec.exec("/usr/local/bin/netscape");

    // Run commands, printing results
    Exec.execPrint("/usr/bin/ls");
    Exec.execPrint("/usr/bin/cat Test.java");

    // Don't print results, but wait until done
    // before continuing on.
    Exec.execWait("/usr/local/JDK/bin/javac Test.java");

    // There should be Test.class there now
    Exec.execPrint("/usr/bin/ls");
  }
}
```

Listing 8.6   ExecTest Output

```
Unix> java ExecTest
==========================================
Executing '/usr/local/bin/netscape'.
==========================================
Executing '/usr/bin/ls'.
Output: Exec.class
Output: Exec.java
Output: ExecTest.class
Output: ExecTest.java
Output: Test.java
```

| Listing 8.6   ExecTest Output   (continued) |

```
===============================================
Executing '/usr/bin/cat Test.java'.
Output: public class Test {
Output:   public static void main(String[] args) {
Output:       System.out.println("This is a test.");
Output:   }
Output: }
===============================================
Executing '/usr/local/JDK/bin/javac Test.java'.

===============================================
Executing '/usr/bin/ls'.
Output: Exec.class
Output: Exec.java
Output: ExecTest.class
Output: ExecTest.java
Output: Test.class
Output: Test.java
```

8.6 Reference Types

Values that are objects (i.e., class instances or arrays; anything nonprimitive) are known as *reference values* or simply *references*. In the Java world, we normally say that the value of such and such a variable "is" an object. Because Java has no explicit referencing or dereferencing of pointers or pointer arithmetic, it is commonly but erroneously stated that Java does not have pointers. Wrong! In fact, *all* nonprimitive variables in Java are pointers. So a C or C++ programmer might find it clearer to say that such and such a nonprimitive variable "points to" an object. This is the only kind of nonprimitive type in Java; there is no distinction between variables that *are* objects and variables that *point to* objects as in some languages. If you're not familiar with pointers already, be aware that you can pass big complicated objects around efficiently; Java doesn't copy them every time you pass them from one method to another. If you've used pointers extensively in other languages, be aware that Java forbids dereferencing pointers; a method can't change the object that an external variable references. Listing 8.7 gives an example.

Listing 8.7   ReferenceTest.java

```java
import java.awt.Point;

public class ReferenceTest {
  public static void main(String[] args) {
    Point p1 = new Point(1, 2); // Assign Point to p1
    Point p2 = p1; // p2 is new reference to *same* Point
    print("p1", p1); // (1, 2)
    print("p2", p2); // (1, 2)
    triple(p2); // Doesn't change p2
    print("p2", p2); // (1, 2)
    p2 = triple(p2); // Have p2 point to *new* Point
    print("p2", p2); // (3, 6)
    print("p1", p1); // p1 unchanged: (1, 2)
  }

  public static Point triple(Point p) {
    p = new Point(p.x * 3, p.y * 3); // Redirect p
    return(p);
  }

  public static void print(String name, Point p) {
    System.out.println("Point " + name + "= (" +
                       p.x + ", " + p.y + ").");
  }
}
```

Listing 8.8   ReferenceTest Output

```
Point p1= (1, 2).
Point p2= (1, 2).
Point p2= (1, 2).
Point p2= (3, 6).
Point p1= (1, 2).
```

Notice that changing the local variable p in the `triple` method didn't change the variable passed in (p2); it merely made p point someplace new, leaving p2 referring to the original place. To change p2 to a new object, I had to explicitly assign it to the return value of `triple`. Although it is not possible for a method to change where an external variable points (i.e., the *object* to which it refers), it is possible for a method to change the *fields* of an object, assuming that the field's access permissions are appropriate. This is illustrated in Listing 8.9.

Listing 8.9   `ModificationTest.java`

```
import java.awt.Point;

public class ModificationTest extends ReferenceTest {
  public static void main(String[] args) {
    Point p1 = new Point(1, 2); // Assign Point to p1
    Point p2 = p1; // p2 is new reference to *same* Point
    print("p1", p1); // (1, 2)
    print("p2", p2); // (1, 2)
    munge(p2); // Changes fields of the *single* Point
    print("p1", p1); // (5, 10)
    print("p2", p2); // (5, 10)
  }

  public static void munge(Point p) {
    p.x = 5;
    p.y = 10;
  }
}
```

Listing 8.10   Modification Test Output

```
Point p1= (1, 2).
Point p2= (1, 2).
Point p1= (5, 10).
Point p2= (5, 10).
```

Java Argument-Passing Conventions

Now, if you are already familiar with the terms "call by value" and "call by reference," you may be puzzled as to which scheme Java uses. It cannot be call by reference, because the change to p in `triple` didn't change the external value. But it doesn't look like call by value either, because the munge method showed that methods don't get copies of objects. I recommend that you not worry about the definitions, and simply remember the following rule.

Core Note

---

*If you pass a variable to a method in Java, the method cannot change which **object** the variable references, but might be able to change the **fields** of that object.*

If you are absolutely determined to pin the definition down, then you can say that Java uses call by value, but that the values themselves are references (restricted pointers).

The Instanceof Operator

The `instanceof` operator returns `true` or `false` depending on whether the left-hand argument is a direct or indirect instance of the class named by the right-hand argument. Listing 8.11 gives an example; output is shown in Listing 8.12. Use this operator with caution; many applications of `instanceof` can be replaced by overloading, yielding a simpler and more maintainable result.

Listing 8.11   `InstanceOf.java`

```java
class One {}

class Two extends One {}

class Three extends Two {}

class Four extends Three {}

public class InstanceOf {
  public static void main(String[] args) {
    Two test1 = new Two();
    Four test2 = new Four();
    report(test1, "test1");
    report(test2, "test2");
  }

  public static void report(Object object, String name) {
    System.out.println(name + " is One: " +
                        (object instanceof One));
    System.out.println(name + " is Two: " +
                        (object instanceof Two));
    System.out.println(name + " is Three: " +
                        (object instanceof Three));
    System.out.println(name + " is Four: " +
                        (object instanceof Four));
  }
}
```

Listing 8.12   InstanceOf Output

```
test1 is One: true
test1 is Two: true
test1 is Three: false
test1 is Four: false
test2 is One: true
test2 is Two: true
test2 is Three: true
test2 is Four: true
```

Java 1.1 has a dynamic version: the isInstance method of java.lang.Object. The idea is to turn an object into a Class using getClass then compare potential instances of subclasses to this. Listing 8.13 gives an example: the code shown prints true when executed.

Listing 8.13   IsInstance.java

```java
class Foo {}

class Bar extends Foo {}

public class IsInstance {
  public static void main(String[] args) {
    Foo f = new Foo();
    Bar b = new Bar();
    // Is b an instance of the class f belongs to? (Yes)
    System.out.println(f.getClass().isInstance(b));
  }
}
```

8.7 Strings

In Java, strings are real objects, members of the java.lang.String class. However, because they are so frequently used, you are allowed to create them simply by using double quotes, as follows:

```java
String s1 = "This is a String";
```

The normal object-creation approach of using new is legal also, but is rarely used. E.g.:

```
String s2 = new String("This is a String too");
```

The most unusual thing about the `String` class is that strings are immutable; once created they cannot be changed. "Hold on," you say, "I know there is no `setCharacterAt` method, but I've seen string concatenation used lots of places." This is a good point, the "+" character can be used to concatenate strings, as follows:

```
String test = "foo" + "bar"; // "foobar"
```

However, in this example *three* strings are created: `"foo"`, `"bar"`, and a new third string `"foobar"`. This distinction doesn't seem important here, but is very significant in the following example:

```
String foo = "foo";
String bar = "bar";
String test = foo + bar;
```

The key point here is that neither `foo` nor `bar` are modified by the concatenation performed on the third line. This is a convenient feature; it means that it is safe to pass strings to arbitrary methods without worrying about them being modified. On the other hand, to implement this nonchangeable nature Java has to copy the strings when concatenation is performed. This can be expensive, so Java supplies a `StringBuffer` class that is mutable. See Section 18.9 (Decoding URL-Encoded Values) for an example of the cost of repeated concatenation and the use of `StringBuffer`.

Note that "+" is one of the few overloaded operators in Java; it has a totally different meaning for strings than it has for numbers. You cannot define your own operators or overload existing ones.

Methods in the String Class

Java provides a number of useful methods for working with strings. They are summarized below.

Instance Methods

These "normal" methods can be called on `String` instances:

public char charAt(int index)
This returns the character at the specified location.

public int compareTo(String comparison)

This method compares the current string to the supplied one character by character, checking Unicode ordering. It returns 0 if the strings are equal (have the same characters), a negative number if the current string is lexicographically less than the comparison, a positive number otherwise. This is generally used for determining if strings are in order. The actual number is the difference in Unicode values between the first nonmatching characters, or the difference in lengths if the shorter string is a prefix of the longer one.

public String concat(String suffix)

The following two forms are identical:

```
String result = someString.concat(someOtherString);
String result = someString + someOtherString;
```

public boolean endsWith(String suffix)

This checks for a suffix of a string.

public boolean equals(Object comparison)

If the comparison object is not a String, this returns false. Otherwise it compares character by character. Thus, two different strings with the same characters will be equals but not ==. For example, Listing 8.14 compares the first input argument to a fixed string using equals and ==. As Listing 8.15 shows, the == test fails but the equals test succeeds. Also note that different occurrences of literal strings may or may not be == since the compiler may collapse such constants.

Listing 8.14   StringCompare.java

```java
public class StringCompare {
  public static void main(String[] args) {
    String s1 = "This is a test";
    if (args.length > 0) {
      System.out.println(s1 == args[0]);
      System.out.println(s1.equals(args[0]));
    }
  }
}
```

Listing 8.15   StringCompare Output

```
prompt> java StringCompare "This is a test"
false
true
```

Core Warning

Two different String *objects that contain the same characters will not be*
==. *They will, however, be* equals. *In general, two different objects are*
not == even when their fields have identical values.

public boolean equalsIgnoreCase(String comparison)
This does a case insensitive character-by-character comparison.

public void getBytes(int sourceStart, int sourceEnd,
                           byte[ ] destination, int destinationStart)
public byte[ ] getBytes() [Java 1.1]
public byte[ ] getBytes(String encoding) [Java 1.1]
These methods convert strings to bytes. In the first method (deprecated
in Java 1.1), you supply the target array and it is filled. In the other two
methods (new in Java 1.1), the byte array is returned.

public void getChars(int sourceStart, int sourceEnd,
                           char[ ] destination, int destinationStart)
This copies the characters from sourceStart (inclusive) to
sourceEnd (exclusive) into the specified part of the destination array.

public int indexOf(int character)
public int indexOf(int character, int startIndex)
public int indexOf(String subString)
public int indexOf(String subString, int startIndex)
These methods return the index of the first occurrence of the specified
target.

public native String intern()
This returns a canonical String containing the same characters as the
supplied string. The interned result of two strings are == if and only if
the strings themselves are equals.

public int lastIndexOf(int character)
public int lastIndexOf(int character, int startIndex)
public int lastIndexOf(String subString)
public int lastIndexOf(String subString, int startIndex)
These methods return the index of the last occurrence of the specified target.

public int length()
This gives the length of the string. Note that this is a method call, not an instance variable. So don't forget that for strings you have to do:
```
int len = someString.length(); // length()
```
while for arrays you do
```
int len = someArray.length; // No parens
```

public boolean regionMatches(int startIndex1, String string2,
                                                    int startIndex2, int count)
public boolean regionMatches(boolean ignoreCase,
                                        int startIndex1, String string2,
                                        int startIndex2, int count)
These methods do a case sensitive or insensitive comparison of two substrings.

public String replace(char oldChar, char newChar)
This returns a *new* String that is the result of replacing all occurrences of oldChar by newChar. The original string is not modified.

public boolean startsWith(String prefix)
public boolean startsWith(String prefix, int startIndex)
These check for string prefixes.

public String subString(int startIndex, int endIndex)
public String subString(int startIndex)
These return substrings in the specified range. If no ending index is supplied, the substring goes to the end of the original string.

public char[ ] toCharArray()
This generates a character array.

public String toLowerCase()
public String toLowerCase(Locale locale) [Java 1.1]
This converts the entire string to lowercase, optionally using the rules of the specified locale (for Java 1.1 internationalized code).

public String toUpperCase()
public String toUpperCase(Locale locale) [Java 1.1]
This converts the entire string to uppercase, optionally using the rules of the specified locale (for Java 1.1 internationalized code).

public String trim()
This returns a *new* String with leading and trailing whitespace and control characters removed. The original String is not modified.

Class Methods

These static methods can be called without having a String instance.

public static String copyValueOf(char[ ] characters)
public static String copyValueOf(char[ ] data, int startIndex,
int count)
These convert character arrays to strings.

public static String valueOf(boolean b)
public static String valueOf(char c)
public static String valueOf(char[ ] data)
public static String valueOf(char[ ] data, int startIndex,
int count)
public static String valueOf(double d)
public static String valueOf(float f)
public static String valueOf(int i)
public static String valueOf(long l)
These convert the specified primitive values to strings.

public Static String valueOf(Object o)
This uses the object's toString method to generate a string.

Constructors

public String()
This builds a zero-length but non-null string.

public String(byte[ ] bytes) [Java 1.1]
public String(byte[ ] bytes, String encoding) [Java 1.1]
public String(byte[ ] bytes, int startIndex, int count) [Java 1.1]

public String(byte[ ] bytes, int startIndex, int count,
        String encoding) [Java 1.1]
public String(byte[ ] lowBytes, int hiByte)
public String(byte[ ] lowBytes, int hiByte, int startIndex,
        int count)

These constructors build a string from byte arrays. If the array came from reading ASCII data, supply 0 for the `hiByte` in the Java 1.0 methods.

public String(char[ ] chars)
public String(char[ ] chars, int startIndex, int count)

These build a string from character arrays.

public String(String string)

This copies the string. The result is `equals` but not `==` to the input.

public String(StringBuffer stringBuffer)

This converts a `StringBuffer` to a `String`. See Section 18.9 (Decoding URL-Encoded Values) for an example.

8.8 Vectors

Java provides a "stretchable" array class: `java.util.Vector`. It is used for many of the same purposes as linked lists because you can insert or remove elements at any location. However, because arrays are used for the underlying implementation, it takes only constant time to access a specified location, but takes time proportional to the number of elements contained to insert elements at the beginning of the `Vector`. Following is a summary of the `Vector` methods; see Section 8.9 for an example. Notice that the insertion and retrieval methods return elements of type `Object`, and that most methods are `final`. This makes it difficult, but not impossible, to make vectors that can only hold objects of a particular type and that let you retrieve values without typecasting the return value. See Listing 18.16 (`StringVector.java`) for a class that creates a `Vector` of strings.

Constructors

public Vector()
public Vector(int initialCapacity)
public Vector(int initialCapacity, int capacityIncrement)

This builds an empty `Vector`. The initial capacity (size of the underlying array) is 10 if not specified, but Java will automatically copy vectors into bigger arrays if they grow too big.

Methods

public final void addElement(Object object)
public final void insertElementAt(Object object, int index)
public final void setElementAt(Object object, int index)

These methods add elements to the `Vector`. The `addElement` method inserts at the end; the other two methods use the location specified. With `insertElementAt`, the objects at and to the right of the specified location are shuffled down. With `setElementAt`, the object at the specified location is replaced.

public final int capacity()

This returns the size of the underlying array, i.e. the number of elements the `Vector` can hold before it will be resized.

public final boolean contains(Object object)

This determines if the `Vector` contains an object that is `equals` to the one specified.

public final void copyInto(Object[ ] newArray)

This copies the object references into the specified array, in order.

public final Object elementAt(int index)

This returns the element at the specified location.

public final Enumeration elements()

The `java.util.Enumeration` class defines an interface used by several enumerable classes. You can use `elements` to get an Enumeration object.

public final void ensureCapacity(int minimum)

This guarantees that the underlying array has at least the specified number of elements.

public final Object firstElement()
public final Object lastElement()

These methods return the first and last entry in the Vector, respectively.

public final int indexOf(Object object)
public final int indexOf(Object object, int startIndex)
public final int lastIndexOf(Object object)
public final int lastIndexOf(Object object, int startIndex)

These methods return the leftmost or rightmost index holding an element that is equals to the object specified.

public final boolean isEmpty()

This returns false if the Vector has any elements; true otherwise.

public final boolean removeElement(Object object)
public final void removeElementAt(int index)
public final void removeAllElements()

These methods let you remove entries from the Vector.

public final void setSize(int newSize)

This sets a specific size for the Vector. It differs from ensureCapacity in that it will truncate the Vector if it is larger than the specified size.

public final int size()

This returns the number of elements in the Vector (not the size of the underlying array, which might be larger than this).

public final void trimToSize()

This sets the underlying array to be exactly the same size as the current number of elements. You should avoid this method while elements are being added and removed, but it might save memory if used once the Vector elements are fixed.

8.9 Example: A Simple Binary Tree

Listing 8.16 shows how reference values can be used to create a binary tree. This data structure includes a `depthFirstSearch` method, which traverses the tree in depth first order (staying to the left and going as deep as possible until having to backtrack). Notice that this method is recursive; recursion is natural for depth-first search. The `depthFirstSearch` method also uses the `NodeOperator` interface to generalize the operation that will be performed on each node. This lets you change what to do with a tree without changing the `Node` class. The data structure also includes a `breadthFirstSearch` method that uses a `Vector` to build a queue used to traverse the tree in breadth first order (visiting all nodes on a given level before moving on to the next).

Note that many data structures like this have already been put in third-party libraries. In particular, ObjectSpace's Java Generic Library (JGL) contains a large number of optimized data structures for sets, maps, queues, sorting, etc. It is distributed with a number of commercial development environments and is available for free download and use (even in commercial products). See `http://www.objectspace.com/jgl/`. Java 1.2 is expected to add a variety of new data structures as well. For a preview, see `http://www.javasoft.com/products/jdk/preview/docs/guide/collections/`.

Listing 8.16 `Node.java`

```
import java.util.Vector;

/** A data structure representing a node in a binary
 *  tree. It contains a node value and a reference
 *  (pointer) to the left and right subtrees.
 */

public class Node {
  private Object nodeValue;
  private Node leftChild, rightChild;
```

Listing 8.16 `Node.java` (continued)

```java
/** Build Node with specified value and subtrees. */

public Node(Object nodeValue,
            Node leftChild, Node rightChild) {
  this.nodeValue = nodeValue;
  this.leftChild = leftChild;
  this.rightChild = rightChild;
}

/** Build Node with specified value and L subtree.
 *  R child will be null. If you want both children
 *  to be null, use the Leaf constructor.
 *
 * @see Leaf
 */

public Node(Object nodeValue, Node leftChild) {
  this(nodeValue, leftChild, null);
}

/** Return the value of this node. */

public Object getNodeValue() {
  return(nodeValue);
}

/** Specify the value of this node. */

public void setNodeValue(Object nodeValue) {
  this.nodeValue = nodeValue;
}


/** Return the L subtree. */

public Node getLeftChild() {
  return(leftChild);
}

/** Specify the L subtree. */

public void setLeftChild(Node leftChild) {
  this.leftChild = leftChild;
}
```

Listing 8.16   `Node.java`   (continued)

```java
/** Return the R subtree. */

public Node getRightChild() {
  return(rightChild);
}

/** Specify the R subtree. */

public void setRightChild(Node rightChild) {
  this.rightChild = rightChild;
}

/** Traverse the tree in depth-first order, applying
 *  the specified operation to each node along the way.
 */

public void depthFirstSearch(NodeOperator op) {
  op.operateOn(this);
  if (leftChild != null)
    leftChild.depthFirstSearch(op);
  if (rightChild != null)
    rightChild.depthFirstSearch(op);
}

/** Traverse the tree in breadth-first order, applying
 *  the specified operation to each node along the way.
 */


public void breadthFirstSearch(NodeOperator op) {
  Vector nodeQueue = new Vector();
  nodeQueue.addElement(this);
  Node node;
  while(!nodeQueue.isEmpty()) {
    node = (Node)nodeQueue.elementAt(0);
    nodeQueue.removeElementAt(0);
    op.operateOn(node);
    if (node.getLeftChild() != null)
      nodeQueue.addElement(node.getLeftChild());
    if (node.getRightChild() != null)
      nodeQueue.addElement(node.getRightChild());
  }
}
}
```

Listing 8.17 `NodeOperator.java`

```
/** An interface used in the Node class to ensure that
 *  an object has an operateOn method.
 */

public interface NodeOperator {
  void operateOn(Node node);
}
```

Listing 8.18 `Leaf.java`

```
/** Leaf node: a node with no subtrees. */

public class Leaf extends Node {
  public Leaf(Object value) {
    super(value, null, null);
  }
}
```

Now that we have a general data structure, let's build a specific test case. Figure 8–1 shows a simple tree; Listing 8.19 represents it using the `Node` and `Leaf` classes just shown and makes a `NodeOperator` that does nothing but print the value of each node it visits. Listing 8.20 shows the results.

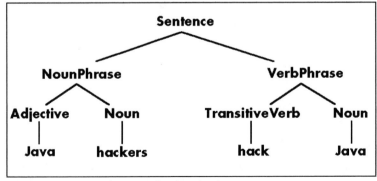

Figure 8-1   Parse tree for "Java hackers hack Java."

Listing 8.19   `TreeTest.java`

```java
/** A NodeOperator that prints each node. */

class PrintOperator implements NodeOperator {
  public void operateOn(Node node) {
    System.out.println(node.getNodeValue());
  }
}


/** A sample tree representing a parse tree of
 *  the sentence "Java hackers hack Java" using
 *  some simple Context Free Grammar.
 */

public class TreeTest {
  public static void main(String[] args) {
    Node adjective =
      new Node(" Adjective", new Leaf("  Java"));
    Node noun1 =
      new Node(" Noun", new Leaf("   hackers"));
    Node verb =
      new Node(" TransitiveVerb", new Leaf("  hack"));
    Node noun2 =
      new Node(" Noun", new Leaf("  Java"));
    Node np = new Node(" NounPhrase", adjective, noun1);
    Node vp = new Node(" VerbPhrase", verb, noun2);
    Node sentence = new Node("Sentence", np, vp);
    PrintOperator printOp = new PrintOperator();
    System.out.println("Depth first traversal:");
    sentence.depthFirstSearch(printOp);
    System.out.println("\nBreadth first traversal:");
    sentence.breadthFirstSearch(printOp);
  }
}
```

Listing 8.20   TreeTest Output

```
Depth first traversal:
Sentence
 NounPhrase
  Adjective
   Java
  Noun
   hackers
 VerbPhrase
  TransitiveVerb
   hack
  Noun
   Java

Breadth first traversal:
Sentence
 NounPhrase
 VerbPhrase
  Adjective
  Noun
  TransitiveVerb
  Noun
   Java
   hackers
   hack
   Java
```

8.10 Arrays

In Java, arrays are real objects. They have a `length` instance variable and can be assigned to variables of type `Object` as well as to variables of their specific type.

Two-Step Array Allocation

Arrays are normally created in two steps. In the first step, an array of the proper size is allocated:

```
int[] values = new int[2]; // a 2-element array
Point[] points = new Point[5]; // a 5-element array
int numNames = askHowManyNames(); // Set at run-time
String[] names = new String[numNames];
```

This step does not build any of the objects that actually go into the array. That is done in a separate step using the `arrayReference[index]` notation to access array locations. For example:

```
values[0] = 10;
values[1] = 100;
for(int i=0; i<points.length; i++)
  points[i] = new Point(i*2, i*4);
for(int j=0; j<names.length; j++)
  names[j] = "Name " + j;
```

It is a common error to forget the second step. If you get a `NullPointerException` whenever you access an array element, check for this problem first.

Core Warning

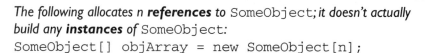

The following allocates n **references** *to* `SomeObject`; *it doesn't actually build any* **instances** *of* `SomeObject`:
`SomeObject[] objArray = new SomeObject[n];`

If you are a die-hard C hacker, you are permitted to declare arrays via

```
Type someVar[] = ...
```

instead of

```
Type[] someVar = ...
```

Just be aware that this reduces your JHF (Java Hipness Factor) by 2.5 units.

One-Step Array Allocation

Arrays can also be allocated and assigned in one fell swoop by specifying comma-separated elements inside curly braces in the initialization portion of a variable declaration. For instance:

```
int[] values = { 10, 100 };
Point[] points = { new Point(0, 0),
                   new Point(2, 4),
                   new Point(4, 8),
                   ... };
```

Multidimensional Arrays

In Java, multidimensional arrays are implemented using arrays-of-arrays, just as in C. For instance, the following allocates and fills a 12x14 array.

```
int[][] values = new int[12][14];
for(int i=0; i<12; i++)
  for(int j=0; j<14; j++)
    values[i][j] = someFunctionOf(i, j);
```

You can access individual elements as follows:

```
int someVal = values[i][j]; // i<12, j<14
values[i][j] = someInt;
```

You can also access entire rows by omitting the second subscript:

```
int[] someArray = values[i]; // 0<=i<=11
values[i] = someOtherArray;
```

You can generalize this process to dimensions higher than 2. Also, the internal arrays need not be of the same length. To implement nonrectangular arrays, omit the rightmost size declarations. Here is an example:

```
String[][] names = new String[3][];
String[] name0 = { "John", "Q.", "Public" };
String[] name1 = { "Jane", "Doe" };
String[] name2 = { "Pele" };
names[0] = name0; // 3 elements
names[1] = name1; // 2 elements
names[2] = name2; // 1 element
```

The "shorthand" array declaration is legal with multidimensional arrays also:

```
String[][] altNames = { { "John", "Q.", "Public" },
                        { "Jane", "Doe" },
                        { "Pele" } };
```

8.11 Exceptions

Java has a very nice error-handling system: *exceptions*. Exceptions can be "thrown" (generated) in one block of code and "caught" (handled) in an outer block or in a method that called the current one. Java exceptions differ from C++ exceptions in two major ways. The first major difference is that the exception-handling construct (try/catch) has a `finally` clause that always gets executed, regardless of whether or not an exception was thrown. The second significant difference is that you can *require* users of your methods to handle exceptions your methods generate. If they don't, their code will not compile. On the other hand, if you feel an exception is lower-priority, you can declare that handling it be optional, as in C++.

Basic Form

The simplest form of exception handling is a block of the following form:

```
try {
  statement1;
  statement2;
  ...
} catch(SomeException someVar) {
  handleTheException(someVar);
}
```

For example, the constructor for `java.net.URL` potentially generates a `java.net.MalformedURLException`, and the `readLine` method of `java.io.DataInputStream` potentially generates a `java.io.IOException`. Listing 8.21 uses both the URL constructor and the `readLine` method to read a URL from the user and print descriptive information about it, so it needs to catch both possible exceptions. As Listing 8.22 shows, `MalformedURLException` verifies that the URL is in legal format; it doesn't retrieve the referenced file or even check that it exists. You can see plenty of examples of reading the contents of such files in Chapter 15, "Client-Server Programming in Java."

```java
import java.net.*; // For URL, MalformedURLException
import java.io.*;  // For DataInputStream

/** A small class to demonstrate try/catch blocks. */

public class URLTest {
  public static void main(String[] args) {
    URLTest test = new URLTest();
    test.getURL();
    test.printURL();
  }

  private URL url = null;

  /** Read a string from user and create URL from it.
   *  If reading fails, give up and report error.
   *  If reading succeeds but URL is illegal, try again.
   */

  public URL getURL() {
    if (url != null)
      return(url);
    System.out.print("Enter URL: ");
    System.out.flush();
    DataInputStream in = new DataInputStream(System.in);
    String urlString;
    try {
      urlString = in.readLine();
    } catch(IOException ioe) {
      System.out.println("IOError when reading input: " +
                         ioe);
      ioe.printStackTrace(); // Show stack dump
      return(null);
    }
    try {
      url = new URL(urlString);
    } catch(MalformedURLException mue) {
      System.out.println(urlString + " is not valid.\n" +
                         "Try again.");
      getURL();
    }
    return(url);
  }
```

Listing 8.21 URLTest.java (continued)

```
/** Print info on URL. */

  public void printURL() {
    if (url == null)
      System.out.println("No URL.");
    else {
      String protocol = url.getProtocol();
      String host = url.getHost();
      int port = url.getPort();
      if (protocol.equals("http") && (port == -1))
        port = 80;
      String file = url.getFile();
      System.out.println("Protocol: " + protocol +
                         "\nHost: " + host +
                         "\nPort: " + port +
                         "\nFile: " + file);
    }
  }
}
```

Listing 8.22 URLTest Output

```
Prompt> java URLTest
Enter URL: http://java.sun.com/ConvertingToActiveX.html
Protocol: http
Host: java.sun.com
Port: 80
File: /ConvertingToActiveX.html
```

Note the use of the printStackTrace method in getURL. This shows the method call stack at the point the exception occurred. In many implementations it even includes line numbers in the source files. This is such a useful debugging tool that it is sometimes used even when there are no exceptions generated. For instance, the following simply prints a stack dump:

```
new Throwable().printStackTrace();
```

Multiple Catch Clauses

A single `try` can have more than one `catch`. If an exception is generated, Java executes the first `catch` clause that matches the type of exception thrown. Since exceptions can be created hierarchically like other Java classes, you should catch more specific exception types before more general ones. For instance, although the `getURL` method could be simplified to use a single `try` block with two `catch` clauses (Listing 8.23), the order of the `catch` clauses needs to be reversed since a `MalformedURLException` is a subclass of `IOException`.

Core Approach

If you have multiple `catch` *clauses, order them from the most specific to the most general.*

Listing 8.23   Simplified getURL method

```
public URL getURL() {
  if (url != null)
    return(url);
  System.out.print("Enter URL: ");
  System.out.flush();
  DataInputStream in = new DataInputStream(System.in);
  String urlString = null;
  try {
    urlString = in.readLine();
    url = new URL(urlString);
  } catch(MalformedURLException mue) {
    System.out.println(urlString + " is not valid.\n" +
                       "Try again.");
    getURL();
  } catch(IOException ioe) {
    System.out.println("IOError when reading input: " +
                       ioe);
    ioe.printStackTrace(); // Show stack dump
    return(null);
  }
  return(url);
}
```

The Finally Clause

After the last catch clause, you are permitted a finally clause that *always* gets executed, regardless of whether or not exceptions are thrown. It is executed even if break, continue, or return is used within the try or catch clauses. Listing 8.24 shows a third version of getURL that uses this approach.

Listing 8.24   Further simplified getURL method

```
public URL getURL() {
  if (url != null)
    return(url);
  System.out.print("Enter URL: ");
  System.out.flush();
  DataInputStream in = new DataInputStream(System.in);
  String urlString = null;
  try {
    urlString = in.readLine();
    url = new URL(urlString);
  } catch(MalformedURLException mue) {
    System.out.println(urlString + " is not valid.\n" +
                       "Try again.");
    getURL();
  } catch(IOException ioe) {
    System.out.println("IOError when reading input: " +
                       ioe);
    ioe.printStackTrace(); // Can skip return(null) now
  } finally {
    return(url);
  }
}
```

Throwing Exceptions

If you write a method that potentially generates one or more exceptions and you don't handle them explicitly, you need to declare them using the throws construct as follows:

```
public SomeType someMethod(...) throws SomeException
{
```

or

```
public SomeType someMethod(...)
```

```
throws ExceptionType1, ExceptionType2 {
```

This lets you do two things. First, it permits you to write methods that have enforced safety checking; users are required to handle the exception when calling them. Second, it permits you to postpone exception handling to a method higher in the method call chain by declaring them in the method declaration but ignoring them in the method body.

If you want to explicitly generate an exception, use the `throw` construct as illustrated:

```
throw new IOException();
throw
    new MalformedURLException("Blocked by firewall");
```

Using `throw` is most common with exceptions you define yourself. You can make your own exception classes by subclassing any of the existing exception types. Listing 8.25 gives an example of an exception type you might use when creating geometric objects that require nonnegative widths, heights, radii, and so forth.

Listing 8.25   `NegativeLengthException.java`

```java
public class NegativeLengthException extends Exception {
  public NegativeLengthException() {
    super("Negative dimensions not permitted.");
  }

  public NegativeLengthException(String message) {
    super(message);
  }
}
```

Unchecked Exceptions

The exceptions discussed so far have been *checked exceptions*; exceptions that you are required to handle. Java also includes two classes of *unchecked exceptions*: `Error` and `RuntimeException`. You are permitted to handle these exceptions, but are not required to since the number of places they could be generated are too large. For instance, members of the `Error` class include `OutOfMemoryError` (e.g., array allocation or call to new failed due to insufficient memory) and `ClassFormatError` (e.g., a .class file in illegal format, perhaps due to using text mode instead of binary mode when FTP'ing it). `RuntimeException` subclasses include `ArithmeticEx-`

ception (e.g., an integer division-by-zero) and `ArrayIndexOutOf-BoundsException` (e.g., you forget to bound a loop at the array's length). A catch-all `RuntimeException` often extended in user code is `IllegalArgumentException`. This lets you create hooks in your code for the handling of unusual cases without requiring users to catch the exceptions.

8.12 Summary

This chapter gave a quick overview of the fundamental syntax of Java programs: primitive and reference types, operators, the `Math` class, strings, vectors, and exceptions. Once you have a handle on this and the object-oriented programming covered in Chapter 7, you can focus on the more specific Java topics covered in the next seven chapters.

APPLETS, GRAPHICAL APPLICATIONS, AND BASIC DRAWING

Topics in This Chapter

- Creating *applets*: Java programs that are embedded in Web pages
- The applet life cycle
- Methods in the Applet class
- Customizing applets via parameters embedded in HTML
- Creating graphical *applications*: Java programs that run independently of a Web page or browser
- Basic drawing, color, font, and clipping area operations
- Extending the built-in drawing operations to support pen widths
- Loading and drawing images
- Preloading images
- Controlling image loading with MediaTracker

Chapter 9

This chapter discusses the two basic types of graphical Java programs: "applets" and "applications." For applets, it explains how to create them, how to associate them with Web pages, and how to pass customization parameters via the PARAM element. For applications, it discusses one common approach to creating windows, postponing alternatives until Chapter 11, "Windows." Finally, it covers the basic drawing operations that can be performed in applets and applications, looks at extensions to support line thicknesses, and discusses methods for loading and displaying images.

9.1 What Are Applets?

An "applet" is a particular type of Java program that is intended to be embedded in a Web page. When a user opens a Web page containing an applet, the applet runs *locally* (on the client machine that is running the Web browser), not *remotely* (on the system running the HTTP server). Consequently, security considerations are paramount, and applets are restricted from performing various operations that are allowed in general Java programs ("applications"). For instance, you might need to write a stand-alone program that deletes files, but you certainly don't want to let applets that come in over the Web delete your files. These restrictions are enforced by a Security-Manager class on the client system. In the 1.1 version of Java, classes can be digitally signed, and the user can tell this security manager to allow various restricted operations in classes signed by certain individuals or organizations. Even in 1.02, the precise restrictions placed upon applets depend on the `SecurityManager`. However, in version 3 and earlier of Netscape and Internet Explorer, the default manager verifies that applets:

Don't read from the local (client) disk.

That is, they cannot read arbitrary files. Applets can, however, instruct the browser to display pages that are generally accessible on the Web, which might include some local files.

Don't write to the local (client) disk.

The browser may choose to cache certain files, including some loaded by applets, but this is not under direct control of the applet.

Don't open network connections other than to the server from which the applet was loaded.

This is to prevent applets from browsing behind network firewalls.

Do not call local programs.

Ordinary Java applications can invoke locally installed programs (via the `exec` method of the `Runtime` class) as well as link to local C/C++ modules ("native" methods). This is prohibited in applets because there is no way to determine whether the operations these local programs perform are safe.

Cannot discover private information about the user.

Applets should not be able to discover the username of the person running them, nor specific system information such as current users, directory names or listings, system software, and so forth. However, applets *can* determine the name of the host they are on; this information is already reported to the HTTP server that delivered the applet.

9.2 Creating an Applet

Creating an applet involves two steps: making the Java class and making the associated HTML document. The Java class defines the actual behavior of the applet, while the HTML document associates the applet with a particular rectangular region of the Web page.

Java Template

Listing 9.1 shows the typical organization of a Java applet. It contains a section for declaring instance variables, an `init` method, and a `paint` method. The `init` method is automatically called by the browser when the APPLET is first created. Then, when it is ready to be drawn, `paint` is called. The `paint` method is automatically called again whenever the image has been obscured and is reexposed, when graphical components are added, or it can be invoked programmatically. The default implementations of `init` and `paint` don't do anything; they are just provided as placeholders for the programmer to override. Although there are additional placeholders for user code (see Section 9.4, "The Applet Life Cycle"), this basic structure (declarations, `init`, `paint`) is a good starting point for most applets. Although Java, unlike C++, allows direct initialization of instance variables when they are declared in the body of the class, this is not recommended for applets. Prior to `init`, the applet does not have everything set up that it needs to initialize certain types of graphical objects. So rather than trying to remember which variables can be directly initialized (strings) and which must be done in `init` (images), a good rule of thumb is to simply declare them in the main body of the applet and initialize them in `init`. Of course, variables that are only needed in `init` can be local to `init` rather than instance variables available to the whole class.

Listing 9.1   Java applet template

```java
import java.applet.Applet;
import java.awt.*;

public class AppletTemplate extends Applet {

  // Variable declarations

  public void init() {
    // Variable initializations, image loading, etc.
  }

  public void paint(Graphics g) {
    // Drawing operations
  }
}
```

HTML Template

Once an applet has been created and compiled, the resultant class file must be associated with a Web page. The APPLET element is used for this, as shown in Listing 9.2. This element is discussed further in Section 9.6, but for now note that CODE, WIDTH, and HEIGHT are required attributes, and that you need to use CODEBASE if the applet is being loaded from somewhere other than the place the associated HTML document resides. After the applet has been compiled and associated with a Web page, loading the Web page in a Java-enabled browser executes the applet. You sometimes name the HTML file with the same prefix as the Java file (e.g., AppletTemplate.html to correspond to AppletTemplate.class), but the name is arbitrary, and in fact a single HTML document can load multiple applets.

Although the compiled file (*file*.class) for your applet must be available on the Web, the source code (*file*.java) need not be. If you put the source and class files in different locations, remember that *all* non-system class files used by your applet need to be WWW accessible, and should be either in the same directory as the applet or in subdirectories corresponding to their package. So if your applet uses four custom classes, those class files need to be moved along with applet. On the other hand, for security reasons system classes are always loaded from the client machine, even if you try to make them available on the server along with your applet. Applets have the same rules as normal programs regarding multiple classes in a single source file; this is permitted as long as only one (the applet) is declared public, but it will still result in multiple class files. If you move class files from one system to another using FTP, be sure to use binary (raw) mode, not text mode.

Finally, some Java systems have the concept of a CLASSPATH that tells the system where to look for classes. If your system uses this, note that CLASSPATH settings apply only to local programs; a remote user accessing your applet won't know anything about your CLASSPATH. Also, since both Netscape and Internet Explorer grant extra privileges to class files that are listed in your CLASSPATH, you want to be sure your CLASSPATH is *not* set in the process that starts your browser. This prevents people who know your CLASSPATH from using your own classes to attack you.

Core Security

Make sure your CLASSPATH is not set when you start your browser.

Listing 9.2   HTML applet template

```
<!DOCTYPE HTML PUBLIC "-//W3C//DTD HTML 3.2//EN">
<HTML>
<HEAD>
  <TITLE>A Template for Loading Applets</TITLE>
</HEAD>

<BODY>
<H1>A Template for Loading Applets</H1>
<P>
<APPLET CODE="AppletTemplate.class" WIDTH=120 HEIGHT=60>
  <B>Error! You must use a Java enabled browser.</B>
</APPLET>

</BODY>
</HTML>
```

The <P> between the heading and the applet should not be necessary, but in Internet Explorer, a paragraph break is not automatically inserted after a heading that is followed by an applet. Because inserting the <P> makes little difference in browsers that do not suffer from this bug, it is a good standard practice.

Core Approach

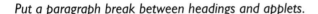

Put a paragraph break between headings and applets.

9.3 An Example Applet

Listing 9.3 presents an applet that follows the pattern shown in the previous section. The details of the various steps the applet performs will be covered in later sections, but the basic approach is what is important here. The variable declaration section declares a variable of type Image. The init method sets the default color and font, loads an image file from the network and assigns it to the Image declared earlier, adds a label to the applet, then performs an informational printout. The paint method draws the image, placing its top 25 pixels from the top of the applet. Listing 9.4 shows the associated HTML document; the result in Netscape 3.01 (Windows 95) is shown in Figure 9–1.

Listing 9.3   `JavaJump.java`

```java
import java.applet.Applet;
import java.awt.*;

/** An applet that draws an image. */

public class JavaJump extends Applet {
  private Image jumpingJava;

  public void init() {
    setBackground(Color.white);
    setFont(new Font("Helvetica", Font.BOLD, 18));
    jumpingJava = getImage(getDocumentBase(),
                           "images/Jumping-Java.gif");
    add(new Label("Great Jumping Java!"));
    System.out.println("Yow! I'm jiving with Java.");
  }

  public void paint(Graphics g) {
    g.drawImage(jumpingJava, 0, 25, this);
  }
}
```

Listing 9.4   `JavaJump.html`

```html
<!DOCTYPE HTML PUBLIC "-//W3C//DTD HTML 3.2//EN">
<HTML>
<HEAD>
  <TITLE>Jumping Java</TITLE>
</HEAD>

<BODY BGCOLOR="BLACK" TEXT="WHITE">
<H1>Jumping Java</H1>
<P>
<APPLET CODE="JavaJump.class" WIDTH=400 HEIGHT=500>
  <B>Sorry, this example requires Java.</B>
</APPLET>

</BODY>
</HTML>
```

Figure 9–1   Many applets follow a similar pattern: declarations, `init`, `paint`.

Automatic Redrawing

In most applets (and graphical applications, for that matter), the main drawing is done in `paint`. If something changes that requires the drawing to change, you can call the `repaint` method, which calls `update`, which normally clears the screen and then calls `paint`. We'll give more details on `repaint` and `update` later, but the point is that they are called whenever the *programmer* wants the screen to be redrawn. The *system* may also want to redraw the screen; this is typical when part of it has been covered up by some other window and then reexposed. In the vast majority of cases, you don't care why `paint` is called; you do the same thing either way. However, when the system calls `paint`, it sets the clipping region of the `Graphics` object to be the part that was obscured. This means that in the unlikely case that `paint` draws something different every time it is called, but `repaint` isn't invoked, the screen won't be redrawn correctly unless you adjust the clipping region (see Section 9.9, "Graphics Operations"). For instance, Listing 9.5 shows an applet that changes color every time `paint` is called. Although it tries to redraw the entire applet in the new color, as Figures 9–2 through 9–4 show, only the part that was obscured actually gets updated.

Listing 9.5 `Clip.java`

```java
import java.applet.Applet;
import java.awt.*;

/** A demonstration of the fact that the system
 *  calls <CODE>paint</CODE> with a clipping region
 *  set if a window is partially obscured and
 *  reexposed. Try covering up just part of the applet.
 *  When it is uncovered, only the previously
 *  covered part will change color. So in the unusual
 *  case that the result of paint is different every
 *  time (but repaint isn't being called), this will
 *  fail unless you change the clipping region.
 */

public class Clip extends Applet {
  private int paintCount = 0;
  private Color[] colors =
    { Color.lightGray, Color.gray, Color.darkGray };

  public void paint(Graphics g) {
    g.setColor(colors[paintCount]);
    g.fillRect(0, 0, size().width, size().height);
    paintCount = (paintCount + 1)%3;
  }
}
```

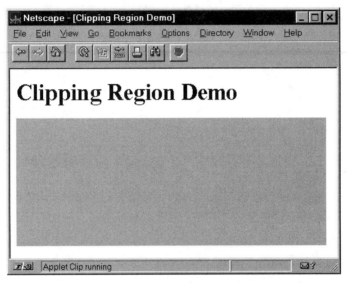

Figure 9-2   The `Clip` class displays a solid rectangle in a given color.

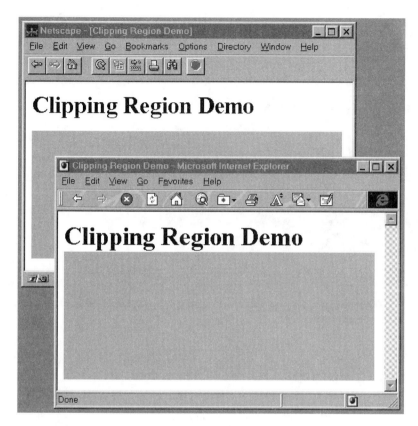

Figure 9-3 Part of the original applet is obscured.

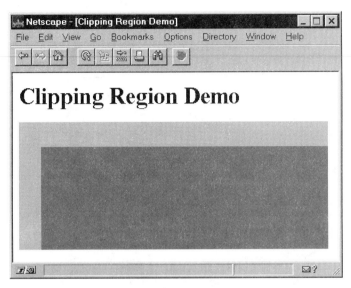

Figure 9–4   When the obscuring window is removed, only the part of the applet that was covered up gets redrawn.

Reloading Applets During Development

Netscape versions 2 and 3 and Internet Explorer version 3 have a significant bug in the way in which they cache applets. Due to this problem, reloading a Web page containing a modified applet often results in the *original* applet being executed. Holding down the shift key when clicking the Reload button sometimes, but not always, cures the problem (this works reliably in Netscape Communicator, however). Furthermore, because the browsers cache applets in a different place than regular documents, clearing the disk and/or memory cache does not necessarily fix the problem either. Nor does altering the modification date of the associated HTML file. The only reliable way to be sure the page reflects changes during development is to quit the browser and restart it. Even without this problem, the fact is that Netscape and Internet Explorer usually take a few seconds to start up, and consume moderate system resources. As a result, many Java systems include "appletviewer," a lightweight mini-browser that ignores all HTML in a page except for the APPLET part. Appletviewer is included with JDK 1.02 and 1.1 from Sun on all supported platforms, and by third-party IDE vendors as well. Using appletviewer is very useful for frequent testing during initial development, with the complete browsers being reserved for more occasional testing. An alternative is to use

Sun's HotJava browser, a full-blown browser that does not suffer from the applet reload problem. However, although HotJava supports HTML 3.2 plus extensions such as https (Secure Sockets Layer) and frames, it doesn't support JavaScript, cascading style sheets, ActiveX, or plug ins.

> **Core Warning**
>
> *In Netscape Navigator and Internet Explorer, reloading a page after recompiling an associated applet does **not** usually result in the new class file being used. A cached version of the previous applet is usually used instead.*

Getting Standard Output

For output in "production" applets, you normally create a text area or other GUI control to display results. This will be covered at length in Chapter 13, "Graphical User Interface Controls." You can also send a single line of debugging results to the status line by using the applet's `showStatus` method. However, during development it is often convenient to print multiple lines of debugging output using `System.out.println`. When you print this way from an applet, where do you see the result? The answer depends on the browser being used.

Standard Output in Netscape

In Netscape version 2, 3, or 4, the user can select "Show Java Console" from the "Options" menu (or the "Communicator" menu in Netscape 4.01) to get a pop-up window in which to see output. For example, Figure 9–5 shows the Java Console after running the `JavaJump` example.

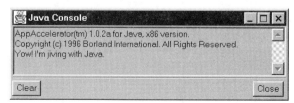

Figure 9–5 In Netscape, standard output is sent to a separate window: the Java Console.

Table 9.1 lists several little-known commands that customize the behavior of the Java console.

Table 9.1	Customization Commands in the Netscape Java Console

Keystroke	*Result*
1 2 ... 9	Set the debugging level. 1 gives the least information, 9 gives the most. Running an applet with a debug level of 9 describes many of the internal workings of the Netscape virtual machine.
d or D	Dumps the current applet state, giving the value of several internal variables. The exact details vary across Netscape releases.
g or G	Perform garbage collection.
f or F	Perform finalization.

Standard Output in Internet Explorer

In Internet Explorer, printing is a bit less convenient. From the "View" menu, select "Options," then choose the "Advanced" screen. There, select "Enable Java Logging," quit Internet Explorer, and restart. Now, any output from Java programs gets sent to a log file (`C:\Windows\Java\java-log.txt` on Windows 95).

Standard Output in Appletviewer

In appletviewer on Windows and Unix platforms, the output gets sent to the window that started appletviewer. On a Mac, a separate window pops up when output is sent to `System.out`.

9.4 The Applet Life Cycle

`Applet` is an unusual class since the browser automatically creates an instance of it and calls certain methods at certain times. The `main` method is never called by the browser. Instead, the following placeholder methods are called at various times. The methods are empty unless overridden by the author.

public void init()

This method is called after the applet instance is first created by the browser. It is not called again if the applet is stopped and restarted unless the applet has been "trimmed" (deleted from memory) by the browser.

public void start()

The start method is called after init is completed, but before the first invocation of paint. If the applet is stopped and restarted, start is called again each time. This makes start a good place to restart animation that gets paused when the user leaves the page or minimizes (iconifies) the browser. Netscape versions 2, 3, and 4 also call start and stop when the browser window is resized; Internet Explorer, appletviewer, and HotJava don't.

public void paint(Graphics g)

This is where user-level drawing is placed. It is invoked by the browser after init and start have completed, and again whenever the browser thinks the screen needs to be redrawn, typically when part of the screen has been obscured and then reexposed. From another method, you can call repaint with no arguments to tell the browser's graphics thread to call paint at its first opportunity.

public void stop()

The browser calls stop when the user leaves the page containing the applet or minimizes the browser. It can be used to halt animation that will be restarted in start. In Netscape, this method is also called when the browser window is resized.

public void destroy()

The destroy method is called when the applet is about to be permanently destroyed (e.g., when the browser is shut down or when it "trims" the applet from memory to keep the browser image size from growing too large). It can be used for bookkeeping or to free up shared resources, but is not used frequently.

9.5 Other Applet Methods

The built-in versions of the methods described in Section 9.4 don't actually *do* anything; they are simply placeholders for the user to override. Applet also contains a number of methods that perform common useful tasks, with

the most frequently used ones summarized below. `Applet` inherits from
`Panel`, `Container`, and `Component`; full details of these classes are given
in Chapter 11, "Windows."

public void add(Component c)
public void add(String location, Component c)
public void add(PopupMenu menu) [Java 1.1]

These methods insert graphical components into the applet window.
They are discussed in Chapter 11, "Windows" and Chapter 12, "Arranging Windows Using Layout Managers."

public Image createImage(int width, int height)
public Image createImage(ImageProducer producer)

The `createImage` method is used to make an off-screen pixmap.
Like `getImage`, `createImage` will fail if used prior to `init`. So it
should not be used to directly initialize instance variables. It is discussed
in the context of double-buffering in Chapter 14, "Concurrent Programming Using Java Threads."

public String getAppletInfo()

You can override this method to return a string describing the author,
version, and other information about the applet.

public AudioClip getAudioClip(URL audioFile)
public AudioClip getAudioClip(URL base,
String audioFilename)

These methods retrieve an audio file in .au format from a remote file
and assign it to an `AudioClip` object. The `AudioClip` `play`, `loop`,
and `stop` methods can then be used. Other types of audio files must be
converted to .au format before they can be used in an applet. One good
free utility for doing this is Lance Norskog's Sound Exchange, available
at `http://www.spies.com/Sox/`.

public Color getBackground()
public void setBackground(Color bgColor)

These methods get and set the background color of the applet. Colors
can be created by calling the `Color` constructor, as follows:

```
Color someColor = new Color(red, green, blue);
```

The red, green, and blue parameters should be ints from 0 to 255 or floats from 0.0 to 1.0. Colors can also be created using `Color.get-HSBColor(hue, saturation, brightness)`, where the arguments are floats between 0.0 and 1.0. Alternatively, there are thirteen predefined colors, listed in Table 9.2.

Table 9.2   Predefined Java Colors

Color	Red	Green	Blue
Color.black	0	0	0
Color.blue	0	0	255
Color.cyan	0	255	255
Color.darkGray	64	64	64
Color.gray	128	128	128
Color.green	0	255	0
Color.lightGray	192	192	192
Color.magenta	255	0	255
Color.orange	255	200	0
Color.pink	255	175	175
Color.red	255	0	0
Color.white	255	255	255
Color.yellow	255	255	0

In JDK 1.1, there is also a `SystemColor` class that provides access to the desktop colors. This lets you create applets that conform to the user's current color scheme. For instance, in `paint` you could do `g.setColor(SystemColor.windowText)` before doing `drawString`. Table 9.3 lists the options available.

Table 9.3 System Colors in JDK 1.1

Color (Static variables in SystemColor class)	Meaning
activeCaption	The background color for captions of active windows.
activeCaption-Border	The border color for captions of active windows.
control	The background color for control objects ("widgets").
controlDkShadow	The dark shadow color used to give a 3D effect.
controlHighlight	The emphasis color.
controlLtHighlight	A lighter emphasis color.
controlShadow	The light shadow color used to give a 3D effect.
controlText	The text color.
desktop	The desktop background color.
inactiveCaption	The background color for captions of inactive windows.
inactiveCaption-Border	The border color for captions of inactive windows.
inactiveCaption-Text	The text color for captions of inactive windows.
info	The background color for help text ("tool tips").
infoText	The text color for help text ("tool tips").
menu	The background color of deselected menu items. Selected menu items should use textHighlight.
menuText	The text color of deselected menu items. Selected menu items should use textHighlightText.
scrollbar	The background color for scrollbars.

Table 9.3	System Colors in JDK 1.1 (continued)
textHighlight	The background color for highlighted text such as selected text in a textfield, selected menu items, etc.
textHighlightText	The text color for highlighted text.
textInactiveText	The text color of inactive components.
textText	The text color for text components.
window	The background color for windows.
windowBorder	The border color for windows.
windowText	The text color for windows.

public URL getCodeBase()
public URL getDocumentBase()
These methods return the directories containing the applet (get-
CodeBase) and the HTML document using the applet (getDocu-
mentBase).

public Cursor getCursor() [Java 1.1]
public void setCursor(Cursor cursor) [Java 1.1]
These methods get and set the cursor. They are available only in JDK
1.1; in 1.02, cursors have to be set in the enclosing Frame (see get-
Parent).

public Font getFont()
public void setFont(Font defaultFont)
These methods get and set the default font for the applet. Unless overridden explicitly, the default font is used for labels, buttons, textfields,
and other such components, and when strings are drawn use the draw-
String method of Graphics. Fonts are created via the Font constructor, which takes a family, style, and size as follows:

```
String family = "TimesRoman";
int style = Font.BOLD;
int size = 18;
Font font = new Font(family, style, size);
setFont(font);
```

In JDK 1.02, the family can be TimesRoman, Helvetica, Courier, Dialog, DialogInput, and ZapfDingbats. In JDK 1.1, ZapfDingbats is dropped and the generic names Serif, Sans-Serif, Monospaced, Dialog, and DialogInput are used. The style should be one of Font.PLAIN, Font.BOLD, Font.ITALIC, or Font.BOLD|Font.ITALIC. The size must be an integer. Use Toolkit.getDefaultToolkit().getFontList to obtain an array of available font families. On most Java systems, nonstandard fonts cannot be used even if they are locally installed, with one exception. In Java 1.1, you can generally change the mapping between the font names and the actual font used by editing the font.properties file in the lib subdirectory of the installation directory. However, that only affects the fonts *you* see, not the fonts that *users* of your programs see. There is *no* portable method for specifying fonts beyond the standard set. Fortunately, the upcoming Graphics2D class (expected to be part of Java 1.2) has extensive font support. See http://java.sun.com/products/java-media/2D/ for more details.

public FontMetrics getFontMetrics(Font f)

This returns an object that can be used to determine the size of strings (stringWidth) or individual characters (charWidth) in a given font.

public Color getForeground()
public Color setForeground(Color fgColor)

These methods get and set the default foreground color for the applet. See getBackground for a discussion of colors.

public Graphics getGraphics()

The getGraphics method returns the current graphics context object for the applet. You need to use this method if you want to perform drawing operations from a method that is not directly called from paint. The paint method gets the graphics context supplied automatically.

public Image getImage(URL imageFile)
public Image getImage(URL base, String imageFilename)

These methods "register" a remote image file with an Image object. Java does not actually load the image file until you try to draw it or ask the system to start loading it via prepareImage or with a Media-Tracker. For more details, see Section 9.11 (Drawing Images).

public Locale getLocale() [Java 1.1]
public void setLocale(Locale locale) [Java 1.1]
These methods are available only in JDK 1.1; they get and retrieve the current locale for use in internationalized code.

public String getParameter(String parameterName)
This method retrieves the value of parameters set in the PARAM tag inside the APPLET element in the HTML document. For details, see Section 9.7   (Reading Applet Parameters).

public String[ ][ ] getParameterInfo()
This method can be used to supply documentation on the parameters an applet recognizes. Each element in the top-level array should be an array containing the parameter name, its type, and a short description.

public Container getParent()
In general, getParent returns the enclosing window. In the particular case of applets, it returns the enclosing Frame. Access to the Frame is needed to set the cursor in JDK 1.02. See the discussion of frames in Chapter 11, "Windows."

public boolean inside(int x, int y)
public boolean contains(int x, int y) [Java 1.1]
public boolean contains(Point p) [Java 1.1]
The inside (JDK 1.02, supported but "deprecated" in 1.1) or contains (JDK 1.1) method determines if the specified location is contained inside the applet. That is, it returns true if and only if the x coordinate is less than or equal to the applet's width and the y coordinate is less than or equal to the applet's height.

public boolean isActive()
This determines if the applet is "active." Applets are inactive before start is called and after stop is called; otherwise they are active.

public Component locate(int x, int y)
public Component getComponentAt(int x, int y) [Java 1.1]
The locate (JDK 1.02) or getComponentAt (JDK 1.1) method returns the top-most component at the specified location. This will be the applet itself if no other component is at this location; null will be returned if x and y are off the applet.

public void play(URL audioFile)
public void play(URL base, String audioFilename)
These methods retrieve and play an audio file in .au format. Also see
`getAudioClip`.

public void repaint()
public void repaint(long millisecondDelay)
public void repaint(int x, int y, int width, int height)
public void repaint(long msDelay, int x, int y, int width,
                     int height)
This method asks the AWT update thread to call `update`, either immediately or after the specified number of milliseconds. In either case,
control is returned immediately; the actual updating and painting is
done in a separate thread. You can also ask the system to only repaint a
portion of the screen. This results in `update` and `paint` getting a
`Graphics` context with the specified clipping region set.

public void showDocument(URL htmlDoc)
   [in class AppletContext]
public void showDocument(URL htmlDoc, String frameName)
   [in class AppletContext]
These methods ask the browser to retrieve and display a Web page.
They are actually part of the `AppletContext` class, not `Applet`, but
they are used from applets in a similar way to the other methods
described here. To use them, you have to call `getAppletCon-`
`text().showDocument(...)`, not just `showDocument(...)`.
The `showDocument` method is ignored by appletviewer.

public void showStatus(String message)
The `showStatus` method displays a string in the status line at the bottom of the browser.

public Dimension size()
public Dimension getSize() [Java 1.1]
The `size` (JDK 1.02) or `getSize` (JDK 1.1) method can be used to
retrieve a `Dimension` object describing the size of the applet.
`Dimension` has `width` and `height` fields. Thus, to get the width of
the applet, use `size().width` (JDK 1.02) or `getSize().width`
(JDK 1.1). Technically, applets also have a `resize` (JDK 1.02) or `set-`
`Size` (JDK 1.1) method. However, in practice this is ignored by most

browsers other than appletviewer, and the size specified in the `WIDTH` and `HEIGHT` attributes of the `APPLET` element are used as the *permanent* dimensions.

public void update(Graphics g)

This method is called by the AWT thread after `repaint` is called. The default implementation of `update` clears the screen then calls `paint`. Animation and double buffering applications typically override `update` to simply call `paint`, omitting the screen-clearing step. This will be discussed further in Chapter 14, "Concurrent Programming Using Java Threads."

handleEvent, action, mouseDown, mouseUp, mouseMove, mouseDrag, keyDown, keyUp, addComponentListener, addFocusListener, addKeyListener, addMouseListener, addMouseMotionListener

These methods are used to catch various events. They are discussed in Chapter 10, "Handling Mouse and Keyboard Events."

9.6 The HTML APPLET Tag

HTML Element: `<APPLET CODE="..." WIDTH=xxx`
`                    HEIGHT=xxx ...>`
`         ... </APPLET>`

Attributes: `CODE` (required), `WIDTH` (required), `HEIGHT` (required), `CODEBASE`, `ALT`, `ALIGN`, `HSPACE`, `VSPACE`, `NAME`, `OBJECT` (nonstandard), `ARCHIVE` (nonstandard), `MAYSCRIPT` (nonstandard)

The `APPLET` element is used to associate a class file with a Web page. The referenced class file must extend the `Applet` class. `CODE`, `WIDTH`, and `HEIGHT` are required in JDK 1.02; in 1.1 `OBJECT` can be substituted for `CODE`.

CODE

`CODE` designates the filename of the Java class file to load. This is not an absolute URL; it is interpreted with respect to the current document's base directory unless `CODEBASE` is supplied. It is required in JDK 1.02 and in JDK 1.1.1 unless `OBJECT` is present. Although the class file must be Web accessible, the Java source file need not be.

Core Note

CODE cannot be used to give an absolute URL. Use CODEBASE if you want to load applets from someplace other than the current document's location.

WIDTH, HEIGHT

WIDTH and HEIGHT specify the area the applet will occupy. They can be specified in pixels or as a percentage of the browser window width. However, appletviewer cannot handle percentages because there is no preexisting window for the percentage to refer to. These attributes are required in all applets.

Core Alert

Sun's appletviewer cannot handle WIDTH and HEIGHT attributes as percentages.

CODEBASE

This designates the base URL. The entry in CODE is taken with respect to this directory. The default behavior is to use the directory that the main HTML document came from.

ALT

Java-enabled browsers ignore markup between <APPLET ...> and </APPLET>, so alternative text for these browsers is normally placed there. The ALT attribute was intended for browsers that support Java but have it disabled, but is not widely supported. I recommend avoiding it.

ALIGN

This specifies alignment options, and has the same possible values (LEFT, RIGHT, TOP, BOTTOM, MIDDLE) and interpretation of values as the IMG element (see Section 3.4, "Embedded Images").

HSPACE

HSPACE specifies the empty space at the left and right of the applet (in pixels).

VSPACE

VSPACE specifies the empty space at the top and bottom of the applet (in pixels).

NAME

NAME gives a name to the applet. It is used in Java for inter-applet communication and by JavaScript to reference an applet by name instead of
using an index in the applet array. However, a bug in Netscape prevents
it from recognizing applets that contain uppercase characters in their
names. So if you want two applets to talk to each other, use lowercase
names.

Core Approach

If you supply a NAME for the applet, use all lowercase letters.

OBJECT

The OBJECT attribute can be used to supply a serialized applet that was
saved using JDK 1.1's object serialization facility.

ARCHIVE

ARCHIVE is used in JDK 1.1.1 and by some 1.02 browsers to specify an
archive of class files to be preloaded. The archive eventually will be in
Java Archive (.jar) format, but Netscape 3.01 allows *uncompressed* Zip
(.zip) archives.

MAYSCRIPT

Netscape 3 and 4 use this attribute to determine if JavaScript is permitted to control the applet.

9.7 Reading Applet Parameters

HTML Element: `<PARAM NAME="..." VALUE="...">`
                  (No End Tag)

Attributes: NAME (required), VALUE (required)

An applet does not receive the `String[]` argument list that applications get
in the `main` method. However, an applet can be customized by supplying
information inside `PARAM` tags located between `<APPLET ...>` and
`</APPLET>`. These parameters are declared as follows:

```
<PARAM NAME="Parameter Name"
       VALUE="Parameter Value">
```

They are read from within an applet via `getParameter("Parameter Name")`, which returns `"Parameter Value"` as a `String`, or `null` if the parameter is not found. Note that `getParameter` is case sensitive, but as with HTML in general, the `PARAM`, `NAME`, and `VALUE` element and attribute names themselves are case insensitive. Note also that strings should not be compared with `==`, because `==` simply checks if the two strings are the same object. Use the `equals` (case sensitive) or `equalsIgnoreCase` (case insensitive) method of `String` for this.

Although the return value of `getParameter` is always a `String`, you can convert that into an `int` by using the static `parseInt` method of the `Integer` class. Section 9.8 (Graphical Applications) gives an example of `Integer.parseInt` as well as listing methods to convert strings to bytes, shorts, longs, floats, and doubles.

Finally, be aware that `PARAM` names of `WIDTH` or `HEIGHT` override the `WIDTH` and `HEIGHT` values supplied in the `APPLET` tag itself, so should be avoided.

Core Alert

Never use `WIDTH` *or* `HEIGHT` *as* `PARAM` *names.*

Reading Applet Parameters: An Example

Listing 9.6 gives a variation of the `HelloWWW` applet (Section 6.5) that allows the applet to be customized in the HTML document via a `PARAM` entry of the form

```
<PARAM NAME="BACKGROUND" VALUE="LIGHT">
```

or

```
<PARAM NAME="BACKGROUND" VALUE="DARK">
```

Note the check to see if the `backgroundType` is `null`, which would happen if the `PARAM` entry was missing or had a `NAME` other than `"BACKGROUND"` in all uppercase. If this test was not performed, and the value was `null`, the `backgroundType.equals(...)` call would crash since `null` does not have an `equals` method (or any other method, for that matter). This could be avoided by doing

```
if ("LIGHT".equals(backgroundType))
```

instead of

```
if (backgroundType.equals("LIGHT"))
```

but many authors prefer to have an explicit test for `null`.

Core Approach

If you read applet parameters, be sure you handle the case when the parameter is not found.

Listing 9.7 shows an HTML document that loads the same applet three different times with different configuration parameters. Figure 9–6 shows the result in Internet Explorer 3.01 on Windows 95.

Listing 9.6   `HelloWWW2.java`

```java
import java.applet.Applet;
import java.awt.*;

public class HelloWWW2 extends Applet {
  public void init() {
    setFont(new Font("Helvetica", Font.BOLD, 30));
    String backgroundType = getParameter("BACKGROUND");
    if (backgroundType != null &&
        backgroundType.equals("LIGHT")) {
      setBackground(Color.white);
      setForeground(Color.black);
    } else if (backgroundType != null &&
               backgroundType.equals("DARK")) {
      setBackground(Color.black);
      setForeground(Color.white);
    } else {
      setBackground(Color.gray);
      setForeground(Color.darkGray);
    }
  }

  public void paint(Graphics g) {
    g.drawString("Hello, World Wide Web.", 5, 35);
  }
}
```

Listing 9.7 `HelloWWW2.html`

```
<!DOCTYPE HTML PUBLIC "-//W3C//DTD HTML 3.2//EN">
<HTML>
<HEAD>
  <TITLE>Customizable HelloWWW Applet</TITLE>
</HEAD>

<BODY>
<H1>Customizable HelloWWW Applet</H1>
<P>
<APPLET CODE="HelloWWW2.class" WIDTH=400 HEIGHT=40>
  <PARAM NAME="BACKGROUND" VALUE="LIGHT">
  <B>Error! You must use a Java-enabled browser.</B>
</APPLET>
<P>
<APPLET CODE="HelloWWW2.class" WIDTH=400 HEIGHT=40>
  <PARAM NAME="BACKGROUND" VALUE="DARK">
  <B>Error! You must use a Java-enabled browser.</B>
</APPLET>
<P>
<APPLET CODE="HelloWWW2.class" WIDTH=400 HEIGHT=40>
  <B>Error! You must use a Java-enabled browser.</B>
</APPLET>

</BODY>
</HTML>
```

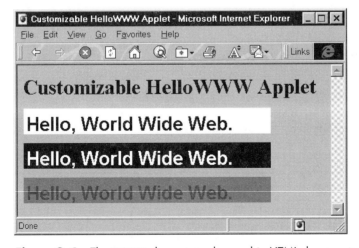

Figure 9-6 The PARAM element can be used in HTML documents to pass customizations parameters to applets.

9.8 Graphical Applications

The previous examples used applets: Java programs that run within a Web browser. Local Java programs can use windows as well. Stand-alone graphical Java programs start with a Java `Frame`. For example, Listing 9.8 shows a simple `Frame` that tiles an image across the background, taking the image size from command line arguments if available. In this use of frames, I give it a title by calling the `Frame` constructor (`super`), give it a width and height using `resize` (`setSize` in JDK 1.1), then pop it up using `show` (`setVisible` in JDK 1.1). Customizing frames is particularly easy; you simply supply command line arguments to the program. For instance, Figures 9–7 and 9–8 show the results of Listing 9.8 with no command line arguments and when invoked with `java JavaJump2 50 60`.

Note the use of `Integer.parseInt` to convert a command line argument (a string) to an integer in Listing 9.8. This is a useful trick when reading customization parameters in applets via `getParameter` as well. The `parseInt` method can optionally take a second argument that signifies the radix. Also, `parseInt` throws a `NumberFormatException` if it gets something that does not represent an integer; you are not required to catch it since it is a `RuntimeException`, but it is a good idea for "production" code. There are other built-in number parsing routines: `Long.parseLong`, `Short.parseShort` (Java 1.1), `Byte.parseByte` (Java 1.1), `Double.valueOf`, and `Float.valueOf`. These all throw `NumberFormatException` as well.

Core Approach

To convert a string to a number, use one of the `parseXxx` *or* `valueOf`
methods in `Integer, Short, Long, Byte, Float,` *or* `Double`.

One of the surprising things about frames is that the user cannot quit them unless you explicitly put in code to let them. That's the purpose of the `handleEvent` method in the example. Don't worry if you don't follow all the details; copy `handleEvent` verbatim for now, but we'll explain it more fully in the following chapters. There are a variety of other ways frames that can be created and used. One common approach is to place the code that lets the user quit the window (i.e., the `handleEvent` method) in a custom class, then extend that class instead of `Frame`. For instance, we'll make a `QuittableFrame` in Chapter 11, "Windows," then use it instead of a standard `Frame` throughout much of the rest of the book. Another approach is to create programs that can be run as either applets *or* applications. This technique is discussed in Chapter 11 as well.

Listing 9.8   `JavaJump2.java`

```java
import java.awt.*;

/** An application that tiles an image using either
 *  a default width/height or values supplied via
 *  command line arguments.
 */

public class JavaJump2 extends Frame {
  public static void main(String[] args) {
    // Parse input parameters
    int imageWidth = 100;
    if (args.length > 0)
      imageWidth = Integer.parseInt(args[0]);
    int imageHeight = 120;
    if (args.length > 1)
      imageHeight = Integer.parseInt(args[1]);
    // Build the class
    new JavaJump2(imageWidth, imageHeight);
  }

  private Image jumpingJava;
  private int imageWidth, imageHeight;
  private int top = 0;

  public JavaJump2(int imageWidth, int imageHeight) {
    super("Great Jumping Java!"); // Frame constructor
    String imageFile = System.getProperty("user.dir") +
                       "/images/Jumping-Java.gif";
    jumpingJava = getToolkit().getImage(imageFile);
    this.imageWidth = imageWidth;
    this.imageHeight = imageHeight;
    setBackground(Color.white);
    resize(700, 500);
    show();
  }
```

Listing 9.8   `JavaJump2.java`

```
public void paint(Graphics g) {
  int width = size().width;
  int height = size().height;
  for(int y=0; y<height; y=y+imageHeight)
    for(int x=0; x<width; x=x+imageWidth)
      g.drawImage(jumpingJava,
                  x, y, imageWidth, imageHeight, this);
}

/** Honor requests to quit the window. */

public boolean handleEvent(Event event) {
  if (event.id == Event.WINDOW_DESTROY)
    System.exit(0);
  return(super.handleEvent(event));
}
}
```

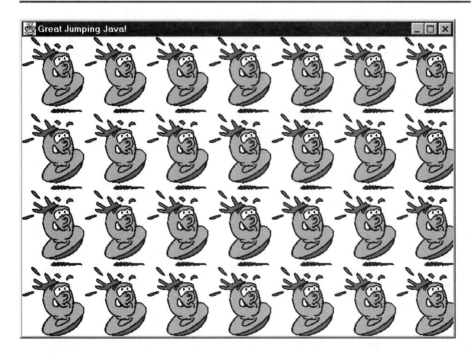

Figure 9-7   A `Frame` is the starting point for graphical programs that run independently of Web pages. This one was invoked with no command line arguments.

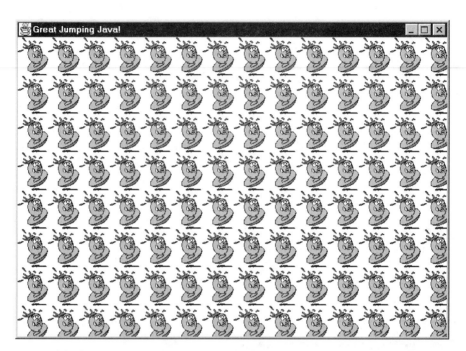

Figure 9-8   Frames can be customized by providing command line arguments. This one was invoked with command line arguments of 50 and 60, used as the width and height of the tiled image.

9.9 Graphics Operations

In both applets and applications, the paint method is used to implement custom drawing. It takes a Graphics object as an argument; this object is used to draw onto the window. Methods outside paint can obtain the current Graphics object by calling getGraphics(). Note that it is not reliable to simply call getGraphics once and store the Graphics object in an instance variable because subsequent invocations of paint get new versions. However, it *is* reliable to pass the Graphics object to other methods that draw and then return before paint returns.

The drawing methods discussed as follows can be used in windows such as Panel, Canvas, Frame, and so forth, in addition to Applet. These other components will be discussed in Chapter 11, "Windows." Java does not supply any method to find the absolute location of an applet in the browser window, although you can discover the location of a frame. In any case, all coordinates in the following methods are relative, not absolute, interpreted with respect to (0,0) being the top left corner of the window, with x increasing to the right and y increasing downward. As with many graphical systems, coordinates in Java are considered to be between the screen pixels. Operations that draw the outline of figures draw the pixels down and to the right of the coordinates, while operations that fill a figure fill the interior of the coordinates. This means that drawing the outline of a rectangle will take one extra pixel on the bottom and right sides compared to filling the same rectangle.

The current AWT does not support pen widths (line thicknesses) or fill patterns. However, Java 1.2 should include the Java Foundation Classes (`http://java.sun.com/products/jfc/`) which includes a much improved version of `Graphics` called `Graphics2D`. This will include pen widths, stroke styles (dashed, dotted, etc.), fill patterns, antialiasing, greatly improved font support, and much more. For more information, see `http://java.sun.com/products/java-media/2D/`. In the meantime, Section 9.10 presents a class that adds pen widths to the basic drawing functions of the `Graphics` class.

The following summarizes the methods supported by `Graphics`. All of the methods are declared `public void` unless stated otherwise.

Drawing Operations

clearRect(int left, int top, int width, int height)
The `clearRect` method draws a solid rectangle in the current background color.

copyArea(int left, int top, int width, int height, int deltaX, int deltaY)
This method copies all pixels from the rectangle defined by (left, top, width, height) to (left+deltaX, top+deltaY, width, height).

public Graphics create()
public Graphics create(int left, int top, int width, int height)
This creates a new graphics context. If a rectangle is specified, the context is translated to the designated location and its clipping region set to the specified width and height.

draw3DRect(int left, int top, int width, int height, boolean raised)
This draws a 1 pixel-wide outline around the specified rectangle. If `raised` is `true`, the left and top edges will be lighter, giving the appearance of the rectangle being above the surface of the window. If

`raised` is `false`, the rectangle is drawn with the top and left edges darker, giving the appearance of an indented rectangle. In most cases, it is a good idea to set the foreground color to be the same as the background color before calling this method so that the shading is calculated based on the background.

fill3DRect(int left, int top, int width, int height, boolean raised)

This makes a solid rectangle with a 3D outline.

drawArc(int left, int top, int width, int height, int startAngle, int deltaAngle)

This draws a curve taken from a portion of the outside of an oval. The first four parameters specify the bounding rectangle for an oval. The angles specify what part of the oval will be drawn; 0 means east (3 o'clock) and angles go counterclockwise. Unlike the trig functions in the `Math` class, angles are in degrees, not radians.

fillArc(int left, int top, int width, int height, int startAngle, int deltaAngle)

This draws a solid "pie wedge" from an oval pie. See `drawArc`.

drawImage(Image image, int left, int top, ImageObserver observer)

This draws an image in its original size. Create the image via the `getImage` method of `Applet` or `Toolkit`, but note that `getImage` operates asynchronously, so calls to `drawImage` immediately after `getImage` may draw blank images. Pass the applet or window (via `this`) as the argument for observer. See Section 9.11 for details on using images.

drawImage(Image image, int left, int top, int width, int height, ImageObserver observer)

This draws an image scaled to fit in the rectangle defined by (left, top, width, height).

drawImage(Image image, int left, int top, Color bgColor, ImageObserver observer)
drawImage(Image image, int left, int top, int width, int height, Color bgColor, ImageObserver observer)

These are variations of the two previous methods for transparent images. The specified background color is used for transparent pixels.

drawLine(int x1, int y1, int x2, int y2)
This draws a 1-pixel thick line.

drawOval(int left, int top, int width, int height)
This draws the outline of an oval. Arguments describe the rectangle that the oval is inside. For example, `drawOval(75, 75, 50, 50)` specifies a circle of radius 50 centered at (100, 100).

fillOval(int left, int top, int width, int height)
This draws a solid oval bounded by the specified rectangle.

drawPolygon(int[ ] xArray, int[ ] yArray, int numPoints)
drawPolygon(Polygon polygon)
These methods draw the outline of a polygon defined by the arrays or `Polygon` (a nongraphic data structure). The polygon is not closed by default. To make a closed polygon, specify the same location for the first and last points.

fillPolygon(int[ ] xArray, int[ ] yArray, int numPoints)
fillPolygon(Polygon polygon)
This draws a solid polygon. The polygon is closed by default; a connection is automatically made between the first and last points.

drawRect(int left, int top, int width, int height)
This draws a hollow rectangle (1-pixel border) in the current color. See also `draw3DRect` and `drawRoundRect` for variations on the theme.

fillRect(int left, int top, int width, int height)
This draws a solid rectangle in the current color. The current AWT has no provision for setting fill patterns or images, so that would have to be reproduced manually. See also `fill3DRect` and `fillRoundRect`.

drawRoundRect(int left, int top, int width, int height, int arcWidth, int arcHeight)
This draws the outline of a rectangle with rounded corners. The `arcWidth` and `arcHeight` parameters specify the amount of curve (in degrees) on the top/bottom and left/right sides. If either is zero, square corners are used.

drawString(String string, int left, int bottom)

This draws a string in the current font and color with the *bottom* left corner at the specified location. This is one of the few methods where the y coordinate refers to the bottom, not the top. There are also drawChars and drawBytes methods that take arrays of char or byte.

Colors and Fonts

public Color getColor()

This returns the current Color. For more information on using custom and built-in colors, see the discussion of getBackground and set-Background in Section 9.5 (Other Applet Methods).

setColor(Color color)

This sets the foreground color. When the Graphics object is created, the default drawing color is the foreground color of the window. Color changes made by calling setColor on the Graphics object do not change the default, so the next time paint or getGraphics is called, the new Graphics is reinitialized with the window defaults. Permanent changes can be recorded by calling the applet's or frame's setForeground method, but this only affects drawing done with Graphics objects created *after* the call to setForeground.

public Font getFont()

This returns the current Font. See the discussion of getFont and setFont in Section 9.5 (Other Applet Methods) for more information on fonts. Both Component (and thus Applet, which inherits from it) and Graphics have a getFontMetrics method that takes a Font as an argument. This FontMetrics object can then be used to find out the size of characters (charWidth) and strings (stringWidth) in that font.

setFont(Font font)

This sets the font to be used by the drawString method. The font changes specified by the setFont method of the Graphics object do not persist to the next invocation of paint or to the next time get-Graphics is called. Permanent font changes can be specified via the setFont method of the applet or other associated component.

Drawing Modes

setXORMode(Color color)

This specifies that subsequent drawing operations will use XOR: the color of each pixel in the result will be determined by bitwise XORing the specified color with the color of the pixel at the location being drawn. Thus, a line drawn in XOR mode over a multicolor background will be in multiple colors. The resultant color at each pixel is unpredictable, since the XOR is done on the bits as they appear in the internal representation, which may vary from machine to machine. But drawing something using XOR twice in a row will return it to the original condition. This is useful for rubberbanding or other short-term erasable drawing done over top of some more complex drawing. Note that many platforms do not support drawing erasable images in XOR mode. You should avoid using `Color.black` as the specified color, since this will be represented internally by all zeros on many (but not all) platforms, so the XOR results in the original color, and your drawing will be invisible. Set the drawing mode back to normal with `setPaintMode()`.

setPaintMode()

This sets the drawing mode back to normal (vs. XOR mode). That is, drawing will be done using the normal foreground color only.

Coordinates and Clipping Rectangles

clipRect(int left, int top, int width, int height)

This shrinks the clipping region to the intersection of the current clipping region and the specified rectangle.

public Rectangle getClipRect()
public Rectangle getClipBounds() [Java 1.1]

This returns the current clipping rectangle, which may be `null`. The `getClipRect` method of JDK 1.02 is deprecated in JDK 1.1. Use `getClipBounds` instead.

public Shape getClip() [Java 1.1]

This returns a Shape object describing the clipping region.

setClip(Shape clippingRegion) [Java 1.1]

This designates a new clipping region.

translate(int deltaX, int deltaY)

This method moves the origin by the specified amount.

9.10 Setting Line Thicknesses: The GraphicsUtil Class

The standard `Graphics` class does not support pen widths for drawing operations. This is such a commonly requested feature that this section presents a class to add this capability. Thick rectangles can be created simply by drawing nested 1-pixel-thick rectangles. Thick lines can be drawn by using the built-in trig functions to find the corners of the rectangle that will represent the line, then using `fillPolygon`. Ovals and arcs are more problematic. Simple nested ovals can leave missing pixels since the underlying pixel representation has limited resolution. So you need to draw multiple arcs or ovals offset by 1 pixel in each direction. This makes for worse drawing performance, and, more importantly, means that XOR drawing of thick ovals or arcs will not be reliable due to the overlapping pixels. Unfortunately, that is the best available option given the current AWT. `GraphicsUtil` also adds `drawCircle` and `fillCircle` methods, and lets you pass colors and fonts to the drawing operations rather than setting the `Graphics` object in a separate step. To illustrate this class, Listing 9.9 shows a test case that draws thick arcs, rectangles, ovals, rounded rectangles, 3D rectangles, and lines. Figure 9–9 shows the result.

Listing 9.9   `GraphicsUtilTest.java`

```java
import java.awt.*;

/** An example to illustrate the GraphicsUtil package.
 *  The thick lines, rectangles, etc. have a normal
 *  sized one drawn in the center for comparison.
 */

public class GraphicsUtilTest extends Frame{

  public static void main(String[] args) {
    new GraphicsUtilTest();
  }


  public GraphicsUtilTest() {
    super("GraphicsUtilTest");
    setBackground(Color.white);
    resize(900, 700);
    show();
  }
```

Listing 9.9   `GraphicsUtilTest.java`   **(continued)**

```java
public void paint(Graphics g) {
 int x=50, top=30;
 for(int i=0; i<10; i++) {
   x = 50;
   // Thick arc
   GraphicsUtil.drawArc(g, x, 60*i+top, 75, 75,
                        30*i, 90, 2*i+1,
                        Color.lightGray);
   // Regular arc
   g.drawArc(x, 60*i+top, 75, 75, 30*i, 90);
   x = x + 100;
   // Thick rectangle
   GraphicsUtil.drawRect(g, x, 60*i+top, 75, 35,
                         2*i+1, Color.gray);
   // Regular rectangle
   g.drawRect(x, 60*i+top, 75, 35);
   x = x + 100;
   // Thick oval
   GraphicsUtil.drawOval(g, x, 60*i+top, 75, 35,
                         2*i+1, Color.darkGray);
   // Regular oval
   g.drawOval(x, 60*i+top, 75, 35);
   x = x + 100;
   // Thick rounded rectangle
   GraphicsUtil.drawRoundRect(g, x, 60*i+top, 75, 35,
                              20, 10,
                              2*i+1, Color.lightGray);
   // Regular rounded rectangle
   g.drawRoundRect(x, 60*i+top, 75, 35, 20, 10);
   x = x + 100;
   // Thick 3D rectangle
   GraphicsUtil.draw3DRect(g, x, 60*i+top, 75, 35,
                           true, 2*i+1, Color.gray);
 }
 for(x=-150; x<=150; x=x+75)
   for(int y=-250; y<=250; y=y+100)
     // Thick line
     GraphicsUtil.drawLine(g, 700, 350, 700+x, 350+y,
                           20, Color.gray);
 for(x=-150; x<=150; x=x+75)
   for(int y=-250; y<=250; y=y+100)
     // Regular line
     g.drawLine(700, 350, 700+x, 350+y);
}
```

continued

Listing 9.9 `GraphicsUtilTest.java` (continued)

```
/** Honor requests to quit the window */

public boolean handleEvent(Event event) {
  if (event.id == Event.WINDOW_DESTROY)
    System.exit(0);
  return(super.handleEvent(event));
  }
}
```

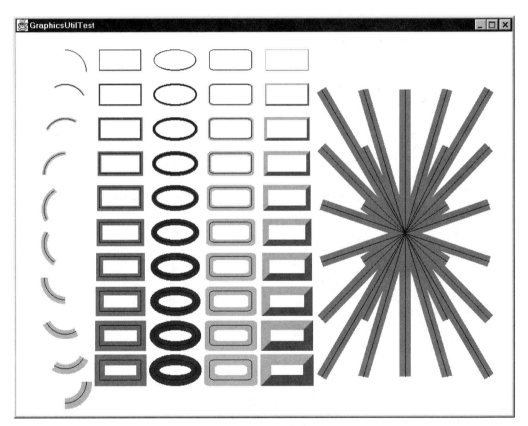

Figure 9–9 The `GraphicsUtil` class simplifies drawing thick lines.

The source code to GraphicsUtil is presented in Listing 9.10. Note the use of javadoc comments throughout. Although javadoc may seem like overkill for small test programs, it is very valuable for larger programs, and well worth the time invested. This is especially true for libraries that will be used by multiple people. Figures 9–10 and 9–11 show the kind of information javadoc generates. Note that this is *exactly* the same format used by Sun for their on-line API to Java 1.1 (http://java.sun.com/products/jdk/1.1/docs/api/packages.html, in case you foolishly don't already have it bookmarked or have a local copy installed). In fact, the API was generated by javadoc from the source code. The 1.02 API (http://java.sun.com/products/jdk/1.0.2/api/packages.html) is a variation of the javadoc-generated version, made when the API was published in hardcopy form.

Core Approach

*If you make a class that will be used at **all** widely, document it using javadoc.*

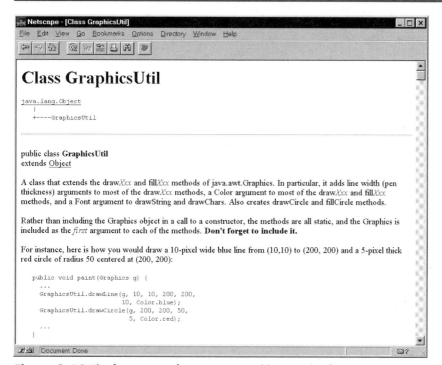

Figure 9–10 The first screen of page generated by javadoc from GraphicsUtil.java.

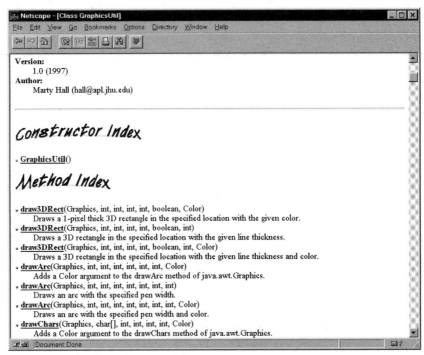

Figure 9–11 The second screen of page generated by javadoc from
`GraphicsUtil.java`.

Listing 9.10 `GraphicsUtil.java`

```java
import java.awt.*;

/**
 * A class that extends the draw<I>Xxx</I> and
 * fill<I>Xxx</I> methods of java.awt.Graphics. In
 * particular, it adds line width (pen thickness)
 * arguments to most of the draw<I>Xxx</I> methods,
 * a Color argument to most of the draw<I>Xxx</I> and
 * fill<I>Xxx</I> methods, and a Font argument to
 * drawString and drawChars. Also creates drawCircle
 * and fillCircle methods.
 * <P>
 * Rather than including the Graphics object in a call
 * to a constructor, the methods are all static, and
```

Listing 9.10 GraphicsUtil.java (continued)

```
 * the Graphics is included as the <I>first</I>
 * argument to each of the methods.
 * <B>Don't forget to include it.</B>
 * <P>
 * For instance, here is how you would draw a 10-pixel
 * wide blue line from (10,10) to (200, 200) and a
 * 5-pixel thick red circle of radius 50 centered at
 * (200, 200):
 * <PRE>
 *    public void paint(Graphics g) {
 *       ...
 *       GraphicsUtil.drawLine(g, 10, 10, 200, 200,
 *                             10, Color.blue);
 *       GraphicsUtil.drawCircle(g, 200, 200, 50,
 *                             5, Color.red);
 *       ...
 *    }
 * </PRE>
 *
 * @author Marty Hall (hall@apl.jhu.edu)
 * @version 1.0 (1997)
 */

public class GraphicsUtil {

  //-------------------------------------------------------
  /** Draws an arc with the specified pen width. Note
   *  that the rectangle specified falls in the
   *  <B>middle</B> of the thick line (half inside it,
   *  half outside).
   *
   * @param g The Graphics object.
   * @param left The left side of the bounding rectangle
   * @param top The top of the bounding rectangle
   * @param width The width of the bounding rectangle
   * @param height The height of the bounding rectangle
   * @param startAngle The beginning angle
   *                   <B>in degrees.</B> 0 is 3
   *                   o'clock, increasing
   *                   counterclockwise.
   * @param deltaAngle The sweep angle in degrees
   *                   (going counterclockwise).
   * @param lineWidth The pen width (thickness of
   *                   line drawn).
   */
```

continued

Listing 9.10 `GraphicsUtil.java` (continued)

```
public static void drawArc(Graphics g,
                           int left, int top,
                           int width, int height,
                           int startAngle,
                           int deltaAngle,
                           int lineWidth) {
  left = left - lineWidth/2;
  top = top - lineWidth/2;
  width = width + lineWidth;
  height = height + lineWidth;
  for(int i=0; i<lineWidth; i++) {
    g.drawArc(left, top, width, height,
              startAngle, deltaAngle);
    if((i+1)<lineWidth) {
      g.drawArc(left, top, width-1, height-1,
                startAngle, deltaAngle);
      g.drawArc(left+1, top, width-1, height-1,
                startAngle, deltaAngle);
      g.drawArc(left, top+1, width-1, height-1,
                startAngle, deltaAngle);
      g.drawArc(left+1, top+1, width-1, height-1,
                startAngle, deltaAngle);
      left = left + 1;
      top = top + 1;
      width = width - 2;
      height = height - 2;
    }
  }
}

/** Draws an arc with the specified pen width
 *   and color.
 *
 * @param g The Graphics object.
 * @param left The left side of the bounding rectangle
 * @param top The top of the bounding rectangle
 * @param width The width of the bounding rectangle
 * @param height The height of the bounding rectangle
 * @param startAngle The beginning angle
 *                   <B>in degrees.</B> 0 is 3
 *                   o'clock, increasing
 *                   counterclockwise.
 * @param deltaAngle The sweep angle in degrees
 *                   (going counterclockwise).
 * @param lineWidth The pen width (thickness of
 *                   line drawn).
 * @param c The Color in which to draw.
 */
```

Listing 9.10 GraphicsUtil.java (continued)

```java
public static void drawArc(Graphics g,
                           int left, int top,
                           int width, int height,
                           int startAngle,
                           int deltaAngle,
                           int lineWidth, Color c) {
  Color origColor = g.getColor();
  g.setColor(c);
  drawArc(g, left, top, width, height,
          startAngle, deltaAngle, lineWidth);
  g.setColor(origColor);
}

/** Adds a Color argument to the drawArc method of
 *  java.awt.Graphics.
 *
 * @param g The Graphics object.
 * @param left The left side of the bounding rectangle
 * @param top The top of the bounding rectangle
 * @param width The width of the bounding rectangle
 * @param height The height of the bounding rectangle
 * @param deltaAngle The sweep angle in degrees
 *                   (going counterclockwise).
 * @param lineWidth The pen width (thickness of
 *                  line drawn).
 * @param c The color in which to draw the arc.
 */

public static void drawArc(Graphics g,
                           int left, int top,
                           int width, int height,
                           int startAngle,
                           int deltaAngle,
                           Color c) {
  Color origColor = g.getColor();
  g.setColor(c);
  g.drawArc(left, top, width, height,
            startAngle, deltaAngle);
  g.setColor(origColor);
}

//-----------------------------------------------------
/** Adds a Color argument to the fillArc method of
 *  java.awt.Graphics.
 *
 * @param g The Graphics object.
```

continued

Listing 9.10 GraphicsUtil.java (continued)

```
 * @param x The left side of the bounding rectangle
 * @param y The top of the bounding rectangle
 * @param width The width of the bounding rectangle
 * @param height The height of the bounding rectangle
 * @param startAngle The beginning angle
 *                    <B>in degrees.</B> 0 is 3
 *                    o'clock, increasing
 *                    counterclockwise.
 * @param deltaAngle The sweep angle in degrees
 *                    (going counterclockwise).
 * @param c The color in which to draw the arc.
 */

public static void fillArc(Graphics g,
                           int left, int top,
                           int width, int height,
                           int startAngle,
                           int deltaAngle,
                           Color c) {
  Color origColor = g.getColor();
  g.setColor(c);
  g.fillArc(left, top, width, height,
            startAngle, deltaAngle);
  g.setColor(origColor);
}


//-----------------------------------------------------
/** Adds a Color argument to the drawChars method of
 *  java.awt.Graphics.
 *
 * @param g The Graphics object.
 * @param chars An array of characters.
 * @param start The index in chars at which the
 *              string starts.
 * @param numChars Number of characters to draw
 *                 (starting at start).
 * @param x The left side of the string that gets drawn
 * @param y The <B>bottom</B> (not top) of the string.
 * @param c The color in which to draw the string.
 */
```

Listing 9.10 `GraphicsUtil.java` (continued)

```
public static void drawChars(Graphics g, char[] chars,
                             int start, int numChars,
                             int x, int y,
                             Color c) {
  Color origColor = g.getColor();
  g.setColor(c);
  g.drawChars(chars, start, numChars, x, y);
  g.setColor(origColor);
}

/** Adds a Font argument to the drawChars method of
 *  java.awt.Graphics.
 *
 * @param g The Graphics object.
 * @param chars An array of characters.
 * @param start The index in chars at which the
 *              string starts.
 * @param numChars Number of characters to draw
 *                 (starting at start).
 * @param x The left side of the string that gets drawn
 * @param y The <B>bottom</B> (not top) of the string.
 * @param f The font in which to draw the string.
 */

public static void drawChars(Graphics g, char[] chars,
                             int start, int numChars,
                             int x, int y,
                             Font f) {
  Font origFont = g.getFont();
  g.setFont(f);
  g.drawChars(chars, start, numChars, x, y);
  g.setFont(origFont);
}

/** Adds Font and Color arguments to the drawChars
 *  method of java.awt.Graphics.
 *
 * @param g The Graphics object.
 * @param chars An array of characters.
 * @param start The index in chars at which the
 *              string starts.
 * @param numChars Number of characters to draw
 *                 (starting at start).
```

continued

Listing 9.10 `GraphicsUtil.java` (continued)

```
 * @param x The left side of the string that gets drawn
 * @param y The <B>bottom</B> (not top) of the string.
 * @param f The font in which to draw the string.
 * @param c The color in which to draw the string.
 */

public static void drawChars(Graphics g, char[] chars,
                             int start, int numChars,
                             int x, int y,
                             Font f, Color c) {
  Font origFont = g.getFont();
  g.setFont(f);
  drawChars(g, chars, start, numChars, x, y, c);
  g.setFont(origFont);
}

//----------------------------------------------------
/** Calls the drawOval method of java.awt.Graphics
 *  with a square bounding box centered at specified
 *  location with width/height of 2r.
 *
 * @param g The Graphics object.
 * @param x The x-coordinate of the center of the
 *          circle.
 * @param y The y-coordinate of the center of the
 *          circle.
 * @param r The radius of the circle.
 */

public static void drawCircle(Graphics g,
                              int x, int y, int r) {
  g.drawOval(x-r, y-r, 2*r, 2*r);
}

// Calling drawOval directly would save having to do
// x-r, 2*r calculations each time, but that time is
// insignificant compared to the drawing time,
// and it is easier and more extensible to use
// existing drawCircle method.
//
// Unfortunately, drawOval calls with concentric
// radii do not exactly fall next to each other in
```

Listing 9.10 `GraphicsUtil.java` (continued)

```
// all cases, since ovals are being approximated by
// filling in pixels in a rectangular grid. So
// occasional pixels will get omitted.
// If you knew nothing was inside your circle, you
// could avoid this by implementing line thickness
// by two consecutive calls to fillOval (the second
// using the current background color), but this
// would require the circle drawing to be done
// first when things are inside it, prevent
// overlapping circles, etc. So instead 4 offset
// inner circles are drawn before each centered
// inner circle.

/** Draws a circle of radius r at location (x,y) with
 *  the specified line width. Note that the radius r
 *  is to the <B>center</B> of the doughnut drawn.
 *  The outside radius will be r+lineWidth/2 (rounded
 *  down). Inside radius will be r-lineWidth/2
 *  (rounded down).
 *
 *  @param g The Graphics object.
 *  @param x The x-coordinate of the center of the
 *           circle.
 *  @param y The y-coordinate of the center of the
 *           circle.
 *  @param r The radius of the circle.
 *  @param lineWidth Pen thickness of circle drawn.
 */

public static void drawCircle(Graphics g,
                              int x, int y, int r,
                              int lineWidth) {
  r = r+lineWidth/2;
  for(int i=0; i<lineWidth; i++) {
    drawCircle(g, x, y, r);
    if ((i+1)<lineWidth) {
      drawCircle(g, x+1, y, r-1);
      drawCircle(g, x-1, y, r-1);
      drawCircle(g, x, y+1, r-1);
      drawCircle(g, x, y-1, r-1);
      r = r-1;
    }
  }
}
```

continued

Listing 9.10 `GraphicsUtil.java` (continued)

```java
/** Draws a circle of radius r at location (x,y) with
 *  the specified line width and color. Note that
 *  the radius r is to the <B>center</B> of the
 *  doughnut drawn. The outside radius will
 *  be r+lineWidth/2 (rounded down). Inside radius
 *  will be r-lineWidth/2 (rounded down).
 *
 * @param g The Graphics object.
 * @param x The x-coordinate of the center of the
 *          circle.
 * @param y The y-coordinate of the center of the
 *          circle.
 * @param r The radius of the circle.
 * @param lineWidth Pen thickness of circle drawn.
 * @param c The color in which to draw.
 */

public static void drawCircle(Graphics g,
                              int x, int y, int r,
                              int lineWidth, Color c) {
  Color origColor = g.getColor();
  g.setColor(c);
  drawCircle(g, x, y, r, lineWidth);
  g.setColor(origColor);
}

/** Calls the drawOval method of java.awt.Graphics
 *  with a square bounding box centered at specified
 *  location with width/height of 2r. Draws in the
 *  color specified.
 *
 * @param g The Graphics object.
 * @param x The x-coordinate of the center of the
 *          circle.
 * @param y The y-coordinate of the center of the
 *          circle.
 * @param r The radius of the circle.
 * @param c The color in which to draw.
 */

public static void drawCircle(Graphics g,
                              int x, int y, int r,
                              Color c) {
  drawCircle(g, x, y, r, 1, c);
}
```

Listing 9.10 `GraphicsUtil.java` (continued)

```java
//----------------------------------------------------
/** Calls the fillOval method of java.awt.Graphics
 *  with a square bounding box centered at specified
 *  location with width/height of 2r.
 *
 * @param g The Graphics object.
 * @param x The x-coordinate of the center of the
 *          circle.
 * @param y The y-coordinate of the center of the
 *          circle.
 * @param r The radius of the circle.
 */

public static void fillCircle(Graphics g,
                                int x, int y, int r) {
  g.fillOval(x-r, y-r, 2*r, 2*r);
}


/** Calls the fillOval method of java.awt.Graphics
 *  with a square bounding box centered at specified
 *  location with width/height of 2r. Draws in the
 *  color specified.
 *
 * @param g The Graphics object.
 * @param x The x-coordinate of the center of the
 *          circle.
 * @param y The y-coordinate of the center of the
 *          circle.
 * @param r The radius of the circle.
 * @param c The color in which to draw.
 */

public static void fillCircle(Graphics g,
                                int x, int y, int r,
                                Color c) {
  Color origColor = g.getColor();
  g.setColor(c);
  fillCircle(g, x, y, r);
  g.setColor(origColor);
}

//----------------------------------------------------
```

continued

Listing 9.10 `GraphicsUtil.java` (continued)

```
/** Draws a line from (x1, y1) to (x2, y2) using the
 *  specified pen thickness.
 *
 * @param g The Graphics object.
 * @param x1 x position of start of line.
 * @param y1 y position of start of line.
 * @param x2 x position of end of line.
 * @param y2 y position of end of line.
 * @param lineWidth Thickness of line drawn.
 */

public static void drawLine(Graphics g,
                            int x1, int y1,
                            int x2, int y2,
                            int lineWidth) {
  double angle;
  double halfWidth = ((double)lineWidth)/2.0;
  double deltaX = (double)(x2 - x1);
  double deltaY = (double)(y2 - y1);
  if (x1 == x2)
    angle=Math.PI;
  else
    angle=Math.atan(deltaY/deltaX)+Math.PI/2;
  int xOffset = (int)(halfWidth*Math.cos(angle));
  int yOffset = (int)(halfWidth*Math.sin(angle));
  int[] xCorners = { x1-xOffset, x2-xOffset,
                     x2+xOffset, x1+xOffset };
  int[] yCorners = { y1-yOffset, y2-yOffset,
                     y2+yOffset, y1+yOffset };
  g.fillPolygon(xCorners, yCorners, 4);
}

/** Draws a line from (x1, y1) to (x2, y2) using the
 *  specified pen thickness and color.
 *
 * @param g The Graphics object.
 * @param x1 x position of start of line.
 * @param y1 y position of start of line.
 * @param x2 x position of end of line.
 * @param y2 y position of end of line.
 * @param lineWidth Thickness of line drawn.
 * @param c The color in which to draw.
 */
```

Listing 9.10 GraphicsUtil.java (continued)

```java
public static void drawLine(Graphics g,
                            int x1, int y1,
                            int x2, int y2,
                            int lineWidth, Color c) {
  Color origColor = g.getColor();
  g.setColor(c);
  drawLine(g, x1, y1, x2, y2, lineWidth);
  g.setColor(origColor);
}


/** Draws a 1-pixel wide line from (x1, y1) to
 *  (x2, y2) using the specified color.
 *
 * @param g The Graphics object.
 * @param x1 x position of start of line.
 * @param y1 y position of start of line.
 * @param x2 x position of end of line.
 * @param y2 y position of end of line.
 * @param c The color in which to draw.
 */

public static void drawLine(Graphics g,
                            int x1, int y1,
                            int x2, int y2,
                            Color c) {
  drawLine(g, x1, y1, x2, y2, 1, c);
}


//----------------------------------------------------
/** Draws an oval in the specified bounding rectangle
 *   with the specified pen thickness. Note that the
 *   rectangle bounds the <B>center</B> (not the
 *   outside) of the oval. So the oval will really go
 *   lineWidth/2 pixels inside and outside the
 *   bounding rectangle. Specifying a width of 1 has
 *   the identical effect to
 *   g.drawOval(left, top, width, height).
 *
 * @param g The Graphics object.
 * @param left The left side of the bounding rectangle.
 * @param top The y-coordinate of the top of the
 *            bounding rectangle.
 * @param width The width of the bounding rectangle.
 * @param height The height of the bounding rectangle.
 * @param lineWidth The pen thickness.
 */
```

continued

Listing 9.10 `GraphicsUtil.java` (continued)

```java
public static void drawOval(Graphics g,
                            int left, int top,
                            int width, int height,
                            int lineWidth) {
  left = left - lineWidth/2;
  top = top - lineWidth/2;
  width = width + lineWidth;
  height = height + lineWidth;
  for(int i=0; i<lineWidth; i++) {
    g.drawOval(left, top, width, height);
    if((i+1)<lineWidth) {
      g.drawOval(left,   top,   width-1, height-1);
      g.drawOval(left+1, top,   width-1, height-1);
      g.drawOval(left,   top+1, width-1, height-1);
      g.drawOval(left+1, top+1, width-1, height-1);
      left = left + 1;
      top = top + 1;
      width = width - 2;
      height = height - 2;
    }
  }
}

/** Draws an oval in the specified bounding rectangle
 *  with the specified pen thickness and color. Note
 *  that the rectangle bounds the <B>center</B> (not
 *  the outside) of the oval. So the oval will really
 *  go lineWidth/2 pixels inside and outside the
 *  bounding rectangle. Specifying a width of 1 has
 *  the identical effect to
 *  g.drawOval(left, top, width, height).
 *
 * @param g The Graphics object.
 * @param left The left side of the bounding rectangle.
 * @param top The y-coordinate of the top of the
 *             bounding rectangle.
 * @param width The width of the bounding rectangle.
 * @param height The height of the bounding rectangle.
 * @param lineWidth The pen thickness.
 * @param c The color in which to draw.
 */
```

Listing 9.10 `GraphicsUtil.java` (continued)

```java
public static void drawOval(Graphics g,
                            int left, int top,
                            int width, int height,
                            int lineWidth, Color c) {
  Color origColor = g.getColor();
  g.setColor(c);
  drawOval(g, left, top, width, height, lineWidth);
  g.setColor(origColor);
}


/** Draws a 1-pixel thick oval in the specified
 *  bounding rectangle with the specified color.
 *
 * @param g The Graphics object.
 * @param left The left side of the bounding rectangle.
 * @param top The y-coordinate of the top of the
 *            bounding rectangle.
 * @param width The width of the bounding rectangle.
 * @param height The height of the bounding rectangle.
 * @param c The color in which to draw.
 */

public static void drawOval(Graphics g,
                            int left, int top,
                            int width, int height,
                            Color c) {
  drawOval(g, left, top, width, height, 1, c);
}


//----------------------------------------------------
/** Calls g.fillOval(left, top, width, height)
 *  after setting the color appropriately. Resets
 *  color after drawing.
 *
 * @param g The Graphics object.
 * @param left The left side of the bounding rectangle.
 * @param top The y-coordinate of the top of the
 *            bounding rectangle.
 * @param width The width of the bounding rectangle.
 * @param height The height of the bounding rectangle.
 * @param c The color in which to draw.
 */
```

continued

Listing 9.10 `GraphicsUtil.java` (continued)

```java
public static void fillOval(Graphics g,
                             int left, int top,
                             int width, int height,
                             Color c) {
  Color origColor = g.getColor();
  g.setColor(c);
  g.fillOval(left, top, width, height);
  g.setColor(origColor);
}

//-----------------------------------------------------
/** Draws a polygon in the specified color.
 *  Having a drawPolygon with a line width argument
 *  would be nice, but you can't just do it by
 *  drawing thick lines, since you could have jagged
 *  corners. Filling in those corners takes more
 *  work, so is postponed. If someone wants to
 *  implement this and send it to me, it would
 *  be great.
 */

public static void drawPolygon(Graphics g,
                                int[] xPoints,
                                int[] yPoints,
                                int numPoints,
                                Color c) {
  Color origColor = g.getColor();
  g.setColor(c);
  g.drawPolygon(xPoints, yPoints, numPoints);
  g.setColor(origColor);
}

/** Draws a polygon in the specified color. */

public static void drawPolygon(Graphics g,
                                Polygon p, Color c) {
  Color origColor = g.getColor();
  g.setColor(c);
  g.drawPolygon(p);
  g.setColor(origColor);
}
```

Listing 9.10 GraphicsUtil.java (continued)

```java
//-------------------------------------------------------
/** Draws a solid polygon in the specified color. */

public static void fillPolygon(Graphics g,
                               int[] xs, int[] ys,
                               int numPoints,
                               Color c) {
  Color origColor = g.getColor();
  g.setColor(c);
  g.fillPolygon(xs, ys, numPoints);
  g.setColor(origColor);
}

/** Draws a solid polygon in the specified color. */

public static void fillPolygon(Graphics g,
                               Polygon p, Color c) {
  Color origColor = g.getColor();
  g.setColor(c);
  g.fillPolygon(p);
  g.setColor(origColor);
}

//-------------------------------------------------------
/** Draws a rectangle at the specified location
 *   with the supplied pen thickness. Left/top are
 *   the <B>center</B> of the lines drawn. Ie
 *   width/height are from the center of one side
 *   to the center of the other. So the inside
 *   width/heights are really lineWidth less than
 *   the values of width and height.
 *
 * @param g The Graphics object.
 * @param left Center of left side edge.
 * @param top Center of the top edge.
 * @param width Distance from center of L side to
 *              center of R side.
 * @param height Distance from center of top side to
 *              center of bottom side.
 * @param lineWidth Pen thickness.
 */
```

continued

Listing 9.10 `GraphicsUtil.java` (continued)

```java
public static void drawRect(Graphics g,
                            int left, int top,
                            int width, int height,
                            int lineWidth) {
  left = left - lineWidth/2;
  top = top - lineWidth/2;
  width = width + lineWidth;
  height = height + lineWidth;
  for(int i=0; i<lineWidth; i++) {
    g.drawRect(left, top, width, height);
    left = left + 1;
    top = top + 1;
    width = width - 2;
    height = height - 2;
  }
}

/** Draws a rectangle at the specified location
 *  with the supplied pen thickness and color.
 *  Left/top are the <B>center</B> of the lines drawn.
 *  Ie width/height are from the center of one side
 *  to the center of the other. So the inside
 *  width/heights are really lineWidth less than
 *  the values of width and height.
 *
 * @param g The Graphics object.
 * @param left Center of left side edge.
 * @param top Center of the top edge.
 * @param width Distance from center of L side to
 *              center of R side.
 * @param height Distance from center of top side to
 *              center of bottom side.
 * @param lineWidth Pen thickness.
 * @param c The color in which to draw.
 */

public static void drawRect(Graphics g,
                            int left, int top,
                            int width, int height,
                            int lineWidth, Color c) {
  Color origColor = g.getColor();
  g.setColor(c);
  drawRect(g, left, top, width, height, lineWidth);
  g.setColor(origColor);
}
```

Listing 9.10 `GraphicsUtil.java` (continued)

```java
/** Draws a 1-pixel thick rectangle at the specified
 *  location with the supplied color.
 *
 * @param g The Graphics object.
 * @param left The x-coordinate of left side edge.
 * @param top The y-coordinate of the top edge.
 * @param width width of rectangle.
 * @param height height of rectangle.
 * @param c The color in which to draw.
 */

public static void drawRect(Graphics g,
                            int left, int top,
                            int width, int height,
                            Color c) {
  drawRect(g, left, top, width, height, 1, c);
}


//------------------------------------------------------
/** Calls g.fillRect(left, top, width, height) after
 *  setting the color appropriately. Resets the color
 *  when done.
 */

public static void fillRect(Graphics g,
                            int left, int top,
                            int width, int height,
                            Color c) {
  Color origColor = g.getColor();
  g.setColor(c);
  g.fillRect(left, top, width, height);
  g.setColor(origColor);
}


//------------------------------------------------------
/** Draws a rounded rectangle at the specified
 *  location with the supplied pen thickness.
 *  Left/top are the <B>center</B> of the lines
 *  drawn. Ie width/height are from the center of one
 *  side to the center of the other. So the inside
 *  width/heights are really lineWidth less than the
 *  values of width and height, and the
 *  outside width/heights are lineWidth more.
 *
```

continued

Listing 9.10 `GraphicsUtil.java` **(continued)**

```
 * @param g The Graphics object.
 * @param left Center of left side edge.
 * @param top Center of the top edge.
 * @param width Distance from center of L side to
 *               center of R side.
 * @param height Distance from center of top side to
 *               center of bottom side.
 * @param arcWidth Horizontal diameter of arc at
 *                  corners.
 * @param arcHeight Vertical diameter of arc at
 *                  corners.
 * @param lineWidth Pen thickness.
 */

public static void drawRoundRect(Graphics g,
                                 int left,
                                 int top,
                                 int width,
                                 int height,
                                 int arcWidth,
                                 int arcHeight,
                                 int lineWidth) {
  left = left - lineWidth/2;
  top = top - lineWidth/2;
  width = width + lineWidth;
  height = height + lineWidth;
  for(int i=0; i<lineWidth; i++) {
    g.drawRoundRect(left, top, width, height,
                    arcWidth, arcHeight);
    if((i+1)<lineWidth) {
      g.drawRoundRect(left, top, width-1, height-1,
                      arcWidth, arcHeight);
      g.drawRoundRect(left+1, top, width-1, height-1,
                      arcWidth, arcHeight);
      g.drawRoundRect(left, top+1, width-1, height-1,
                      arcWidth, arcHeight);
      g.drawRoundRect(left+1, top+1, width-1, height-1,
                      arcWidth, arcHeight);
      left = left + 1;
      top = top + 1;
      width = width - 2;
      height = height - 2;
    }
  }
}
```

Listing 9.10 `GraphicsUtil.java` (continued)

```
/** Draws a rounded rectangle at the specified
 *   location with the supplied pen thickness and color.
 *   Left/top are the <B>center</B> of the lines
 *   drawn. Ie width/height are from the center of one
 *   side to the center of the other. So the inside
 *   width/heights are really lineWidth less than the
 *   values of width and height, and the
 *   outside width/heights are lineWidth more.
 *
 * @param g The Graphics object.
 * @param left Center of left side edge.
 * @param top Center of the top edge.
 * @param width Distance from center of L side to
 *              center of R side.
 * @param height Distance from center of top side to
 *               center of bottom side.
 * @param arcWidth Horizontal diameter of arc at
 *                 corners.
 * @param arcHeight Vertical diameter of arc at
 *                  corners.
 * @param lineWidth Pen thickness.
 * @param c Pen color.
 */

public static void drawRoundRect(Graphics g,
                                 int left,
                                 int top,
                                 int width,
                                 int height,
                                 int arcWidth,
                                 int arcHeight,
                                 int lineWidth,
                                 Color c) {
  Color origColor = g.getColor();
  g.setColor(c);
  drawRoundRect(g, left, top, width, height,
                arcWidth, arcHeight, lineWidth);
  g.setColor(origColor);
}

/** Draws a 1-pixel wide rounded rectangle with the
 *   specified color. Same as g.drawRoundRect except
 *   for the color.
 *
```

continued

Listing 9.10 `GraphicsUtil.java` (continued)

```
 * @param g The Graphics object.
 * @param left The x-coordinate of left edge.
 * @param top The y-coordinate of the top edge.
 * @param width Distance from L side to R side.
 * @param height Distance from top side to bottom side.
 * @param arcWidth Horizontal diameter of arc at
 *                 corners.
 * @param arcHeight Vertical diameter of arc at
 *                  corners.
 * @param c Pen color.
 */

public static void drawRoundRect(Graphics g,
                                 int left,
                                 int top,
                                 int width,
                                 int height,
                                 int arcWidth,
                                 int arcHeight,
                                 Color c) {
  drawRoundRect(g, left, top, width, height,
          arcWidth, arcHeight, 1, c);
}

//-------------------------------------------------------
/** Draws a solid rounded rectangle with the
 *  specified color. Same as g.fillRoundRect except
 *  for the color.
 *
 * @param g The Graphics object.
 * @param left Center of left side edge.
 * @param top Center of the top edge.
 * @param width Distance from center of L side to
 *              center of R side.
 * @param height Distance from center of top side to
 *               center of bottom side.
 * @param arcWidth Horizontal diameter of arc at
 *                 corners.
 * @param arcHeight Vertical diameter of arc at
 *                  corners.
 * @param c Pen color.
 */
```

Listing 9.10 `GraphicsUtil.java` (continued)

```java
public static void fillRoundRect(Graphics g,
                                 int left,
                                 int top,
                                 int width,
                                 int height,
                                 int arcWidth,
                                 int arcHeight,
                                 Color c) {
  Color origColor = g.getColor();
  g.setColor(c);
  g.fillRoundRect(left, top, width, height,
                  arcWidth, arcHeight);
  g.setColor(origColor);
}

//-----------------------------------------------------
/** Draws a 3D rectangle in the specified location
 *  with the given line thickness. Left/top
 *  are the <B>center</B> of the lines drawn.
 *  Ie width/height are from the center of one side
 *  to the center of the other. So the inside
 *  width/heights are really lineWidth less than
 *  the values of width and height; the
 *  outside width/heights are lineWidth more.
 *
 * @param g The Graphics object.
 * @param left Center of left side edge.
 * @param top Center of the top edge.
 * @param width Distance from center of L side to
 *              center of R side.
 * @param height Distance from center of top side to
 *               center of bottom side.
 * @param isRaised A boolean variable that determines
 *                 if the right and bottom sides are
 *                 shaded to try to make the rectangle
 *                 look like it is higher than
 *                 background (true) or lower (false).
 *                 Works best with relatively thin
 *                 lines and gray colors.
 * @param lineWidth The pen thickness.
 */
```

continued

Listing 9.10 `GraphicsUtil.java` (continued)

```
public static void draw3DRect(Graphics g,
                                int left, int top,
                                int width, int height,
                                boolean isRaised,
                                int lineWidth) {
  left = left - lineWidth/2;
  top = top - lineWidth/2;
  width = width + lineWidth;
  height = height + lineWidth;
  for(int i=0; i<lineWidth; i++) {
    g.draw3DRect(left, top, width, height, isRaised);
    left = left + 1;
    top = top + 1;
    width = width - 2;
    height = height - 2;
  }
}

/** Draws a 3D rectangle in the specified location
 *  with the given line thickness and color. Left/top
 *  are the <B>center</B> of the lines drawn.
 *  Ie width/height are from the center of one side
 *  to the center of the other. So the inside
 *  width/heights are really lineWidth less than
 *  the values of width and height; the
 *  outside width/heights are lineWidth more.
 *
 * @param g The Graphics object.
 * @param left Center of left side edge.
 * @param top Center of the top edge.
 * @param width Distance from center of L side to
 *              center of R side.
 * @param height Distance from center of top side to
 *              center of bottom side.
 * @param isRaised A boolean variable that determines
 *              if the right and bottom sides are
 *              shaded to try to make the rectangle
 *              look like it is higher than
 *              background (true) or lower (false).
 *              Works best with relatively thin
 *              lines and gray colors.
 * @param lineWidth The pen thickness.
 * @param c The pen color.
 */
```

Listing 9.10 GraphicsUtil.java (continued)

```
public static void draw3DRect(Graphics g,
                              int left, int top,
                              int width, int height,
                              boolean isRaised,
                              int lineWidth, Color c) {
  Color origColor = g.getColor();
  g.setColor(c);
  draw3DRect(g, left, top, width, height,
             isRaised, lineWidth);
  g.setColor(origColor);
}

/** Draws a 1-pixel thick 3D rectangle in the
 *   specified location with the given color.
 *
 * @param g The Graphics object.
 * @param left The x-coordinate of left side edge.
 * @param top The y-coordinate of the top edge.
 * @param width Distance from L side to R side.
 * @param height Distance from top side to bottom side.
 * @param isRaised A boolean variable that determines
 *                 if the right and bottom sides are
 *                 shaded to try to make the rectangle
 *                 look like it is higher than
 *                 background (true) or lower (false).
 *                 Works best with gray colors.
 * @param c The pen color.
 */

public static void draw3DRect(Graphics g,
                              int left, int top,
                              int width, int height,
                              boolean isRaised,
                              Color c) {
  draw3DRect(g, left, top, width, height,
             isRaised, 1, c);
}

//----------------------------------------------------
/** Makes a solid 3D rectangle in the given color.
 *
 * @param g The Graphics object.
```

continued

Listing 9.10 `GraphicsUtil.java`   (continued)

```
 * @param left The x-coordinate of left side edge.
 * @param top The y-coordinate of the top edge.
 * @param width Distance from L side to R side.
 * @param height Distance from top side to bottom side.
 * @param isRaised A boolean variable that determines
 *                 if the right and bottom sides are
 *                 shaded to try to make the rectangle
 *                 look like it is higher than
 *                 background (true) or lower (false).
 *                 Works best with gray colors.
 * @param c The pen color.
 */

public static void fill3DRect(Graphics g,
                              int left, int top,
                              int width, int height,
                              boolean isRaised,
                              Color c) {
  Color origColor = g.getColor();
  g.setColor(c);
  g.fill3DRect(left, top, width, height, isRaised);
  g.setColor(origColor);
}


//-------------------------------------------------------
/** Calls g.drawString(s, x, y) after setting the
 *  color to c. Resets the color after drawing.
 *
 * @param g The Graphics object.
 * @param s The string to be drawn.
 * @param x The left side of the string.
 * @param y The <B>bottom</B> (not top) of the string.
 * @param c The color in which to draw the string.
 */

public static void drawString(Graphics g,
                              String s,
                              int x, int y,
                              Color c) {
  Color origColor = g.getColor();
  g.setColor(c);
  g.drawString(s, x, y);
  g.setColor(origColor);
}
```

Listing 9.10 `GraphicsUtil.java` **(continued)**

```java
/** Calls g.drawString(s, x, y) after setting the
 *  font to f. Resets the font after drawing.
 *
 * @param g The Graphics object.
 * @param s The string to be drawn.
 * @param x The left side of the string
 * @param y The <B>bottom</B> (not top) of the string.
 * @param f The font in which to draw the string.
 */

public static void drawString(Graphics g,
                              String s,
                              int x, int y,
                              Font f) {
  Font origFont = g.getFont();
  g.setFont(f);
  g.drawString(s, x, y);
  g.setFont(origFont);
}

/** Calls g.drawString(s, x, y) after setting the
 *  font to f and the color to c. Resets the font
 *  and color after drawing.
 *
 * @param g The Graphics object.
 * @param s The string to be drawn.
 * @param x The left side of the string
 * @param y The <B>bottom</B> (not top) of the string.
 * @param f The font in which to draw the string.
 * @param c The color in which to draw the string.
 */

public static void drawString(Graphics g,
                              String s,
                              int x, int y,
                              Font f, Color c) {
  Font origFont = g.getFont();
  g.setFont(f);
  drawString(g, s, x, y, c);
  g.setFont(origFont);
}

//----------------------------------------------------
}
```

9.11 Drawing Images

Java applets and applications can load and display static images in GIF or JPEG format. This includes GIF89A (a.k.a. "animated GIF") files, but only the first frame of the animation will be shown. Besides, Java lets you control animation much better than do GIF89A files, so there wouldn't be that much use for them even if Java supported them. Image drawing is done in two steps. First, a remote or local image is registered using the `getImage` method of `Applet` or `Toolkit`. Secondly, it is drawn on the screen using the `drawImage` method of `Graphics`. You can draw the image at its regular size or supply an explicit width and height. The key point to remember is that calls to `getImage` don't actually initiate image loading. Instead, Java doesn't start loading the image until it is needed. Instead of waiting until you try to draw the image, you can tell Java to load it in advance by calling `prepareImage` or using a `MediaTracker` object. The first approach (`prepareImage`) loads the image in the background, returning control to you immediately. This is normally an advantage because processing can continue while the program might otherwise be waiting for a slow network connection. However, if `drawImage` is called before the image is done loading, it just draws the portion that has arrived (possibly none) without giving any error messages. The `paint` method will get called once the image is done, so assuming `drawImage` is being invoked from `paint`, the image will get drawn in its entirety eventually. In the meantime, however, partial images may be drawn and the width and height of the image may be incorrect. If you want to be sure the image is finished before you do any drawing, you can use the second approach: the `MediaTracker` class.

Loading Applet Images from Relative URLs

The `Applet` class contains a `getImage` method that takes two arguments: a URL corresponding to a directory and a string corresponding to a filename relative to that URL. For the relative URLs, supply `getCodeBase()` (the applet's home directory) or `getDocumentBase()` (the Web page's home directory) for the URL argument. Note that `getImage` will not succeed until the applet's context is set up. This means that you should call `getImage` in `init` rather than trying to directly initialize the `Image` instance variable via:

```
private Image myImage = getImage(...); // fails
```

Core Warning

Trying to declare and initialize `Image` instance variables in the body of an applet will fail. Initialize them in `init` or a method that runs after `init`.

To actually draw the image, use the `drawImage` of the `Graphics` class. If you're in a method other than `paint` (which is passed the current `Graphics` context automatically), you can obtain the window's `Graphics` context by calling `getGraphics`. There are two variations of `drawImage`:

```
drawImage(image, left, top, window)
```

and

```
drawImage(image, left, top, width, height, window)
```

The first uses the image's normal size; the second stretches it to fit in the specified area. Technically, the last argument is an `ImageObserver`; in ordinary cases, you just use the current window (the applet in this case). So for image drawing being performed in the paint method, "`this`" is almost always used as the last argument to `drawImage`. Listings 9.11 and 9.12 show an applet that loads images from the `images` subdirectory of the applet's home directory. The result is shown in Figure 9–12.

Listing 9.11 JavaMan1.java

```java
import java.applet.Applet;
import java.awt.*;

/** An applet that loads an image from a relative URL */

public class JavaMan1 extends Applet {
  private Image javaMan;

  public void init() {
    javaMan = getImage(getCodeBase(),
                       "images/Java-Man.gif");
  }

  public void paint(Graphics g) {
    g.drawImage(javaMan, 0, 0, this);
  }
}
```

Listing 9.12 JavaMan1.html

```html
<!DOCTYPE HTML PUBLIC "-//W3C//DTD HTML 3.2//EN">
<HTML>
<HEAD>
  <TITLE>JavaMan1</TITLE>
</HEAD>

<BODY BGCOLOR="WHITE">
<H1>JavaMan1</H1>

<APPLET CODE="JavaMan1.class" WIDTH=494 HEIGHT=488>
  <B>Sorry, you have a Java-challenged browser.</B>
</APPLET>

</BODY>
</HTML>
```

Figure 9–12 The most common way to load images in applets is using `getImage(getCodeBase(), path)` or `getImage(getDocumentBase(), path)`.

Loading Applet Images from Absolute URLs

Using absolute URLs is a bit more cumbersome than using relative ones because making a URL object requires catching the exception that would result if the URL is in an illegal format. Furthermore, because the `Securi-tyManager` of most browsers only allows an applet to load images off the machine that served the applet, this approach is not particularly common. However, it is quite possible that you store images in a different location than the applets and their associated HTML documents, and using an absolute URL would be more convenient. Listings 9.13 and 9.14 give an example applet and associated HTML document, with the result shown in Figure 9–13. In addition to the `try/catch` block around the URL constructor, note that the `java.net` package is imported; it contains the URL and `Mal-formed-URLException` classes. Using this approach does not change the fact that the image loading is postponed until the image is needed, so the image might appear to flicker into view as progressively larger pieces are drawn. If this is a problem for your application, the following sections will discuss how to partially or completely preload the image.

Listing 9.13 JavaMan2.java

```java
import java.applet.Applet;
import java.awt.*;
import java.net.*;

/** An applet that loads an image from an absolute
 *  URL on the same machine that the applet came from.
 */

public class JavaMan2 extends Applet {
  private Image javaMan;

  public void init() {
    try {
      URL imageFile =
        new URL("http://www.apl.jhu.edu/~hall" +
                "/images/Java-Man.gif");
      javaMan = getImage(imageFile);
    } catch(MalformedURLException mue) {
      showStatus("Bogus image URL.");
      System.out.println("Bogus URL");
    }
  }

  public void paint(Graphics g) {
    g.drawImage(javaMan, 0, 0, this);
  }
}
```

Listing 9.14 `JavaMan2.html`

```html
<!DOCTYPE HTML PUBLIC "-//W3C//DTD HTML 3.2//EN">
<HTML>
<HEAD>
  <TITLE>JavaMan2</TITLE>
</HEAD>

<BODY BGCOLOR="WHITE">
<H1>JavaMan2</H1>

<APPLET CODE="JavaMan2.class" WIDTH=494 HEIGHT=488>
  <B>Sorry, you have a Java-challenged browser.</B>
</APPLET>

</BODY>
</HTML>
```

Figure 9–13 Applets can load images from absolute URLs, but security restrictions apply.

Loading Images in Applications

Graphical applications can load images from absolute URLs or from local files using the getImage method of the Toolkit class. The concept of a relative URL is not completely applicable because applications are not normally associated with a Web page. Nevertheless, even though applications do not have a two-argument version of getImage like applets do, a URL object can be created from an existing URL and a filename. You can use this if, for instance, you want to load multiple images from the same directory. The current Toolkit can be obtained from any graphical object by calling getToolkit(), or from an arbitrary object by calling Toolkit.get-DefaultToolkit(). For instance, Listing 9.15 creates a simple Frame and draws an Image in it. Note the use of System.getProp-erty("user.dir") in order to make the filename relative to the directory containing the application. This makes it easier to move directories around or to move the application from machine to machine. Figure 9–14 shows the result.

Core Approach

Whenever possible, refer to local files using pathnames relative to the application's directory.

Listing 9.15 JavaMan3.java

```java
import java.awt.*;

/** An application that loads an image from a
 *  local file. Applets are not permitted to do this.
 */

public class JavaMan3 extends Frame {
  public static void main(String[] args) {
    new JavaMan3();
  }

  private Image javaMan;


  public JavaMan3() {
    super("JavaMan3");
    String imageFile = System.getProperty("user.dir") +
                       "/images/Java-Man.gif";
    javaMan = getToolkit().getImage(imageFile);
    setBackground(Color.white);
    resize(500, 520);
    show();
  }

  public void paint(Graphics g) {
    g.drawImage(javaMan, 0, 0, this);
  }

  public boolean handleEvent(Event event) {
    if (event.id == Event.WINDOW_DESTROY)
      System.exit(0);
    return(super.handleEvent(event));
  }
}
```

Figure 9–14 Images can be loaded in applications via
`getToolkit().getImage(arg)` or
`Toolkit.getDefaultToolkit().getImage(arg)`.
The `arg` can be a URL or local filename.

9.12 Preloading Images

In many cases, you'd like the system to start loading the images as soon as possible, rather than waiting until you try to draw them with `drawImage`. This is particularly true if the images will not be drawn until the user initiates some action such as clicking on a button or choosing a menu option. That way, if the user doesn't act right away, the image might arrive before action is taken. The `prepareImage` method can be used for this purpose. It starts the image loading in a background process, giving you control back immediately. There are two versions of `prepareImage`, one for each version of `drawImage`:

```
prepareImage(image, window)
```

and

```
prepareImage(image, width, height, window)
```

Each time you stretch the image it counts as a new one, so be sure to call `prepareImage` once for each size at which you plan to draw. For example, Listing 9.16 shows an application that draws an image only when the user presses a button. The time from when the user presses the button to the time the drawing is completed is printed in a textfield. If a `-preload` command line argument is supplied, `prepareImage` is called. Figure 9–15 shows the result when `prepareImage` is not used, while Figure 9–16 shows what happens when the same image is loaded, `-preload` is specified, and the button is not clicked until several seconds have gone by. Of course, the time shown in Figure 9–15 could be much smaller or much larger, depending upon the speed of your network connection, but the fact remains that the time before the button is pressed is wasted. For now, don't worry about the details of Listing 9.16; we'll cover user interfaces at length in the upcoming chapters. For now, concentrate on what goes on in the `registerImage` method, which is called from the `Preload` constructor.

Listing 9.16 `Preload.java`

```java
import java.awt.*;
import java.net.*;

/** A class that compares the time to draw an image
 *  preloaded (getImage, prepareImage, and drawImage) vs.
 *  regularly. (getImage and drawImage).
 *  <P>
 *  The answer you get the regular way is dependent
 *  on the network speed and the size of the image, but
 *  if you assume you load the applet "long" (compared
 *  to the time the image loading requires) before
 *  pressing the button, the drawing time in the
 *  preloaded version depends only on the speed of
 *  the local machine.
 */
```

Listing 9.16 `Preload.java` (continued)

```java
public class Preload extends Frame {
  public static void main(String[] args) {
    if (args.length == 0) {
      System.out.println("Must provide URL");
      System.exit(0);
    }
    if (args.length == 2 && args[1].equals("-preload"))
      new Preload(args[0], true);
    else
      new Preload(args[0], false);
  }

  private TextField timeField;
  private long start = 0;
  private boolean draw = false;
  private Image plate;

  public Preload(String imageFile, boolean preload) {
    super("Preloading Images");
    Panel buttonPanel = new Panel();
    buttonPanel.add(new Button("Display Image"));
    timeField = new TextField(25);
    timeField.setEditable(false);
    buttonPanel.add(timeField);
    add("South", buttonPanel);
    registerImage(imageFile, preload);
    resize(1000, 750);
    show();
  }

  /** If button has been clicked, draw image and
   *  show elapsed time. Otherwise do nothing.
   */
  public void paint(Graphics g) {
    if (draw) {
      g.drawImage(plate, 0, 0, this);
      showTime();
    }
  }

  /** No need to check which object caused this,
   *  since the button is the only possibility.
   */
```

Listing 9.16 `Preload.java` (continued)

```
public boolean action(Event event, Object object) {
  draw = true;
  start = System.currentTimeMillis();
  repaint();
  return(true);
}

/** Honor requests to quit the window. */

public boolean handleEvent(Event event) {
  if (event.id == Event.WINDOW_DESTROY)
    System.exit(0);
  return(super.handleEvent(event));
}

// Do getImage, optionally starting the loading.

private void registerImage(String imageFile,
                           boolean preload) {
  try {
    plate = getToolkit().getImage(new URL(imageFile));
    if (preload)
      prepareImage(plate, this);
  } catch(MalformedURLException mue) {
    System.out.println("Bad URL: " + mue);
  }
}

// Show elapsed time in textfield.

private void showTime() {
  timeField.setText("Elapsed Time: " + elapsedTime()
                    + " seconds.");
}

// Time in seconds since button clicked.

private double elapsedTime() {
  double delta =
    (double)(System.currentTimeMillis() - start);
  return(delta/1000.0);
}
}
```

Figure 9-15 Results when no preload argument is supplied. If you use `getImage` and `drawImage` only, the image does not get loaded over the network until the system tries to draw it.

Figure 9–16 Results when a preload argument is supplied. If you use `prepareImage` the system starts loading the image immediately.

9.13 Controlling Image Loading: Waiting for Images and Checking Status

Even if you preload images, you often want to be sure that the images are done loading before you perform certain tasks. For instance, because you cannot determine an image's width and height until it is done loading, programs that try to draw outlines around images must be careful how they go about it. As an example of a common but incorrect approach, consider Listings 9.17 and 9.18, which record the image's width and height in `init`, then draw a rectangle in `paint` based on these dimensions. Figure 9–17 shows the result in the HotJava browser on Solaris; the rectangle is missing because the height is –1.

Listing 9.17 `ImageBox.java`

```java
import java.applet.Applet;
import java.awt.*;

/** A class that incorrectly tries to load an
 *   image and draw an outline around it.
 *   Don't try this at home.
 */
public class ImageBox extends Applet {
  private int imageWidth, imageHeight;
  private Image image;

  public void init() {
    String imageName = getParameter("IMAGE");
    if (imageName != null)
      image = getImage(getDocumentBase(), imageName);
    else
      image = getImage(getDocumentBase(), "error.gif");
    setBackground(Color.white);

    // The following is wrong, since the image
    // won't be done loading, and -1 will be
    // returned.
    imageWidth = image.getWidth(this);
    imageHeight = image.getHeight(this);
  }

  public void paint(Graphics g) {
    g.drawImage(image, 0, 0, this);
    g.drawRect(0, 0, imageWidth, imageHeight);
  }
}
```

Listing 9.18 `ImageBox.html`

```html
<!DOCTYPE HTML PUBLIC "-//W3C//DTD HTML 3.2//EN">
<HTML>
<HEAD>
  <TITLE>ImageBox</TITLE>
</HEAD>

<BODY>
<H1>ImageBox</H1>

<APPLET CODE="ImageBox.class" WIDTH=400 HEIGHT=500>
  <PARAM NAME="IMAGE" VALUE="images/Java-Lightning.gif">
  Sorry, you need a <B>real</B> browser.
</APPLET>

</BODY>
</HTML>
```

Figure 9–17 Trying to determine an image's size when you aren't sure it is done loading can lead to bad results.

The solution to this problem is to use the `MediaTracker` class. This lets you start to load one or more images, register them with a `MediaTracker` using `addImage`, then at some point explicitly wait until all the images are done loading by calling `waitForID` or `waitForAll`. `MediaTracker` also has various methods for checking if the image file was not found or if other errors occurred. These methods are summarized below.

MediaTracker

public void addImage(Image image, int id)
public void addImage(Image image, int id, int width, int height)
This registers a normal or scaled image with a given ID. You can register one or more images with a particular ID, then either check the status of, or wait for, images with a given ID. You can also wait for all images; when doing so the system tries to load the images with lower IDs first.

public boolean checkAll()
public boolean checkAll(boolean startLoading)
These methods return `true` if all the images registered with the `MediaTracker` are done loading. They return `false` otherwise. If you supply `true` for the `startLoading` argument, the system will begin loading the images if it wasn't doing so already. Note that you should not normally put `CheckAll` inside a loop to wait until images are done. Instead, use `waitForAll`, which accomplishes the same goal without consuming nearly as much cpu resources.

public boolean checkID(int id)
public boolean checkID(int id, boolean startLoading)
These methods are similar to `checkForAll`, but only report the status of images registered under a particular ID.

public Object[ ] getErrorsAny()
public Object[ ] getErrorsID(int id)
This returns an array of images that have encountered an error while loading.

public boolean isErrorAny()
public boolean isErrorID(int id)
This returns `true` if any image encountered an error while loading, `false` otherwise.

public void removeImage(Image image) [Java 1.1]
public void removeImage(Image image, int id) [Java 1.1]
public void removeImage(Image image, int id, int width,
                                       int height) [Java 1.1]
These Java 1.1 methods let you "unregister" an image.

public int statusAll()
public int statusID(int id, boolean startLoading)
These methods return the bitwise inclusive OR of the status flags of all images being loaded. The status flag options are `Media-Tracker.LOADING`, `MediaTracker.ABORTED`, `Media-Tracker.ERRORED`, and `MediaTracker.COMPLETE`. Images that haven't started loading have zero for their status. If you supply `true` for the `startLoading` argument, the system will begin loading the images if it wasn't doing so already.

public void waitForAll()
public boolean waitForAll(long milliseconds)
These methods start loading any images that are not already loading, and do not return until all of them are done or the specified time has elapsed. The system starts loading images with lower IDs before those with higher ones. The methods throw an `InterruptedException` when done; you are required to catch it.

public void waitForID(int id)
public boolean waitForID(int id, long milliseconds)
These methods start loading any images registered under the specified ID that are not already loading, and do not return until all of them are done or the specified time has elapsed. They throw an `Interrupted-Exception` when done; you are required to catch it.

Listings 9.19 and 9.20 show a corrected version of the `ImageBox` applet that waits until the image is done loading before trying to determine its size. Figure 9–18 shows the result.

Listing 9.19 `BetterImageBox.java`

```java
import java.applet.Applet;
import java.awt.*;

/** This version fixes the problems associated with
 *  ImageBox by using a MediaTracker to be sure the
 *  image is done loading before you try to get
 *  its dimensions
 */

public class BetterImageBox extends Applet {
  private int imageWidth, imageHeight;
  private Image image;
```

continued

Listing 9.19 `BetterImageBox.java` (continued)

```java
  public void init() {
    String imageName = getParameter("IMAGE");
    if (imageName != null)
      image = getImage(getDocumentBase(), imageName);
    else
      image = getImage(getDocumentBase(), "error.gif");
    setBackground(Color.white);
    MediaTracker tracker = new MediaTracker(this);
    tracker.addImage(image, 0);
    try {
      tracker.waitForAll();
    } catch(InterruptedException ie) {}
    if (tracker.isErrorAny())
      System.out.println("Error while loading image");

    // This is safe: image is fully loaded
    imageWidth = image.getWidth(this);
    imageHeight = image.getHeight(this);
  }

  public void paint(Graphics g) {
    g.drawImage(image, 0, 0, this);
    g.drawRect(0, 0, imageWidth, imageHeight);
  }

}
```

Listing 9.20 `BetterImageBox.html`

```html
<!DOCTYPE HTML PUBLIC "-//W3C//DTD HTML 3.2//EN">
<HTML>
<HEAD>
  <TITLE>ImageBox</TITLE>
</HEAD>

<BODY>
<H1>ImageBox</H1>

<APPLET CODE="BetterImageBox.class" WIDTH=400 HEIGHT=500>
  <PARAM NAME="IMAGE" VALUE="images/Java-Lightning.gif">
  Sorry, you need a <B>real</B>browser.
</APPLET>

</BODY>
</HTML>
```

Figure 9–18 `MediaTracker` can be used to wait until images are done loading.

Because waiting for images and checking for errors is the most common use of `MediaTracker`, it is convenient to combine these two tasks into a single method. Listing 9.21 defines a `TrackerUtil` class with two static methods: `waitForImage` and `waitForImages`. The `waitForImage` method can be used as follows:

```
someImage = getImage(...);
doSomeOtherStuff();
if (TrackerUtil.waitForImage(someImage, this))
  // someImage finished loading
else
  // error loading someImage
```

Similarly, the `waitForImages` method can be used as follows:

```
image1 = getImage(...);
image2 = getImage(...);
...
imageN = getImage(...);
doSomeOtherStuff();
Image[] images = { image1, image2, ... , imageN };
if (TrackerUtil.waitForImages(images, this))
    // all images finished loading
else
    // error loading an image
```

If you want more control over image loading than `MediaTracker` provides, you can override the `imageUpdate` method of the window. See the API for details.

Listing 9.21 `TrackerUtil.java`

```java
import java.awt.*;

/** A utility class that lets you load and wait
 *  for an image or images in one fell swoop.
 *  If you are loading multiple images, only
 *  use multiple calls to waitForImage if you
 *  <B>need</B> loading to be done serially.
 *  Otherwise use waitForImages, which loads
 *  concurrently, which can be much faster.
 */

public class TrackerUtil {
  public static boolean waitForImage(Image image,
                                     Component c) {
    MediaTracker tracker = new MediaTracker(c);
    tracker.addImage(image, 0);
    try {
      tracker.waitForAll();
    } catch(InterruptedException ie) {}
    if (tracker.isErrorAny())
      return(false);
    else
      return(true);
  }
```

Listing 9.21 `TrackerUtil.java` (continued)

```
public static boolean waitForImages(Image[] images,
                                     Component c) {
  MediaTracker tracker = new MediaTracker(c);
  for(int i=0; i<images.length; i++)
    tracker.addImage(images[i], 0);
  try {
    tracker.waitForAll();
  } catch(InterruptedException ie) {}
  if (tracker.isErrorAny())
    return(false);
  else
    return(true);
}
}
```

9.14 Summary

An applet is a type of graphical Java program that can be embedded in a Web page. Applets run on the client machine, and consequently have various security restrictions. They are created by extending the `java.applet.Applet` class, and associated with a Web page via the `APPLET` element. Graphical Java programs that will not be run in a Web browser are created by using the `Frame` class. In either case, drawing is typically performed in the `paint` method. This method takes a `Graphics` object as an argument; the `Graphics` class has a variety of drawing operations. However, this class does not support pen thicknesses, so the `GraphicsUtil` class was developed to add this capability. Another graphics operation of particular interest is `drawImage`, which can be used to draw GIF or JPEG images loaded earlier via the `getImage` method of `Applet` or `Toolkit`. Images loaded this way are loaded in a background thread, and may be drawn in incremental pieces unless loading is explicitly controlled by use of a `MediaTracker`.

Drawing lines, polygons, text, and images is nice, but for a complete user interface, you need to be able to react to actions taken by the user, create other types of windows, and insert user interface controls such as buttons, textfields, and the like. These topics are discussed in the following three chapters.

HANDLING
MOUSE AND
KEYBOARD
EVENTS

Topics in This Chapter

- The approach to processing events in Java 1.02

- The Event class

- Event-handling helper methods in Java 1.02

- Java 1.02 event types

- Doing drawing and other graphics operations from event-handling methods

- The Java 1.1 event model

- Inner classes

- Java 1.1 event listeners, event classes, and low-level event-processing methods

Chapter 10

Certain user actions are classified as *events*. These include such actions as clicking the mouse, typing a key, or minimizing or moving the window. Java automatically sets up a thread of execution to monitor these events, and they can be processed in one of two distinct ways. In version 1.02 of Java, all events are first delivered to the graphical component they apply to, then can be passed to the containing window, that window's containing window, and so on. In Java 1.1, event processing is much more flexible; a component can specify which events get delivered and which object or objects receive the event report.

10.1 Handling Events in Java 1.02

In Java 1.02, events are initially sent to the `handleEvent` method of the top-most graphical component that the event applies to. This is usually the top-most component under the mouse. If `handleEvent` returns `true`, processing of that event is terminated. If `false` is returned, the event location coordinates are translated to the enclosing window's frame of reference, and then the event is passed to that window's event-handling methods. The built-in version of `handleEvent` returns `false`, so by default events are passed up the containment hierarchy to the outermost window. This gives you the option of having each component handle its own events or performing the event handling for all nested components in the window that holds them. However, this also means that a window has no way to guarantee that it gets events reported to it; components inside the window can ignore events and return `true` without the containing window ever knowing about it.

Core Approach

Return `true` *from event-handling methods if you've finished handling the event. Return* `false` *otherwise.*

It is possible to process all events in the `handleEvent` method. However, such centralized processing can be difficult if there are many different event types of interest, so Java provides a set of helping methods. The default implementation of `handleEvent` checks the `id` field of the `Event` and passes the event and some extra data to methods such as `mouseMove`, `keyDown`, or `lostFocus` as appropriate. These helper methods are where most event handling takes place. If you're interested in how Java decides which helper method to call, Listing 10.1 gives a representative built-in implementation of the `handleEvent` method.

Listing 10.1   The handleEvent method of `java.awt.Component`

```java
public boolean handleEvent(Event event) {
  switch(event.id) {
    case Event.MOUSE_DOWN:
      return(mouseDown(event, event.x, event.y));
    case Event.MOUSE_UP:
      return(mouseUp(event, event.x, event.y));
    ...
    case Event.KEY_PRESS:
    case Event.KEY_ACTION:
      return(keyDown(event, event.key));
    ...
    default: return(false);
  }
}
```

Decentralizing event processing by using these helping methods generally simplifies things, and it is usually best to handle events in helper methods whenever such methods are available. Unfortunately, not all events have such helping methods, so decentralized processing is not always possible.

Core Approach

Whenever possible, override the event-handling helper methods such as `mouseDown`, `keyDown`, `gotFocus`, *and* `action`, *not* `handleEvent`.

As an example, consider Listing 10.2, which creates a `Frame` with five nested windows. Each of these inner windows is a `MouseDownPanel`, which prints out the location of all mouse clicks, returning `false` so that the containing window gets the event as well. The processing is done in the `mouseDown` method, as shown in Listing 10.3. The `Frame` itself overrides the `handleEvent` method in order to accept quit requests, because there is no corresponding helper method for `WINDOW_DESTROY`. The result is shown in Figure 10–1. When the mouse is clicked at the location shown, the output shown in Figure 10–2 is generated. Note two things about these results. First, the innermost windows get the events first. Second, the coordinates of the click are printed with respect to each window's top-left corner, so are different in each case.

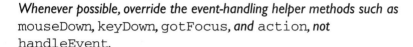

Listing 10.2 `MouseDownFrame.java`

```java
import java.awt.*;

/** A window that contains five nested MouseDownPanel's.
 *  Each of these report the position of mouse clicks
 *  then pass the event on to the enclosing window.
 */

public class MouseDownFrame extends Frame {
  public static void main(String[] args) {
    new MouseDownFrame();
  }
```

continued

Listing 10.2 MouseDownFrame.java (continued)

```
public MouseDownFrame() {
  super("MouseDownFrame");
  MouseDownPanel inner = null, outer=null;
  int minSize = 100, size = 0, nestingLevel = 5;
  Color[] colors = { Color.black, Color.darkGray,
                     Color.gray, Color.lightGray,
                     Color.white };
  String[] names = {"Black", "Dark gray", "Gray",
                    "Light gray", "White" };
  for(int i=0; i<nestingLevel; i++) {
    size = size + minSize;
    outer = new MouseDownPanel(names[i], colors[i]);
    outer.resize(size, size);
    if (inner != null) {
      outer.add(inner);
      inner.move(minSize/2, minSize/2);
    }
    inner = outer;
  }
  resize(size, size);
  add("Center", outer);
  show();
}

public boolean handleEvent(Event event) {
  if (event.id == Event.MOUSE_DOWN) {
    System.out.println("Frame: mouse clicked at (" +
                       event.x + "," + event.y +
                       ").");
    return(true);
  } else if (event.id == Event.WINDOW_DESTROY)
    System.exit(0);
  return(super.handleEvent(event));
}
}
```

Listing 10.3   `MouseDownPanel.java`

```
import java.awt.*;

/** A custom Panel (borderless window) that
 *  reports where the mouse was clicked.
 */

public class MouseDownPanel extends Panel {
  private String name;

  public MouseDownPanel(String name, Color bgColor) {
    setBackground(bgColor);
    this.name = name;
    setLayout(null);
  }

  public boolean mouseDown(Event event, int x, int y) {
    System.out.println(name + ": mouse clicked at (" +
                       x + "," + y + ").");
    return(false); // Pass event to  containing window
  }
}
```

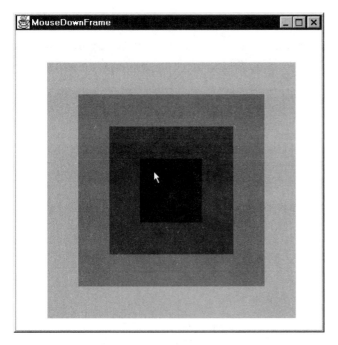

Figure 10–1   A `Frame` with nested `MouseDownPanel`s.

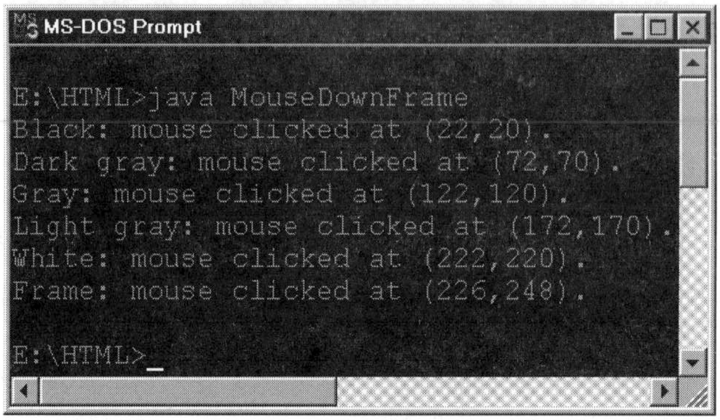

Figure 10–2   Events can be propagated up the window containment hierarchy.

The Event Class

The event-handling methods (handleEvent, mouseDown, keyDown, and so forth) each take an Event as an argument. The Event class contains the following fields:

public Object arg
This is an arbitrary argument associated with the event. It is most often used with action events; for instance, for button action events this field contains the button's label.

public int clickCount
For mouse button events this contains the number of clicks (single, double, triple, and so on).

public int id
This returns the event type. It will be equal to one of the following static variables in the Event class: ACTION_EVENT, GOT_FOCUS, KEY_ACTION, KEY_ACTION_RELEASE, KEY_PRESS, KEY_RELEASE, LIST_DESELECT, LIST_SELECT, LOST_FOCUS, MOUSE_DOWN, MOUSE_DRAG, MOUSE_ENTER, MOUSE_EXIT, MOUSE_MOVE, MOUSE_UP, SCROLL_ABSOLUTE, SCROLL_LINE_DOWN, SCROLL_LINE_UP, SCROLL_PAGE_DOWN,

SCROLL_PAGE_UP, WINDOW_DEICONIFY, WINDOW_DESTROY, WINDOW_EXPOSE, WINDOW_ICONIFY, or WINDOW_MOVED. For more details, see Section 10.3 (Java 1.02 Event Types).

public int key

If a keystroke generated the event, the key is recorded here. See Listing 10.12 (Whiteboard.java) for an example of its use. Non-ASCII keys can be detected by comparison to the following static variables: DOWN, END, F1, F2, F3, F4, F5, F6, F7, F8, F9, F10, F11, F12, HOME, LEFT, PGDN, PGUP, RIGHT, and UP. See the functionKeyName method of Listing 10.7 (EventPanel.java) for an example.

public int modifiers

This field describes the modifier keys that were down when a key or mouse event was generated. The value is a combination of the following static variables: ALT_MASK, CTRL_MASK, META_MASK, and SHIFT_MASK. Clicking the secondary or tertiary mouse button results in these fields being set; see the discussion of mouseDown in Section 10.2 (Event-Handling Helper Methods in Java 1.02) for more details. For regular keys, you can also use the controlDown, metaDown, and shiftDown methods.

public long when

This field contains the event's time in the same units as System.currentTimeMillis (i.e., milliseconds since the epoch). It can be turned into a normal date by passing it to the Date constructor.

public int x

This stores the x location of the event, if applicable, in pixels relative to the left side of the component. You can modify the x and y fields by using the translate method if you want to pass the event to another window.

public int y

This stores the y location of the event, if applicable, in pixels relative to the top of the component.

10.2 Event-Handling Helper Methods in Java 1.02

Rather than processing events in `handleEvent`, it is often easier to use the helping methods Java provides for mouse, keyboard, focus, and action events. This section summarizes these methods.

In Java 1.02, the GUI control components (buttons, scrollbars, and the like) are not supposed to receive normal mouse events. Keyboard events are sent only to text components. Most user interface controls get focus events, and some (such as `Button` and `TextField`) get "action" events signifying that the control was acted upon by the user. All components receive the full complement of events in Java 1.1, but if you need to rely on this behavior, you are better off using the 1.1 event model anyhow. You should also avoid relying on GUI controls *not* getting mouse events, even though they are not supposed to. For instance, Mac implementations usually send extra mouse events to GUI controls in 1.02, and several Windows and Unix implementations occasionally send extras (e.g., to `Scrollbar`). So it is most common to use the mouse event helper methods for regular windows, not for GUI "widgets."

Mouse Events

The following methods are called when the user moves or clicks the mouse. Note that there is no `getMousePosition` method; if you need to know where the mouse pointer is, you have to record it in the methods described next. Also, there is no `setMousePosition` method; Java has no method to warp the cursor position or to prevent it from being moved.

public boolean mouseEnter(Event event, int x, int y)

This method is called when the cursor first moves over a window or a window pops up in a location containing the cursor. The `Event` is often ignored; in many cases, the x and y values are the only important parameters. However, if events for sub-components are being processed in an enclosing window, you will need the value of `event.target` to determine which `Object` originally got the mouse click. Note that if the cursor is moved quickly into a window, the x and y locations might not be precisely on the border of the component, but could be a number of pixels inside. If you drag the mouse into a window with a button already down, `mouseEnter` may or may not be called prior to release of the mouse button, depending on the operating system. For instance, it typically is called immediately on Unix systems, and not called until the mouse is released on Windows or MacOS.

Because Java 1.02 does not have per-window cursors, mouseEnter is often used to change the cursor, with mouseExit used to reset it if there are multiple Java windows with different cursors. However, set-Cursor is only defined for frames, so nested windows in applets and applications need to call getParent repeatedly until they find the enclosing Frame. To illustrate this, Listing 10.4 presents a Cursor-Canvas window that defines a getFrame method that uses this approach. The CursorCanvas is initialized with a width, height, cursor, and background color. This cursor is used on mouseEnter, and the original cursor is used on mouseExit. Listings 10.5 and 10.6 show a simple applet that uses two of these windows, specifying a "busy cursor" for the left one, and a "crosshair cursor" for the right one. The result is shown in Figure 10–3. For more information on cursors in Java 1.02, see the discussion of Frame in Chapter 11, "Windows."

Listing 10.4   CursorCanvas.java

```
import java.awt.*;

/** A Canvas (borderless window that can't hold
 *  other graphical components) that lets you
 *  specify what cursor should be used when
 *  the mouse is inside it.
 */

public class CursorCanvas extends Canvas {
  private int cursor, origCursor = Frame.DEFAULT_CURSOR;
  private Frame frame = null;

  /** Build a Canvas, recording cursor of interest. */

  public CursorCanvas(int width, int height,
                      int cursor, Color bgColor) {
    resize(width, height);
    setBackground(bgColor);
    this.cursor = cursor;
  }
```
continued

Listing 10.4   `CursorCanvas.java` (continued)

```java
/** When mouse enters the Canvas, set cursor. */

public boolean mouseEnter(Event event, int x, int y) {
  origCursor = getCursor();
  setCursor(cursor);
  return(false);
}

/** When mouse leaves, reset cursor to whatever
 *  it was when mouse entered.
 */

public boolean mouseExit(Event event, int x, int y) {
  setCursor(origCursor);
  return(false);
}

private int getCursor() {
  if (getFrame() != null)
    return(frame.getCursorType());
  else
    return Frame.DEFAULT_CURSOR;
}

private void setCursor(int cursor) {
  if (getFrame() != null)
    frame.setCursor(cursor);
}

// Find the Frame holding the Canvas. Keep looking
// at the enclosing window until you find a Frame.
// This works in both applets and applications.

private Frame getFrame() {
  if (frame == null) {
    Container containingWin = getParent();
    while (containingWin != null) {
      if (containingWin instanceof Frame) {
        frame = (Frame)containingWin;
        break;
      } else
        containingWin = containingWin.getParent();
    }
  }
  return(frame);
}
}
```

Listing 10.5   CursorTest.java

```java
import java.applet.Applet;
import java.awt.*;

/** Put two canvases with custom cursors side by side. */

public class CursorTest extends Applet {
  public void init() {
    int width = size().width*4/10;
    int height = size().height*9/10;
    setBackground(Color.lightGray);
    add(new CursorCanvas(width, height,
                         Frame.WAIT_CURSOR,
                         Color.white));
    add(new CursorCanvas(width, height,
                         Frame.CROSSHAIR_CURSOR,
                         Color.white));
  }
}
```

Listing 10.6   CursorTest.html

```html
<!DOCTYPE HTML PUBLIC "-//W3C//DTD HTML 3.2//EN">
<HTML>
<HEAD>
  <TITLE>CursorTest</TITLE>
</HEAD>

<BODY BGCOLOR="WHITE">
<H1>CursorTest</H1>
<P>
<APPLET CODE="CursorTest.class" WIDTH=300 HEIGHT=200>
  <B>Ha. You think pure HTML can change cursors?</B>
</APPLET>

</BODY>
</HTML>
```

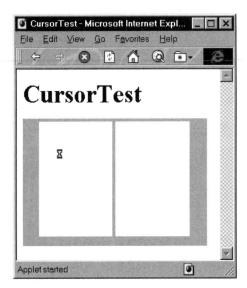

Figure 10–3   The `mouseEnter` and `mouseExit` methods can be used to implement per-window cursors.

public boolean mouseExit(Event event, int x, int y)

This method is called when the cursor moves off a window. If you move the mouse quickly off of the window, the x and y values may be outside the window borders. They will still be relative to the top-left corner of the component, but could be negative (mouse exited to left/top) or positive but greater than the width/height of the component (mouse exited to right/bottom). Also, `mouseExit` may not necessarily be the last mouse event received when you move the mouse off a window. For instance, on Windows 95/NT, `mouseExit` is called when the user drags the mouse off the window, but `mouseDrag` events continue to be reported until the mouse is released.

public boolean mouseDown(Event event, int x, int y)

The `mouseDown` method is called when any mouse button is pressed. Java runs on systems that use a 1-button mouse (MacOS), a 2-button mouse (Windows), or a 3-button mouse (Unix), so doesn't have separate events for selections with the primary mouse button, the secondary button, and so on. However, on a multimouse-button system, `event.modifiers` will be equal to `Event.ALT_MASK` for a middle click and equal to `Event.META_MASK` for a right (secondary button) click. To allow for multiple modifiers, you generally just check that the flag is set, rather than checking if

```
(event.modifiers == Event.ALT_MASK)
```

or if

```
(event.modifiers == Event.META_MASK)
```

Thus, to check for a middle click, you would check

```
((event.modifiers & Event.ALT_MASK) != 0)
```

Multiple clicks can be detected by checking the event's `clickCount` field. The determination of what constitutes a double click versus what should be interpreted as two consecutive single clicks is made by the operating system (often based on user settings), not by Java. However, all events have a `when` field, so you could determine this yourself if you really wanted to. Note that for a double click, `mouseDown` will be called *twice*, first with `event.clickCount` equal to 1, then with `event.clickCount` equal to 2. This is a standard procedure so that the system doesn't have to wait for the multiclick time to expire before reporting the first click, but catches many first-time users off guard. Triple and quadruple clicks are handled similarly. Note that you cannot rely on getting a `mouseUp` for every `mouseDown`, because on some operating systems (Unix, MacOS), if you drag the mouse off a window, `mouseUp` is never called.

See the `EventPanel` of Listing 10.7 and Figure 10–4 for an example of differentiating buttons and numbers of clicks.

public boolean mouseUp(Event event, int x, int y)

This is called when the mouse button is released. In principle, buttons can be distinguished in the same manner as with `mouseDown`. However, in practice you cannot determine which button was released on Windows 95 or Windows NT. In Netscape (versions 2, 3, and 4), Internet Explorer 3, and appletviewer, the `modifiers` field is left unset on `mouseUp` in Windows 95, regardless of which button was pressed. It is reported properly on Unix. Macintosh systems have only a single mouse button.

Core Warning

On Windows 95/NT, most Java implementations do not correctly set the event `modifiers` *field in* `mouseUp`.

Note that you cannot rely on `mouseDown` preceding each `mouseUp`. For instance, on Unix and MacOS, if you drag the mouse into the win-

dow, you get a mouseUp when the mouse is released. No mouseUp is
reported in such a case in Windows 95/NT. Also, clickCount will *not*
generally be greater than 1, even if it was 2 or more during the corresponding mouseDown.

public boolean mouseMove(Event event, int x, int y)

This is called when the mouse is moved while no button is down. Many
Java systems on MacOS, including Netscape 2 and 3, suffer from a bug
whereby mouseMove gets continually reported, even when the mouse
is not moving.

public boolean mouseDrag(Event event, int x, int y)

This is called when the mouse is moved while a button is down. Note
that on Unix it is possible to have mouseDrag without first getting
mouseDown if the mouse button is already depressed when the pointer
is dragged into the window. On Windows 95/NT and MacOS, no mouse
events are reported in such a case until you release the button. On Windows 95/NT and some Unix/X implementations, the x and y locations
may be outside the Java window, because if the user drags the mouse off
the screen, mouseDrag continues to be called until the mouse button
is released.

Keyboard Events

The following methods are called when the user types a key when the component has the input focus. Note that in Java 1.1, a window has to explicitly
request the input focus in order to get keystroke events. In Java 1.02, the
window under the mouse gets these events automatically unless a text-oriented component (e.g., a textfield) already has the focus, or unless another
window has explicitly taken it.

public boolean keyDown(Event event, int key)

The keyDown method is called when a key is pressed while the mouse
pointer is over the window. Note that the key is an int, not a char. To
handle the event, you should first distinguish a regular key (event.id
== Event.KEY_PRESS) from a function key (event.id ==
Event.KEY_ACTION). A regular key can be turned into a String by
the String.valueOf((char)key). Function keys can be differ-
entiated by comparison to the constants Event.DOWN, Event.END,
Event.F1, Event.F2, Event.F3, Event.F4, Event.F5,

`Event.F6`, `Event.F7`, `Event.F8`, `Event.F9`, `Event.HOME`, `Event.LEFT`, `Event.PGDN`, `Event.PGUP`, `Event.RIGHT`, and `Event.UP`. See the `EventPanel` of Listing 10.7 and Figure 10–4 for an example.

public boolean keyUp(Event event, int key)
This is called when a key is released. The key can be processed in the same manner as with `keyDown`.

Focus Events

These methods are called when a component gets the input focus. This could be caused by mouse movement, or by keyboard actions like hitting TAB.

public boolean gotFocus(Event event, Object ignore)
This is called when the component gets the input focus. You can ask for the input focus by calling `requestFocus`, which changes the focus but not the mouse cursor location. The second argument is always `null`.

public boolean lostFocus(Event event, Object ignore)
This is called when the component loses the input focus. The second argument is always `null`.

Action Events

public boolean action(Event event, Object object)
The `action` method is called when a GUI control is acted upon. For instance, `action` is called when a button is clicked or ENTER is hit while a button has the input focus, when ENTER is hit in a textfield, and so forth. If processing is done in an enclosing window, the `target` field of the event can be used to determine which component was acted upon, plus the second argument contains related information. For instance, if you click on a `Button`, the second argument to `action` contains the button's label. For more details, see Chapter 13, "Graphical User Interface Controls."

An Event Recorder Using Java 1.02

To illustrate the helping methods used in Java 1.02 (and still available in Java 1.1), Listing 10.7 shows an `EventPanel` class. This creates a simple window that monitors the type and location of the simple mouse and keyboard events. If this window is created with an empty constructor, the results are printed to System.out. If a TextArea is supplied, results are displayed there. The use of the Panel and TextArea classes is discussed in Chapter 11, "Windows" and Chapter 13, "Graphical User Interface Controls." For now, however, the point is that a Panel is a simple window, TextArea can be used to display scrolling text, and both can be used in either applets or applications. For instance, Listing 10.8 shows an applet that uses the BorderLayout layout manager (Section 12.2) to place a TextArea at the right of the window and an EventPanel at the left. The associated HTML document is shown in Listing 10.9, with the result on Windows 95 shown in Figure 10–4. Notice that the background color of the EventPanel is different than the Web page background. This is a good practice when first experimenting with event handling, because it makes it easy to determine when the mouse enters and leaves the window.

Listing 10.7   EventPanel.java

```java
import java.awt.*;

/** A Panel that reports mouse, keyboard and focus
 *  events to a TextArea (if available) or to
 *  standard output (if no TextArea is available).
 */

public class EventPanel extends Panel {

  /** The TextArea messages can be reported in. */

  protected TextArea reportArea = null;

  /** Build EventPanel; reports get sent to TextArea. */

  public EventPanel(TextArea reportArea) {
    this.reportArea = reportArea;
  }

  /** Build EventPanel; reports get printed. */

  public EventPanel() {}

  /** Report that mouse was pressed. */
```

Listing 10.7 `EventPanel.java` **(continued)**

```java
public boolean mouseDown(Event event, int x, int y) {
  return(mouseClick("mouseDown", event, x, y));
}

/** Report that mouse was released. */

public boolean mouseUp(Event event, int x, int y) {
  return(mouseClick("mouseUp", event, x, y));
}

/** Determine button and number of clicks. */

protected boolean mouseClick(String type, Event event,
                             int x, int y) {
  String description = type + "[";
  if ((event.modifiers & Event.ALT_MASK) != 0)
    description = description + "middle, ";
  else if ((event.modifiers & Event.META_MASK) != 0)
    description = description + "right, ";
  else
    description = description + "left, ";
  if (event.clickCount > 1)
    description = description + event.clickCount + "]";
  else
    description = description + "single]";
  return(report(description, x, y));
}

/** Report that mouse was moved (no buttons down). */

public boolean mouseMove(Event event, int x, int y) {
  return(report("mouseMove", x, y));
}

/** Report that mouse was moved (with button down). */

public boolean mouseDrag(Event event, int x, int y) {
  return(report("mouseDrag", x, y));
}

/** Report that mouse entered panel. */

public boolean mouseEnter(Event event, int x, int y) {
  return(report("mouseEnter", x, y));
}
```

continued

Listing 10.7   `EventPanel.java` (continued)

```
/** Report that mouse left panel. */

public boolean mouseExit(Event event, int x, int y) {
  return(report("mouseExit", x, y));
}

/** Report that panel got input focus. */

public boolean gotFocus(Event event, Object ignore) {
  return(report("gotFocus", event.x, event.y));
}

/** Report that panel lost input focus. */

public boolean lostFocus(Event event, Object ignore) {
  return(report("lostFocus", event.x, event.y));
}

/** Report that a key was pressed. */

public boolean keyDown(Event event, int key) {
  return(keyStroke("keyDown", event, key));
}

/** Report that a key was released. */

public boolean keyUp(Event event, int key) {
  return(keyStroke("keyUp", event, key));
}

/** Separate regular keys from function keys. */

protected boolean keyStroke(String type,
                            Event event, int key) {
  String description = ": " + type;
  if (event.id == Event.KEY_ACTION ||
      event.id == Event.KEY_ACTION_RELEASE)
    description = functionKeyName(key) + description;
  else
    description = keyName(key) + description;
  return(report(description, event.x, event.y));
}
```

Listing 10.7   `EventPanel.java`   **(continued)**

```java
/** Give name of function-key code. */

protected String functionKeyName(int key) {
  switch(key) {
    case Event.DOWN: return("Down Arrow");
    case Event.END: return("END");
    case Event.F1: return("F1");
    case Event.F2: return("F2");
    case Event.F3: return("F3");
    case Event.F4: return("F4");
    case Event.F5: return("F5");
    case Event.F6: return("F6");
    case Event.F7: return("F7");
    case Event.F8: return("F8");
    case Event.F9: return("F9");
    case Event.HOME: return("HOME");
    case Event.LEFT: return("Left Arrow");
    case Event.PGDN: return("Page Down");
    case Event.PGUP: return("Page Up");
    case Event.RIGHT: return("Right Arrow");
    case Event.UP: return("Up Arrow");
    default: return("Unknown Function Key");
  }
}

/** Give name of normal-key code. */

protected String keyName(int key) {
  switch(key) {
    case 8: return("BACKSPACE");
    case 9: return("TAB");
    case 10: return("LF");
    case 13: return("CR");
    case 27: return("ESCAPE");
    case 32: return("SPACE");
    case 127: return("DELETE");
  }
  if (key<33)
    return("Control-" +
           String.valueOf((char)(64+key)));
  else
    return(String.valueOf((char)key));
}
```

continued

Listing 10.7 `EventPanel.java` (continued)

```java
/** Report on event and return true. */

protected boolean report(String methodName,
                         int x, int y) {
  String message = methodName + "("
                   + x + "," + y + ").\n";
  if (reportArea != null)
    reportArea.appendText(message);
  else
    System.out.print(message);
  return(true);
}
}
```

Listing 10.8 `Events.java`

```java
import java.applet.Applet;
import java.awt.*;

/** Create an EventPanel and a TextArea to get
 *  the EventPanel's reports.
 */

public class Events extends Applet {
  public void init() {
    setBackground(Color.lightGray);
    setLayout(new BorderLayout());
    TextArea reportArea = new TextArea(20, 30);
    reportArea.setEditable(false);
    add("East", reportArea);
    add("Center", new EventPanel(reportArea));
  }
}
```

Listing 10.9   Events.html

```
<!DOCTYPE HTML PUBLIC "-//W3C//DTD HTML 3.2//EN">
<HTML>
<HEAD>
  <TITLE>Mouse and Keyboard Events in Java 1.02</TITLE>
</HEAD>

<BODY BGCOLOR="WHITE">
<H1>Mouse and Keyboard Events in Java 1.02</H1>
Hit any key or move, click, or drag the mouse in the
lefthand window below.

<APPLET CODE="Events.class" WIDTH=700 HEIGHT=500>
  <B>Get a clue^H^H^H^H^H^HJava.</B>
</APPLET>

</BODY>

</HTML>
```

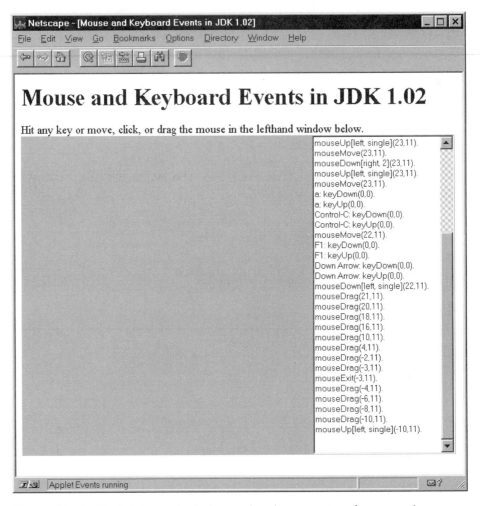

Figure 10–4   The helping methods decentralize the processing of mouse and keyboard events.

10.3 Java 1.02 Event Types

Whenever possible, it is best to process events in the helping methods discussed in Section 10.2. However, many events have no such helping methods, and must be processed in `handleEvent`. This requires particular care, because mistakes can have serious consequences. If you goof in `mouseUp`, you might prevent mouse release events from propagating. But if you goof in handleEvent, you can stop *all* event processing. Consequently, whenever you are finished processing specific events of interest, you should call super.handleEvent so that the remaining events get processed normally. This approach was used in Listings 9.8 (JavaJump2.java), 9.9 (GraphicsUtilTest.java), 9.15 (JavaMan3.java), and 10.2 (MouseDownFrame.java), and a generic version is illustrated as follows:

```java
public boolean handleEvent(Event event) {
  switch(event.id) {
    case Event.TYPE1:
      doType1Action();
      return(true);
    case Event.TYPE2:
      doType2Action();
      return(true);
    ...
    default: return(super.handleEvent(event));
  }
}
```

Core Approach

If you override handleEvent, *be sure to call* super.handleEvent *at the end of the method.*

The following sections list the standard event types. All are integers declared as static final fields in the Event class.

ACTION_EVENT

This event is generated when actions are performed on user interface controls. For instance, pressing buttons, selecting or deselecting checkboxes, or double clicking combo-box entries generates an Event.ACTION_EVENT. In most cases, this is handled in action, not directly in handleEvent.

GOT_FOCUS

The Event.GOT_FOCUS event is generated when an element gains the input focus. This is one of the few events that does not require the mouse to be over the component. It is usually handled in the lostFocus helper method, not directly in handleEvent.

KEY_PRESS, KEY_ACTION

These two events are generated when a regular key or function key is pressed. They are usually handled in `keyDown`.

KEY_RELEASE, KEY_ACTION_RELEASE

These two events are generated when a regular key or function key is released. They are usually handled in `keyUp`.

LIST_SELECT, LIST_DESELECT

These two events are generated when a `List` entry (i.e., an entry in a drop down list box or combo-box) is selected or deselected. There is no helping method for these events.

LOAD_FILE, SAVE_FILE

These events are intended to be used when the user selects a filename from a file selection dialog. They are currently ignored.

LOST_FOCUS

The `Event.LOST_FOCUS` event is generated when an element loses the input focus. As with `GOT_FOCUS`, this event does not require the mouse to be over the component. It is usually handled in the `gotFocus` helper method, not directly in `handleEvent`.

MOUSE_DOWN

This event is generated when any mouse button is pressed. The various buttons can be distinguished via the `modifiers` field of the event, and multiple clicks can be detected via the `clickCount` field. This event is typically handled in `mouseDown`.

MOUSE_DRAG

`Event.MOUSE_DRAG` is generated when the mouse is moved while any button is held down. It is generally handled in `mouseDrag`.

MOUSE_ENTER

This event is generated when the mouse first enters a window. It is normally processed in `mouseEnter`.

MOUSE_EXIT

This event is generated when the mouse exits a window. It is normally processed in `mouseExit`.

MOUSE_MOVE

`Event.MOUSE_MOVE` is generated when the mouse is moved while all buttons are up. It is generally handled in `mouseMove`.

MOUSE_UP

This event is generated when a mouse button is released. It is typically processed in the `mouseUp` method.

SCROLL_ABSOLUTE, SCROLL_LINE_UP, SCROLL_LINE_DOWN, SCROLL_PAGE_UP, SCROLL_PAGE_DOWN

These events are generated when a scrollbar "thumb" is dragged (`SCROLL_ABSOLUTE`), when the arrows at the top/left (`SCROLL_LINE_UP`) or bottom/right (`SCROLL_LINE_DOWN`) are selected, or when the trough above/left (`SCROLL_PAGE_UP`) or below/right (`SCROLL_PAGE_DOWN`) is clicked. There are no helping methods for these events.

WINDOW_ICONIFY, WINDOW_DEICONIFY

These events are generated when a window is iconified (minimized) or restored. There are no helping methods for these events.

WINDOW_DESTROY

This event is generated when the user tries to quit a window. For instance, this event will be generated by clicking on the X at the top right corner of a window in Windows 95, clicking on the square button in the top left corner of a window in MacOS, or choosing "Quit" from the right-mouse menu on window borders in Unix/X. Due to a questionable design decision, a `Frame` will ignore this event by default, so if you create a `Frame` you have to explicitly catch the event or your window cannot be closed. `Event.WINDOW_DESTROY` has no associated helping method.

WINDOW_EXPOSE

This event is generated when all or part of a window is exposed after being covered. There is no corresponding helping method.

WINDOW_MOVED

This event is generated when the window is moved. There is no associated helping method.

10.4 Performing Graphics Operations in Event-Handling Methods

When you override the `paint` method, you are automatically supplied a `Graphics` object to use for drawing. To draw in event-handling methods, however, you need to call `getGraphics` to get the current `Graphics` object. However, this drawing will not persist beyond the next invocation of `paint`. "Permanent" drawing can be done by having these helping methods set some information known to `paint`, then calling `repaint`. This can be done by changing nongraphic data that `paint` relies on (such as the positions of various objects), or by drawing into an off-screen pixmap that `paint` uses. These approaches are discussed in Chapter 14, "Concurrent Programming Using Java Threads." The `repaint` method schedules a call to `update`, whose default implementation clears the screen and calls `paint`. There are three things to note about `repaint`. First, `repaint` returns immediately: It tells the AWT thread to schedule a call to `update`, but does not wait for `update` to actually finish. Second, the calls do not queue, but simply set a flag telling the system that repainting is necessary. For instance, suppose that `mouseDown` stores the location of the mouse click, then calls `repaint` so that a circle can be drawn at that location. Now suppose that you click the mouse five times before the system has a chance to redraw the screen. In such a case, the screen will get redrawn once, not five times. Third, although `repaint` is often called with no arguments, it can also be called as `repaint(x, y, width, height)`, specifying the portion of the screen that should be repainted. In such a case, Java calls `update` and `paint` with the appropriate clipping region of the `Graphics` object specified.

To obtain smooth performance, it is important that the event-handling routines and `paint` execute very quickly. If they have significant processing to do, it should be spun off to a separate thread so that the main graphics thread does not have long pauses. If `mouseDown`, for instance, takes five seconds to execute, then the rest of the interface will not respond to any events for five seconds. Similarly, if `paint` takes 10 seconds, no GUI controls will respond for 10 seconds. For more information on threads, see Chapter 14, "Concurrent Programming Using Java Threads."

Core Performance Tip

If event-handling routines need to perform time-consuming actions, they should execute such actions in a separate thread.

Example: Whiteboard Applet

Listings 10.10 and 10.11 show an applet that uses the mouse-event methods to let the user create freehand diagrams. After that, we'll show how to extend it to accept typed text by overriding `keyDown`. The idea is to record the initial x and y position whenever the user presses the mouse (`mouseDown`) and then to connect line segments starting from that position as the pointer moves (`mouseDrag`). However, the initial position should also be set when the pointer enters the applet, because it is possible to get a `mouseDrag` without a corresponding `mouseDown` if the mouse button is already depressed as the mouse is dragged onto the applet. Figure 10–5 shows an attempt to draw a map indicating how to find the Johns Hopkins University Applied Physics Laboratory, and where to park once there.

Listing 10.10 `SimpleWhiteboard.java`

```java
import java.applet.Applet;
import java.awt.*;

/** An applet that lets you perform freehand drawing. */

public class SimpleWhiteboard extends Applet {
  protected int lastX=0, lastY=0;

  public void init() {
    setBackground(Color.white);
  }

  public boolean mouseEnter(Event e, int x, int y) {
    return(record(x, y));
  }

  public boolean mouseDown(Event e, int x, int y) {
    return(record(x, y));
  }
```

continued

Listing 10.10 `SimpleWhiteboard.java` (continued)

```java
public boolean mouseDrag(Event e, int x, int y) {
  getGraphics().drawLine(lastX, lastY, x, y);
  return(record(x, y));
}

protected boolean record(int x, int y) {
  lastX = x;
  lastY = y;
  return(true);
}

)
```

Listing 10.11 `SimpleWhiteboard.html`

```html
<!DOCTYPE HTML PUBLIC "-//W3C//DTD HTML 3.2//EN">
<HTML>
<HEAD>
  <TITLE>The Simple Whiteboard Applet</TITLE>
</HEAD>

<BODY>
<H1>The Simple Whiteboard Applet</H1>

<TABLE BORDER=5 CELLPADDING=0>
  <TR>
    <TD BGCOLOR="WHITE">
      <APPLET CODE="SimpleWhiteboard.class"
              WIDTH=300 HEIGHT=200>
        <B>Sorry, Java is required.</B>
      </APPLET>
</TABLE>

</BODY>
</HTML>
```

Figure 10–5 A simple whiteboard; drawing is performed when the mouse is dragged.

A Better Whiteboard

Next, we add the ability to insert typed text (Listing 10.12). Whenever a key is hit, `keyDown` converts the `int` to a `String`, draws the `String` at the current location, then the current location is shifted to the right based on the width of the `String` in the current font. Note that, because inherited methods override methods in the parent classes, `init` in `Whiteboard` has to call `super.init` in order to get the original `init` to run. Figure 10–6 shows the result.

Listing 10.12 Whiteboard.java

```java
import java.applet.Applet;
import java.awt.*;

/** A better whiteboard that lets you enter
 *  text in addition to freehand drawing.
 */

public class Whiteboard extends SimpleWhiteboard {
  private FontMetrics fm;

  public void init() {
    super.init();
    Font font = new Font("Helvetica", Font.BOLD, 20);
    setFont(font);
    fm = getFontMetrics(font);
  }

  public boolean keyDown(Event e, int key) {
    String s = String.valueOf((char)key);
    getGraphics().drawString(s, lastX, lastY);
    return(record(lastX + fm.stringWidth(s), lastY));
  }
}
```

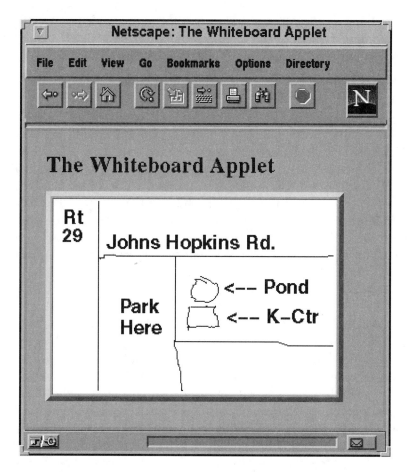

Figure 10-6   A better whiteboard; text is drawn when keys are typed.

Now, this whiteboard is not too bad for such a small amount of code, but it is lacking in several ways. First of all, there are no options for choosing colors or fonts, or for specifying the type of drawing operation (freehand, straight lines, circles, rectangles, and so forth). Chapter 13, "Graphical User Interface Controls" will cover the combo-boxes, pulldown menus, and other GUI widgets needed to create such an interface. Secondly, because drawing is done directly to the window, it is transient. If another window is moved over the browser and then removed, the drawing is lost. In Chapter 14, "Concurrent Programming Using Java Threads," we will discuss *double buffering*, a technique for drawing into off-screen arrays that overcomes this problem. Finally, for whiteboards to be most useful they should be shareable. We will discuss methods for making a server that would permit this in Chapter 15, "Client-Server Programming in Java."

10.5 Handling Events in Java 1.1

Version 1.1 brought significant improvements in the way events are processed. Rather than having all events propagate up the tree of nested components, you can choose which events get sent, and can specify which object or objects receive the events. This "delegation" model makes event handling much more efficient, because the flood of 1.02 events can be slowed to a trickle if only a few events are of particular interest. Furthermore, because any object can receive events (not just graphical components as in 1.02), it is straightforward to separate the GUI from the event-handling modules. This simplifies design, and allows the same interface to be reused multiple places with different behaviors. Also, in Java 1.02, event-handling methods had to know enough of the overall picture to know whether the event was completely processed (and thus `true` should be returned), or if containing windows still needed access to it (and thus `false` should be returned). With the 1.1 model, event handlers simply do whatever local action they need to take without having to know the global picture. Finally, 1.1 adds the option to consume events before they are noticed by the native window system object ("peer"). This supports capabilities not possible in 1.02, such as textfields that ignore nonnumeric keystrokes, buttons that can only be depressed in certain situations, multiple-selection combo-boxes that have restrictions on which items can be selected together, and so forth. The main disadvantage of the 1.1 model is its lack of support in current browsers. Netscape Communicator 4.01 does not support the 1.1 event model; hopefully Netscape 4.02 and Internet Explorer 4.0 will. Hopefully, they both will support it in an incremental release such as 4.1. In the meantime, however, use of 1.1 event handling is restricted to applications and to applets that will be run in HotJava or appletviewer.

Listeners and Adapters

AWT events in Java 1.1 are grouped into categories such as key events, mouse events, action events, and the like. Each category of events can be processed by an associated type of *listener*: a class with methods specific to that category of event. This involves two steps: making the listener and registering it with the component.

Make an EventListener

The actual listener object can be defined by creating an object that implements the *Type*Listener interface where *Type* is one of the eleven AWT event types such as Action, Adjustment, Key, Mouse, and the like. For example:

```
public class MyActionListener implements ActionListener {
    public void actionPerformed(ActionEvent event) {
        ...
    }
}
```

or

```
public class MyKeyListener implements KeyListener {
    public void keyPressed(KeyEvent event) { ... }
    public void keyReleased(KeyEvent event) { ... }
    public void keyTyped(KeyEvent event) { ... }
}
```

If this interface contains more than one method, then Java also supplies a *Type*Adapter class with empty implementations of all the methods. This lets you override one of the methods while ignoring the others. For instance:

```
public void AnotherKeyListener extends KeyAdapter {
    public void keyTyped(KeyEvent event) { ... }
    // ignore keyPressed and keyReleased
}
```

Associate the Listener with the Component

A listener is registered with a component by calling add*Type*Listener(*type*Listener). For instance, to handle keyboard events you would call addKeyboardListener with a KeyboardListener as an argument. Similarly, to handle mouse events you would call addMouseListener with a MouseListener as an argument. A component can register more than one listener for the same event, and the same listener can process events from more than one component. For backwards compatibility, events are propagated up the tree in the Java 1.02 style *if and only if* no listeners are registered with the component.

For example, the following simplified example uses a listener that directly implements the ActionListener interface:

```
import java.applet.Applet;
import java.awt.*;
import java.awt.event.*;

class MyActionListener implements ActionListener {
  public void actionPerformed(ActionEvent event) {
    doSomeAction();
  }
}

public class MyApplet extends Applet {
  public void init() {
    Button b1 = new Button("Button 1");
    b1.addActionListener(new MyActionListener());
    ...
  }
  ...
}
```

An advantage of using the interface approach is that an existing class can become a listener. For instance, a `Frame` could implement *Xxx*`Listener`, then call `add`*Xxx*`Listener(this)` on some component. However, an adapter class saves you from implementing all the methods in the interface if you only care about one. The following outlines the use of an adapter class:

```
import java.applet.Applet;
import java.awt.*;
import java.awt.event.*;

class MyMouseListener extends MouseAdapter {
  public void mouseClicked(MouseEvent event) {
    doSomeAction();
  }
}

public class MyApplet extends Applet {
  public void init() {
    addMouseListener(new MyMouseListener());
    ...
  }
  ...
}
```

For a more complete example, Listing 10.13 presents an applet with two equal-sized textfields. The textfields share a common `KeyListener`. When you type in *either* textfield, this listener consumes the event to prevent the keystroke from showing up, then sends a copy to *both* textfields. The effect is identical text in both textfields, regardless of where input is typed. Figure 10–7 shows the result.

Listing 10.13 `Mirror.java`

```java
import java.applet.Applet;
import java.awt.*;
import java.awt.event.*;

/** A listener used to send identical text to
 *  two text areas. Used in the Mirror class below.
 */

class MirrorListener extends KeyAdapter {
  private TextArea area1, area2;

  public MirrorListener(TextArea area1,
                        TextArea area2) {
    this.area1 = area1;
    this.area2 = area2;
  }

  public void keyPressed(KeyEvent event) {
    String key = String.valueOf(event.getKeyChar());
    area1.append(key);
    area2.append(key);
    event.consume();
  }
}

/** An applet that creates two text areas and
 *  attaches the same KeyListener to both.
 */

public class Mirror extends Applet {
  public void init() {
    setLayout(new GridLayout(1, 2));
    TextArea area1 = new TextArea();
    TextArea area2 = new TextArea();
    MirrorListener mirror =
      new MirrorListener(area1, area2);
    area1.addKeyListener(mirror);
    area2.addKeyListener(mirror);
    add(area1);
    add(area2);
  }
}
```

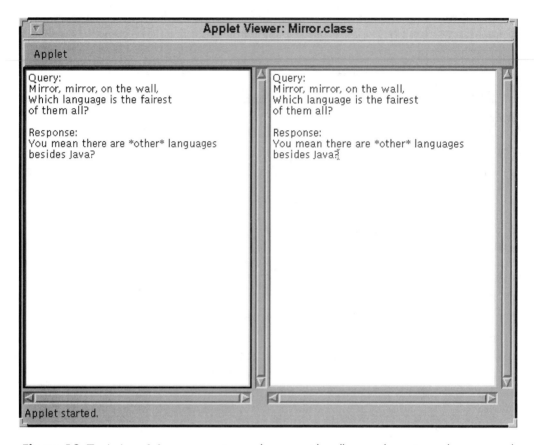

Figure 10-7   In Java 1.1, components can share event handlers, and events can be consumed before being seen by the underlying graphical object.

Inner Classes

Java 1.1 introduced a new capability: inner classes. See `http://java.sun.com/products/jdk/1.1/docs/guide/inner-classes/` for the full specification, but the key points are that they allow you to create *nested* and *anonymous* classes. Nested classes let you create classes that have full access to protected (but not private) data and methods in the enclosing class, as follows:

```
public class Outer {
  protected void foo() { ... }

  class Inner {
    public void bar() {
      doSomethingWith(foo());
    }
  }

  private Inner test = new Inner();
  ...
}
```

Inner could implement an interface or extend an arbitrary superclass, just like a regular class could. If you used the this reference within Inner it would refer to the inner class, but a reference to the outer class could be obtained via Outer.this.

Anonymous classes also let you define and create a class within an expression. To do this, you make what looks like a call to a class constructor, but you include the definition of the class right after the parens, as in the following three examples:

```
SomeType st =
  new SomeType() {
    // Class definition
  };
doSomethingWith(st);

Color someColor = pickColor();
add(new Panel() {
    public Color origColor = someColor;
    public void init() {
      setBackground(origColor);
    }
  });

KeyAdapter myAdapter =
  new KeyAdapter() {
    public void keyPressed(KeyEvent event) {
      // keyPressed definition
    }
  };
addKeyListener(myAdapter);
```

When compiled, each inner class generates a separate class file, even if the class is anonymous. In many cases, the file for the inner class will be a variation of the name of the file for the outer class (e.g., `Outer$1.class`). In many cases, you don't care, but if you move the class files to a different location than the source files, it is easy to overlook the files for the inner classes.

Core Warning

If you move the `.class` _file of a class containing inner classes, don't forget to also move the_ `.class` _files for the inner classes._

Inner classes are convenient for defining listeners. In particular, they let an enclosing window attach listeners to components where the listeners perform graphics operations on the enclosing window, but without the need to make all the needed parameters `public`. Listings 10.14 and 10.15 illustrate this approach by creating a local `MouseAdapter` that calls `getGraphics`; a method not normally available in `MouseAdapter` but that is in the outer `Applet` class. In this particular case, because `getGraphics` is public, a regular class could have been used and the `Applet`'s `Graphics` object obtained via

```
event.getComponent().getGraphics()
```

Even so, using inner classes is a convenience here, and would have been necessary if access to protected resources was required. Figure 10–8 shows the result.

Listing 10.14 `Circles.java`

```java
import java.applet.Applet;
import java.awt.*;
import java.awt.event.*;

/** Draw circles centered where the user clicks. */

public class Circles extends Applet {
  public void init() {
    MouseListener circleListener =
      // An inner class.
      new MouseAdapter() {
        public void mouseClicked(MouseEvent event) {
          getGraphics().fillOval(event.getX()-25,
                                 event.getY()-25,
                                 50, 50);
        }
      };

    // Attach the class just defined to the Applet.
    addMouseListener(circleListener);
  }
}
```

Listing 10.15 `Circles.html`

```html
<!DOCTYPE HTML PUBLIC "-//W3C//DTD HTML 3.2//EN">
<HTML>
<HEAD>
  <TITLE>Using Inner Classes in Event Handling</TITLE>
</HEAD>

<BODY BGCOLOR="WHITE">
<H1>Using Inner Classes in Event Handling</H1>
Click in the applet to draw circles.
<TABLE BORDER=5>
  <TR><TD>
      <APPLET CODE="Circles.class" WIDTH=400 HEIGHT=400>
      </APPLET>
</TABLE>

</BODY>
</HTML>
```

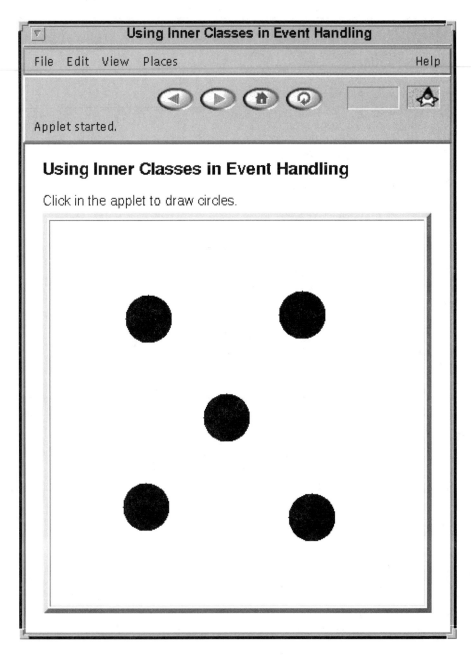

Figure 10–8   Inner classes give listeners access to the fields and methods of the creating class.

Low-Level Event Processing

In addition to the high-level event listeners, Java 1.1 still lets you process events within the component similarly to the way the event-handling helper methods are used in Java 1.02. Each of the 11 AWT event listeners (MouseListener, KeyListener, FocusListener, and so on; see the following section for details) has a corresponding process*Xxx*Event method that can be used to handle events within the component. For instance, to handle mouse button events, override processMouseEvent; for key events, use processKeyEvent; for focus events, use process-FocusEvent. These methods do not return a boolean like their 1.02 counterparts; Java 1.1 has dispensed with the containment model for propagating events. Also, you almost always want to call super.process*Xxx*-Event from within the body of process*Xxx*Event, because it is process*Xxx*Event that calls any attached listeners. If you forget to do this and later come back and add some listeners, they will be ignored. You usually call the superclass version at the end of your method, but if you want the listeners to be activated before your code, you can call it first.

Core Approach

If you override processMouseEvent, *call* super.processMouseEvent *from within the method. Similarly, if you override any other* processWhateverEvent *method, call* super.processWhateverEvent *from inside it.*

For efficiency, Java does not send events to these methods unless you ask it to. The way to do this is to call enableEvents on a mask in the AWTEvent class corresponding to the type of event. For instance, to enable the reporting of mouse button events to processMouseEvent, use

```
enableEvents(AWTEvent.MOUSE_EVENT_MASK);
```

Similarly, for key events use

```
enableEvents(AWTEvent.KEY_EVENT_MASK);
```

and for focus events use

```
enableEvents(AWTEvent.FOCUS_EVENT_MASK);
```

To enable multiple events within a single call, use the bitwise OR of the masks. For example:

```
enableEvents(AWTEvent.MOUSE_EVENT_MASK |
             AWTEvent.KEY_EVENT_MASK |
             AWTEvent.FOCUS_EVENT_MASK);
```

In general, the processXxxEvent methods take an argument of type XxxEvent. For instance, processMouseEvent gets a MouseEvent, processKeyEvent gets a KeyEvent, processFocusEvent gets a FocusEvent, processItemEvent gets an ItemEvent, processActionEvent gets an ActionEvent, and so forth. There is one exception however: processMouseMotionEvent does not have its own event type, but instead shares MouseEvent with processMouseEvent. Also, there is a disableEvents method corresponding to enableEvents; it is used to undo inherited settings. Finally, note that AWTEvent is in the java.awt package, while MouseEvent and the other specific event types are in java.awt.event. So you need to import both packages.

For example, Listing 10.16 shows an applet that reports mouse enter, mouse exit, and mouse press/release events in processMouseEvent, and reports mouse move and drag events in processMouseMotionEvent.

Listing 10.16 MouseReporter.java

```java
import java.applet.Applet;
import java.awt.*;
import java.awt.event.*; // For MouseEvent

/** Prints non-detailed reports of mouse events.
 *  Java 1.1 only.
 */

public class MouseReporter extends Applet {
  public void init() {
    enableEvents(AWTEvent.MOUSE_EVENT_MASK |
                 AWTEvent.MOUSE_MOTION_EVENT_MASK);
  }

  public void processMouseEvent(MouseEvent event) {
    System.out.println("Mouse enter/exit or click at (" +
                       event.getX() + "," +
                       event.getY() + ").");
    // In case there are MouseListeners attached:
    super.processMouseEvent(event);
  }
```

Listing 10.16 `MouseReporter.java` (continued)

```
public void processMouseMotionEvent(MouseEvent event) {
    System.out.println("Mouse move/drag at (" +
                        event.getX() + "," +
                        event.getY() + ").");
    // In case there are MouseMotionListeners attached:
    super.processMouseMotionEvent(event);
}
```

Table 10.1 summarizes the low-level event-processing methods available in Java 1.1.

Table 10.1 Event-processing methods in Java 1.1.

Low-Level Event Method	Corresponding Event Type	Mask for enableEvents (Static var in AWTEvent)
processActionEvent	ActionEvent	ACTION_EVENT_MASK
processAdjustment-Event	Adjustment-Event	ADJUSTMENT_EVENT_ MASK
processComponent-Event	Compo-nentEvent	COMPONENT_EVENT_ MASK
processContainer-Event	Container-Event	CONTAINER_EVENT_ MASK
processFocusEvent	FocusEvent	FOCUS_EVENT_MASK
processItemEvent	ItemEvent	ITEM_EVENT_MASK
processKeyEvent	KeyEvent	KEY_EVENT_MASK
processMouseEvent	MouseEvent	MOUSE_EVENT_MASK
processMouseMotion-Event	**MouseEvent**	MOUSE_MOTION_EVENT_ MASK
processTextEvent	TextEvent	TEXT_EVENT_MASK
processWindowEvent	WindowEvent	WINDOW_EVENT_MASK

10.6 Event Listeners in Java 1.1

Table 10.2 summarizes the 11 AWT event listeners available in Java 1.1. Each is described in more detail later in this section. The method to register a listener has the same name as the listener, but with "add" on the front. For example, use `addMouseListener` to attach a `MouseListener`, `addComponentListener` to attach a `ComponentListener`, etc. Finally, for each `addXxxListener` there is a corresponding `removeXxx-Listener` method.

Table 10.2   Event Listeners in `java.awt.event`

Listener	Adapter Class (If Any)	Registration Method
`ActionListener`		`addActionListener`
`AdjustmentListener`		`addAdjustment-` `Listener`
`ComponentListener`	`Component-` `Adapter`	`addComponentListener`
`ContainerListener`	`Container-` `Adapter`	`addContainerListener`
`FocusListener`	`FocusAdapter`	`addFocusListener`
`ItemListener`		`addItemListener`
`KeyListener`	`KeyAdapter`	`addKeyListener`
`MouseListener`	`MouseAdapter`	`addMouseListener`
`MouseMotion-` `Listener`	`MouseMotion-` `Adapter`	`addMouseMotion-` `Listener`
`TextListener`		`addTextListener`
`WindowListener`	`WindowAdapter`	`addWindowListener`

The listeners define methods that you can override to handle certain types of situations. Each of those methods takes a single argument that is a subclass of AWTEvent. AWTEvent contains four important methods: consume (delete the event), isConsumed (a boolean designating if the event has already been consumed by another listener on the same source), getID (an int representing the event type), and getSource (the Object that the event came from). The Event class used in Java 1.02 has no equivalent to consume and isConsumed, but the getID and getSource methods in AWTEvent are analogous to the id and target fields in Event.

ActionListener

This interface defines a single method:

```
public void actionPerformed(ActionEvent event)
```

Because there is only a single method, no adapter class is provided. This listener applies to buttons, list items, menu items, and textfields only, and actionPerformed is invoked when the user clicks on the button, hits ENTER in the textfield, and so forth. In addition to the standard methods of AWTEvent, ActionEvent has two additional methods: getActionCommand (return the command field of the source as a String) and getModifiers (return an int with SHIFT, CONTROL and other modifier flags set). However, in most cases the most important thing is the getSource method, which specifies the particular component that generated the event. See Chapter 13, "Graphical User Interface Controls" for additional details.

AdjustmentListener

This interface defines a single method:

```
public void adjustmentValueChanged
  (AdjustmentEvent event)
```

Because there is only a single method, no adapter class is provided. This listener applies only to scrollbars, and adjustmentValueChanged is invoked when the scrollbar is moved. AdjustmentEvent has several new methods in addition to the standard AWTEvent methods. In particular, getAdjustable returns the source scrollbar; getAdjustmentType returns one of the static constants UNIT_DECREMENT, UNIT_INCREMENT, BLOCK_DECREMENT, BLOCK_INCREMENT, or TRACK; and getValue returns the current setting.

ComponentListener

This interface defines four methods:

```
public void componentResized(ComponentEvent event)
public void componentMoved(ComponentEvent event)
public void componentShown(ComponentEvent event)
public void componentHidden(ComponentEvent event)
```

Java provides a class called `ComponentAdapter` that has empty implementations of each of these four methods. This allows you to override one without bothering to implement the others. These methods are called when a component is resized, moved, made visible, or hidden, respectively. The `getComponent` method of `ComponentEvent` returns the originating `Component`. Using it is easier than calling `getSource` and casting the result to a `Component`.

ContainerListener

This interface defines two methods:

```
public void componentAdded(ContainerEvent event)
public void componentRemoved(ContainerEvent event)
```

The `ContainerAdapter` class provides empty implementations of both of these. A `ContainerListener` is invoked when components are added to or removed from a `Container`. The `ContainerEvent` class defines `getContainer` and `getChild` for accessing the window and its associated component.

FocusListener

This interface defines two methods:

```
public void focusGained(FocusEvent event)
public void focusLost(FocusEvent event)
```

`FocusAdapter` provides empty versions of these. The `FocusEvent` class has a boolean `isTemporary` method that determines if the focus change was temporary or permanent.

ItemListener

This interface defines a single method:

```
public void itemStateChange(ItemEvent event)
```

No adapter is provided. This listener applies to `Checkbox`, `CheckboxMenuItem`, `Choice`, and `List`, and is invoked when an item is changed. The `ItemEvent` class defines three methods:

`getItemSelectable` (the source object), `getItem` (the item selected), and `getStateChange` (an `int` that is either `ItemEvent.SELECTED` or `ItemEvent.DESELECTED`).

KeyListener

This interface defines three methods:

```
public void keyPressed(KeyEvent event)
public void keyReleased(KeyEvent event)
public void keyTyped(KeyEvent event)
```

The `KeyAdapter` class provides empty versions of these so that you can override one or more without implementing all three. This listener is invoked when a key is typed while the component has the input focus. In Java 1.1, ordinary windows such as `Panel` or `Canvas` have to explicitly request the focus (via `requestFocus`) in order to get key events. This was not necessary in Java 1.02. The `keyPressed` and `keyReleased` methods are used to catch lower-level actions, where SHIFT, CONTROL, and so forth, are sent separately from the key they modify. Use `consume` in `keyPressed` if you want to prevent a component from seeing the keystroke. This lets you restrict textfields to certain formats, for instance. If you are only interested in the key that was typed, override `keyTyped` instead. The `KeyEvent` class defines a variety of methods and constants. Two methods of particular importance are `getKeyChar` and `setKeyChar`. The first returns the character typed, and the second can be used to replace the character with a different one. This lets you do things like map tabs and newlines to spaces, convert lowercase to uppercase, and so forth. There are also `getModifiers` and `setModifiers` methods that let you retrieve and/or replace the modifier keys, and a boolean `isActionKey` method that differentiates function and arrow keys from normal keys. You can also use one of four related methods inherited from `InputEvent`: `isAltDown`, `isControlDown`, `isMetaDown`, and `isShiftDown`. Rather than acting on characters with `getKeyChar`, you can retrieve an integer with `getKeyCode`, then pass that to `get-KeyText` to find the associated string. This is useful in internationalized code. There is a corresponding `setKeyCode` as well. Finally, you can obtain the `Component` receiving the event via `getComponent`, and the time the key was hit via `getWhen`.

MouseListener

This interface defines five methods:

```
public void mouseEntered(MouseEvent event)
public void mouseExited(MouseEvent event)
public void mousePressed(MouseEvent event)
public void mouseReleased(MouseEvent event)
public void mouseClicked(MouseEvent event)
```

You can use the MouseAdapter class if you want to override some but not all of these. If you consume the event in mousePressed, the associated graphical component will not see the mouse click. You can call getModifiers to determine which button was clicked, just as with Java 1.02. Similarly, getClickCount lets you differentiate single clicks from multiclicks. The getX, getY, and getPoint methods determine the location of the click. The isPopupTrigger method is used to determine if the user hit the platform-specific key that requested a PopupMenu. Like KeyEvent, MouseEvent inherits from InputEvent, getting isAltDown, isControlDown, isMetaDown, isShiftDown, getComponent, and getWhen methods.

MouseMotionListener

This interface defines two methods:

```
public void mouseMoved(MouseEvent event)
public void mouseDragged(MouseEvent event)
```

MouseMotionAdapter provides empty versions of these two methods. A MouseMotionListener is invoked when the mouse is moved. Note that in Java 1.1, unlike in 1.02, buttons, scrollbars, and the like receive mouse motion events as well as action events. The Mouse-Event class is described in the previous MouseListener section.

TextListener

This interface defines a single method:

```
public void textValueChanged(TextEvent event)
```

There is no associated adapter. This listener applies only to TextArea, TextField, and any custom subclasses of TextComponent. The textValueChanged method is invoked when text changes, regardless of whether this is from user action or from the program (e.g., via setText or append).

WindowListener

This final interface defines seven methods:

```
public void windowOpened(WindowEvent event)
public void windowClosing(WindowEvent event)
public void windowClosed(WindowEvent event)
public void windowIconified(WindowEvent event)
public void windowDeiconified(WindowEvent event)
public void windowActivated(WindowEvent event)
public void windowDeactivated(WindowEvent event)
```

If you are only concerned with one or two of these methods, you can extend a `WindowAdapter` class, which comes with empty versions of all seven of these. The `windowOpened` method is called when a window is first opened; `windowClosing` is called when the user tries to quit the window; `windowClosed` is called when it actually is closed; `window-Iconified` and `windowDeiconified` are called when the window is minimized and restored; and `windowActivated` and `windowDe-activated` are called when the window is brought to the front and either buried, iconified, or otherwise deactivated. The `getWindow` method of `WindowEvent` returns the `Window` being acted upon.

10.7 Summary

Event handling is one of the most significant areas of change from Java 1.02 to Java 1.1. In version 1.02 of Java, events are first sent to the `handleEvent` method, then, if their `id` is appropriate, to helper methods such as `mouse-Down` or `keyDown`. If `false` is returned, the events are then sent to the enclosing window, where this procedure is repeated. Processing events in the helping methods is generally easier than in `handleEvent`, but not all events have associated helper methods. Version 1.1 of Java introduces a delegation event model, whereby events are sent only to objects that are registered to receive them. To use this model, you create a "listener" object of one of eleven predefined classes, then associate it with a class of events by calling one of the `addXxxListener` methods. You then override particular methods in the listener object to get the desired behavior. This approach to events is a significant improvement over Java 1.02, but most Web browsers do not yet support it.

Low-level mouse events are usually applied to windows. Java windows are covered in the next chapter, "Windows." Higher-level mouse and keyboard events typically apply to user interface widgets. They are discussed in Chapter 13, "Graphical User Interface Controls."

WINDOWS

Topics in This Chapter

- Creating and using canvases for drawing or implementing custom graphical components
- The Component class
- Using "lightweight" components in Java 1.1 to implement partially transparent graphical objects
- Creating and using panels for holding other components or implementing composite graphical components
- The Container class
- Using "lightweight" containers in Java 1.1 to implement partially transparent windows
- Where Applet fits in the window hierarchy
- Java 1.1 scrollable windows
- Creating and using frames (popup windows)
- Putting menus in frames
- Using object serialization to save windows to disk and reload them in later sessions
- Creating and using dialog boxes
- Using file dialogs to load or save files
- Using the low-level Window class
- Creating an ImageLabel class

Chapter 11

J ava's Abstract Window Toolkit (AWT) has eight major types of windows that the developer can use for user interfaces: `Canvas`, `Panel`, `Applet`, `ScrollPane`, `Frame`, `Dialog`, `FileDialog`, and `Window`. Some windows (such as `Panel` and `ScrollPane`) are borderless and can only be placed in other windows, while others (such as, `Frame`, and `Dialog`) have borders and title bars and can pop up anywhere on the screen. `Applet` is the starting point for Web-embedded applets; `Frame` is the base window for graphical applications.

Most windows can contain other graphical components, but a few (e.g., `Canvas`, `FileDialog`) cannot. Except for `ScrollPane`, all the windows that can contain other components have a `LayoutManager` that helps arrange the nested components. This topic is so important that the entire next chapter is devoted to layout managers. Except for `FileDialog`, all the windows receive the mouse and keyboard events described in Chapter 10, "Handling Mouse and Keyboard Events." In the following sections, I'll describe each of the eight window types, summarizing their major purposes, their standard layout manager, the steps required to create and use them, and an example of their use. Separate sections are devoted to the `Component` and `Container` classes, the bases on which the windows are built. Finally, I will cover *lightweight* components and containers, new windows provided by Java 1.1 that support transparent regions.

Learning how to create and arrange windows and user interface controls is a bit of a chicken and egg problem. It is hard to give practical examples of window usage without adding buttons, text areas, and the like. On the other hand, you can't use a textfield or scrollbar without having a window to put it in. So the order is up to you. Most people prefer to get the basics of at least a couple of window types first. If you're in this category, read this chapter and the next first, but don't get too hung up on the details of how we create the few interface controls needed. Then go on to the GUI control chapter. If you'd rather read about the widgets first, skip ahead to Chapter 13, "Graphical User Interface Controls," skimming over the window creation part, then come back here when you're done.

11.1   Canvas

A `Canvas` is the simplest window type in Java. It cannot contain any GUI controls or nested windows. Also, it is not a stand-alone window; you need an existing window to put it in. The examples here will illustrate putting canvases into an `Applet` (because applets have been relatively thoroughly described already), but if you are more interested in regular graphical applications, skip ahead to Section 11.9 for details on using `Frame`.

Major Purposes

A Drawing Area.

Suppose that you are creating a `Frame` or `Applet` that has some user-interface controls (radio buttons, checkboxes, etc.) as well as an area that will show a graph or image. In a multiplatform environment, these widgets will vary somewhat in size, and it might be difficult to decide exactly where to draw the graph or image. Rather than trying to have a single window that contains the controls and the drawing, it may be more convenient to insert a separate `Canvas` on which to do the drawing. Note, however, that the `Canvas` should draw *itself* by overriding the `paint` method. This requires you to subclass `Canvas`, so specialized extensions to the `Canvas` class are used more commonly than direct instances of `Canvas` itself. Due to interaction with the `Canvas'` default `update` and `paint` methods, it is not reliable for a method in an external class to try to look up the `Canvas'` `Graphics` object (e.g., with `getGraphics`) and draw into it. Instead, the external routines should set some data that the Canvas knows about, then invoke the Canvas' repaint method when drawing is needed.

Core Approach

Windows that need to draw should override paint *to draw themselves. Don't try to get the* Graphics *object of another window and draw into it.*

A Custom Component That Does Not Need to Contain Other Components.

The Canvas is also the starting place for many custom components. For instance, if you want to define an ImageLabel or ImageButton, subclassing Canvas is a convenient starting place.

Default LayoutManager: None

Most windows (Panel, Frame, and others) can contain other windows and GUI controls such as buttons and text areas. These windows have a LayoutManager associated with them that helps arrange the enclosed components. A Canvas cannot contain any other component, and thus does not have a layout manager.

Creating and Using

Create the Canvas

```
Canvas canvas = new Canvas();
```

Or, since you typically use Canvas subclasses that know how to draw themselves, this might look like:

```
SpecializedCanvas canvas = new SpecializedCanvas();
```

Resize the Canvas

```
canvas.resize(width, height); //Java 1.02
```

or

```
canvas.setSize(width, height); // Java 1.1
```

Because this step is often not needed with other window types, it is frequently forgotten when using a Canvas. The default size is 0 pixels by 0 pixels, so in most cases your Canvas won't show up if you forget to resize it. There are a few exceptions to this rule, such as when you put a `Canvas` into the `Center` region of a `BorderLayout` (see Chapter 12, "Arranging Windows Using Layout Managers"), but forgetting to give a size to the `Canvas` is one of the most common sources of problems when first using them.

Core Alert

Don't forget to give a size to your `Canvas`.

Add the Canvas to the Container

```
add(canvas);
```

The last statement assumes the current container is not using `Border-Layout`, otherwise it would be

```
add("Region", canvas);
```

The use of `BorderLayout` is discussed briefly in the section on frames (Section 11.9); lots more detail is provided in Chapter 12, "Arranging Windows Using Layout Managers."

Example: A Circle Component

One of the uses of `Canvas` is to implement custom components: windows with a predefined type of drawing inside. For instance, Listing 11.1 gives an example of a `Circle` class. Using it does not require any modifications to the `paint` method of the window using it. Instead, you simply add it to a window (Listing 11.2) and let Java take care of the rest. It is automatically redrawn whenever the window is covered and reexposed, and can get moved around by layout managers if the enclosing window uses one. Figure 11–1 shows the result.

Listing 11.1   Circle.java

```java
import java.awt.*;

/** A Circle component built using a Canvas. */

public class Circle extends Canvas {
  public Circle(Color foreground, int radius) {
    setForeground(foreground);
    resize(2*radius, 2*radius);
  }

  public void paint(Graphics g) {
    g.fillOval(0, 0, size().width, size().height);
  }

  public void setCenter(int x, int y) {
    move(x - size().width/2, y - size().height/2);
  }
}
```

Listing 11.2   CircleTest.java

```java
import java.awt.*;
import java.applet.Applet;

/** Insert three circles into an Applet using FlowLayout.
 * @see Circle
 */

public class CircleTest extends Applet {
  public void init() {
    setBackground(Color.lightGray);
    add(new Circle(Color.white, 30));
    add(new Circle(Color.gray, 40));
    add(new Circle(Color.black, 50));
  }
}
```

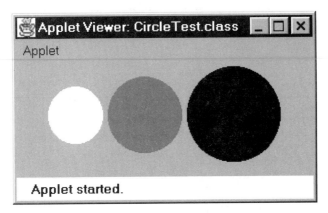

Figure 11-1   A `Canvas` can be used to create a new type of graphical component.

Here, we let the `Applet` decide where the circles were placed in this example, but we'll show how to control this in Chapter 12, "Arranging Windows Using Layout Managers." However, there is a significant restriction: a `Canvas` is always rectangular and opaque. This means that the circles cannot overlap or even be arbitrarily close together without interfering with each other. To illustrate this, Listing 11.3 creates diagonally aligned circles packed together. As can be seen in Figure 11–2, the corners of the underlying `Canvas` block part of the neighboring circles. This problem is not limited to `Canvas`. In fact, in Java 1.02, *all* graphical components are rectangular and opaque. In Java 1.1, you can create "lightweight" components and containers that are transparent, and Section 11.3 shows how to use this capability to make a `BetterCircle` class that can be used to create circles that are overlapping or arbitrarily close to each other without interference. Even in Java 1.1, however, components are still rectangular. This, for instance, means that an event handler for a circle would need to filter out mouse clicks that fell outside the circle and explicitly pass them to the enclosing window. This restriction will be dropped in the upcoming Java Foundation Classes (`http://java.sun.com/products/jfc/`), which are expected to be part of Java 1.2.

Core Note

In Java 1.02, all windows and graphical components are rectangular and opaque.

Listing 11.3   CircleTest2.java

```java
import java.awt.*;
import java.applet.Applet;

/** Position circles down the diagonal so that
 *  their borders just touch. Illustrates that
 *  Java 1.0 components are rectangular and opaque.
 * @see Circle
 */

public class CircleTest2 extends Applet {
  public void init() {
    setBackground(Color.lightGray);
    setLayout(null);
    Circle circle;
    int radius = size().width/6;
    int deltaX =
      round(2.0 * (double)radius / Math.sqrt(2.0));
    for (int x=radius; x<6*radius; x=x+deltaX) {
      circle = new Circle(Color.black, radius);
      add(circle);
      circle.setCenter(x, x);
    }
  }

  private int round(double num) {
    return((int)Math.round(num));
  }
}
```

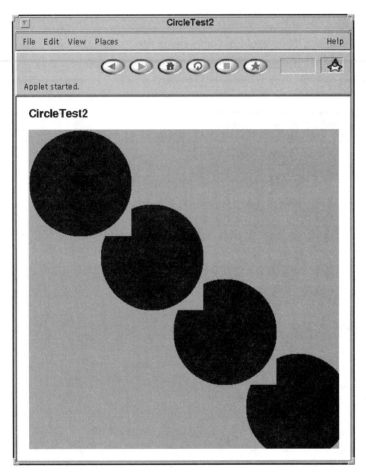

Figure 11-2   In Java 1.02, windows and GUI controls are rectangular and opaque.

Example: An ImageLabel Class

For a more serious example, consider the task of creating a window to hold images. By default, we will size this window to exactly fit the image, but enable the user to supply an explicit size to stretch the image. Rather than messing around with getImage and drawImage and MediaTracker, you can simply drop one of these objects in an existing window. I'll call this class ImageLabel by analogy with the built-in Label class, which is used to create text that will be redrawn automatically and can be moved around by layout managers. Listing 11.4 shows an example of its use, with the result shown in Figure 11–3. The code for `ImageLabel` is a bit long, so rather than including it here, it is postponed until the end of the chapter (Section 11.14). We'll build on `ImageLabel` to create an `ImageButton` class in Chapter 13, "Graphical User Interface Controls."

Listing 11.4 `ImageLabelTest.java`

```
import java.applet.Applet;
import java.awt.*;

/** Create a couple of ImageLabels with identical
 *  images but different borders and sizes.
 * @see ImageLabel
 */

public class ImageLabelTest extends Applet {
  public void init() {
    setBackground(Color.white);
    ImageLabel imageLabel1 =
      new ImageLabel(getCodeBase(),
                     "images/Java-Logo.gif");
    ImageLabel imageLabel2 =
      new ImageLabel(getCodeBase(),
                     "images/Java-Logo.gif");
    ImageLabel imageLabel3 =
      new ImageLabel(getCodeBase(),
                     "images/Java-Logo.gif");
    ImageLabel imageLabel4 =
      new ImageLabel(getCodeBase(),
                     "images/Java-Logo.gif");

    imageLabel2.resize(220, 202);
    imageLabel3.setBorder(5);
    imageLabel4.setBorder(3);
    imageLabel4.setBorderColor(Color.lightGray);

    add(imageLabel1);
    add(imageLabel2);
    add(imageLabel3);
    add(imageLabel4);
  }

}
```

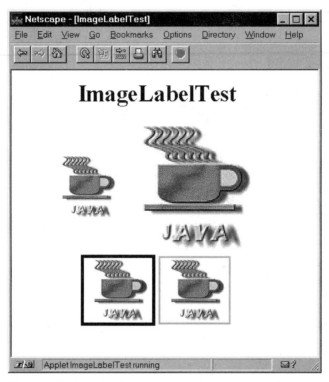

Figure 11–3   A `Canvas` is a good starting point for an `ImageLabel`.

11.2 The Component Class

All windows and GUI controls are built on top of `Component`. So the following methods can be used with all the classes discussed in this chapter and in Chapter 13, "Graphical User Interface Controls."

public boolean action(Event event, Object object)

This is an event-handling helper method used by `handleEvent`. For more details, see Section 10.2, "Event-Handling Helper Methods in Java 1.02."

public void add(PopupMenu menu) [Java 1.1]

This associates a `PopupMenu` with the component. It won't pop up automatically; you have to monitor keyboard events to decide when to invoke it.

public void addComponentListener
  (ComponentListener listener) [Java 1.1]
public void addFocusListener(FocusListener listener) [Java 1.1]
public void addKeyListener(KeyListener listener) [Java 1.1]
public void addMouseListener(MouseListener listener) [Java 1.1]
public void addMouseMotionListener
  (MouseMotionListener listener) [Java 1.1]

These methods add event listeners to the component. See Section 10.6 (Event Listeners in Java 1.1) for more information.

public void addNotify()

This creates the component's "peer," the native window-system object associated with it. If your custom component needs to be sure the peer exists before performing some action, you can call this method. If you do, be sure to call `super.addNotify`. The method name is a bit unintuitive; the `addNotify` and `removeNotify` methods probably should have been called `createPeer` and `destroyPeer`.

public Rectangle bounds()
public Rectangle getBounds() [Java 1.1]

This returns a `Rectangle` object describing the outside edges of the component. A `Rectangle` is a nongraphical data structure with x, y, width, and height fields.

public int checkImage(Image image, ImageObserver observer)
public int checkImage(Image image, int width, int height,
                ImageObserver observer)

This returns an `int` that combines the flags in the `ImageObserver` interface to give information on an image that is being loaded. In general, `MediaTracker` is a better option. For more information on using images, see Section 9.11 (Drawing Images).

public Image createImage(int width, int height)
public Image createImage(ImageProducer producer)

These methods create images. The first method makes an empty image of the given size, and is usually used for double-buffering applications. The second method is used to programmatically create images, typically by image filters.

public void deliverEvent(Event event)

This is the lowest-level event-handling method in Java 1.02. The default version just passes the event to postEvent. I recommend not messing around at this level.

public void disable()
public void setEnabled(boolean enabledFlag) [Java 1.1]

These methods prevent a component from responding to user input. On most operating systems, disabling a GUI control such as a button results in the component being grayed out. In Java 1.1, use setEnabled(false) in lieu of disable().

protected final void disableEvents(long eventsToDisable) [Java 1.1]

This turns off the specified events.

public final void dispatchEvent(AWTEvent event)

This is a low-level event-handling method in Java 1.1, approximately equivalent to postEvent in Java 1.02.

public void enable()
public void enable(boolean enableFlag)

These methods enable (or, with a value of false, disable) a component. In Java 1.1, use setEnable(true) instead of enable() (see disable).

protected final void enableEvents(long eventsToEnable) [Java 1.1]

This turns on the specified events. Available in Java 1.1 only.

public float getAlignmentX() [Java 1.1[
public float getAlignmentY() [Java 1.1]

These methods can be overridden to provide alignment information, where a value of 0.0f should be interpreted to align the side closest to the X or Y axis (i.e., left and top, respectively), 0.5f should be interpreted to align the centers, and 1.0f to align the side furthest from the axis (i.e. right and bottom). The default value for both is 0.5f. There are also five associated constants:
Component.TOP_ALIGNMENT (0.0f),
Component.CENTER_ALIGNMENT (0.5f),
Component.BOTTOM_ALIGNMENT (1.0f),
Component.LEFT_ALIGNMENT (0.0f), and
Component.RIGHT_ALIGNMENT (1.0f).

public Color getBackground()

This returns the background color of the component.

public ColorModel getColorModel()

This returns the `ColorModel` being used. If no peer yet exists, it returns the `Toolkit`'s default `ColorModel`.

public Cursor getCursor() [Java 1.1]

The `getCursor` method returns the current cursor. It is available in Java 1.1 only.

public Font getFont()

This returns the current font, either from a `setFont` call or inherited from the enclosing window.

public FontMetrics getFontMetrics(Font f)

Given a `Font`, `getFontMetrics` returns a `FontMetrics` object. As illustrated in the `Whiteboard` class (Listing 10.12), this object can be used to find the width and height of characters or strings in the specified font.

public Color getForeground()

This returns the foreground color of the component.

public Graphics getGraphics()

This returns a `Graphics` object that can be used to draw onto the component. The `Graphics` object is initialized with the component's font and foreground and background colors.

public Locale getLocale() [Java 1.1]

This method is used in internationalized Java 1.1 code to get the `Locale`.

public Point getLocationOnScreen() [Java 1.1]

This returns the absolute location of the component's top left corner. In Java 1.02, you can calculate this value in applications by looking up a component's location, adding in the enclosing window's location, and so on up to the top-level frame. For applets, however, there is no reliable way to do this. For instance, both Netscape and Internet Explorer always report (0,0) for the applet `Frame`'s location.

public String getName() [Java 1.1]

Java 1.1 allows you to name components. This returns the name; set-Name sets it.

public Container getParent()

This returns the enclosing window (null in the case of a Frame or a Component not yet associated with a window).

public Toolkit getToolkit()

This returns the Toolkit, which can be used to load images (getImage), find the available fonts (getFontList), look up the screen size (getScreenSize) and resolution (getScreenResolution), and so forth.

public final Object getTreeLock() [Java 1.1]

In Java 1.1, this returns the Object holding the thread lock for tree and layout operations.

public boolean gotFocus(Event event, Object object)

This is an event-handling helper method used by handleEvent. For more details, see Section 10.2, "Event-Handling Helper Methods in Java 1.02."

public boolean handleEvent(Event event)

This is the starting point for user-level event handling in Java 1.02. For more details, see Section 10.1, "Handling Events in Java 1.02."

public void hide()
public void setVisible(boolean visibleFlag) [Java 1.1]

The hide method makes an AWT component invisible. Using set-Visible(false) is preferred in Java 1.1.

public boolean inside(int x, int y)
public boolean contains(int x, int y) [Java 1.1]
public boolean contains(Point p) [Java 1.1]

These methods determine if the specified location is inside the component. However, several early Java implementations, including the applet-viewer with Java 1.0 (not 1.02) and Netscape version 2, implemented this incorrectly, using the parent window's coordinate system instead of the local one. If your code is likely to run in Netscape 2.02 and earlier, you might consider reimplementing `inside` as follows:

```
public synchronized boolean inside(int x, int y) {
   return((x >= 0) && (x <= width)
          && (y >= 0) && (y <= height));
}
```

Since `locate` depends on `inside`, it is also broken in Netscape 2.

Core Warning

The `inside` *and* `locate` *methods are incorrect in Netscape 2.0, 2.01, and 2.02.*

public void invalidate()
This specifies that a component is invalid. Validating (see `validate`) an invalid component will redo the layout of the component and all nested components.

public boolean isEnabled()
This determines if a component is enabled. See `enable` and `disable` (`setEnabled` in Java 1.1).

public boolean isFocusTraversable() [Java 1.1]
This Java 1.1 method determines if the component will get the input focus when the user uses TAB or Shift-TAB. If not, it can still explicitly request the focus with `requestFocus`.

public boolean isShowing()
This method determines if the component is visible and that the window holding it is showing.

public boolean isValid()
The `isValid` method determines if the component is valid. See `validate` and `invalidate`.

public boolean isVisible()
This method determines if the component is currently visible. Even if this method returns `true`, the component won't appear if the containing window is not visible. See `isShowing`.

public boolean keyDown(Event event, int key)
public boolean keyUp(Event event, int key)

These are event-handling helper methods used by `handleEvent`. For more details, see Section 10.2, "Event-Handling Helper Methods in Java 1.02."

public void layout()
public void doLayout() [Java 1.1]

These methods tell the associated `LayoutManager` (available only for `Containers`) to lay the component out.

public void list()
public void list(PrintStream stream)
public void list(PrintStream stream, int indentation)
public void list(PrintWriter writer) [Java 1.1]
public void list(PrintWriter writer, int indentation) [Java 1.1]

These methods print information about the component and subcomponents, traversing the tree in depth-first order and printing nested components indented relative to their parents. This is a very useful tool during development, since calling `list` on the top-level window (i.e., the `Applet` or `Frame`) gives information on every other component in the application. For debugging, you can trigger it in a number of ways: by pressing a button (see Chapter 13, "Graphical User Interface Controls"), clicking a mouse in an empty window (see Chapter 10, "Handling Mouse and Keyboard Events"), or even by calling it from the `paint` method (see Chapter 9, "Applets, Graphical Applications, and Basic Drawing").

Core Approach

The `list` method is a valuable debugging tool, especially when first learning about windows and GUI controls.

public Component locate(int x, int y)
public Component getComponentAt(int x, int y) [Java 1.1]
public Component getComponentAt(Point p) [Java 1.1]

These methods return the top-most component at the specified location. The component itself will be returned if there is no nested component at the location; `null` will be returned for coordinates outside the component. Note that this works incorrectly in version 2 of Netscape. See `inside` for details.

public Point location()
public Point getLocation() [Java 1.1]

This returns a `Point` object (with x and y fields) describing the top left corner of the window, *in the enclosing window's coordinate system.* See `getLocationOnScreen` (Java 1.1 only) for retrieving the absolute coordinates.

public boolean lostFocus(Event event, Object object)

This is an event-handling helper method used by `handleEvent`. For more details, see Section 10.2, "Event-Handling Helper Methods in Java 1.02."

public Dimension minimumSize()
public Dimension getMinimumSize() [Java 1.1]
public Dimension getMaximumSize() [Java 1.1]

These methods return a `Dimension` object (with x, y, `width`, and `height` fields) describing the smallest or largest size the component should be. Layout managers should not resize components beyond these bounds if it can be avoided.

public boolean mouseDown(Event event, int x, int y)
public boolean mouseUp(Event event, int x, int y)
public boolean mouseEnter(Event event, int x, int y)
public boolean mouseExit(Event event, int x, int y)
public boolean mouseMove(Event event, int x, int y)
public boolean mouseDrag(Event event, int x, int y)

These are event-handling helper methods used by `handleEvent`. For more details, see Section 10.2, "Event-Handling Helper Methods in Java 1.02."

public void move(int x, int y)
public void setLocation(int x, int y)
public void setLocation(Point p)

These methods move the top left corner of the component to the specified position in the enclosing window's coordinate system. Note that if the parent window is using one of the normal layout managers, it may undo the effects of this.

public void nextFocus()
public void transferFocus() [Java 1.1]
This method passes the input focus to the next component in the TAB order.

public void paint(Graphics g)
This method is called whenever the user calls `repaint` or when the component has been obscured and reexposed. This is the method to override to perform graphics operations in a component. If `paint` is called because part of the component has been covered, the clipping region of the `Graphics` object will be set to that area.

public void paintAll(Graphics g)
This method paints the component and any nested components.

protected String paramString()
This returns a debugging string describing the component's state.

public boolean postEvent(Event event)
This is a low-level event-handling method used in Java 1.02. It passes the event to `handleEvent`, passing it on to the containing window if `false` is returned.

public Dimension preferredSize()
public Dimension getPreferredSize() [Java 1.1]
These methods return a `Dimension` object (`x`, `y`, `width`, `height` fields) describing the preferred size of the component. Layout managers such as `FlowLayout` use this value.

public boolean prepareImage(Image image,
                          ImageObserver observer)
public boolean prepareImage(Image image, int width, int height,
                          ImageObserver observer)
This method starts the loading of the image data for the associated `Image`. It is used to preload images prior to drawing them with `Graphics.drawImage`. For more information, see Section 9.11 (Drawing Images). Note that scaled images are treated as new images, so if you are going to draw an image at a size other than the default, you have to call `prepareImage` with that size. It returns `true` if all the image data is already available, `false` otherwise.

public void print(Graphics g)
public void printAll(Graphics g)

In the 1.02 release of Java, these methods have little value. However, in Java 1.1, these methods can be used to print the component if the `Graphics` object implements the `PrintGraphics` interface. The default implementations do nothing but call `paint` and `paintAll`.

public void processEvent(AWTEvent event) [Java 1.1]
public void processComponentEvent(ComponentEvent event)
  [Java 1.1]
public void processFocusEvent(FocusEvent event) [Java 1.1]
public void processKeyEvent(KeyEvent event) [Java 1.1]
public void processMouseEvent(MouseEvent event) [Java 1.1]
public void processMouseMotionEvent
  (MouseMotionEvent event) [Java 1.1]

If the associated events are enabled, these methods can process them. They are available in Java 1.1 only; for more information see Chapter 10, "Handling Mouse and Keyboard Events."

public void remove(MenuComponent menu) [Java 1.1]

This method removes a popup menu.

public void removeComponentListener
  (ComponentListener listener) [Java 1.1]
public void removeFocusListener(FocusListener listener)
  [Java 1.1]
public void removeKeyListener(KeyListener listener) [Java 1.1]
public void removeMouseListener(MouseListener listener)
  [Java 1.1]
public void removeMouseMotionListener
  (MouseMotionListener listener) [Java 1.1]

These methods remove event listeners for the component. See Section 10.6 (Event Listeners in Java 1.1) for more information.

public void removeNotify()

This method destroys the component's peer (native window-system object). The `addNotify` and `removeNotify` methods really should have been called `createPeer` and `destroyPeer`.

public void repaint()
public void repaint(int x, int y, int width, int height)
public void repaint(long milliseconds)
public void repaint(long milliseconds, int x, int y, int width,
                            int height)
These methods ask the AWT thread to asynchronously call update as
soon as possible (or after the specified number of milliseconds). This
normally results in the screen being cleared and paint being called. If
a rectangular region is specified, it is used for the clipping region of the
Graphics object in update and paint.

public void requestFocus()
This method is called when you want the component to get the input
focus, but when it wouldn't have gotten it otherwise. For instance, you
could use requestFocus so that clicking on a certain Button
resulted in a given TextField getting the focus.

public void reshape(int x, int y, int width, int height)
public void setBounds(int x, int y, int width, int height) [Java 1.1]
public void setBounds(boundingRectangle) [Java 1.1]
The reshape method (or setBounds, as is preferred in Java 1.1) is
used to change both the size and location of a component. For instance,
in Java 1.02, calling resize(width, height) and move(top,
left) is equivalent to doing reshape(top, left, width,
height). In release 1.1 of Java, the combination of setSize and
setLocation can be replaced by setBounds.

public void resize(int width, int height)
public void resize(Dimension d)
public void setSize(int width, int height) [Java 1.1]
public void setSize(Dimension d) [Java 1.1]
The resize (setSize in Java 1.1) method changes the width and
height of the component by calling reshape (setBounds) with the
specified width and height and the current top left corner location.

public void setBackground(Color bgColor)
This sets the background color of the component.

public void setCursor(Cursor c) [Java 1.1]

In Java 1.02, you can only set the cursor in a Frame. In Java 1.1, setCursor can be used in any Component. To use it, call setCursor(Cursor.getPredefinedCursor(type)), where type is one of Cursor.CROSSHAIR_CURSOR, Cursor.DEFAULT_CURSOR, Cursor.E_RESIZE_CURSOR, Cursor.HAND_CURSOR, Cursor.MOVE_CURSOR, Cursor.N_RESIZE_CURSOR, Cursor.NE_RESIZE_CURSOR, Cursor.NW_RESIZE_CURSOR, Cursor.S_RESIZE_CURSOR, Cursor.SE_RESIZE_CURSOR, Cursor.SW_RESIZE_CURSOR, Cursor.TEXT_CURSOR, Cursor.W_RESIZE_CURSOR, or Cursor.WAIT_CURSOR. Neither Java 1.02 nor 1.1 let you define your own cursor images.

public void setFont(Font f)

This sets the default font for the component. It is inherited by nested windows and the Graphics object used in paint and update (and returned by getGraphics).

public void setForeground(Color fgColor)

This sets the foreground color of the component.

public void setLocale(Locale locale) [Java 1.1]

In internationalized Java 1.1 code, setLocale can be used to change the component's Locale.

public void setName(String name) [Java 1.1]

Java 1.1 allows you to name components. This sets the name; getName returns it.

public void show()
public void show(boolean visibleFlag)

These methods are used in Java 1.02 to make a component visible. In Java 1.1, setVisible is preferred; see hide.

public Dimension size()
public Dimension getSize() [Java 1.1]
These methods return the current size of the component, as a Dimension object. A Dimension has width and height fields, so, for instance, someComponent.size().width returns the width of someComponent.

public String toString()
The toString method generates a String for use in debugging. It is not necessarily very informative, however. See list.

public void update(Graphics g)
This method is called by the AWT thread after the user calls repaint. The default implementation clears the screen and then calls paint(g), but it is common to override update to simply call paint. This is particularly common when drawing into an offscreen pixmap; for more details, see the discussion of double buffering in Chapter 14, "Concurrent Programming Using Java Threads."

public void validate()
This will make a component valid. Validating an invalid component (see invalidate) will redo the layout of the component and all nested components.

11.3 Lightweight Components in Java 1.1

In the 1.0 release of Java, all of the methods of Component are available for use in any Component subclass, but Component itself cannot be directly extended. The standard approach is to use Canvas as a starting point, but this has the drawback that a Canvas is rectangular and opaque, plus that the underlying peer is relatively expensive to create. For instance, in Section 11.1, we looked at using Canvas to make Circle and ImageLabel classes. As Figure 11–2 illustrated, the Circle class suffered from being rectangular and opaque. This problem is less serious for ImageLabel because images are already rectangular, but even there, it would be nice to let underlying colors or images show through when ImageLabel is used with a partially transparent image.

Java 1.1 introduces "lightweight" components that provide the ability to make a direct subclass of Component with no associated native window-system "peer." Any region not directly drawn in the paint method will let the underlying component show through. For instance, Listing 11.5 shows a BetterCircle class that uses this approach. The code is very similar to the version that used Canvas (Listing 11.1), with the exception that here we have to override getPreferredSize and getMinimumSize to do what Canvas already does: simply report its current size. In general, these two methods should be used to calculate the optimum and minimum sizes for the component. Listing 11.6 shows BetterCircle used in the same way as Circle was used in Section 11.1. As Figure 11–4 shows, the overlapping corners no longer cut into the underlying circle.

If you use lightweight components in a Container that has a custom paint method, this paint method *must* call super.paint or the lightweight components will not be drawn. See Section 11.6 (Lightweight Containers in Java 1.1) for more details.

Listing 11.5   BetterCircle.java

```java
import java.awt.*;

/** An improved variation of the Circle class that
 *  uses Java 1.1 lightweight components instead
 *  of Canvas.
 * @see Circle
 */

public class BetterCircle extends Component {
  private Dimension preferredDimension;

  public BetterCircle(Color foreground, int radius) {
    setForeground(foreground);
    preferredDimension =
      new Dimension(2*radius, 2*radius);
    setSize(preferredDimension);
  }

  public void paint(Graphics g) {
    g.fillOval(0, 0, getSize().width, getSize().height);
  }

  public void setCenter(int x, int y) {
    setLocation(x - getSize().width/2,
                y - getSize().height/2);
  }

  /** Report the original size as the preferred size.
   *  That way, the BetterCircle doesn't get
   *  shrunk by layout managers.
   */

  public Dimension getPreferredSize() {
    return(preferredDimension);
  }

  /** Report same thing for minimum size as
   *  preferred size.
   */

  public Dimension getMinimumSize() {
    return(preferredDimension);
  }
}
```

Listing 11.6   BetterCircleTest2.java

```java
import java.awt.*;
import java.applet.Applet;

/** Position circles down the diagonal so that
 *  their borders just touch. Illustrates that
 *  Java 1.1 lightweight components can be
 *  partially transparent.
 * @see BetterCircle
 */

public class BetterCircleTest2 extends Applet {
  public void init() {
    setBackground(Color.lightGray);
    setLayout(null);
    BetterCircle circle;
    int radius = getSize().width/6;
    int deltaX =
      round(2.0 * (double)radius / Math.sqrt(2.0));
    for (int x=radius; x<6*radius; x=x+deltaX) {
      circle = new BetterCircle(Color.black, radius);
      add(circle);
      circle.setCenter(x, x);
    }
  }

  private int round(double num) {
    return((int)Math.round(num));
  }
}
```

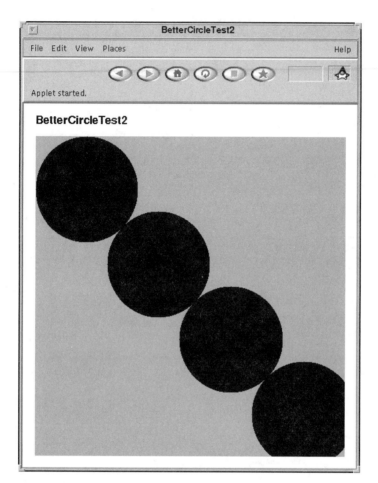

Figure 11–4   In Java 1.1, lightweight components can be transparent.

11.4 Panel

A Panel is a borderless window that can contain GUI controls and nested windows. Like Canvas, it is not a stand-alone window; you need an existing window to put it in. This section illustrates putting panels in an Applet, but if you are more interested in regular graphical applications, skip ahead to Section 11.9 for details on using Frame.

Major Purposes

To group/organize other components.

For simple GUI designs, it may be straightforward to design a single layout that positions all components in their desired locations. For more complex layouts, however, it is generally much easier to break the display into rectangular regions, embedding each in a `Panel`. Each `Panel` is then in charge of laying out the components it contains, and the top-level layout simply has to put the panels in the proper positions.

To create a custom component that requires embedded components.

In Section 11.1 (Canvas) we used a `Canvas` to implement `Circle` and `ImageLabel` components. However, since a `Canvas` is not a `Container`, it cannot be used for components that need to hold other components. A `Panel` can. For example, a `Panel` could be used to create a `Slider` class that includes a `Scrollbar` and a `TextField` that displays the currently selected value.

Default LayoutManager: FlowLayout

Windows that can hold other components (i.e., that are in the `Container` class) get a `LayoutManager` that helps them arrange the components. This generally simplifies layout when components are added or removed, the window size changes, or the components are different sizes on different operating systems. The `FlowLayout` layout manager places components in rows, adding as many as possible to the current row before going on to the next row. By default, the rows are centered horizontally and vertically. Before placing the components into the rows, the layout manager asks each component their "preferred" (really minimum) size, and then resizes them to that size. In Chapter 12, "Arranging Windows Using Layout Managers," we'll see how to change or disable this, but the normal behavior is that if you place a `Button`, `Label`, `Scrollbar`, or another `Panel` into a `Panel` (or other `Container`) that uses `FlowLayout`, you do not have direct control over its size. This can be quite disconcerting to beginners who wonder why all the `resize` (`setSize` in Java 1.1) calls on their `Panel`'s components seem to be ignored. A `Canvas` is an exception to this rule, because it reports its current size whenever asked for its preferred size.

Core Approach

Except for canvases, if you want to give exact sizes to components that are in a `Panel`, *you have to change the layout manager first.*

Furthermore, a `Panel`'s *own* preferred size is calculated to be just barely large enough to enclose the components that it contains. This means that if you put a `Panel` into some other window that is using `FlowLayout`, it may get shrunk or stretched. In fact, if you put an *empty* `Panel` into a Container that is using `FlowLayout`, your `Panel` will be shrunk to a width and height of zero, and not show up.

Core Warning

Never put an empty `Panel` *into a* `Container` *that is using* `FlowLayout`. *Your* `Panel` *will disappear.*

Creating and Using

As mentioned in the preceding section, if a `Panel` is placed in a Container that is using `FlowLayout`, it will be shrunk to its preferred size regardless of what size it was given initially. In addition, few other layout managers use the current size for anything, relying on the preferred size or the dimensions of the enclosing window instead. As a result, a `Panel` (unlike a `Canvas`) is usually not given an explicit size before being added to its `Container`.

Create the Panel

```
Panel panel = new Panel();
```

Add Components to Panel

```
panel.add(someComponent);
panel.add(someOtherComponent);
. . .
```

Add Panel to Current Container

To an external container not using `BorderLayout`:

```
container.add(panel);
```

From within a container (e.g., from within `init` in an `Applet` or in the constructor of a `Frame`) not using `BorderLayout`:

```
add(panel);
```

To an external container that is using `BorderLayout`:

```
container.add("Region", panel);
// E.g. add("South", ...);
```

From within a container that is using `BorderLayout`:

```
add("Region", panel); // E.g. add("Center", ...);
```

Example: Using a Panel for Grouping

Here's an example of using a `Panel` to group buttons. In the first example (Listing 11.7), eight buttons are added to an `Applet` that is wide enough to hold five side-by-side. So the first five buttons are placed in the first row, with the final three going into the second row (Figure 11–5). This is not the best layout, however, since the first four are related to one topic, and the second four are related to another. The second example (Listing 11.8) shows a way to group them this way by placing each set of buttons in a different panel. Figure 11–6 shows the result. A similar effect could have been obtained by using a layout manager called `GridLayout`, but the `Panel` approach has the advantage of keeping the sets of buttons together even if the window is too narrow to allow four buttons in a row.

Listing 11.7   ButtonTest1.java

```java
import java.applet.Applet;
import java.awt.*;

/** 8 ungrouped buttons in an Applet using FlowLayout. */

public class ButtonTest1 extends Applet {
  public void init() {
    String[] labelPrefixes = { "Start", "Stop",
                               "Pause", "Resume" };
    for (int i=0; i<4; i++)
      add(new Button(labelPrefixes[i] + " Thread1"));
    for (int i=0; i<4; i++)
      add(new Button(labelPrefixes[i] + " Thread2"));
  }
}
```

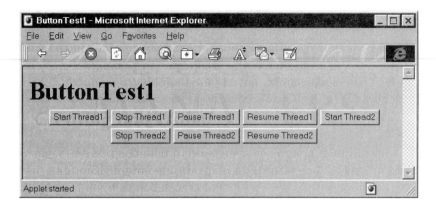

Figure 11-5   Without nested panels, as many components as can fit get packed into each row.

Listing II.8   ButtonTest2.java

```java
import java.applet.Applet;
import java.awt.*;

/** 8 buttons: 4 each in 2 panels. */

public class ButtonTest2 extends Applet {
  public void init() {
    String[] labelPrefixes = { "Start", "Stop",
                               "Pause", "Resume" };
    Panel p1 = new Panel();
    for (int i=0; i<4; i++)
      p1.add(new Button(labelPrefixes[i] + " Thread1"));
    Panel p2 = new Panel();
    for (int i=0; i<4; i++)
      p2.add(new Button(labelPrefixes[i] + " Thread2"));
    add(p1);
    add(p2);
  }

}
```

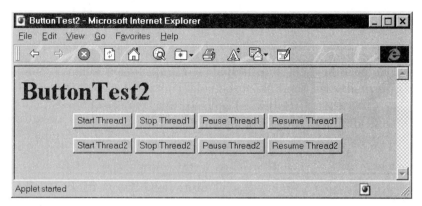

Figure 11–6   Nested panels can be used to group components together.

11.5 The Container Class

As we saw in Section 11.1, a Canvas is Java's basic blank window, used to draw into or to implement custom components. However, as a Component (Section 11.2) Canvas cannot contain any other window or a GUI control such as a label, button, or textfield (although in Java 1.1 it can contain a popup menu). In Section 11.4 we looked at Panel, Java's basic window used to hold other components. Windows that can hold other components are part of the Container class. In addition to all of the characteristics of Component, containers have the following methods. Methods that are overridden in Container but that perform the same abstract task as in the Component description are not repeated here.

> **public Component add(Component c)**
> **public Component add(Component c, int position)**
> **public Component add(String region, Component c)**
> **public Component add(Component c, Object constraints)**
>   **[Java 1.1]**
> **public Component add(Component c, Object constraints,**
>   **int position) [Java 1.1]**
> **protected void addImpl(Component c, Object constraints,**
>   **int position) [Java 1.1]**

These methods are used to add components to the window. The most common one is the first, which simply inserts the component in the last position in the component array. It is used with all standard layout man-

agers except `BorderLayout`, where you must specify a region of
`"North"`, `"South"`, `"East"`, `"West"`, or `"Center"`. You can also
supply a position; in such a case the other components are shifted down
the array to make room. Specify –1 or omit the index to put a component in the last position. Note that adjusting the order of components is
not a reliable way to control the stacking order of overlapping components. For instance on Unix, later components are stacked above earlier
ones. It is the other way around in most Windows 95/NT implementations. Lightweight components are always below regular ones. The
`Object` is used in Java 1.1 to specify layout constraints, and `addImpl`
was added to Java 1.1 to allow you to track all `add` requests.

Core Warning

*If you overlap components in a window, be aware that Java does not have a
portable method for controlling their z-order. The standard layout managers
will not overlap components, however.*

public void addContainerListener(ContainerListener listener) [Java 1.1]

This method is used in Java 1.1 to add an event listener. See Section
10.6 (Event Listeners in Java 1.1) for more information.

public int countComponents()
public int getComponentCount() [Java 1.1]

These methods return the number of components contained in the window. Components are counted even if they are not visible (see the
`isVisible` method of `Component`).

public Component getComponent(int position)

The `getComponent` method returns the *N*th element contained in
the window, where 0 corresponds to the first one added. It throws an
`ArrayIndexOutOfBoundsException` if you supply an *N* greater
than or equal to the value of `countComponents` (`getComponent-
Count`).

public Component[ ] getComponents()

This returns an array of the components contained in the window. The
array might have zero length, but will not be `null`.

public LayoutManager getLayout()

This returns the layout manager instance being used, `null` if there is none.

public Insets insets()
public Insets getInsets() [Java 1.1]

This returns an `Insets` object (`top`, `bottom`, `left`, and `right` fields) describing the margins of the window. The standard layout managers will never draw into these margins. There is no corresponding `setInsets` method; you have to override `insets` (`getInsets` in Java 1.1) to change it.

public boolean isAncestorOf
(Component possibleSubComponent) [Java 1.1]

This Java 1.1 method determines if the specified component is contained *anywhere* in the window's containment hierarchy.

public void paint(Graphics g)
public void print(Graphics g)

These methods are inherited from `Component`. However, there is an important difference in how they are used in containers. If your window contains any lightweight components and you override `paint` or `print`, you must call `super.paint(g)` or `super.print(g)` to make sure they are drawn properly. Since you never know if a lightweight component will be added later, it is a good idea to always call them at the end of `paint` or `print`.

public void paintComponents(Graphics g)
public void printComponents(Graphics g)

These methods can be called to print the component hierarchy. They are of little value; use `paintAll` or `printAll` (see `Component`) instead.

public void processContainerEvent(ContainerEvent event)
[Java 1.1]

If container events are enabled, this method can monitor them. See Section 10.5 (Handling Events in Java 1.1) for more information.

public void remove(Component c)
public void remove(int position) [Java 1.1]
The remove method can be used to take a specified component out of
the window. In Java 1.1, you can also remove the Nth component in the
window's component array. Assuming you used the normal version of
add, 0 corresponds to the first component added; getComponent-
Count()-1 corresponds to the last one.

public void setLayout(LayoutManager manager)
This method is used to change the layout manager. For instance, you
could change BorderLayout to FlowLayout for a Frame or tell an
Applet to use FlowLayout with a horizontal and vertical gap of 10
pixels instead of 5.

protected void validateTree() [Java 1.1]
This is called by the validate method (see Component) in Java 1.1.
You can override it if you want to customize the way you descend the
container tree and recompute layouts for subcomponents.

11.6 Lightweight Containers in Java 1.1

In Section 11.3 we saw that Java 1.1 introduced lightweight components that
can be partially transparent. Java 1.1 supports lightweight containers as well.
To illustrate why this is useful, consider Listing 11.9, which creates a Panel,
places some buttons in it, then puts that Panel in an Applet that contains

a background pattern. As Figure 11–7 illustrates, this `Panel` occludes the underlying `Applet`, even in the gaps between the buttons.

Listing 11.9   HeavyPanel.java

```
import java.applet.Applet;
import java.awt.*;

/** Illustrates that Panels are opaque. Java 1.1 only.
 * @see LightPanel
 */

public class HeavyPanel extends Applet {
  public void init() {
    setFont(new Font("TimesRoman", Font.BOLD, 18));
    Panel heavy = new Panel();
    heavy.add(new Button("Button 1"));
    heavy.add(new Button("Button 2"));
    add(heavy);
  }

  public void paint(Graphics g) {
    int width = getSize().width,
        height = getSize().height;
    for(int y=5; y<height; y=y+5)
      g.drawLine(0, y, width, y);
  }

}
```

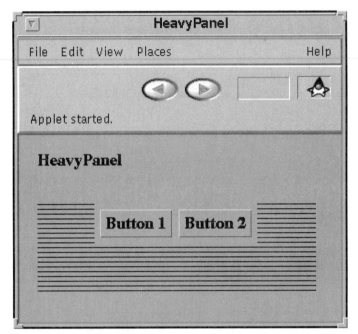

Figure 11–7   The built-in containers are rectangular and opaque.

With a lightweight container (Listing 11.10, Figure 11–8), however, the background applet is only occluded in the area reserved for the buttons themselves (the drawn area and the empty space reserved to show the input focus). Creating lightweight containers is quite easy: simply extend `Container`, set a layout manager, and you are ready to go. However, there is a very important change that needs to be made to the window that *holds* the lightweight container: if it overrides `paint` it now needs to call `super.paint` or any lightweight components it contains will not be drawn. In Java 1.1, because you may not be sure if a lightweight component will be added later, it is a good practice to always call `super.paint` at the bottom of a `paint` method in an `Applet`, `Panel`, `Frame`, or other `Container`.

Core Approach

If you override `paint` *in a* `Container` *that holds a lightweight component, you must call* `super.paint` *for the component to be drawn. In Java 1.1, it is good practice to call* `super.paint` *at the bottom of the* `paint` *method of all containers.*

Listing 11.10 `LightPanel.java`

```java
import java.applet.Applet;
import java.awt.*;

/** Illustrates that Java 1.1 lightweight containers
 *  can be transparent.
 * @see HeavyPanel
 */

class LightweightPanel extends Container {
  public LightweightPanel() {
     setLayout(new FlowLayout());
  }
}

public class LightPanel extends Applet {
  public void init() {
    setFont(new Font("TimesRoman", Font.BOLD, 18));
    LightweightPanel light = new LightweightPanel();
    light.add(new Button("Button 1"));
    light.add(new Button("Button 2"));
    add(light);
  }

  public void paint(Graphics g) {
    int width = getSize().width,
        height = getSize().height;
    for(int y=5; y<height; y=y+5)
      g.drawLine(0, y, width, y);
    super.paint(g); // Don't forget this
  }

}
```

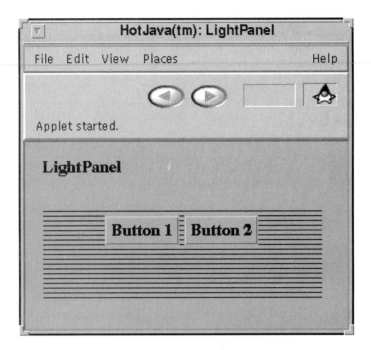

Figure 11-8   Lightweight containers can be partially transparent.

11.7 Applet

An `Applet` is a subclass of `Panel`, and can be used in stand-alone Java programs as well as Java programs embedded in Web pages. So we need to distinguish an `Applet` (a Java window type) from an "applet" (a Java program that runs in a Web browser as part of a WWW page). The following gives a very brief summary of `Applet`; for more details, see Chapter 9, "Applets, Graphical Applications, and Basic Drawing."

Major Purpose

The `Applet` class is for Java programs that will run exclusively in Web pages (applets) or that will be run as both applets and applications. These double-duty programs will be explained further in Section 11.9 (Frame).

Default LayoutManager: FlowLayout

This is unchanged from the parent `Panel` class.

Creating and Using

See Chapter 9, "Applets, Graphical Applications, and Basic Drawing."

11.8 ScrollPane

A `ScrollPane` is a scrollable `Container` added to the AWT in Java 1.1.

Major Purpose

A `ScrollPane` is a borderless window used to contain something too large to show all at once.

Default LayoutManager: None

Although a `Container`, it can only contain a *single* component. However, this one component could be a `Panel` containing many other components.

Core Alert

A `ScrollPane` *can only hold one component.*

Creating and Using

Although there are several options for controlling scrolling and scrolling programmatically, the most common use is to simply place a large `Component` or `Container` in the `ScrollPane`, letting the user scroll as needed.

Create the ScrollPane

The main option here is to designate whether or not scrollbars will be present. A `ScrollPane` made with the empty constructor only uses scrollbars when they are needed.

```
ScrollPane pane = new ScrollPane();
ScrollPane pane =
  new ScrollPane(ScrollPane.SCROLLBARS_ALWAYS);
ScrollPane pane =
  new ScrollPane(ScrollPane.SCROLLBARS_AS_NEEDED);
ScrollPane pane =
  new ScrollPane(ScrollPane.SCROLLBARS_NEVER);
```

Size the ScrollPane and Add It to a Container

A ScrollPane, like a Canvas, reports its current size as its preferredSize. So if it is going in a Container using FlowLayout, you might do

```
pane.setSize(width, height);
add(pane);
```

If BorderLayout is being used, you might simply do

```
add("Center", pane);
```

Example

Listing 11.11 shows a simple ScrollPane containing a 100-button Panel. Figures 11–9 and 11–10 show the result. It makes use of the Closeable-Frame class (Listing 11.13), a minor variation of Frame with built-in code to let you quit. See Section 11.9 (Frame) for details.

Listing 11.11 ScrollPaneTest.java

```java
import java.awt.*;

/** Places a Panel holding 100 buttons in a ScrollPane
 *  that is too small to hold it. Java 1.1 only.
 */

public class ScrollPaneTest extends CloseableFrame {
  public static void main(String[] args) {
    new ScrollPaneTest();
  }

  public ScrollPaneTest() {
    super("ScrollPane Test");
    ScrollPane pane = new ScrollPane();
    Panel bigPanel = new Panel();
    bigPanel.setLayout(new GridLayout(10, 10));
    for(int i=0; i<100; i++)
      bigPanel.add(new Button("Button " + i));
    pane.add(bigPanel);
    add("Center", pane);
    setSize(300, 300);
    setVisible(true);
  }
}
```

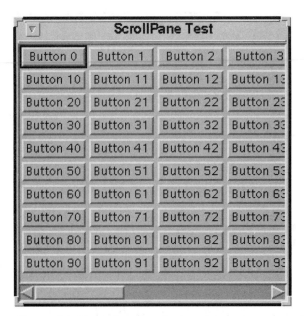

Figure 11-9 When first displayed, a ScrollPane shows the top left corner of the Component it contains.

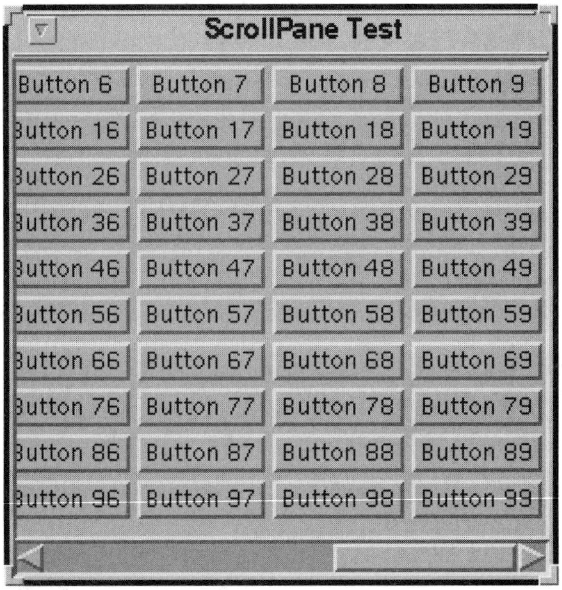

Figure 11-10 A ScrollPane can be scrolled to reveal any part of the enclosed Component that is beyond the bounds of the window.

11.9 Frame

A `Frame` is the starting point for graphical applications and can be used for popup windows in applets. It can contain other GUI components.

Major Purpose

A `Frame` is used to create a stand-alone window with its own title and menu bar, border, cursor, and icon image.

Default LayoutManager: BorderLayout

This layout manager divides the screen into five regions: `North`, `South`, `East`, `West`, and `Center`. Each region can contain at most one component, and you specify the region when adding the component to the window (e.g., `add("South", component)`). A component placed in the `North` or `South` region will be placed at the top or bottom of the frame, shrunk to its preferred height (see the `preferredSize` method of `Component`), and stretched to the full width of the frame, minus any margins (see the `insets` or `getInsets` method of `Container`). Components placed in the `East` or `West` region are placed at the right or left sides, shrunk to their preferred widths, and stretched to the full frame height, minus any margins and space for `North` and `South`. The `Center` region gets whatever is left. If you are already familiar with applets but not frames, the thing you will probably find most confusing is the layout manager. To switch the layout manager to the more familiar one that applets use, perform the following command:

```
setLayout(new FlowLayout());
```

For more details, see the discussion of `BorderLayout` in Chapter 12, "Arranging Windows Using Layout Managers."

Creating and Using: Option 1—A Fixed Size Frame

Create Frame:

```
Frame frame = new Frame(titleString);
```

Add any components to Frame

```
frame.add("Center", somePanel);
...
```

One of the most common errors when first starting out with frames is to forget the region in the call to add. If you simply do `frame.add(some-Component)`, nothing will show up. Alternatively, you can switch the layout manager to `FlowLayout` (which is what applets use) by using `setLayout`, as described in the previous subsection.

Resize the Frame

```
frame.resize(width, height); // Java 1.02
frame.setSize(width, height); // Java 1.1
```

or (at a specific location)

```
frame.reshape(left, top, width, height); // Java 1.02
frame.setBounds(left, top, width, height); // Java 1.1
```

Pop Up the Frame

```
frame.show(); // Java 1.02
frame.setVisible(true); // Java 1.1
```

Note that you can pop up frames from applets, but they will generally be annotated with some marking like "Unsigned Java Applet Window" (Netscape; see Figure 11–11) or "Warning: Applet Window" (Internet Explorer). This is to prevent applets from popping up official looking windows that say "Reestablishing lost network connection. Please enter username and password below," then reporting the password found to the applet's author.

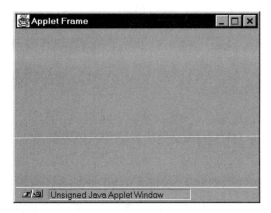

Figure 11–11 Frames started by applets typically have warning labels at the bottom.

Creating and Using: Option 2—A Frame That Stretches Depending on What It Contains

Create Frame:
```
Frame frame = new Frame(titleString);
```

Position the Frame (Optional)
```
frame.move(left, top); // Java 1.02
frame.setLocation(left, top); // Java 1.1
```

Add any components to Frame
```
frame.add("Center", somePanel);
...
```

Stretch the Frame
```
frame.pack();
```

Pop Up the Frame
```
frame.show(); // Java 1.02
frame.setVisible(true); // Java 1.1
```

Example 1: A Quittable Frame

By default, a `Frame` ignores all events including window-destroy events. So window-destroy events have to trapped explicitly in `handleEvent` (Java 1.02), or it will be difficult for the user to kill the `Frame`. A Frame that cannot be quit is of little use other than to annoy users, so the first thing to do when working with frames is to change this behavior. Listing 11.12 shows a `QuittableFrame` that calls `System.exit` when the user tries to quit it. This class will be used as the starting point for graphical applications throughout much of the rest of the book. Frames that are popped up from existing windows (e.g., from applets or other frames) should call `dispose`, not `System.exit`, when the user tries to close them. Also, since the title bar is part of the `Frame`, drawing that goes in the top several pixels will be covered up. So to draw reliably in frames you should either read the `insets()` (`getInsets()` in Java 1.1) values to determine where to start the drawing, or add a `Container` (e.g., `Panel`) to the `Center` and do the drawing there.

Listing 11.12 `QuittableFrame.java`

```java
import java.awt.*;

/** A Frame that you can actually quit. Used as
 *  the starting point for most Java 1.0 graphical
 *  applications. CloseableFrame is the Java 1.1 version.
 *  @see CloseableFrame
 */

public class QuittableFrame extends Frame {
  public QuittableFrame(String title) {
    super(title);
  }

  /** Catch window destroy events. Pass all other
   *  events to the original handler.
   */

  public boolean handleEvent(Event event) {
    if (event.id == Event.WINDOW_DESTROY)
      System.exit(0);
    return(super.handleEvent(event));
  }
}
```

`QuittableFrame` uses the Java 1.0 event-handling approach to catch the window-destroy events. Listing 11.13 shows a Java 1.1 version.

Listing 11.13 `CloseableFrame.java`

```java
import java.awt.*;
import java.awt.event.*;

/** A Frame that you can actually quit. Used as
 *  the starting point for most Java 1.1 graphical
 *  applications. QuittableFrame is the Java 1.0 version.
 * @see QuittableFrame
 */

public class CloseableFrame extends Frame {
  public CloseableFrame(String title) {
    super(title);
    enableEvents(AWTEvent.WINDOW_EVENT_MASK);
  }

  /** Since we are doing something permanent, we need
   *  to call super.processWindowEvent <B>first</B>.
   */

  public void processWindowEvent(WindowEvent event) {
    super.processWindowEvent(event); // Handle listeners
    if (event.getID() == WindowEvent.WINDOW_CLOSING)
      System.exit(0);
  }
}
```

Example 2: A Class that Can Be Run as an Applet or an Application

When an applet is loaded by a browser, the `main` method is ignored. By making a `main` method that imitates what the browser does (stick the `Applet` in a `Frame`, initialize it, display it), you can create an `Applet` that can be run either stand-alone *or* embedded in a Web page. (See Listing 11.14 and Figures 11–12 and 11–13.)

Listing 11.14 `DualUse.java`

```
import java.applet.Applet;
import java.awt.*;

/** A class that runs as an applet or an application. */

public class DualUse extends Applet {

  /** The main method is ignored by applets. */

  public static void main(String[] args) {
    Frame mainFrame = new QuittableFrame("DualUse");
    DualUse app = new DualUse();
    app.init();
    app.start();
    mainFrame.resize(420,120); // Match <APPLET> values
    mainFrame.add("Center", app);
    mainFrame.show();
  }

  public void paint(Graphics g) {
    Font font = new Font("TimesRoman", Font.BOLD, 60);
    g.setFont(font);
    g.drawString("DualUse Applet", 0, 70);
  }
}
```

Figure 11–12   The `DualUse` class can run as an applet.

Figure 11–13   The `DualUse` class can run as an application.

Unfortunately, most of the useful methods of the `Applet` class are only available once the browser sets up the appropriate context. You can fix a few of these yourself, for example, overriding `getImage` to call `getToolkit.getImage`. Other methods such as `getParameter`, `showDocument`, and `getDocumentBase` would be difficult to replace. One of the most serious losses is `getAudioClip`. Amazingly, Java has no support for audio in applications, only in applets! Using the `Applet` class in an application won't help. If you are *really* desperate for audio in applications, you can try the following trick (Listing 11.15). It is absolutely, positively not guaranteed to be portable (don't say I didn't warn you!), but happens to work in most 1.0 Java implementations. Fortunately, the Java Media Framework, due in 1997 or 1998, will have extensive audio support. See `http://java.sun.com/products/java-media/jmf/` for more information.

See `http://www.apl.jhu.edu/~hall/java/JavaStub.html` for a Java application that uses this approach to automatically generate stub Java classes that can be run as either applets or applications. Given "Foo" as input, it generates `Foo.java`, that can be compiled and then run either standalone or by loading `Foo.html` (also generated automatically), which references `Foo.class`.

Listing 11.15   `DualUseWithAudio.java`

```java
import java.applet.Applet;
import java.awt.*;

import java.net.*;    // for getImage & getAudioClip
import sun.applet.AppletAudioClip; // for AppletAudioClip

/** <B>Warning!</B> This is not portable, but happens
 *  to work on most Java 1.0 implementations.
 *  There is <B>no</B> portable way to play audio
 *  from non-applets in Java 1.0.
 */

public class DualUseWithAudio extends Applet {
  public static void main(String[] args) {
    Frame mainFrame = new Frame("DualUseWithAudio");
    DualUseWithAudio app = new DualUseWithAudio();
    app.start();
    app.init();
    mainFrame.resize(500,400);
    mainFrame.add("Center", app);
    mainFrame.show();
    mainFrame.repaint();
  }

  public java.applet.AudioClip getAudioClip(URL url) {
    return new AppletAudioClip(url);
  }
  ...
}
```

Menus

Frames let you add menu bars that contain one or more menus. To use menus, first create a MenuBar, then one or more Menu objects. You can add a String (a label), another Menu (a cascading choice), or a CheckboxMenuItem (a choice with a checkbox) to a Menu. Once you have your menus, place them in the MenuBar using the MenuBar's add (to put them left to right) or setHelpMenu (to put a menu at the far right corner) method. Finally, put the MenuBar in the Frame via the Frame's set-MenuBar method. Handling menu selections in Java 1.0 is a bit inconvenient: the action events are sent to the Frame, not to the Menu or MenuBar. In Java 1.0, this means that you have to override the very low-level postEvent method in the Menu, or use the action helping method in the Frame. Listing 11.16 gives an example that creates a menu of color choices, using the Java 1.0 event model to set the background of the Frame whenever a choice is selected. Figure 11–14 shows the result. For use of the Java 1.1 event model with menus, see the discussion of PopupMenu in Chapter 13, "Graphical User Interface Controls."

Listing 11.16 ColorMenu.java

```java
import java.awt.*;

/** Illustrates the insertion of menu entries in
 *  Frame menubars.
 */

public class ColorMenu extends QuittableFrame {
  public static void main(String[] args) {
    new ColorMenu();
  }

  private String[] colorNames =
    { "Black", "White",
      "Light Gray", "Medium Gray", "Dark Gray" };
  private Color[] colorValues =
    { Color.black, Color.white,
      Color.lightGray, Color.gray, Color.darkGray };

  public ColorMenu() {
    super("ColorMenu");
    MenuBar bar = new MenuBar();
    Menu colorMenu = new Menu("Colors");
    for(int i=0; i<2; i++)
      colorMenu.add(colorNames[i]);
    Menu grayMenu = new Menu("Gray");
    for(int i=2; i<colorNames.length; i++)
      grayMenu.add(colorNames[i]);
    colorMenu.add(grayMenu);
    bar.add(colorMenu);
    setMenuBar(bar);
    setBackground(Color.lightGray);
    resize(400, 200);
    show();
  }
```

continued

Listing 11.16 `ColorMenu.java` (continued)

```
/** Catch menu events in the containing Frame. */

public boolean action(Event event, Object label) {
  if (event.target instanceof MenuItem) {
    setBackground(getMenuColor(label));
    repaint();
    return(true);
  } else
    return(false);
}

private Color getMenuColor(Object label) {
  for(int i=0; i<colorNames.length; i++)
    if(label.equals(colorNames[i]))
      return(colorValues[i]);
  return(Color.red);
}
}
```

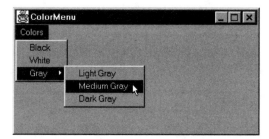

Figure 11-14 Frames can contain menu bars.

Since menu bars can only be added to frames, nested components need to find the enclosing frame before creating the menu bar. Listing 11.17 shows a getFrame method that can be used to accomplish this. Although a few browsers (appletviewer, Netscape on Unix) let you use this trick to add menu bars to applets, most do not. So in Java 1.02, menus should be reserved for applications. Java 1.1 introduces popup menus, which can be added to any component.

Listing 11.17   Finding the enclosing Frame

```
public class SomeComponent extends SomeOtherComponent {
  ...
  private Frame frame = null;

  private Frame getFrame() {
    if (frame == null) {
      Container containingWin = getParent();
      while (containingWin != null) {
        if (containingWin instanceof Frame) {
          frame = (Frame)containingWin;
          break;
        } else
          containingWin = containingWin.getParent();
      }
    }
    return(frame);
  }
}
```

Other Useful Frame Methods

The following gives a quick overview of the methods available specifically in the Frame class. All of the Component and Container methods are available as well, of course.

public void dispose()

This method destroys the Frame's peer (actual native window) and those of all nested components. Since you cannot call System.exit from applets, a quittable frame launched from an applet should dispose itself when it gets WINDOW_DESTROY events.

public int getCursorType()
public void setCursor(int cursorType)

These methods get and set the current cursor in Java 1.02, as illustrated in the discussion of mouseEnter in Section 10.2 (Event-Handling Helper Methods in Java 1.02). In Java 1.1, use the setCursor and getCursor methods of Component instead. The cursor type can be one of Frame.CROSSHAIR_CURSOR, Frame.DEFAULT_CURSOR, Frame.E_RESIZE_CURSOR, Frame.HAND_CURSOR, Frame.MOVE_CURSOR, Frame.N_RESIZE_CURSOR,

Frame.NE_RESIZE_CURSOR, Frame.NW_RESIZE_CURSOR,
Frame.S_RESIZE_CURSOR, Frame.SE_RESIZE_CURSOR,
Frame.SW_RESIZE_CURSOR, Frame.TEXT_CURSOR,
Frame.W_RESIZE_CURSOR, or Frame.WAIT_CURSOR. Note that
on most Windows 95/NT implementations, the HAND_CURSOR is
drawn as an upward pointing arrow instead of a pointing hand. Neither
Java 1.0 nor 1.1 let you define your own cursor images.

public Image getIconImage()
public void setIconImage(Image icon)

These methods let you retrieve or change the image that will be used
when the Frame is iconified. The return value of getIconImage will
be null if you haven't explicitly called setIconImage.

public MenuBar getMenuBar()
public void setMenuBar(MenuBar menuBar)
public void remove(MenuComponent menuBar)

These methods let you retrieve or change the menu bar, as illustrated
earlier in this section.

public String getTitle()
public void setTitle(String title)

These methods let you retrieve or change the label in the Frame's title
bar.

public boolean isResizable()
public void setResizable(boolean resizeFlag)

By default, users can interactively stretch or shrink frames you create.
Calling setResizable(false) will suppress this; isResizable
will report the current setting. However, note that setResizable is
ignored on most Solaris implementations in both Java 1.0 and 1.1.

public void pack()

The pack method resizes the Frame based on the preferred sizes of
the components it contains.

public void toBack()
public void toFront()
These methods move the `Frame` to the back or front of the display (i.e., behind or on top of any overlapping windows).

11.10 Serializing Windows

Java 1.1 introduced an extremely useful capability: *serialization*. This lets you save the state of Java objects to disk or to send them over the network. In particular, with a single command (`writeObject`), we can save the state of a frame or other window, including all subwindows, sizes, locations, colors, and GUI controls. The only restriction is that any objects the window references must be serializable if you want them to be saved with the window. All AWT objects are already serializable, and making other objects serializable is a trivial matter of having the class implement the `Serializable` interface. This interface does not declare any methods, so implementing it is a simple matter of tacking "implements `Serializable`" onto the class definition. If you have a field you don't want to bother saving, you can declare it `transient`. The frame can be reconstituted later with a single command (`readObject`).

Writing a Window to Disk

A standard approach to saving a window is as follows, assuming your code imports `java.io.*`:

```
try {
  FileOutputStream fileOut =
    new FileOutputStream("SaveFilename");
  ObjectOutputStream out =
    new ObjectOutputStream(fileOut);
  out.writeObject(someWindow);
  out.flush();
  out.close();
} catch(IOException ioe) {
  System.out.println("Error saving window: " + ioe);
}
```

If you are concerned about disk space, you can interpose a `GZIPOut-`
`putStream` (in `java.util.zip`) between the `FileOutputStream`
and the `ObjectOutputStream`, but serialized windows are relatively
compact even without compression.

Reading a Window from Disk

Reading the window back in is equally easy:

```
try {
  File saveFile = new File("SaveFilename");
  FileInputStream fileIn =
    new FileInputStream(saveFile);
  ObjectInputStream in =
    new ObjectInputStream(fileIn);
  someWindow = (WindowType)in.readObject();
  doSomethingWith(someWindow); // E.g. setVisible
} catch(IOException ioe) {
  System.out.println("Error reading file: " + ioe);
} catch(ClassNotFoundException cnfe) {
  System.out.println("No such class: " + cnfe);
}
```

If the window was compressed when saved, you should put a `GZIPIn-`
`putStream` between the `FileInputStream` and the `ObjectInput-`
`Stream`.

Example: A Saveable Frame

Listing 11.18 creates a `Frame` that lets you draw circles by clicking the
mouse. After drawing circles, moving the `Frame` around, and stretching it
interactively, you can press "Save" to store the result on disk. Next time you
run the same program, the saved version is automatically loaded: circles, buttons, location, size, and all. Figure 11–15 shows the result after adding some
circles, quitting, and restarting in a later session. The `SavedFrame` class
makes use of two helper classes. `CirclePanel` is shown in Listing 11.19; it
is simply a `Panel` with a `MouseListener` that adds circles wherever the

mouse is clicked. The circles themselves are instances of the `BetterCir-cle` class. This was shown earlier in Listing 11.5.

Listing 11.18 `SavedFrame.java`

```java
import java.awt.*;
import java.awt.event.*;
import java.io.*;

/** A Frame that lets you draw circles with mouse
 *  clicks and then save the Frame and all circles to
 *  disk. Java 1.1 only.
 */

public class SavedFrame extends CloseableFrame
                        implements ActionListener {
  //-------------------------------------------------
  /** If a saved version exists, use it. Otherwise
   *  create a new one.
   */

  public static void main(String[] args) {
    SavedFrame frame;
    File serializeFile = new File(serializeFilename);
    if (serializeFile.exists())
      try {
        FileInputStream fileIn =
          new FileInputStream(serializeFile);
        ObjectInputStream in =
          new ObjectInputStream(fileIn);
        frame = (SavedFrame)in.readObject();
        frame.setVisible(true);
      } catch(IOException ioe) {
        System.out.println("Error reading file: " + ioe);
      } catch(ClassNotFoundException cnfe) {
        System.out.println("No such class: " + cnfe);
      }
    else
      frame = new SavedFrame();
  }
```

continued

Listing 11.18 `SavedFrame.java` **(continued)**

```
//-----------------------------------------------------
private static String serializeFilename =
  "SavedFrame.ser";
private CirclePanel circlePanel;
private Button clearButton, saveButton;

//-----------------------------------------------------
/** Build a frame with CirclePanel and buttons. */

public SavedFrame() {
  super("SavedFrame");
  setBackground(Color.white);
  setFont(new Font("Serif", Font.BOLD, 18));
  circlePanel = new CirclePanel();
  add("Center", circlePanel);
  Panel buttonPanel = new Panel();
  buttonPanel.setBackground(Color.lightGray);
  clearButton = new Button("Clear");
  saveButton = new Button("Save");
  buttonPanel.add(clearButton);
  buttonPanel.add(saveButton);
  add("South", buttonPanel);
  clearButton.addActionListener(this);
  saveButton.addActionListener(this);
  setSize(500, 500);
  setVisible(true);
}
```

Listing 11.18 `SavedFrame.java` **(continued)**

```java
/** If "Clear" clicked, delete all existing circles.
 *  If "Save" clicked, save existing frame
 *  configuration (size, location, circles, etc.)
 *  to disk.
 */

public void actionPerformed(ActionEvent event) {
  if (event.getSource() == clearButton) {
    circlePanel.removeAll();
    circlePanel.repaint();
  } else if (event.getSource() == saveButton) {
    try {
      FileOutputStream fileOut =
        new FileOutputStream("SavedFrame.ser");
      ObjectOutputStream out =
        new ObjectOutputStream(fileOut);
      out.writeObject(this);
      out.flush();
      out.close();
    } catch(IOException ioe) {
      System.out.println("Error saving frame: " + ioe);
    }
  }
}
}
```

Listing 11.19   `CirclePanel.java`

```java
import java.awt.*;
import java.awt.event.*;
import java.io.*;

/** A Panel that draws circles centered wherever
 *  the user clicks the mouse. <B>Uses a null
 *  layout manager.</B>.
 */

public class CirclePanel extends Panel {
  class ClickAdapter extends MouseAdapter
                      implements Serializable {
    public void mouseClicked(MouseEvent event) {
      BetterCircle circle =
        new BetterCircle(Color.black, 50);
      add(circle);
      circle.setCenter(event.getX(), event.getY());
      invalidate();
      validate();
    }
  }

  public CirclePanel() {
    setLayout(null);
    addMouseListener(new ClickAdapter());
  }
}
```

Figure 11-15 Serialization lets you save the complete frame configuration to disk. The saved version is automatically used in later sessions.

11.11 Dialog

A Dialog is a stripped down Frame, useful for applications that don't need all of the capabilities of a Frame.

Major Purposes

A Simplified Frame (no cursor, menu, icon image).

A nonmodal dialog can be used in a similar manner to a Frame, but requires less resources and is faster to pop up.

A modal Dialog that freezes interaction with other AWT components until it is closed.

A modal dialog can be used in situations that require the user to respond before other processing can continue.

Default LayoutManager: BorderLayout

This layout manager divides the screen into five regions: North, South, East, West, and Center. See the discussion of BorderLayout in Chapter 12, "Arranging Windows Using Layout Managers."

Creating and Using

Using a Dialog is similar to using a Frame except that the constructor takes two additional arguments: the parent Frame and a boolean specifying whether or not it is modal, as below:

```
Dialog dialog =
  new Dialog(parentFrame, titleString, false);
Dialog modalDialog =
  new Dialog(parentFrame, titleString, true);
```

To use dialog boxes from applets, you need to find the parent frame (e.g., using the getFrame method shown in Listing 11.17). Modal dialogs will freeze all mouse/keyboard interaction with other Java components, but in Java 1.02 they will not necessarily suspend the calling frame's thread. That is, in Java 1.02, the following is not necessarily safe (it generally works in Windows implementations, generally fails on Unix):

```
modalDialog.show(); // Should wait here
doSomethingDependingOnDialogResults();
```

In Java 1.1, the above approach is safe.

Core Warning

In Java 1.02, modal dialogs may not properly freeze the calling thread. They work properly in Java 1.1.

Example: A Quit Confirmation Dialog

Listing 11.20 presents a dialog box with two buttons, asking you if you really want to quit. Clicking the "Yes" button quits the entire application, while clicking the "No" closes the dialog box itself, but leaves the rest of the application alone. Listing 11.21 associates this with the WINDOW_DESTROY event, so that the dialog box pops up when the user tries to quit the window. Figure 11–16 shows the result.

Listing 11.20 `Confirm.java`

```java
import java.awt.*;

/** A modal dialog box with two buttons: Yes and No.
 *  Clicking Yes exits Java. Clicking No exits the
 *  dialog. Used for confirmed quits from frames.
 */

class Confirm extends Dialog {
  private Button yes, no;

  public Confirm(Frame parent) {
    super(parent, "Confirmation", true);
    setLayout(new FlowLayout());
    add(new Label("Really quit?"));
    yes = new Button("Yes");
    no  = new Button("No");
    add(yes);
    add(no);
    pack();
    show();
  }

  public boolean action(Event event, Object object) {
    if (event.target == yes) {
      System.exit(0);
      return(true);
    } else {
      dispose();
      return(true);
    }
  }
}
```

Listing 11.21 ConfirmTest.java

```java
import java.awt.*;

/** A Frame that uses the Confirm dialog to
 *  verify that users really want to quit.
 * @see Confirm
 */

public class ConfirmTest extends Frame {
  public static void main(String[] args) {
    new ConfirmTest();
  }

  public ConfirmTest() {
    super("Confirming QUIT");
    resize(200, 200);
    show();
  }

  public ConfirmTest(String title) {
    super(title);
  }

  public boolean handleEvent(Event event) {
    if (event.id == Event.WINDOW_DESTROY)
      new Confirm(this);
    return(super.handleEvent(event));
  }
}
```

Figure 11-16 Modal dialogs freeze interaction with all other Java components.

11.12 FileDialog

A `FileDialog` is a type of modal dialog that can be used to load or save files.

Major Purpose

`FileDialog` is used for loading or saving files. Use this with applications; normal applets cannot access the local disk.

Default LayoutManager: None

Although a `FileDialog` is technically a `Container`, it cannot hold any other components, and has no layout manager.

Creating and Using

Make the FileDialog

```
FileDialog fileLoader =
  new FileDialog(frame, title, FileDialog.LOAD);
FileDialog fileSaver =
  new FileDialog(frame, title, FileDialog.SAVE);
```

Set a Default File or File Type

```
fileLoader.setFile("*.txt");
```

Pop Up the FileDialog

```
fileLoader.show();
```

Look Up the Filename Chosen

```
String filename = fileLoader.getFile();
```

Example: Displaying Files in a TextArea

Listing 11.22 shows a Frame that is mostly filled with a large TextArea, but that also contains one button at the bottom (see Figure 11–17). When the button is pressed, a FileDialog appears (Figure 11–18) to let the user choose a filename. Once that filename is chosen, a FileInputStream is opened and the file contents are placed in the TextArea (Figure 11–19).

Listing 11.22 `DisplayFile.java`

```java
import java.awt.*;
import java.io.*;

/** Uses a FileDialog to choose the file to display. */

public class DisplayFile extends QuittableFrame {
  public static void main(String[] args) {
    new DisplayFile();
  }

  private Button loadButton;
  private TextArea fileArea;
  private FileDialog loader;

  public DisplayFile() {
    super("Using FileDialog");
    loadButton = new Button("Display File");
    Panel buttonPanel = new Panel();
    buttonPanel.add(loadButton);
    add("South", buttonPanel);
    fileArea = new TextArea();
    add("Center", fileArea);
    loader =
      new FileDialog(this, "Browse", FileDialog.LOAD);
    // Default file extension: .java
    loader.setFile("*.java");
    resize(500, 700);
    show();
  }
```

continued

Listing 11.22 `DisplayFile.java` **(continued)**

```java
/** When the button is clicked, a file dialog is opened.
 *  When file dialog is closed, load the file it
 *  referenced.
 */

public boolean action(Event event, Object object) {
  if (event.target == loadButton) {
    loader.show();
    displayFile(loader.getFile());
    return(true);
  } else
    return(false);
}

public void displayFile(String filename) {
  try {
    File file = new File(filename);
    FileInputStream in = new FileInputStream(file);
    int fileLength = (int)file.length();
    byte[] fileContents = new byte[fileLength];
    in.read(fileContents);
    // Supply hiByte of 0 to turn byte[] into String
    String fileContentsString =
      new String(fileContents, 0);
    fileArea.setText(fileContentsString);
  } catch(IOException ioe) {
    fileArea.setText("IOError: " + ioe);
  }
}
}
```

Figure 11-17 The initial Frame shows a Button and an empty TextArea.

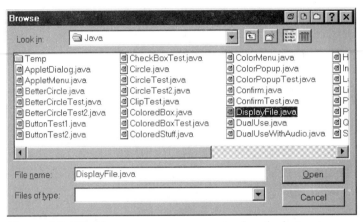

Figure 11-18 The `FileDialog` pops up when the button is pressed.

```
import java.awt.*;
import java.io.*;

public class DisplayFile extends QuittableFrame {
  public static void main(String[] args) {
    new DisplayFile();
  }

  private Button loadButton;
  private TextArea fileArea;
  private FileDialog loader;

  public DisplayFile() {
    super("Using FileDialog");
    loadButton = new Button("Display File");
    Panel buttonPanel = new Panel();
    buttonPanel.add(loadButton);
    add("South", buttonPanel);
    fileArea = new TextArea();
    add("Center", fileArea);
    loader =
      new FileDialog(this, "Browse", FileDialog.LOAD);
    loader.setFile("*.java");
    resize(500, 700);
    show();
  }

  public boolean action(Event event, Object object) {
    if (event.target == loadButton) {
      loader.show();
      displayFile(loader.getFile());
      return(true);
    } else
      return(false);
  }

  public void displayFile(String filename) {
```

Figure 11-19 After choosing a file, it is displayed in the `TextArea`.

11.13 Window

`Window` is the underlying class that `Frame` is built upon. It is used less frequently than the other window types.

Major Purpose

The `Window` class is used to create popup windows with no border or title bar.

Default LayoutManager: BorderLayout

This layout manager divides the screen into five regions: `North`, `South`, `East`, `West`, and `Center`. See the discussion of `BorderLayout` in Chapter 12, "Arranging Windows Using Layout Managers."

Creating and Using: Option 1—A Fixed Size Window

Create Window:

```
Window win = new Window(parentFrame);
```

Add any components to Window

```
win.add("Center", somePanel);
...
```

Resize the Window

```
win.resize(width, height); // Java 1.02
win.setSize(width, height); // Java 1.1
```

or (at a specific location)

```
win.reshape(left, top, width, height); // Java 1.02
win.setBounds(left, top, width, height); // Java 1.1
```

Pop Up the Window

```
win.show(); // Java 1.02
win.setVisible(true); // Java 1.1
```

Creating and Using: Option 2—A Window That Stretches Depending on What It Contains

Create Window:
```
Window win = new Window(parentFrame);
```

Position the Window (Optional)
```
win.move(left, top); // Java 1.02
win.setLocation(left, top); // Java 1.1
```

Add any components to Window
```
win.add("Center", somePanel);
...
```

Stretch the Window
```
win.pack();
```

Pop Up the Window
```
win.show(); // Java 1.02
win.setVisible(true); // Java 1.1
```

Example

Java 1.1 contains a PopupMenu class. Java 1.02 doesn't. However, you can fake a popup menu in 1.02 by using the Window class. The idea is to pop up a window containing a scrolling listbox when the secondary mouse button is clicked. The window will be closed whenever the user selects an item or moves the mouse off the window. Before exiting, the doAction method will be called. The basic Popup class is shown in Listing 11.23. A subclass called ColorPopup is shown in Listing 11.24. This class overrides the doAction method to set the background color of the window. Finally, Listing 11.25 shows an applet that displays a ColorPopup whenever the secondary mouse button is pressed. Figures 11–20 and 11–21 show the results. This is a far from perfect solution. For one thing, the List object does not work quite like a normal popup menu. For another, Netscape and Internet Explorer do not give you a way to find out the absolute location of the mouse on the screen, so there is no way to guarantee that this "menu" pops up under the mouse in applets. Fortunately, popup menus are standard in Java 1.1 (see Chapter 13, "Graphical User Interface Controls").

Listing 11.23 Popup.java

```java
import java.awt.*;

/** A pseudo-popup-menu to use in Java 1.0, which
 *  doesn't have a real one. It is really a listbox
 *  in a borderless window, with mouse tracking so
 *  it is closed when you move off it.
 */

public class Popup extends Window {
  private Component source;
  private List list;

  public Popup(Frame source) {
    super(source);
    resize(100, 100);
    this.source = source;
  }

  public void display(String[] labels, int x, int y) {
    list = new List();
    for(int i=0; i<labels.length; i++)
      list.addItem(labels[i]);
    list.select(0);
    add("Center", list);
    pack();
    move(source.bounds().x + x,
         source.bounds().y + y);
    show();
  }

  /** Clicking an entry or moving off the menu
   *  counts as activating the menu.
   */

  public boolean handleEvent(Event event) {
    switch(event.id) {
      case Event.ACTION_EVENT:
      case Event.LIST_SELECT:
      case Event.MOUSE_EXIT:
        doAction();
        dispose();
        return(true);
      default: return(super.handleEvent(event));
    }
  }
}
```

continued

Listing 11.23 Popup.java (continued)

```
/** This is the method you override in subclasses
 *   to put the action that should be taken
 *   when a menu entry is selected. Use
 *   getList().getSelectedItem() or
 *   getList.getSelectedIndex() to determine which
 *   entry was chosen.
 */

public void doAction() {} // override in subclass

protected List getList() {
  return(list);
}
}
```

Listing 11.24   ColorPopup.java

```java
import java.awt.*;

/** A Popup that takes an array of colornames and
 *   an array of colors, setting a specified
 *   component to the corresponding color when
 *   a colorname is chosen.
 */

public class ColorPopup extends Popup {
  private Component target;
  private String[] colorNames;
  private Color[] colors;

  public ColorPopup(Frame source) {
    super(source);
  }

  public void display(Component target,
                      String[] colorNames,
                      Color[] colors,
                      int x, int y) {
    this.target = target;
    this.colorNames = colorNames;
    this.colors = colors;
    display(colorNames, x, y);
  }

  public void doAction() {
    int colorIndex = getList().getSelectedIndex();
    if (colorIndex >= 0)
      target.setBackground(colors[colorIndex]);
    target.repaint();
  }
}
```

Listing 11.25 `ColorPopupTest.java`

```
import java.applet.Applet;
import java.awt.*;

/** Tries out the ColorPopUp pseudo-menu class. */

public class ColorPopupTest extends Applet {
  private ColorPopup popup;

  public void init() {
    popup = new ColorPopup(getFrame());
    setBackground(Color.lightGray);
  }

  /** Pop up "menu" when right mouse button clicked. */

  public boolean mouseDown(Event event, int x, int y) {
    if ((event.modifiers & Event.META_MASK) != 0) {
      String[] colorNames = { "White", "Light Gray",
                              "Gray", "Dark Gray",
                              "Black" };
      Color[] colors = { Color.white, Color.lightGray,
                         Color.gray, Color.darkGray,
                         Color.black };
      popup.display(this, colorNames, colors, x, y);
      return(true);
    } else
      return(false);
  }

  private Frame frame = null;

  private Frame getFrame() {
    if (frame == null) {
      Container containingWin = getParent();
      while (containingWin != null) {
        if (containingWin instanceof Frame) {
          frame = (Frame)containingWin;
          break;
        } else
          containingWin = containingWin.getParent();
      }
    }
    return(frame);
  }
}
```

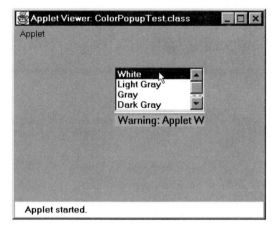

Figure 11-20   The popup "menu" is displayed when the right mouse button is clicked.

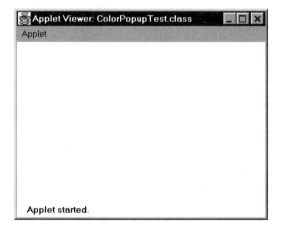

Figure 11-21   When the popup "menu" is closed, its doAction method is called. Here, that method changes the applet's background color.

11.14 The ImageLabel Class

In Section 11.1 (Canvas), I mentioned that Canvas is a good starting place for custom components, and showed an example of an ImageLabel class. This section gives more details on this class and presents the source code.

Major Purposes

Displaying an image in its own window, a base class for an image button (see Section 13.3).

Creating and Using

Create an `ImageLabel` by supplying an image to its constructor. Then simply drop it in a window. If you want to resize it, do so before it is first displayed.

Constructors

public ImageLabel(URL imageFile)
public ImageLabel(URL imageDirectory, String imageFile)
This creates an `ImageLabel` from the specified file, which should be in GIF or JPEG format.

public ImageLabel(Image image)
If you already have an `Image`, you can turn it into an `ImageLabel` using this constructor.

public ImageLabel()
This creates an `ImageLabel` from the file specified in `getDefault-ImageString`.

Other ImageButton Methods

public void centerAt(int x, int y)
This moves the `ImageLabel` so that its center is at the specified x and y. Note that explicit positioning will be undone by most layout managers.

public int getBorder()
public void setBorder(int borderWidth)
This retrieves or specifies the size of the border around the outside of the image.

public Color getBorderColor()
public void setBorderColor(Color borderColor)
This retrieves or specifies the color of the `ImageLabel` border. This may be distinct from the background color, since a partially transparent image will let the background color show through. Note that the get-

`Background` and `setBackground` methods are inherited from `Component`.

public static String getDefaultImageString()
public static void setDefaultImageString(String imageFile)
These static methods retrieve or specify the default image file. Use with caution, if at all.

public Image getImage()
This returns the `Image` used in the `ImageLabel`. If you want to pre-load the image before the `ImageLabel` is actually drawn, call `prepareImage` on this value.

public String getImageString()
If you created the `ImageLabel` from a file, this will show the file name. Used mainly for debugging.

public int getWidth()
public int getHeight()
These report the width/height of the `ImageLabel`. If no explicit `resize`/`reshape` call was performed, this will be the image width/height plus twice the border thickness.

public boolean hasExplicitSize()
This determines if the user has called `resize` or `reshape` on the `ImageLabel` before it was displayed. If so, that size will be maintained. Otherwise the `ImageLabel` will be shrunk to just fit the image (plus the borders).

public void waitForImage(boolean doLayout)
This starts loading the image, not returning until done. Supply a value of `true` for `doLayout`.

Example

See Section 11.1 (Canvas).

Source Code

Listing 11.26 presents the source code for the `ImageLabel` class.

Listing 11.26   `ImageLabel.java`

```java
import java.awt.*;
import java.net.*;

//========================================================
/**
 * A class for displaying images. It places the Image
 * into a canvas so that it can be moved around by layout
 * managers, will get repainted automatically, etc.
 * No mouseXXX or action events are defined, so it is
 * most similar to the Label Component.
 * <P>
 * By default, with FlowLayout the ImageLabel takes
 * its minimum size (just enclosing the image). The
 * default with BorderLayout is to expand to fill
 * the region in width (North/South), height
 * (East/West) or both (Center). This is the same
 * behavior as with the builtin Label class. If you
 * give an explicit resize or
 * reshape call <B>before</B> adding the
 * ImageLabel to the Container, this size will
 * override the defaults.
 * <P>
 * Here is an example of its use:
 * <P>
 * <PRE>
 * public class ShowImages extends Applet {
 *    private ImageLabel image1, image2;
 *
 *    public void init() {
 *       image1 = new ImageLabel(getCodeBase(),
 *                               "some-image.gif");
 *       image2 = new ImageLabel(getCodeBase(),
 *                               "other-image.jpg");
 *       add(image1);
 *       add(image2);
 *    }
 * }
 * </PRE>
 *
 * @author Marty Hall (hall@apl.jhu.edu)
 * @see Icon
 * @see ImageButton
 * @version 1.0 (1997)
 */
```

Listing 11.26 `ImageLabel.java` (continued)

```java
public class ImageLabel extends Canvas {
//----------------------------------------------------
// Instance variables.

// The actual Image drawn on the canvas.
private Image image;

// A String corresponding to the URL of the image
// you will get if you call the constructor with
// no arguments.
private static String defaultImageString
    = "http://java.sun.com/lib/images/" +
      "logo.java.color-transp.55x60.gif";

// The URL of the image. But sometimes we will use
// an existing image object (e.g. made by
// createImage) for which this info will not be
// available, so a default string is used here.
private String imageString = "<Existing Image>";

// Turn this on to get verbose debugging messages.
private boolean debug = false;

/** Amount of extra space around the image. */
private int border = 0;

/** If there is a non-zero border, what color should
 *  it be? Default is to use the background color
 *  of the Container.
 */
private Color borderColor = null;

// Width and height of the Canvas. This is the
//  width/height of the image plus twice the border.
private int width, height;
```

continued

Listing 11.26 `ImageLabel.java` (continued)

```java
/** Determines if it will be sized automatically.
 *  If the user issues a resize() or reshape()
 *  call before adding the label to the Container,
 *  or if the LayoutManager resizes before
 *  drawing (as with BorderLayout), then those sizes
 *  override the default, which is to make the label
 *  the same size as the image it holds (after
 *  reserving space for the border, if any).
 *  This flag notes this, so subclasses that
 *  override ImageLabel need to check this flag, and
 *  if it is true, and they draw modified image,
 *  then they need to draw them based on the width
 *  height variables, not just blindly drawing them
 *  full size.
 */
private boolean explicitSize = false;
private int explicitWidth=0, explicitHeight=0;

// The MediaTracker that can tell if image has been
// loaded before trying to paint it or resize
// based on its size.
private MediaTracker tracker;

// Used by MediaTracker to be sure image is loaded
// before paint & resize, since you can't find out
// the size until it is done loading.
private static int lastTrackerID=0;
private int currentTrackerID;
private boolean doneLoading = false;

private Container parentContainer;

//-----------------------------------------------------
/** Create an ImageLabel with the default image.
 *
 * @see #getDefaultImageString
 * @see #setDefaultImageString
 */
// Remember that the funny "this()" syntax calls
// constructor of same class
public ImageLabel() {
  this(defaultImageString);
}
```

Listing 11.26   `ImageLabel.java`   (continued)

```java
/** Create an ImageLabel using the image at URL
 *   specified by the string.
 *
 * @param imageURLString A String specifying the
 *   URL of the image.
 */
public ImageLabel(String imageURLString) {
  this(makeURL(imageURLString));
}

/** Create an ImageLabel using the image at URL
 *   specified.
 *
 * @param imageURL The URL of the image.
 */
public ImageLabel(URL imageURL) {
  this(loadImage(imageURL));
  imageString = imageURL.toExternalForm();
}

/** Create an ImageLabel using the image in the file
 *   in the specified directory.
 *
 * @param imageDirectory Directory containing image
 * @param file Filename of image
 */
public ImageLabel(URL imageDirectory, String file) {
  this(makeURL(imageDirectory, file));
  imageString = file;
}

/** Create an ImageLabel using the image specified.
 *   The other constructors eventually call this one,
 *   but you may want to call it directly if you
 *   already have an image (e.g. created via
 *   createImage).
 *
 * @param image The image
 */
public ImageLabel(Image image) {
  this.image = image;
  tracker = new MediaTracker(this);
  currentTrackerID = lastTrackerID++;
  tracker.addImage(image, currentTrackerID);
}
```

continued

Listing 11.26 `ImageLabel.java` (continued)

```
//----------------------------------------------------
/** Makes sure that the Image associated with the
 *  Canvas is done loading before returning, since
 *  loadImage spins off a separate thread to do the
 *  loading. Once you get around to drawing the
 *  image, this will make sure it is loaded,
 *  waiting if not. The user does not need to call
 *  this at all, but if several ImageLabels are used
 *  in the same Container, this can cause
 *  several repeated layouts, so users might want to
 *  explicitly call this themselves before adding
 *  the ImageLabel to the Container. Another
 *  alternative is to start asynchronous loading by
 *  calling prepareImage on the ImageLabel's
 *  image (see getImage).
 *
 * @param doLayout Determines if the Container
 *    should be re-laid out after you are finished
 *    waiting. <B>This should be true when called
 *    from user functions</B>, but is set to false
 *    when called from preferredSize to avoid an
 *    infinite loop. This is needed when
 *    using BorderLayout, which calls preferredSize
 *    <B>before</B> calling paint.
 */
public void waitForImage(boolean doLayout) {
  if (!doneLoading) {
    debug("[waitForImage] - Resizing and waiting for "
          + imageString);
    try { tracker.waitForID(currentTrackerID); }
    catch (InterruptedException ie) {}
    catch (Exception e) {
      System.out.println("Error loading "
                          + imageString + ": "
                          + e.getMessage());
      e.printStackTrace();
    }
```

Listing 11.26   `ImageLabel.java`   (continued)

```
      if (tracker.isErrorID(0))
        new Throwable("Error loading image "
                        + imageString).printStackTrace();
      doneLoading = true;
      if (explicitWidth != 0)
        width = explicitWidth;
      else
        width = image.getWidth(this) + 2*border;
      if (explicitHeight != 0)
        height = explicitHeight;
      else
        height = image.getHeight(this) + 2*border;
      resize(width, height);
      debug("[waitForImage] - " + imageString + " is "
            + width + "x" + height + ".");

      // If no parent, you are OK, since it will have
      // been resized before being added. But if
      // parent exists, you have already been added,
      // and the change in size requires re-layout.
      if (((parentContainer = getParent()) != null)
          && doLayout) {
        setBackground(parentContainer.getBackground());
        parentContainer.layout();
      }
    }
  }
}


//-----------------------------------------------------
/** Moves the image so that it is <I>centered</I> at
 *  the specified location, as opposed to the move
 *  method of Component which places the top left
 *  corner at the specified location.
 *  <P>
 *  <B>Note:</B> The effects of this could be undone
 *  by the LayoutManager of the parent Container, if
 *  it is using one. So this is normally only used
 *  in conjunction with a null LayoutManager.
 *
 *  @param x The X coord of center of the image
 *           (in parent's coordinate system)
 *  @param y The Y coord of center of the image
 *           (in parent's coordinate system)
 *  @see java.awt.Component#move
 */
```

continued

Listing 11.26 `ImageLabel.java` **(continued)**

```java
public void centerAt(int x, int y) {
  debug("Placing center of " + imageString + " at ("
        + x + "," + y + ")");
  move(x - width/2, y - height/2);
}


//-------------------------------------------------------
/** Determines if the x and y <B>(in the ImageLabel's
 *  own coordinate system)</B> is inside the
 *  ImageLabel. Put here because Netscape 2.02 has
 *  a bug in which it doesn't process inside() and
 *  locate() tests correctly.
 */
public synchronized boolean inside(int x, int y) {
  return((x >= 0) && (x <= width)
        && (y >= 0) && (y <= height));
}


//-------------------------------------------------------
/** Draws the image. If you override this in a
 *  subclass, be sure to call super.paint.
 */
public void paint(Graphics g) {
  if (!doneLoading)
    waitForImage(true);
  else {
    if (explicitSize)
      g.drawImage(image, border, border,
                  width-2*border, height-2*border,
                  this);
    else
      g.drawImage(image, border, border, this);
    drawRect(g, 0, 0, width-1, height-1,
             border, borderColor);
  }
}


//-------------------------------------------------------
/** Used by layout managers to calculate the usual
 *  size allocated for the Component. Since some
 *  layout managers (e.g. BorderLayout) may
 *  call this before paint is called, you need to
 *  make sure that the image is done loading, which
 *  will force a resize, which determines the values
 *  returned.
 */
```

Listing 11.26 `ImageLabel.java` (continued)

```java
public Dimension preferredSize() {
  if (!doneLoading)
    waitForImage(false);
  return(super.preferredSize());
}

//-----------------------------------------------------
/** Used by layout managers to calculate the smallest
 *  size allocated for the Component. Since some
 *  layout managers (e.g. BorderLayout) may
 *  call this before paint is called, you need to
 *  make sure that the image is done loading, which
 *  will force a resize, which determines the values
 *  returned.
 */
public Dimension minimumSize() {
  if (!doneLoading)
    waitForImage(false);
  return(super.minimumSize());
}

//-----------------------------------------------------
// LayoutManagers (such as BorderLayout) might call
// resize or reshape with only 1 dimension of
// width/height non-zero. In such a case, you still
// want the other dimension to come from the image
// itself.

/** Resizes the ImageLabel. If you don't resize the
 *  label explicitly, then what happens depends on
 *  the layout manager. With FlowLayout, as with
 *  FlowLayout for Labels, the ImageLabel takes its
 *  minimum size, just enclosing the image. With
 *  BorderLayout, as with BorderLayout for Labels,
 *  the ImageLabel is expanded to fill the
 *  section. Stretching GIF/JPG files does not always
 *  result in clear looking images. <B>So just as
 *  with builtin Labels and Buttons, don't
 *  use FlowLayout if you don't want the Buttons to
 *  get resized.</B> If you don't use any
 *  LayoutManager, then the ImageLabel will also
 *  just fit the image.
 *  <P>
 *  Note that if you resize explicitly, you must do
```

continued

Listing 11.26   `ImageLabel.java`   (continued)

```
 *   it <B>before</B> the ImageLabel is added to the
 *   Container. In such a case, the explicit size
 *   overrides the image dimensions.
 *
 * @see #reshape
 */
public void resize(int width, int height) {
  if (!doneLoading) {
    explicitSize=true;
    if (width > 0)
      explicitWidth=width;
    if (height > 0)
      explicitHeight=height;
  }
  super.resize(width, height);
}


/** Resizes the ImageLabel. If you don't resize the
 *   label explicitly, then what happens depends on
 *   the layout manager. With FlowLayout, as with
 *   FlowLayout for Labels, the ImageLabel takes its
 *   minimum size, just enclosing the image. With
 *   BorderLayout, as with BorderLayout for Labels,
 *   the ImageLabel is expanded to fill the
 *   section. Stretching GIF/JPG files does not always
 *   result in clear looking images. <B>So just as
 *   with builtin Labels and Buttons, don't
 *   use FlowLayout if you don't want the Buttons to
 *   get resized.</B> If you don't use any
 *   LayoutManager, then the ImageLabel will also
 *   just fit the image.
 *   <P>
 *   Note that if you resize explicitly, you must do
 *   it <B>before</B> the ImageLabel is added to the
 *   Container. In such a case, the explicit size
 *   overrides the image dimensions.
 *
 * @see #resize
 */
```

Listing 11.26 `ImageLabel.java` (continued)

```java
public void reshape(int x, int y,
                    int width, int height) {
  if (!doneLoading) {
    explicitSize=true;
    if (width > 0)
      explicitWidth=width;
    if (height > 0)
      explicitHeight=height;
  }
  super.reshape(x, y, width, height);
}

//---------------------------------------------------
// You can't just set the background color to
// the borderColor and skip drawing the border,
// since it messes up transparent gifs. You
// need the background color to be the same as
// the container.

/** Draws a rectangle with the specified OUTSIDE
 *  left, top, width, and height.
 *  Used to draw the border.
 */
protected void drawRect(Graphics g,
                        int left, int top,
                        int width, int height,
                        int lineThickness,
                        Color rectangleColor) {
  g.setColor(rectangleColor);
  for(int i=0; i<lineThickness; i++) {
    g.drawRect(left, top, width, height);
    if (i < lineThickness-1) {  // Skip last iteration
      left = left + 1;
      top = top + 1;
      width = width - 2;
      height = height - 2;
    }
  }
}
```

continued

Listing 11.26 `ImageLabel.java` **(continued)**

```
//-----------------------------------------------------
/** Calls System.out.println if the debug variable
 *  is true; does nothing otherwise.
 *
 * @param message The String to be printed.
 */
protected void debug(String message) {
  if (debug)
    System.out.println(message);
}


//-----------------------------------------------------
// Creates the URL with some error checking.

private static URL makeURL(String s) {
  URL u = null;
  try { u = new URL(s); }
  catch (MalformedURLException mue) {
    System.out.println("Bad URL " + s + ": " + mue);
    mue.printStackTrace();
  }
  return(u);
}

private static URL makeURL(URL directory,
                           String file) {
  URL u = null;
  try { u = new URL(directory, file); }
  catch (MalformedURLException mue) {
    System.out.println("Bad URL " +
                       directory.toExternalForm() +
                       ", " + file + ": " + mue);
    mue.printStackTrace();
  }
  return(u);
}


//-----------------------------------------------------
// Loads the image. Needs to be static since it is
// called by the constructor.

private static Image loadImage(URL url) {
  return(Toolkit.getDefaultToolkit().getImage(url));
}
```

Listing 11.26 `ImageLabel.java` (continued)

```java
//---------------------------------------------------
/** The Image associated with the ImageLabel. */

public Image getImage() {
  return(image);
}

//---------------------------------------------------
/** Gets the border width. */

public int getBorder() {
  return(border);
}

/** Sets the border thickness. */

public void setBorder(int border) {
  this.border = border;
}

//---------------------------------------------------
/** Gets the border color. */

public Color getBorderColor() {
  return(borderColor);
}

/** Sets the border color. */

public void setBorderColor(Color borderColor) {
  this.borderColor = borderColor;
}

//---------------------------------------------------
// You could just call size().width and size().height,
// but since we've overridden resize to record
// this, we might as well use it.

/** Gets the width (image width plus twice border). */

public int getWidth() {
  return(width);
}
```

continued

Listing 11.26   `ImageLabel.java`   **(continued)**

```java
  /** Gets the height (image height plus 2x border). */

  public int getHeight() {
    return(height);
  }

  //-------------------------------------------------------
  /** Has the ImageLabel been given an explicit size?
   *  This is used to decide if the image should be
   *  stretched or not. This will be true if you
   *  call resize or reshape on the ImageLabel before
   *  adding it to a Container. It will be false
   *  otherwise.
   */
  protected boolean hasExplicitSize() {
    return(explicitSize);
  }

  //-------------------------------------------------------
  /** Returns the string representing the URL that
   *  will be used if none is supplied in the
   *  constructor.
   */
  public static String getDefaultImageString() {
    return(defaultImageString);
  }

  /** Sets the string representing the URL that
   *  will be used if none is supplied in the
   *  constructor. Note that this is static,
   *  so is shared by all ImageLabels. Using this
   *  might be convenient in testing, but "real"
   *  applications should avoid it.
   */
  public static void setDefaultImageString(String file) {
    defaultImageString = file;
  }

  //-------------------------------------------------------
  /** Returns the string representing the URL
   *  of image.
   */
  protected String getImageString() {
    return(imageString);
  }
```

Listing 11.26 `ImageLabel.java` (continued)

```
//---------------------------------------------------
/** Is the debugging flag set? */

public boolean isDebugging() {
  return(debug);
}

/** Set the debugging flag. Verbose messages
 *  will be printed to System.out if this is true.
 */
public void setIsDebugging(boolean debug) {
  this.debug = debug;
}

//---------------------------------------------------
}
```

11.15 Summary

Java has eight major types of windows that the developer can use for user interfaces: Canvas, Panel, Applet, ScrollPane, Frame, Dialog, FileDialog, and Window. This chapter explained the differences among these and described the basics of their use. One topic that was introduced but not covered thoroughly was the use of layout managers, the class used by many windows to help arrange the components they contain. Chapter 12 covers this topic in depth, explaining how to use layout managers to simplify user interface design, how to make them work most effectively, how to turn them off when they get in the way, and how to design your own. Next, Chapter 13 describes the user interface controls Java provides: buttons, textfields, combo boxes, popup menus, scrollbars, and the like. You start with the windows, then add GUI controls, using the layout managers to keep everything organized. Voila! An effective cross-platform user interface.

ARRANGING WINDOWS USING LAYOUT MANAGERS

Chapter 12

W hen a `Container` is created in Java, it automatically gets an associated object to help position components inside it. This helper object is known as a *layout manager*. It is intended to free the programmer from the burden of positioning each component pixel-by-pixel when the components may be different sizes on different platforms, when the main windows may be interactively resized or customized based on parameters in the HTML file, or when the design changes several times during development.

Although this idea is a good one, in practice the built-in layout managers are good for basic layouts but not flexible enough for many complex arrangements. However, by using nested containers that each have their own layout manager, relatively complex layouts can be achieved even with the simplest layout managers. Besides, you can always turn the layout manager off if you'd rather do things by hand. You can also design your own layout manager to fit your specific requirements or favored look.

To use a layout manager, you first associate it with the container using `setLayout` (or by simply accepting the window's default), then insert components into the window using `add`. In an `Applet`, this is usually performed in `init`. In an application, it is usually done in the constructor.

In this chapter, we first cover the five standard layout managers: `FlowLayout`, `BorderLayout`, `GridLayout`, `CardLayout`, and `GridBagLayout`. We then discuss turning off the layout manager, tips for getting the layout managers to work for you (instead of the other way around), and writing your own layout manager.

12.1 FlowLayout

This layout manager resizes components to their "preferred" (minimum) size then arranges them in rows in the window. The first component is placed in the left-most position in the top row, the second component next, and so on until the next component would not fit in the current row, in which case the process is repeated in the next row for the remaining components. By default, each row is centered and five pixels are left between components in a row and between rows. The constructor options described later in this section let you make left-aligned or right-aligned rows or to change the spacing between components. This is the default layout manager for a `Panel` or an `Applet`.

Listing 12.1 shows an example that places five buttons in a window that is wide enough to hold only four. As Figure 12–1 shows, the group containing the first four is centered on the top row of the applet while the last button is centered in a row directly underneath. Note that because `FlowLayout` is the default layout manager for `Applet`, there is no need for an explicit `setLayout` call.

Listing 12.1   FlowTest.java

```
import java.applet.Applet;
import java.awt.*;

/** FlowLayout puts components in rows. */

public class FlowTest extends Applet {
  public void init() {
    // Default: setLayout(new FlowLayout());
    for(int i=1; i<6; i++)
      add(new Button("Button " + i));
  }
}
```

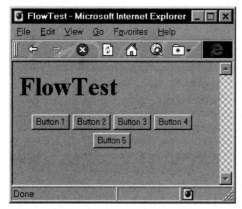

Figure 12–1 `FlowLayout` puts components in rows, moving to a new row only when the component won't fit in the current row.

FlowLayout Constructor Options

public FlowLayout()
This builds a `FlowLayout` layout manager that centers each row and keeps five pixels between entries in a row and between rows.

public FlowLayout(int alignment)
This builds a `FlowLayout` with left-aligned, right-aligned, or centered rows, depending on the value of the alignment argument (`FlowLayout.LEFT`, `FlowLayout.RIGHT`, or `FlowLayout.CENTER`). The horizontal and vertical gap is five pixels.

public FlowLayout(int alignment, int hGap, int vGap)
This builds a `FlowLayout` that uses the specified alignment, keeps hGap pixels between entries in a row, and reserves vGap pixels between rows.

Other FlowLayout Methods

The following methods are available in Java 1.1 only.

> **public int getAlignment() [Java 1.1]**
> **public void setAlignment(int alignment)**
> These methods let you look up or modify the row alignment. As in the constructor, the alignment can be FlowLayout.LEFT, FlowLayout.RIGHT, or FlowLayout.CENTER.

> **public int getHgap() [Java 1.1]**
> **public void setHgap(int hGap) [Java 1.1]**
> These methods let you look up or change the empty space kept between entries in a row.

> **public int getVgap() [Java 1.1]**
> **public void setVgap(int vGap) [Java 1.1]**
> These methods let you look up or change the amount of empty space between rows.

In Java 1.02, you cannot change the characteristics of a FlowLayout object once it is created, so it is not significant that the default FlowLayout instance used by panels is stored in a static (shared) variable in the Panel class. In Java 1.1, however, you have to exercise caution to avoid unintended side effects. Although the shared FlowLayout is stored in a final variable, that only means that the *reference* is constant: that it cannot be redirected to refer to a new object. It does not mean that the *fields* of the object are unmodifiable. In this regard, Java has the equivalent of C++'s const pointers, but not the equivalent of const objects. For instance, if you want to change the horizontal gap in a Panel, you should do

```
Panel p = new Panel();
p.setLayout(new FlowLayout(FlowLayout.CENTER,
            10, 5));
```

not

```
Panel p = new Panel();
FlowLayout layout = (FlowLayout)p.getLayout();
layout.setHgap(10);
```

You might think that the latter is more efficient because it does not allocate a new `FlowLayout` instance, but the consequences of this fact mean that changes to the shared `FlowLayout` instance can affect other panels. For example, Listing 12.2 shows a `Frame` containing two panels holding 20 buttons each. Because no layout manager is explicitly given to the panels, the rows are centered and five pixels are reserved between buttons and between rows, as shown in Figure 12–2. In Listing 12.3, this process is repeated with one twist: a third `Panel` is allocated and its layout manager changed to left-align the rows, keep 30 pixels between buttons, and reserve 20 pixels between rows. As Figure 12–3 shows, even though this `Panel` is unrelated to the other two (in fact, it is not even added to a window), the layout manager changes propagate to the other panels.

Core Approach

If a window is using the default layout manager and you want to change its characteristics, assign a new layout manager. Don't do `setXxx` *operations on the return value of* `getLayout` *unless you know the window has been explicitly assigned a layout manager.*

Listing 12.2   `NormalFlow.java`

```java
import java.awt.*;

/** A bunch of buttons in a Panel that uses the
 *   default version of FlowLayout.
 *   Java 1.1 only.
 * @see ModifiedFlow
 */

public class NormalFlow extends CloseableFrame {
  public static void main(String[] args) {
    new NormalFlow("Default FlowLayout Configuration",
                   475, 300, 2);
  }

  public NormalFlow(String title,
                    int width, int height,
                    int numPanels) {
    super(title);
    setLayout(new GridLayout(1, numPanels));
    Panel p;
    for(int i=0; i<numPanels; i++) {
      p = new Panel();
      addButtons(p, i, 20);
      add(p);
    }
    setSize(width, height);
    setVisible(true);
  }

  public void addButtons(Panel p,
                         int prefix, int numButtons) {
    for(int i=0; i<numButtons; i++)
      p.add(new Button("Button " + prefix + "-" + i));
  }
}
```

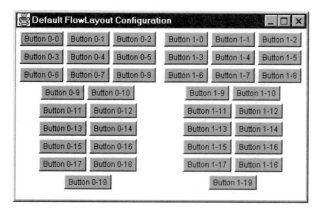

Figure 12–2   A Frame with two panels: both use the default FlowLayout characteristics.

Listing 12.3   ModifiedFlow.java

```java
import java.awt.*;

/** This example illustrates that retrieving the
 *  default layout manager using getLayout and then
 *  changing its characteristics can have global
 *  effects in Java 1.1.
 */

public class ModifiedFlow extends NormalFlow {
  public static void main(String[] args) {
    Panel p = new Panel();
    FlowLayout panelManager = (FlowLayout)p.getLayout();
    panelManager.setAlignment(FlowLayout.LEFT);
    panelManager.setHgap(30);
    panelManager.setVgap(20);
    new ModifiedFlow("Modified FlowLayout Configuration",
                475, 300, 2);
  }

  public ModifiedFlow(String title,
                int width, int height,
                int numPanels) {
    super(title, width, height, numPanels);
  }
}
```

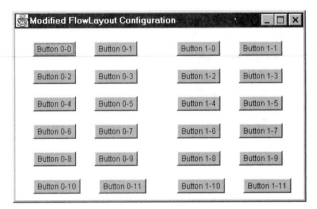

Figure 12–3   Changing the return value of `getLayout` can have global side effects.

12.2 BorderLayout

This layout manager divides the window into five sections: `North`, `South`, `East`, `West`, and `Center`. You add a component to a region by using a version of the add method that takes two arguments instead of the normal one. The first argument is a string naming the region that should hold the component specified in the second argument, as follows:

```
add("North", buttonForTop);
add("East", scrollbarForRightSide);
add("Center", panelForRemainingSpace);
```

Components added to `North` or `South` are resized to be the full width of the `Container`, but to be their "preferred" (minimum) heights. Components added to `East` or `West` are resized to take the full height of the `Container` (minus any space taken by `North` and `South`), and to be their minimum widths. A component in the `Center` region is expanded to take whatever space is remaining. The `BorderLayout` constructor also allows specification of the gaps between the areas; the default is zero. This is the default layout manager for `Frame`, `Dialog`, and `Window`.

Listing 12.4 shows an applet using `BorderLayout` that places a button in each of the five regions. As Figure 12–4 shows, these buttons are stretched based on the size of the window, rather than remaining their preferred size as when using `FlowLayout`.

Listing 12.4   `BorderTest.java`

```java
import java.applet.Applet;
import java.awt.*;

/** An example of BorderLayout. */

public class BorderTest extends Applet {
  public void init() {
    setLayout(new BorderLayout());
    add("North",  new Button("Button 1"));
    add("South",  new Button("Button 2"));
    add("East",   new Button("Button 3"));
    add("West",   new Button("Button 4"));
    add("Center", new Button("Button 5"));
  }
}
```

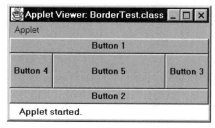

Figure 12–4   `BorderLayout` divides the window into five regions.

The single most common error made when first using `BorderLayout` is forgetting to use:

       `add("Region", component);`

and instead doing the more familiar but incorrect:

       `add(component);`

If you do this, your component won't be displayed, but no warning will be given when compiling or running.

Core Warning

> If you forget to specify a region when adding a component to a window that uses `BorderLayout`, the component won't show up. The same thing happens if you misspell a region name. Either way, no warning will be issued.

You should also remember that you should have at most one component per region when using `BorderLayout`. Otherwise the top component will obscure the one underneath. If you want several components in a region, group them in a `Panel` (or possibly a lightweight container in Java 1.1), then put the `Panel` in the desired region.

Core Approach

Add at most one component to each region of a `BorderLayout`. To have multiple components in a region, group them in a `Panel` or other `Container`.

BorderLayout Constructor Options

public BorderLayout()
This builds a `BorderLayout` object with regions that touch each other.

public BorderLayout(int hGap, int vGap)
This builds a `BorderLayout` object that reserves hGap empty pixels between the `West` and `Center` regions and between `Center` and `East`. It also keeps vGap blank pixels between the `North` and `Center` regions and between `Center` and `South`.

Other BorderLayout Methods

These methods are available only in Java 1.1. You should be careful not to use `setHgap` or `setVgap` on the return value of `getLayout` when applied to a `Frame` or `Dialog` that has no explicit layout manager set. See the example in Section 12.1 (FlowLayout) for more details.

public int getHgap() [Java 1.1]
public void setHgap(int hGap) [Java 1.1]
These methods are used to report and specify the empty space between horizontally adjacent regions.

public int getVgap() [Java 1.1]
public void setVgap(int vGap) [Java 1.1]
These methods are used to report and specify the empty space between vertically adjacent regions.

public float getLayoutAlignmentX(Container c) [Java 1.1]
public float getLayoutAlignmentY(Container c) [Java 1.1]
These methods tell you how the `Container` wants to be aligned. For more details, see `getAlignmentX` and `getAlignmentY` in Section 11.2 (The Component Class).

12.3 GridLayout

This layout manager divides the window into equal-sized rectangles based upon the number of rows and columns specified. Items are placed into the cells left to right, top to bottom, based upon the order they are added. Each component is resized to fit into its grid cell without regard to its current or preferred sizes. A constructor option lets you specify the gaps between the rows and columns.

Listing 12.5 presents an applet divided into two rows and three columns, with a button placed into each cell. Figure 12–5 shows the result.

Listing 12.5 `GridTest.java`

```java
import java.applet.Applet;
import java.awt.*;

/** An example of GridLayout. */

public class GridTest extends Applet {
  public void init() {
    setLayout(new GridLayout(2,3)); // 2 rows, 3 cols
    add(new Button("Button One"));
    add(new Button("Button Two"));
    add(new Button("Button Three"));
    add(new Button("Button Four"));
    add(new Button("Button Five"));
    add(new Button("Button Six"));
  }
}
```

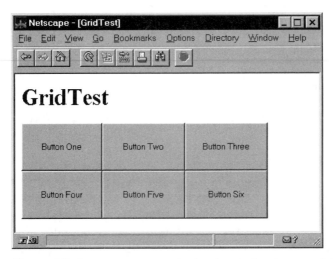

Figure 12–5   GridLayout divides the window into equal-sized rectangles.

GridLayout Constructor Options

public GridLayout() [Java 1.1]
This creates a single row with one column allocated per component. It is available only in Java 1.1, but you can get the same effect in Java 1.02 by specifying one row and zero columns.

public GridLayout(int rows, int cols)
This creates a GridLayout object that divides the window into the specified number of rows and columns, with each grid cell flush against the neighboring cell. Either rows or cols (but not both) can be zero. If you specify zero for the number of rows, Java will try to set the number of rows so that each column has approximately the same number of elements. Similarly, if you specify zero for the column count, Java will try to choose the number of columns so that each row gets approximately an even number of components. To illustrate this, Listing 12.6 places 11 buttons in a window that specifies zero columns, taking the number of

rows as a command line argument. Figures 12–6 and 12–7 show the result when two and three rows are chosen, respectively.

Listing 12.6 `ElevenButtons.java`

```java
import java.awt.*;

/** This illustrates the effect of specifying 0 for
 *  the number of columns. The number of rows
 *  is read from the command line (default 2), and
 *  the column number is chosen by the system to get
 *  as even a layout as possible.
 */

public class ElevenButtons extends QuittableFrame {
  public static void main(String[] args) {
    int numRows = 2;
    if (args.length > 0)
      numRows = Integer.parseInt(args[0]);
    new ElevenButtons(numRows);
  }

  public ElevenButtons(int numRows) {
    super("11 Buttons using GridLayout("
        + numRows + ", 0).");
    setLayout(new GridLayout(numRows, 0));
    for(int i=0; i<11; i++)
      add(new Button("Button " + i));
    resize(600, 400);
    show();
  }
}
```

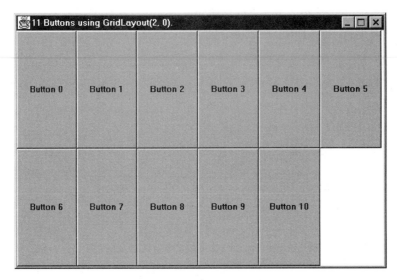

Figure 12–6   When specifying two rows and zero columns, Java chooses six columns for an eleven-component window.

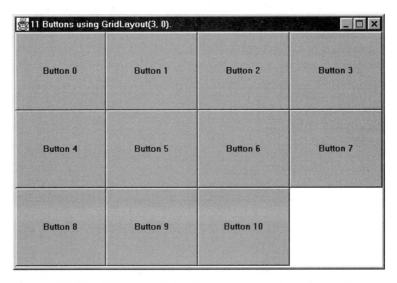

Figure 12–7   When specifying three rows and zero columns, Java chooses four columns for an eleven-component window.

public GridLayout(int rows, int cols, int hGap, int vGap)
This divides the window into the specified number of rows and columns, leaving hGap and vGap empty pixels between columns and rows. Either the row count or the column count can be zero, but not both. A value of zero is interpreted as "any number," as illustrated with the description of the previous constructor.

Other GridLayout Methods

These methods are available in Java 1.1 only.

public int getRows() [Java 1.1]
public void setRows(int rows) [Java 1.1]
These methods let you look up and modify the number of rows.

public int getColumns() [Java 1.1]
public void setColumns(int cols) [Java 1.1]
These methods let you read and change the number of columns.

public int getHgap() [Java 1.1]
public void setHgap(int hGap) [Java 1.1]
These methods are used to report and specify the empty space between columns.

public int getVgap() [Java 1.1]
public void setVgap(int vGap) [Java 1.1]
These methods are used to report and specify the empty space between rows.

12.4 CardLayout

This layout manager stacks components on top of each other, displaying one at a time. To use it, you create a CardLayout instance, telling the window to use it but also saving the reference in a variable:

```
Panel cardPanel;
CardLayout layout;
...
layout = new CardLayout();
cardPanel.setLayout(layout);
```

Don't forget to save a reference to the layout manager; you'll need it later. You then associate a name with each component you add to the window, as below:

```
cardPanel.add("Card 1", component1);
cardPanel.add("Card 2", component2);
...
```

The first component added is shown by default. You tell the layout manager to display a particular component in a number of ways: by specifying the name with a call to show, or by calling first, last, previous, or next. In all cases, the Container using the layout manager must be supplied as an argument, as follows:

```
layout.show(cardPanel, "Card 1");
layout.first(cardPanel);
layout.next(cardPanel);
```

By way of example, consider Listing 12.7. It places a Panel using Card-Layout in the right-hand portion of the window and a column of buttons in the left-hand region. The Panel contains four versions of a CardPanel (Listing 12.8), which is a Panel that holds a Label and an ImageLabel (Section 11.14) showing a picture of a playing card. Depending on which button is selected, a different card is shown. Figures 12–8 and 12–9 show two of the four possible configurations.

Listing 12.7   CardDemo.java

```
import java.applet.Applet;
import java.awt.*;

/** An example of CardLayout. The right side of the
 *  window holds a Panel that uses CardLayout to control
 *  four possible sub-panels (each of which is a
 *  CardPanel that shows a picture of a playing card).
 *  The buttons on the left side of the window manipulate
 *  the "cards" in this layout by calling methods in
 *  the right-hand panel's layout manager.
 *  @see CardPanel
 */
```

Listing 12.7 `CardDemo.java` **(continued)**

```java
public class CardDemo extends Applet {
  private Button first, last, previous, next;
  private String[] cardLabels = { "Jack", "Queen",
                                  "King", "Ace" };
  private CardPanel[] cardPanels = new CardPanel[4];
  private CardLayout layout;
  private Panel cardDisplayPanel;

  public void init() {
    setBackground(Color.white);
    setLayout(new BorderLayout());
    addButtonPanel();
    addCardDisplayPanel();
  }

  private void addButtonPanel() {
    Panel buttonPanel = new Panel();
    buttonPanel.setLayout(new GridLayout(9, 1));
    Font buttonFont =
      new Font("Helvetica", Font.BOLD, 18);
    buttonPanel.setFont(buttonFont);
    for(int i=0; i<cardLabels.length; i++)
      buttonPanel.add(new Button(cardLabels[i]));
    first = new Button("First");
    last = new Button("Last");
    previous = new Button("Previous");
    next = new Button("Next");
    buttonPanel.add(new Label("------------",
                             Label.CENTER));
    buttonPanel.add(first);
    buttonPanel.add(last);
    buttonPanel.add(previous);
    buttonPanel.add(next);
    add("West", buttonPanel);
  }
```

continued

Listing 12.7   CardDemo.java   (continued)

```java
private void addCardDisplayPanel() {
    cardDisplayPanel = new Panel();
    layout = new CardLayout();
    cardDisplayPanel.setLayout(layout);
    String cardName;
    for(int i=0; i<cardLabels.length; i++) {
        cardName = cardLabels[i];
        cardPanels[i] =
            new CardPanel(cardName, getCodeBase(),
                        "images/" + cardName + ".gif");
        cardDisplayPanel.add(cardName, cardPanels[i]);
    }
    add("Center", cardDisplayPanel);
}

public boolean action(Event event, Object object) {
    if (event.target == first)
        layout.first(cardDisplayPanel);
    else if (event.target == last)
        layout.last(cardDisplayPanel);
    else if (event.target == previous)
        layout.previous(cardDisplayPanel);
    else if (event.target == next)
        layout.next(cardDisplayPanel);
    else
        layout.show(cardDisplayPanel, (String)object);
    return(true);
}
}
```

Listing 12.8   `CardPanel.java`

```java
import java.awt.*;
import java.net.*;

/** A Panel that displays a playing card. This window
 *  does <B>not</B> use CardLayout. Rather, instances
 *  of CardPanel are contained in another window
 *  used in the CardDemo example. It is this enclosing
 *  window that uses CardLayout to manipulate which
 *  CardPanel it shows.
 * @see CardDemo
 */

public class CardPanel extends Panel {
  private Label name;
  private ImageLabel picture;

  public CardPanel(String cardName,
                   URL directory, String imageFile) {
    setLayout(new BorderLayout());
    name = new Label(cardName, Label.CENTER);
    name.setFont(new Font("TimesRoman", Font.BOLD, 50));
    add("North", name);
    picture = new ImageLabel(directory, imageFile);
    Panel picturePanel = new Panel();
    picturePanel.add(picture);
    add("Center", picturePanel);
    resize(preferredSize());
  }

  public Label getLabel() {
    return(name);
  }

  public ImageLabel getImageLabel() {
    return(picture);
  }
}
```

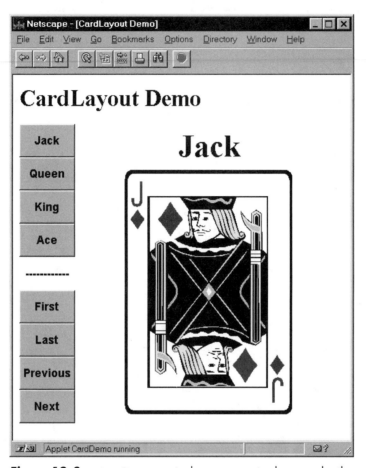

Figure 12-8   CardLayout stacks components above each other.

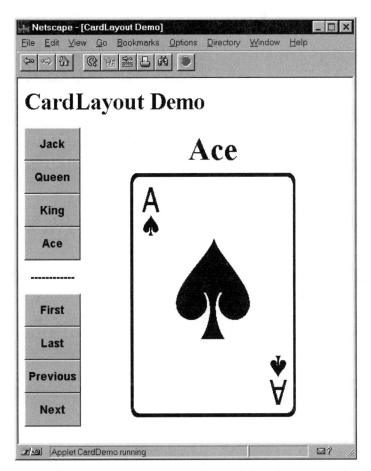

Figure 12–9 You can switch among cards by selecting a card's label or by choosing the first, last, previous, or next card in the layout.

CardLayout Constructor Options

public CardLayout()

This creates a CardLayout instance that places components in the top-left corner of the window.

public CardLayout(int sideMargins, int topMargins)

This creates a CardLayout object that reserves the specified number of empty pixels on the sides and top/bottom of the window.

Other CardLayout Methods

The following methods are available in both the 1.0 and 1.1 versions of Java.
Note that the Container argument is referring to the window that is using
the CardLayout, not to the card (Component) itself.

public void show(Container c, String cardName)
This displays the card that was given the specified name when added to
the Container.

public void first(Container c)
public void last(Container c)
These methods display the card that was added first and last, respectively.

public void previous(Container c)
public void next(Container c)
These methods display the previous or next card in the sequence.
Unless you use a version of add that lets you specify a position in the
component array, the sequence is arranged in the order components
were added.

The following methods are available in Java 1.1 only.

public int getHgap()
public void setHgap(int hGap)
These methods are used to report and specify the empty space reserved
at the left and right sides. The names getSideMargins and
setSideMargins might have been clearer in this case, but these
names were chosen for consistency with other layout managers.

public int getVgap()
public void setVgap(int vGap)
These methods are used to report and specify the empty space reserved
at the top and bottom of the window. The names getTopMargins
and setTopMargins might have been clearer in this case, but these
names were chosen for consistency with other layout managers.

public float getLayoutAlignmentX(Container c)
public float getLayoutAlignmentY(Container c)

These methods tell you how the `Container` wants to be aligned. For more details, see `getAlignmentX` and `getAlignmentY` in Section 11.2 (The Component Class).

12.5 GridBagLayout

This layout manager is about three times more flexible than any of the other standard layout managers. Unfortunately, it is also about *nine* times harder to use. The basic idea is that you chop the window up into grids, then each component specifies which cell it starts and ends in. You can also specify how objects stretch when there is extra room and alignment within cells.

The basic steps to using `GridBagLayout` are:

Set the layout, saving a reference to it

```
GridBagLayout layout = new GridBagLayout();
setLayout(layout);
```

Allocate a GridBagConstraints object

```
GridBagConstraints constraints =
  new GridBagConstraints();
```

Set up the GridBagConstraints for component 1

```
constraints.gridx = x1;
constraints.gridy = y1;
constraints.gridwidth = width1;
constraints.gridheight = height1;

...
```

Tell the layout about the constraints

```
layout.setConstraints(component1, constraints);
```

Add first component to the window

```
add(component1);
```

Repeat the last three steps for each remaining component

The GridBagConstraints Object

In addition to setting the layout in the Container, you also need to allocate a GridBagConstraints object, set it up, then call the layout's setConstraints method to specify the location and size of the components that you add. Once you record the values via setConstraints, you can reset the GridBagConstraints values, so it is not necessary to allocate one GridBagConstraints for each component. The GridBagConstraints class has many fields, most of which need to be set for every component added. Consequently, it is valuable to create a helping method that sets these fields, rather than setting them individually each time (see the setPosition method in Listing 12.9). The available fields are listed as follows.

public int gridx
public int gridy
These variables specify the top-left corner of the component.

public int gridwidth
public int gridheight
These variables determine the number of columns and rows the Component occupies. Note that you do not specify the total number of rows or columns in the layout; the GridBagLayout determines this automatically. In fact, you can set gridwidth and gridheight to GridBagConstraints.RELATIVE and then add the components left to right, top to bottom, and let the layout manager try to figure out the widths/heights. If you use this approach, use the value GridBag-Constraints.REMAINDER for the *last* entry in a row or column. The default value is 1.

public int anchor
If the fill field is set to GridBagConstraints.NONE, then the anchor field determines where the element gets placed. Use Grid-BagConstraints.CENTER to center it, or GridBagConstraints.NORTH, GridBagConstraints.NORTHEAST, GridBagConstraints.EAST, GridBagConstraints.SOUTH-EAST, GridBagConstraints.SOUTH, GridBagConstraints.SOUTHWEST, GridBagConstraints.WEST, or GridBagConstraints.NORTHWEST to position one side/corner in the allocated box.

public int fill

The size of the row/column is determined by the widest/tallest element in it. The `fill` field specifies what to do to an element that is smaller than this size. `GridBagConstraints.NONE` (the default) means not to expand it at all, `GridBagConstraints.HORIZONTAL` means to expand horizontally but not vertically, `GridBagConstraints.VER-TICAL` means to expand vertically but not horizontally, and `GridBag-Constraints.BOTH` means to expand it both horizontally and vertically.

public Insets insets

You can use this field to supply an `Insets` object that specifies margins to go on all four sides of the component.

public int ipadx
public int ipady

These values specify internal padding to add to the component's minimum size. The new size will be the old size plus twice the padding.

public int weightx
public int weighty

These fields determine how much the `Component` will "stretch" in the x or y direction if there is space left over after sizing each column based on the widest object and each row based on the tallest. Specifying 0 means that the `Component` will stay at its preferred size. Specifying 100 means that it will share extra space equally with other objects that have a weight of 100 specified. Values in between result in pro-rating.

Example

As an example, consider the task of arranging an applet with a column of buttons down the left side and with the remainder of the space reserved for drawing space (with a `Label` as a title). All the buttons should be the same width, determined by width of the widest button. The heights of the buttons should be adjusted to just fill the height of the window. Listing 12.9 shows the code; Figure 12–10 shows the result. Other than `GridBagLayout`, there is no other standard layout manager that will achieve this effect. However, before you leap to the conclusion that `GridBagLayout` is appropriate for this job, let me preview the advice of Section 12.7 (Using Layout Managers Effectively)—consider using multiple nested layouts instead of one huge layout. In fact, in Section 12.7 you'll see how this exact layout can be achieved more easily using nested containers. If you want to evaluate the difficulty of using GridBagLayout, Listing 12.10 shows an empirical model that gives a remarkably accurate estimate of the number of lines required, given the number of components that need to be arranged.

Listing 12.9   GridBagTest.java

```java
import java.applet.Applet;
import java.awt.*;

/** An example of GridBagLayout. This is actually
 *  relatively simple as far as GridBagLayout usage
 *  goes.
 */

public class GridBagTest extends Applet {
  private GridBagLayout layout;
  private GridBagConstraints constraints;

  public void init() {
    layout = new GridBagLayout();
    setLayout(layout);
    constraints = new GridBagConstraints();
    Label buttonLabel = new Label("Buttons");
    setPosition(buttonLabel, 0, 0, 1, 1, 0, 100,
            GridBagConstraints.VERTICAL);
    add(buttonLabel);
    Button button1 = new Button("Button One");
    setPosition(button1, 0, 1, 1, 1, 0, 100,
            GridBagConstraints.BOTH);
    add(button1);
    Button button2 = new Button("Button Two");
    setPosition(button2, 0, 2, 1, 1, 0, 100,
            GridBagConstraints.BOTH);
    add(button2);
    Button button3 = new Button("Button Three");
    setPosition(button3, 0, 3, 1, 1, 0, 100,
            GridBagConstraints.BOTH);
    add(button3);
    Button button4 = new Button("Button Four");
    setPosition(button4, 0, 4, 1, 1, 0, 100,
            GridBagConstraints.BOTH);
```

Listing 12.9 `GridBagTest.java` **(continued)**

```java
    add(button4);
    Button button5 = new Button("Button Five");
    setPosition(button5, 0, 5, 1, 1, 0, 100,
                GridBagConstraints.BOTH);
    add(button5);
    Label restLabel
      = new Label("Everything Else");
    setPosition(restLabel, 1, 0, 2, 1, 100, 100,
                GridBagConstraints.VERTICAL);
    add(restLabel);
  }

  /** If you use GridBagLayout, you'll want a helper
   *  method like this to help set values in
   *  the GridBagConstraints object.
   */

  public void setPosition(Component component,
                          int x, int y,
                          int width, int height,
                          int weightx, int weighty,
                          int fill) {
    constraints.weightx = 100;
    constraints.weighty = 100;
    constraints.gridx = x;
    constraints.gridy = y;
    constraints.gridwidth = width;
    constraints.gridheight = height;
    constraints.weightx = weightx;
    constraints.weighty = weighty;
    constraints.fill = fill;
    layout.setConstraints(component, constraints);
  }
}
```

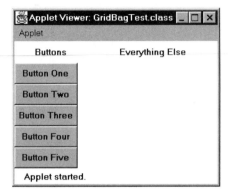

Figure 12–10   Using `GridBagConstraints` gives you more control, but at a significant cost in code complexity.

Listing 12.10   `GridBagCost.java`

```java
/** Given the number of components an application
 *  will take, this estimates the number of
 *  lines of GridBagLayout code required.
 *  OK, so "remarkably" accurate was an exaggeration.
 *  Sue me.
 */

public class GridBagCost {
  public static void main(String[] args) {
    if (args.length != 1)
      System.out.println("You can't even pass command "
                       + "line args correctly.\nHow "
                       + "do you *ever* expect to "
                       + "use GridBagLayout?");
    else {
      int numComponents = Integer.parseInt(args[0]);
      System.out.println("Lines of code required: "
                       + gridBagLines(numComponents));
    }
  }

  public static long gridBagLines(int numComponents) {
    return(Math.round(15.0 + 2.0 * Math.PI *
                      numComponents *
                      (1.0 + Math.random())));
  }
}
```

GridBagLayout Constructor Options

public GridBagLayout()
This is the only GridBagLayout constructor. Options are provided via the GridBagConstraints object.

Other GridBagLayout Methods

Following are the public methods of GridBagLayout. Except for set-Constraints, they are not commonly used.

public GridBagConstraints getConstraints(Component c)
This returns a copy of the GridBagConstraints object used to set up the specified component.

public float getLayoutAlignmentX(Container c)
public float getLayoutAlignmentY(Container c)
These methods tell you how the Container wants to be aligned. For more details, see getAlignmentX and getAlignmentY in Section 11.2 (The Component Class).

public int[ ][ ] getLayoutDimensions()
This returns an array containing the dimensions of each row and column in the window.

public Point getLayoutOrigin()
This returns the location of the top-left corner of the GridBagLayout relative to its containing window.

public double[ ][ ] getLayoutWeights
This retrieves the weightx and weighty values.

public void setConstraints(Component component,
GridBagConstraints constraints)
This method registers the specified constraints with the given component. This is the key method in the entire class.

12.6 Turning Off the LayoutManager

Layout managers are supposed to make your life easier. If you find they're getting in the way, just turn them off. This is no sin, although with a little experience you'll find that you want to do this less often than you might think at first. If the layout is set to `null`, then components can be (in fact *must* be) positioned by hand using (in Java 1.02) `resize(width, height)` and `move(left, top)` or `reshape(left, top, width, height)`. In Java 1.1, you would use either `setSize` and `setLocation`, or `setBounds`. Although this sounds tedious, if the window with the layout manager turned off contains only a few components (possibly other windows with nonnull layout managers), it is quite tractable. Listing 12.11 gives an example, with the result shown in Figure 12–11. As we'll see in Section 12.7 (Using Layout Managers Effectively), using nested containers and basing dimensions on the current window size rather than on absolute pixels makes this approach significantly more flexible while requiring very little extra work.

Listing 12.11   `NullTest.java`

```java
import java.applet.Applet;
import java.awt.*;

/** Layout managers are intended to help you, but there
 *  is no law saying you <B>have</B> to use them.
 *  Set the layout to null to turn them off.
 */

public class NullTest extends Applet {
  public void init() {
    setLayout(null);
    Button b1 = new Button("Button 1");
    Button b2 = new Button("Button 2");
    Button b3 = new Button("Button 3");
    Button b4 = new Button("Button 4");
    Button b5 = new Button("Button 5");
    b1.reshape(0, 0, 150, 50);
    b2.reshape(150, 0, 75, 50);
    b3.reshape(225, 0, 75, 50);
    b4.reshape(25, 60, 100, 40);
    b5.reshape(175, 60, 100, 40);
    add(b1);
    add(b2);
    add(b3);
    add(b4);
    add(b5);
  }
}
```

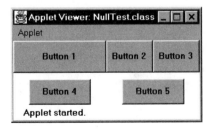

Figure 12-11   You can position elements by hand if you set
the layout manager to `null`.

12.7 Using Layout Managers Effectively

The idea of a layout manager is a good one. In principle, it relieves the developer of the requirement to specify the positions of each and every component and simplifies the development of many interfaces. In practice, however, many developers feel that the layout managers are hindering more than helping them. Although it is true that some layout managers such as GridBagLayout require more effort than they should, a few basic strategies for harnessing the power of layout managers will significantly simplify the UI layout process:

Use Nested Containers

There's no law that says you have to use a single layout manager for everything. Divide and conquer!

Turn Off the LayoutManager for Some Containers

In a pinch, don't be afraid to position a few things by hand.

Use a Custom LayoutManager

Don't like the standard layout managers? Write your own.

Adjust the Empty Space Around Components

If your layout is almost perfect except for some empty space, there are a few small tweaks you can use to fix up those last details.

Use Nested Containers

Rather than struggling to fit your design into a single layout, try dividing the design into rectangular sections. Let each section be a panel with its own layout manager. For instance, a common problem is to create a row of buttons along one side of the visible area. In Section 12.5 (GridBagLayout) we showed how to do this with a single GridBagLayout, but as Listing 12.12 shows, it can be done more easily by setting the overall layout to Border-Layout, inserting a panel in the West for the buttons and another in the Center for everything else. The Panel in the West would then use a GridLayout with a single column and the appropriate number of rows. Figure 12–12 shows the result.

Listing 12.12 ButtonCol.java

```java
import java.applet.Applet;
import java.awt.*;

/** An applet with a column of buttons down the L side */

public class ButtonCol extends Applet {
  public void init() {
    setLayout(new BorderLayout());
    Panel buttonPanel = new Panel();
    buttonPanel.setLayout(new GridLayout(6, 1));
    buttonPanel.add(new Label("Buttons", Label.CENTER));
    buttonPanel.add(new Button("Button One"));
    buttonPanel.add(new Button("Button Two"));
    buttonPanel.add(new Button("Button Three"));
    buttonPanel.add(new Button("Button Four"));
    buttonPanel.add(new Button("Button Five"));
    add("West", buttonPanel);
    Panel everythingElse = new Panel();
    everythingElse.add(new Label("Everything Else"));
    add("Center", everythingElse);
  }
}
```

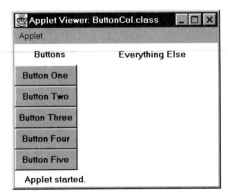

Figure 12-12   Nested containers generally simplify complex layouts.

Turn Off the LayoutManager for Some Containers

Positioning components individually is not always particularly difficult, especially if this is combined with the use of nested windows. For instance, suppose that you wanted to do something similar to the above example, except that you wanted the button column to take up exactly 40% of the width of the applet, rather than a width independent of the Container size (enough space for the widest button). This can be done by allocating two Panels as before, but positioning them using reshape after turning off the layout manager for the overall applet. Because each Panel still has its own layout manager, components inside of them do *not* need to be positioned manually.

Listing 12.13 `ButtonCol2.java`

```java
import java.applet.Applet;
import java.awt.*;

/** A variation of ButtonCol that adjusts the width
 *  taken by the column of buttons. The top-level
 *  panels are positioned by hand. Since applets can't
 *  be resized in most browsers, setting the size
 *  once when the applet is created is sufficient.
 * @see ButtonCol
 */

public class ButtonCol2 extends Applet {
  public void init() {
    setLayout(null);
    int width1 = size().width*4/10,
        width2 = size().width - width1,
        height = size().height;
    Panel buttonPanel = new Panel();
    buttonPanel.reshape(0, 0, width1, height);
    buttonPanel.setLayout(new GridLayout(6, 1));
    buttonPanel.add(new Label("Buttons", Label.CENTER));
    buttonPanel.add(new Button("Button One"));
    buttonPanel.add(new Button("Button Two"));
    buttonPanel.add(new Button("Button Three"));
    buttonPanel.add(new Button("Button Four"));
    buttonPanel.add(new Button("Button Five"));
    add(buttonPanel);
    Panel everythingElse = new Panel();
    everythingElse.reshape(width1+1, 0, width2, height);
    everythingElse.add(new Label("Everything Else"));
    add(everythingElse);
  }
}
```

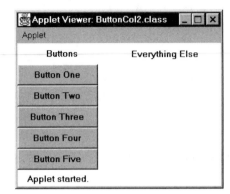

Figure 12-13 Position top-level windows by hand, not individual components.

Use a Custom LayoutManager

As discussed in the following section (Section 12.8), designing a special-purpose layout manager, although nontrivial, is not overly difficult, and the result can be reused many times. In addition, there are many third-party layout managers available on sites such as Gamelan (`http://java.devel-oper.com/pages/Gamelan.programming.ui.layout.html`).

Adjust the Empty Space Around Components

Change the Space Allocated by the LayoutManager

All the standard layout managers except for `GridBagLayout` have a constructor option that lets you specify the amount of space that will be reserved between components. With `GridBagLayout`, you can specify this using the `insets` or `ipadx` and `ipady` fields of the `Grid-BagConstraints` object.

Override insets in the Container

`Insets` are designed to be empty margins around the inside of a `Container`. All built-in layout managers respect them, as should any custom layout managers. This allows for borders around components. Unfortunately, however, a `Container` does not provide a way to change its insets. So a subclass of `Container` (probably a `Panel` subclass) must be created that overrides the `insets` (`getInsets` in Java 1.1) method.

Use a Canvas as a Spacer

A `Canvas` that does not draw or handle mouse events can be used as an "empty" component for spacing in windows that `FlowLayout`, `Grid-`

Layout, GridBagLayout, or in the noncenter region of a window using BorderLayout. Unlike a Panel, where the Container's layout manager typically undoes the effects of any calls to reshape, calling reshape (setShape in Java 1.1) on a Canvas is reliable. This is because a Canvas reports its current size when asked its preferredSize, while a Panel calculates it based on the components it contains.

12.8 Writing a Custom LayoutManager

If the standard layout managers are not sufficient, and positioning components individually is not feasible, you can use a custom layout manager. Create an object that implements the LayoutManager interface, then use it in setLayout calls just like the standard layout managers. It's a bit of effort, but you can use your new layout managers over and over.

The LayoutManager Interface

A layout manager must implement the LayoutManager interface, providing an implementation for the following five methods:

public void addLayoutComponent(String name, Component c)
This is called when an item is added to the Container. It is often left empty and all appropriate actions are handled in layoutContainer instead. Also, note that this method only gets called when a two-argument version of add is called. This is a poor design for two reasons. First of all, most often simply add(Component) is used. There is no way to monitor this call from the layout manager, only from the Container. Secondly, if a custom version of add were being designed, it might want a two-argument version where the first argument is something other than a String. But that's the design Java uses, so we have to live with it.

public void removeLayoutComponent(Component c)
This is called when an item is deleted from the Container. Again, it is often left empty, and all appropriate actions are handled in layoutContainer instead.

public Dimension preferredLayoutSize(Container container)
If you place a `Panel` in a `FlowLayout`, the `Panel` shrinks itself to just barely accommodate the components inside. This is because the `FlowLayout` asks the `Panel` for its `preferredSize` (`getPreferredSize` in Java 1.1), then calls `reshape` (`setBounds`) on it appropriately. The `Panel`, in responding to the request for `preferredSize`, asks its layout manager for its `preferredLayoutSize`. So `preferredLayoutSize` should look up the preferred sizes of the components inside and return the optimum `Dimension` to accommodate them.

public Dimension minimumLayoutSize(Container container)
This is similar to `preferredLayoutSize`, but is intended to return the minimum `Dimension`, not the optimum. As with the standard components, it is usually set to return the same value as `preferredLayoutSize`.

public void layoutContainer(Container container)
This method is the one that does the real work of positioning and sizing the components contained inside the `Container`. It should ignore any `Component` that is not currently visible, and should check the `Container` for any `Insets` (reserved empty space) when computing the space available.

The LayoutManager2 Interface

In Java 1.1, there is a `LayoutManager2` interface that extends `LayoutManager`. All of the standard layout managers use this, and it would be a good idea for your custom ones to use it as well. It provides the following additonal method placeholders, none of which are yet being used by the standard methods in the AWT:

**public void addLayoutComponent(Component c,
                                 Object constraints)**

public float getLayoutAlignmentX(Container container)

public float getLayoutAlignmentY(Container container)

public void invalidateLayout(Container container)

public Dimension maximumLayoutSize ()

Example: RowLayout

As an example, consider a new LayoutManager called RowLayout that puts equal-width components into a single row. Given the window size, it will space each Component equally in the available width (and with each using the full available height), just like GridLayout(1, 0) would do. The layoutContainer method would need to count the number of visible Components, divide the available width by this number, then resize each Component accordingly. When a window using RowLayout is asked its preferredSize, it will respond with a width equal to the width of the widest component times the number of components in the window, plus any horizontal spacing the user requested. The height will be the height of the tallest component (plus any top/bottom padding). This will allow the Container to be shrunk to this size yet still allow all components to have identical widths without squeezing any below their preferred width. The following summarizes the implementation; the actual code is given in Listing 12.16.

addLayoutComponent
This method is empty; we do all the work in layoutContainer.

```
public void addLayoutComponent(String s, Component c)
{
}
```

removeLayoutComponent
This method is empty; we do all the work in layoutContainer.

```
public void removeLayoutComponent(Component c) {
}
```

preferredLayoutSize
This simplified version gives the basic idea: calculate N times the width of widest component for the width, the height of the tallest component for the height. The actual version (Listing 12.16) does a bit more. First of all, it only counts a component if it is visible, since hidden components should not affect the window in any way. Secondly, it adds in any insets used by the container. Finally, it accounts for any horizontal and vertical gaps specified by the user.

```
public Dimension preferredLayoutSize(Container cont)
{
   int count=0, maxWidth=0, maxHeight=0;
   Dimension componentSize;
```

```
Component[] components = cont.getComponents();
Component c;
for(int i=0; i<components.length; i++) {
  c = components[i];
  componentSize = c.preferredSize();
 maxWidth = Math.max(componentSize.width, maxWidth);
  maxHeight = Math.max(componentSize.height,
                         maxHeight);
  count++;
}
return(new Dimension(count*maxWidth, maxHeight));
}
```

minimumLayoutSize

The minimum size is the same as the preferred size.

```
public Dimension minimumLayoutSize(Container cont) {
  return(preferredLayoutSize(cont));
}
```

layoutContainer

This simplified version gives the basic idea: find the width of the window, divide by the number of components, then use that as the individual component width. Use the window height as the height of individual components. To lay out the window, position the first component at the left of the window, resizing it to the width and height just calculated. Then move one component width to the right and repeat the process on the next component. The actual version (Listing 12.16) does a bit more. As with `preferredLayoutSize`, it only counts visible components and takes the window's insets and the horizontal and vertical gaps into account. In addition, it compensates for the possibility that the window width divided by the number of visible components may not come out evenly. The left over pixels are added back in one pixel at a time to the first several components. That way, up to $N-1$ components could be 1 pixel wider than the final component, but there will be no large gap.

```
public void layoutContainer(Container cont) {
  Component[] components = cont.getComponents();
  int width = cont.size().width/components.length,
      height= cont.size().height, left=0, top=0;
  Component c;
  for(int i=0; i<components.length; i++) {
    c = components[i];
```

```
        c.reshape(left, top, width, height);
        left = left + width;
    }
}
```

Listing 12.14 shows RowLayout in action. In this example, three buttons are added to an applet that uses RowLayout. The RowLayout layout manager sizes all of them to 1/3 of the available width. Figure 12–14 shows the result.

Listing 12.14 RowLayoutTest.java

```
import java.applet.Applet;
import java.awt.*;

/** The RowLayout layout manager in action.
 * @see RowLayout
 */

public class RowLayoutTest extends Applet {
  public void init() {
    setLayout(new RowLayout(5, 5));
    add(new Button("Test One"));
    add(new Button("Test Two"));
    add(new Button("Test Three"));
  }
}
```

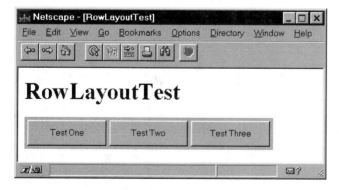

Figure 12–14   RowLayout gives each button 1/3 of the width of the window.

Listing 12.15 gives a second example. In this case, a `Panel` is added to an `Applet`, and the `Panel` uses `RowLayout`. Since the default layout manager for an `Applet` is `FlowLayout`, and `FlowLayout` tries to keep components as small as possible, the `Panel` will be asked its preferred size, which it will get from the `RowLayout`. It will use three times the width of the largest button ("Test Three") for this width, plus add in 20 pixels for the space to the left of the first button, between the buttons, and to the right of the last button. Figure 12–15 shows the result.

Listing 12.15 `RowLayoutTest2.java`

```java
import java.applet.Applet;
import java.awt.*;

/** An example of RowLayout calculating preferred size.
 * @see RowLayout
 */

public class RowLayoutTest2 extends Applet {
  public void init() {
    Panel p = new Panel();
    p.setBackground(Color.gray);
    p.setLayout(new RowLayout(5, 5));
    p.add(new Button("Test One"));
    p.add(new Button("Test Two"));
    p.add(new Button("Test Three"));
    add(p);
  }
}
```

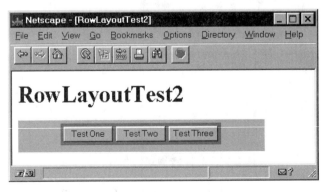

Figure 12–15 The `preferredSize` of a `Panel` using `RowLayout` is *N* times the width of the widest component.

Listing 12.16 gives the code for `RowLayout`.

Listing 12.16   RowLayout.java

```java
import java.awt.*;

/**
 * A layout manager that distributes all components
 * evenly across the width of the Container, with an
 * optional spacing in between each.
 * <P>
 * Its effect is very similar to GridLayout with 1 row
 * and 0 columns.
 *
 * @author Marty Hall (hall@apl.jhu.edu)
 * @version 1.0 (1997)
 */

public class RowLayout implements LayoutManager {
  private int hGap = 0, vGap = 0;

  //-----------------------------------------------------
  /** Build a RowLayout with 0 pixel hGap and vGap */
  public RowLayout() {
  }

  /** Build a RowLayout with the specified
   *   horizontal and vertical gaps.
   *
   * @param hGap The horizontal space at the left and
   *             right of components.
   * @param vGap The vertical space above and below
   *             components.
   */
  public RowLayout(int hGap, int vGap) {
    this.hGap = hGap;
    this.vGap = vGap;
  }


  //-----------------------------------------------------
  /** An empty method. */
  public void addLayoutComponent(String s, Component c) {
  }

  /** An empty method */
  public void removeLayoutComponent(Component c) {
  }
```

continued

Listing 12.16   `RowLayout.java`   (continued)

```
//-------------------------------------------------
/** This gives the preferred width/height of the window
 *  using this layout manager. The width is
 * calculated by finding the widest visible Component
 * and multiplying that width by the number of visible
 * Components, plus extra space between Components
 * (i.e. hGap between each, plus at the far left
 * and right of the row), plus the left and right
 * insets of the Container. The height is simply the
 * height of the tallest Component, plus twice the
 * vGap.
 *
 * @param cont The window using RowLayout.
 * @return A Dimension object giving the width
 *         and height.
 * @see #setVgap
 * @see #setHgap
 */
public Dimension preferredLayoutSize(Container cont) {
  int count=0, totalWidth, totalHeight, maxWidth=0,
      maxHeight=0;
  Dimension componentSize;
  Component[] components = cont.getComponents();
  Component c;
  for(int i=0; i<components.length; i++) {
    c = components[i];
    if (c.isVisible()) {
      componentSize = c.preferredSize();
      maxWidth = Math.max(componentSize.width,
                          maxWidth);
      maxHeight = Math.max(componentSize.height,
                           maxHeight);
      count++;
    }
  }
  Insets margins = cont.insets();
  totalWidth = count*maxWidth + (count+1)*hGap +
               margins.left + margins.right;
  totalHeight = maxHeight + 2*vGap +
                margins.top + margins.bottom;
  return(new Dimension(totalWidth, totalHeight));
}
```

Listing 12.16 `RowLayout.java` (continued)

```
//-----------------------------------------------------
/** This is identical to preferredLayoutSize
 * @see #preferredLayoutSize
 */
public Dimension minimumLayoutSize(Container cont) {
  return(preferredLayoutSize(cont));
}


//-----------------------------------------------------
/** This resizes all visible components to have
 *  the same width (1/Nth of the available space
 * after accounting for insets and hGap) and height
 * (the full available height after accounting for
 * insets and vGap).
 */
public void layoutContainer(Container cont) {
  Insets margins = cont.insets();
  Component[] components = cont.getComponents();
  int left = margins.left + hGap,
      top = margins.top + vGap,
      count = countVisibleComponents(components),
      totalWidth = cont.size().width -
                   (count+1)*hGap -
                   margins.left - margins.right,
      totalHeight = cont.size().height - 2*vGap -
                    margins.top - margins.bottom,
      componentWidth = totalWidth/count,
      extra = totalWidth - componentWidth*count,
      width;
  Component c;
  for(int i=0; i<components.length; i++) {
    c = components[i];
    if (c.isVisible()) {
      if (extra>0) {
        width = componentWidth + 1;
        extra--;
      } else
        width = componentWidth;
      c.reshape(left, top, width, totalHeight);
      left = left + width + hGap;
    }
  }
}
```

continued

Listing 12.16 `RowLayout.java` (continued)

```java
//------------------------------------------------------
/** The horizontal gap as specified in the constructor
 *   or by setHgap.
 * @see #setHgap
 */
public int getHgap() {
  return(hGap);
}

/** Sets the horizontal gap between components.
 * @param hGap The horizontal gap in pixels.
 * @see #getHgap
 */
public void setHgap(int hGap) {
  this.hGap = hGap;
}

//------------------------------------------------------
/** The vertical gap as specified in the constructor
 *   or by setVgap.
 * @see #setVgap
 */
public int getVgap() {
  return(vGap);
}

/** Sets the vertical gap between components.
 * @param vGap The vertical gap in pixels.
 * @see #getVgap
 */
public void setVgap(int vGap) {
  this.vGap = vGap;
}

//------------------------------------------------------

private int countVisibleComponents(Component[] comps) {
  int count=0;
  for(int i=0; i<comps.length; i++)
    if(comps[i].isVisible())
      count++;
  return(count);
}
}
```

12.9 Summary

Layout managers help you position components in the window. They are particularly helpful when you resize the window, add components, or move the program among operating systems. There are five standard layout managers: `FlowLayout`, `BorderLayout`, `GridLayout`, `CardLayout`, and `GridBagLayout`. If you don't like any of those, you can always turn off the layout manager, but clever use of nested containers often makes this unnecessary. If you have a layout that you want to repeat several places but that isn't easily obtained with the built-in layout managers, you can roll your own.

Okay, so you've got windows galore. You're a layout manager pro. But it would be nice to put something *in* the windows. Read on: Chapter 13 covers buttons, checkboxes, radio buttons, scrollbars, and other GUI controls.

GRAPHICAL USER INTERFACE CONTROLS

Topics in This Chapter

Chapter 13

I n the previous three chapters, we discussed the basic window types provided by the Abstract Window Toolkit (AWT) and how to process the events that occur in them. These windows differ in whether or not they have borders or can contain other graphical components. However, they are essentially similar in the way that they handle mouse and keyboard events and the way in which drawing is done (usually by overriding `paint`). The GUI controls (or "widgets") discussed in this chapter are not like this. First of all, in Java 1.0, scrollbars, checkboxes, buttons, and the like do not receive the mouse and keyboard events that windows do. They do in Java 1.1, but even so, those events are not of primary concern. Instead, Java defines higher-level events based on when a button was clicked, a checkbox was checked or unchecked, a slider was adjusted, and so forth. Secondly, these GUI controls have their own graphical representation that the user should not attempt to tamper directly with; the `paint` method is not used at all. Instead, they adopt the look and feel of the operating system on which they are running (via a native "peer"), leaving interfaces that allow the user to change only certain aspects of their appearance. This is a two-edged sword. On the one hand, it lets you easily adapt to multiple platforms and saves you from the myriad details that implementing GUI controls yourself would require. On the other hand, you have only limited control over these graphical objects. For instance, you can always change the labels of buttons, may or may not be able to change their color (depending on operating system), and can never change their shape, border thickness, or what constitutes clicking them. However, in many cases you can implement your own user interface control from scratch; I'll give a complete implementation of an image button to illustrate this.

Despite the promise of cross-platform support, there are a few inconsistencies in the way various features are implemented on different platforms, especially with regard to color usage. Except for scrollbars, these differences are not all that significant, but it is still important to be aware of them when developing multiplatform applications. I'll alert you to them throughout the chapter.

13.1 Handling Action Events in GUI Controls

After you create a component and add it to a window, you probably want to make it actually *do* something when the user interacts with it. In Java 1.02, you do this primarily by watching for "action" events, typically by overriding the `action` method in the component or its enclosing window. There are a few other events of interest (list selection and deselection events, keyboard events for textfields and text areas, scrolling events), but action events are the most important. In Java 1.1, action events are still important, but other important high-level events are generated as well. Action events are generated by `Button`, `List`, `MenuItem`, and `TextField`, and are handled either in `processActionEvent` or in another object designated via `addActionListener`. Item selection events are generated by `Checkbox`, `CheckboxMenuItem`, `Choice`, and `List`, and are handled in `processItemEvent` or in an object designated via `addItemListener`. Textfields and text areas generate both keyboard events and text events; they are handled in `processKeyEvent` and `processTextEvent` or in an object designated with `addKeyListener` or `addTextListener`. Scrollbars generate adjustment events; they are handled in `processAdjustmentEvent` or in an object designated with `addAdjustmentListener`. Furthermore, the mouse and keyboard events discussed in Chapter 10 are delivered to Java 1.1 GUI components, unlike in Java 1.0. Nevertheless, the higher-level events are still the primary event types of concern.

There are two basic approaches to handling action events: letting each component process its own events, or handling the events in a centralized location such as the enclosing window. The following four sections give an example of each of these approaches in Java 1.02 and Java 1.1. Except for the frame title, all four result in an identical interface and in identical behavior: a frame with three buttons that resize the frame when pressed. Figures 13–1 through 13–3 show the result after each of the three buttons is clicked.

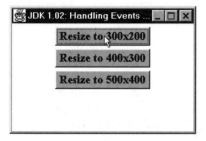

Figure 13–1   Frame after pressing the first button.

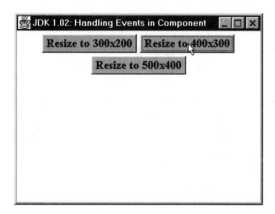

Figure 13–2   Frame after pressing the second button.

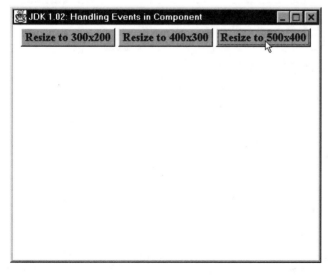

Figure 13–3   Frame after pressing the third button.

Processing Action Events in Individual Components in Java 1.0

The first possible approach to handling user interface events is to have a GUI element handle its own events. It does this by overriding the action method. For instance, in Listings 13.1 and 13.2, a custom subclass of Button (ResizeButton) is added to a Frame. When pressed, each of these buttons behave according to their *own* copy of action (which accesses per-button instance variables), resizing the frame as shown in Figures 13–1 through 13–3. This type of decentralized processing is advantageous in that it lets developers build components with behaviors independently of the application in which the components will be used. This can simplify development and maintenance. On the other hand, if the component's behavior affects the window the component is in, it has to gain access to it in order to carry out the action. In Listing 13.2, this was done by calling getParent. However, this is not always so easy. For one thing, that assumed the buttons wanted to act on their directly enclosing window. If an intermediate Panel was introduced, the getParent call would have to change. The ResizeButton could plan for this eventuality by finding the topmost Frame instead of just using getParent, but the point remains that it often needs to know something about the environment in which it will be used. Secondly, this approach will not work when the action to be carried out requires access to protected data in the enclosing window.

Listing 13.1 `ActionExample1.java`

```java
import java.awt.*;

public class ActionExample1 extends QuittableFrame {
  public static void main(String[] args) {
    new ActionExample1();
  }

  public ActionExample1() {
    super("JDK 1.02: Handling Events in Component");
    setLayout(new FlowLayout());
    setFont(new Font("TimesRoman", Font.BOLD, 18));
    add(new ResizeButton(300, 200));
    add(new ResizeButton(400, 300));
    add(new ResizeButton(500, 400));
    resize(400, 300);
    show();
  }
}
```

Listing 13.2 `ResizeButton.java`

```java
import java.awt.*;

public class ResizeButton extends Button {
  private int width, height;

  public ResizeButton(int width, int height) {
    super("Resize to " + width + "x" + height);
    this.width = width;
    this.height = height;
  }

  public boolean action(Event event, Object object) {
    getParent().resize(width, height);
    getParent().layout();
    return(true);
  }
}
```

Processing Action Events in Containers in Java 1.0

The second possible way to handle GUI control events in Java 1.0 is to have a window handle events for the elements it contains. You do this by overriding the `action` method in the window, then checking the event's target field to find the GUI elements of interest. Listing 13.3 gives an example of such a centralized event-processing routine. Here, `action` is overridden in the window holding the buttons, rather than in the `Button` class itself. The effect is the same however; the frame is resized according to which button is selected, as in Figures 13–1 through 13–3. In the `ResizeButton` class (Listing 13.2), the action could be taken whenever the `action` method was invoked. Here, however, you have to first determine which button was pressed before knowing which action should be performed. This kind of centralized processing does not require you to make a custom `Component` subclass, plus it lets the behavior be based on protected methods or data in the window. On the other hand, it makes it more difficult to build components separately from the applications in which they will be used. In many cases, it is a simple matter of preference. Try it both ways a few times and see which you prefer.

Listing 13.3   `ActionExample2.java`

```java
import java.awt.*;

public class ActionExample2 extends QuittableFrame {
  public static void main(String[] args) {
    new ActionExample2();
  }

  private Button button1, button2, button3;

  public ActionExample2() {
    super("JDK 1.02: Handling Events in Container");
    setLayout(new FlowLayout());
    setFont(new Font("TimesRoman", Font.BOLD, 18));
    button1 = new Button("Resize to 300x200");
    button2 = new Button("Resize to 400x300");
    button3 = new Button("Resize to 500x400");
    add(button1);
    add(button2);
    add(button3);
    resize(400, 300);
    show();
  }

  public boolean action(Event event, Object object) {
    if (event.target == button1) {
      resize(300, 200);
      layout();
      return(true);
    } else if (event.target == button2) {
      resize(400, 300);
      layout();
      return(true);
    } else if (event.target == button3) {
      resize(500, 400);
      layout();
      return(true);
    } else
      return(false);
  }
}
```

Processing Action Events in Individual Components in Java 1.1

In Java 1.1, the first alternative for handling GUI control events is to have an element handle its own events. You do this by primarily overriding `proc-essActionEvent`, but some interface elements generate events other than action events. In such a case, you'd override `processXxxEvent` instead (e.g., `processItemEvent`, `processTextEvent`, and so forth). For example, Listings 13.4 and 13.5 show the Java 1.1 version of decentralized event handling. Except for the frame title, it generates the same interface and behavior as the previous two examples. It has similar advantages and disadvantages to the 1.0 version. Don't forget to enable events via `enableEvents` before trying to process them; Java 1.1 doesn't send events unless you ask for them. Also, you want to call `super.processAction-Event` from within `processActionEvent`, so that any action listeners attached to the control will still be activated normally. Finally, remember to import `java.awt.event.*`; that's where all the event types are defined. For details on enabling and processing events, see Section 10.5 (Handling Events in Java 1.1).

Listing 13.4   `ActionExample3.java`

```java
import java.awt.*;

// JDK 1.1 Only

public class ActionExample3 extends CloseableFrame {
  public static void main(String[] args) {
    new ActionExample3();
  }

  public ActionExample3() {
    super("JDK 1.1: Handling Events in Component");
    setLayout(new FlowLayout());
    setFont(new Font("TimesRoman", Font.BOLD, 18));
    add(new SetSizeButton(300, 200));
    add(new SetSizeButton(400, 300));
    add(new SetSizeButton(500, 400));
    setSize(400, 300);
    setVisible(true);
  }
}
```

Listing 13.5   `SetSizeButton.java`

```java
import java.awt.*;
import java.awt.event.*;

public class SetSizeButton extends Button {
  private int width, height;

  public SetSizeButton(int width, int height) {
    super("Resize to " + width + "x" + height);
    this.width = width;
    this.height = height;
    enableEvents(AWTEvent.ACTION_EVENT_MASK);
  }

  public void processActionEvent(ActionEvent event) {
    getParent().setSize(width, height);
    getParent().doLayout();
    super.processActionEvent(event); // Handle listeners
  }
}
```

Processing Action Events in Other Objects in Java 1.1

In Java 1.1, the second way to process GUI element events is to pass the events to an external object. You first create an object that implements the `ActionListener` interface, defining a method called `actionPerformed` that takes an `ActionEvent` as an argument. You then associate this object with the button via `addActionListener`. Listing 13.6 gives an example of this. In this particular case, the object was the window itself, but there is no reason it has to be. Although it is sometimes convenient to handle events in the window itself, inner classes let you pass events to external objects and still access protected data in the window. See Section 10.5 (Handling Events in Java 1.1) for more details on using inner classes for event handling, plus I'll give several examples in this chapter.

Listing 13.6 `ActionExample4.java`

```java
import java.awt.*;
import java.awt.event.*;

// JDK 1.1 Only

public class ActionExample4 extends CloseableFrame
                            implements ActionListener {
  public static void main(String[] args) {
    new ActionExample4();
  }

  private Button button1, button2, button3;

  public ActionExample4() {
    super("JDK 1.1: Handling Events in Other Object");
    setLayout(new FlowLayout());
    setFont(new Font("TimesRoman", Font.BOLD, 18));
    button1 = new Button("Resize to 300x200");
    button2 = new Button("Resize to 400x300");
    button3 = new Button("Resize to 500x400");
    button1.addActionListener(this);
    button2.addActionListener(this);
    button3.addActionListener(this);
    add(button1);
    add(button2);
    add(button3);
    setSize(400, 300);
    setVisible(true);
  }

  public void actionPerformed(ActionEvent event) {
    if (event.getSource() == button1) {
      setSize(300, 200);
      doLayout();
    } else if (event.getSource() == button2) {
      setSize(400, 300);
      doLayout();
    } else if (event.getSource() == button3) {
      setSize(500, 400);
      doLayout();
    }
  }
}
```

13.2 Buttons

The Button class creates pushbuttons with text labels. Java doesn't have a built-in class that supports buttons with images, but in Section 13.3 we'll build one by extending the Canvas class. The most common usage is to simply create one with a specified label, drop it in a window, then watch for action events to see if it has been pressed. For instance, to create a button and add it to the current window, you'd do something like the following:

```
Button button = new Button("...");
add(button);
```

Constructors

public Button(String buttonLabel)

This creates a button with the specified label. Its preferredSize (used by layout managers like FlowLayout and BorderLayout) is based on the height and width of the label in the current font, plus some extra space that varies depending on the window system being used.

public Button()

This creates a button with no label. One can be added later via set-Label. The width reported by preferredSize is greater than zero even when there is no label, because the border requires some space.

Example

Listing 13.7 shows an applet that contains three buttons. In this particular case, because we don't ever do anything with the buttons, there is no need to assign the Button objects to separate instance variables. It is sufficient to simply do add(new Button(...)). However, you will want access to the buttons when you go to give them behavior, so you might as well plan ahead and store the button references somewhere that will be accessible in other methods.

One of the key features of user interface controls in Java is that they take on the look and feel of the operating system they are running on. Figures 13–4, 13–5, and 13–6 show the results of Listing 13.7 in Netscape 3 on Windows 95, MacOS, and Solaris, respectively.

Listing 13.7   Buttons.java

```java
import java.applet.Applet;
import java.awt.*;

public class Buttons extends Applet {
  private Button button1, button2, button3;
```

Listing 13.7 `Buttons.java` (continued)

```java
public void init() {
  button1 = new Button("Button One");
  button2 = new Button("Button Two");
  button3 = new Button("Button Three");
  add(button1);
  add(button2);
  add(button3);
}
}
```

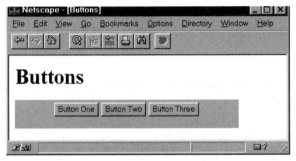

Figure 13–4 Java buttons in Windows 95.

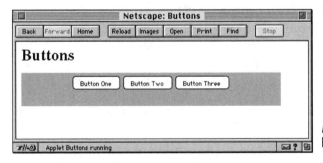

Figure 13–5 Java buttons in MacOS.

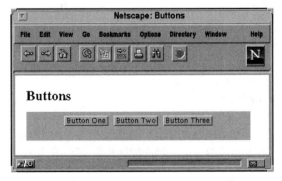

Figure 13–6 Java buttons in Solaris.

Other Button Methods

public String getLabel()
The getLabel method retrieves the current label.

public void setLabel(String newLabel)
The setLabel method changes the button's label. If the button is already displayed, doing this does not automatically resize it in its Container. So the containing window should be invalidated and validated to force a fresh layout, as below:

```
someButton.setLabel("A New Label");
someButton.getParent().invalidate();
someButton.getParent().validate();
```

public void addActionListener(ActionListener listener) [Java 1.1]
public void removeActionListener(ActionListener listener) [Java 1.1]
These methods add and remove objects that process action events. See the following subsection for a discussion of their use.

public String getActionCommand() [Java 1.1]
public void setActionCommand(String command) [Java 1.1]
These Java 1.1 methods are used to associate a string with the button. The idea is that this string stays the same even when the label changes in internationalized code. The string can be retrieved in event-processing code by calling the getActionCommand method of Action-Event. The default string is simply the label of the button.

public void processActionEvent(ActionEvent event) [Java 1.1]
This is a low-level event-processing routine used when you want a button to handle its own events. If you use it, don't forget to enable events first with enableEvents, and to call super.processAction-Event from within the body of the method. See the following section for examples.

Also, as with every Component (Section 11.2), buttons have getFore-ground, setForeground, getBackground, setBackground, get-Font, setFont, and a variety of other inherited methods. However, setForeground and setBackground are ignored on many Windows and MacOS implementations. In particular, Netscape version 2 and 3, Internet Explorer version 3, and Sun JDK 1.02 all ignore button foreground and background colors on Windows 95 and NT. JDK 1.1.3 and Netscape 4.01 honor them on Windows 95/NT. They work on virtually all Unix implementations.

Core Warning

Most 1.02 Java implementations and browsers ignore button foreground and background colors on Windows 95/NT and MacOS.

Handling Button Events

Precisely how Java determines that a button has been activated depends on the operating system. However, typically activation is either when the user clicks and releases the mouse on a button or when the user enters a carriage return while the button has the input focus.

Button Events in Java 1.0

In Java 1.0, events can be handled in the `action` method of the button itself by making a `Button` subclass. If not, the event gets passed to the `Container`, which can handle it there. But because the `Container` may contain more than one `Component`, if the event is handled there it first needs to determine which component was activated before acting upon it, as in the following example:

```
public boolean action(Event event, Object object) {
  if (event.target == button1) {
    doActionForButton1();
    return(true);
  } else ...
}
```

When `action` is called for a button, Java passes the button's label as the second argument. It has become common practice to determine which `Button` was activated by comparing the label to this argument (i.e. by checking if `object.equals("Button Label")`), rather than comparing `event.target` to the instance variable storing the `Button`. Although this can be a tiny bit shorter since you don't have to have a `Button` instance variable, I recommend against using this approach in production code for the following reasons:

- Changing the label requires changes to code in two separate places (e.g. `init` or constructor and `action`), and the second change can easily be overlooked. <FACETIOUS>Normally, you might argue that comparing to the label is good for job security for this very reason (nobody except you will be able to maintain the code). Fortunately, the demand for Java programmers is so high right now that we can dispense with this argument.</FACETIOUS>
- Labels can change at run-time.
- Two buttons could have the same label.
- Comparing to labels in internationalized Java 1.1 code is much more difficult.
- The `String` comparison is more expensive.

Core Approach

When handling action events in the enclosing window's `action` method, determine which button was selected by checking the button object reference, not by comparing to the button's label.

Button Events in Java 1.1

Like other action events, you can handle button events one of two ways. To handle events in the `Button` object itself, first enable action events via

```
enableEvents(AWTEvent.ACTION_EVENT_MASK);
```

Next, override `processActionEvent` to perform the specific behavior you want. You should call `super.processActionEvent` in the body so that, if anyone else attaches listeners to your button, they will still be invoked. Following is an abstract example; for specifics see `SetSizeButton` (Listing 13.5):

```
public void processActionEvent(ActionEvent event) {
  takeSomeAction(...);
  super.processActionEvent(event); // Handle listeners
}
```

That's the first possible approach: processing events in the `Button` itself. The next option is to attach one or more `ActionListeners` to the button. To do that, create an object that implements the `ActionListener` interface, put the action to be taken in the `actionPerformed` method, then associate it with the button via `addActionListener`. In Listing 13.6, the window itself was the `ActionListener`, but you can do this a variety of ways. For instance, Listing 13.8 creates three buttons, each with one to three different ActionListeners attached. It associates an FgReporter (Listing 13.9) with the first button, an FgReporter and a BgReporter (Listing 13.10) with the second, and an FgReporter, a BgReporter, and a Size-Reporter (Listing 13.11) with the third. Each of these reporters is an ActionListener that simply prints some information about the component that was the source of the action. Figure 13–7 shows the result, with the output after clicking on the three buttons once each shown in Listing 13.12.

Listing 13.8 ButtonExample.java

```java
import java.awt.*;
import java.awt.event.*;

// JDK 1.1 Only

public class ButtonExample extends CloseableFrame {
  public static void main(String[] args) {
    new ButtonExample();
  }

  public ButtonExample() {
    super("Using ActionListeners in JDK 1.1");
    setLayout(new FlowLayout());
    Button b1 = new Button("Button 1");
    Button b2 = new Button("Button 2");
    Button b3 = new Button("Button 3");
    b1.setBackground(Color.lightGray);
    b2.setBackground(Color.gray);
    b3.setBackground(Color.darkGray);
    FgReporter fgReporter = new FgReporter();
    BgReporter bgReporter = new BgReporter();
    SizeReporter sizeReporter = new SizeReporter();
    b1.addActionListener(fgReporter);
    b2.addActionListener(fgReporter);
    b2.addActionListener(bgReporter);
    b3.addActionListener(fgReporter);
    b3.addActionListener(bgReporter);
    b3.addActionListener(sizeReporter);
    add(b1);
    add(b2);
    add(b3);
    setSize(350, 100);
    setVisible(true);
  }
}
```

Listing 13.9   `FgReporter.java`

```
import java.awt.event.*;
import java.awt.*;

// JDK 1.1 Only

public class FgReporter implements ActionListener {
  public void actionPerformed(ActionEvent event) {
    Component c = (Component)event.getSource();
    System.out.println("Foreground: " +
                       c.getForeground());
  }
}
```

Listing 13.10   `BgReporter.java`

```
import java.awt.event.*;
import java.awt.*;

// JDK 1.1 Only

public class BgReporter implements ActionListener {
  public void actionPerformed(ActionEvent event) {
    Component c = (Component)event.getSource();
    System.out.println("Background: " +
                       c.getBackground());
  }
}
```

Listing 13.11   `SizeReporter.java`

```
import java.awt.event.*;
import java.awt.*;

// JDK 1.1 Only

public class SizeReporter implements ActionListener {
  public void actionPerformed(ActionEvent event) {
    Component c = (Component)event.getSource();
    Dimension d = c.getSize();
    System.out.println("Size: " + d.width + "x" +
                       d.height);
  }
}
```

Figure 13–7   You can attach more than one `ActionListener`
to a 1.1 component.

Listing 13.12 ButtonExample output after pressing Button 1, Button 2, and Button 3 once each in that order.

```
Foreground: java.awt.Color[r=0,g=0,b=0]
Foreground: java.awt.Color[r=0,g=0,b=0]
Background: java.awt.Color[r=128,g=128,b=128]
Foreground: java.awt.Color[r=0,g=0,b=0]
Background: java.awt.Color[r=64,g=64,b=64]
Size: 59x23
```

13.3 An Image Button Class

One of the most frequently requested additions to the AWT is a button that can contain an image, rather than just text. Unfortunately, the 1.1 release of the AWT did not add such a component, but it is not too difficult to implement a decent version ourselves. The idea is to start with the `ImageLabel` developed in Section 11.14. If you recall, this was simply a `Canvas` that resized itself to fit around a supplied image. Options let you stretch the image or leave empty margins around it. To make this into a button, you first draw a 3D border in the margin. Next, you monitor mouse events, inverting the 3D border and displaying a grayed-out image when the button is pressed. Finally, when the button is released, you generate action events so that `ImageButton` and `Button` event-handling code can be identical.

The following subsections describe the behavior of the `ImageButton` class; Listing 13.14 gives the source code.

Constructors

public ImageButton(URL imageFile)
This creates an `ImageButton` from the specified GIF or JPEG file.

public ImageButton(String imageFile)

This constructor turns the specified `String` into a URL, then creates an `ImageButton` as above.

public ImageButton(Image buttonImage)

If you already have an `Image`, you can use this constructor to place it in a button.

public ImageButton()

This makes an `ImageButton` using the default image of the `Image-Label` class (Section 11.14).

Example

Listing 13.13 creates four rows of image buttons. The first and third have varying border thicknesses and are sized to exactly fit the image they display. The second and fourth vary the button size in addition to varying the border width. Figures 13–8 and 13–9 show the results on Windows 95 and Solaris.

Listing 13.13 `ImageButtons.java`

```
import java.applet.Applet;
import java.awt.*;

public class ImageButtons extends Applet {
  public void init() {
    addButtons("images/Marty-Plate-Small.gif", 75, 39);
    addButtons("images/Java-Logo.gif", 55, 50);
  }

  private void addButtons(String file,
                          int width, int height) {
    Panel panel = new Panel();
    ImageButton button;
    for(int i=0; i<3; i++) {
      button = new ImageButton(getCodeBase(), file);
      button.setBorder(button.getBorder() + 4*i);
      panel.add(button);
    }
```

Listing 13.13 `ImageButtons.java` (continued)

```
    add(panel);
    panel = new Panel();
    for(int i=0; i<3; i++) {
      button = new ImageButton(getCodeBase(), file);
      button.setBorder(button.getBorder() + 4*i);
      button.resize(width*(i+1), height*(i+1));
      panel.add(button);
    }
    add(panel);
  }
}
```

Figure 13–8 Image buttons with varying border thicknesses and sizes, shown on Windows 95. One button is being clicked.

Figure 13–9   Image buttons with varying border thicknesses and sizes, shown on Solaris. One button is being clicked.

Other ImageButton Methods

ImageButton inherits a number of methods such as getBorder, set-Border, getBorderColor, and setBorderColor from the ImageLa-bel class (Section 11.14). It also inherits methods like getBackground, setBackground, and resize from the Component class. If you resize the button, be sure to do so before displaying it. In addition, you can use the following methods:

public int getDarkness()

This returns an int that is combined via logical "and" with the red, green, and blue values of the image to create the grayed out version.

The default is `0xffafafaf`, where the last three bytes represent the parts that will go with red, green, and blue values, respectively.

public Image getGrayImage()
This returns the `Image` that is being used when the button is pressed down. For instance, the middle button of the third row of Figures 13–8 and 13–9 show the gray image (since that button is pressed).

public void setDarkness(int darkMask)
This changes the darkness value described above.

public void setGrayImage(Image grayImage)
In general, you want to let `ImageButton` automatically determine the image that should be displayed when the button is pressed, using a grayed-out version of the normal image. However, you can supply it explicitly using this method.

Handling ImageButton Events

You handle events exactly the same way as with regular buttons in Java 1.0.

Source Code

Listing 13.14 presents the source code for the `ImageButton`.

Listing 13.14 `ImageButton.java`

```
import java.awt.*;
import java.net.*;
import java.awt.image.*;      // For ImageFilter stuff


//=========================================================
/**
 * A button class that uses an image instead of a
 * textual label. Clicking and releasing the mouse over
 * the button triggers an ACTION_EVENT, so you can add
 * behavior in the same two ways as you would with a normal
 * Button (in Java 1.0):
 * <OL>
 *   <LI>Make an ImageButton subclass and put the
```

continued

Listing 13.14 `ImageButton.java` (continued)

```
 *         behavior in the action method of that subclass.
 *   <LI>Use the main ImageButton class but then catch
 *         the events in the action method of the Container.
 * </OL>
 * <P>
 * Normally, the ImageButton's preferredSize (used,
 * for instance, by FlowLayout) is just big enough
 * to hold the image. However, if you give an explicit
 * resize or reshape call <B>before</B> adding the
 * ImageButton to the Container, this size will
 * override the defaults.
 * <P>
 * @author Marty Hall (hall@apl.jhu.edu)
 * @see Icon
 * @see GrayFilter
 * @version 1.0 (1997)
 */

public class ImageButton extends ImageLabel {
  //-----------------------------------------------------

  /** Default width of 3D border around image.
   *   Currently 4.
   * @see ImageLabel#setBorder
   * @see ImageLabel#getBorder
   */
  protected static final int defaultBorderWidth = 4;

  /** Default color of 3D border around image.
   *   Currently a gray with R/G/B of 160/160/160.
   *   Light grays look best.
   * @see ImageLabel#setBorderColor
   * @see ImageLabel#getBorderColor
   */
  protected static final Color defaultBorderColor =
    new Color(160, 160, 160);

  private boolean mouseIsDown = false;

  //-----------------------------------------------------
  // Constructors
```

Listing 13.14 `ImageButton.java` **(continued)**

```java
/** Create an ImageButton with the default image.
 * @see ImageLabel#getDefaultImageString
 */
public ImageButton() {
  super();
  setBorders();
}

/** Create an ImageButton using the image at URL
 *   specified by the string.
 * @param imageURLString A String specifying the URL
 *         of the image.
 */
public ImageButton(String imageURLString) {
  super(imageURLString);
  setBorders();
}

/** Create an ImageButton using the image at URL
 *   specified.
 * @param imageURL The URL of the image.
 */
public ImageButton(URL imageURL) {
  super(imageURL);
  setBorders();
}

/** Create an ImageButton using the file in
 *   the directory specified.
 * @param imageDirectory The URL of a directory
 * @param imageFile File in the above directory
 */
public ImageButton(URL imageDirectory,
                   String imageFile) {
  super(imageDirectory, imageFile);
  setBorders();
}

/** Create an ImageButton using the image specified.
 *   You would only want to use this if you already
 *   have an image (e.g., created via createImage).
 * @param image The image.
 */
public ImageButton(Image image) {
  super(image);
  setBorders();
}
```

continued

Listing 13.14 `ImageButton.java` (continued)

```
//-----------------------------------------------------
/** Draws the image with the border around it. If you
 *  override this in a subclass, call super.paint().
 */
public void paint(Graphics g) {
  super.paint(g);
  if (grayImage == null)
    createGrayImage(g);
  drawBorder(true);
}


//-----------------------------------------------------
// You only want mouseExit to repaint when mouse
// is down, so you have to set that flag here.

/** When the mouse is clicked, reverse the 3D border
 *  and draw a dark-gray version of the image.
 *  The action is not triggered until mouseUp.
 */
public boolean mouseDown(Event event, int x, int y) {
  mouseIsDown = true;
  Graphics g = getGraphics();
  int border = getBorder();
  if (hasExplicitSize())
    g.drawImage(grayImage, border, border,
                getWidth()-2*border,
                getHeight()-2*border,
                this);
  else
    g.drawImage(grayImage, border, border, this);
  drawBorder(false);
  return(true);
}


//-----------------------------------------------------
/** If cursor is still inside, trigger the action
 *  event and redraw the image (non-gray, button
 *  "out"). Otherwise ignore this.
 */
```

Listing 13.14 `ImageButton.java` (continued)

```
public boolean mouseUp(Event event, int x, int y) {
  mouseIsDown = false;
  if (inside(x,y)) {
    paint(getGraphics());
    event.id = Event.ACTION_EVENT;
    event.arg = (Object)getImage();
    return(action(event, event.arg));
  } else
    return(false);
}

//----------------------------------------------------
/** Generated when the button is clicked and released.
 *  Override this in subclasses to give behavior to
 *  the button. Alternatively, since the default
 *  behavior is to pass the ACTION_EVENT along to the
 *  Container, you can catch events for a bunch of
 *  buttons there.
 * @see Component#action
 */

public boolean action(Event event, Object arg) {
  debug("Clicked on button for " +
        getImageString() + ".");
  return(false);
}

//----------------------------------------------------
/** If you move the mouse off the button while the
 *  mouse is down, abort and do <B>not</B> trigger
 *  the action. Ignore this if button was not
 *  already down.
 */
public boolean mouseExit(Event event, int x, int y) {
  if (mouseIsDown)
    paint(getGraphics());
  return(true);
}

//----------------------------------------------------

/** The darkness value to use for grayed images.
 * @see #setDarkness
 */
public int getDarkness() {
  return(darkness);
}
```

continued

Listing 13.14 `ImageButton.java` (continued)

```java
/** An int whose bits are combined via "and" ("&")
 *  with the alpha, red, green, and blue bits of the
 *  pixels of the image to produce the grayed-out
 *  image to use when button is depressed.
 *  Default is 0xffafafaf: af combines with r/g/b
 *  to darken image.
 */

public void setDarkness(int darkness) {
  this.darkness = darkness;
}

// Changing darker is consistent with regular buttons

private int darkness = 0xffafafaf;

//-----------------------------------------------------
/** The gray image used when button is down.
 * @see #setGrayImage
 */

public Image getGrayImage() {
  return(grayImage);
}

/** Sets gray image created automatically from regular
 *  image via an image filter to use when button is
 *  depressed. You won't normally use this directly.
 */
public void setGrayImage(Image grayImage) {
  this.grayImage = grayImage;
}

private Image grayImage = null;

//-----------------------------------------------------

private void drawBorder(boolean isUp) {
  Graphics g = getGraphics();
  g.setColor(getBorderColor());
  int left = 0;
  int top = 0;
  int width = getWidth();
```

Listing 13.14 `ImageButton.java` **(continued)**

```java
    int height = getHeight();
    int border = getBorder();
    for(int i=0; i<border; i++) {
      g.draw3DRect(left, top, width, height, isUp);
      left++;
      top++;
      width = width - 2;
      height = height - 2;
    }
  }

  //-----------------------------------------------------

  private void setBorders() {
    setBorder(defaultBorderWidth);
    setBorderColor(defaultBorderColor);
  }

  //-----------------------------------------------------
  // The first time the image is drawn, update() is
  // called, and the result does not come out correctly.
  // So this forces a brief draw on loadup, replaced
  // by real, non-gray image.

  private void createGrayImage(Graphics g) {
    ImageFilter filter = new GrayFilter(darkness);
    ImageProducer producer =
      new FilteredImageSource(getImage().getSource(),
                              filter);
    grayImage = createImage(producer);
    int border = getBorder();
    if (hasExplicitSize())
      prepareImage(grayImage, getWidth()-2*border,
                   getHeight()-2*border, this);
    else
      prepareImage(grayImage, this);
    super.paint(g);
  }

  //-----------------------------------------------------
}

//                                                    continued
//=====================================================
```

Listing 13.14 `ImageButton.java` (continued)

```java
/** Builds an image filter that can be used to gray-out
 *  the image.
 * @see ImageButton
 */

class GrayFilter extends RGBImageFilter {

  //----------------------------------------------------

  private int darkness = 0xffafafaf;

  //----------------------------------------------------

  public GrayFilter() {
    canFilterIndexColorModel = true;
  }

  public GrayFilter(int darkness) {
    this();
    this.darkness = darkness;
  }

  //----------------------------------------------------

  public int filterRGB(int x, int y, int rgb) {
    return(rgb & darkness);
  }

  //----------------------------------------------------
}

//======================================================
```

13.4 Checkboxes

This section describes checkboxes (toggle buttons) that operate independently of other checkboxes. In the next section, I'll show how to put checkboxes into a group so that they operate like radio buttons (where pressing one raises the previous selection). The most common usage is to create one with a specified label and then drop it into a window. You can watch for action events in Java 1.0, item selection events in Java 1.1, or simply wait until you need the value then look it up via getState. Creating a checkbox and placing it in a nested window would look something like the following:

```
Checkbox cb = new Checkbox("...");
somePanel.add(cb);
```

Constructors

These three constructors apply to checkboxes that operate independently of each other. The following section will introduce two more that are used with radio buttons.

public Checkbox(String checkboxLabel)
This creates a checkbox with the specified label. It is initially unchecked; see setState for changing it.

public Checkbox()
This creates an initially unchecked checkbox with no label.

public Checkbox(String checkboxLabel, boolean state) [Java 1.1]
This creates a checkbox with the specified label. It can be checked or unchecked depending on the boolean value provided. A value of true means it is checked.

Example

Listing 13.15 creates twelve checkboxes, placing them in a two-column layout with the even-numbered ones initially checked. Figure 13–10 shows the result on Windows 95. For examples in MacOS and Unix/X, see Section 13.5, "Checkbox Groups (Radio Buttons)."

Listing 13.15   Checkboxes.java

```java
import java.awt.*;

public class Checkboxes extends QuittableFrame {
  public static void main(String[] args) {
    new Checkboxes();
  }

  public Checkboxes() {
    super("Checkboxes");
    setFont(new Font("Helvetica", Font.BOLD, 18));
    setLayout(new GridLayout(0, 2));
    Checkbox box;
    for(int i=0; i<12; i++) {
      box = new Checkbox("Checkbox " + i);
      if (i%2 == 0)
        box.setState(true);
      add(box);
    }
    pack();
    show();
  }
}
```

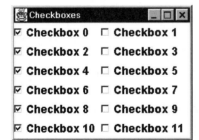

Figure 13-10 Checkboxes in Java.

Other Checkbox Methods

public boolean getState()

This determines if the checkbox is checked (`true`) or unchecked (`false`).

public void setState(boolean checkedState)

This method sets the checkbox to be checked (`true`) or unchecked (`false`).

public String getLabel()

This retrieves the current label.

public void setLabel(String newLabel)

The setLabel method changes the label. As with buttons, if the checkbox is already displayed, doing this does not automatically resize it in its Container. So the containing window should be invalidated and validated to force a new layout, as illustrated here:

```
someCheckbox.setLabel("A New Label");
someCheckbox.getParent().invalidate();
someCheckbox.getParent().validate();
```

public void addItemListener(ItemListener listener) [Java 1.1]
public void removeItemListener(ItemListener listener) [Java 1.1]

These methods associate or unassociate ItemListeners with the checkbox. They are discussed further in the following subsection.

public void processItemEvent(ItemEvent event) [Java 1.1]

This is a lower-level event-processing method. If you use this, enable events first and call super.processItemEvent from within the method. See the following subsection for details.

public Object[ ] getSelectedObjects() [Java 1.1]

This method returns an array containing a single item: either the checkbox label (if the checkbox is checked) or null (if unchecked).

Like the other GUI controls, Checkbox inherits all of the Component methods listed in Section 11.2. However, the foreground color (setForeground) is implemented inconsistently on Windows 95 and MacOS. For instance, JDK 1.02, Netscape 2.02, and Internet Explorer 3.01 support background but not foreground colors for checkboxes on Windows 95. JDK 1.1, Netscape 3.01, and Netscape 4.01 support both foreground and background colors on Windows. Netscape 3 supports background but not foreground colors on MacOS.

Core Warning

Many Windows and Mac implementations ignore foreground colors for checkboxes.

Handling Events

Checkbox Events in Java 1.0

In Java 1.02, checkboxes generate action events when selected or deselected. You can process these events in the checkbox or in the enclosing window, just as with buttons. You can check the status of a checkbox by looking at the result of the `getState` method. Alternatively, the second argument to `action` is a `Boolean` (not `boolean`) representing the current state, but using it adds little if any benefit over simply checking the state with `get-State`. For instance, to process events in the `Container`, you might do something like the following:

```
public boolean action(Event event, Object object) {
   if (event.target == checkbox1) {
     if (checkbox1.getState()) {
       doActionForCheckedBox();
       return(true);
     } else {
       doActionForUncheckedBox();
       return(true);
     }
   } ...
}
```

It is also common to ignore the action event when it occurs, and simply look up the status of the `Checkbox` (using `getState`) when it is needed. Other times, however, you want to take action immediately. For instance, a GUI might present some image-editing options, and the checkbox might allow the user to specify whether or not the image is in color. In such a case, you might want to enable the color palette when the checkbox is selected and disable the palette when the checkbox is deselected.

Checkbox Events in Java 1.1

In JDK 1.1, checkboxes do not generate action events. They generate item-selection events instead. To handle events in the checkbox itself, you first enable events:

```
enableEvents(AWTEvent.ITEM_EVENT_MASK);
```

Next, you override `processItemEvent`, which takes an `ItemEvent` as an argument. You should call `super.processItemEvent` in the body of `processItemEvent` in case any `ItemListeners` have been attached.

The `ItemEvent` class has two useful methods above and beyond those in the `AWTEvent` class: `getItemSelectable` and `getStateChange`. The first of these returns the checkbox as an `ItemSelectable` (an interface `Checkbox` implements), while the second returns either `Item-Event.SELECTED` or `ItemEvent.DESELECTED`.

To process events in another object, attach an `ItemListener` to the checkbox via `addItemListener`. An `ItemListener` *must* implement the `itemStateChanged` method, which takes an `ItemEvent` as an argument.

13.5 Checkbox Groups (Radio Buttons)

If you combine checkboxes into a `CheckboxGroup`, you get versions with a different graphical look where only one can be selected at any one time. Selecting a new entry results in the previously selected entry becoming unselected. Just as with radio button input forms in HTML (see Section 17.3, "FORM Input Elements"), there is no requirement that all the checkboxes in a given group be placed near each other. However, this is almost always what you want. This is typically accomplished by grouping them in a `Panel` or choosing an appropriate layout manager. The most common usage is to first create the `CheckboxGroup` object, then to create the checkboxes that belong to the group. These checkboxes will also contain an argument specifying if they are initially checked. This is summarized as follows:

```
CheckboxGroup cbGroup = new CheckboxGroup();
Checkbox cb1 = new Checkbox("...", cbGroup, true);
add(cb1);
Checkbox cb2 = new Checkbox("...", cbGroup, false);
add(cb2);
...
```

Constructors

CheckboxGroup

public CheckboxGroup()

This creates a non-graphical object used as a "tag" to group checkboxes together into a set of radio buttons. Checkboxes that are associated with a tag will look and act like radio buttons rather than like normal checkboxes. Only one checkbox associated with a particular tag can be selected at any given time.

Checkbox

public Checkbox(String label, CheckboxGroup group, boolean state)

This creates a radio button associated with the specified group, with the given label and initial state. If you specify an initial state of `true` for more than one `Checkbox` in a group, the last one will be shown selected.

public Checkbox(String label, boolean state, CheckboxGroup group) [Java 1.1]

This JDK 1.1 constructor has the same effect as the above, but takes the final two arguments in the opposite order.

Example

Listing 13.16 presents an applet that illustrates the difference between normal checkboxes and those made into radio buttons via a `CheckboxGroup`. The left column shows radio buttons; the right shows regular checkboxes. Figures 13–11, 13–12, and 13–13 show the results on Windows 95, MacOS, and Solaris, respectively.

Listing 13.16 CheckboxGroups.java

```
import java.applet.Applet;
import java.awt.*;

public class CheckboxGroups extends Applet {
  public void init() {
    setLayout(new GridLayout(4, 2));
    setBackground(Color.lightGray);
    setFont(new Font("TimesRoman", Font.BOLD, 16));
    add(new Label("Flavor", Label.CENTER));
    add(new Label("Toppings", Label.CENTER));
    CheckboxGroup flavorGroup = new CheckboxGroup();
    add(new Checkbox("Vanilla", flavorGroup, true));
    add(new Checkbox("Colored Sprinkles"));
    add(new Checkbox("Chocolate", flavorGroup, false));
    add(new Checkbox("Cashews"));
    add(new Checkbox("Strawberry", flavorGroup, false));
    add(new Checkbox("Kiwi"));
  }
}
```

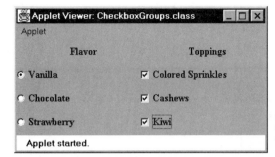

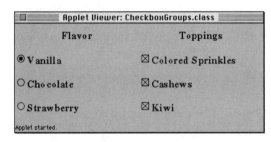

Figure 13-11 Radio buttons (left) vs. regular checkboxes (right) in Windows 95.

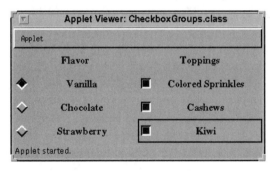

Figure 13-12 Radio buttons vs. regular checkboxes in MacOS.

Figure 13-13 Radio buttons vs. regular checkboxes in Solaris.

Other CheckboxGroup and Checkbox Methods

CheckboxGroup

public Checkbox getCurrent()
public Checkbox getSelectedCheckbox() [Java 1.1]

These methods return the radio button (Checkbox) that is currently selected. They return null if none is checked.

public void setCurrent(Checkbox boxToSelect)
public void setSelectedCheckbox(Checkbox boxToSelect)
  [Java 1.1]
This sets the radio button that is currently selected. If you specify a
radio button that is not part of the current group, the method call is
ignored. Supplying null as an argument results in all radio buttons in
the group becoming unselected.

Checkbox

In addition to the general methods described in Section 13.4 (Checkboxes),
Checkbox has the following two methods specific to CheckboxGroups.

public CheckboxGroup getCheckboxGroup()
This determines the group that the radio button is associated with.

public void setCheckboxGroup(CheckboxGroup newGroup)
This registers the checkbox with a new group.

Handling CheckboxGroup Events

Putting checkboxes into a CheckboxGroup does not change the basic way
in which events are handled, so you should refer to Section 13.4 (Checkboxes) for details. However, there is one small variation. As with ungrouped
checkboxes, it is common to ignore the events when they occur, and simply
look up the state when it is needed. Rather than cycling through the various
checkboxes in a group and checking getState on each, it is easier to call
the getCurrent (getSelectedCheckbox in Java 1.1) method of the
associated CheckboxGroup, which returns a reference to the currently
selected Checkbox.

13.6 Choice Menus (Combo Boxes)

Choice entries produce pull-down menus with a single selection showing,
but where the other options get displayed when the user clicks with the
mouse. These are sometimes known as "combo boxes," "drop-down list
boxes," or "option menus," depending on the operating/windowing system
you are using. Unlike buttons and checkboxes, the entire Choice is not cre-

ated using the constructor. Instead, there is a two-step process. The first step builds an empty menu, and the second adds elements to it using `addItem` (Java 1.0) or `add` (Java 1.1). Creating a `Choice` menu and adding it to a panel is illustrated as follows:

```
Choice choice = new Choice();
choice.addItem("...");
choice.addItem("...");
...
somePanel.add(choice);
```

Constructor

public Choice()

This creates an empty combo box. Menu entries are not added in the constructor, but in a separate step via `addItem` (Java 1.0) or `add` (Java 1.1).

Example

Listing 13.17 creates a simple `Choice` with three entries. Figures 13–14 through 13–17 show the results in appletviewer on various operating systems.

Listing 13.17 `ChoiceTest.java`

```java
import java.applet.Applet;
import java.awt.*;

public class ChoiceTest extends Applet {
  private Choice choice;

  public void init() {
    setFont(new Font("Helvetica", Font.BOLD, 36));
    choice = new Choice();
    choice.addItem("Choice 1");
    choice.addItem("Choice 2");
    choice.addItem("Choice 3");
    add(choice);
  }
}
```

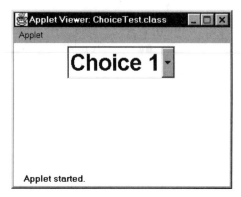

Figure 13–14 A Choice menu (unselected) on Windows 95.

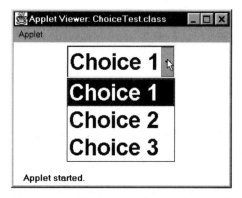

Figure 13–15 A Choice menu (selected) on Windows 95.

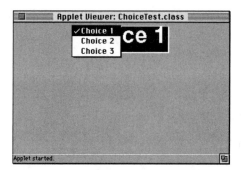

Figure 13–16 A Choice menu (selected) on MacOS.

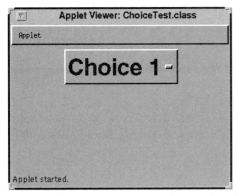

Figure 13–17 A Choice menu (unselected) on Solaris.

Other Choice Methods

public void addItem(String menuItem)
public void add(String menuItem) [Java 1.1]
A Choice menu is built in two steps. First, an empty menu is created using the empty constructor. Second, entries are added to the menu via addItem (or by add in Java 1.1). By default, the first item added is the one initially displayed, but you can override this by using select. In JDK 1.02 there is no mechanism for removing entries once they are added, but in JDK 1.1 you can use remove or removeAll.

public void addItemListener(ItemListener listener) [Java 1.1]
public void removeItemListener(ItemListener listener) [Java 1.1]
These methods let you attach/detach an ItemListener to process selection events.

public int countItems()
public int getItemCount() [Java 1.1]
These methods return the number of entries in the Choice.

public String getItem(int itemIndex)
This returns the label of the item at the specified index.

public int getSelectedIndex()
This returns the index of the item that is currently selected. –1 is returned if the Choice has no entries.

public String getSelectedItem()

This returns the label of the currently-selected item.

public Object[ ] getSelectedObjects() [Java 1.1]

This Java 1.1 method returns an array containing either the selected entry or `null` if no entry is selected.

public void insert(String menuItem, int itemIndex) [Java 1.1]

The insert method adds an entry to the specified location in the list. This is in contrast to `add` or `addItem`, which add to the end of the list only.

public void processItemEvent(ItemEvent event) [Java 1.1]

You can override this lower-level event-processing method if you want to have the `Choice` handle its own events.

public void remove(String menuItem) [Java 1.1]
public void remove(int itemIndex) [Java 1.1]
public void removeAll() [Java 1.1]

These methods remove entries from the combo box. Surprisingly, there is no way to do this in version 1.0 of Java.

public void select(int itemIndex)

This selects the item at the specified index. Recall that Java uses zero-based indexing.

public void select(String itemLabel)

Select the first item with the specified label. No action is taken if no such label exists.

As usual, recall that the color, font, size, visibility, etc., methods of `Component` (Section 11.2) are inherited. Also as usual, note that the use of color varies greatly across implementations. For instance, on Windows 95/NT, neither Netscape 2, Internet Explorer 3, nor Sun JDK 1.02 support colors for `Choice` menus. Netscape 3 on Windows supports colors for the initial display, but uses the default colors for the popup menu when the `Choice` is selected. Netscape 4 and Sun JDK 1.1 fully support `Choice` colors on Windows. Netscape 3 on MacOS supports neither colors nor custom fonts for `Choice` menus. On Solaris, neither Netscape 2 nor 3 supports `Choice` colors. Sun/Solaris JDK 1.02 supports background colors only; JDK 1.1 fully supports `Choice` colors.

Handling Choice Events

Events are handled in a manner very similar to checkboxes. In Java 1.02, you override the `action` method in the `Choice` or in an enclosing window. In release 1.1 of Java, you override `processItemEvent` or use `addItem-Listener` to attach an external listener. The main difference is that with checkboxes you have only two possible values (selected or deselected). With choice menus, you can have an arbitrary number of options. So after determining that the checkbox was acted upon, you have to next decide which entry was chosen. Listing 13.18 gives an expanded version of the `ChoiceTest` class shown earlier. Here, the Java 1.0 event-processing model is used to print out which entry was selected. Note that the second argument to the `action` method is the label of the `Choice`; you can use that instead of `getSelectedItem` if you want. Also, as with checkboxes, it is quite common to ignore the selection event when it occurs and simply determine which item is selected via `getSelectedItem` or `getSelectedIndex` when it is needed.

Listing 13.18 `ChoiceTest.java`

```java
import java.applet.Applet;
import java.awt.*;

public class ChoiceTest extends Applet {
  private Choice choice;

  public void init() {
    setFont(new Font("Helvetica", Font.BOLD, 36));
    choice = new Choice();
    choice.addItem("Choice 1");
    choice.addItem("Choice 2");
    choice.addItem("Choice 3");
    add(choice);
  }

  public boolean action(Event event, Object object) {
    if (event.target == choice) {
      String selection = choice.getSelectedItem();
      if (selection.equals("Choice 1"))
        doChoice1Action();
      else if (selection.equals("Choice 2"))
        doChoice2Action();                          continued
```

continued

Listing 13.18 `ChoiceTest.java` (continued)

```
            else if (selection.equals("Choice 3"))
              doChoice3Action();
          return(true);
       } else
          return(false);
    }

  private void doChoice1Action() {
    System.out.println("Choice 1 Action");
  }

  private void doChoice2Action() {
    System.out.println("Choice 2 Action");
  }

  private void doChoice3Action() {
    System.out.println("Choice 3 Action");
  }
}
```

13.7 List Boxes

These present scrolling lists (list boxes) where the user can select an item
(single-selectable lists) or several items (multi-selectable lists). Like `Choice`
menus, you first create an empty one, then add items to it via `addItem` (Java
1.0) or `add` (Java 1.1), as below:

```
        List list = new List();
        list.addItem("...");
        list.addItem("...");
        ...
        add(list);
```

Constructors

public List(int rows, boolean multiSelectable)
This creates a listbox with the specified number of visible rows. The
number of rows specified affects the height of the `List` box, not the
maximum number of possible entries. If more are added, a scrollbar is

automatically created. The second argument determines if the List is multiselectable. As with Choice menus, an empty List is created, then items are added to it with addItem or add. The preferred width is set to a platform-dependent value, and is typically *not* directly related to the width of the widest entry. Of course, you can always resize it explicitly if your layout manager permits it.

public List()
This creates a single-selectable list box with a platform-dependent number of rows and a platform-dependent width.

public List(int rows) [Java 1.1]
This creates a single-selectable list box with the specified number of rows and a platform-dependent width.

Example

Listing 13.19 creates two lists. The first allows a single selection only, while the second permits multiple selections. Figures 13–18, 13–19, and 13–20 show the results on Windows 95, MacOS, and Solaris.

Listing 13.19 Lists.java

```java
import java.awt.*;

public class Lists extends QuittableFrame {
  public static void main(String[] args) {
    new Lists();
  }

  public Lists() {
    super("Lists");
    setLayout(new FlowLayout());
    setBackground(Color.lightGray);
    setFont(new Font("Helvetica", Font.BOLD, 18));
    List list1 = new List(3, false);
    list1.addItem("Vanilla");
    list1.addItem("Chocolate");
    list1.addItem("Strawberry");
    add(list1);
    List list2 = new List(3, true);
```

continued

Listing 13.19 `Lists.java` (continued)

```
        list2.addItem("Colored Sprinkles");
        list2.addItem("Cashews");
        list2.addItem("Kiwi");
        add(list2);
        pack();
        show();
    }
}
```

Figure 13–18 List boxes can allow single or multiple selections. This shows both kinds on Windows 95.

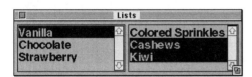

Figure 13–19 Single- and multiple-selection lists on MacOS.

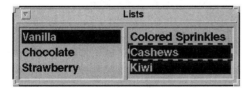

Figure 13–20 Single- and multiple-selection lists on Solaris.

Other List Methods

public void addItem(String itemLabel)
public void add(String itemLabel) [Java 1.1]
This adds an item with the specified label to the end of the list box.

public void addItem(String itemLabel, int itemIndex)
public void add(String itemLabel, int itemIndex) [Java 1.1]

This adds an item with the specified label at the specified position in the list box. All items at that index or later get moved down.

public void addActionListener(ActionListener listener)
public void addItemListener(ItemListener listener)
public void removeActionListener(ActionListener listener)
public void removeItemListener(ItemListener listener)

These Java 1.1 methods let you attach/detach an `ActionListener` or an `ItemListener`. Item events are generated whenever you select or deselect an entry. Action events occur only when you double click an entry or hit RETURN while an entry is selected. They apply only to single-selectable list boxes.

public boolean allowsMultipleSelections()
public boolean isMultipleMode()[Java 1.1]

This determines if the list is multiple selectable (`true`) or single selectable (`false`).

public synchronized void clear()
public void removeAll() [Java 1.1]

These methods remove all items from the list.

public int countItems()
public int getItemCount() [Java 1.1]

These return the number of items in the list.

public void delItem(int itemIndex)
public void remove(String menuItem) [Java 1.1]
public void remove(int itemIndex) [Java 1.1]

These methods remove entries from the list.

public void delItems(int startIndex, int endIndex)

This removes all the items from the starting index through and including the ending index. It is deprecated in Java 1.1; use multiple calls to `remove` instead.

public void deselect(int itemIndex)

If the item at the specified index is selected, this deselects it. Otherwise it does nothing.

public String getItem(int itemIndex)
This returns the label at the specified location.

public String[] getItems() [Java 1.1]
This returns an array of the labels, in order.

public int getRows()
This returns the number of rows (visible height) of the list box, which does not change during the life of the list box. This is in contrast to countItems (or getItemCount), which returns the number of items in the list, which can change over time and be less than or greater than the number of rows. A vertical scrollbar is automatically added if the number of items is greater than the number of rows.

public int getSelectedIndex()
For a single-selectable list, this returns the index of the selected item. It returns –1 if nothing is selected or if the list permits multiple selections.

public int[] getSelectedIndexes()
This returns an array of the indices of all selected items. It works for single- or multi-selectable lists. If no items are selected, a zero-length (but non-null) array is returned.

public String getSelectedItem()
For a single-selectable list, this returns the label of the selected item. It returns null if nothing is selected or if the list permits multiple selections.

public String[ ] getSelectedItems()
This returns an array of all selected items. It works for single- or multi-selectable lists. If no items are selected, a zero-length (but non-null) array is returned.

public Object[ ] getSelectedObjects() [Java 1.1]
This Java 1.1 method returns an array of the selected labels. It returns null if nothing is selected.

public int getVisibleIndex()
This returns the index of the most recent item made visible via make-Visible. Zero is returned if makeVisible has never been called.

public boolean isSelected(int itemIndex)
public boolean isIndexSelected(int itemIndex) [Java 1.1]

This determines if the item at the specified index is currently selected.

public void makeVisible(int itemIndex)

If necessary, this scrolls the list to make the item at the given index visible. It is not reliable in all implementations. In particular, this method is erratic in Java 1.0 Windows 95/NT versions.

public void processItemEvent(ItemEvent event) [Java 1.1]
public void processActionEvent(ActionEvent event) [Java 1.1]

You can override these lower-level event-processing methods if you want to have the List handle its own events. Item events are generated every time an entry is selected or deselected. Action events are generated when you double click on an entry in a single-selectable list box, or hit ENTER while an entry is selected.

public void replaceItem(String newItemLabel, int itemIndex)

This overwrites the item at the specified index.

public void select(int itemIndex)

This selects the item at the current index. If the list does not permit multiple selections, then the previously selected item, if any, is also deselected. Note that unlike a Choice, a List does not have a select method that lets you supply the label to be selected; you must supply the index.

public void setMultipleSelections(boolean multipleSelectable)
public void setMultipleMode(boolean multipleSelectable)
    [Java 1.1]

This permits (true) or prohibits (false) the list from allowing multiple selections.

As a subclass of Component (Section 11.2), List has access to all Component methods. Unlike most of the GUI controls discussed so far, color support for lists is consistent across platforms. Foreground and background colors are supported in Netscape (2, 3, and 4, where released), Internet Explorer (version 3), and Sun's JDK (1.0 and 1.1) on Windows 95/NT, MacOS, and Unix/X11.

Handling List Events

Lists are interesting in that they generate two main kinds of events. Item selection events are generated whenever an item is selected or deselected by the user. Calling `select` from the program does not generate selection events. Action events apply only to single-selectable list boxes, and are generated when the user *double* clicks on an entry or hits RETURN while an entry is selected. In Java 1.0, these are the only two types of events. In Java 1.1, however, the `List` also gets all mouse, keyboard, or focus events that occur over it.

List Events in Java 1.0

You can monitor item selection events by watching for `Event.LIST_SELECT` and `Event.LIST_DESELECT`. Unfortunately, there is no event-handling helper method for these events, so you have to override `handleEvent`. Action events, on the other hand, can be monitored in `action`, just as with buttons and combo boxes (`Choice` menus). On the other hand, if you are looking for both types of events, you might want to watch for `Event.ACTION_EVENT` in `handleEvent` seeing as you have to put code there anyhow. Listing 13.20 shows an example that monitors both types of events, placing the results in textfields (Section 13.8). Figure 13–21 shows the result after activating "Pascal" by clicking twice on it, then selecting but not activating "Java" by clicking once on it.

Listing 13.20 `ListEvents1.java`

```
import java.awt.*;

/** A class to demonstrate list selection/deselection
 *  and action events in Java 1.0.
 */

public class ListEvents1 extends QuittableFrame {
  public static void main(String[] args) {
    new ListEvents1();
  }

  private List languageList;
  private TextField selectionField, actionField;
  private String selection = "[NONE]", action;
```

Listing 13.20 ListEvents1.java (continued)

```java
/** Build a Frame with list of language choices
 *  and two textfields to show the last selected
 *  and last activated items from this list.
 */
public ListEvents1() {
  super("List Events in Java 1.0");
  setFont(new Font("TimesRoman", Font.BOLD, 16));
  add("West", makeLanguagePanel());
  add("Center", makeReportPanel());
  pack();
  show();
}

/** Watches for Event.LIST_SELECT and
 *  Event.LIST_DESELECT events in textfield.
 */
public boolean handleEvent(Event event) {
  if (event.target == languageList) {
    if (event.id == Event.LIST_SELECT) {
      selection = languageList.getSelectedItem();
      selectionField.setText(selection);
      System.out.println("Selected " + selection);
      return(true);
    } else if (event.id == Event.LIST_DESELECT) {
      selectionField.setText("");
      System.out.println("Deselected " + selection);
      return(true);
    }
  }
  return(super.handleEvent(event));
}

/** Reports when list item is activated. Item
 *  is either (String)object or the list's
 *  getSelectedItem.
 */
public boolean action(Event event, Object object) {
  if (event.target == languageList) {
    action = languageList.getSelectedItem();
    actionField.setText(action);
    System.out.println("Activated " + action);
    return(true);
  } else
    return(false);
}
```

continued

Listing 13.20 `ListEvents1.java` (continued)

```
// Create Panel containing List with language choices.
// Constructor puts this at left side of Frame.

private Panel makeLanguagePanel() {
  Panel languagePanel = new Panel();
  languagePanel.setLayout(new BorderLayout());
  languagePanel.add("North",
                    new Label("Choose Language"));
  languageList = new List(3, false);
  String[] languages =
    { "Ada", "C", "C++", "Common Lisp", "Eiffel",
      "Forth", "Fortran", "Java", "Pascal",
      "Perl", "Scheme", "Smalltalk" };
  for(int i=0; i<languages.length; i++)
    languageList.addItem(languages[i]);
  showJava();
  languagePanel.add("Center", languageList);
  return(languagePanel);
}

// Create Panel with two labels and two textfields.
// The first will show the last selection in List; the
// second the last item activated. The constructor puts
// this Panel at the right of Frame.

private Panel makeReportPanel() {
  Panel reportPanel = new Panel();
  reportPanel.setLayout(new GridLayout(4, 1));
  reportPanel.add(new Label("Last Selection:"));
  selectionField = new TextField();
  reportPanel.add(selectionField);
  reportPanel.add(new Label("Last Action:"));
  actionField = new TextField();
  reportPanel.add(actionField);
  return(reportPanel);
}

// Select and show "Java".

private void showJava() {
  languageList.select(7);
  languageList.makeVisible(7);
}
}
```

Figure 13–21 Result after double-clicking "Pascal" then single-clicking "Java."

List Events in Java 1.1

In Java 1.1, you have two choices. If you want the List to handle its own events, you can enable AWTEvent.ITEM_EVENT_MASK and AWTEvent. ACTION_EVENT_MASK, then override processItemEvent and pro-cessActionEvent to handle item selection and action events. In general, however, it is more flexible to pass the events to an external object to process. You do this by registering an ItemListener via addItemLis-tener and an ActionListener via addActionListener. Listing 13.21 shows an example of the second approach, using the helper classes of Listings 13.22 (an ItemListener) and 13.23 (an ActionListener). Figure 13–22 shows the result, which, except for the frame title, looks and acts just like the Java 1.0 version.

Listing 13.21 ListEvents2.java

```
import java.awt.*;
import java.awt.event.*;

/** A class to demonstrate list selection/deselection
 *  and action events in Java 1.1.
 */

public class ListEvents2 extends CloseableFrame {
  public static void main(String[] args) {
    new ListEvents2();
  }

  protected List languageList;
  private TextField selectionField, actionField;
  private String selection = "[NONE]", action;
```

continued

Listing 13.21 `ListEvents2.java` (continued)

```java
/** Build a Frame with list of language choices
 *   and two textfields to show the last selected
 *   and last activated items from this list.
 */
public ListEvents2() {
  super("List Events in Java 1.1");
  setFont(new Font("Serif", Font.BOLD, 16));
  add("West", makeLanguagePanel());
  add("Center", makeReportPanel());
  pack();
  setVisible(true);
}

// Create Panel containing List with language choices.
// Constructor puts this at left side of Frame.

private Panel makeLanguagePanel() {
  Panel languagePanel = new Panel();
  languagePanel.setLayout(new BorderLayout());
  languagePanel.add("North",
                    new Label("Choose Language"));
  languageList = new List(3);
  String[] languages =
    { "Ada", "C", "C++", "Common Lisp", "Eiffel",
      "Forth", "Fortran", "Java", "Pascal",
      "Perl", "Scheme", "Smalltalk" };
  for(int i=0; i<languages.length; i++)
    languageList.add(languages[i]);
  showJava();
  languagePanel.add("Center", languageList);
  return(languagePanel);
}

// Create Panel with two labels and two textfields.
// The first will show the last selection in List; the
// second the last item activated. The constructor puts
// this Panel at the right of Frame.

private Panel makeReportPanel() {
  Panel reportPanel = new Panel();
  reportPanel.setLayout(new GridLayout(4, 1));
  reportPanel.add(new Label("Last Selection:"));
  selectionField = new TextField();
```

Listing 13.21 `ListEvents2.java` (continued)

```java
    SelectionReporter selectionReporter =
      new SelectionReporter(selectionField);
    languageList.addItemListener(selectionReporter);
    reportPanel.add(selectionField);
    reportPanel.add(new Label("Last Action:"));
    actionField = new TextField();
    ActionReporter actionReporter =
      new ActionReporter(actionField);
    languageList.addActionListener(actionReporter);
    reportPanel.add(actionField);
    return(reportPanel);
  }

  /** Select and show "Java". */

  protected void showJava() {
    languageList.select(7);
    languageList.makeVisible(7);
  }
}
```

Listing 13.22 `SelectionReporter.java`

```java
import java.awt.*;
import java.awt.event.*;

/** Whenever an item is selected, it is displayed
 *  in the textfield that was supplied to the
 *  SelectionReporter constructor
 */

public class SelectionReporter implements ItemListener {
  private TextField selectionField;

  public SelectionReporter(TextField selectionField) {
    this.selectionField = selectionField;
  }

  public void itemStateChanged(ItemEvent event) {
    if (event.getStateChange() == event.SELECTED) {
      List source = (List)event.getSource();
      selectionField.setText(source.getSelectedItem());
    } else
      selectionField.setText("");
  }
}
```

Listing 13.23 `ActionReporter.java`

```java
import java.awt.*;
import java.awt.event.*;

/** Whenever an item is activated, it is displayed
 *  in the textfield that was supplied to the
 *  ActionReporter constructor
 */

public class ActionReporter implements ActionListener {
  private TextField actionField;

  public ActionReporter(TextField actionField) {
    this.actionField = actionField;
  }

  public void actionPerformed(ActionEvent event) {
    List source = (List)event.getSource();
    actionField.setText(source.getSelectedItem());
  }
}
```

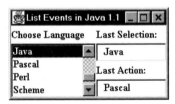

Figure 13–22 Result after double-clicking "Pascal" then single-clicking "Java."

In Java 1.0, item selection and action events are the only types of events a `List` is supposed to generate. In Java 1.1, however, they generate mouse, keyboard, and focus events as well. To demonstrate this, Listing 13.24 shows a variation of the previous example where typing any of the letters in "Java" (upper or lowercase) results in the "Java" entry being selected and made visible. Note the use of an inner class to accomplish this. Instead of creating a separate `KeyAdapter` class, a nested version is made. Besides being more convenient in such a short class, it lets the `showJava` method of `ListEvents2` remain protected.

Listing 13.24 `ListEvents3.java`

```java
import java.awt.event.*;

public class ListEvents3 extends ListEvents2 {
  public static void main(String[] args) {
    new ListEvents3();
  }

  /** Extends ListEvents2 with the twist that
   *  typing any of the letters of "JAVA" or "java"
   *  over the language list will result in "Java"
   *  being selected
   */
  public ListEvents3() {
    super();
    // Create a KeyAdapter and attach it to languageList.
    // Since this is an inner class, it has access
    // to nonpublic data (such as the ListEvent2's
    // protected showJava method).
    KeyAdapter javaChooser =
      new KeyAdapter() {
        public void keyPressed(KeyEvent event) {
          int key = event.getKeyChar();
          if ("JAVAjava".indexOf(key) != -1)
            showJava();
        }
      };
    languageList.addKeyListener(javaChooser);
  }
}
```

13.8   TextFields

Textfields create boxed areas to display and/or read a single line of text. See `TextArea` (Section 13.9) for a component that can display multiple lines. Java textfields do not permit mixed fonts or colors within a single textfield. If a textfield is being used for input, you typically allocate it (perhaps with a default entry and/or size) by specifying everything in the constructor, as follows:

```java
TextField lastNameField = new TextField(15);
add(lastNameField);
TextField langField = new TextField("Java");
add(langField);
```

Textfields used only for display are similar, but require a call to `setEditable` to turn off input capability. Also, the value is often filled in via a separate step, since it might not be available when the textfield is first created. Here's the idea:

```
TextField temperatureField = new TextField(4);
temperatureField.setEditable(false);
statusPanel.add(temperatureField);
...
temperatureString = simulationTemperature("F");
temperatureField.setText(temperatureString);
```

Constructors

public TextField()
This creates an empty textfield with a platform-dependent width (often one character).

public TextField(int numChars)
This creates an empty textfield that is the specified number of characters wide. Note that if a proportional-spaced font is being used, the definition of "the space required for *N* characters" is ambiguous. So the *average* character width is used.

public TextField(String initialString)
This creates a textfield filled with an initial string. It will be just wide enough to hold the string.

public TextField(String initialString, int numChars)
This creates a textfield of the specified width, filled with an initial string. As before, the width is based on the *average* width of characters in the font the textfield is using.

Example

Listing 13.25 creates a TextField with each of the four constructors. The result is shown in Figure 13–23.

Listing 13.25 `TextFields.java`

```java
import java.applet.Applet;
import java.awt.*;

/** A TextField from each of the four constructors */

public class TextFields extends Applet {
  public void init() {
    add(new TextField());
    add(new TextField(30));
    add(new TextField("Initial String"));
    add(new TextField("Initial", 30));
  }
}
```

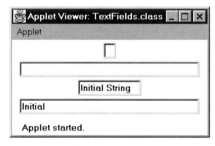

Figure 13–23 A `TextField` from each of the four constructors.

Other TextField Methods

A `TextField` is a subclass of `TextComponent`. The following two subsections list the methods of `TextComponent` and of `TextField`. Some of the most commonly used methods are `getText` and `setText` (for retrieving and specifying `TextField` contents), `setEditable` (for allowing or disallowing user input), `getColumns` and `setColumns` (for looking up and setting the `TextField` width) and `setEchoChar` (for specifying that "*" or some other character be displayed when text is entered, as for password fields).

TextComponent Methods

public void addTextListener(TextListener listener) [Java 1.1]
public void removeTextListener(TextListener listener) [Java 1.1]
These Java 1.1 methods let you add or remove a TextListener for
processing text events. Recall that Component (Section 11.2) already
supplies addKeyListener and removeKeyListener methods,
but text events occur whenever the text value changes, even if the
change is programmatic (i.e. via setText). A TextListener needs
to implement a single method: textValueChanged. This method
takes a TextEvent as an argument. To get the component's string
from this event, use getSource to find the source object, cast the
result to a TextComponent, and do getText on that.

public int getCaretPosition() [Java 1.1]
This lets you look up the position of the text insertion caret.

public String getSelectedText()
This returns the selected text. If no text is currently selected, a zero-
length (but non-null) string is returned.

public int getSelectionEnd()
This returns the index of the first character *after* the end of the selected
text. Zero is returned if no text is selected.

public int getSelectionStart()
This returns the index of the first character of any selected text. Zero is
returned if no text is selected.

public String getText()
This returns the text in the textfield, if any. If there is no text, a zero-
length (but non-null) string is returned.

public boolean isEditable()
This determines if the textfield allows user input (true) or if it is just
for display (false).

public void processTextEvent(TextEvent event) [Java 1.1]

This lower-level event-processing method can be overridden to handle text events. See `addTextListener` for more details. You can also handle individual keyboard events, since `processKeyEvent` is inherited from the `Component` class (Section 11.2). Don't forget to enable text events, call `super.processTextEvent` from within the method, and import `java.awt.event.*`.

public void select(int startIndex, int endIndex)

This selects the text starting at `startIndex`, up through but *not* including `endIndex`. Selected text is highlighted on most operating systems. If the ending index is longer than the length of the text, the entire text is selected.

public void selectAll()

This selects all the text.

public void setCaretPosition(int index) [Java 1.1]

This sets the position of the text insertion caret.

public void setEditable(boolean editableStatus)

This permits (`true`) or prohibits (`false`) the user from typing into the textfield.

public void setSelectionEnd(int startIndex) [Java 1.1]

This sets the index of the first character *after* the end of the selected text.

public void setSelectionStart(int endIndex) [Java 1.1]

This sets the index of the first character of selected text.

public void setText(String newText)

This method replaces any text with the supplied string. An input value of `null` is the same as `" "`.

TextField Methods

In addition to the TextComponent methods, the following methods are available:

public void addActionListener(ActionListener listener) [Java 1.1]
public void removeActionListener(ActionListener listener) [Java 1.1]

Action events are generated when the user hits RETURN while the textfield has the focus. These methods let you attach or remove an ActionListener to process them. In many cases, addTextListener and removeTextListener (inherited from TextComponent) or addKeyListener and removeKeyListener (inherited from Component) are of more interest.

public boolean echoCharIsSet()

This determines if an echo character been specified. See setEchoCharacter.

public int getColumns()

This method tells you the number of columns in the textfield. If you are using a proportional font, this is no guarantee that this number of characters will really fit in the textfield, however, because the value is based on the *average* width of characters in the current font.

public char getEchoChar()

This returns the current echo character. This value is only meaningful if echoCharIsSet is true.

public void processActionEvent(ActionEvent event) [Java 1.1]

Action events are generated when the user hits RETURN while the textfield has the focus. If you want the textfield to process its own events, you first enable AWTEvent.ACTION_EVENT_MASK, then override this method. Be sure to call super.processActionEvent in case any listeners are attached.

public void setColumns(int cols) [Java 1.1]

In Java 1.0, you cannot change the width of a textfield after it is created, aside from resizing it with resize or reshape, which is based on pixels, not characters. Java 1.1 lets you specify the width directly.

Note that the width is in terms of the *average* width of characters in the textfield's font.

public void setEchoCharacter(char echoChar)
public void setEchoChar(char echoChar) [Java 1.1]
This specifies a character to display for each character the user types in. The actual text entered is still available from `getText`. The "`*`" character is often used for implementing fields to gather passwords or other sensitive data.

Because `TextField` is a subclass of `Component` (Section 11.2), it has access to all `Component` methods. Color support for textfields is relatively consistent across platforms. The only major platform not supporting colors is Netscape for MacOS, which supports neither foreground nor background colors.

Handling TextField Events

In Java 1.0, there are three event types of interest: focus events, keyboard events, and action events. Focus events happen when the textfield acquires or loses the input focus, keyboard events when the user hits a key while the textfield has the focus, and action events when the user hits RETURN while it has the focus. These events are of interest in Java 1.1 as well, plus a basic text event is generated whenever the textfield contents change due to user input *or* from a call to `setText`.

TextField Events in Java 1.0

In Java 1.0, you can monitor focus events with `gotFocus` and `lostFocus`; keyboard events with `keyDown` and `keyUp`, and action events with `action`. You can catch the events in the textfield itself or centralize the processing in an enclosing window. In many cases, you don't bother to catch these events at all, but simply look up the textfield contents via `getText` when some other event occurs (e.g., when the user clicks a button). In fact, if the textfield is being used only for display and input has been disabled via `setEditable(false)`, *no* events are available.

For example, Listing 13.26 implements a spelling-corrected `TextField` that lets the user enter the name of a good programming language. The `keyUp` method is used to read the text entered so far. If the text does not match an entry in the program's database, the text is replaced by a legal sub-

string of the same length. The gotFocus method is used to flash a sublimi-
nal hint to the user, before returning the text to the previous value. Finally, if
the user hits RETURN, the text is filled in with the full name of the appropriate programming language most closely matching the text entered so far. The
action method is used for this task. Figure 13–24 shows one possible result.

Listing 13.26 JavaTextField.java

```java
import java.applet.Applet;
import java.awt.*;

/** Lets the user enter the name of <B>any</B>
 *  good programming language. Or does it?
 */

public class JavaTextField extends Applet {
  private TextField langField;
  private String[] substrings =
    { "", "J", "Ja", "Jav", "Java" };

  public void init() {
    setFont(new Font("TimesRoman", Font.BOLD, 14));
    setLayout(new GridLayout(2, 1));
    add(new Label("Enter a Good Programming Language",
                  Label.CENTER));
    langField = new TextField();
    Font langFont = new Font("Helvetica", Font.BOLD, 18);
    langField.setFont(langFont);
    add(langField);
  }

  /** Monitor/correct spelling as user types */

  public boolean keyUp(Event event, int key) {
    if (event.target == langField) {
      setLanguage();
      return(true);
    } else
      return(false);
  }
```

Listing 13.26 `JavaTextField.java` (continued)

```java
// "Correct" the user's spelling if they've
// made a typo.


private void setLanguage() {
  int length = langField.getText().length();
  if (length <= 4)
    langField.setText(substrings[length]);
  else
    langField.setText("Java");
}

/** When they hit RETURN, fill in the right answer. */

public boolean action(Event event, Object object) {
  if (event.target == langField) {
    langField.setText("Java");
    return(true);
  } else
    return(false);
}

/** Subliminal advertising! Give the user a hint. */

public boolean gotFocus(Event event, Object ignore) {
  if (event.target == langField) {
    String text = langField.getText();
    for(int i=0; i<5; i++) {
      langField.setText("Hint: Java");
      langField.setText(text);
    }
    return(true);
  } else
    return(false);
}
}
```

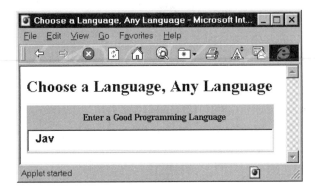

Figure 13–24 Textfield after "C++" entered (an obvious typo). The name will be completed when the user hits RETURN.

TextField Events in Java 1.1

In Java 1.1, there are four event types of interest: focus events, keyboard events, text events, and action events. The difference between keyboard events and text events are that text events are generated even when someone calls `setText` programmatically; keyboard events don't. As usual, you have the choice of handling events in the component itself using the lower-level `processXxxEvent` methods, or of attaching an external listener to process them. Listing 13.27 creates a Java 1.1 applet with the identical look and behavior to the `JavaTextField` just shown. It uses a `LanguageField` (Listing 13.28), which overrides `processKeyEvent`, `processAction-Event`, and `processFocusEvent` to implement the spelling-correction and hints. Note that the `processXxxEvent` of the super class is called in case a class using the `LanguageField` also attaches a listener to it.

Listing 13.27 `JavaTextField2.java`

```java
import java.applet.Applet;
import java.awt.*;

/** Lets the user enter the name of <B>any</B>
 *  good programming language. Or does it?
 */

public class JavaTextField2 extends Applet {
  public void init() {
    setFont(new Font("Serif", Font.BOLD, 14));
    setLayout(new GridLayout(2, 1));
    add(new Label("Enter a Good Programming Language",
                  Label.CENTER));
    LanguageField langField = new LanguageField();
    Font langFont = new Font("SansSerif", Font.BOLD, 18);
    langField.setFont(langFont);
    add(langField);
  }
}
```

Listing 13.28 `LanguageField.java`

```java
import java.awt.*;
import java.awt.event.*;

/** A spelling-correcting TextField for entering
 *  a language name.
 */

public class LanguageField extends TextField {
  private String[] substrings =
    { "", "J", "Ja", "Jav", "Java" };

  public LanguageField() {
    super();
    enableEvents(AWTEvent.KEY_EVENT_MASK |
                 AWTEvent.ACTION_EVENT_MASK |
                 AWTEvent.FOCUS_EVENT_MASK);

  }
```

continued

Listing 13.28 LanguageField.java (continued)

```java
/** Monitor/correct spelling as user types */

public void processKeyEvent(KeyEvent event) {
  if (event.getID() == event.KEY_RELEASED)
    setLanguage();
  super.processKeyEvent(event);
}

// "Correct" the user's spelling if they've
// made a typo.

private void setLanguage() {
  int length = getText().length();
  if (length <= 4)
    setText(substrings[length]);
  else
    setText("Java");
}

/** When they hit RETURN, fill in the right answer. */

public void processActionEvent(ActionEvent event) {
  setText("Java");
  super.processActionEvent(event);
}

/** Subliminal advertising! Give the user a hint. */

public void processFocusEvent(FocusEvent event) {
  if (event.getID() == event.FOCUS_GAINED) {
    String text = getText();
    for(int i=0; i<5; i++) {
      setText("Hint: Java");
      setText(text);
    }
  }
  super.processFocusEvent(event);
}
}
```

13.9 TextAreas

A TextArea is similar to a TextField, except that it can have multiple lines and action events are not generated. Here are some typical examples:

```
TextArea inputArea = new TextArea(4, 15);
add(inputArea);
TextArea resultsArea =
  new TextArea("No Results Yet", 2, 10);
resultsArea.setEditable(false);
add(resultsArea);
```

Constructors

public TextArea()
This creates an empty text area with a platform-dependent number of rows and columns and both vertical and horizontal scrollbars. The default size may be very large, so use this constructor with caution if you're not using a layout manager that will size it for you.

public TextArea(int rows, int cols)
This creates an empty text area with the specified number of rows and columns. The column value is set based on the average width of characters in whatever font the TextArea is using. Vertical and horizontal scrollbars are included.

public TextArea(String initialString)
This creates an initialized text area with a platform-dependent size and both types of scrollbars. The initial string can contain explicit line breaks (\n) to force it to span multiple lines.

public TextArea(String initialString, int rows, int cols)
This creates an initialized text area with the specified size and both types of scrollbars.

public TextArea(String initialString, int rows, int cols, int scrollbarType) [Java 1.1]
This creates an initialized text area with the specified size. If the scrollbar type is TextArea.SCROLLBARS_BOTH, the result is the same as with the previous constructor. If TextArea.SCROLLBARS_VERTICAL_ONLY is specified, the text

area will have vertical but not horizontal scrollbars, and words will wrap to the next line if the user enters text that would otherwise extend past the right side of the text area. If `TextArea.SCROLLBARS_HORIZONTAL_ONLY` is supplied, the text area will have horizontal but not vertical scrollbars. Finally, if you specify `TextArea.SCROLLBARS_NEITHER`, no scrollbars will be included. Again, text will wrap as it is entered. Java 1.0 text areas always have both scrollbars and never automatically wraps words.

Example

Listing 13.29 creates two text areas; an empty one and another filled with three initial lines. Figures 13–25, 13–26, and 13–27 show the results on Windows 95, MacOS, and Solaris.

Listing 13.29 `TextAreas.java`

```
import java.applet.Applet;
import java.awt.*;

public class TextAreas extends Applet {
  public void init() {
    setBackground(Color.lightGray);
    add(new TextArea(3, 10));
    add(new TextArea("Some\nInitial\nText", 3, 10));
  }
}
```

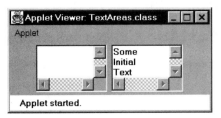

Figure 13–25 Text areas in Windows 95.

Figure 13–26 Text areas in MacOS.

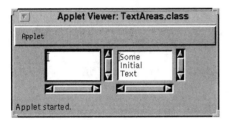

Figure 13–27 Text areas in Solaris.

Other TextArea Methods

TextArea inherits getText, setText, setEditable, select, and all of the other methods of TextComponent described in Section 13.8 (Text-Fields). In addition, they support the following methods.

public void appendText(String additionalText)
public void append(String additionalText) [Java 1.1]

This adds the specified text to the end of the text area.

public int getColumns()

This returns the number of columns in the text area.

public int getRows()

This returns the number of rows used to create the text area.

public void insertText(String additionalText, int index)
public void insert(String additionalText, int index) [Java 1.1]

These methods insert the specified text at the given index. Any text at that location or later is moved down.

**public void replaceText(String replacement, int startIndex,
int endIndex)**
**public void replaceRange(String replacement, int startIndex,
int endIndex) [Java 1.1]**

This replaces the text starting at `startIndex`, up through but *not* including `endIndex`, with the specified string. The replacement string need not be the same length as the text being replaced.

As a subclass of `Component` (Section 11.2), `TextArea` has access to all `Component` methods. Color support for text areas is quite consistent across platforms. Foreground and background colors are supported in Netscape (2, 3, and 4, where released), Internet Explorer (version 3), and Sun's JDK (1.0 and 1.1) on Windows 95/NT, MacOS, and Unix/X11.

Handling Events

Text areas do not generate action events. Keyboard, text (Java 1.1 only), and focus events are handled in exactly the same manner as with textfields.

13.10 Labels

Labels are simple textual displays, without any associated actions, at least in Java 1.0. It is often more convenient to use them than to draw text with the `drawString` method of `Graphics` because labels get redisplayed automatically and can be moved around by layout managers. You can just create one with designated text and drop it in a window, as follows:

```
Label label = new Label("...");
add(label);
```

Frequently, however, I want the Label to describe some other object, and want to be sure the label is aligned with it. So I may use the label with a layout manager other than `FlowLayout`. Changing the label font and/or alignment is common as well. For instance, the following might be used to make a title on a panel:

```
Panel resultsPanel = new Panel();
resultsPanel.setLayout(new BorderLayout());
Label title = new Label("Results", Label.CENTER);
title.setFont(new Font("Helvetica", Font.BOLD, 18));
resultsPanel.add("North", title);
TextArea resultsArea = new TextArea();
resultsPanel.add("Center", resultsArea);
```

Constructors

public Label(String labelString)

This creates a label displaying the specified string.

public Label(String labelString, int alignment)

This creates a label with the specified alignment. The alignment is one of Label.LEFT (default), Label.RIGHT, and Label.CENTER. The alignment is not particularly important if the label is used in a window that is using FlowLayout or in the East or West regions of a BorderLayout. That is because the preferred width of a Label is only a little bit bigger than the text it contains, and there's not much aligning left to be done. However, alignment is quite important if you resize a Label by hand or use one in a GridLayout, GridBagLayout, or the North or South regions of a BorderLayout. In such a case, the width of the Label might be much larger than the text it contains, and Java needs to know where to place the text in that area.

public Label()

This creates a blank label. You can specify the text later via setText.

Example

Listing 13.30 creates four labels with various fonts and alignment options. Figure 13–28 shows the result.

Listing 13.30 `Labels.java`

```java
import java.applet.Applet;
import java.awt.*;

public class Labels extends Applet {
  public void init() {
    setLayout(new GridLayout(4,1));
    Label label1, label2, label3, label4;
    label1 = new Label("Label 1");
    label2 = new Label("Label 2", Label.LEFT);
    label3 = new Label("Label 3", Label.RIGHT);
    label4 = new Label("Label 4", Label.CENTER);
    Font bigFont = new Font("Helvetica",
                              Font.BOLD, 25);
    label2.setFont(bigFont);
    label3.setFont(bigFont);
    label4.setFont(bigFont);
    add(label1);
    add(label2);
    add(label3);
    add(label4);
  }
}
```

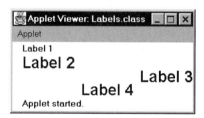

Figure 13-28 Labels can have different fonts and can be left-aligned, right-aligned, or centered.

Other Label Methods

public int getAlignment()
This returns the current alignment, which will be one of Label.LEFT, Label.RIGHT, or Label.CENTER.

public String getText()
This returns the text of the label. If none has been set, a zero-length (but non-null) string is returned.

public void setAlignment(int alignment)
This sets the alignment.

public void setText(String newLabel)
This method changes the label's text. If the label is already displayed, doing this does not automatically resize it in its Container. So the containing window should be invalidated and validated to force a new layout, as follows.

```
someLabel.setText("A Different Label");
someLabel.getParent().invalidate();
someLabel.getParent().validate();
```

As a Component subclass, Label inherits all the color, font, and resizing methods of Component (Section 11.2). However, as with several other GUI controls, support for colors is spotty on Windows 95/NT implementations. In particular, neither Netscape 2, Internet Explorer 3, nor Sun JDK 1.02 support background or foreground colors for labels on Windows. Label colors are supported in Netscape 3, Netscape 4 (i.e. Netscape Communicator), and JDK 1.1 on Windows, as well as in virtually all MacOS and Unix implementations.

Handling Events

In Java 1.0, no events are generated for labels; mouse and keyboard events are suppressed. In Java 1.1, the normal mouse and keyboard events are generated, but there are no selection or action events. Listing 13.31 shows a frame that inserts two "reversible" labels (Listing 13.32); labels with attached mouse listeners that switch the foreground and background colors when the mouse enters the label, switching back when the mouse leaves. Figures 13–29, 13–30, and 13–31 show the original result, the result after moving the mouse over the first ReversibleLabel, and the result after moving the mouse over the second ReversibleLabel, respectively.

Listing 13.31 ReverseLabels.java

```java
import java.awt.*;

// Java 1.1 Only

public class ReverseLabels extends CloseableFrame {
  public static void main(String[] args) {
    new ReverseLabels();
  }

  public ReverseLabels() {
    super("Reversible Labels");
    setLayout(new FlowLayout());
    setBackground(Color.lightGray);
    setFont(new Font("Serif", Font.BOLD, 18));
    ReversibleLabel label1 =
      new ReversibleLabel("Black on White",
                          Color.white, Color.black);
    add(label1);
    ReversibleLabel label2 =
      new ReversibleLabel("White on Black",
                          Color.black, Color.white);
    add(label2);
    pack();
    setVisible(true);
  }
}
```

Listing 13.32 ReversibleLabel.java

```java
import java.awt.*;
import java.awt.event.*;

/** A Label that reverses its background and
 *  foreground colors when the mouse is over it.
 *  Java 1.1 Only
 */
public class ReversibleLabel extends Label {
  public ReversibleLabel(String text,
                         Color bgColor, Color fgColor) {
    super(text);
    MouseAdapter reverser =
      new MouseAdapter() {
        public void mouseEntered(MouseEvent event) {
          reverseColors();
        }

        public void mouseExited(MouseEvent event) {
          reverseColors(); // or mouseEntered(event);
        }
      };
    addMouseListener(reverser);
    setText(text);
    setBackground(bgColor);
    setForeground(fgColor);
  }

  protected void reverseColors() {
    Color fg = getForeground();
    Color bg = getBackground();
    setForeground(bg);
    setBackground(fg);
  }
}
```

Figure 13–29 ReverseLabels: original appearance.

Figure 13–30 ReverseLabels: after moving mouse over left label.

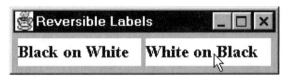

Figure 13–31 ReverseLabels: after moving mouse over right label.

13.11 Scrollbars and Sliders

The AWT uses the same basic component for scrollbars (used to scroll windows) and sliders (used to interactively select values), the Scrollbar class. This is a bit inconvenient when using them for sliders, so in Section 13.12 we will develop a Slider class that combines a Scrollbar with a Text-Field to show the current value. The "preferred" size and shape of a Scrollbar is not generally usable, so they are not usually placed in a window that uses FlowLayout. Instead, they are typically placed in the east or south sections of a BorderLayout, used in a GridLayout, or resized by hand.

Unfortunately, there are a number of bugs in the way scrollbars are implemented in the most widely used Java systems, so creating reliable scrollbars for multiplatform applications requires significantly more effort than necessary. The situation is so bad, in fact, that you really cannot count on scrollbars working in a cross-platform environment unless you thoroughly test on all the platforms your application is likely to run on. Fortunately, if you are using scrollbars for scrolling (rather than for selecting values), many applications can be replaced by ScrollPane in Java 1.1, which works reliably. For simple scrolling text, TextArea is an even easier alternative, and is available in both Java 1.0 and Java 1.1.

Core Warning

In current implementations, scrollbars are the least reliable interface element. If you use them, test thoroughly on all platforms on which you will be delivering.

Constructors

public Scrollbar()
This creates a vertical scrollbar. The "bubble" (or "thumb," the part that actually moves) size defaults to 10% of the trough length. The internal min and max values (see below) are set to zero.

public Scrollbar(int orientation)
This creates a horizontal or vertical scrollbar. The orientation can be either Scrollbar.HORIZONTAL or Scrollbar.VERTICAL. The "bubble" ("thumb") size defaults to 10% of the trough length. The internal min and max values (see below) are set to zero.

public Scrollbar(int orientation, int initialValue,
int bubbleSize, int min, int max)
This constructor is the one you use when you want to make a "slider" for interactively selecting values (see Section 13.12 for a slider implementation). It creates a horizontal or vertical slider or scrollbar with a customized bubble (or "thumb," -- i.e., the part that actually moves) thickness and a specific internal range of values. The bubble thickness is in terms of the scrollbar's range of values, not in pixels, so that if max minus min was 5, a bubble size of 1 would specify 20% of the trough length. Note, however, that some operating systems (MacOS, in particular) do not support varying sizes to scrollbar thumbs, nor does Netscape Navigator 2 or 3 on Windows 95 or Windows NT. Also, the value corresponds to the location of the *left* (horizontal sliders) or *top* (vertical sliders) edge of the bubble, not its center. Unfortunately, Java 1.1 implementations tend to interpret the maximum value differently than in Java 1.0. For a horizontal scrollbar, rather than having the maximum correspond to the highest value the left side of the slider can reach, it is the highest value

the right side of the slider can reach. Similarly for vertical scrollbars. This means that in current 1.1 implementations the actual values that can be set range from the minimum value to the bubble size *less* than the maximum value. For example, in Java 1.0, the following would make a scrollbar that can range from 0 to 50, with the initial value at 25 and a bubble size of 5:

```
new Scrollbar(Scrollbar.HORIZONTAL, 25, 5, 0, 50);
```

In Java 1.1, however, the same code makes a scrollbar that can range only from 0 to 45. It is not clear from the 1.1 specification if this is the new intended behavior (a strange design, if so) or if it is simply an implementation bug (strange that it has persisted to JDK 1.1.3, then). But in any case, this happens in Sun's JDK 1.1.1 through 1.1.3 on Unix and Windows platforms. This is illustrated in Figures 13–32 and 13–33, which show the exact same code (Listing 13.33) run in JDK 1.02 and JDK 1.1.3 on Windows 95.

Core Warning

In Java 1.1, to get a scrollbar with a thumb size of t that can range in value from min to max, you have to create it with a maximum value of max+t.

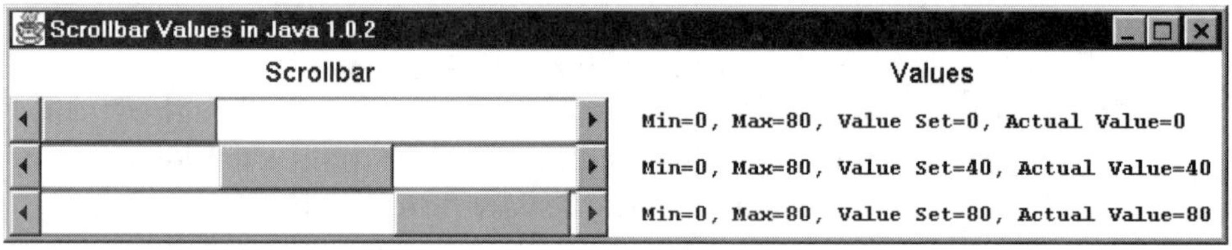

Figure 13–32 In Java 1.02, scrollbar max values are interpreted the way most people would expect.

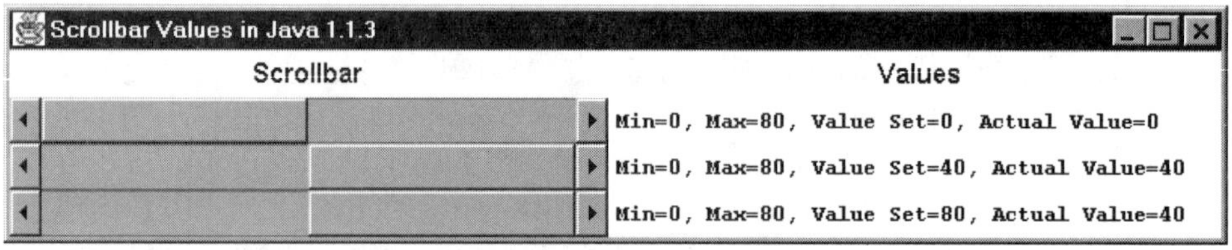

Figure 13–33 In Java 1.1, scrollbar max values are interpreted strangely.

Listing 13.33 `ScrollbarValues.java`

```java
import java.awt.*;

public class ScrollbarValues extends QuittableFrame {
  public static void main(String[] args) {
    new ScrollbarValues(0, 80, 40);
  }

  private Font headingFont =
    new Font("Helvetica", Font.BOLD, 16);
  private Font bodyFont =
    new Font("Courier", Font.BOLD, 14);

  public ScrollbarValues(int min, int max, int bubble) {
    super("Scrollbar Values in Java " +
          System.getProperty("java.version"));
    setLayout(new GridLayout(4, 2, 5, 0));
    add(makeHeadingLabel("Scrollbar"));
    add(makeHeadingLabel("Values"));
    Scrollbar bar;
    for(int i=0; i<3; i++) {
      bar = new Scrollbar(Scrollbar.HORIZONTAL,
                          bubble*i, bubble, min, max);
      add(bar);
      add(makeScrollbarLabel(bar, bubble*i));
    }
    pack();
    show();
  }

  private Label makeHeadingLabel(String heading) {
    Label headingLabel =
      new Label(heading, Label.CENTER);
    headingLabel.setFont(headingFont);
    return(headingLabel);
  }

  private Label makeScrollbarLabel(Scrollbar bar,
                                   int valueSet) {
    Label scrollbarLabel =
      new Label("Min=" + bar.getMinimum() +
                ", Max=" + bar.getMaximum() +
                ", Value Set=" + valueSet +
                ", Actual Value=" + bar.getValue() +
                " ");
    scrollbarLabel.setFont(bodyFont);
    return(scrollbarLabel);
  }
}
```

Note the small amount of empty space to the right of the bottom scrollbar in Figure 13–32. This, unfortunately, is common in Windows 95/NT implementations of Java 1.0. It appears in Internet Explorer 3, Netscape Communicator, and Sun's JDK. Interestingly, neither Netscape 2 nor 3 suffer from the problem, however. The percent of the total scrollbar length wasted this way tends to be proportional to the range of scrollbar values, with a shorter range having more serious problems. Listing 13.34 creates a scrollbar with range from only 1 to 4, at its maximum value of 4. Figure 13–34 shows the result in JDK 1.02 on Windows 95.

Listing 13.34 WastedSpace.java

```java
import java.applet.Applet;
import java.awt.*;

public class WastedSpace extends Applet {
  public void init() {
    setLayout(new BorderLayout());
    Label label =
      new Label("Scrollbar is at its maximum value",
                Label.CENTER);
    add("North", label);
    Scrollbar bar =
      new Scrollbar(Scrollbar.HORIZONTAL, 4, 1, 1, 4);
    add("Center", bar);
  }
}
```

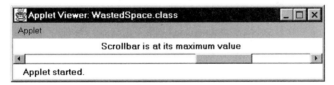

Figure 13–34 Java 1.0 scrollbar with a range of only three values has a lot of dead space at the right.

Core Warning

If you create a scrollbar with a small range in Internet Explorer, Netscape Communicator, or JDK 1.02 on Windows 95/NT, you will have a large amount of wasted space at the right or bottom.

Example

Listing 13.35 creates a variety of horizontal and vertical sliders (scrollbars for selecting values). The values range from 0 to 100 with an initial value of 50 and various different bubble thicknesses. Figures 13–35, 13–36, and 13–37 show the results in Java 1.0 on Windows 95, MacOS, and Solaris. Figure 13–38 shows the result on Solaris in Java 1.1.

Listing 13.35 `Scrollbars.java`

```
import java.applet.Applet;
import java.awt.*;

public class Scrollbars extends Applet {
  public void init() {
    int i;
    setLayout(new GridLayout(1, 2));
    Panel left = new Panel(), right = new Panel();
    left.setLayout(new GridLayout(10, 1));
    for(i=5; i<55; i=i+5)
      left.add(new Scrollbar(Scrollbar.HORIZONTAL,
                             50, i, 0, 100));
    right.setLayout(new GridLayout(1, 10));
    for(i=5; i<55; i=i+5)
      right.add(new Scrollbar(Scrollbar.VERTICAL,
                              50, i, 0, 100));
    add(left);
    add(right);
  }
}
```

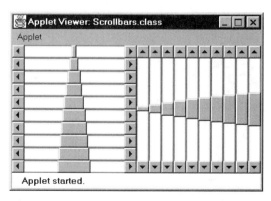

Figure 13–35 Scrollbars with varying bubble sizes but constant ranges and initial values, shown in Java 1.0 on Windows 95.

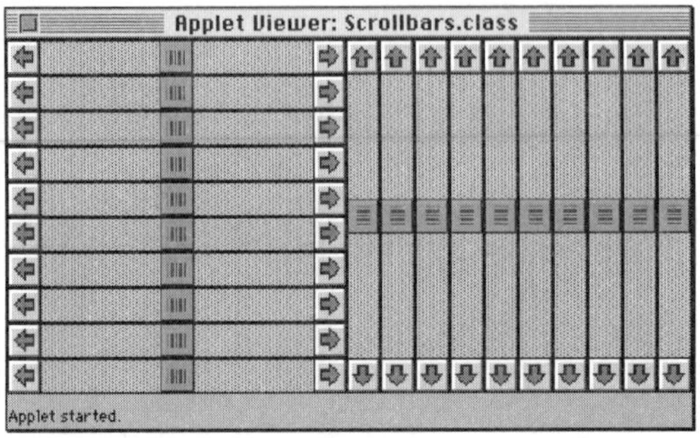

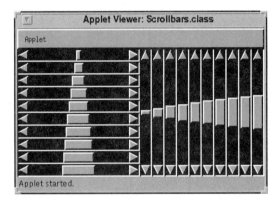

Figure 13–36 Scrollbars in MacOS always have the same bubble size.

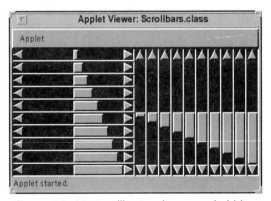

Figure 13–37 Scrollbars with varying bubble sizes but constant ranges and initial values, shown in Java 1.0 on Solaris.

Figure 13–38 Scrollbars with varying bubble sizes but constant ranges and initial values, shown in Java 1.1 on Solaris.

Other Scrollbar Methods

public void addAdjustmentListener
(AdjustmentListener listener) [Java 1.1]
public void removeAdjustmentListener
(AdjustmentListener listener) [Java 1.1]

These Java 1.1 methods add/remove an AdjustmentListener to the scrollbar, used to monitor when the user adjusts the scrollbar. An AdjustmentListener needs to implement adjustmentValueChanged, which takes an AdjustmentEvent as an argument. The AdjustmentEvent class contains a getAdjustmentType method that returns one of AdjustmentEvent.UNIT_INCREMENT (the right or down arrow was clicked), Adjustment-Event.UNIT_DECREMENT (the left or up arrow was clicked), AdjustmentEvent.BLOCK_INCREMENT (the trough to the right of or below the bubble was clicked), Adjustment-Event.BLOCK_DECREMENT (the trough to the left of or above the bubble was clicked), or AdjustmentEvent.TRACK (the bubble was dragged).

public int getLineIncrement()
public int getUnitIncrement() [Java 1.1]

These methods are intended to return the amount that the value will be adjusted when the arrows at either end of the scrollbar are pressed. It is usually 1 if the you haven't specified anything different with setLine-Increment (Java 1.0) or setUnitIncrement (Java 1.1). Unfortunately, however, many implementations ignore this. For instance, the line increment value has no effect on Solaris in JDK 1.02 or 1.1, or on Windows 95/NT in JDK 1.02. For many applications it is possible to fix this yourself, however. See Listing 13.36 for an example.

public int getMaximum()

This returns the scrollbar's maximum possible value. Recall that this is the largest value that can be selected in Java 1.0, but in most Java 1.1 implementations it is getVisibleAmount *more* than the largest possible selectable value.

public int getMinimum()

This returns the scrollbar's minimum possible value.

public int getOrientation()

This returns either `Scrollbar.HORIZONTAL` or `Scrollbar.VERTICAL`.

public int getPageIncrement()
public int getBlockIncrement() [Java 1.1]

This supposedly tells you how much the value will change when the user clicks inside the trough above or below the scrollbar bubble. The default is platform dependent; common defaults are 10 (Win95) or the bubble size (Solaris). Unfortunately, many implementations ignore this value. For instance, it has no effect in JDK 1.02 on either Solaris or Windows 95/NT. For many applications it is possible to fix this yourself, however. See Listing 13.36 for an example.

public int getValue()

This returns the current value.

public int getVisible()
public int getVisibleAmount() [Java 1.1]

This returns the size of the bubble (thumb), represented in terms of the units used for the scrollbar range, not in terms of pixels.

public void processAdjustmentEvent(AdjustmentEvent event) [Java 1.1]

In Java 1.1, if you want to have a scrollbar handle its own events, you first enable adjustment events as follows:

```
enableEvents(AWTEvent.ADJUSTMENT_EVENT_MASK);
```

Next, you override `processAdjustmentEvent`, which takes an `AdjustmentEvent` as an argument. Remember to call `super.processAdjustmentEvent` in case there are listeners on the scrollbar. See the following subsection for an example.

public void setLineIncrement(int increment)
public void setUnitIncrement(int increment) [Java 1.1]

This supposedly changes the amount the scrollbar will move when you click on the arrows, but is poorly supported. See `getLineIncrement`.

public void setPageIncrement(int increment)
public void setBlockIncrement(int increment) [Java 1.1]

This supposedly changes the amount the scrollbar will move when you click in the trough above or below the scrollbar bubble, but is poorly supported. See `getPageIncrement`.

public void setMaximum(int maxValue) [Java 1.1]

This changes the maximum possible value. Recall that in Java 1.1 implementations, the maximum selectable value is this maximum *minus* the bubble size (see `getVisible`). In Java 1.0, `setMaximum` is not available; you have to use `setValues` instead.

public void setMinimum(int minValue) [Java 1.1]

This changes the minimum possible value. In Java 1.0, you have to use `setValues` instead of this.

public void setOrientation(int orientation) [Java 1.1]

This changes orientation of the scrollbar. In Java 1.0, you have to use `setValues` instead of this.

public void setValue(int value)

This changes the stored value and moves the scrollbar appropriately. Specifying a value below the minimum value does not cause an error; the minimum value is simply stored. Specifying a value above the maximum (or above the maximum minus the thumb size in Java 1.1) does not cause an error either. Instead, the scrollbar takes on either the maximum value (Java 1.0) or the maximum minus the thumb size (Java 1.1).

public void setValues(int value, int bubbleSize, int min, int max)

This changes several parameters in one fell swoop. In Java 1.0, this is the only way to change the bubble size, the minimum value, or the maximum value.

As a subclass of `Component`, the `setForeground` and `setBackground` methods are available, but `setForeground` is not generally supported. On Windows 95/NT, `setBackground` sets the color of the scrollbar trough. On Solaris, it sets the color of the bubble and the arrows. Current MacOS implementations do not support scrollbar colors.

Handling Scrollbar Events

In Java 1.0, you process scrolling events in handleEvent. In Java 1.1, you can either use processAdjustmentEvent or attach an AdjustmentListener.

Scrollbar Events in Java 1.0

Unfortunately, in Java 1.0 the Scrollbar class does not generate events that are passed onto a "helper" method like action or mouseDown. So the events need to be trapped in handleEvent. There are 5 different types of events that can be generated: Event.SCROLL_LINE_DOWN (when the right/bottom arrow is clicked), Event.SCROLL_LINE_UP (when the left/top arrow is clicked), Event.SCROLL_PAGE_DOWN (when the right/bottom trough is clicked), Event.SCROLL_PAGE_UP (when the left/top trough is clicked), and Event.SCROLL_ABSOLUTE (when the bubble is dragged). There is rarely a reason to handle each of these events separately, especially since page and line increments are implemented inconsistently. Instead you can simply look at the current value, which can be obtained by the getValue method or from the arg instance variable of the event, which is an Integer. However, since Java 1.1 implementations and some 1.0 implementations send mouse and/or keyboard events to scrollbars, you should at least check that the event was one of the specified five before taking action. Here's the basic idea, shown assuming you are capturing events in an enclosing window.

```
public boolean handleEvent(Event event) {
  if (event.target == scrollbar &&
      isScrollEvent(event.id)) {
    doAction(scrollbar.getValue());
    return(true);
  } else
    return(super.handleEvent(event));
}

private boolean isScrollEvent(int eventID) {
  return(eventID == Event.SCROLL_LINE_UP ||
         eventID == Event.SCROLL_LINE_DOWN ||
         eventID == Event.SCROLL_PAGE_UP ||
         eventID == Event.SCROLL_PAGE_DOWN ||
         eventID == Event.SCROLL_ABSOLUTE);
}
```

Unfortunately, there is still another bug we need to be concerned about. In many Windows 95/NT implementations (including both Java 1.0 and 1.1), scrollbars will sometimes "pop" back to their original position when you release the mouse after dragging them. In many cases, this can be fixed by sleeping (`Thread.sleep`) for a short time after each `Event.SCROLL_ABSOLUTE` event. I add this ugly but necessary hack to the `Slider` class shown in the Section 13.12.

Slider Events in Java 1.1

The Java 1.1 event model simplifies things considerably. Rather than trying to sort through the various events to figure out which are the scrolling events, Java will decide for you. If you override `processAdjustment-Event`, you can let a scrollbar handle its own events. If you attach an `AdjustmentListener`, an external object can handle the events. In either case, note that the `AdjustmentEvent` class has two methods of particular import: `getValue` and `getAdjustmentType`. The first returns an int giving the scrollbar's current value, while the second returns one of `AdjustmentEvent.UNIT_INCREMENT`, `Adjustment-Event.UNIT_DECREMENT`, `AdjustmentEvent.BLOCK_INCREMENT`, `AdjustmentEvent.BLOCK_DECREMENT`, or `AdjustmentEvent.TRACK`. For instance, Listing 13.36 shows how you could use `processAdjust-mentEvent` to make a scrollbar that honors the unit increment and block increment values, regardless of whether the underlying implementation already does. Note, however, that it only works if all scrollbar adjustment is by the user. Calling `setValue` will not properly update the `lastValue` variable, but there is no way around this since you cannot tell the difference between a system-generated `setValue` call (when the scrollbar is adjusted) and a user-generated one.

Listing 13.36 `BetterScrollbar.java`

```
import java.awt.*;
import java.awt.event.*;

/** The beginnings of a better Scrollbar. This one
 *  adjusts for the fact that many implementations
 *  ignore the line and/or page increment. Created
 *  to demonstrate low-level 1.1 scrollbar events.
 */
```

continued

Listing 13.36 `BetterScrollbar.java` **(continued)**

```
public class BetterScrollbar extends Scrollbar {
  private int lastValue;

  public BetterScrollbar(int orientation,
                         int initialValue,
                         int bubbleSize,
                         int min,
                         int max) {
    super(orientation, initialValue, bubbleSize,
          min, max);
    enableEvents(AWTEvent.ADJUSTMENT_EVENT_MASK);
    lastValue = initialValue;
  }

  public void processAdjustmentEvent(AdjustmentEvent e) {
    int type = e.getAdjustmentType();
    switch(type) {
      case e.UNIT_INCREMENT:
        setValue(lastValue + getUnitIncrement());
        break;
      case e.UNIT_DECREMENT:
        setValue(lastValue - getUnitIncrement());
        break;
      case e.BLOCK_INCREMENT:
        setValue(lastValue + getBlockIncrement());
        break;
      case e.BLOCK_DECREMENT:
        setValue(lastValue - getBlockIncrement());
        break;
    }
    lastValue = getValue();
    super.processAdjustmentEvent(e);
  }
}
```

13.12 A Slider Class

Scrollbars are frequently used for creating scrolling windows or graphics. In some windowing packages, there is a separate "slider" class that is used for interactively choosing values in an integral range. In Java, `Scrollbar` doubles for both. This is inconvenient, and I find a separate slider quite useful. The class presented here places a textfield to the right of a horizontal scrollbar. When the scrollbar value is changed, it is displayed right-justified in the textfield, which is just wide enough to hold the largest value. Optionally, the text area can accept input, letting you enter an integer to be used to set the slider value. The preferred width is 250 pixels, but can be changed. The preferred height is based on the textfield height (which uses 12-point Courier by default), but top and bottom margins can be set to make it thinner than the text area. Min and max values are interpreted identically in Java 1.0 and 1.1, and the Windows 95 drag-bug is prevented by use of a small pause between absolute scroll events.

The most common usage is to simply drop one in a window, let the user manipulate it, then read the value with `getValue` whenever you need it. The `setEditable` method can be used to let the user enter values in the textfield as well as by dragging the slider. For example:

```
setLayout(new BorderLayout());
Slider simulationRunsSlider = new Slider(1, 25, 5);
simulationRunsSlider.setEditable(true);
add(simulationRunsSlider);
...
startSimulation(simulationRunsSlider.getValue());
```

The following subsections describe the `Slider` behavior; Listing 13.38 presents the source code.

Constructors

public Slider(int min, int max, int initialValue)
This creates a slider with the specified min, max, and initial values. The bubble size is set to one tenth of the slider range, top/bottom margins are set to 4, and the preferred width is set to 250.

public Slider(int min, int max, int initialValue, int bubbleSize)
This creates a slider with the specified min, max, initial value, and bubble size. The top/bottom margins are set to 4, and the preferred width is set to 250.

Example

Listing 13.37 creates several sliders with values that range from 0 to 120, cycling through three different top and bottom margin settings: the default, the default plus one, and the default plus two. Figures 13–39 and 13–40 show the results in Windows 95 and Solaris, respectively.

Listing 13.37 `Sliders.java`

```java
import java.awt.*;

public class Sliders extends QuittableFrame {
  public static void main(String[] args) {
    new Sliders();
  }

  public Sliders() {
    super("Sliders with Varying Margins");
    setLayout(new FlowLayout());
    setFont(new Font("TimesRoman", Font.BOLD, 14));
    setBackground(Color.lightGray);
    add(makeSliderPanel(10));
    add(makeSliderPanel(12));
    add(makeSliderPanel(14));
    pack();
    show();
  }

  private Panel makeSliderPanel(int fontSize) {
    Panel panel = new Panel();
    panel.setLayout(new GridLayout(0, 1));
    panel.add(new Label("Font size: " + fontSize,
                        Label.CENTER));
    Slider slider;
    for(int i=0; i<6; i++) {
      slider = new Slider(0, 50, 10*i);
      slider.setFontSize(fontSize);
      slider.setMargins(slider.getMargins() + i-2);
      panel.add(slider);
    }
    return(panel);
  }
}
```

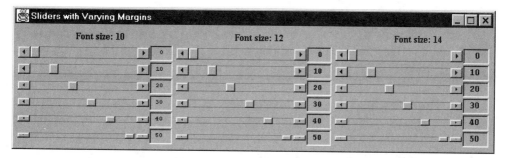

Figure 13–39 Sliders with various margins, font sizes, and initial values in Windows 95.

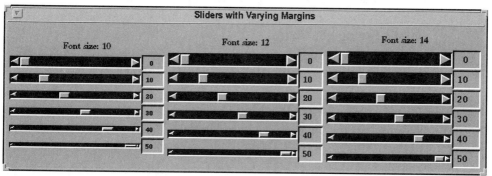

Figure 13–40 Sliders with various margins, font sizes, and initial values in Solaris.

Other Slider Methods

public void doAction()

This is a placeholder that you can override in `Slider` subclasses to put side effects that you want to take place every time the slider value changes.

public Font getFont()

This returns the font used in the textfield, 12 point bold monospaced is the default.

public int getFontSize()

This returns the size of the current textfield font.

public int getMargins()

This returns the value of the top and bottom margins. This is empty space reserved above and below the scrollbar so that it is not as tall as the textfield. The default is 4.

public int getPreferredWidth()

This returns the width part of the `preferredSize`.

public Scrollbar getScrollbar()

This returns the `Scrollbar` used in the left part of the `Slider`. All of the normal `Scrollbar` methods are available with it.

public String getText()

This calls the scrollbar's `getText` method. The string returned will represent an integer, but will be padded with blanks.

public TextField getTextField()

This returns the `TextField` used in the right part of the `Slider`. All of the normal `TextField` methods are available with it.

public int getValue()

This returns the scrollbar value.

public boolean isEditable()

This determines if you can enter an integer in the textfield to change the scrollbar value, in addition to dragging the slider. Noninteger values are ignored when entered.

public void setEditable(boolean editFlag)

This lets you specify whether or not the user can enter values into the textfield.

public void setFont(Font textFieldFont)

This lets you change the textfield font. Be careful; proportional fonts may not display numeric values as well as Courier.

public void setFontSize(int size)

This sets the textfield font to Courier, bold, and the specified size.

public void setMargins(int topAndBottomMargin)

This changes the amount of empty space at the top and bottom of the scrollbar. The default is 4.

public void setPreferredWidth(int preferredWidth)

The normal `preferredSize` of a `Scrollbar` is too small to be usable. The height part will be taken from the `TextField`. This method sets the width portion; the default is 250. Of course, as with other graphical components you can always enforce exact sizes instead of relying on the preferred size.

public void setText(String text)

This changes the value in the `TextField`. In general, you want to use `setValue` instead, since that will make sure the value is an integer in the proper range and will right-justify the string.

public void setValue(int value)

This changes the slider value. Out of bound values do not generate errors; the minimum or maximum value is set instead.

Handling Slider Events

`Scrollbar` and `TextField` events are already handled by the `Slider` class; dragging the scrollbar updates the textfield, and entering a value in the textfield (if it is editable) changes the slider value. In most cases, if you have additional actions you want to take place when the slider changes, the only thing you need to do is to override `doAction`. However, if you need to customize `handleEvent` or `action`, be sure to call `super.handleEvent` or `super.action` when done.

Source Code

Listing 13.38 presents the source code for the `Slider` class. To enforce top/bottom margins for the scrollbar part, it uses `ScrollbarPanel`, a small helping class shown in Listing 13.39.

Listing 13.38 `Slider.java`

```java
import java.awt.*;

/** A class that combines a horizontal Scrollbar and
 *  a TextField (to the right of the Scrollbar).
 *  The TextField shows the current scrollbar value,
 *  plus, if setEditable(true) is set, it can be used
 *  to change the value as well.
 *
 *  @author Marty Hall (hall@apl.jhu.edu)
 */

public class Slider extends Panel {
  private Scrollbar scrollbar;
  private TextField textfield;
  private ScrollbarPanel scrollbarPanel;
  private int preferredWidth = 250;

  //----------------------------------------------------
  /** Construct a slider with the specified min, max
   *  and initial values. The "bubble" (thumb)
   *  size is set to 1/10th the scrollbar range.
   *  In JDK 1.1.x, it tries to adjust for the max
   *  value bug by adding the bubble thickness to
   *  the max value.
   */
  public Slider(int minValue, int maxValue,
                int initialValue) {
    this(minValue, maxValue, initialValue,
         (maxValue - minValue)/10);
  }

  /** Construct a slider with the specified min, max,
   *  and initial values, plus the specified "bubble"
   *  (thumb) value. This bubbleSize should be
   *  specified in the units that min and max use,
   *  not in pixels. Thus, if min is 20 and max is
   *  320, then a bubbleSize of 30 is 10% of the
   *  visible range.
   */
  public Slider(int minValue, int maxValue,
                int initialValue, int bubbleSize) {
    setLayout(new BorderLayout());
```

Listing 13.38 Slider.java (continued)

```
      maxValue = adjustFor1_1(maxValue, bubbleSize);
      scrollbar = new Scrollbar(Scrollbar.HORIZONTAL,
                                initialValue,
                                bubbleSize,
                                minValue, maxValue);
      scrollbarPanel = new ScrollbarPanel(6);
      scrollbarPanel.add("Center", scrollbar);
      add("Center", scrollbarPanel);
      textfield = new TextField(numDigits(maxValue) + 1);
      setFontSize(12);
      textfield.setEditable(false);
      setTextFieldValue();
      add("East", textfield);
   }

   //-----------------------------------------------------
   /** A placeholder to override for action to be taken
    *  when scrollbar changes
    */
   public void doAction(int value) {
   }

   //-----------------------------------------------------
   /** When scrollbar changes, sets the textfield */

   public boolean handleEvent(Event event) {
      if (event.target == scrollbar &&
          isScrollEvent(event.id)) {
         setTextFieldValue();
         doAction(scrollbar.getValue());
         fixWindowsProblem(event.id);
         return(true);
      } else
         return(super.handleEvent(event));
   }

   //-----------------------------------------------------
   /** When textfield changes, sets the scrollbar */
```

continued

Listing 13.38 `Slider.java` (continued)

```java
public boolean action(Event event, Object object) {
  if (event.target == textfield) {
    String value = textfield.getText();
    int oldValue = getValue();
    try {
      setValue(Integer.parseInt(value.trim()));
    } catch(NumberFormatException nfe) {
      setValue(oldValue);
    }
    return(true);
  } else
    return(false);
}

//----------------------------------------------------
/** Returns the Scrollbar part of the Slider. */

public Scrollbar getScrollbar() {
  return(scrollbar);
}

/** Returns the TextField part of the Slider */

public TextField getTextField() {
  return(textfield);
}

//----------------------------------------------------
/** Changes the preferredSize to take a minimum
 *  width, since super-tiny scrollbars are
 *  hard to manipulate.
 *
 * @see #getPreferredWidth
 * @see #setPreferredWidth
 */
public Dimension preferredSize() {
  Dimension d = super.preferredSize();
  d.height = textfield.preferredSize().height;
  d.width = Math.max(d.width, preferredWidth);
  return(d);
}

/** This just calls preferredSize */

public Dimension minimumSize() {
  return(preferredSize());
}
```

Listing 13.38 `Slider.java` **(continued)**

```java
//----------------------------------------------------
/** To keep scrollbars legible, a minimum width is
 *  set. This returns the current value (default is
 *  150).
 *
 *  @see #setPreferredWidth
 */
public int getPreferredWidth() {
  return(preferredWidth);
}

/** To keep scrollbars legible, a minimum width is
 *  set. This sets the current value (default is
 *  150).
 *
 *  @see #getPreferredWidth
 */
public void setPreferredWidth(int preferredWidth) {
  this.preferredWidth = preferredWidth;
}

//----------------------------------------------------
/** This returns the current scrollbar value */

public int getValue() {
  return(scrollbar.getValue());
}

/** This assigns the scrollbar value. If it is below
 *  the minimum value or above the maximum, the value
 *  is set to the min and max value, respectively.
 */
public void setValue(int value) {
  scrollbar.setValue(value);
  setTextFieldValue();
}

//----------------------------------------------------
/** Sometimes horizontal scrollbars look odd if they
 *  are very tall. So empty top/bottom margins
 *  can be set. This returns the margin setting.
 *  The default is four.
 *
 *  @see setMargins
 */
```

continued

Listing 13.38 Slider.java (continued)

```java
public int getMargins() {
  return(scrollbarPanel.getMargins());
}

/** Sometimes horizontal scrollbars look odd if they
 *  are very tall. So empty top/bottom margins
 *  can be set. This sets the margin setting.
 *
 * @see getMargins
 */
public void setMargins(int margins) {
  scrollbarPanel.setMargins(margins);
}


//---------------------------------------------------
/** Returns the current textfield string. In most
 *  cases this is just the same as a String version
 *  of getValue, except that there may be padded
 *  blank spaces at the left.
 */
public String getText() {
  return(textfield.getText());
}

/** This sets the TextField value directly. Use with
 *  extreme caution since it does not right-align
 *  or check if value is numeric.
 */
public void setText(String text) {
  textfield.setText(text);
}


//---------------------------------------------------
/** Returns the Font being used by the textfield.
 *  Courier bold 12 is the default.
 */

public Font getFont() {
  return(textfield.getFont());
}

/** Changes the Font being used by the textfield. */
```

Listing 13.38 Slider.java (continued)

```java
public void setFont(Font textFieldFont) {
  textfield.setFont(textFieldFont);
}

//----------------------------------------------------
/** The size of the current font */

public int getFontSize() {
  return(getFont().getSize());
}

/** Rather than setting the whole font, you can
 *  just set the size (Courier bold will be used
 *  for the family/face).
 */
public void setFontSize(int size) {
  setFont(new Font("Courier", Font.BOLD, size));
}

//----------------------------------------------------
/** Determines if the textfield is editable. If it
 *  is, you can enter a number to change the
 *  scrollbar value. In such a case, entering a value
 *  outside the legal range results in the min or
 *  max legal value. A non-integer is ignored.
 *
 *  @see #setEditable
 */
public boolean isEditable() {
  return(textfield.isEditable());
}

/** Determines if you can enter values directly
 *  into the textfield to change the scrollbar.
 *
 *  @see #isEditable
 */
public void setEditable(boolean editable) {
  textfield.setEditable(editable);
}

//----------------------------------------------------
// Sets a right-aligned textfield number.
```

Listing 13.38 `Slider.java` (continued)

```java
private void setTextFieldValue() {
  int value = scrollbar.getValue();
  int digits = numDigits(scrollbar.getMaximum());
  String valueString = padString(value, digits);
  textfield.setText(valueString);
}

//-------------------------------------------------------
// Repeated String concatenation is expensive, but
// this is only used to add a small amount of
// padding, so converting to a StringBuffer would
// not pay off.

private String padString(int value, int digits) {
  String result = String.valueOf(value);
  for(int i=result.length(); i<digits; i++)
    result = " " + result;
  return(result + " ");
}

//-------------------------------------------------------
// Determines the number of digits in a decimal
// number.

private static final double LN10 = Math.log(10.0);

private static int numDigits(int num) {
  return(1 +
         (int)Math.floor(Math.log((double)num)/LN10));
}

//-------------------------------------------------------
// Since several implementations generate extraneous
// scrollbar events, you shouldn't just check
// the event target, but verify a correct
// event type also. Used by handleEvent.

private boolean isScrollEvent(int eventID) {
  return(eventID == Event.SCROLL_LINE_UP ||
         eventID == Event.SCROLL_LINE_DOWN ||
         eventID == Event.SCROLL_PAGE_UP ||
         eventID == Event.SCROLL_PAGE_DOWN ||
         eventID == Event.SCROLL_ABSOLUTE);
}

//-------------------------------------------------------
```

Listing 13.38 `Slider.java` (continued)

```
// KLUDGE ALERT!
// Many Windows 95 Java implementations (including
// most browsers and Sun's JDK through version 1.1.3)
// fail when you drag the "thumb", often bouncing back
// to their original location when the button is
// released. Enforcing short pauses between the events
// appears to solve the problem in many cases, but
// it slows things down, the exact sleep amount
// needed depends on the system speed, and there is
// absolutely no guarantee that this will always work.
// The only "real" solution is to get the vendors to
// fix the implementations.

private void fixWindowsProblem(int eventID) {
  if (eventID == Event.SCROLL_ABSOLUTE)
    pause(100);
}

private void pause(long millis) {
  try {
    Thread.sleep(millis);
  } catch(InterruptedException ie) {}
}

//-----------------------------------------------------
// KLUDGE ALERT!
// In all or most Java 1.02 implementations (JDK,
// Netscape 2, 3, 4, Internet Explorer 3.01),
// the max value is the largest possible value that
// can be set. But in JDK 1.1.1-1.1.3 on Unix and
// Windows, you can only set values as big
// as max-bubble (ie getMaximum() *minus*
// getVisible()), despite what getMaximum()
// returns. This adjusts for that, but of course
// has the problem that a 1.1 implementation that
// *was* consistent with 1.02 would no longer work.
// Trying to fix bugs on a per-implementation basis
// is a risky proposition indeed; this is not the
// high point of Java's platform independence.

private int adjustFor1_1(int max, int bubble) {
  String version = System.getProperty("java.version");
  if (version.startsWith("1.1"))
    return(max+bubble);
  else
    return(max);
}

//-----------------------------------------------------
}
```

continued

Listing 13.39 `ScrollbarPanel.java`

```java
import java.awt.*;

/** A Panel with adjustable top/bottom insets value.
 *  Used to hold a Scrollbar in the Slider class
 */

public class ScrollbarPanel extends Panel {
  private Insets insets;

  public ScrollbarPanel(int margins) {
    setLayout(new BorderLayout());
    setMargins(margins);
  }

  public Insets insets() {
    return(insets);
  }

  public int getMargins() {
    return(insets.top);
  }

  public void setMargins(int margins) {
    this.insets = new Insets(margins, 0, margins, 0);
  }
}
```

13.13 Popup Menus

Java 1.1 adds a long-awaited feature: popup menus. They are remarkably simple to use: allocate a `PopupMenu`, add some `MenuItem`'s to it, then watch for the popup trigger in a `Component` by checking mouse events with `isPopupTrigger`. When the trigger is received, `show` the menu. This will trigger an action event in the selected menu item.

Constructors

public PopupMenu()
This creates an untitled popup menu.

public PopupMenu(String title)
This creates a popup menu with the specified title. However, most current Windows 95/NT implementations do not display the title.

Example

Listing 13.40 creates a popup menu in an applet. It then watches the mouse events until one occurs that is a "popup trigger" (whatever mouse action normally displays menus in the current operating system), in which case the menu is displayed. By implementing the `ActionListener` interface and adding itself as a listener on each item in the menu, the applet's own `actionPerformed` method is called when items are selected. Figure 13–41 shows the result on Windows 95.

Listing 13.40 ColorPopupMenu.java

```
import java.applet.Applet;
import java.awt.*;
import java.awt.event.*;

/** Simple demo of popup menus in Java 1.1 */

public class ColorPopupMenu extends Applet
                      implements ActionListener {
  private String[] colorNames =
    { "White", "Light Gray", "Gray",
      "Dark Gray", "Black" };
  private Color[] colors =
    { Color.white, Color.lightGray, Color.gray,
      Color.darkGray, Color.black };
  private PopupMenu menu;

  /** Create PopupMenu and add MenuItems */

  public void init() {
    setBackground(Color.gray);
    menu = new PopupMenu("Background Color");
    enableEvents(AWTEvent.MOUSE_EVENT_MASK);
    MenuItem colorName;
    for(int i=0; i<colorNames.length; i++) {
      colorName = new MenuItem(colorNames[i]);
      menu.add(colorName);
      colorName.addActionListener(this);
      menu.addSeparator();
    }
    add(menu);
  }
```

continued

Listing 13.40 `ColorPopupMenu.java` **(continued)**

```java
/** Don't use a MouseListener, since in Win95/NT
 *  you have to check isPopupTrigger in
 *  mouseReleased, but do it in mousePressed in
 *  Solaris (boo!).
 */
public void processMouseEvent(MouseEvent event) {
  if (event.isPopupTrigger())
    menu.show(event.getComponent(),
              event.getX(), event.getY());
  super.processMouseEvent(event);
}

public void actionPerformed(ActionEvent event) {
  setBackground(colorNamed(event.getActionCommand()));
  repaint();
}

private Color colorNamed(String colorName) {
  for(int i=0; i<colorNames.length; i++)
    if(colorNames[i].equals(colorName))
      return(colors[i]);
  return(Color.white);
}
}
```

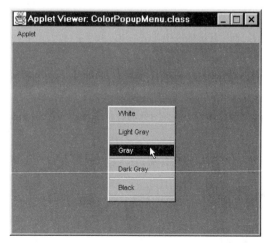

Figure 13–41 Popup menus on Windows 95 appear without titles.

Other PopupMenu Methods

The only method directly in the PopupMenu class is show, which displays the menu. Selected methods from the ancestor classes Menu and MenuItem are listed here as well.

public void add(MenuItem item)
public void add(String label)

This adds an entry to the menu. Rather than adding a string directly, it is usually better to turn it into a MenuItem first via new Menu-Item(label). This lets you add an ActionListener on the label.

public void addActionListener(ActionListener listener)

This method is normally applied to MenuItems within the popup menu, and lets you add a listener to take action when the item is selected. Note that the label is available in the ActionEvent class via getAction-Command().

public void addSeparator()

This adds a nonselectable horizontal line to the menu. In Figure 13–41, there is a separator after every entry.

public void setShortcut(MenuShortcut shortcut)
public MenuShortcut getShortcut()
public void deleteShortcut()

In Java 1.0, there was no portable way to associate keyboard shortcuts with menu items. However, most Windows 95/NT implementations let you preface labels with "&" to make the next character be a shortcut. This was not satisfactory, however, since the "&" appeared in the label on other operating systems, and you had to remember to include the ampersand when comparing to labels. Java 1.1 lets you create portable shortcuts. Simply create a MenuShortcut via

```
MenuShortcut shortcut = new MenuShortcut(int key);
```

Next, add the shortcut to a MenuItem via setShortcut. The get-Shortcut and deleteShortcut methods retrieve and delete the shortcut associated with a menu item.

public void show(Component c, int x, int y)
This displays the popup menu at the specified location relative to the top-left corner of the component.

Strictly speaking, PopupMenu is a Component. However, you should not rely on custom colors or fonts being supported.

Handling PopupMenu Events

There are two types of events you need to worry about with popup menus. The first is the mouse click that brings up the menu in the first place. The second is the event that occurs when an entry is actually selected.

Rather than having to remember what types of mouse clicks are supposed to initiate popup menus on different platforms, Java provides a convenient method in the MouseEvent class: isPopupTrigger. However, since some operating systems invoke the menu when the mouse is first pressed (e.g., Solaris) but others when it is released (e.g., Windows 95 and Windows NT), you probably want to watch mouse events in processMouseEvent rather than in a MouseListener. If you do use a MouseListener, be sure to check *both* mousePressed and mouseReleased. So the process of popping up the menu would go something like this:

```
PopupMenu menu = new PopupMenu("[Title]");
...
enableEvents(AWTEvent.MOUSE_EVENT_MASK);
...
public void processMouseEvent(MouseEvent event) {
  if (event.isPopupTrigger())
    menu.show(event.getComponent(),
              event.getX(), event.getY());
  super.processMouseEvent(event);
}
```

To process the selections, add an ActionListener to each as it is created, as follows:

```
MenuItem item = new MenuItem("[Label]");
menu.add(item);
item.addActionListener(someListener);
```

Recall that an ActionListener needs to implement the actionPerformed method, which takes an ActionEvent as an argument. The getActionCommand method of ActionEvent returns the label of the MenuItem.

13.14 Summary

The major GUI controls available in Java are Button, Checkbox (which can create regular checkboxes or radio buttons), Choice, List, Text-Field, TextArea, Label, Scrollbar (used for scrolling and for selecting values), and PopupMenu. This is in addition to the bordered and borderless windows, dialog boxes, and file dialogs covered in Chapter 11, "Windows." In addition, two new components were created: ImageButton and Slider. The first illustrated how to build new components from scratch, while the second showed how to combine existing widgets into a composite interface control. To use built-in or custom GUI components, there are two things you need to know: how to create them with the look you want, and how to process the events that occur when the user interacts with them. In most cases, the main look is specified in the interface element's constructor, but some elements (Choice, List, PopupMenu) are created empty then filled later. Action events are perhaps the most important type of event that applies to GUI elements, but item selection events, keyboard events, text events (Java 1.1 only), and scrolling events are important as well.

Now, perhaps you wondered how Java was able to monitor and generate events for you. How do they do this while your code is performing other tasks? The answer is that Java is multithreaded; different lightweight processes can handle different tasks concurrently. Multithreading makes it easy for Java to monitor GUI events, and it can simplify many of *your* tasks as well. In some cases, it can also significantly speed up your application. That's the topic of the next chapter.

CONCURRENT PROGRAMMING USING JAVA THREADS

Chapter 14

J ava has one of the most powerful and usable concurrent programming packages of any modern programming language: the `Thread` class. Threads are sometimes known as "lightweight processes": processes that share the heap but have their own stack. They provide three distinct advantages.

Efficiency

Some tasks can be performed much more quickly in a multithreaded manner. For instance, consider the task of downloading and analyzing five text files from various URLs. Suppose that it took 12 seconds to establish the network connection, and 1 second to download the file once the connection was open. Doing this serially would take 5x13=65 seconds. But if done in separate threads, the waiting could be done in parallel, and it might take about 13+5=18 seconds. In fact, the efficiency benefits of this type of approach are so great that Java *automatically* downloads images in separate threads. For more information, see Section 9.11 (Drawing Images).

Convenience

Some tasks are simpler to visualize and implement when various pieces are considered separately. For instance, in a simulation system it might be easier to give each object its own behavior and let it run in a separate thread than to try to have a centralized routine that updates all of the simulation objects.

New Capabilities

Finally, some tasks simply cannot be done without multiprocessing. For instance, an HTTP server needs to listen on a given network port for a connection. When it obtains one, it passes the connection to a different process that actually handles the request. If it didn't do this, the original port would be tied up until the request was finished, only very light loads could be supported, and it would be unusable for real-life applications. In fact, in Chapter 15, "Client-Server Programming in Java," I'll present code for a simple multithreaded HTTP server based on the socket techniques discussed in that chapter and the threading techniques explained here.

However, a word of caution is in order. Threads in Java are more convenient than threads or "heavyweight" processes in other languages (e.g., when using `fork` in C). They add significant capability in some situations. Nevertheless, it is much harder to test and debug a program where multiple things are going on at once, than a program where only one thing is happening at a time. So weigh the pros and cons of using threads carefully before using them, and be prepared for extra development and debugging time when you do, especially until you gain experience.

14.1 Starting Threads

The Java implementation provides two convenient mechanisms for thread programming: (1) making a separate subclass of the `Thread` class that contains the code that will be run, and (2) using a `Thread` instance to call back to code in an ordinary object.

Mechanism 1: Put Behavior in a Separate Thread Object

The first way to run threads in Java is to make a separate subclass of `Thread`, put the actions to be performed in the `run` method of the subclass, create an instance of it, and call that instance's `start` method. This is illustrated in Listings 14.1 and 14.2.

Listing 14.1 DriverClass.java

```java
public class DriverClass extends SomeClass {
  ...
  public void startAThread() {
    // Create a Thread object
    ThreadClass thread = new ThreadClass();
    // Start it in a separate process
    thread.start();
    ...
  }
}
```

Listing 14.2 ThreadClass.java

```java
public class ThreadClass extends Thread {
  public void run() {
    // Thread behavior here
  }
}
```

If a class extends `Thread`, it will inherit a `start` method that calls the `run` method in a separate thread of execution. The author of the class is responsible for implementing `run`, and the thread dies when `run` ends. So even though you put your code in `run`, you call `start`, not `run`. If you call `run` directly, the code will be executed in the current thread, just like a normal method. Data that is to be local to that thread is normally kept in local variables of `run` or in private instance variables of that object. Outside data is only accessible to the thread if it is passed to the thread's constructor, or if publicly available static variables or methods are used.

Core Warning

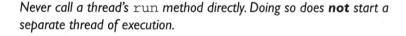

Never call a thread's `run` *method directly. Doing so does **not** start a separate thread of execution.*

For example, Listing 14.3 gives a `Counter` class that counts from 0 to *N* with random pauses in between. The driver class (Listing 14.4) can create and start multiple instances of `Counter`, resulting in interleaved execution (Listing 14.5).

Listing 14.3   `Counter.java`

```java
/** A subclass of Thread that counts up to a specified
 *  limit with random pauses in between each count.
 */

public class Counter extends Thread {
  private static int totalNum = 0;
  private int currentNum, loopLimit;

  public Counter(int loopLimit) {
    this.loopLimit = loopLimit;
    currentNum = totalNum++;
  }

  private void pause(double seconds) {
    try { Thread.sleep(Math.round(1000.0*seconds)); }
    catch(InterruptedException ie) {}
  }

  /** When run finishes, the thread exits. */

  public void run() {
    for(int i=0; i<loopLimit; i++) {
      System.out.println("Counter " + currentNum
                            + ": " + i);
      pause(Math.random()); // Sleep for up to 1 second
    }
  }
}
```

Listing 14.4   `CounterTest.java`

```java
/** Try out a few instances of the Counter class. */

public class CounterTest {
  public static void main(String[] args) {
    Counter c1 = new Counter(5);
    Counter c2 = new Counter(5);
    Counter c3 = new Counter(5);
    c1.start();
    c2.start();
    c3.start();
  }
}
```

Listing 14.5	CounterTest Output

```
Counter 0: 0
Counter 1: 0
Counter 2: 0
Counter 1: 1
Counter 2: 1
Counter 1: 2
Counter 0: 1
Counter 0: 2
Counter 1: 3
Counter 2: 2
Counter 0: 3
Counter 1: 4
Counter 0: 4
Counter 2: 3
Counter 2: 4
```

Mechanism 2: Put Behavior in the Driver Class, Which Must Implement Runnable

The second way to perform multithreaded computation is to implement the Runnable interface, construct an instance of Thread passing the current class (i.e., the Runnable) as an argument, and call that Thread's start method. You put the actions you want executed in the run method of the main class; the thread's run method is ignored. This means that run has full access to the variables and methods of the object containing it. The thread decides whether to execute its own run method based on what is passed to the constructor. If a Runnable is supplied, the thread's start method will use the Runnable's run method instead of its own. Declaring that you implement Runnable serves as a guarantee to the thread that you have a public run method. Listing 14.6 shows an outline of this approach.

Listing 14.6   `ThreadedClass.java`

```
public class ThreadedClass extends AnyClass
                              implements Runnable {
  public void run() {
    // Thread behavior here
    // If you want to access thread instance (e.g. to
    // get private per-thread data), use
    // Thread.currentThread().
  }

  public void startThread() {
    Thread t = new Thread(this);
    t.start(); // Calls back to run method in "this"
  }


    . . .
}
```

Note that there is no requirement that an object only invoke a *single* Thread that calls back to its run method. However, when starting more than one Thread that share a class, you have to worry about contention for common data. This is discussed in Section 14.2 (Race Conditions).

Listing 14.7 gives an example of this process. Note that the driver class (Listing 14.8) does not call start on the Counter2's that it creates, because Counter2 is not a Thread, and does thus does not necessarily have a start method. The result (Listing 14.9) is substantially the same as with the original Counter.

Listing 14.7 `Counter2.java`

```java
/** A Runnable that counts up to a specified
 *  limit with random pauses in between each count.
 */

public class Counter2 implements Runnable {
  private static int totalNum = 0;
  private int currentNum, loopLimit;

  public Counter2(int loopLimit) {
    this.loopLimit = loopLimit;
    currentNum = totalNum++;
    Thread t = new Thread(this);
    t.start();
  }

  private void pause(double seconds) {
    try { Thread.sleep(Math.round(1000.0*seconds)); }
    catch(InterruptedException ie) {}
  }

  public void run() {
    for(int i=0; i<loopLimit; i++) {
      System.out.println("Counter " + currentNum
                          + ": " + i);
      pause(Math.random()); // Sleep for up to 1 second
    }
  }
}
```

Listing 14.8 `Counter2Test.java`

```java
/** Try out a few instances of the Counter2 class. */

public class Counter2Test {
  public static void main(String[] args) {
    Counter2 c1 = new Counter2(5);
    Counter2 c2 = new Counter2(5);
    Counter2 c3 = new Counter2(5);
  }
}
```

Listing 14.9   Counter2Test Output

```
Counter 0: 0
Counter 1: 0
Counter 2: 0
Counter 1: 1
Counter 1: 2
Counter 0: 1
Counter 1: 3
Counter 2: 1
Counter 0: 2
Counter 0: 3
Counter 1: 4
Counter 2: 2
Counter 2: 3
Counter 0: 4
Counter 2: 4
```

In this particular instance, this approach probably seems more cumbersome than making a separate subclass of `Thread`. However, because Java does not have multiple inheritance, if your class already is a subclass of something else (say `Applet`), it cannot also be a subclass of `Thread`. In such a case, if the thread needs access to the instance variables and methods of the main class, this approach works well, while the previous approach (a separate `Thread` subclass) requires some extra work to give the `Thread` subclass access to the applet's variables/methods (perhaps by passing along a reference to the `Applet`). When doing this from an `Applet`, the applet's `start` method is usually the place to create and start the threads.

14.2 Race Conditions

A class that implements `Runnable` could start more than one thread per instance. However, all of the threads started from that object will be looking at the *same* instance of that object. Per-thread data can be in local variables of `run`, but care must be taken when using more permanent data because multiple threads may try to access the same instance variables. For instance, Listing 14.10 shows an *incorrect* counter applet. Before reading further, take a look at the `run` method and see if you can see what is wrong.

Listing 14.10 BuggyCounterApplet.java

```java
import java.applet.Applet;
import java.awt.*;

/** Emulates the Counter and Counter2 classes, but
 *  this time from an applet that invokes multiple
 *  versions of its own run method. This version is
 *  likely to work correctly <B>except</B> when
 *  an important customer is visiting.
 */

public class BuggyCounterApplet extends Applet
                              implements Runnable{
  private static int totalNum = 0;
  private int loopLimit = 5;

  public void start() {
    Thread t;
    for(int i=0; i<3; i++) {
      t = new Thread(this);
      t.start();
    }
  }

  private void pause(double seconds) {
    try { Thread.sleep(Math.round(1000.0*seconds)); }
    catch(InterruptedException ie) {}
  }

  public void run() {
    int currentNum = totalNum;
    System.out.println("Setting currentNum to "
                       + currentNum);
    totalNum = totalNum + 1;
    for(int i=0; i<loopLimit; i++) {
      System.out.println("Counter "
                         + currentNum + ": " + i);
      pause(Math.random());
    }
  }
}
```

Listing 14.11   Usual BuggyCounterApplet Output

```
> appletviewer BuggyCounterApplet.html
Setting currentNum to 0
Counter 0: 0
Setting currentNum to 1
Counter 1: 0
Setting currentNum to 2
Counter 2: 0
Counter 2: 1
Counter 1: 1
Counter 0: 1
Counter 2: 2
Counter 0: 2
Counter 1: 2
Counter 1: 3
Counter 0: 3
Counter 2: 3
Counter 1: 4
Counter 2: 4
Counter 0: 4
```

In the vast majority of cases, the output (Listing 14.11) is correct, and the temptation would be to assume that the class is indeed correct, and leave it as it stands. In fact, however, it suffers from the flawed assumption that the new thread will be created and read totalNum between the time the previous thread reads it and that same thread increments it. That is, the operation of this code depends on the already-activated thread "winning the race" to the increment operation. This is an unsafe assumption, and in fact a small percent of the time it will lose the race, as shown in Listing 14.12, obtained after running the same applet over and over *many* times.

Listing 14.12 Occasional BuggyCounterApplet Output

```
> appletviewer BuggyCounterApplet.html
Setting currentNum to 0
Counter 0: 0
Setting currentNum to 1
Setting currentNum to 1
Counter 0: 1
Counter 1: 0
Counter 1: 0
Counter 0: 2
Counter 0: 3
Counter 1: 1
Counter 0: 4
Counter 1: 1
Counter 1: 2
Counter 1: 3
Counter 1: 2
Counter 1: 3
Counter 1: 4
Counter 1: 4
```

Now, one obvious "solution" is to perform the updating of the thread number in a single step, as follows, rather than first reading the value, then incrementing it a couple of lines later.

```
public void run() {
    int currentNum = totalNum++;
    System.out.println("Setting currentNum to "
                    + currentNum);
    for(int i=0; i<loopLimit; i++) {
        System.out.println("Counter "
                        + currentNum + ": " + i);
        pause(Math.random());
    }
}
```

Although the idea of performing the update in a single step is a good one, there is no guarantee that this code really *will* be done in a single step. Sure, it is a single line of Java source code, but who knows what goes on behind the scenes? The most likely scenario is that this simply shortens the race so the error occurs less frequently. Less frequent errors are *worse*, not better, because they are more likely to survive unnoticed until some critical moment. Fortunately, Java has a construct (synchronized) that lets you guarantee that a thread can complete a designated series of operations before another thread gets to execute any of them. This topic is so important that the entire next section is devoted to it.

14.3 Synchronization

Synchronization is the way to arbitrate contention for shared resources. When you synchronize a section of code, a "lock" (or "monitor") is set when the first thread enters that section of code. Unless the thread explicitly gives up the lock, no other thread can enter that section of code until the first one exits it. In fact, synchronization can be even stronger than this. A synchronized block has an Object as a tag, and once a thread enters a synchronized section of code, no other thread can enter *any* other section of code that is locked with the same tag.

Synchronizing a Section of Code

The way to protect a section of code that accesses shared resources is to place it inside a synchronized block, as follows:

```
synchronized(someObject) {
  code
}
```

This tells the system to perform the section of code atomically. That is, once a thread enters the enclosed code, no other thread will be allowed to enter until the first thread exits or voluntarily gives up the lock via wait. Note that this does *not* mean that the designated code is executed uninterrupted; it is still perfectly possible that the thread scheduler suspends a thread in the middle of the synchronized section in order to let another thread run. The key point is that the other thread will be executing a *different* section of code. Also note that you lock sections of *code*, not *objects*. Using someObject as a label on the lock in no way "locks" someObject. Other threads can still access it, and race conditions are still possible if a different section of code accesses the same resources as those inside the synchronized block. However, you are permitted to use the same label on more than one block of code. Thus, once a thread enters a block that is synchronized on someObject, no other section of code that is also synchronized on someObject can run until either the first thread exits the synchronized section, or it explicitly gives up the lock. In fact, a single thread is allowed to hold the same lock multiple times as when one synchronized block calls another that is synchronized using the same lock.

Core Note

The synchronized *construct locks sections of code, not objects.*

Synchronizing an Entire Method

If you want to synchronize all of the code in a method, Java provides a short-hand method: using the synchronized keyword, as follows:

```
public synchronized void someMethod() {
    body
}
```

This tells the system to perform someMethod atomically, using the current object instance (i.e., this) as the lock label. That is, once a thread starts executing someMethod, no other thread can enter it or any other section of code that is synchronized on the current object (this) until the current thread exits from someMethod or gives up the lock explicitly via wait. Thus, the following are equivalent.

```
public synchronized void someMethod() {
    body
}

public void someMethod() {
    synchronized(this) {
        body
    }
}
```

Now, after all the dire warnings about race conditions, programmers are sometimes tempted to synchronize everything in sight. Unfortunately, this can have performance penalties, and can result in coarser grained threading. For an extreme case, consider what would happen if you marked the run method as synchronized: you'd be forcing your code to run completely serially!

Note that a static method that specifies synchronized has the same effect as one whose body is synchronized on the class object (getClass()). Also note that synchronized declarations are *not* inherited, so if someMethod is overridden in a subclass, it would not be atomic unless the synchronized keyword was repeated.

Core Warning

Overridden methods in subclasses do not inherit the synchronized *declaration.*

14.4 Thread Methods

The following subsections summarize the constructors, constants, and methods in the Thread class. Included also are the wait, notify, and notifyAll methods (which really belong to Object, not just to Thread), and a discussion of the unusual way Netscape 3 treats threads.

Constructors

public Thread()
Using this constructor on the original Thread class is not very useful, because once the thread is started it will call its own run method, which is empty. However, a zero-argument constructor is commonly used for thread *subclasses* that have overridden the run method. Calling new Thread() is equivalent to calling new Thread(null, null, "Thread-N"), where *N* is automatically chosen by the system.

public Thread(Runnable target)
When you create a thread with a Runnable as a target, the target's run method will be used when start is called. This constructor is equivalent to Thread(null, target, "Thread-N").

public Thread(ThreadGroup group, Runnable target)
This creates a thread with the specified target (whose run method will be used), placing it in the designated ThreadGroup as long as that group's checkAccess method permits it. A ThreadGroup is a collection of threads that can be operated on as a set; see Section 14.5 for details. In fact, *all* threads belong to a ThreadGroup; if one is not specified, the ThreadGroup of the thread creating the new thread is used. This constructor is equivalent to Thread(group, target, "Thread-N").

public Thread(String name)
When threads are created, they are automatically given a name of the form "Thread-N" if a name is not specified. This lets you supply your

own name. Thread names can be retrieved via the `getName` method. This constructor is equivalent to `Thread(null, null, name)`, meaning that the calling thread's `ThreadGroup` will be used, and the new thread's own `run` method will be called when the thread is started.

public Thread(ThreadGroup group, String name)

This creates a thread in the given group with the specified name. The thread's own `run` method will be used when the thread is started. It is equivalent to `Thread(group, null, name)`.

public Thread(Runnable target, String name)

This creates a thread with the specified target and name. The target's `run` method will be used when the thread is started; it is equivalent to `Thread(null, target, name)`.

public Thread(ThreadGroup group, Runnable target, String name)

This creates a thread with the given group, target and name. If the group is not `null`, the new thread is placed in specified group unless the group's `checkAccess` method throws a `SecurityException`. If the group is `null`, the calling thread's group is used. If the target is not `null`, its `run` method is used when the thread is started; if the target is `null`, the thread's own `run` is used.

Constants

public final int MAX_PRIORITY

This is the highest value a thread priority can have, and is equal to 10.

public final int MIN_PRIORITY

This is the lowest value a thread priority can have, and is equal to 1.

public final int NORM_PRIORITY

This is the priority given to the first user thread, and is equal to 5. Subsequent threads are automatically given the priority of their creating thread.

Methods

public static int activeCount()

This returns the number of active threads in the thread's `Thread-Group` (and all subgroups).

public void checkAccess()

This determines if the thread that is currently running has permission to modify the thread. It is used in applets and other applications that implement a `SecurityManager`.

public native int countStackFrames()

This gives the number of stack frames being used by the thread. You can only call this method on suspended threads.

public static native Thread currentThread()

This returns a reference to the currently executing thread. Note that this is a static method, so can be called by arbitrary methods, not just from within a `Thread` object.

public void destroy() [Java 1.1]

This kills the thread without performing any cleanup operations. If the thread locked any locks, they remain locked.

public static void dumpStack()

This prints a stack trace to `System.err`.

public static int enumerate(Thread[ ] groupThreads)

This finds all active threads in the `ThreadGroup` belonging to the *currently executing* thread (not a particular specified thread), placing the references in the designated array. Use `activeCount` to determine the size of the array needed.

public final String getName()

This gives the thread's name.

public final int getPriority()

This gives the thread's priority. See `setPriority` for a discussion of the way Java schedules threads of different priorities.

public final ThreadGroup getThreadGroup()

This gives the `ThreadGroup` to which the thread belongs. All threads belong to a group; if none is specified in the `Thread` constructor, the calling thread's group is used.

public void interrupt()

This sets a flag in the thread that can be detected by `isInterrupted`. It does not actually "interrupt" the thread in the normal sense; the thread is responsible for checking the status of the interrupted flag and taking action if desired. Furthermore, since there is no way to reset the flag, this method has limited value.

public static boolean interrupted()

This static method checks if the *currently executing* thread is interrupted (i.e. has its interrupted flag set via `interrupt`). It differs from `isInterrupted`, which checks if the *specified* thread is interrupted. In fact, `Thread.interrupted()` is equivalent to `Thread.currentThread().isInterrupted()`.

public final native boolean isAlive()

This returns `true` for running or suspended threads, `false` for threads that have been stopped. A thread calling `isAlive` on itself is not too useful, since if you can call *any* method you are obviously alive. It is used by external methods to check the liveness of thread references they hold.

public final boolean isDaemon()

This determines if the thread is a "daemon" thread. Java will exit when the only active threads remaining are daemon threads. A thread initially has the same status as the thread that created it, but this can be changed via `setDaemon`.

public boolean isInterrupted()

This checks if the thread's interrupt flag has been set by means of the `interrupt` method. Unfortunately, there is no way to reset the flag.

public final void join() throws InterruptedException
public final synchronized join(long milliseconds)
   throws InterruptedException
public final synchronized join(long milliseconds, int nanoseconds)
   throws InterruptedException

This suspends the calling thread until either the specified timeout has elapsed, or the thread on which `join` was called has terminated (i.e. would return `false` for `isAlive`). For those not familiar with the terminology of "thread joining," calling this method `sleepUntilDead` would have been clearer. This provides a convenient way to wait until one thread has finished before starting another, but without polling or consuming too many CPU cycles. A thread should never try to `join` itself; this simply waits forever (a bit boring, don't you think?).

For more complex conditions, use `wait` and `notify` instead.

public final native void notify()
public final native void notifyAll()

Like `wait`, this is really a method of `Object`, not just of `Thread`. It wakes up a single thread (`notify`) or all threads (`notifyAll`) that are waiting for the specified object's lock. Only code that holds an object's lock (i.e. is inside a block of code synchronized on the object) can send it a `notify` or `notifyAll` request, and the thread or threads being notified will not actually get restarted until the process issuing the notify request gives up the lock. See the discussion of `wait` for more details.

public final void resume()

If a thread has been suspended, this resumes it. Otherwise no action is taken. Note that resuming a suspended thread does not necessarily make it start executing. That depends on the thread scheduler being used and the priorities of the other active threads.

public void run()

This is where the user places the actions to be performed. When `run` finishes, the thread exits. The method creating the thread should not call this directly; it should call `start` instead.

public final void setDaemon(boolean becomeDaemon)

This sets the daemon status of the thread. A thread initially has the same status as the thread that created it, but this can be changed via `setDaemon`. Java will exit when the only active threads remaining are daemon threads.

public final void setName(String threadName)

This changes the name of the thread. Also, note that Netscape 3 disallows changing names of threads that do not belong to the applet's `ThreadGroup`. See the following subsection (Using Threads in Netscape 3.0x) for details.

public final void setPriority(int threadPriority)

This changes the thread's priority; higher-priority threads are supposed to be executed in favor of lower-priority ones. Legal values range from `Thread.MIN_PRIORITY` to `Thread.MAX_PRIORITY`. A thread's default priority is the priority of whatever thread created it. Be careful, as starvation can occur; almost all current implementations use a completely preemptive scheduler where lower-priority threads will *never* get executed unless the higher-priority threads terminate, sleep, or wait for I/O. Also, note that Netscape 3 disallows the setting of priorities for threads that do not belong to the applet's `Thread-Group`. See the following subsection (Using Threads in Netscape 3.0x) for details.

public static native void sleep(long milliseconds)
throws InterruptedException
public static native void sleep(long milliseconds, int nanoseconds)
throws InterruptedException

This does a nonbusy wait for the specified amount of time, then throws an `InterruptedException`. Since it is a static method, it is used by nonthreaded applications as well. In most Java 1.0 implementations, the nanoseconds argument is rounded to the nearest millisecond, so is not useful.

Core Approach

You can use `Thread.sleep` *from any method, not just in threads.*

public synchronized native void start()

This is called to initialize the thread and then call `run`. If the thread is created with a `null` target (see the constructors earlier in this section), then it calls its own `run` method. But if some `Runnable` is supplied, it calls the `run` method of that `Runnable`.

Note that applets also have a `start` method that gets called after `init` is finished and before the first call to `paint`. Don't confuse it with the `start` method of threads, although it is a convenient place for applets to initiate threads.

public final void stop()
public final synchronized void stop(Throwable stopError)

This terminates the thread. The action being performed by the thread is permanently stopped, and the thread will now return `false` from `isAlive`. However, it can still be restarted at the beginning (not at the point at which it was halted, as with `suspend`) by calling `start`.

The default version of `stop` throws a `ThreadDeath` exception, which is automatically caught by the Java run-time system, which terminates the thread. Unless you are absolutely sure you know what you are doing, you don't want to catch `ThreadDeath` explicitly. It is also possible, but rarely recommended, to throw a different exception instead; that is the purpose of the second variation of `stop`.

Applets also have a `stop` method that gets called whenever the Web page is exited or, in the case of Netscape, when the browser is resized. Threads do not get stopped automatically, so you should normally put code in the applet's `stop` method that stops (perhaps via `suspend`, not `stop`, however) all active threads.

Core Approach

If you make a multithreaded applet, you should halt the threads in the applet's `stop` *method, restarting them in the applet's* `start` *method.*

public final void suspend()

This pauses a thread. The `suspend` method is temporary, in contrast to the `stop` method which is permanent. When `resume` is called the thread restarts at the point at which it was paused.

public final void wait() throws InterruptedException
public final void wait(long milliseconds)
   throws InterruptedException
public final void wait(long milliseconds, int nanoseconds)
   throws InterruptedException

This gives up the lock and suspends the current thread. The thread is restarted by `notify` or `notifyAll`. This is actually a method of `Object`, not just of `Thread`, but can only be called from within a synchronized method or block of code. For example,

```
public synchronized void someMethod() {
  doSomePreliminaries();
  while (!someContinueCondition()) {
    try {
      // Give up the lock and suspend ourself. We'll
      // rely on somebody else to wake us up, but
      // will check someContinueCondition before
      // proceeding, just in case we get woken up
      // for the wrong reason.
      wait();
    } catch(InterruptedException ie) {}
  }
  continueOperations();
}
```

You call `wait` on the object that is used to tag the synchronized block, so if that is not the current object (`this`), you need to supply it explicitly, as in the following example.

```
public void someOtherMethod() {
  doSomeUnsynchronizedStuff();
  synchronized(someObject) {
    doSomePreliminaries();
    while (!someContinueCondition()) {
      try {
        someObject.wait();
      } catch(InterruptedException ie) {}
    }
    continueOperations();
  }
  doSomeMoreUnsynchronizedStuff();
}
```

public static native void yield()

If two threads of the same priority are running and neither sleeps or waits for I/O, they may or may not alternate execution. In particular, they often are *not* time sliced on Unix implementations, although they are in virtually all Windows 95/NT and MacOS versions. Using `yield` gives up execution to any other process of the same priority that is waiting, and is a good practice to ensure that time slicing takes place. Although it is appropriate to leave the details of time slicing to the implementation, in my opinion not requiring that threads be time sliced is a significant drawback in an otherwise excellent thread specification.

Core Approach

If your code needs to run on Unix platforms and your threads never sleep or wait for I/O, you should insert calls to `yield` *in your code.*

Using Threads in Netscape 3.0x

The behavior of threads in Netscape 3 is a little unusual. If you have a thread that does not belong to the applet's `ThreadGroup`, you get a `SecurityException` if you call `suspend`, `resume`, `interrupt`, `destroy`, `setPriority`, `setName`, or `setDaemon`. However, threads that are created from event-handling methods (e.g., from inside `mouseDown` or `action`) are placed in the AWT `ThreadGroup`, not the applet's. This means that if you do nothing special, you cannot suspend, resume, or change characteristics of threads that are created from event handlers! The solution is to look up a reference to the applet's group in `init`, as follows:

```
public class SomeApplet extends Applet {
  private ThreadGroup appletGroup;

  public void init() {
    appletGroup =
      Thread.currentThread().getThreadGroup();
    . . .
  }


  . . .
}
```

Then, whenever you need to create a thread, place it explicitly in the group by passing the `ThreadGroup` to the thread constructor. Since this does no harm even if not necessary (Netscape 2, 4, Internet Explorer), it is a good standard practice when making threads in applets that must run on multiple browsers.

Core Approach

If you are creating threaded cross-platform applets that need to be suspended or have custom priorities or names, be sure to place the threads in the applet's `ThreadGroup`.

14.5 Thread Groups

The ThreadGroup class provides a convenient mechanism for controlling sets of threads. A ThreadGroup can contain other thread groups in addition to a thread, letting you arrange groups hierarchically. Its constructors and methods are summarized in the following subsections.

Constructors

public ThreadGroup(String groupName)

This creates a named ThreadGroup that belongs to the same group as does the thread that called the constructor.

public ThreadGroup(ThreadGroup parent, String groupName)

This creates a named ThreadGroup that belongs to the specified parent group.

Methods

public synchronized int activeCount()

This gives the number of active threads directly or indirectly in the thread group, as of the time the method call was initiated.

public synchronized int activeGroupCount()

This gives the number of active thread groups in the group, as of the time the method call was initiated.

public final void checkAccess()

This determines if the calling thread is allowed to modify the group. It is used by applets and applications with a custom SecurityManager.

public final synchronized void destroy()

If the group contains no threads, it destroys the group (and any empty subgroups) and removes the group from its parent's group. It throws an IllegalThreadStateException if it contains any threads when called.

public int enumerate(Thread[ ] threads)
public int enumerate(Thread[ ] groupThreads, boolean recurse)
public int enumerate(ThreadGroup[ ] groups)
public int enumerate(ThreadGroup[ ] groups, boolean recurse)

This copies the references of active threads or thread groups into the specified array. If the `recurse` flag is `true`, it recursively descends child groups.

public final int getMaxPriority()

This returns the maximum priority threads in the group are allowed to be given via their `setPriority` method. However, their initial priority, derived from the priority of the creating thread, can be anything up to `Thread.MAX_PRIORITY`, regardless of the group's `getMaxPriority` value. See `setMaxPriority` for setting the value.

public final String getName()

This returns the name of the group.

public final ThreadGroup getParent()

This returns the parent group. Its value will be `null` for the first group created in the system.

public final boolean isDaemon()

This tells you if the group is a daemon group. Daemon groups are automatically destroyed when they are empty.

public synchronized void list()

This prints all the threads and subgroups in the group to `System.out`, and is a useful debugging tool.

public final boolean parentOf(ThreadGroup descendant)

This determines if the group is an ancestor (not necessarily the direct parent) of the specified descendant group.

public final synchronized void resume()

This calls resume on all threads directly or indirectly in the group.

public final void setDaemon(boolean becomeDaemon)

A group automatically gets the daemon status of its parent group; this method can change that initial status. A daemon group is automatically destroyed when it becomes empty.

public final synchronized void setMaxPriority(int max)

This gives the maximum priority any thread in the group can be explicitly given via `setPriority`. They can still inherit a higher priority from their creating thread, however.

public final synchronized void stop()

This stops all threads that are directly or indirectly in the group.

public final synchronized void suspend()

This suspends all threads that are directly or indirectly in the group.

public void uncaughtException(Thread thread, Throwable error)

When a thread throws an exception that is not caught, it comes here first. The default behavior is to print a stack trace for any error except for `ThreadDeath` (which is thrown by the `stop` method).

14.6 Multithreaded Graphics and Double Buffering

One common application of threads is to develop dynamic graphics. There are various standard approaches to doing this that have various advantages and disadvantages.

- *Redraw Everything in Paint.* This is simple and easy, but if things change quickly it is slow and can result in a flickering display.
- *Implement the Dynamic Part as a Separate Component.* This is relatively easy and eliminates the flickering problem, but requires a `null` layout manager, can be quite slow, and, in Java 1.0, works poorly with graphics whose rectangular bounding boxes overlap.

- *Have Routines Other Than Paint Do Drawing Operations Directly.* This is easy, efficient, and flicker free, but results in "transient" drawing that is lost next time the screen is redrawn.
- *Override Update and Have Paint Do Incremental Updating.* This eliminates the flicker and improves efficiency somewhat, but requires the graphics to be nonoverlapping.
- *Double Buffering.* This is the most efficient option, and has no problem with overlapping graphics. However, it is more complex and requires additional memory resources.

Redraw Everything in Paint

A common technique in graphical Java programs is to have processes set parameters that describe the appearance of the window, rather than drawing the graphics themselves. The various routines call `repaint` to schedule a call to `paint`, and `paint` does the necessary drawing based on the parameters that have been set. The `repaint` method actually calls `update`, which clears the screen then calls `paint` with the appropriate `Graphics` object. The `paint` method also gets called automatically after the applet is initialized, whenever part of the applet is obscured and reexposed, and when certain other resizing or layout events occur. It is also possible to supply a rectangular area to the `repaint` method, which determines the clipping region given to the `Graphics` object used in `update` and `paint`. However, it can be difficult to determine the proper area, and it is still the case that an entire region gets redrawn, not just some particular graphical items.

For instance, suppose that you are developing a user interface for a naval simulation system, and need to animate the icons that represent the ships. A background thread (or threads) could be updating the positions, then periodically invoking `repaint`. The `paint` method simply loops over all the simulation objects drawing them in their current positions, as shown in the simplified example of Listing 14.13.

Listing 14.13 `ShipSimulation.java`

```java
import java.applet.Applet;
import java.awt.*;

public class ShipSimulation extends Applet
                            implements Runnable {
  ...

  public void run() {
    Ship s;
    for(int i=0; i<ships.length; i++) {
      s = ships[i];
      s.move(); // Update location
    }
    repaint();
  }

  ...

  public void paint(Graphics g) {
    Ship s;
    for(int i=0; i<ships.length; i++) {
      s = ships[i];
      s.draw(s); // draws at current location
    }
  }
}
```

Alternatively, you might only initiate changes to the interface at user request, but still redraw everything each time. For example, suppose that you want to draw some sort of image wherever the user clicks the mouse. Listing 14.14 shows a solution using the "store and redraw" approach, with a sample result shown in Figure 14–1. It makes use of the `QuittableFrame` class developed in Listing 11.12.

Listing 14.14 `DrawCircles.java`

```java
import java.awt.*;
import java.util.Vector;

/** A frame that draws a small circle where you click.*/

public class DrawCircles extends QuittableFrame {
  public static void main(String[] args) {
    new DrawCircles();
  }

  private Vector circles;

  public DrawCircles() {
    super("Drawing Circles");
    circles = new Vector();
    setBackground(Color.white);
    resize(500, 300);
    show();
  }

  /** When you click the mouse, create a SimpleCircle,
   *  put it in the Vector, and tell the system
   *  to repaint (which calls update, which clears
   *  the screen and calls paint).
   */
  public boolean mouseDown(Event event, int x, int y) {
    circles.addElement(new SimpleCircle(x, y, 25));
    repaint();
    return(true);
  }

  /** This loops down the available SimpleCircle objects,
   *  drawing each one.
   */
  public void paint(Graphics g) {
    SimpleCircle circle;
    for(int i=0; i<circles.size(); i++) {
      circle = (SimpleCircle)circles.elementAt(i);
      circle.draw(g);
    }
  }
}
```

Listing 14.15 presents the `SimpleCircle` class used in `DrawCircles`.

Listing 14.15 `SimpleCircle.java`

```java
import java.awt.*;

/** A class to store an x, y, and radius, plus a
 *  draw method.
 */

public class SimpleCircle {
  private int x, y, radius;

  public SimpleCircle(int x, int y, int radius) {
    setX(x);
    setY(y);
    setRadius(radius);
  }

  /** Given a Graphics, draw the SimpleCircle
   *  centered around its current position.
   */
  public void draw(Graphics g) {
    g.fillOval(x - radius, y - radius,
               radius * 2, radius * 2);
  }

  public int getX() { return(x); }
  public void setX(int x) { this.x = x; }

  public int getY() { return(y); }
  public void setY(int y) { this.y = y; }

  public int getRadius() { return(radius); }
  public void setRadius(int radius) {
    this.radius = radius;
  }
}
```

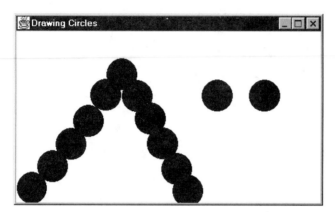

Figure 14–1   By storing results in a permanent data structure and redrawing the whole structure every time `paint` is invoked, the drawing will persist even after the window is covered up and reexposed.

Pros and Cons

This approach is quite simple, but is not well suited to applications that have complicated time-consuming graphics (because all or part of the window gets redrawn each time), or for ones that have frequent changes (because of the flicker caused by the clearing of the screen).

Implement the Dynamic Part as a Separate Component

Components know how to update themselves, so the `Container` that uses a `Component` need not explicitly draw them. For instance, in the simulation example mentioned above, the ships could be implemented as custom subclasses of `Canvas`, and placed in a window with a `null` layout manager. To update the positions, the main simulation process could simply call `move` on the components. Similarly, drawing triggered by user events is a simple matter of creating a `Component`, setting its x and y locations, and adding it to the current `Container`. An example of drawing circles this way is shown in Section 11.10 (Serializing Windows).

Pros and Cons

In some situations, this is easier than doing things explicitly in `paint`, as it lets the movement be controlled by the `Component` with few changes required in the code for the Container. However, it suffers from the same disadvantages as redrawing everything in paint: slow updates and flickering. In addition, because a Component is rectangular and opaque in Java 1.0, it precludes closely packed or overlapping components.

Have Routines Other Than Paint Do Drawing Operations Directly

In some cases, you don't want to bother to call paint *at all*, but want to do drawing directly. This can be done by getting the Graphics object using getGraphics, setting the drawing mode to use XOR, then directly calling the drawXxx methods of the Graphics object. This drawing can be erased by drawing in the same location a second time, at least as long as multiple drawing does not overlap. To illustrate this, Listing 14.16 creates a simple Frame that lets the user create and stretch "rubberband" rectangles. Figure 14–2 shows a typical result.

Listing 14.16 Rubberband.java

```java
import java.awt.*;

/** Draw "rubberband" rectangles when the user drags
 *  the mouse. Ignore problems with dragging into
 *  or out of the window.
 */

public class Rubberband extends QuittableFrame {
  public static void main(String[] args) {
    new Rubberband();
  }

  private int startX, startY, lastX, lastY;

  public Rubberband() {
    super("Click and drag to show rubberbanding");
    setBackground(Color.white);
    resize(500, 300);
    show();
  }
```

continued

Listing 14.16 `Rubberband.java` (continued)

```java
/** When the user presses the mouse, record the
 *  location of the top-left corner of rectangle.
 */
public boolean mouseDown(Event e, int x, int y) {
  startX = x;
  startY = y;
  lastX = startX;
  lastY = startY;
  return(true);
}

/** This draws a rubberband rectangle, assuming
 *  you first choose the top-left corner, then draw
 *  down and to the right.
 */
public boolean mouseDrag(Event e, int x, int y) {
  Graphics g = getGraphics();
  g.setXORMode(Color.lightGray);
  g.drawRect(startX, startY,
             lastX - startX, lastY - startY);
  g.drawRect(startX, startY,
             x - startX, y - startY);
  lastX = x;
  lastY = y;
  return(true);
}

/** Erase the last rectangle when the user releases
 *  the mouse.
 */

public boolean mouseUp(Event e, int x, int y) {
  Graphics g = getGraphics();
  g.setXORMode(Color.lightGray);
  g.drawRect(startX, startY,
             lastX - startX, lastY - startY);
  return(true);
}
}
```

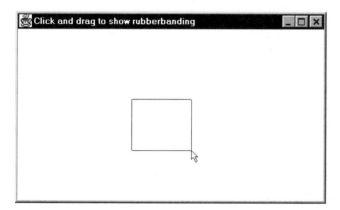

Figure 14–2 Direct drawing from threads or event handlers is easy to implement and very fast, but gives transient results.

Pros and Cons

This approach (direct drawing instead of setting variables that `paint` will use) is very appropriate for "temporary" drawing; it is simple and efficient. However, if `paint` is ever triggered, this drawing will be lost. So it is not appropriate for "permanent" drawing.

Override Update and Have Paint Do Incremental Updating

Suppose that some graphical objects need to be moved around on the screen. Suppose further that the objects never overlap one another. In such a case, rather than clearing the screen and completely redrawing the new situation, the `paint` method could erase the object at its old location (say by drawing a solid rectangle in the background color) and then redraw it at the new location, saving the time required to redraw the rest of the window. The `paint` method could be triggered from some mouse or keyboard event, or by a background thread calling the applet's `repaint` method. For this to work without flickering, however, a new version of `update` has to be defined that does not clear the screen before calling `paint`.

```
public void update(Graphics g) {
    paint(g);
}
```

Also, because `paint` runs from the same foreground thread that watches for mouse and keyboard events, it is important to keep the time spent in `paint` as short as possible in order to prevent the system from being unresponsive to buttons, scrollbars, and the like.

To illustrate this approach, Listing 14.17 shows an applet that lets you create any number of small circles that bounce around in the window. As can be seen in Figure 14–3, the incremental drawing works well everywhere except where the circles overlap, where erasing one circle can accidentally erase part of another circle.

Listing 14.17 `Bounce.java`

```java
import java.applet.Applet;
import java.awt.*;
import java.util.Vector;

//-------------------------------------------------------
/** Bounce circles around on the screen.
 *  Doesn't use double buffering so has problems
 *  with overlapping circles. Overrides update
 *  to avoid flicker problems.
 */

public class Bounce extends Applet
                    implements Runnable {
  private Vector circles;
  private int width, height;
  private Button startButton, stopButton;
  private Thread animationThread = null;
  private ThreadGroup appletThreadGroup;

  public void init() {
    setBackground(Color.white);
    width = size().width;
    height = size().height;
    circles = new Vector();
    startButton = new Button("Start a circle");
    add(startButton);
    stopButton = new Button("Stop all circles");
    add(stopButton);
    // For Netscape-3 problems
    appletThreadGroup =
      Thread.currentThread().getThreadGroup();
  }
```

Listing 14.17 `Bounce.java` **(continued)**

```java
//------------------------------------------------------
/** When the "start" button is pressed, start the
 *  animation thread if it is not already started.
 *  Either way, add a circle to the Vector of
 *  circles that are being bounced.
 *  <P>
 *  When the "stop" button is pressed, stop
 *  the thread and clear the Vector of circles.
 */
public boolean action(Event event, Object object) {
  if (event.target == startButton) {
    if (circles.size() == 0) {
      animationThread =
        new Thread(appletThreadGroup, this);
      animationThread.start();
    }
    int radius = 25;
    int x = radius + randomInt(width - 2 * radius);
    int y = radius + randomInt(height - 2 * radius);
    int deltaX = 1 + randomInt(10);
    int deltaY = 1 + randomInt(10);
    circles.addElement(new MovingCircle(x, y, radius,
                                        deltaX,
                                        deltaY));
  } else if (event.target == stopButton) {
    if (animationThread != null) {
      animationThread.stop();
      circles.removeAllElements();
    }
  }
  repaint();
  return(true);
}

//------------------------------------------------------
/** Each time around the loop, call paint and then
 *  take a short pause. The paint method will
 *  move the circles and draw them.
 */
public void run() {
  MovingCircle circle;
  while(true) { // Really while thread not stopped
    repaint();
    pause(100);
  }
}
```

continued

Listing 14.17 `Bounce.java` **(continued)**

```java
//-------------------------------------------------------
/** Skip the usual screen-clearing step of update
 *  so that there is no "flicker" between each
 *  drawing step.
 */
public void update(Graphics g) {
  paint(g);
}

//-------------------------------------------------------
/** Erase each circle's old position, move it,
 *  then draw it in new location.
 */
public void paint(Graphics g) {
  MovingCircle circle;
  for(int i=0; i<circles.size(); i++) {
    circle = (MovingCircle)circles.elementAt(i);
    g.setColor(getBackground());
    circle.draw(g);
    circle.move(width, height);
    g.setColor(getForeground());
    circle.draw(g);
  }
}

//-------------------------------------------------------
// Returns an int from 0 to max (inclusive),
// yielding max + 1 possible values.

private int randomInt(int max) {
  double x =
    Math.floor((double)(max + 1) * Math.random());
  return((int)(Math.round(x)));
}

//-------------------------------------------------------
// Sleep for the specified amount of time.

private void pause(int milliseconds) {
  try {
    Thread.sleep((long)milliseconds);
  } catch(InterruptedException ie) {}
}
}
```

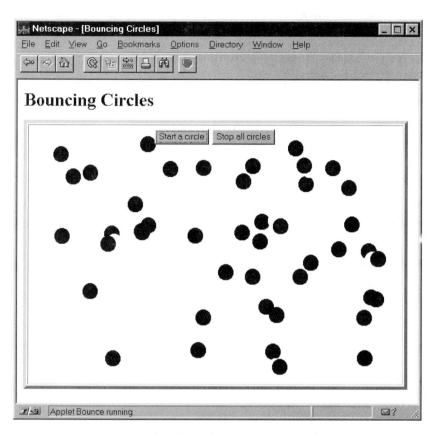

Figure 14–3 Incremental updating from `paint` can be flicker-free and relatively fast, but it does not easily handle overlapping items.

`Bounce` makes use of `MovingCircle`, a class that encapsulates the movement of the circle as well as its position and size, which are inherited from `SimpleCircle`. `MovingCircle`, is shown in Listing 14.18.

Listing 14.18 `MovingCircle.java`

```
/** An extension of SimpleCircle that can be moved
 *  around based on deltaX and deltaY values. Movement
 *  will continue in a given direction until the
 *  edge of the circle reaches a wall, in which case it
 *  will "bounce" and move the other direction.
 */
```

continued

Listing 14.18 `MovingCircle.java` (continued)

```java
public class MovingCircle extends SimpleCircle {
  private int deltaX, deltaY;

  public MovingCircle(int x, int y, int radius,
                      int deltaX, int deltaY) {
    super(x, y, radius);
    this.deltaX = deltaX;
    this.deltaY = deltaY;
  }

  public void move(int windowWidth, int windowHeight) {
    setX(getX() + getDeltaX());
    setY(getY() + getDeltaY());
    bounce(windowWidth, windowHeight);
  }

  private void bounce(int windowWidth,
                      int windowHeight) {
    int x = getX(), y = getY(), radius = getRadius(),
        deltaX = getDeltaX(), deltaY = getDeltaY();
    if ((x - radius < 0) && (deltaX < 0))
      setDeltaX(-deltaX);
    else if ((x + radius > windowWidth) && (deltaX > 0))
      setDeltaX(-deltaX);
    if ((y -radius < 0) && (deltaY < 0))
      setDeltaY(-deltaY);
    else if((y + radius > windowHeight) && (deltaY > 0))
      setDeltaY(-deltaY);
  }

  public int getDeltaX() {
    return(deltaX);
  }

  public void setDeltaX(int deltaX) {
    this.deltaX = deltaX;
  }

  public int getDeltaY() {
    return(deltaY);
  }

  public void setDeltaY(int deltaY) {
    this.deltaY = deltaY;
  }
}
```

Pros and Cons

This approach takes a bit more effort than previous ones, and requires that your objects be nonoverlapping. However, it lets you implement "permanent" drawing more quickly than redrawing everything every time.

Double Buffering

Consider a scenario that involves many different moving objects and/or where the objects overlap. Drawing several different objects individually is expensive, and if the objects overlap it is difficult to reliably erase them in their old positions. In such a situation, double buffering is often employed. In this approach, an offscreen image (pixmap) is created, and all of the drawing operations are done into this image. The actual "drawing" of the window consists of a single step: draw the image on the screen. As before, the update method is overridden to avoid clearing the screen, because the offscreen image completely replaces what is underneath it each time it is drawn. Although there are several variations of double buffering, the basic approach involves five steps.

1. *Override update to simply call paint.* This prevents the flicker that would normally occur each time update clears the screen before calling paint.

2. *Allocate an Image using createImage.* Note that since this image uses native window-system support, it cannot be done until a window actually appears. For instance, you should call createImage in an applet from init (or later), not in the direct initialization of an instance variable. For an application, you should wait until after the initial frame has been displayed (e.g., by show or setVisible) before calling createImage. However, calling it earlier will not result in an error message; null will simply be returned.

Core Warning

Calling createImage *from a component that is not visible results in* null.

3. *Look up its Graphics object using getGraphics.* Unlike with windows, where you need to look up the `Graphics` context each time you draw, with images it is reliable to look it up once, store it, and reuse the same reference thereafter.
4. *For each step, clear the image and redraw all objects onto it.* This will be dramatically faster than drawing onto a visible window.
5. *Draw the offscreen image onto the window.* Use `drawImage` for this.

Listing 14.19 shows a concrete implementation of this approach. It changes the previous `Bounce` applet to use double buffering, resulting in improved performance and eliminating the problems with overlapping circles. Figure 14–4 shows the result.

Listing 14.19 `DoubleBufferBounce.java`

```java
import java.applet.Applet;
import java.awt.*;
import java.util.Vector;

//-----------------------------------------------------
/** Bounce circles around on the screen, using
 *  double buffering for speed and to avoid problems
 *  with overlapping circles. Override update to
 *  to avoid flicker problems.
 */

public class DoubleBufferBounce extends Applet
                                implements Runnable {
  private Vector circles;
  private int width, height;
  private Image offScreenImage;
  private Graphics offScreenGraphics;
  private Button startButton, stopButton;
  private Thread animationThread = null;
  private ThreadGroup appletThreadGroup;

  public void init() {
    setBackground(Color.white);
    width = size().width;
    height = size().height;
```

Listing 14.19 DoubleBufferBounce.java (continued)

```java
    offScreenImage = createImage(width, height);
    offScreenGraphics = offScreenImage.getGraphics();
    // Automatic in some systems, not in others
    offScreenGraphics.setColor(Color.black);
    circles = new Vector();
    startButton = new Button("Start a circle");
    add(startButton);
    stopButton = new Button("Stop all circles");
    add(stopButton);
    // For Netscape-3 problems
    appletThreadGroup =
      Thread.currentThread().getThreadGroup();
  }

  //------------------------------------------------------
  /** When the "start" button is pressed, start the
   *  animation thread if it is not already started.
   *  Either way, add a circle to the Vector of
   *  circles that are being bounced.
   *  <P>
   *  When the "stop" button is pressed, stop
   *  the thread and clear the Vector of circles.
   */
  public boolean action(Event event, Object object) {
    if (event.target == startButton) {
      if (circles.size() == 0) {
        animationThread =
          new Thread(appletThreadGroup, this);
        animationThread.start();
      }
      int radius = 25;
      int x = radius + randomInt(width - 2 * radius);
      int y = radius + randomInt(height - 2 * radius);
      int deltaX = 1 + randomInt(10);
      int deltaY = 1 + randomInt(10);
      circles.addElement(new MovingCircle(x, y, radius,
                                          deltaX,
                                          deltaY));
    } else if (event.target == stopButton) {
      if (animationThread != null) {
        animationThread.stop();
        circles.removeAllElements();
      }
    }
```

continued

Listing 14.19 `DoubleBufferBounce.java` **(continued)**

```
    repaint();
    return(true);
  }


  //----------------------------------------------------
  /** Each time around the loop, move each circle
   *  based on its current position and deltaX/deltaY
   *  values. These values reverse when the circles
   *  reach the edge of the window.
   */
  public void run() {
    MovingCircle circle;
    while(true) { // Really while thread not stopped
      for(int j=0; j<circles.size(); j++) {
        circle = (MovingCircle)circles.elementAt(j);
        circle.move(width, height);
      }
      repaint();
      pause(100);
    }
  }


  //----------------------------------------------------
  /** Skip the usual screen-clearing step of update
   *  so that there is no "flicker" between each
   *  drawing step.
   */
  public void update(Graphics g) {
    paint(g);
  }
```

Listing 14.19 DoubleBufferBounce.java (continued)

```java
//-----------------------------------------------------
/** Clear the offscreen pixmap, draw each circle
 *  onto it, then draw that pixmap onto the
 *  applet window.
 */
public void paint(Graphics g) {
  offScreenGraphics.clearRect(0, 0, width, height);
  MovingCircle circle;
  for(int i=0; i<circles.size(); i++) {
    circle = (MovingCircle)circles.elementAt(i);
    circle.draw(offScreenGraphics);
  }
  g.drawImage(offScreenImage, 0, 0, this);
}

//-----------------------------------------------------
// Returns an int from 0 to max (inclusive),
// yielding max + 1 possible values.

private int randomInt(int max) {
  double x =
    Math.floor((double)(max + 1) * Math.random());
  return((int)(Math.round(x)));
}

//-----------------------------------------------------
// Sleep for the specified amount of time.

private void pause(int milliseconds) {
  try {
    Thread.sleep((long)milliseconds);
  } catch(InterruptedException ie) {}
}
}
```

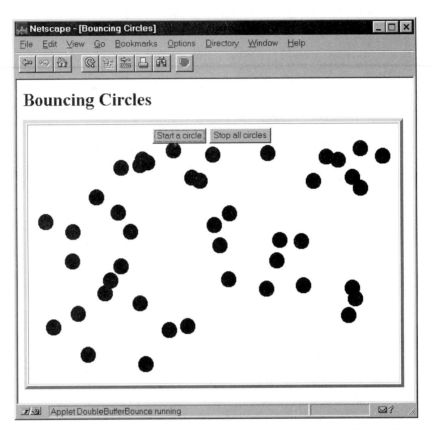

Figure 14–4   Double buffering allows fast, flicker-free updating of possibly overlapping images, but at the cost of some complexity and additional memory usage.

Pros and Cons

Drawing into an offscreen image then drawing that image once to the screen is much faster than doing the drawing directly to the screen. Double buffering allows fast, flicker-free updating even when there is no reliable way to erase the old graphics. However, it is more complex than most of the previously discussed options, and requires extra memory for the offscreen image.

14.7 Summary

Threads can be used for a variety of applications. In some cases, using threads makes software design simpler by letting you separate various pieces of work into independent chunks, rather than coordinating them in a central routine. In other cases, threads can improve efficiency by letting you continue processing while a routine is waiting for user input or a network connection. However, threaded programs tend to be more difficult to understand and debug, and improper synchronization can lead to inconsistent results. So threads should be used with some caution. An area that is particularly difficult is when threads are used for animation or when graphics change dynamically based on user interaction. There are a variety of potential solutions, but one of the most generally applicable ones is double buffering, where graphics operations are performed in an off-screen pixmap, then that pixmap is drawn to the screen. Another area where concurrent processing can be beneficial is in the area of network programming. The next chapter discusses a variety of issues under that topic, including how servers should be made multithreaded.

CLIENT-SERVER PROGRAMMING IN JAVA

Topics in This Chapter

- The basic steps to implementing network clients in Java
- A generic network client implementation
- Using the StringTokenizer class to process strings
- A network client that validates e-mail addresses
- A network client that retrieves files from an HTTP server
- Using the URL class to retrieve Web documents
- The basic steps to implementing network servers in Java
- A generic network server implementation
- A simple HTTP server
- Making servers multithreaded
- Invoking distributed objects using RMI
- Accessing remote databases using JDBC

Chapter 15

Client-server programming is the way in which software systems communicate with each other over the network. A *client* is the program that connects to a system to request services. A *server* is a program that runs on a machine listening on a designated part of the network (a "port"), waiting for other programs to connect. When it gets a connection, it provides some service to the connecting program. Servers often provide services to more than one connecting program, either one after the other or to several concurrently. If the distinction between who is requesting the service and who is providing it seems blurry, just remember that the server starts first and doesn't need to know which host will be connecting, while the client starts second and has to specify a particular host to talk to.

Core Note

Remember that the security manager of most browsers prohibits applets from making network connections to machines other than the one from which they are loaded.

In the first part of this chapter, you'll see how to directly implement clients and servers using network "sockets." Although this is the lowest-level type of network programming in Java, if you've used sockets in other languages you may be surprised at how simple they are to use in Java. In addition to sockets, which can communicate with general-purpose programs in arbitrary languages, Java 1.1 provides two higher-level packages for communicating with specific types of systems. The Remote Method Invocation package lets you easily access methods in remote Java objects, and includes the ability to send and receive general Java objects. The Java DataBase Connectivity API provides access to a wide variety of relational databases using a standard interface, letting you easily create Java programs that are integrated with databases on local or remote systems. These two packages are discussed in the second part of the chapter.

15.1 Implementing a Client

The client is the program that initiates a network connection. Implementing a client consists of five basic steps:

1. Create a Socket object.
2. Create an output stream that can be used to send info to the Socket.
3. Create an input stream to read the response from the server.
4. Do I/O with input and output streams.
5. Close the socket when done.

   Each of these steps is described in the sections that follow. Note that most of the methods described in these sections throw an `IOException`, so need to be wrapped in a `try/catch` block.

Create a Socket object

A `Socket` is the Java object corresponding to a network connection. A client connects to an existing server that is listening on a numbered network "port" for a connection. The standard way of making a socket is to supply a hostname and port as follows:

```
Socket client = new Socket("hostname", portNumber);
```

If you only have an IP address (e.g., 198.4.155.21), you can turn it into an `InetAddress` object by calling `getByName`, then pass that to the `Socket` constructor:

```
InetAddress address =
  InetAddress.getByName("IP Address");
Socket client = new Socket(address, portNumber)
```

If you are already familiar with network programming, note that this creates a connection-oriented socket. Java also supports connectionless (UDP) sockets. In Java 1.02, add a third argument of `true` to the `Socket` constructors; in Java 1.1 use the `DatagramSocket` constructor.

Create an output stream that can be used to send info to the Socket

Java does not have separate methods to send data to files, sockets, and standard output. Instead, it starts with different underlying objects, then layers standard output streams on top of them. So any variety of `OutputStream` available for files is also available for sockets. In Java 1.0, a common one is `PrintStream`, the stream type of `System.out`. This lets you use `print` and `println` on the socket in exactly the same way as you would print to the screen. The `PrintStream` constructor takes a generic `OutputStream` as an argument, which you can obtain from the `Socket` via `getOutputStream`. Here's an example:

```
PrintStream out =
   new PrintStream(client.getOutputStream());
```

In Java 1.1, you would use `PrintWriter` instead. This gives you everything `PrintStream` does, but has better Unicode support.

```
PrintWriter out =
   new PrintWriter(client.getOutputStream());
```

Java 1.1 also lets you use `ObjectOutputStream` to send complex Java objects over the network to be reassembled at the other end. An `ObjectOutputStream` connected to the network is used in exactly the same way as one connected to a file; simply use `writeObject` to send a serializable object and all serializable objects it references. The server on the other end would use an `ObjectInputStream`'s `readObject` method to reassemble it. Note that all AWT components are automatically serializable, and making other objects serializable is a simple matter of declaring that they implement the `Serializable` interface. See Section 11.10 (Serializing Windows) for more details and an example. Also see Section 15.8 (RMI: Remote Method Invocation) for a high-level interface that uses serialization to let you distribute Java objects across networks.

Create an input stream to read the response from the server

Once you send data to the server, you will want to read the server's response. Again, there is no socket-specific way of doing this; you use a standard input stream layered on top of the socket. The most common one is `DataInputStream`; its constructor takes a generic `Input-Stream`. Here is a sample:

```
DataInputStream in =
    new DataInputStream(client.getInputStream());
```

Although this is the simplest approach, in most cases it is better to put a `BufferedInputStream` between the socket's generic `Input-Stream` and the `DataInputStream`. This causes Java to read the data in blocks behind the scenes, rather than reading the underlying stream every time the user performs a read. This usually results in significantly improved performance at the cost of a small increase in memory usage (the buffer size, which defaults to 512 bytes). Here's the idea:

```
BufferedInputStream buffered =
    new BufferedInputStream(client.getInputStream());
DataInputStream in = new DataInputStream(buffered);
```

Core Performance Tip

If you are going to read from a socket multiple times, a buffered input stream can speed things up considerably.

In a few cases, you might want to send data to a server but not read anything back. You could imagine a simple e-mail client working this way. In that case, you can skip this step. In other cases, you might want to read data without sending anything first. For instance, you might connect to a network "clock" to read the time. In such a case, you would skip the output stream and just follow this step. In most cases, however, you will want to both send and receive data, so will follow both steps. Also, if you are using Java 1.1 and the server is sending complex Java objects, you will want to open an `ObjectInputStream` and use `readObject` to receive data.

Do I/O with input and output streams

A `PrintStream` has `print` and `println` methods that let you send a single primitive value, `String`, or `Object` over the network. Most likely you are already familiar with these methods, since `System.out` is in fact an instance of `PrintStream`. `PrintStream` also inherits some simple `write` methods from `OutputStream`. These let you send all or part of a `byte` array; see the on-line API for details.

`DataInputStream` has two particularly useful methods: `readChar` and `readLine`. The `readChar` method returns a single `char`; `readLine` returns a `String`. Both of these methods are *blocking*; they do not return until data is available. Because `readLine` will wait if it does not get a carriage return or an EOF (the server closed the connection), it should be used only when you are sure the server will close the socket when done transmitting or when you know the number of lines that will be sent by the server. **It returns** `null` **if there was an** EOF. `DataInputStream` also has a `read` method that will read a single byte or fill in a byte array. This lets you read a large chunk of data in one fell swoop. The `read` method blocks until at least one byte of data is available. It specifies the actual number of bytes read as its return value. If you know how much data will be sent, you can use `read-Fully`, which fills in a byte array, blocking until *all* of the data is available. Also note that there are two `String` constructors that convert byte arrays to strings, as follows:

```
String fullString = new String(byteArray, 0);
String partialString =
  new String(byteArray, 0, startIndex, numBytes);
```

Close the socket when done

When you are done, close the socket using the `close` method:

```
client.close();
```

This closes the associated input and output streams as well.

Example: A Generic Network Client

Listing 15.1 illustrates the approach outlined in the preceding section. Processing starts with the `connect` method, which initiates the connection, then passes the socket to `handleConnection` to do the actual communication. This version of `handleConnection` simply reports who it connected to, sends a single line to the server ("`Generic  Network Client`"), reads and prints a single response line, and exits. "Real" clients would override `handleConnection` to implement their desired behavior.

Listing 15.1   `NetworkClient.java`

```java
import java.net.*;
import java.io.*;

/** A starting point for network clients. You'll need to
 *  override handleConnection, but in many cases
 *  connect can remain unchanged. It uses
 *  SocketUtil to simplify the creation of the
 *  PrintStream and DataInputStream.
 * @see SocketUtil
 */

public class NetworkClient {
  protected String host;
  protected int port;

  //-----------------------------------------------------
  /** Register host and port. The connection won't
   *  actually be established until you call
   *  connect.
   *
   * @see #connect
   */

  public NetworkClient(String host, int port) {
    this.host = host;
    this.port = port;
  }

  //-----------------------------------------------------
  /** Establishes the connection, then passes the socket
   *  to handleConnection.
   *
   * @see #handleConnection
   */

  public void connect() {
    try {
      Socket client = new Socket(host, port);
      handleConnection(client);
    } catch(UnknownHostException uhe) {
      System.out.println("Unknown host: " + host);
      uhe.printStackTrace();
    } catch(IOException ioe) {
      System.out.println("IOException: " + ioe);
      ioe.printStackTrace();
    }
  }
```

Listing 15.1 `NetworkClient.java` (continued)

```
//-------------------------------------------------------
/** This is the method you will override when
 *  making a network client for your task.
 *  The default version sends a single line
 *  ("Generic Network Client") to the server,
 *  reads one line of response, prints it, then exits.
 */

protected void handleConnection(Socket client)
    throws IOException {
  SocketUtil s = new SocketUtil(client);
  PrintStream out = s.getPrintStream();
  DataInputStream in = s.getDataStream();
  out.println("Generic Network Client");
  System.out.println
    ("Generic Network Client:\n" +
     "Made connection to " + host +
     " and got '" + in.readLine() + "' in response");
  client.close();
}

//-------------------------------------------------------
/** The hostname of the server we're contacting. */

public String getHost() {
  return(host);
}

/** The port connection will be made on. */

public int getPort() {
  return(port);
}

//-------------------------------------------------------
}
```

The `SocketUtil` class is just a simple interface to the `DataInput-Stream` and `PrintStream` constructors, and is given in Listing 15.2.

Listing 15.2   `SocketUtil.java`

```java
import java.net.*;
import java.io.*;

/** A shorthand way to create PrintStreams and
 *  buffered/unbuffered DataInputStreams associated
 *  with a socket.
 */

public class SocketUtil {
  private Socket s;

  public SocketUtil(Socket s) {
    this.s = s;
  }

  public DataInputStream getDataStream()
      throws IOException {
    return(new DataInputStream(
               new BufferedInputStream(
                   s.getInputStream())));
  }

  public DataInputStream getUnbufferedDataStream()
      throws IOException {
    return(new DataInputStream(s.getInputStream()));
  }

  public PrintStream getPrintStream()
      throws IOException {
    return(new PrintStream(s.getOutputStream()));
  }
}
```

Finally, the `NetworkClientTest` class, shown in Listing 15.3, provides a way to use the `NetworkClient` class with any hostname and any port.

Listing 15.3   `NetworkClientTest.java`

```java
/** Make simple connection to host and port specified. */

public class NetworkClientTest {
  public static void main(String[] args) {
    String host = "localhost";
    if (args.length > 0)
      host = args[0];
    int port = 5555;
    if (args.length > 1)
      port = Integer.parseInt(args[1]);
    NetworkClient nwClient
      = new NetworkClient(host, port);
    nwClient.connect();
  }
}
```

Output: Connecting to an FTP server

Let's use the test program in Listing 15.3 to connect to Netscape's public FTP server, which listens on port 21. Assume "> " is the DOS or Unix prompt.

```
> java NetworkClientTest ftp.netscape.com 21
Generic Network Client:
Made connection to ftp.netscape.com and got '220
ftp26 FTP server (UNIX(r) System V Release 4.0)
ready.' in response
```

15.2 Parsing Strings Using StringTokenizer

A common task when doing network programming is to break a large string down into various constituents. A developer could do this using low-level `String` methods such as `indexOf`, and `substring` to return substrings bounded by certain delimiters. However, Java has a built-in class to simplify this process: the `StringTokenizer` class. This class isn't specific to network programming (it's in `java.util`, not `java.net`), but because string processing tends to be a large part of client-server programming, I will discuss it here.

The java.util.StringTokenizer Class

The idea is that you build a tokenizer from an initial string, then retrieve tokens one at a time via `nextToken` either based on a set of delimiters defined when the tokenizer was created, or as an optional argument to `nextToken`. You can also see how many tokens are remaining (`countTokens`) or simply test if the number of tokens remaining is nonzero (`hasMoreTokens`). The most common methods are summarized as follows.

Constructors

public StringTokenizer(String input)
This builds a tokenizer from the input string using whitespace (space, tab, newline, return) as the set of delimiters. The delimiters will not be included as part of the tokens returned.

public StringTokenizer(String input, String delimiters)
This creates a tokenizer from the input string using the specified delimiters. The delimiters will not be included as part of the tokens returned.

public StringTokenizer(String input, String delimiters, boolean includeDelimiters)
This constructor builds a tokenizer from the input string using the specified delimiters. The delimiters *will* be included as part of the tokens returned if the third argument is `true`.

Methods

public String nextToken()
This returns the next token. It throws a `NoSuchElementException` if there are no characters or only delimiter characters remaining.

public String nextToken(String delimiters)
This changes the set of delimiters, then returns the next token. It throws a `NoSuchElementException` if there are no characters or only delimiter characters remaining.

public int countTokens()
This returns the number of tokens remaining based on the current set of delimiters.

public boolean hasMoreTokens()
This determines whether there are any tokens remaining based on the
current set of delimiters. Most applications should either check this
before calling nextToken, or catch a NoSuchElementException
when calling nextToken. Note that hasMoreTokens has the side
effect of advancing the internal counter, which yields unexpected
results when doing the rare but possible sequence of checking has-
MoreTokens with one delimiter set, then calling nextToken with
another delimiter set.

Example: Interactive Tokenizer

A good way to get a feel for how StringTokenizer works is to try a bunch
of test cases. Listing 15.4 gives a simple class that lets you enter an input
string and a set of delimiters on the command line and prints the resultant
tokens one to a line.

Listing 15.4   TokTest.java

```java
import java.util.StringTokenizer;

/** Prints the tokens resulting from treating the first
 *  command-line argument as the string to be tokenized
 *  and the second as the delimiter set.
 */

public class TokTest {
  public static void main(String[] args) {
    if (args.length == 2) {
      String input = args[0], delimiters = args[1];
      StringTokenizer tok
        = new StringTokenizer(input, delimiters);
      while (tok.hasMoreTokens())
        System.out.println(tok.nextToken());
    } else
      System.out.println
        ("Usage: java TokTest string delimiters");
  }
}
```

Here is TokTest in action:

```
> java TokTest http://www.microsoft.com/~gates/ :/.
http
www
microsoft
com
~gates
> java TokTest "if (tok.hasMoreTokens()) {" "(){. "
if
tok
hasMoreTokens
```

15.3   Example: A Client to Verify E-Mail Addresses

Next, let's make a network client that will talk to a mail server to verify the correctness of potential e-mail addresses. To do this, we need to know that SMTP (Simple Mail Transfer Protocol) servers generally listen on port 25, send one or more lines of data after receiving a connection, accept commands of the form "expn *username*" to expand usernames, and use "quit" as the command to terminate the connection. Commands are case insensitive. For instance, Listing 15.5 shows an interaction with the mail server at apl.jhu.edu.

Listing 15.5   Talking to a Mail Server

```
> telnet apl.jhu.edu 25
Trying 128.220.101.100 ...
Connected to apl.jhu.edu.
Escape character is '^]'.
220 aplcenmp.apl.jhu.edu Sendmail SMI-8.6/SMI-SVR4 ready at
Fri, 2 May 1997 15:19:34 -0400
expn hall
250 Marty Hall <hall@aplcenmp.apl.jhu.edu>
quit
221 aplcenmp.apl.jhu.edu closing connection
Connection closed by foreign host.
```

For a network client to verify an e-mail address, it needs to break it up into username and hostname sections, connect to port 25 of the host, read the initial connection message, send an `expn` on the username, read and print the result, then send a `quit`. However, unlike with the `UriRetriever`, the client cannot safely call `readLine` a fixed number of times. This is because there is no guarantee that the responses from the server will consist of only one line. Because `readLine` blocks if the connection is still open but no line of data has been sent, we cannot call `readLine` more than once. So rather than using `readLine` at all, we use `read` to populate a byte array large enough to hold the likely response, record how many bytes were read, then use `write` to print out that number of bytes. This process is shown in Listing 15.6, with Listing 15.7 showing the helper class that breaks an e-mail address into separate username and hostname components.

Listing 15.6   `AddressVerifier.java`

```
import java.net.*;
import java.io.*;

/** Given an email address of the form user@host,
 *  connect to port 25 of the host and issue an
 *  'expn' request for the user. Print the results.
 */

public class AddressVerifier extends NetworkClient {
  private String username;

  public static void main(String[] args) {
    if (args.length != 1)
      usage();
    MailAddress address = new MailAddress(args[0]);
    AddressVerifier verifier
      = new AddressVerifier(address.getUsername(),
                            address.getHostname(),
                            25);
    verifier.connect();
  }

  public AddressVerifier(String username,
                         String hostname,
                         int port) {
    super(hostname, port);
    this.username = username;
  }
```

continued

Listing 15.6 `AddressVerifier.java` (continued)

```java
protected void handleConnection(Socket client) {
  try {
    SocketUtil s = new SocketUtil(client);
    PrintStream out = s.getPrintStream();
    InputStream in = client.getInputStream();
    byte[] response = new byte[1000];
    in.read(response);
    out.println("EXPN " + username);
    int numBytes = in.read(response);
    System.out.write(response, 0, numBytes);
    out.println("QUIT");
    client.close();
  } catch(IOException ioe) {
    System.out.println("Couldn't make connection: "
                        + ioe);
  }
}

public static void usage() {
  System.out.println
    ("You must supply an email address " +
     "of the form 'username@hostname'.");
  System.exit(-1);
}
}
```

Listing 15.7   `MailAddress.java`

```java
import java.util.*;

/** Takes a string of the form "user@host" and
 *  separates it into the "user" and "host" parts.
 */

public class MailAddress {
  private String username, hostname;

  public MailAddress(String emailAddress) {
    StringTokenizer tokenizer
      = new StringTokenizer(emailAddress, "@");
    this.username = getArg(tokenizer);
    this.hostname = getArg(tokenizer);
  }

  private static String getArg(StringTokenizer tok) {
    try { return(tok.nextToken()); }
    catch (NoSuchElementException nsee) {
      System.out.println("Illegal email address");
      System.exit(-1);
      return(null);
    }
  }

  public String getUsername() {
    return(username);
  }

  public String getHostname() {
    return(hostname);
  }
}
```

Finally, here is an example of the address verifier in action, looking for the addresses of the main originators of the WWW and Java.

```
> java AddressVerifier tbl@w3.org
250 <timbl@hq.lcs.mit.edu>
> java AddressVerifier timbl@hq.lcs.mit.edu
250 Tim Berners-Lee <timbl>
> java AddressVerifier gosling@mail.javasoft.com
550 gosling... User unknown
```

15.4 Example: A Network Client That Retrieves URLs

Retrieving a document via HTTP is remarkably simple. You open a connection to the HTTP port of the machine hosting the page, send the string "GET" followed by the address of the document, followed by the string "HTTP/1.0", followed by a blank line. You then read the result a line at a time. Reading a line at a time was not safe with the mail client of Section 15.3, because the server sent an indeterminate number of lines but kept the connection open. Here, however, it is safe because the server closes the connection when done, yielding null as the return value of readLine. Although quite simple, even this is slightly harder than necessary, because Java has built-in classes (URL and URLConnection) that simplify the process even further. These classes will be demonstrated in Section 15.5, but doing it "by hand" is a useful exercise to prepare yourself for dealing with protocols that don't have built-in helping methods as well as to gain familiarity with the HTTP protocol. For instance, a link validator is an important class of network program that verifies that the links in a specified Web page point to "live" documents. Writing such a program in Java is relatively straightforward, but to limit load on your servers you probably want it to use HEAD instead of GET (see Section 16.3, "HTTP Request Headers"). Java has no helping class for this, but it is only a trivial change in the following code.

A Class to Retrieve a Given URI from a Given Host

Listing 15.8 presents a class that retrieves a file given the host, port, and URI (the filename part of the URL) as separate arguments. It uses the Network-Client shown earlier in Listing 15.1 to send a single GET line to the specified host and port, then reads the result a line at a time, printing each line to the standard output.

Listing 15.8   `UriRetriever.java`

```java
import java.net.*;
import java.io.*;

/** Retrieve a URL given the host, port, and file
 *  as three separate command-line arguments.
 * @see SocketUtil
 */

public class UriRetriever extends NetworkClient {
  private String uri;

  public static void main(String[] args) {
    UriRetriever uriClient
      = new UriRetriever(args[0],
                         Integer.parseInt(args[1]),
                         args[2]);
    uriClient.connect();
  }

  public UriRetriever(String host, int port,
                      String uri) {
    super(host, port);
    this.uri = uri;
  }

  /** Send one GET line, then read the results
   *  one line at a time, printing each to
   *  standard output.
   */

  protected void handleConnection(Socket uriSocket)
      throws IOException {
    SocketUtil s = new SocketUtil(uriSocket);
    PrintStream out = s.getPrintStream();
    DataInputStream in = s.getDataStream();
    out.println("GET " + uri + " HTTP/1.0\n");
    String line;
    while ((line = in.readLine()) != null)
      System.out.println("> " + line);
  }
}
```

A Class to Retrieve a Given URL

The previous program requires the user to pass the hostname, port, and URI as three separate command-line arguments. Listing 15.9 improves on this by making a front end that parses a whole URL using `StringTokenizer` (Section 15.2) then passes the appropriate pieces to the `UriRetriever`.

Listing 15.9 `UrlRetriever.java`

```java
import java.util.*;

/** This parses the input to get a host, port,
 *  and file, then passes these three values to
 *  the UriRetriever class to grab the URL
 *  from the Web.
 */

public class UrlRetriever {
  public static void main(String[] args) {
    checkUsage(args);
    StringTokenizer tok = new StringTokenizer(args[0]);
    String protocol = tok.nextToken(":");
    checkProtocol(protocol);
    String host = tok.nextToken(":/");
    String uri;
    int port = 80;
    try {
      uri = tok.nextToken("");
      if (uri.charAt(0) == ':') {
        tok = new StringTokenizer(uri);
        port = Integer.parseInt(tok.nextToken(":/"));
        uri = tok.nextToken("");
      }
    } catch(NoSuchElementException nsee) {
      uri = "/";
    }
    UriRetriever uriClient
      = new UriRetriever(host, port, uri);
    uriClient.connect();
  }

  // Warn user if they forgot the URL
```

Listing 15.9   `UrlRetriever.java` (continued)

```
private static void checkUsage(String[] args) {
  if (args.length != 1) {
    System.out.println("Usage: UrlRetriever <URL>");
    System.exit(-1);
  }
}

// This can only handle HTTP.

private static void checkProtocol(String protocol) {
  if (!protocol.equals("http")) {
    System.out.println("Don't understand protocol "
                       + protocol);
    System.exit(-1);
  }
}
}
```

UrlRetriever Output

No explicit port number:

Prompt> **java UrlRetriever**
http://www.microsoft.com/netscape-beats-ie.html
> HTTP/1.0 404 Object Not Found
> Content-Type: text/html
>
> <body><h1>HTTP/1.0 404 Object Not Found
> </h1></body>

Explicit port number:

Prompt> **java UrlRetriever**
http://home.netscape.com:80/ie-beats-netscape.html
> HTTP/1.0 404 Not found
> Server: Netscape-Enterprise/2.01
> Date: Wed, 12 Mar 1997 21:17:50 GMT
> Content-length: 207
> Content-type: text/html
>
> <TITLE>Not Found</TITLE><H1>Not Found</H1> The
requested object does not exist on this server. The
link you followed is either outdated, inaccurate, or
the server has been instructed not to let you have it.

Hey! We just wrote a browser. OK, not quite, seeing as there is still the small matter of formatting the result. Still, not bad for two pages of code. We'll add a very simple graphical user interface in Chapter 16, " The Hyper-Text Transfer Protocol." Section 15.7 will show how to build an equally simple HTTP server.

DILBERT© United Features Syndicate. Reprinted with permission.

15.5   The URL Class

The URL class provides simple access to URLs. It automatically parses a string for you, letting you retrieve the protocol (e.g., "http"), host (e.g., "java.sun.com"), port (e.g., 80) and filename (e.g., "/reports/earnings.html") separately. It also provides an easy to use interface for reading remote files.

Reading from a URL

Although writing a client to explicitly connect to an HTTP server and retrieve a URL was quite simple, it is such a common task that Java provides a helper class for this: `java.net.URL`. We saw this class when looking at applets (see Section 9.5, "Other Applet Methods"); it was an object of this type that needed to be passed to `getAppletContext().showDocument`. However, it can also be used to parse a string representing a URL and reading the contents. An example of this is shown in Listing 15.10. Note the use of a

BufferedInputStream instead of a normal InputStream. This can speed up some connections by a factor of three or more.

Listing 15.10 UrlRetriever2.java

```java
import java.net.*;
import java.io.*;

/** Read a remote file using the standard URL class
 *  instead of connecting explicitly to the HTTP server.
 */

public class UrlRetriever2 {
  public static void main(String[] args) {
    checkUsage(args);
    try {
      URL url = new URL(args[0]);
      BufferedInputStream buffer =
        new BufferedInputStream(url.openStream());
      DataInputStream in =
        new DataInputStream(buffer);
      String line;
      while ((line = in.readLine()) != null)
        System.out.println("> " + line);
      in.close();
    } catch(MalformedURLException mue) { // URL c'tor
      System.out.println(args[0] + "is an invalid URL: "
                         + mue);
    } catch(IOException ioe) { // Stream constructors
      System.out.println("IOException: " + ioe);
    }
  }

  private static void checkUsage(String[] args) {
    if (args.length != 1) {
      System.out.println("Usage: UrlRetriever2 <URL>");
      System.exit(-1);
    }
  }
}
```

Here is the `UrlRetriever2` in action:

```
Prompt> java UrlRetriever2 http://www.white-
house.gov/
> <HTML>
> <HEAD>
> <TITLE>Welcome To The White House</TITLE>
> </HEAD>
> ... Remainder of HTML document omitted ...
> </HTML>
```

This implementation just prints out the resultant document, not the HTTP response lines included in the original "raw" `UrlRetriever` class. However, Java has another class called `URLConnection` that will supply this information. Create a `URLConnection` object by calling the `openConnection` method of an existing `URL`, then use methods such as `getContentType` and `getLastModified` to retrieve the response header information. See the on-line API for `java.net.URLConnection` for more details.

Other Useful Methods of the URL Class

The most valuable use of a `URL` object is to use the constructor to parse a string representation and then to use `openStream` to provide an `InputStream` for reading. However, it is useful in a number of other ways, as outlined in the following sections.

public URL(String absoluteSpec)
public URL(URL base, String relativeSpec)
public URL(String protocol, String host, String file)
public URL(String protocol, String host, int port, String file)

These four constructors build a `URL` in different ways. All throw a `MalformedURLException`.

public String getFile()
This returns the filename part of the URL. See the output following Listing 15.11.

public String getHost()
This returns the hostname part of the URL. See the output following Listing 15.11.

public int getPort()
This returns the port, if one was explicitly specified. If not, it returns –1 (*not* 80). See the output following Listing 15.11.

public String getProtocol()
This returns the protocol part of the URL. See the output following Listing 15.11.

public String getRef()
Returns the "reference" (i.e., section heading) part of the URL. See the output following Listing 15.11.

public final InputStream openStream()
This returns the input stream that can be used for reading, as used in the UrlRetriever2 class. Throws an IOException.

public URLConnection openConnection()
This method yields a URLConnection that can be used to retrieve header lines and (for POST requests) supply data to the HTTP server. See Chapter 17 (CGI Programming and Beyond—The Client Side) for an example. The POST method is discussed in Chapter 16 (The Hyper-Text Transfer Protocol).

public String toExternalForm()
This gives the string representation of the URL, useful for printouts. It is identical to toString.

Listing 15.11 gives an example of some of these methods.

Listing 15.11 `UrlTest.java`

```java
import java.net.*;

/** Read a URL from the command line, then print
 *  the various components.
 */

public class UrlTest {
  public static void main(String[] args) {
    if (args.length == 1) {
      try {
        URL url = new URL(args[0]);
        System.out.println
          ("URL: " + url.toExternalForm() + "\n" +
          "  File:      " + url.getFile() + "\n" +
          "  Host:      " + url.getHost() + "\n" +
          "  Port:      " + url.getPort() + "\n" +
          "  Protocol:  " + url.getProtocol() + "\n" +
          "  Reference: " + url.getRef());
      } catch(MalformedURLException mue) {
        System.out.println("Bad URL.");
      }
    } else
      System.out.println("Usage: UrlTest <URL>");
  }
}
```

Here's `UrlTest` in action:

```
> java UrlTest http://www.irs.gov/mission/#squeez-
ing-them-dry
URL: http://www.irs.gov/mission/#squeezing-them-dry
  File:      /mission/
  Host:      www.irs.gov
  Port:      -1
  Protocol:  http
  Reference: squeezing-them-dry
```

15.6 Implementing a Server

The server is the program that starts first and waits for incoming connections. Implementing a server consists of six basic steps:

1. Create a SocketServer object
2. Create a Socket object from the ServerSocket
3. Create an input stream to read input from the client
4. Create an output stream that can be used to send info back to the client
5. Do I/O with input and output streams
6. Close the socket when done

Each of these steps is described in more detail in the following sections. As with the client, note that most of the methods described throw an `IOException`, so need to be wrapped inside a `try/catch` block in an actual implementation.

Create a SocketServer object

With a client socket, you actively go out and connect to a particular system. With a server, however, you more passively sit and wait for someone to come to you. So creation requires a port number but not a host, as follows:

```
ServerSocket listenSocket =
  new ServerSocket(portNumber);
```

On Unix, if you are a nonprivileged user, this port number *must* be greater than 1023 (lower numbers are reserved), and *should* be greater than 5000 (numbers from 1024 to 5000 are more likely to already be in use). In addition, you should check `/etc/services` to make sure it doesn't conflict with any other port number. If you try to listen on a socket that is already in use, an `IOException` will be thrown.

Create a Socket object from the ServerSocket

Many servers will allow multiple connections, continuing to accept connections until some termination condition is reached. The `ServerSocket` accept method blocks until a connection is established, then returns a normal `Socket` object. Here is the basic idea:

```
while(someCondition) {
  Socket server = listenSocket.accept();
  doSomethingWith(server);
}
```

If you want to allow multiple simultaneous connections to the socket, you will want to pass this socket to a separate thread to create the input/output streams. I'll give an example of this in the next section.

Create an input stream to read input from the client

Once you have a `Socket`, you can use it in the same way as with the client code shown in Section 15.1. The example here shows the creation of an input stream before an output stream, assuming that most servers will read data before transmitting a reply. You can switch the order of this step and the next if you send data before reading, and even omit this step if your server only transmits information. As shown in the client section, one of the most common input streams is `DataInput-Stream`, which you create as follows:

```
DataInputStream in =
  new DataInputStream(server.getInputStream());
```

As was also discussed in the client section, it is often more efficient to use a `BufferedInputStream` underneath the `DataInput-Stream`, as follows:

```
BufferedInputStream buffered =
  new BufferedInputStream(client.getInputStream());
DataInputStream in = new DataInputStream(buffered);
```

Java 1.1 also lets you use `ObjectInputStream` to receive complex objects from another Java program. An `ObjectInputStream` connected to the network is used in exactly the same way as one connected to a file; simply use `readObject` and cast the result to the appropriate type. See Section 11.10 (Serializing Windows) for more details and an example. Also see Section 15.8 (RMI: Remote Method Invocation) for a high-level interface that uses serialization to let you distribute Java objects across networks.

Create an output stream that can be used to send info back to the client

You can use a generic `OutputStream` if you want to send binary data. If you want to use the familiar `print` and `println` commands, create a `PrintStream` (Java 1.0) or `PrintWriter` (Java 1.1). Here is an example of creating a `PrintStream`:

```
PrintStream out =
    new PrintStream(server.getOutputStream());
```

In Java 1.1, you can use an `ObjectOutputStream` if the client is written in Java and is expecting complex Java objects.

Do I/O with input and output streams

The `DataInputStream` and `PrintStream` (or `PrintWriter`) can be used in the same ways as discussed in the client section earlier in this chapter. `DataInputStream` has `read` and `readFully` methods for reading a single byte or a byte array, and `readChar` and `read-Line` for reading characters or strings. Use `print` and `println` for sending high-level data via a `PrintStream` or `PrintWriter`, `write` to send a byte or byte array.

Close the socket when done

When finished, close the socket:

```
server.close();
```

This closes the associated input and output streams, but does *not* terminate any loop that listens for additional incoming connections.

Example: A Generic Network Server

Listing 15.12 gives an sample implementation of the approach outlined in Section 15.6. Processing starts with the `listen` method, which waits until it gets a connection, then passes the socket to `handleConnection` to do the actual communication. "Real" servers might have `handleConnection` operate in a separate thread to allow multiple simultaneous connections, but even if not they would override it to provide the server with their desired behavior. The generic version of `handleConnection` simply reports the hostname of the system that made the connection, shows the first line of input received from the client, sends a single line to the client ("Generic Network Server"), then closes the connection.

Listing 15.12 `NetworkServer.java`

```java
import java.net.*;
import java.io.*;

/** A starting point for network servers. You'll need to
 *  override handleConnection, but in many cases
 *  listen can remain unchanged. It uses
 *  SocketUtil to simplify the creation of the
 *  PrintStream and DataInputStream.
 * @see SocketUtil
 */

public class NetworkServer {
  protected int port, maxConnections;

  //-------------------------------------------------------
  /** Build a server on specified port. It will continue
   *  to accept connections (passing each to
   *  handleConnection) until an explicit exit
   *  command is sent (e.g. System.exit) or the
   *  maximum number of connections is reached. Specify
   *  0 for maxConnections if you want the server
   *  to run indefinitely.
   */

  public NetworkServer(int port, int maxConnections) {
    this.port = port;
    this.maxConnections = maxConnections;
  }

  //-------------------------------------------------------
  /** Monitor a port for connections. Each time one
   *  is established, pass resulting Socket to
   *  handleConnection.
   */

  public void listen() {
    int i=0;
    try {
      ServerSocket listener = new ServerSocket(port);
      Socket server;
      while((i++ < maxConnections) ||
            (maxConnections == 0)) {
        server = listener.accept();
        handleConnection(server);
      }
    } catch (IOException ioe) {
      System.out.println("IOException: " + ioe);
      ioe.printStackTrace();
    }
  }
```

Listing 15.12 `NetworkServer.java` (continued)

```
//-----------------------------------------------------
/** This is the method that provides the behavior
 *   to the server, since it determines what is
 *   done with the resulting socket. <B>Override this
 *   method in servers you write.</B>
 *   <P>
 *   This generic version simply reports the host
 *   that made the connection, shows the first line
 *   the client sent, and sends a single line
 *   in response.
 */

protected void handleConnection(Socket server)
    throws IOException{
  SocketUtil s = new SocketUtil(server);
  DataInputStream in = s.getDataStream();
  PrintStream out = s.getPrintStream();
  System.out.println
    ("Generic Network Server:\n" +
     "got connection from " +
     server.getInetAddress().getHostName() + "\n" +
     "with first line '" +
     in.readLine() + "'");
  out.println("Generic Network Server");
  server.close();
}
}
```

Finally, the `NetworkServerTest` class provides a way to invoke the `NetworkServer` class on a specified port.

Listing 15.13 `NetworkServerTest.java`

```
public class NetworkServerTest {
  public static void main(String[] args) {
    int port = 5555;
    if (args.length > 0)
      port = Integer.parseInt(args[0]);
    NetworkServer nwServer = new NetworkServer(port, 1);
    nwServer.listen();
  }
}
```

Output: Accepting a Connection from a WWW Browser

Suppose the test program in Listing 15.13 is started up on port 5555 of system1.com:

```
system1> java NetworkServerTest
```

Then, a standard Web browser (Netscape Navigator in this case) on system2.com requests http://system1.com:5555/foo/:, yielding the following back on system1.com:

```
Generic Network Server:
got connection from system2.com
with first line 'GET /foo/ HTTP/1.0'
```

Connecting NetworkClient and NetworkServer Together

OK, we showed the NetworkClient and NetworkServer classes tested separately, with the client talking to a standard FTP server and the server talking to a standard Web browser. However, we can also connect them to each other. No changes in the source code are required; simply specify the appropriate hostnames and port. The test server is started on port 6666 of system1.com, then the client on system2.com, yielding the following results:

Time t_0, system1:

```
system1> java NetworkServerTest 6666
```

Time t_1, system2:

```
system2> java NetworkClientTest system1.com 6666
```

Time t_2, system1:

```
Generic Network Server:
got connection from system2.com
with first line 'Generic Network Client'
```

Time t_3, system2:

```
Generic Network Client:
Made connection to system1.com and got 'Generic Net-
work Server' in response
```

15.7 Example: A Simple HTTP Server

Let's adapt the `NetworkServer` class to act as an HTTP server. Rather than returning files, however, we will have it simply echo back the input that it receives by storing all of the input lines, then transmitting an HTML file that shows them. Although it seems a bit odd to be writing programs that output HTML, in Chapters 18 "CGI Programming and Beyond—The Server Side" and 19 "JavaScript: Adding Dynamic Content to Web Pages" you'll see that this is actually common practice. Furthermore, having a program that can act as an HTTP server but returns a Web page showing the input it received is a useful debugging tool when working with HTTP clients and CGI programming. You'll see this class used many times in the HTTP and CGI chapters.

Listing 15.14 `EchoServer.java`

```java
import java.net.*;
import java.io.*;
import java.util.StringTokenizer;

/** A simple HTTP server that generates a Web page
 *  showing all of the data that it received from
 *  the Web client (usually a browser). To use this,
 *  start it on the system of your choice, supplying
 *  a port number if you want something other than
 *  port 5555. Call this system server.com. Next,
 *  start a Web browser on the same or a different
 *  system, and connect to
 *  http://server.com:5555/whatever. The resultant
 *  Web page will show the data that your browser
 *  sent. For CGI programming, specify
 *  http://server.com:5555/whatever as the
 *  ACTION of your CGI form. You can send GET
 *  or POST data; either way the resultant page
 *  will show what your browser sent.
 */

public class EchoServer extends NetworkServer {
  protected int maxInputLines = 25;
  protected String serverName = "EchoServer 1.0";     continued
```

Listing 15.14 `EchoServer.java` (continued)

```java
//-------------------------------------------------------
/** Supply a port number as a command-line
 *  argument. Otherwise port 5555 will be used.
 */

public static void main(String[] args) {
  int port = 5555;
  if (args.length > 0)
    port = Integer.parseInt(args[0]);
  EchoServer echoServer = new EchoServer(port, 0);
  echoServer.listen();
}

public EchoServer(int port, int maxConnections) {
  super(port, maxConnections);
}

//-------------------------------------------------------
/** Overrides the NetworkServer handleConnection
 *  to read each line of data received, save it
 *  into an array of strings, then send it
 *  back embedded inside a PRE element in an
 *  HTML page.
 */

public void handleConnection(Socket server)
    throws IOException{
  System.out.println
      (serverName + ": got connection from " +
       server.getInetAddress().getHostName());
    SocketUtil s = new SocketUtil(server);
  DataInputStream in = s.getDataStream();
  PrintStream out = s.getPrintStream();
  String[] inputLines = new String[maxInputLines];
  int i;
  for (i=0; i<maxInputLines; i++) {
    inputLines[i] = in.readLine();
    if (inputLines[i] == null)
      break;
    if (inputLines[i].length() == 0) {
      if (usingPost(inputLines)) {
        readPostData(inputLines, i, in);
        i = i + 2;
      }
      break;
    }
  }
}
```

Listing 15.14 EchoServer.java (continued)

```java
    printHeader(out);
    for (int j=0; j<i; j++)
      out.println(inputLines[j]);
    printTrailer(out);
    server.close();
  }
  //---------------------------------------------------
  // Print top of a "standard" Web page.

  private void printHeader(PrintStream stream) {
    stream.println
      ("HTTP/1.0 200 Document follows\r\n" +
       "Server: " + serverName + "\r\n" +
       "Content-Type: text/html\r\n" +
       "\r\n" +
       "<!DOCTYPE HTML PUBLIC " +
                 "\"-//W3C//DTD HTML 3.2//EN\">\n" +
       "<HTML>\n" +
       "<HEAD>\n" +
       "  <TITLE>" + serverName + " Results</TITLE>\n" +
       "</HEAD>\n" +
       "\n" +
       "<BODY>\n" +
       "<H1>" + serverName + " Results</H1>\n" +
       "Here is the request line and request headers\n" +
       "sent by your browser:\n" +
       "<PRE>");
  }

  //---------------------------------------------------
  // Print bottom of a "standard" Web page.

  private void printTrailer(PrintStream stream) {
    stream.println
      ("</PRE>\n" +
       "</BODY>\n" +
       "</HTML>\n");
  }

  //---------------------------------------------------
  // Normal Web page requests use GET, so this
  // server can simply read a line at a time.
  // However, CGI programs can use POST, in which
  // case we have to determine the number of POST bytes
  // that are sent so we know how much extra data
  // to read after the standard HTTP headers.
```

continued

Listing 15.14 `EchoServer.java` (continued)

```java
private boolean usingPost(String[] inputs) {
  return(inputs[0].toUpperCase().startsWith("POST"));
}

private void readPostData(String[] inputs, int i,
                          DataInputStream in)
    throws IOException {
  int contentLength = contentLength(inputs);
  byte[] postData = new byte[contentLength];
  in.read(postData);
  inputs[++i] = new String(postData, 0);
}

//-----------------------------------------------------
// Given a line that starts with CONTENT-LENGTH,
// this returns the integer value specified.

private int contentLength(String[] inputs) {
  String input;
  for (int i=0; i<inputs.length; i++) {
    if (inputs[i].length() == 0)
      break;
    input = inputs[i].toUpperCase();
    if (input.startsWith("CONTENT-LENGTH"))
      return(getLength(input));
  }
  return(0);
}

private int getLength(String length) {
  StringTokenizer tok = new StringTokenizer(length);
  tok.nextToken();
  return(Integer.parseInt(tok.nextToken()));
}
}
```

Figure 15–1 shows the `EchoServer` in action, displaying the header lines sent by Netscape Navigator 3.01 on Windows 95.

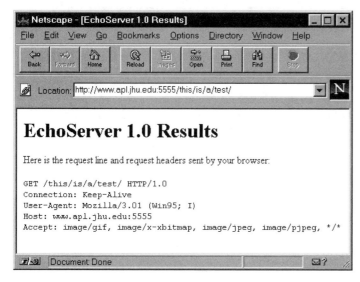

Figure 15-1   The EchoServer shows data sent by the browser

ThreadedEchoServer: Adding Multithreading

The problem with the EchoServer is that it can only accept one connection at a time. If, for instance, it takes 0.001 seconds to establish a connection but 0.01 seconds for the client to transmit the request and 0.01 seconds for the server to return the results, then the entire process takes about 0.02 seconds, and the server can only handle about 50 connections per second. By doing the socket processing in a separate thread, establishing the connection becomes the rate-limiting step, and the server could handle about 1,000 connections per second with these example times. Listing 15.15 shows how to convert the EchoServer into a multithreaded version. The idea is that the new version's handleConnection starts up a thread, which calls back to the original handleConnection. The problem is how to get the Socket object from handleConnection to run, because placing it in an instance variable would be subject to race conditions. So a Connection class is used, which is simply a Thread with a place to store the Socket object.

Listing 15.15 `ThreadedEchoServer.java`

```java
import java.net.*;
import java.io.*;

/** This is just a Thread with a field to store a
 *  Socket object. Used as a thread-safe means to pass
 *  the Socket from handleConnection to run.
 */

class Connection extends Thread {
  protected Socket serverSocket;

  public Connection(Runnable serverObject,
                    Socket serverSocket) {
    super(serverObject);
    this.serverSocket = serverSocket;
  }
}

//------------------------------------------------------
/** A multithreaded variation of EchoServer. */

public class ThreadedEchoServer extends EchoServer
                                implements Runnable {
  public static void main(String[] args) {
    int port = 5555;
    if (args.length > 0)
      port = Integer.parseInt(args[0]);
    ThreadedEchoServer echoServer =
      new ThreadedEchoServer(port, 0);
    echoServer.serverName = "Threaded Echo Server 1.0";
    echoServer.listen();
  }

  public ThreadedEchoServer(int port, int connections) {
    super(port, connections);
  }
```

Listing 15.15 `ThreadedEchoServer.java` (continued)

```
//-----------------------------------------------------
/** The new version of handleConnection starts
 *  a thread. This new thread will call back to the
 *  <I>old</I> version of handleConnection, keeping
 *  the same server behavior in a multithreaded
 *  version. The thread stores the Socket instance
 *  since run doesn't take any arguments, and since
 *  storing the socket in an instance variable risks
 *  having it overwritten if the next thread starts
 *  before the run method gets a chance to
 *  copy the socket reference.
 */

public void handleConnection(Socket server) {
  Connection connectionThread
    = new Connection(this, server);
  connectionThread.start();
}

public void run() {
  Connection currentThread
    = (Connection)Thread.currentThread();
  try {
    super.handleConnection(currentThread.serverSocket);
  } catch(IOException ioe) {
    System.out.println("IOException: " + ioe);
    ioe.printStackTrace();
  }
}
}
```

This server gives the same results as the EchoServer, but allows multiple simultaneous connections. It is used several places in the Chapter 16, "The HyperText Transfer Protocol" to show data sent by browsers in various circumstances.

15.8 RMI: Remote Method Invocation

Java 1.1 introduced an important new capability: Remote Method Invocation. This distributed-objects package simplifies communication among Java applications on multiple machines. If you are already familiar with the Common Object Request Broker Architecture, think of RMI as a simpler but less powerful variation of CORBA that only works with Java systems. If you don't know anything about CORBA, think of RMI as an object-oriented version of remote-procedure calls. The idea is that the client requests an object from the server using a simple high-level request. Once it has the object, it invokes its methods as though it were a normal local object. Behind the scenes, however, the requests are routed to the server, where methods in the "real" object are invoked and the results returned. The beauty of the process is that neither the client nor the server have to do anything explicit with input streams, output streams or sockets. The values that are sent back and forth can be complex Java objects (including windows and other graphical components), but no parsing is required at either end. This is handled by the Java serialization facility.

Now, this seems so convenient that you might wonder why anyone would implement sockets "by hand." First of all, RMI only works among Java systems, so it cannot be used for an HTTP client, an HTTP server, an e-mail client, or other applications where the other end will not necessarily be using Java. Secondly, even for Java-to-Java applications, RMI requires some common code to be installed on both the client and the server. This is in contrast to sockets, where random programs can talk to each other as long as they both understand the types of commands that should be sent. Thirdly, RMI is a bit more taxing on the server than regular sockets, since it requires two versions of the Java virtual machine to be running (one to broker requests for objects, the other to provide the actual object implementation). Finally, RMI wasn't added to Java until version 1.1, so if you want to use RMI from applets or Java 1.02 applications, you will need to download a Java 1.02 RMI add-on (`http://chatsubo.javasoft.com/current/download.html`).

Steps to Building an RMI Application

To use RMI, you will need to build four classes then execute a five-step compilation process. These steps are outlined here. The following subsection fleshes out each step with actual code.

The Four Required Classes

To use RMI, you will need to build four main classes:

1. **An interface for the remote object.** This will be used by both the client and the server.

2. **The RMI client.** This will look up the object on the remote server, cast it to the type of the interface from Step 1, then use it like a local object. Note that as long as there is a "live" reference to the remote object, an open network connection will be maintained. The connection will be automatically closed when the remote object is garbage collected on the client.

3. **The object implementation.** This object needs to implement the interface of Step 1, and will be used by the server.

4. **The RMI server.** This will create an instance of the object from Step 3 and register it with a particular URL.

Compiling and Running the System

Once you have the basic four classes, five further steps are required to actually use the application.

1. **Compile client and server.** This will compile the remote object interface and implementation automatically.

2. **Generate the client stub and the server skeleton.** Use the rmic compiler on the remote object implementation for this. The client system will need the client class, the interface class, and the client stub class. If the client is an applet, these three classes must be available from the applet's home machine. The server system will need the server class, the remote object interface and implementation, and the server skeleton class.

3. **Start the RMI registry.** This only needs to be done once, not for each remote object. The current version of RMI requires this registry to be running on the same system as server.

4. **Start the server.** This must be on the same machine as the registry of Step 3.

5. **Start the client.** This can be on an arbitrary machine.

A Simple Example

Here's a simple example to illustrate the process. The remote object simply returns a message string. See the next subsection for a more realistic example.

The Four Required Classes

The Interface for the Remote Object

The interface should extend `java.rmi.RemoteObject`, and all its methods should throw `java.rmi.RemoteException`. Listing 15.16 shows an example.

Listing 15.16   Rem.java

```java
import java.rmi.*;

/** The RMI client will use this interface directly.
 *  The RMI server will make a real remote object that
 *  implements this, then register an instance of it
 *  with some URL.
 */

public interface Rem extends Remote {
  public String getMessage() throws RemoteException;
}
```

The RMI Client

This should look up the object from the appropriate host using `Naming.lookup`, cast it to the appropriate type, then use it like a local object. Unlike in CORBA, RMI clients must know the host that is providing the remote services. The URL can be specified via `rmi://host/path` or `rmi://host:port/path`. If the port is omitted, 1099 is used. This process can throw three possible exceptions: `RemoteException`, `NotBoundException`, and `MalformedURLException`. You are required to catch all three. You should import `java.rmi.*` for `RemoteException`, `Naming`, and `NotBoundException`. You should import `java.net.*` for `MalformedURLException`. In addition, many clients will pass `Serializable` objects to the remote object, so importing `java.io.*` is a good habit, even though it is not required in this particular case. Listing 15.17 shows an example.

Listing 15.17 `RemClient.java`

```java
import java.rmi.*; // For Naming, RemoteException, etc.
import java.net.*; // For MalformedURLException
import java.io.*;  // For Serializable interface

/** Get a Rem object from the specified remote host.
 *   Use its methods as though it were a local object.
 *  @see Rem
 */

public class RemClient {
  public static void main(String[] args) {
    try {
      String host =
        (args.length > 0) ? args[0] : "localhost";
      // Get the remote object and store it in remObject:
      Rem remObject =
        (Rem)Naming.lookup("rmi://" + host + "/Rem");
      // Call methods in remObject:
      System.out.println(remObject.getMessage());
    } catch(RemoteException re) {
      System.out.println("RemoteException: " + re);
    } catch(NotBoundException nbe) {
      System.out.println("NotBoundException: " + nbe);
    } catch(MalformedURLException mfe) {
      System.out.println("MalformedURLException: "
                          + mfe);
    }
  }
}
```

The Remote Object Implementation

This class must extend `UnicastRemoteObject` and implement the remote object interface defined earlier. The constructor should throw `RemoteException`. Listing 15.18 shows an example.

Listing 15.18 `RemImpl.java`

```java
import java.rmi.*;
import java.rmi.server.UnicastRemoteObject;

/** This is the actual implementation of Rem that
 *  the RMI server uses. The server builds an instance
 *  of this then registers it with a URL. The
 *  client accesses the URL and binds the result to
 *  a Rem (not a RemImpl; it doesn't have this).
 */

public class RemImpl extends UnicastRemoteObject
                     implements Rem {
  public RemImpl() throws RemoteException {}

  public String getMessage() throws RemoteException {
    return("Here is a remote message.");
  }
}
```

The RMI Server

The server's job is to build an object and register it with a particular URL. Use `Naming.rebind` (replace any previous bindings) or `Naming.bind` (throw `AlreadyBoundException` if a previous binding exists) for this. Usage of the term "bind" is a bit different than in the CORBA world; here it means "register" and is performed by the server, not the client. You are required to catch `RemoteException` and `MalformedURLException`. Listing 15.19 shows an example.

Listing 15.19 `RemServer.java`

```java
import java.rmi.*;
import java.net.*;

/** The server creates a RemImpl (which implements
 *  the Rem interface), then registers it with
 *  the URL Rem, where clients can access it.
 */
```

Listing 15.19 `RemServer.java` **(continued)**

```
public class RemServer {
  public static void main(String[] args) {
    try {
      RemImpl localObject = new RemImpl();
      Naming.rebind("rmi:///Rem", localObject);
    } catch(RemoteException re) {
      System.out.println("RemoteException: " + re);
    } catch(MalformedURLException mfe) {
      System.out.println("MalformedURLException: "
                                      + mfe);
    }
  }
}
```

Compiling and Running the System

As outlined earlier in this section, this requires five steps.

Compile the Client and the Server

> Prompt> **javac RemClient.java**

This compiles the Rem interface automatically.

> Prompt> **javac RemServer.java**

This compiles the RemImpl object implementation automatically.

Generate the Client Stub and Server Skeleton.

> Prompt> **rmic RemImpl**

This builds RemImpl_Stub.class and
RemImpl_Skeleton.class. The client machine needs
Rem.class, RemClient.class, and RemImpl_Stub.class.
The server machine needs Rem.class, RemImpl.class, Rem-
Server.class, and RemImpl_Skeleton.class.

Start the RMI Registry

> Server> **rmiregistry**

On Unix systems you would probably add "&" to put the registry process in the background. You can also specify a port number; if omitted, port 1099 is used.

Start the Server

```
Server> java RemServer
```

Again, on Unix systems you would probably add "&" to put the process in the background.

Start the Client

```
Client> java RemClient hostname
Here is a remote message.
```

Example: A Server for Numeric Integration

Listing 15.20 shows a class that provides two methods. The first method, sum, calculates

$$\sum_{x=start}^{stop} f(x)$$

The definition of $f(x)$ is provided by an Evaluatable object (Listing 15.21). The second method, integrate, uses the midpoint rule (Figure 15–2) to approximate

$$\int_{start}^{stop} f(x)dx$$

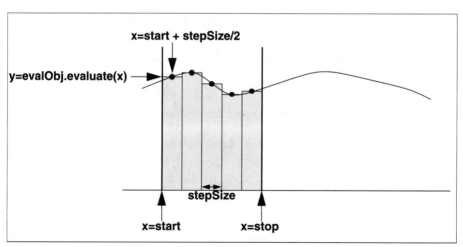

Figure 15–2   The integrate method approximates the area under the curve by adding up the area of many small rectangles which have width stepSize and whose length $y = f(x)$ is evaluated at the midpoint of each width.

Listing 15.20 `Integral.java`

```java
/** A class to calculate summations and numeric
 *  integrals. The integral is calculated using
 *  the simple midpoint rule.
 */

public class Integral {
  /** Returns the sum of f(x) from x=start to x=stop,
   *  where the function f is defined by the evaulate
   *  method of the Evaluatable object.
   */

  public static double sum(double start, double stop,
                           double stepSize,
                           Evaluatable evalObj) {
    double sum = 0.0, current = start;
    while (current <= stop) {
      sum += evalObj.evaluate(current);
      current += stepSize;
    }
    return(sum);
  }

  /** Returns an approximation of the integral of f(x)
   *  from start to stop using the midpoint rule.
   *  The function f is defined by the evaulate method
   *  of the Evaluatable object.
   *  @see #sum
   */

  public static double integrate(double start,
                                 double stop,
                                 int numSteps,
                                 Evaluatable evalObj) {
    double stepSize = (stop - start) / (double)numSteps;
    start = start + stepSize / 2.0;
    return(stepSize *
           sum(start, stop, stepSize, evalObj));
  }

}
```

Listing 15.21 `Evaluatable.java`

```
/** An interface for evaluating functions y = f(x) at
 *   a specific value. Both x and y are double precision
 *   floating point numbers.
 * @see Integral
 */

public interface Evaluatable {
  public double evaluate(double value);
}
```

Now, suppose that you have a big workstation that has very fast floating point capabilities, and a variety of slower PC's that need to run an interface that makes use of numerical integration. A natural approach is to make the workstation the integration server. RMI makes this very simple.

The RemoteIntegral Interface

Listing 15.22 shows the interface that will be shared by the client and server.

Listing 15.22 `RemoteIntegral.java`

```
import java.rmi.*;

/** Interface for remote numeric integration object. */

public interface RemoteIntegral extends Remote {
  public double sum(double start,
                    double stop,
                    double stepSize,
                    Evaluatable evalObj)
    throws RemoteException;

  public double integrate(double start,
                          double stop,
                          int numSteps,
                          Evaluatable evalObj)
    throws RemoteException;
}
```

The RemoteIntegral Client

Listing 15.23 shows the RMI client. It obtains a RemoteIntegral from the specified host, then uses it to approximate a variety of integrals. Note that the Evaluatable instances (Sin, Cos, Square) implement Serializable in addition to Evaluatable so that they can be transmitted over the network.

Listing 15.23 `RemoteIntegralClient.java`

```java
import java.rmi.*;
import java.net.*;
import java.io.*;

/** An evaluatable version sin(x). */

class Sin implements Evaluatable, Serializable {
  public double evaluate(double val) {
    return(Math.sin(val));
  }
}

/** An evaluatable version cos(x). */

class Cos implements Evaluatable, Serializable {
  public double evaluate(double val) {
    return(Math.cos(val));
  }
}

/** An evaluatable version x^2. */

class Square implements Evaluatable, Serializable {
  public double evaluate(double val) {
    return(val * val);
  }
}

/** This class calculates a variety of numerical
 *  integration values, printing the results
 *  of successively more accurate approximations.
 *  The actual computation is performed on a remote
 *  machine whose hostname is specified as a command
 *  line argument.
 */
```

continued

Listing 15.23 `RemoteIntegralClient.java` **(continued)**

```java
public class RemoteIntegralClient {
  public static void main(String[] args) {
    try {
      String host =
        (args.length > 0) ? args[0] : "localhost";
      RemoteIntegral remoteIntegral =
        (RemoteIntegral)Naming.lookup("rmi://" + host +
                                      "/RemoteIntegral");
      for(int steps=10; steps<=10000; steps*=10) {
        System.out.println
          ("Approximated with " + steps + " steps:" +
          "\n  Integral from 0 to pi of sin(x)=" +
          remoteIntegral.integrate(0.0, Math.PI,
                                   steps, new Sin()) +
          "\n  Integral from pi/2 to pi of cos(x)=" +
          remoteIntegral.integrate(Math.PI/2.0, Math.PI,
                                   steps, new Cos()) +
          "\n  Integral from 0 to 5 of x^2=" +
          remoteIntegral.integrate(0.0, 5.0, steps,
                                   new Square()));
      }
      System.out.println
        ("`Correct' answer using Math library:" +
        "\n  Integral from 0 to pi of sin(x)=" +
        (-Math.cos(Math.PI) - -Math.cos(0.0)) +
        "\n  Integral from pi/2 to pi of cos(x)=" +
        (Math.sin(Math.PI) - Math.sin(Math.PI/2.0)) +
        "\n  Integral from 0 to 5 of x^2=" +
        (Math.pow(5.0, 3.0) / 3.0));
    } catch(RemoteException re) {
      System.out.println("RemoteException: " + re);
    } catch(NotBoundException nbe) {
      System.out.println("NotBoundException: " + nbe);
    } catch(MalformedURLException mfe) {
      System.out.println("MalformedURLException: " +
                         mfe);
    }
  }
}
```

The RemoteIntegral Implementation

Listing 15.24 shows the implementation of the `RemoteIntegral` interface. It simply uses methods in the `Integral` class.

Listing 15.24 `RemoteIntegralImpl.java`

```java
import java.rmi.*;
import java.rmi.server.UnicastRemoteObject;

/** The actual implementation of the RemoteIntegral
 *  interface.
 * @see Integral
 */

public class RemoteIntegralImpl
        extends UnicastRemoteObject
        implements RemoteIntegral {

  /** Constructor must throw RemoteException. */

  public RemoteIntegralImpl() throws RemoteException {}

  /** Returns the sum of f(x) from x=start to x=stop,
   *  where the function f is defined by the evaulate
   *  method of the Evaluatable object.
   */

  public double sum(double start, double stop,
                    double stepSize,
                    Evaluatable evalObj) {
    return(Integral.sum(start, stop, stepSize, evalObj));
  }

  /** Returns an approximation of the integral of f(x)
   *  from start to stop using the midpoint rule.
   *  The function f is defined by the evaulate method
   *  of the Evaluatable object.
   * @see #sum
   */

  public double integrate(double start,
                          double stop,
                          int numSteps,
                          Evaluatable evalObj) {
    return(Integral.integrate(start, stop,
                              numSteps, evalObj));
  }
}
```

The RemoteIntegral Server

Listing 15.25 shows the server that creates a `RemoteIntegralImpl` object and registers it with the URL `RemoteIntegral` on the local system.

Listing 15.25 `RemoteIntegralServer.java`

```java
import java.rmi.*;
import java.net.*;

/** Creates a RemoteIntegralImpl object and registers
 *  it under the name 'RemoteIntegral' so that remote
 *  clients can connect to it for numeric integration
 *  results. The idea is to place this server on a
 *  workstation with very fast floating point
 *  capabilities, while slower interfaces can run
 *  on smaller computers but still use the integration
 *  routines.
 */

public class RemoteIntegralServer {
  public static void main(String[] args) {
    try {
      RemoteIntegralImpl integral =
        new RemoteIntegralImpl();
      Naming.rebind("rmi:///RemoteIntegral", integral);
    } catch(RemoteException re) {
      System.out.println("RemoteException: " + re);
    } catch(MalformedURLException mfe) {
      System.out.println("MalformedURLException: " +
                        mfe);
    }
  }
}
```

Compiling the Client and Server

```
Prompt> javac RemoteIntegralClient.java
Prompt> javac RemoteIntegralServer.java
```

Generating the Client Stub and Server Skeleton

```
Prompt> rmic RemoteIntegralImpl
```

`RemoteIntegral.class`, `RemoteIntegralClient.class`, and `RemoteIntegralImpl_Stub.class` are put on the client machines. `RemoteIntegral.class`, `RemoteIntegral-Impl.class`, `RemoteIntegralServer.class`, and `RemoteIntegralImpl_Skeleton.class` are put on the server.

Starting the RMI Registry

```
Server> rmiregistry
```

Starting the Server

```
Server> java RemoteIntegralServer
```

Starting the Client

```
Client> java RemoteIntegralClient hostname
Approximated with 10 steps:
  Integral from 0 to pi of sin(x)=2.0082484079079745
  Integral from pi/2 to pi of cos(x)=-1.0010288241427086
  Integral from 0 to 5 of x^2=41.5625
Approximated with 100 steps:
  Integral from 0 to pi of sin(x)=2.0000822490709877
  Integral from pi/2 to pi of cos(x)=-1.000010280911902
  Integral from 0 to 5 of x^2=41.665624999999906
Approximated with 1000 steps:
  Integral from 0 to pi of sin(x)=2.0000008224672983
  Integral from pi/2 to pi of cos(x)=-1.000000102808351
  Integral from 0 to 5 of x^2=41.666656249998724
Approximated with 10000 steps:
  Integral from 0 to pi of sin(x)=2.00000000822436
  Integral from pi/2 to pi of cos(x)=-1.0000000010278831
  Integral from 0 to 5 of x^2=41.666666562504055
'Correct' answer using Math library:
  Integral from 0 to pi of sin(x)=2.0
  Integral from pi/2 to pi of cos(x)=-0.9999999999999999
  Integral from 0 to 5 of x^2=41.666666666666664
```

15.9 JDBC: Java DataBase Connectivity

In addition to RMI, Java 1.1 added another very important new capability: a standard API to relational databases. Using the Java DataBase Connectivity API, you can access a wide variety of *different* SQL databases using exactly the *same* syntax. You can do this from applications and, with some restrictions, from applets. Although a complete tutorial on database programming is beyond the scope of this chapter, I'll cover the basics of using JDBC here, assuming you are already familiar with SQL. For more details on JDBC, see `http://java.sun.com/products/jdbc/` and the on-line API for `java.sql`. The `java.sun.com` site includes a link for downloading a version of JDBC that works in Java 1.02, including from Netscape and Internet Explorer.

Database Calls: An Overview

There are seven basic steps to querying databases:

1. Load the JDBC driver.
2. Define the connection URL type, host, port, and database.
3. Establish the connection.
4. Create a statement object.
5. Execute a query (`SELECT`) or update (`INSERT`) statement.
6. Process the results.
7. Close the connection.

Here are some details of the process:

Load the driver
The driver is the piece of software that knows how to talk to the actual database server. As in Java in general, `Class.forName` will load a class without actually making an instance. Here's how to load a driver:

```
Class.forName("fully qualified class name");
```

This call could throw a `ClassNotFoundException`, so should be inside a `try`/`catch` block. In my examples I'll use the FastForward driver from Connect Software (`http://www.connectsw.com/`); they supply a free one-connection six-month evaluation version for

Microsoft SQL Server or Sybase SQL Server. So, for example, I would use:

```
String driver = "connect.microsoft.MicrosoftDriver";
Class.forName(driver);
```

For an up-to-date list of drivers for various databases, see `http://java.sun.com/products/jdbc/jdbc.drivers.html`.

Define the connection URL

Connections to databases use the "jdbc:" format and are of the form

```
"jdbc:connectionType://host:port/database"
```

For example, the connection type used with FastForward for Sybase is "ff-sybase", so a URL would be constructed as follows:

```
String url =
  "jdbc:ff-sybase://dbhost.host.com/dbname";
```

If you use JDBC from an applet, this is where the security restrictions come into play. To prevent hostile applets from browsing behind a corporate firewall, applets can only make network connections to the server from which they were loaded. However, it may be inconvenient to require the database server to reside on the same machine as the HTTP server. Fortunately, many JDBC driver vendors provide proxy servers that reroute the request to the actual database server.

Establish the connection

Use the URL plus database username and password to make the network connection to the database using the `DriverManager` class, as illustrated below:

```
String user = "username", password = "password";
Connection connection =
  DriverManager.getConnection(url, user, password);
```

Create a statement

A `Statement` object is created from the `Connection` as follows:

```
Statement statement = connection.createStatement();
```

Other useful methods in the `Connection` class include `prepare-Statement` (create a `PreparedStatement`; discussed later in this section), `prepareCall` (create a `CallableStatement`), `roll-back` (undo statements since last `commit`), `commit` (finalizes operations since last `commit`), `getMetaData` (retrieve information about the database's tables, grammar, stored procedures, and so forth), and `close` (terminate connection).

Execute a statement

Once you have a `Statement` object, you can use it to send SQL queries. Here is an example:

```
String query =
  "SELECT col1, col2, col3 FROM table";
ResultSet results =
  statement.executeQuery(query);
```

To modify the database, use `executeUpdate` instead of `execute-Query`, and supply a string that uses UPDATE, INSERT, or DELETE. Other useful methods in the `Statement` class include `execute` (execute an arbitrary command) and `setQueryTimeout` (set a maximum delay to wait for results).

Process the results

The simplest way to process the results is one row at a time, using the `ResultSet`'s `next` method to move to the next row. Within a row, `ResultSet` provides various `getXxx` methods that take a column index as an argument and return the result as a variety of different Java types. For instance, use `getInt` if the value should be an integer, `getString` for a `String`, and so on for most other data types. However, note that columns are indexed starting at one, not at zero as with most of Java.

Core Warning

The first column in a `ResultSet` *row has index 1, not 0.*

Here is an example, assuming three columns and treating all as strings.

```
while(results.next())
  System.out.println(results.getString(1) + " " +
                     results.getString(2) + " " +
                     results.getString(3));
```

Besides the `getXxx` and `next` methods, other useful methods in the `ResultSet` class include `getMetaData` (get the meta data describing the result; illustrated later in this section), `findColumn` (get the index of the named column), and `wasNull` (last `getXxx` was SQL

NULL; alternatively, for strings you can simply compare the return value to `null`).

Close the Connection

You can omit this step if you continue processing or exit the application, but to close the connection explicitly, you would do:

```
connection.close();
```

Example: A Simple Test Database

Listing 15.26 shows a simple application of the process outlined above, connecting to a Microsoft SQL Server database using the FastForward JDBC driver. Listing 15.27 shows the results.

Listing 15.26 `TestDB.java`

```java
import java.sql.*;

/** A test connecting to and printing a very simple
 *  database. You must use Java 1.1 and obtain and
 *  install the Connect Software driver for this to work.
 */

public class TestDB {
  public static void main(String[] args) {
    // Use driver from Connect SW
    String driver = "connect.microsoft.MicrosoftDriver";
    try {
      Class.forName(driver);
      String url =
        "jdbc:ff-microsoft://" + // FastForward
        "dbtest.apl.jhu.edu:1433/" + // Host:port
        "pubs"; // Database name
      String user = "sa", password="";
      // Establish connection
      Connection connection =
        DriverManager.getConnection(url, user, password);
      // Create a statement
      Statement statement = connection.createStatement();
      // Define query
      String query =
```
continued

Listing 15.26 `TestDB.java` (continued)

```
        "SELECT col1, col2, col3 FROM testDB";
      // Execute query and save results
      ResultSet results =
        statement.executeQuery(query);
      // Print column names
      String divider =   "-----+------+-----";
      System.out.println("Col1 | Col2 | Col3\n" +
                          divider);
      // Print results
      while(results.next())
        System.out.println
          (pad(results.getString(1), 4) + " | " +
           pad(results.getString(2), 4) + " | " +
           results.getString(3) + "\n" +
           divider);
      // If driver class not found
    } catch(ClassNotFoundException cnfe) {
      System.out.println("No such class: " + driver);
      // If other connection/query error
    } catch(SQLException se) {
      System.out.println("SQLException: " + se);
    }
  }

  /** Pad a string with enough spaces to take up
   *  designated size. Assumes original string is
   *  shorter than this originally.
   */

  private static String pad(String val, int spaces) {
    val = " " + val;
    while(val.length() < spaces)
      val = val + " ";
    return(val);
  }
}
```

| Listing 15.27 TestDB Output |

```
Prompt> java TestDB
Col1 | Col2 | Col3
-----+------+-----
 1   | foo  | bar
-----+------+-----
 2   | fee  | fie
-----+------+-----
 3   | fo   | fum
-----+------+-----
```

Using Meta Data

Given only a `ResultSet`, you have to know something about the table to be able to process the results properly. For most specific queries, you do know something about the table in advance. In some cases, however, it is useful to be able to discover information after executing the query. That is the role of the `ResultSetMetaData` class. Given a `ResultSet`, this lets you determine the number, names, and types of the columns. Useful methods include `getColumnCount` (the number of columns), `getColumnName` (a `String`), `getColumnType` (an `int` to compare against entries in `java.sql.Types`), `isReadOnly` (is entry a read-only value?), `isSearchable` (can it be used in a `WHERE` clause?), `isNullable` (is a null value permitted?), and several others that give details on the type and precision of the column. See the on-line API for details. Listing 15.28 presents a class that uses this to present a graphical representation of an arbitrary table, creating a query of the form "`SELECT * FROM table`" given a host, database, and table entered by the user, then formatting the results in a set of textfields. The results are shown in Figures 15–3, 15–4, 15–5, and 15–6.

Listing 15.28 ShowTable.java

```java
import java.awt.*;
import java.awt.event.*;
import java.sql.*;

/** Connect to the specified table on the specified
 *  host and retrieve/display the entire table.
 *  Java 1.1 only.
 */

public class ShowTable extends CloseableFrame
                       implements ActionListener {
  public static void main(String[] args) {
    new ShowTable("ShowTable");
  }

  protected LabeledTextField tableField, hostField,
                             dbNameField;
  protected Button showTableButton;
  protected Panel inputPanel, tablePanel;
  protected Connection connection;
  protected ResultSetMetaData metaData;

  public ShowTable(String title) {
    super(title);
    inputPanel = makeInputPanel();
    add("North", inputPanel);
    pack();
    setVisible(true);
  }

  /** When the user clicks the "Show Table" button,
   *  the specified table is retrieved and
   *  a Panel is created to hold the results.
   */

  public void actionPerformed(ActionEvent event) {
    if (event.getSource() == showTableButton) {
      makeConnection();
      invalidate();
      if (tablePanel != null)
        remove(tablePanel);
      tablePanel = makeTablePanel();
      add("Center", tablePanel);
      pack();
      validate();
    }
  }
```

Listing 15.28 ShowTable.java **(continued)**

```java
// Connect to the specified host and database
// using the Connect SW driver and a preset
// username and password.

private void makeConnection() {
  String driver = "connect.microsoft.MicrosoftDriver";
  try {
    Class.forName(driver);
    String host = hostField.getTextField().getText();
    String url =
      "jdbc:ff-microsoft://" + host + ":1433/" +
      dbNameField.getTextField().getText();
    String user = "sa", password="";
    connection =
      DriverManager.getConnection(url, user, password);
    Statement statement = connection.createStatement();
  } catch(ClassNotFoundException cnfe) {
    System.out.println("No such class: " + driver);
  } catch(SQLException se) {
    System.out.println("SQLException: " + se);
  }
}

// Create a Panel that holds the textfields that
// gather user input, plus the "Show Table" button.

private Panel makeInputPanel() {
  Panel inputPanel = new Panel();
  inputPanel.setBackground(Color.lightGray);
  hostField = new LabeledTextField("Host Name:", 20);
  inputPanel.add(hostField);
  dbNameField = new LabeledTextField("DB Name:", 10);
  inputPanel.add(dbNameField);
  tableField = new LabeledTextField("Table Name:", 15);
  inputPanel.add(tableField);
  showTableButton = new Button("Show Table");
  inputPanel.add(showTableButton);
  showTableButton.addActionListener(this);
  return(inputPanel);
}

// Create a Panel with one TextField for each table
// entry, plus an extra row for the column
// names.
```

continued

Listing 15.28 `ShowTable.java` (continued)

```java
private Panel makeTablePanel() {
  Panel tablePanel = new Panel();
  tablePanel.setBackground(Color.white);
  try {
    // Create statement
    Statement statement = connection.createStatement();
    // Lookup table name
    String table = tableField.getTextField().getText();
    // Ask for everything in that table
    ResultSet results =
      statement.executeQuery("SELECT * FROM " + table);
    // Get MetaData that determines number of columns
    // and column names
    metaData =
      results.getMetaData();
    int cols = metaData.getColumnCount();
    // Layout Panel to hold specified number of
    // columns and whatever number of rows is needed
    tablePanel.setLayout(new GridLayout(0, cols));
    // A boldface textfield for each column name
    TextField field;
    Font headerFont =
      new Font("SansSerif", Font.BOLD, 14);
    for(int i=1; i<=cols; i++) {
      field = new TextField(metaData.getColumnName(i));
      field.setFont(headerFont);
      tablePanel.add(field);
    }
    // A regular-face textfield for each table entry
    Font bodyFont =
      new Font("Serif", Font.PLAIN, 12);
    String value;
    while(results.next())
      for(int i=1; i<=cols; i++) {
        value = results.getString(i);
        if (value == null)
          value = "<null>";
        field = new TextField(value);
        field.setFont(bodyFont);
        tablePanel.add(field);
      }
  } catch(SQLException se) {
    System.out.println("SQL Exception: " + se);
  }
  return(tablePanel);
}
)
```

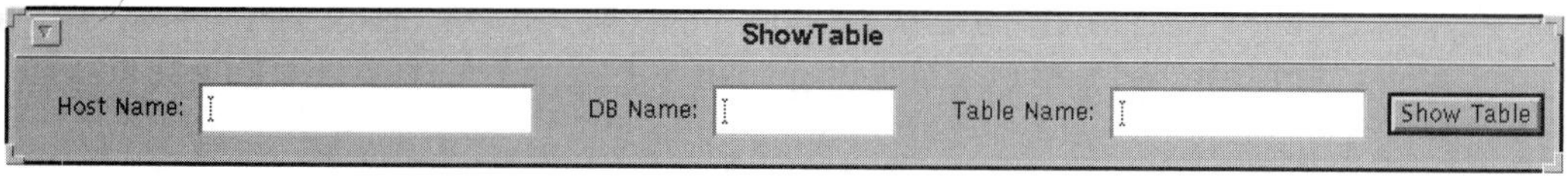

Figure 15–3 Original version of `ShowTable`.

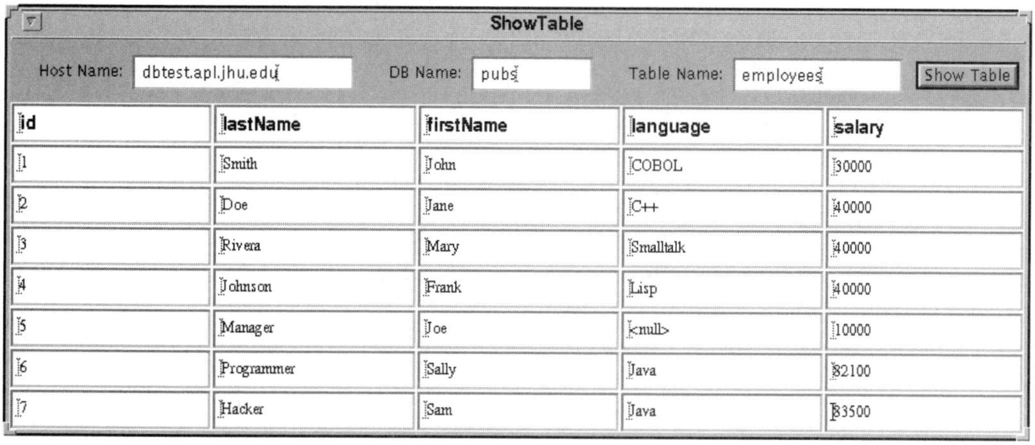

id	lastName	firstName	language	salary
1	Smith	John	COBOL	30000
2	Doe	Jane	C++	40000
3	Rivera	Mary	Smalltalk	40000
4	Johnson	Frank	Lisp	40000
5	Manager	Joe	<null>	10000
6	Programmer	Sally	Java	32100
7	Hacker	Sam	Java	33500

Figure 15–4 `ShowTable` after requesting the employees table.

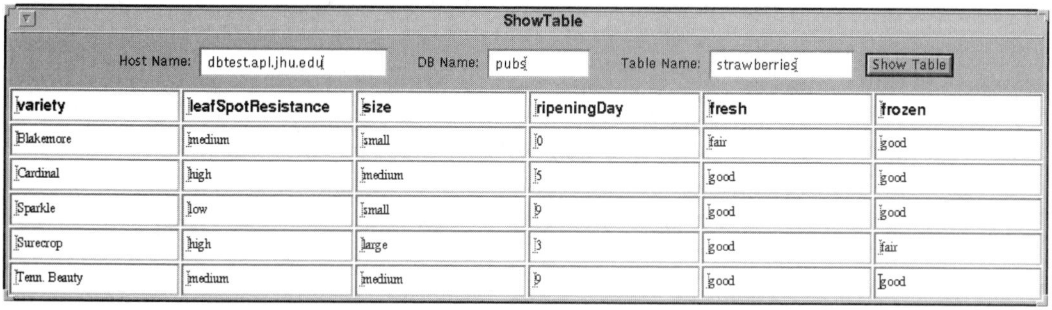

variety	leafSpotResistance	size	ripeningDay	fresh	frozen
Blakemore	medium	small	0	fair	good
Cardinal	high	medium	5	good	good
Sparkle	low	small	9	good	good
Surecrop	high	large	3	good	fair
Tenn. Beauty	medium	medium	9	good	good

Figure 15–5 `ShowTable` after requesting the strawberries table.

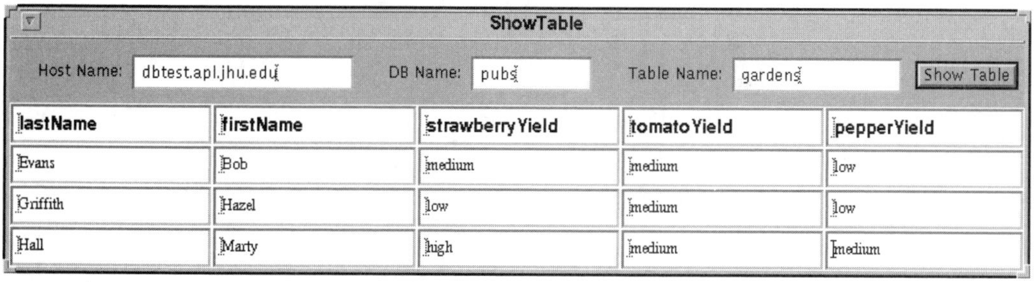

lastName	firstName	strawberryYield	tomatoYield	pepperYield
Evans	Bob	medium	medium	low
Griffith	Hazel	low	medium	low
Hall	Marty	high	medium	medium

Figure 15–6 `ShowTable` after requesting the gardens table.

The `ShowTable` application makes use of a helper class called `LabeledTextField`. It encapsulates a `Label` and a `TextField` in a single component. Listing 15.29 gives the source code.

Listing 15.29 `LabeledTextField.java`

```java
import java.awt.*;
/** A TextField with an associated Label.
 * @see LabeledTextArea
 * @see LabeledChoice
 * @see LabeledList
 * @see LabeledSlider
 */

public class LabeledTextField extends Panel {
  private Label label;
  private TextField textField;

  public LabeledTextField(String labelString,
                          Font labelFont,
                          int textFieldSize,
                          Font textFont) {
    setLayout(new FlowLayout(FlowLayout.LEFT));
    label = new Label(labelString, Label.RIGHT);
    if (labelFont != null)
      label.setFont(labelFont);
    add(label);
    textField = new TextField(textFieldSize);
    if (textFont != null)
      textField.setFont(textFont);
    add(textField);
  }

  public LabeledTextField(String labelString,
                          String textFieldString) {
    this(labelString, null, textFieldString,
        textFieldString.length(), null);
  }

  public LabeledTextField(String labelString,
                          int textFieldSize) {
    this(labelString, null, textFieldSize, null);
  }
```

Listing 15.29   `LabeledTextField.java`   (continued)

```
public LabeledTextField(String labelString,
                        Font labelFont,
                        String textFieldString,
                        int textFieldSize,
                        Font textFont) {
  this(labelString, labelFont,
       textFieldSize, textFont);
  textField.setText(textFieldString);
}

/** The Label at the left side of the LabeledTextField.
 *  To manipulate the Label, do:
 *  <PRE>
 *    LabeledTextField ltf = new LabeledTextField(...);
 *    ltf.getLabel.someLabelMethod(...);
 *  </PRE>
 *
 * @see #getTextField
 */

public Label getLabel() {
  return(label);
}

/** The TextField at the right side of the
 *  LabeledTextField.
 *
 * @see #getLabel
 */

public TextField getTextField() {
  return(textField);
}
}
```

Prepared Statements

If you are going to execute similar SQL statements multiple times, using
"prepared" (parameterized) statements can be more efficient. The idea is to
create a statement in standard form that is sent to the database for compilation before actually being used. Each time you use it, you simply replace
some of the marked parameters using the set*Xxx* methods. For instance, if

you were going to give raises to the personnel in the employees database
you might do something like the following:

```
Connection connection =
   DriverManager.getConnection(url, user, password);
PreparedStatement statement =
   connection.prepareStatement("UPDATE employees " +
                                "SET salary = ? " +
                                "WHERE id = ?");
int[] employeeIDs = getIDs();
int[] newSalaries = getSalaries();
for(int i=0; i<employeeIDs.length; i++) {
  statement.setInt(1, employeeIDs[i]);
  statement.setInt(2, newSalaries[i]);
  statement.execute();
}
```

Listing 15.30 uses this idea to create a version of ShowTable that allows
the addition of database rows as well as viewing of tables. When the "Update"
button is pressed, a new Frame is created. This Frame looks at the current
meta data to create a textfield for each column name. When the user presses
"Execute" in this Frame, the data from these textfields is sent to the database. Rather than using a regular Statement, a PreparedStatement is
used in case the user sends many consecutive updates. Figures 15–7, 15–8,
and 15–9 show the original ShowTable interface, the popup Frame, and
the results after the database is updated, respectively.

Listing 15.30 UpdateTable.java

```java
import java.awt.*;
import java.awt.event.*;
import java.sql.*;

/** Lets you view <B>and</B> update tables. Java 1.1. */

public class UpdateTable extends ShowTable {
  public static void main(String[] args) {
    new UpdateTable("UpdateTable");
  }
```

Listing 15.30 UpdateTable.java (continued)

```java
  private Button updateButton;

  /** Add a button to previous panel. */

  public UpdateTable(String title) {
    super(title);
    invalidate();
    updateButton = new Button("Update");
    updateButton.addActionListener(this);
    inputPanel.add(updateButton);
    pack();
    validate();
  }

  /** When Update button is clicked, pop up a separate
   *  UpdateFrame that lets user enter fields and
   *  send results to the database.
   */

  public void actionPerformed(ActionEvent event) {
    if (event.getSource() == updateButton) {
      String tableName =
        tableField.getTextField().getText();
      new UpdateFrame(connection, metaData, tableName);
    } else
      super.actionPerformed(event);
  }
}
```

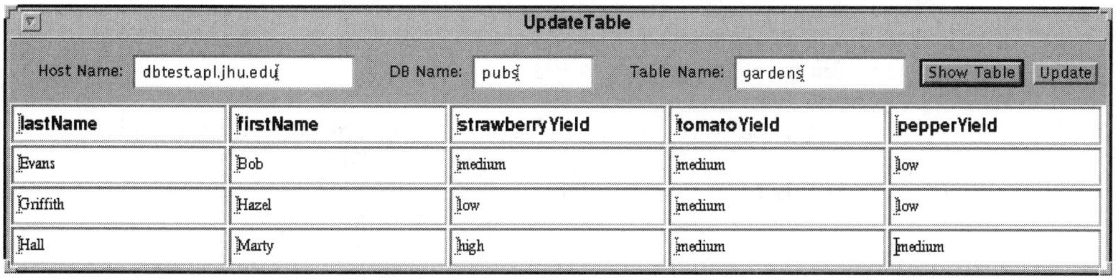

UpdateTable				
Host Name: dbtest.apl.jhu.edu		DB Name: pubs	Table Name: gardens	Show Table Update
lastName	**firstName**	**strawberry Yield**	**tomato Yield**	**pepperYield**
Evans	Bob	medium	medium	low
Griffith	Hazel	low	medium	low
Hall	Marty	high	medium	medium

Figure 15–7   UpdateTable adds one button to the ShowTable interface. Clicking on this button brings up an UpdateFrame (Listing 15.31).

Listing 15.31 `UpdateFrame.java`

```java
import java.awt.*;
import java.awt.event.*;
import java.sql.*;

/** A Frame that pops up to let the user change
 *  database entries. It presents one textfield
 *  for each column name, sending results
 *  to the database when the Execute button is clicked.
 *  @see UpdateTable
 */

public class UpdateFrame extends Frame
                         implements ActionListener {

  private Button executeButton, quitButton;
  private String tableName;
  private Connection connection;
  private ResultSetMetaData metaData;
  private PreparedStatement statement = null;
  private int cols;
  private LabeledTextField[] fields;

  /** Read the meta data to determine the field
   *  names, creating a textfield for each.
   */

  public UpdateFrame(Connection connection,
                     ResultSetMetaData metaData,
                     String tableName) {
    super("Update Table " + tableName);
    this.connection = connection;
    this.metaData = metaData;
    this.tableName = tableName;
    try {
      cols = metaData.getColumnCount();
      setLayout(new GridLayout(cols+1, 1));
      fields = new LabeledTextField[cols];
      LabeledTextField field;
      for(int i=1; i<=cols; i++) {
        field =
          new LabeledTextField(metaData.getColumnName(i)
                               + ":", 15);
        fields[i-1] = field;
        add(field);
      }
    } catch(SQLException se) {
      System.out.println("SQLException Getting Cols: " +
                         se);
```

Listing 15.31 `UpdateFrame.java` **(continued)**

```
}
   Panel buttonPanel = new Panel();
   executeButton = new Button("Execute");
   executeButton.addActionListener(this);
   buttonPanel.add(executeButton);
   quitButton = new Button("Quit");
   quitButton.addActionListener(this);
   buttonPanel.add(quitButton);
   add(buttonPanel);
   pack();
   setVisible(true);
}

/** When the Execute button is clicked, create
 *  a prepared statement <B>if</B> it doesn't
 *  already exist. If it exists, simply change
 *  parameters in existing one. Prepared statement
 *  will look like
 *  <PRE>
 *    INSERT INTO <I>tableName</I>
 *    VALUES (? ? ? ... ?)
 *  </PRE>
 *  For simplicity, assumes that all the columns
 *  are strings, so uses setString throughout.
 *  However, you could discover this information
 *  via metaData.getColumnType(col).
 */

public void actionPerformed(ActionEvent event) {
   if (event.getSource() == executeButton) {
     try {
       if (statement == null) {
         String insert =
           "INSERT INTO " + tableName + " VALUES (";
         for(int i=1; i<cols; i++) {
           insert = insert + "?, ";
         }
         insert = insert + "?)";
         statement =
           connection.prepareStatement(insert);
         System.out.println(insert);
       }
       String value;
       for(int i=1; i<=cols; i++) {
         value = fields[i-1].getTextField().getText();
         statement.setString(i, value);
       }
```

continued

Listing 15.31   `UpdateFrame.java`   (continued)

```
        System.out.println(statement);
        statement.execute();
      } catch(SQLException se) {
        System.out.println("SQLException updating: " +
                            se);
      }
    } else if (event.getSource() == quitButton)
      dispose();
  }
}
```

Figure 15–8   Clicking the "Update" button brings up a frame with a textfield for each column. Clicking "Execute" sends the new data to the database.

UpdateTable				
Host Name: dbtest.apl.jhu.edu DB Name: pubs Table Name: gardens Show Table Update				
lastName	**firstName**	**strawberryYield**	**tomatoYield**	**pepperYield**
Evans	Bob	medium	medium	low
Griffith	Hazel	low	medium	low
Hall	Marty	high	medium	medium
McNamee	Paul	none	medium	high

Figure 15–9   Clicking "Show Table" updates display to show newly-entered data.

15.10 Summary

Java sockets let you create network clients or servers that can communicate with general-purpose network programs written in any language. The process of building a client is straightforward: open a socket, create input and output streams from the socket, use these streams for communication, then close the socket. A server is similar, but waits for an incoming connection before a socket is created. Both types of systems frequently need to parse input they receive, and a `StringTokenizer` is a convenient tool for this. RMI is a powerful and convenient alternative when distributing processing among Java-only systems. If you want to talk to a relational database, Java 1.1 introduced JDBC, a rich API that lets you use standard syntax to communicate with multiple different databases.

This brings the Java-specific part of the book to a close. However, you haven't seen the last of Java. Far from it! The next part discusses CGI programming, the process of connecting a Web page to a remote system. You'll see that Java can be used to make an interface on the Web page as well as to implement the program on the remote system. The final part discusses Java–Script, a scripting language that runs in Web pages. There, you'll see that on Netscape clients, Java can talk to JavaScript and vice versa, giving Java more access to the content of the Web page and JavaScript access to Java's more powerful capabilities. In fact, *the* single most important foundation for Web programming in general is strong Java skills. Hopefully you have them now.

CGI
PROGRAMMING

THE HYPERTEXT TRANSFER PROTOCOL

Topics in this Chapter

- The general structure of a conversation with an HTTP server

- The types of requests that can be sent to an HTTP server

- Possible header lines in HTTP requests

- The HTTP response line and associated status codes

- Possible headers in HTTP responses

- Using cookies to store data on the client

- The response file

- An overview of public-key cryptography

Chapter 16

The HyperText Transfer Protocol (HTTP) is the language used by Web browsers to communicate with WWW servers. An understanding of this protocol is valuable to Web programmers for several reasons. First, CGI programs (Chapter 18) depend on information sent in HTTP requests to determine what action to take, and can manipulate HTTP responses to carry out these actions. Second, JavaScript programs (Chapter 19) can read and manipulate HTTP headers (including "cookies") in order to customize the look of a Web page. Third, browsers are not the only type of HTTP client, and a knowledge of HTTP is critical to writing link checkers, off-line browsers, Web site indexers, WWW spiders, and the like. Finally, although a commercial-quality HTTP server is a significant undertaking, a special-purpose server (Section 15.7) is not necessarily difficult, and can be useful in many situations. Such a server must support the HTTP protocol correctly if it is to communicate with existing browsers.

As of 1997, most servers and browsers support HTTP 1.0, which is the version described in this chapter. Version 3 of Netscape Navigator and Internet Explorer both use HTTP 1.0. However, HTTP 1.1 is starting to gain support, and some of its key features are discussed here as well. The official protocol specifications can be found at the following sites:

HTTP 1.0

    http://ds.internic.net/rfc/rfc1945.txt

HTTP 1.1

    http://www.w3.org/pub/WWW/Protocols/

16.1 Communicating with an HTTP Server

HTTP is a pretty simple protocol. The client first opens a socket connection to an HTTP server, which by default is on port 80. It then issues a command (usually a request for a document) by sending a request line, some optional request headers, and a blank line. In some cases, data for server-side programs is included after the blank line. The HTTP server then sends a response line, some response headers, a blank line, and a document, then closes the connection. Each of these components is summarized as follows and covered in more detail in the following sections.

The Client Request

When contacting a server, an HTTP client first issues a request line, typically using the GET, HEAD, or POST methods. It then sends zero or more HTTP request header lines and a blank line. In the case of GET and HEAD, the server then returns the results. In the case of POST requests, the client can send additional data after the blank line. A request is in the following format.

Request-Method Document-Address **HTTP/Version**

The first thing sent by the client is the request line, which consists of a request method (e.g., GET), the address of a resource, and, in the case of HTTP 1.0, the string "HTTP/1.0". The request methods are discussed in Section 16.2, "The HTTP Request Line."

Request-Header1: Value1
...
Request-HeaderN: ValueN

The next thing sent by the client is a series of zero or more HTTP request headers, each with an associated value. The request headers are discussed in Section 16.3.

Blank Line

Finally, the client ends the request by sending a blank line. In the case of some types of requests (e.g., POST), additional data can be sent after the blank line.

The Server Response

The response consists of a status line, one or more HTTP response header lines, a blank line, and then the requested document.

HTTP/Version Status-Code Message

The first thing returned by the server is a status line consisting (for HTTP version 1.0) of the string "HTTP/1.0", followed by a numeric status code and a short message describing the status code. The status codes are explained in Section 16.4, "The HTTP Response Status Line."

Response-Header1: Value1
...
Response-HeaderN: ValueN

The second thing returned by the server is a series of one or more HTTP response headers, each followed by an associated value. Most of the headers are optional, but at the very least the server should send a Content-Type header identifying the type of data that follows. Section 16.5 describes the response headers.

Blank Line

After the final response header, a blank line is sent.

Response Document

Finally, most responses will end with a document in the format identified by the Content-Type header. However, some types of requests (e.g., HEAD) result in just the status line and the response headers. The response document is discussed in Section 16.7.

An Example Interaction

Figure 16–1 shows a typical interaction with the HTTP server at JavaSoft's main Web site. You can experiment with the request methods and headers and see responses from Web servers at various popular Web sites by opening an interactive socket connection using a telnet client. For example, on Unix "telnet some.random.host.com 80" will connect to the HTTP port of some.random.host.com and let you type a request and see the response. A telnet client comes bundled with Unix (typically in /usr/bin/telnet) and Windows 95 (in C:\Windows) and NT systems, and is widely available separately for Macs. However, using telnet to talk to HTTP servers is inconvenient on Windows and Macintosh systems because many HTML documents end lines with a newline (linefeed) character. This causes the document body to be misaligned, because most non-Unix telnet packages expect a carriage return, not just a newline. Furthermore, the fact that the HTTP server closes the connection when finished often makes it difficult to see more than the last screenful of data. Consequently, I present `WebClient`, a simple graphical interface to HTTP servers used in Figure 16–1 and throughout the chapter. This client reads the request line and headers from the user, then sends them to the server along with a blank line, displaying the result in a scrolling textarea. Downloading is performed in a separate thread so that the user can interrupt the download of long documents. The code for `WebClient` is given in Listing 16.1, with supporting classes given in Listings 16.2 and 16.3. It also makes use of the `NetworkClient` class of Chapter 15, "Client-Server Programming in Java" and the `QuittableFrame` class of Chapter 11, "Windows."

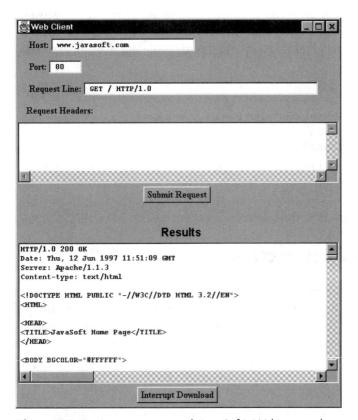

Figure 16–1 A conversation with JavaSoft's Web server shows a typical request and response.

Listing 16.1 `WebClient.java`

```java
import java.awt.*;
import java.util.*;

public class WebClient extends QuittableFrame
                       implements Runnable,
                                  Interruptable {
  public static void main(String[] args) {
    WebClient wc = new WebClient("Web Client");
    wc.resize(600, 700);
    wc.show();
  }

  private LabeledTextField hostField, portField,
          requestLineField;
  private TextArea requestHeadersArea, resultArea;
  private String host, requestLine;
  private int port;
  private String[] requestHeaders = new String[30];
  private Button submitButton, interruptButton;
  private boolean interrupted = false;

  public WebClient(String title) {
    super(title);
    setBackground(Color.lightGray);
    setLayout(new BorderLayout(5, 30));
    int fontSize = 14;
    Font labelFont =
      new Font("TimesRoman", Font.BOLD, fontSize);
    Font headingFont =
      new Font("Helvetica", Font.BOLD, fontSize+4);
    Font textFont =
      new Font("Courier", Font.BOLD, fontSize-2);
    Panel inputPanel = new Panel();
    inputPanel.setLayout(new BorderLayout());
    Panel labelPanel = new Panel();
    labelPanel.setLayout(new GridLayout(4,1));
    hostField = new LabeledTextField("Host:", labelFont,
                                     30, textFont);
    portField = new LabeledTextField("Port:", labelFont,
                                     "80", 5, textFont);
```

continued

Listing 16.1 `WebClient.java` (continued)

```
    requestLineField =
      new LabeledTextField("Request Line:",
                           labelFont,
                           "GET / HTTP/1.0",
                           50,
                           textFont);
  labelPanel.add(hostField);
  labelPanel.add(portField);
  labelPanel.add(requestLineField);
  Label requestHeadersLabel =
    new Label("Request Headers:");
  requestHeadersLabel.setFont(labelFont);
  labelPanel.add(requestHeadersLabel);
  inputPanel.add("North", labelPanel);
  requestHeadersArea = new TextArea(5, 80);
  requestHeadersArea.setFont(textFont);
  inputPanel.add("Center", requestHeadersArea);
  Panel buttonPanel = new Panel();
  submitButton = new Button("Submit Request");
  submitButton.setFont(labelFont);
  buttonPanel.add(submitButton);
  inputPanel.add("South", buttonPanel);
  add("North", inputPanel);
  Panel resultPanel = new Panel();
  resultPanel.setLayout(new BorderLayout());
  Label resultLabel =
    new Label("Results", Label.CENTER);
  resultLabel.setFont(headingFont);
  resultPanel.add("North", resultLabel);
  resultArea = new TextArea();
  resultArea.setFont(textFont);
  resultPanel.add("Center", resultArea);
  Panel interruptPanel = new Panel();
  interruptButton = new Button("Interrupt Download");
  interruptButton.setFont(labelFont);
  interruptPanel.add(interruptButton);
  resultPanel.add("South", interruptPanel);
  add("Center", resultPanel);
}
```

Listing 16.1 WebClient.java **(continued)**

```java
public boolean action(Event event, Object object) {
  if (event.target == submitButton) {
    Thread downloader = new Thread(this);
    downloader.start();
    return(true);
  } else if (event.target == interruptButton) {
    interrupted = true;
    return(true);
  } else
    return(false);
}


public void run() {
  interrupted = false;
  if (checkArgs())
    HttpClient client = new HttpClient(host,
                                       port,
                                       requestLine,
                                       requestHeaders,
                                       resultArea,
                                       this);
}

public boolean interrupted() {
  return(interrupted);
}

private boolean checkArgs() {
  host = hostField.getTextField().getText();
  if (host.length() == 0) {
    report("Missing hostname");
    return(false);
  }
  String portString =
    portField.getTextField().getText();
  if (portString.length() == 0) {
    report("Missing port number");
    return(false);
  }
```

continued

Listing 16.1 `WebClient.java` (continued)

```
  try {
      port = Integer.parseInt(portString);
    } catch(NumberFormatException nfe) {
      report("Illegal port number: " + portString);
      return(false);
    }
  requestLine =
      requestLineField.getTextField().getText();
    if (requestLine.length() == 0) {
      report("Missing request line");
      return(false);
    }
    getRequestHeaders();
    return(true);
  }
  private void report(String s) {
    resultArea.setText(s);
  }

  private void getRequestHeaders() {
    for(int i=0; i<requestHeaders.length; i++)
      requestHeaders[i] = null;
    int headerNum = 0;
    String header =
      requestHeadersArea.getText();
    StringTokenizer tok =
      new StringTokenizer(header, "\r\n");
    while (tok.hasMoreTokens())
      requestHeaders[headerNum++] = tok.nextToken();
  }
}
```

Listing 16.2 `HttpClient.java`

```java
import java.awt.*;
import java.net.*;
import java.io.*;

public class HttpClient extends NetworkClient {
  private String requestLine;
  private String[] requestHeaders;
  private TextArea outputArea;
  private Interruptable app;

  public HttpClient(String host,
                    int port,
                    String requestLine,
                    String[] requestHeaders,
                    TextArea outputArea,
                    Interruptable app) {
    super(host, port);
    this.requestLine = requestLine;
    this.requestHeaders = requestHeaders;
    this.outputArea = outputArea;
    this.app = app;
    if (checkHost(host))
      connect();
  }

  protected void handleConnection(Socket uriSocket)
      throws IOException {
    try {
      SocketUtil s = new SocketUtil(uriSocket);
      PrintStream out = s.getPrintStream();
      DataInputStream in = s.getDataStream();
      outputArea.setText("");
      out.println(requestLine);
      for(int i=0; i<requestHeaders.length; i++) {
        if (requestHeaders[i] == null)
          break;
        else
          out.println(requestHeaders[i]);
      }
      out.println();
      String line;
      while ((line = in.readLine()) != null &&
             !app.interrupted())
        outputArea.appendText(line + "\n");
      if (app.interrupted())
        outputArea.appendText("---- Download " +
                              "Interrupted ----");
```

continued

Listing 16.2 `HttpClient.java` (continued)

```
  } catch(Exception e) {
      outputArea.setText("Error: " + e);
    }
  }

  private boolean checkHost(String host) {
    try {
      InetAddress.getByName(host);
      return(true);
    } catch(UnknownHostException uhe) {
      outputArea.setText("Bogus host: " + host);
      return(false);
    }
  }
}
```

Listing 16.3 `Interruptable.java`

```
public interface Interruptable {
  public boolean interrupted();
}
```

16.2 The HTTP Request Line

An HTTP request consists of a request line, an optional number of request headers, a blank line, and, in the case of POST, some additional data. The request line is of the form:

Request-Method URI **HTTP/*Version***
The request method is a single word taken from the options described later in this section. The URI (Uniform Resource Identifier) is simply the requested URL with the protocol portion (e.g., http://), host-name (e.g., andreesen-pc.netscape.com), and port number (e.g., the "5555" in http://gates-mac.microsoft.com:5555) stripped off. For instance, if a user requests http://www.java-soft.com/~gosling/cobol-users-guide.html, the URI sent by the browser is /~gosling/cobol-users-guide.html.

Technically, the HTTP version could be something other than `HTTP/1.0`, but currently this is usually used. `GET`, `HEAD`, and `POST` are the only HTTP 1.0 request methods. However, as more servers start to support HTTP 1.1, `PUT`, `DELETE`, `OPTIONS`, and `TRACE` may become more widely used. Some examples:

```
GET / HTTP/1.0
GET /~joy/ms-job-application.pdf HTTP/1.0
POST /cgi-bin/search HTTP/1.0
HEAD /reports/notes.html HTTP/1.0
```

HTTP 1.0 Request Methods

The following sections summarize the three standard HTTP 1.0 request methods and the most important HTTP 1.1 additions.

GET

This is the method used by browsers for normal document requests. For instance, if the user requests the URL `http://www.java-soft.com/`, the browser will connect to port 80 of `www.java-soft.com` and issue "`GET / HTTP/1.0`", as shown earlier in Figure 16–1. Data for CGI programs can be attached to the URL after a question mark ("?"); this is discussed in more detail in Chapter 17, "CGI Programming and Beyond—The Client Side."

HEAD

This request method has identical syntax to `GET`, but the server only returns the response headers, omitting the requested document itself. It is used by link verifiers or by clients that want to discover the file size, modification date, or server version without actually retrieving the document. Figure 16–2 gives an example.

POST

With `GET` and `HEAD`, the URI portion of the request line can contain data intended for a server-side program. This is done by attaching the data to the URI after a question mark ("?"). With `POST`, however, the data is sent on a separate line rather than attached to the URI. A client would send the request line, a `Content-Length` line, any additional HTTP headers, a blank line, then the data the CGI program is expecting. For example, Figure 16–3 shows a simple data input form that uses `POST` to send the data in the textfield to the mini-HTTP server created

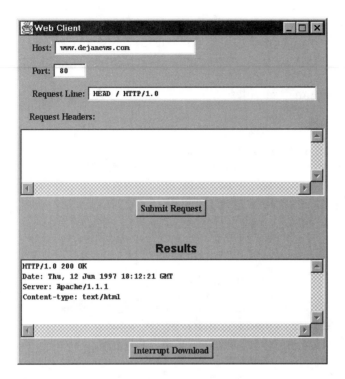

Figure 16–2   HEAD requests yield HTTP headers, but no document.

in Section 15.7. Figure 16–4 shows the request line, HTTP headers, blank line, and data sent when the form is submitted. The CGI program can use the `Content-Length` line to determine how much data to read, or can be a little less cautious, assume that the `POST` request was generated by an HTML form, and read just a single line. Creating HTML forms is discussed in detail in Chapter 17, "CGI Programming and Beyond—The Client Side," and methods for processing `POST` data in CGI programs are covered in Chapter 18, "CGI Programming and Beyond—The Server Side."

PUT

This header is part of HTTP 1.1, and is not yet widely supported. It lets clients supply a document and request the server to store it at the specified URI.

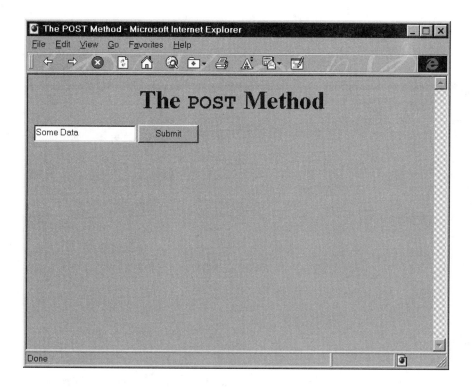

Figure 16–3 An HTML form that sends data via POST.

DELETE

This HTTP 1.1 header requests the server to remove a specified URI.

OPTIONS

This HTTP 1.1 header requests information about what communication options are available for the specified URI. If the URI is replaced by an asterisk ("*"), the request is to be interpreted as asking for options available from the server in general.

TRACE

This HTTP 1.1 header requests that the server return the attached document unchanged; it is used for debugging purposes.

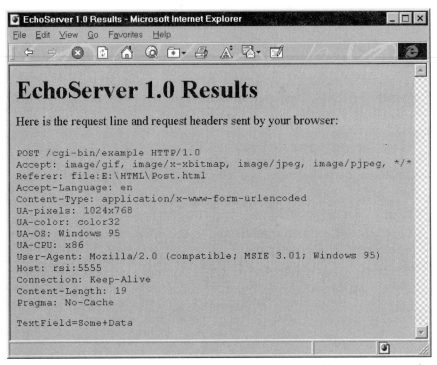

Figure 16–4   POST is used to send data to an HTTP server. This data is sent after the HTTP request headers and a blank line.

16.3 HTTP Request Headers

After the initial request line (the request method, document URI, and "HTTP/1.0"), the client can send several optional headers that provide additional information. For instance, Figure 16–5 uses the simple HTTP server developed in Section 15.7 to echo back the request line and headers sent by Netscape 3.01 when requesting a particular document.

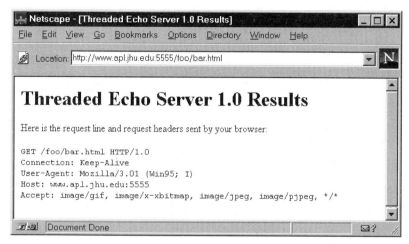

Figure 16–5   HTTP request headers sent by Netscape 3.01 on Windows 95.

This particular example shows `Connection`, `User-Agent`, `Host`, and `Accept` headers. Each of these is described as follows, along with the other standard HTTP request headers.

Accept

This specifies the MIME types that the client is willing to accept, in order of preference. See Table 16.1 in Section 16.5 for more information on MIME types. Multiple options can be given on a single line separated by commas, or placed in separate headers. This information is available to the server or to CGI programs to decide what type of data to return. For instance, in Figure 16–5, Netscape Navigator specifies a preference for GIF images, X11 bitmap files, JPEG images, progressive JPEG images, and any other MIME type, in that order. The `Accept` header can be omitted or

```
Accept: */*
```

can be used to indicate that the client will accept anything.

Authorization: *auth-scheme*: *credentials*

When a requested document requires authentication, usually indicated by a `WWW-Authenticate` response header (see Figure 16–14), the authentication information can be supplied in an `Authorization` header. The most common authorization scheme is `BASIC`, which is followed by *username:password* encoded in base64. In the base64 encoding scheme, the 8-bit encoding of each set of three characters is appended, then broken into four 6-bit sections, each used as the value of one of 64 possible characters (A-Z, a-z, 0-9, +, /, in that order). Padding at the end is indicated with the "=" character. For more details on base64 encoding, see Section 5.2 of RFC 1521, available in plain text at

```
http://ds.internic.net/rfc/rfc1521.txt
```

or at

```
http://ds.internic.net/rfc/rfc1521.ps
```

in PostScript. Note that base64 encoding does not provide protection from an attacker that can intercept network traffic, as the encoding can be easily reversed. Secure Sockets Layer (SSL) would be used in a case needing this level of security, although it should be noted that for users connecting directly through an Internet Service Provider, the difficulty of attackers snooping on the network is roughly akin to that of tapping your phone line. However, many corporate and University sites are vulnerable to users running "packet sniffers" on the local network. SSL provides protection from such attackers as well as from more sophisticated attackers who might have access to ISP systems or teleco phone lines. It is a standard that allows compliant browsers and servers to talk to each other using encrypted data streams. This is known as "secure HTTP," and is generally indicated by "https" instead of "http" in the URL. SSL is supported by both Internet Explorer and Netscape Navigator, and by a variety of commercial HTTP servers. For more information on SSL, see

```
http://www.netscape.com/assist/security/ssl/
```

For a quick summary of cryptographic techniques, see Section 16.8, "An Overview of Public-Key Cryptography."

Core Security

Base64 encoding is not intended to provide cryptographic protection. If you need to restrict access to Web sites and to protect against network eavesdropping, you will need to purchase a server that supports Secure Sockets Layer.

Connection: Keep-Alive

In standard HTTP 1.0, the browser must make a new connection for every document. Thus, each of the image files, Java applets, and so forth contained in a Web page requires a separate network connection. This unnecessarily repeats the time-consuming "handshaking" required to establish the connection. Several servers support an experimental version of persistent connections, whereby the connection is not closed between requests associated with a single Web page. A widely adopted extension to HTTP 1.0 lets clients supply the `Connection:` header with `Keep-Alive` to indicate that this should be used if available. For instance, both Netscape Navigator (Figure 16–5) and Microsoft Internet Explorer (Figure 16–8) use this header in all requests.

Core Note

In HTTP 1.1, persistent connections are the default, and will be used unless the client supplies a header of `Connection: close.`

Content-Length

This header is generally associated with server responses, but it *must* be supplied for `POST` requests. For instance, in the `POST` example of Figure 16–4, a `Content-Length` line is included to indicate that 19 characters will be sent on the data line that follows the HTTP request headers and the blank line.

Cookie: *name1=value1; ... ; nameN=valueN*

This header is used by browsers supporting Netscape's persistent cookie specification. It is used to return information supplied via a `Set-Cookie` header in a previous connection. See Section 16.6 for more details on cookies.

From

This gives an e-mail address of a person responsible for the request. It is sometimes used by Web indexing programs ("robots" or "spiders") to supply a point of contact for problems. For instance, some early spiders used a depth-first algorithm for exploring the Web, resulting in unacceptably heavy loads on servers. However, regular requests from browsers do *not* include this header; the name and e-mail address of the user are deliberately kept private.

Host

The `Host` line gives the host and port as listed in the original URL. Technically, this is an HTTP 1.1 header (in fact, it is *required* in 1.1), but it is widely used by earlier clients. For instance, even version 2.02 of Netscape Navigator supplies this header.

If-Modified-Since

This header is used with GET to conditionally retrieve updated versions of files. The file will only be sent if its modification date is later than the date specified, otherwise a 304 ("Not Modified") response will be sent. The modification date is indicated by the Last-Modified response header (see Section 16.5, "HTTP Response Headers"). The date should be of the form "Weekday, Day Month Year Hr:Min:Sec GMT." For example, Figure 16–6 shows a request for the HTTP reference page at the World Wide Web Consortium.

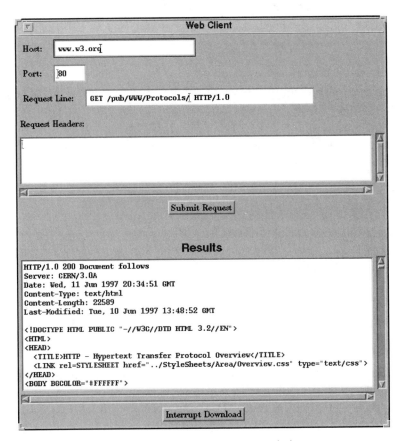

Figure 16–6   Response from the W3C server includes a Last-Modified header.

Note the time given in the Last-Modified header in Figure 16–6. Now, let's look at a similar request that does a conditional GET, asking for the page only if it has been modified after this. The response to this request omits the file, returning a "Not Modified" status line instead, as illustrated in Figure 16–7.

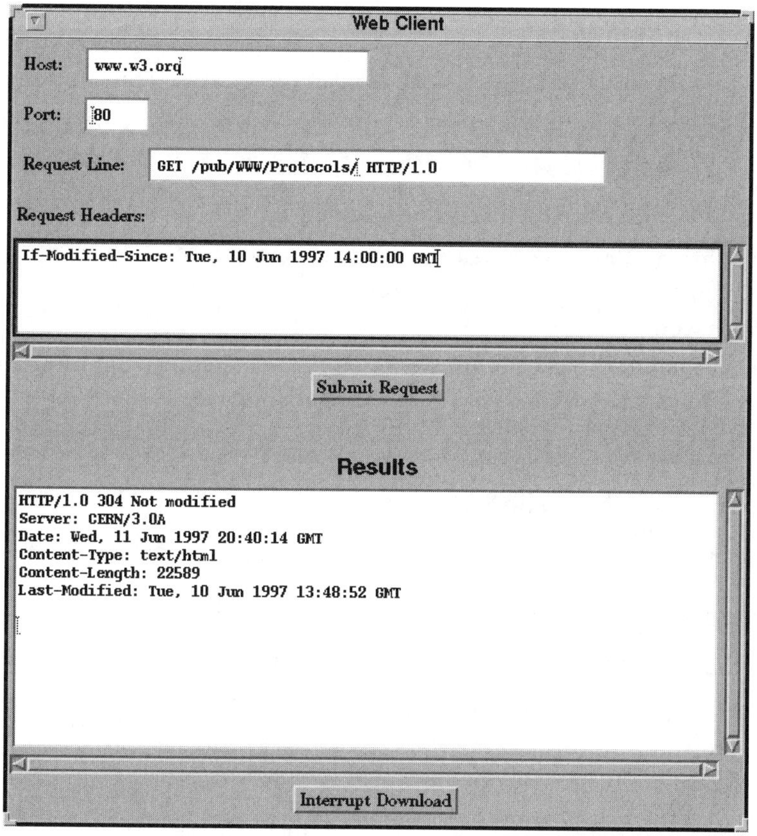

```
┌─────────────────────────────────────────────────────────┐
│  ▽                      Web Client                        │
│                                                           │
│  Host:   www.w3.org                                       │
│                                                           │
│  Port:   80                                               │
│                                                           │
│  Request Line:   GET /pub/WWW/Protocols/ HTTP/1.0         │
│                                                           │
│  Request Headers:                                         │
│ ┌───────────────────────────────────────────────────┐ ▲ │
│ │ If-Modified-Since: Tue, 10 Jun 1997 14:00:00 GMT  │ ▼ │
│ └───────────────────────────────────────────────────┘   │
│                                                           │
│                    Submit Request                         │
│                                                           │
│                      Results                              │
│ ┌───────────────────────────────────────────────────┐ ▲ │
│ │ HTTP/1.0 304 Not modified                         │   │
│ │ Server: CERN/3.0A                                 │   │
│ │ Date: Wed, 11 Jun 1997 20:40:14 GMT               │   │
│ │ Content-Type: text/html                           │   │
│ │ Content-Length: 22589                             │   │
│ │ Last-Modified: Tue, 10 Jun 1997 13:48:52 GMT      │   │
│ │                                                   │ ▼ │
│ └───────────────────────────────────────────────────┘   │
│                   Interrupt Download                      │
└─────────────────────────────────────────────────────────┘
```

Figure 16–7 Response from the W3C server for a conditional GET includes a Not Modified response when the file is older than the specified date.

Pragma: *no-cache*

This directs the server to return a fresh document even if it is a proxy with a locally cached copy. In HTTP 1.1, the Cache-Control: no-cache header can be used instead.

Referer

This specifies the URL of the page, if any, that contained the cross-reference that sent the client to the current document. This information is also normally recorded by servers, and can be used to find out what

WWW pages contain links to your pages. For instance, on Unix with the NCSA server, this may be in

```
/usr/local/etc/httpd/logs/referer_log
```

You can have some fun with people who search this regularly by connecting to the HTTP server with `WebClient` and specifying some unusual URLs such as

```
http://ceo.microsoft.com/~gates/favorite-pages.html
```

or

```
http://most-wanted.fbi.gov/suspects.html
```

User-Agent

This specifies the type of browser. Vendors can choose the format used to fill in this header, but it is often similar to

```
Vendor/version (platform; encryption; os)
```

For instance, Netscape 3.01 sends

```
User-Agent: Mozilla/3.01 (X11; U; SunOS 5.4 sun4m)
```

for the US-encryption version on a Sun platform and

```
User-Agent: Mozilla/3.01 (Win95; I)
```

for the international-encryption version on a Windows 95 platform. Interestingly, Internet Explorer 3.01 sends a "Mozilla" (Netscape) identification :

```
User-Agent: Mozilla/2.0 (compatible; MSIE 3.01; Windows
95)
```

This indicates that it is compatible with JavaScript version 1.0, which was supported in Netscape 2.0. This information is often logged by the server. For instance, on Unix with the NCSA server,

```
/usr/local/etc/httpd/logs/agent_log
```

typically records this information for each connection.

UA-Pixels, UA-Color, UA-OS, UA-CPU

These nonstandard headers are sent by Internet Explorer to indicate the screen size, color depth, operating system, and CPU type used by the browser (i.e., "User Agent," "UA") machine. Figure 16–8 gives an example. These values can be used by CGI programs to customize the types of page they build for users.

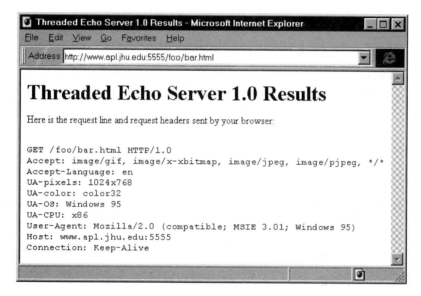

Figure 16–8 HTTP request headers sent by Internet Explorer 3.01 on Windows 95.

Nonstandard Headers

In addition to the standard HTTP 1.0 request headers, many clients transmit proprietary and/or HTTP 1.1 headers. For instance, Netscape 3.01 (Figure 16–5) and Internet Explorer 3.01 (Figure 16–8) send the common but non-HTTP 1.0 Connection and Host headers, Internet Explorer sends proprietary UA-xxx and Accept-Language headers, and Mosaic (Figure 16–9) sends the nonstandard Extension header.

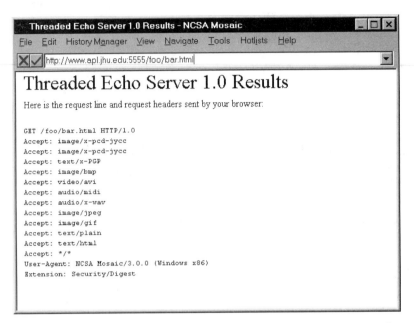

Figure 16–9   HTTP request headers sent by NCSA Mosaic 3.0 on Windows 95.

16.4 The HTTP Response Status Line

After receiving a valid request (request line, optional headers, blank line), the server returns a status line, one or more response headers, a blank line, and the associated document. The status line is of the following form:

HTTP/*Version Status-Code Message*

Currently, the version is usually 1.0. A status code between 200 and 299 indicates success, a value between 300 and 399 indicates the file has moved, a value between 400 and 499 indicates an error by the client, and a value between 500 and 599 indicates a server error. There are only a few predefined codes in HTTP 1.0, but if the browser receives an unrecognized code, it can use the general range to determine what action to take. For instance, a value of 444 should be treated as an error, even though 444 is not a standard HTTP 1.0 status code. The message is a very short string describing the type of error. Some examples include:

```
HTTP/1.0 200 OK

HTTP/1.0 301 Moved Permanently

HTTP/1.0 404 Not Found
```

HTTP 1.0 Status Codes

The predefined HTTP 1.0 status codes are listed in the following paragraphs, along with the usual accompanying message. Although the status codes are standardized, the messages can vary slightly from server to server.

200 OK

This response indicates that the request was successful. If the request method is GET or POST, the resultant document is included after the headers. If HEAD is used, the response includes the headers only. Figure 16–10 shows an example.

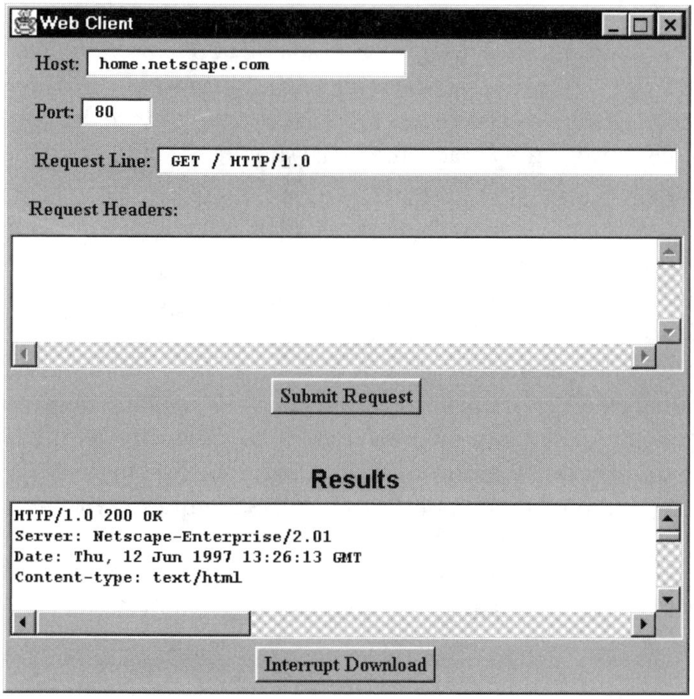

Figure 16–10   A response of 200 indicates a successful request.

201 Created

The 201 response applies to POST requests only; it indicates that a new resource was created as a result of the request. The URL of the new resource is given in the Location header.

202 Accepted

This status code is rarely used, but is intended to indicate that the request has been accepted, but results are not yet available. The body of the response should contain more information in such a case.

204 No Content

A response of 204 is generated when the server has fulfilled the request but has no data to return. Browsers should continue to display the document that generated the request in such a case, rather than updating their document view. This code is sometimes used by CGI programs that have no useful information to return, such as when the user clicks on an unused portion of an image map.

300 Multiple Choices

300 means that the requested resource is available at one or more locations. For GET or POST requests, the body of the response should contain a list of the possible locations in a way that lets the user select one. If the server has a preferred choice, the URL should be supplied in the Location header.

301 Moved Permanently

301 signifies that the requested resource has been assigned a new URL, and that all future requests should use the new location. This new URL should be supplied in the Location header, and for requests other than HEAD, the body of the response should contain a short explanation and a link to the new document. Most browsers will automatically redirect GET requests to the URL specified in the Location header, but should not do so for POST requests without user confirmation. Note that URLs that omit the trailing slash for directories generate either this response (301) or the similar 302, depending on the server. That is, this response is generated for requests such as

```
http://foo.bar.com/some/directory
```

instead of the correct

```
http://foo.bar.com/some/directory/
```

For instance, Figure 16–11 shows the 301 response received when requesting

```
http://www.apl.jhu.edu/~hall/java
```

301 and 302 responses require the browser to read the new URL out of the `Location` field, then to make a *second* connection to retrieve the proper document. This can require significant extra time if the network connection is slow, so you should be careful to explicitly include the trailing slash in hypertext links you create.

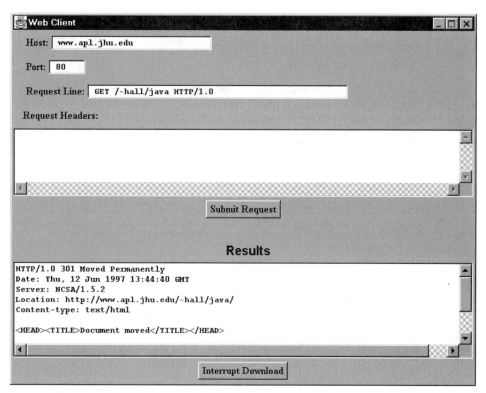

Figure 16–11 A response of 301 means the requested document has permanently moved to the specified location.

302 Moved Temporarily

302 signifies that the requested resource has been temporarily assigned a new URL, but that all future requests should use the original URL. Other than the interpretation of where to go for future requests, it is used identically to the 301 code.

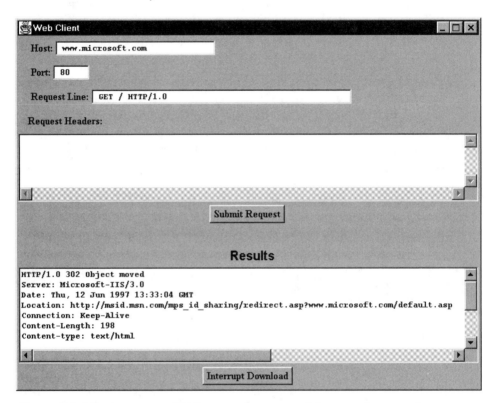

Figure 16–12 A response of 302 means the requested document has moved temporarily to the specified location.

304 Not Modified

If the user requests a document via GET and uses an If-Modified-Since header, then if the document is older than the specified date, a 304 response should be returned. The browser might use its cached copy in such a case.

400 Bad Request

A response of 400 indicates that the server could not understand the request due to a syntax error. For example, Figure 16–13 shows the results when a request line of "A B C D" is sent to the Web server at www.ibm.com.

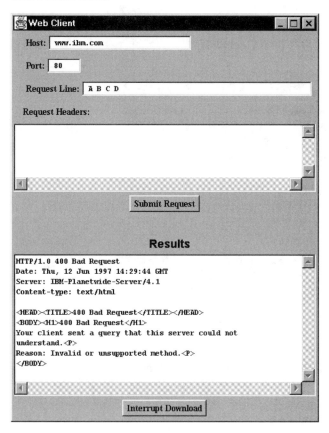

Figure 16–13   A response of 400 indicates a syntax error in the request.

401 Unauthorized

401 specifies that the request did not have the proper authorization, either because the Authorization header was missing, or because the data in it was incorrect. The response should also include a WWW-Authenticate header (see Section 16.2, "The HTTP Request Line"). For example, Figure 16–14 shows the headers returned by Netscape's site when their members-only documentation page is requested.

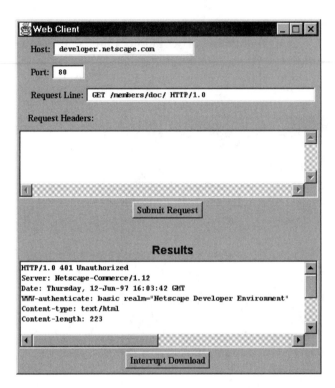

Figure 16–14   A response of 401 indicates a password-protected site.

403 Forbidden

403 is used to indicate that the user cannot access the requested resource, regardless of authorization. It is often used when the file or directory permissions of the resource do not permit access, or when access to a resource is restricted to certain hosts.

404 Not Found

404 indicates that no resource was found at the specified address. It is symptomatic of the dreaded "dead link" problem, where a Web page needs constant monitoring and updating to be sure that links to other pages aren't "dead" (or "broken") because the filename or host machine of the hypertext reference has changed. This is the most common error code. See Figure 16–15 for an example.

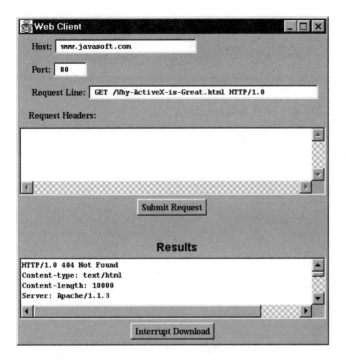

Figure 16–15   A response of 404 indicates a missing document.

500 Internal Server Error

500 is used to designate an unspecified error in the server. It is often the result of CGI programs that crash or return incorrectly formatted headers. How to write CGI programs is discussed in Chapter 18, "CGI Programming and Beyond—The Server Side." For now, note that most CGI programs mimic an HTTP server by generating an HTTP Content-Type line, a blank line, and then a document matching the Content-Type. Listing 16.4 gives an example using the Unix Bourne shell. This example illustrates a common error where whitespace (a single SPACE character, in this case) is generated instead of the blank line, in violation of the HTTP specification. Figure 16–16 shows the result.

Listing 16.4 An Incorrect CGI Program that Doesn't Generate a Blank Line

```sh
#!/bin/sh

echo "Content-Type: text/plain"
echo " "
echo "Oops! Sent a SPACE instead of a blank line"
```

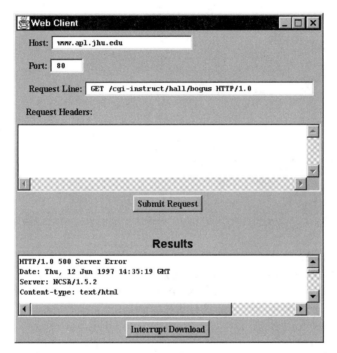

Figure 16–16   A response of 500 could indicate a misconfigured server or an incorrect CGI program.

501 Not Implemented

A 501 response means that the server does not support the functionality needed to fulfill the request. For instance, it cannot handle the request method (POST), or it received an unrecognized method (MUNGE).

502 Bad Gateway

502 is used by servers that act as proxies or gateways; it indicates that the initial server got an invalid response from a remote server.

503 Service Unavailable

503 indicates that the server cannot respond due to maintenance or overloading. When getting this response, the user should reconnect at a later time.

16.5 HTTP Response Headers

In addition to the status line (HTTP/1.0 *Status-Code Message*), there are a number of other headers that can be sent by the server in response to a request. Most are optional, but a Content-Type header should be included in *all* responses so that the client knows what to do with the document.

Allow

This header lists the set of request methods (GET, POST, and so forth) permitted for the specified resource.

Content-Encoding

Content-Encoding describes the decoding mechanism that must be used to obtain the MIME media type specified in the Content-Type header. The predefined HTTP 1.0 types are "x-gzip" (GNU zip) and "x-compress" (Unix "compress").

Content-Length

This specifies the number of bytes contained in the file.

Content-Type

This specifies the MIME type and subtype of the entity being sent (or, in the case of HEAD requests, of the entity requested but not sent) so that the browser knows what to do with the result. For instance, Content-Type: text/html indicates an HTML document. The subtype will begin with "x-" if it is not officially registered, and some media types can be specified either way (e.g., audio/midi or audio/x-midi) because the status changed from unofficial to official after many browsers were released. MIME types are described in RFC 1521, *MIME (Multipurpose Internet Mail Extensions) Part One: Mechanisms for Specifying and Describing the Format of Internet Message Bodies*, available in plain text at

    http://ds.internic.net/rfc/rfc1521.txt

or at

```
http://ds.internic.net/rfc/rfc1521.ps
```

in PostScript. The most important types for Web clients are summarized in Table 16.1.

Table 16.1   Common MIME Types

Type	Meaning
application/octet-stream	Unrecognized or binary data
application/pdf	Acrobat (.pdf) file
application/postscript	PostScript file
audio/basic	Sound file in .au or .snd format
audio/x-aiff	AIFF sound file
audio/x-wav	WAV sound file
audio/midi	MIDI sound file
text/html	HTML document
text/plain	Plain text
image/gif	GIF image
image/jpeg	JPEG image
image/x-xbitmap	X Window bitmap image
video/mpeg	MPEG video clip
video/quicktime	QuickTime video clip

Date

The Date header designates the current time, in Greenwich Mean Time.

Expires

This specifies the time and date after which the information should be considered invalid. The document should not be cached after this date.

Last-Modified

`Last-Modified` gives the time and date at which the document was last changed. The client can supply a date in the `If-Modified-Since` request header in order to prevent downloading of documents that were modified prior to that date. See Figures 16–6 and 16–7 (Section 16.3, "HTTP Request Headers") for an example.

Location

This gives the new location of the requested document. It is usually supplied in conjunction with responses with a status code of 201 (Created), 300 (Multiple Choices), 301 (Moved Permanently), or 302 (Moved Temporarily).

Server

This header supplies descriptive information about the HTTP server. It usually contains vendor and version information. For instance, the `Server` lines of Figures 16–10 through 16–15 show six different HTTP servers used by various sites.

Set-Cookie

This header contains a name/value pair to be stored by browsers such as Netscape Navigator and Microsoft Internet Explorer that support the Netscape persistent "cookie" specification. Optionally, it can contain `expires`, `path`, `domain`, and `secure` attributes. Until the cookie expires, it will be transmitted in the `Cookie` header in future requests to the same URL or to URLs in the specified `path` and `domain`. See Section 16.6 for more details on cookies.

WWW-Authenticate

This header is required for 401 (Unauthorized) responses. It gives an authorization type and realm that the client has to supply in an `Authorization` header in order to gain access to the document. For example:

```
WWW-Authenticate: BASIC realm="Executive-Branch"
```

16.6 Cookies: Storing Persistent Data on the Client

Netscape, Internet Explorer, and several new browsers provide a mechanism that lets server-side programs store simple information on the client machine. Although the etymology of the word is debatable, for some reason the term "cookie" is used for this information. Depending on what parameters are set, the browser may include the cookie data in future requests to the same server, but will not send it to servers in other domains. Cookies allow sites to store user preferences (see Section 18.12, "Using Cookies," for an example), to supply a user-id and/or password that the user need not retype in later sessions, to keep track of purchases, to track a user's activity while at that site, and other similar capabilities.

Netscape's cookie specification can be found at:

```
http://www.netscape.com/newsref/std/cookie_spec.html
```

This document describes the version in use in release 3 of Internet Explorer and by Netscape Navigator in releases 1.1, 2, and 3. Additional information, including pointers to drafts of new cookies specifications, can be found at:

```
http://home.netscape.com/assist/security/faqs/
cookies.html
```

Cookie Syntax

The server asks the client to store a cookie by supplying a `Set-Cookie` header. Multiple cookies (up to 20 per site) can be specified by supplying more than one `Set-Cookie` line. The browser sends previously created cookies back to the server by means of a `Cookie` header. Multiple cookies can be specified by separating them with semicolons on a single `Cookie` line.

The `Set-Cookie` header should contain a cookie name and an associated value, separated by an equals sign. The value can be empty, and additional information can be supplied after a semicolon, but a common form of cookie header looks like the following:

```
Set-Cookie: cookieName=cookieValue
```

For instance, suppose that a Web search engine wanted to allow users to choose how many hits-per-page should be displayed, and whether each hit should be displayed in concise or extended format. To do this, the search service might return the following headers derived from user input:

```
Set-Cookie: hits-per-page=10
Set-Cookie: format=verbose
```

For the remainder of the session, whenever a URL is requested from the same directory as the one that supplied these headers, the browser would send a `Cookie` line of the form:

```
Cookie: hits-per-page=10; format=verbose
```

Sites can also specify that certain cookies be used in later sessions (by using the "`expires`" attribute in the `Set-Cookie` header), that they be shared by multiple URLs at the same site (by using "`path`"), that they be shared by multiple servers in the same domain (by using "`domain`"), or that they only be sent to servers using Secure Sockets Layer (by using "`secure`"). These options are explained in more detail as follows.

expires

This attribute specifies how long the cookie will remain valid. If it is not supplied, the cookie is only valid during the current session. Otherwise it is valid until the date specified. A cookie is deleted by supplying an expiration date in the past. The date must be of the form

```
Weekday, Day-Month-Year Hour:Minute:Second GMT
```

where `Weekday` is spelled out, `Month` is the three-letter abbreviation, and `Year` uses all 4 digits. For example, in the previous search engine example, the site could specify that the preferences persist through all of 1998 by specifying the following. Each header is broken across two lines for readability, but should be on a single line in an actual request.

```
Set-Cookie: hits-per-page=10;
  expires=Friday, 01-Jan-1999 00:00:00 GMT
Set-Cookie: format=verbose;
  expires=Friday, 01-Jan-1999 00:00:00 GMT
```

path

If a site supplies a `path` attribute in the `Set-Cookie` header, then all URLs in the specified path should receive the cookie from the browser. Otherwise the `Cookie` header is sent by the browser only for URLs in the same path (i.e., in same directory or in subdirectories) as the current URL. "`/`" is the most general path. For instance, to create persistent preferences that apply to all URLs at the current site, a search engine might supply

```
Set-Cookie: hits-per-page=10;
  expires=Friday, 01-Jan-1999 00:00:00 GMT;
  path=/
Set-Cookie: format=verbose;
  expires=Friday, 01-Jan-1999 00:00:00 GMT
  path=/
```

Only paths that are a prefix of the current URL will be accepted. If two or more URLs in different directories specify a cookie with the same name, then all applicable cookies are sent by the browser in future requests, ordered from the most specific match to the least specific match.

domain

The `domain` attribute allows cookies to be shared across sites. If the site supplies this attribute, then all the sites in the specified domain receive the cookie. Otherwise it only applies to the current site. The domain must start with a dot and contain at least one additional dot. Only domains that match the domain of the current site will be accepted. Servers on different ports of the same machine count as different domains. For instance, suppose that the search service used in the previous examples was hosted at `main.search-service.com`, and wanted to share cookies with other machines at `search-service.com`. To do so, it could supply a domain of `.search-service.com`, as follows:

```
Set-Cookie: hits-per-page=10;
  expires=Friday, 01-Jan-1999 00:00:00 GMT;
  path=/;
  domain=.search-service.com
Set-Cookie: format=verbose;
  expires=Friday, 01-Jan-1999 00:00:00 GMT;
  path=/;
  domain=.search-service.com
```

Again, note that the `Set-Cookie` header is broken across multiple lines for readability, but would be on a single line in an actual request.

secure

If this attribute is present, then the cookie will only be sent over secure links (i.e., ones that use SSL). This is the only attribute that has no associated value. For instance:

```
Set-Cookie: uid=gates; secure
Set-Cookie: password=iluvmacs; secure
```

A Cookie Example

As a simple illustration of the mechanics of cookies, consider the `choco-late-chip` CGI program illustrated in Figure 16–17. When the URL is contacted, two cookies are returned to the browser: `tried-chocolate-chip` and `last-tasted`.

   Now, after a browser that supports cookies visits this URL, these two cookies are sent with later requests for URLs in the same path, even if the user quits the browser and restarts it in another session. This is illustrated by Figure 16–18, which shows the results of the `ShowCookies` CGI program located in the same directory as `chocolate-chip`. We won't cover the details of writing `chocolate-chip` and `ShowCookies` here, but we cover writing CGI programs, generating `Set-Cookie` headers, and parsing

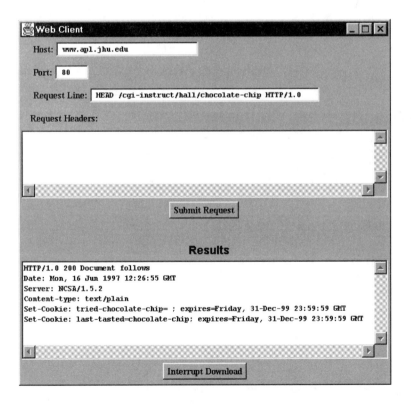

Figure 16–17   The `chocolate-chip` CGI program sends two cookies to the browser.

the `Cookie` line in Chapter 18, "CGI Programming and Beyond—The Server Side." In particular, Section 18.12 gives an example of using cookies, along with the `CookieParser` Java class used in the `ShowCookies` program.

Figure 16–18 shows the cookies sent after visiting only the `chocolate-chip` page. Figures 16–19 and 16–20 show the results after visiting two similar pages: `oatmeal` and `gingersnap`. Each of these pages generates two `Set-Cookie` headers, similarly to `chocolate-chip` in Figure 16–17. One of the cookie names (`tried-oatmeal`, `tried-gingersnap`) is unique to the page, so continues to be sent after other pages are visited. The other name (`last-tasted`) is shared by all three pages, so only the most recently specified value is sent.

Figure 16–18   Cookies sent by Netscape after visiting the `chocolate-chip` page.

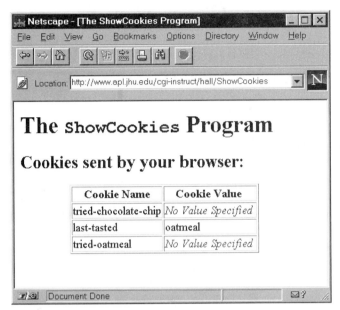

Figure 16–19   Cookies sent by Netscape after visiting the `chocolate-chip` and `oatmeal` pages.

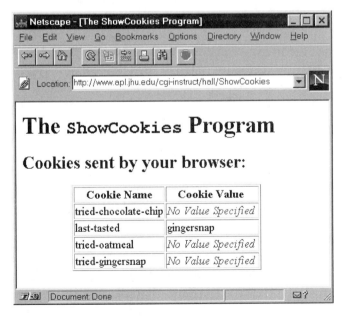

Figure 16–20   Cookies sent by Netscape after visiting the `chocolate-chip`, `oatmeal`, and `gingersnap` pages.

Privacy and Security Issues

Many users are concerned about security and privacy risks associated with cookies. Some of these concerns are based on a misunderstanding of the way that cookies work. For instance, a server can only ask the browser to store information that is already available to the server (e.g., in CGI environment variables); it cannot access the user's hard disk or obtain the user's login name, e-mail address, or current directory unless the user deliberately supplies this information. Cookie data is never "executed" in any way by the client machine, so cannot be used to create viruses or destructive programs. Because each cookie is limited to 4K (name plus value combined) and each site is limited to 20 cookies, cookies cannot be used to fill up a user's disk. Although early systems had flaws in this regard, current browsers do not transmit cookies to sites other than the ones that either set the cookie or are in the domain of the site that set the cookie. So rogue sites cannot read or modify cookies from other sites.

Despite these security features, there are several remaining concerns. A resource can delete cookies supplied by previously visited resources at the same site by supplying a large number of cookies, pushing the browser over the 20-cookie limit. Sites that store password or other security information in cookies introduce the risk of this file being compromised, especially because many users do not know that the cookie file should be protected. Of most concern to most users, however, are the privacy issues assorted with cookies. Even though a cookie can only store information that the site already has access to, the fact that cookies are invisible to the user bothers some people. For instance, a site can track the pages you visit while at their site, the topics you search for in on-line databases, and so forth, accumulating a profile of your interests. And although the restriction that cookies are only sent to the originating domain prevents *hostile* users from stealing cookies, it doesn't prevent *cooperating* sites from sharing cookies across domains. For example, multiple sites could load image files from a single, centralized host. Because images are retrieved via separate HTTP requests, they can have cookies associated with them. All requests to the central host could have a single cookie associated with them, and this host could maintain a database of the user's activities based on data attached to the image URL by the original site. The central host could then share this information with the site that referenced the image. In fact, the Doubleclick Network (`http://www.doubleclick.net/`) performs just such a service for various sites, providing targeted advertisements to sites such as AltaVista (`http://www.altavista.digital.com`), U.S. News Online (`http://www.usnews.com/`), and The Dilbert Zone (`http://www.united-`

media.com/comics/dilbert/). Now, Doubleclick guarantees that it will not gather personal identifying information such as names, e-mail addresses, phone numbers, and so forth, and provides a free option that lets users permanently "opt out" of the network by means of a blank cookie. Nevertheless, the fact that cookies makes this type of application possible bothers some users. For these users, note that both Internet Explorer and Netscape Navigator allow you to set an option that warns you before cookies are downloaded to your machine. Other users prefer to delete the cookies file and then save it in some nonwritable format (e.g., read-only, hidden, system on Windows). Netscape uses a single file (`cookies.txt` on Windows, `cookies` on Unix, `magiccookie` on MacOS) to store the cookie database. Internet Explorer uses one file per site, storing the files in the `C:\Windows\Cookies` directory.

16.7 The Response File

The file itself starts after a single blank line at the end of the response headers and should either be in the format specified in the `Content-Type` header, or in a format that will result in the `Content-Type` format after being decoded according to the method specified by `Content-Encoding`. In the case of an error, a small error file will usually still be sent that the browser displays to the user to indicate an error.

The server will close the connection when done, which means that a client written in Java can safely use `readLine` repeatedly to read the file until the `readLine` returns `null`. Alternatively, if `Content-Length` is provided, a single large `read` of the specified number of bytes could be used.

16.8 An Overview of Public-Key Cryptography

Public-key cryptography underlies much of the security and authentication technology in use on the Internet. For instance, HTTPS (secure HTTP) uses Secure Sockets Layer, a standard that uses public-key cryptography to send a randomly generated session key from the browser to the server. Java 1.1 and ActiveX use public keys for digital signatures to verify the origin of trusted applications. Internet Explorer supports public-key-based personal certificates from Verisign (http://www.verisign.com/), using them to authenticate sites and individuals. PGP (Pretty Good Privacy) uses public-key cryptography as part of its support for secure e-mail. Other applications are growing. With traditional (symmetric) cryptography algorithms, there is a single key used to encrypt or decrypt messages, and this key must be kept secret to prevent messages from being compromised. Using public key cryptography, there are *two* keys associated with encryption. Either can be used to encrypt a message, and applying either key will decrypt messages encrypted with the other key. The keys are generally known as the secret key S, and the public key P, indicating that S is kept secret by the user while P is made public. Encryption/decryption with a secret key will be designated S(), while using a public key will be designated P(). Thus, for some message M and matched set of keys S_i and P_i,

$$M = P_i(S_i(M)) = S_i(P_i(M))$$

The crucial requirement is that the secret key S cannot be determined from the public key P. In practice, this is accomplished by having the secret key be a pair of large prime numbers and having the public key be their product, or some variation of this.

Encryption

Using this approach, Bob (with secret key S_B and public key P_B) can send a message to Alice (with keys S_A and P_A) in such a way that it cannot be read by anyone other than Alice. Bob first creates an encrypted message C from the original message M by using Alice's public key:

$$C = P_A(M)$$

Bob then sends C to Alice, who applies her secret key to obtain the original message:

$$M = S_A(C) = S_A(P_A(M))$$

For Alice to reply to Bob, the process is reversed. Alice encrypts the message with Bob's public key and sends it to Bob, who decrypts with his secret key.

Digital Signatures

Although the scheme described in the last section guarantees to Bob that only Alice can read his message, it does not prove to Alice that the message was really from Bob. Public-key cryptography can accomplish this as well.

For Bob to send a digitally signed message to Alice, he first encrypts his message M with his own secret key, obtaining an encrypted message C.

$$C = S_B(M)$$

Bob then sends both M and C to Alice, who applies Bob's public key to C to verify that

$$M = P_B(C)$$

Digitally Signed Encryption

By combining these two approaches, messages can be sent that combine the security of encryption with the authenticity of digital signatures. For Bob to send an eavesdrop-proof message to Alice that Alice can be sure is really from Bob, Bob first encrypts the message with his own secret key:

$$C_1 = S_B(M)$$

He then encrypts the result with Alice's public key:

$$C_2 = P_A(C_1) = P_A(S_B(M))$$

He sends this to Alice, who first applies her secret key then Bob's public key to obtain the original message:

$$M = P_B(S_A(C_2)) = P_B(S_A(P_A(S_B(M))))$$

Digitally Signed Encryption with Delivery Verification

The approach outlined in the previous section prevents eavesdroppers from reading Bob's message, and authenticates to Alice that the message was really from Bob. However, Bob does not know if Alice has received the message. One verification scheme is for the receiver to decrypt the message, then sign it with their secret key, encrypt it with the public key of the original sender (Bob in this case), then send that result back to the sender. Bob can then decrypt with his secret key and then Alice's public key to confirm that the message is the same as the one he originally sent.

Using Confirmation Messages to Break Encryption

The receiver of an encrypted message has to verify that the message is intelligible before sending a confirmation. Otherwise, an attack is opened that could permit an eavesdropper to decrypt messages from Bob to Alice. Suppose that Mallet obtains a copy of the encrypted, digitally signed message that Bob sent Alice. He can then send it to Alice as though it were from him. If Alice follows the confirmation process automatically, Mallet will get a confirmation message from Alice that he can decrypt to obtain Bob's original message. As described earlier, Bob first encrypts M with his secret key:

$$C_1 = S_B(M)$$

and then encrypts the result with Alice's public key:

$$C_2 = P_A(C_1) = P_A(S_B(M))$$

When Mallet sends C_2 to Alice, she would first try (unsuccessfully) to obtain the original message by applying her secret key followed by Mallet's public key:

$$M_{bogus} = P_M(S_A(C_2)) = P_M(S_A(P_A(S_B(M)))) = P_M(S_B(M))$$

Alice then signs with her secret key and encrypts with Mallet's public key:

$$C_3 = P_M(S_A(M_{bogus})) = P_M(S_A(P_M(S_B(M))))$$

This result is returned to Mallet. He can obtain M by applying his secret key, Alice's public key, his secret key again, and Bob's public key:

$$M = P_B(S_M(P_A(S_M(C_3)))) = P_B(S_M(P_A(S_M(P_M(S_A(P_M(S_B(M))))))))$$

This attack underscores the point that a user should never encrypt a random string with their secret key and return that result to someone else.

Breaking Encryption with Man-in-the-Middle Attacks

Although encryption using public-key cryptography is safe from an eavesdropper (assuming that the underlying cryptographic algorithm is secure), it is not safe from an attacker who controls the communication channel and can intercept and replace messages. Suppose that Bob sends Alice his public key and Alice sends hers to Bob, but that Mallet intercepts both of these, sending his public key both times. Now, whenever Bob sends a message to Alice, it is really encrypted with Mallet's public key, not Alice's. Mallet intercepts the message, decrypts it, stores the original message, encrypts it with Alice's public key, and then passes the result on to Alice. Alice gets a valid message that she can decrypt with her secret key. Her replies are copied then passed on to Bob. Mallet can continue this indefinitely, and Bob and Alice get no indication that the messages have been tampered with. This attack can be prevented in two ways: (1) Instead of directly exchanging keys, retrieve them from a trusted database. This database could digitally sign replies to requests for keys to prevent spoofing. (2) Send messages in multiple pieces with confirmation after each piece using an algorithm such that messages cannot be decrypted except in their entirety (e.g., by sending every other bit). This would require the man-in-the-middle to simulate the replies, a much more difficult task

16.9 Summary

HTTP is the language Web clients use to talk to Web servers. A typical request from a browser starts with a GET, HEAD, or POST request line, followed by zero or more HTTP request lines, followed by a blank line. In the case of POST, additional data will then be sent. HTTP 1.1 defines some additional request methods. Upon receiving the data, the server will normally send a response line giving status information, a Content-Type line, zero or more other HTTP response lines, a blank line, then an associated document of the specified content type. In the case of HEAD requests, the associated document is omitted. Two headers of particular interest are Set-Cookie and Cookie, which let the server supply information to be stored by the browser, and let the browser send the information back in future connections. Some servers and browsers support Secure Sockets Layer, which encrypts the transmissions between the browser and server. SSL and several other Web-related protocols use public-key cryptography, and this chapter ended with a brief overview of this technique. HTTP can be used by custom Web clients and servers, but the most important application for programmers is to connect Web pages to databases and other programs on the server. The next two chapters cover the client and server sides of this process.

CGI PROGRAMMING AND BEYOND— THE CLIENT SIDE

Topics in this Chapter

- How remote programs receive data from Web pages
- Creating user interfaces using HTML forms
- Sending data from HTML forms to remote programs and displaying the resultant page
- Java applets that contact remote programs and display the resultant page
- Java applets that process the results of a remote program
- Bypassing the HTTP server by having an applet communicate directly with a server program.

Chapter 17

The Common Gateway Interface is a method that lets Web pages communicate with programs on an HTTP server. Prior to the advent of Java, this was the only way to get interactive Web pages: An HTML page sent limited information back to the server, which generated a new HTML page and returned it to the client to display. Java replaces some uses of CGI by allowing truly dynamic Web pages, doing the processing on the client instead of the server. However, CGI is still important for three reasons. First of all, it is not always desirable or feasible to do the processing on the client. For instance, downloading the entire Alta Vista database to a user's PC is hardly a reasonable option considering the over a year-per-terabyte download time that a 28.8K baud modem would require. Secondly, difficult as it is to imagine, not everyone is using a Java-enabled browser, and a site might want to make information available to these stone-age users. Thirdly, many existing Web services are already set up with CGI interfaces, and it is useful to know how to send information to them so that you can make use of their services from Web pages and/or Java applets that you write.

In CGI programming, a request is made for a URL from a location reserved by the HTTP server. The HTTP server decides which locations are reserved, but often these special directories are called "cgi-bin," "cgi," or "bin." When a URL in such a reserved location is requested, instead of treating it as a *file* whose *contents* should be returned, the HTTP server treats it as a *program* whose *output* should be returned. Data can be supplied to a CGI program either by appending it to the URL (using HTTP GET) or on a separate line (using HTTP POST).

In this chapter, the client side of this process is discussed: how to collect input from HTML forms or via Java applets, and how to transmit that data to a CGI program using GET or POST. Chapter 18 describes the server side of the process: reading and processing data from CGI clients, and returning the results. Chapter 19 "JavaScript: Adding Dynamic Content to Web Pages" discusses how to use JavaScript to verify that the user has supplied the right type of data before it is transmitted to the server.

17.1 Using HTML Forms to Talk to CGI Programs

A WWW page can gather input in two basic ways: via HTML or via Java. When using HTML for the interface, the author can define various FORM fields that enable the user to enter limited types of data. This data is sent to a CGI program when the user initiates certain actions, such as clicking on a submit button or an image map. Once the data is sent, the CGI program generates a new HTML page describing the result and returns it to the user's browser to be displayed. Java applets can also be used to gather input and send it to CGI programs. Java supports a much richer interface than do HTML forms, but building interfaces in Java is often more difficult than in HTML, especially if the interface contains large amounts of structured text. Once the data is collected, it can be sent to the server and the returned page displayed as is done with HTML interfaces, or in some cases the applet can directly read the results and incorporate them into the existing program. Sections 17.2 through 17.5 discuss building interfaces using HTML, while Sections 17.6 through 17.8 cover doing it in Java.

The general approach to using forms is that the FORM tag specifies the URL of the CGI program, each input element is named (NAME), and some elements are supplied with an initial value (VALUE) either explicitly by the author or from an HTML default. The user can interactively supply additional values by typing into a textfield, selecting a radio button, and so forth. When the user clicks on a "Submit" button or an image map, the active elements are accumulated into a string of the form "name1=val1&name2=val2& ... &nameN=valN," that is then transmitted to the specified URL. The data can be transmitted either by appending it to the URL after a question mark ("?") or by sending it on a separate line. For instance, the Yahoo! search service at http://www.yahoo.com/ uses a CGI program at http://

`search.yahoo.com/bin/search` to process queries, and looks for data after "p=." So directly specifying a URL of `http://search.yahoo.com/bin/search?p=cgi+programming` (Figure 17–1) will give you Yahoo's results page for "cgi programming" (Figure 17–2), bypassing their original data input page at `http://www.yahoo.com`.

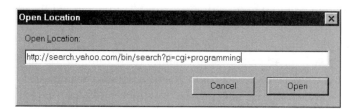

Figure 17–1   Sending data to a CGI program by embedding it in a URL.

Figure 17–2   Result of query shown in Figure 17–1.

17.2 The HTML FORM Element

HTML forms allow you to create a set of data input elements associated with a particular URL. Each of these elements is typically given a name and has a value based on the original HTML and/or user input. When the form is submitted, the names and values of all active elements are collected into a data string with "=" between each name and associated value and with "&" between each name/value pair. This string is then transmitted to the URL designated by the FORM element. The data string is either appended to the URL after a question mark or sent on a separate line, depending on the submission method being used. This section covers the FORM element itself, used primarily to designate the URL and to choose the submission method. The following section (17.3) covers the types of input elements that can be used inside a form to actually collect user input.

HTML Element: `<FORM ACTION="URL" ...> ... </FORM>`
Attributes: ACTION, METHOD, ENCTYPE, TARGET (nonstandard),
NAME (nonstandard), ONSUBMIT (nonstandard),
ONRESET (nonstandard)

The FORM element creates an area for data input elements and designates the URL that any collected data will be transmitted to. For example:

```
<FORM ACTION="http://some.isp.com/cgi-bin/program">
  FORM input elements and regular HTML
</FORM>
```

ACTION

The ACTION attribute specifies the URL of the CGI program that will process the FORM data (e.g., `http://cgi.whitehouse.gov/cgi-bin/schedule-fundraiser`), or an e-mail address where the FORM data will be sent (e.g., `mailto:gingrich@house.congress.gov`). Some sites do not allow ordinary users to create CGI programs, or charge extra for this privilege. In such a case, sending the data via e-mail is a convenient option when creating pages that need to collect data but not return results (e.g., for accepting orders for products). You must use the POST method (see the following section) when using a `mailto` URL. Unfortunately, however, Internet Explorer versions 3.02 and earlier do not properly support `mailto` URLs for form submissions, as they do not automatically include the name/value pairs in the body of the message. It works as expected in Netscape Navigator in version 2.0 and later. However, Netscape 2.0, 2.01, and 2.02 suffer from a privacy flaw in that they transmit to `mailto` URLs without first confirming things with the user, thus revealing the return e-mail address (as specified in "Mail and News Preferences") to potential junk mailers. These "spammers" got even more sophisticated when they discovered that they could submit a form automatically by using Java–Script, thus making a Web page that collected e-mail addresses. The anti-spam crowd fought back by specifying return e-mail addresses of president@whitehouse.gov or "postmaster" at the ISP of the most well-known junk mailers, and this practice mostly died out. Netscape 3.0 and later gives users the best of both worlds, supporting `mailto` URLs for form submission but first warning the user that their e-mail address is being revealed and letting them confirm the transmission.

Core Alert

Specifying an e-mail address as the destination for form data works in Netscape Navigator but not Internet Explorer.

METHOD

The `METHOD` attribute specifies how the data will be transmitted to the HTTP server. When `GET` is used, the data is appended to the end of the designated URL, after a question mark. `GET` is the default and is also the method that is used when a browser requests a normal URL. To illustrate, Listing 17.1 creates a simple input form that uses the `GET` method and contacts a URL connected to the mini HTTP server developed in Section 15.7. Figure 17–3 shows the initial result; Figure 17–4 shows how the data string was sent on the initial HTTP request line. On the other hand, when `POST` is used, the data is sent on a separate line. Listing 17.2 shows the same input form as Listing 17.1 except that `METHOD="POST"` is specified. The initial result is identical to that of Figure 17–3. However, as shown in Figure 17–5, the data is sent to the server on a separate line following the HTTP request headers and a blank line. The advantages of using the `GET` method are that it is simple and that CGI programs that use `GET` can be accessed for testing and debugging without creating a form, simply by typing in a URL with the proper data appended. On the other hand, `GET` requests have limits on the amount of data that can be appended, while `POST` requests do not. Another disadvantage of `GET` is that most browsers show the URL, including the attached data string, in an address bar at the top of the browser. This makes GET inappropriate for sending sensitive data.

Listing 17.1 `Get.html`

```
<!DOCTYPE HTML PUBLIC "-//W3C//DTD HTML 3.2//EN">
<HTML>
<HEAD>
  <TITLE>The ACTION Attribute</TITLE>
</HEAD>

<BODY BGCOLOR="WHITE">
<H1>The <CODE>ACTION</CODE> Attribute</H1>

<FORM ACTION="http://www.apl.jhu.edu:5555/cgi-bin/test">
  Textfield1:
  <INPUT TYPE="TEXT" NAME="Textfield1" VALUE="Entry 1">
  <BR>
  Textfield2:
  <INPUT TYPE="TEXT" NAME="Textfield2" VALUE="Entry 2">
  <BR>
  SubmitButton:
  <INPUT TYPE="SUBMIT" NAME="SubmitButton" VALUE="Send">
</FORM>

</BODY>
</HTML>
```

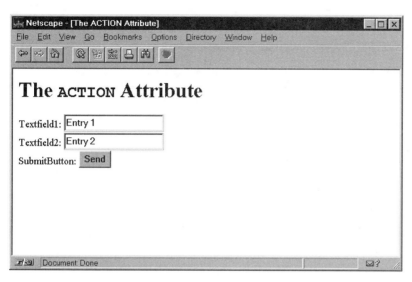

Figure 17–3   A simple input form.

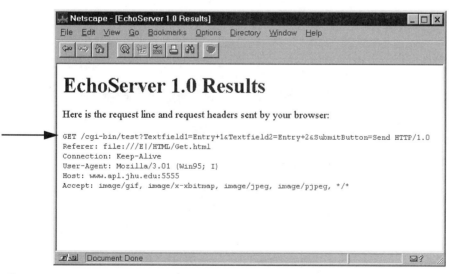

Figure 17–4   Data transmitted via GET is appended to the URL.

Listing 17.2 `Post.html`

```
<!DOCTYPE HTML PUBLIC "-//W3C//DTD HTML 3.2//EN">
<HTML>
<HEAD>
  <TITLE>The ACTION Attribute</TITLE>
</HEAD>

<BODY BGCOLOR="WHITE">
<H1>The <CODE>ACTION</CODE> Attribute</H1>

<FORM ACTION="http://www.apl.jhu.edu:5555/cgi-bin/test"
      METHOD="POST">
  Textfield1:
  <INPUT TYPE="TEXT" NAME="Textfield1" VALUE="Entry 1">
  <BR>
  Textfield2:
  <INPUT TYPE="TEXT" NAME="Textfield2" VALUE="Entry 2">
  <BR>
  SubmitButton:
  <INPUT TYPE="SUBMIT" NAME="SubmitButton" VALUE="Send">
</FORM>

</BODY>
</HTML>
```

Figure 17-5   Data transmitted via `POST` is sent on a separate line.

ENCTYPE

This specifies the way in which the data will be encoded before being transmitted. The default is `application/x-www-form-urlen-coded`, which means that the client converts each space into a plus sign (+) and each other nonalphanumeric characters into a percent sign (%) followed by the two hex digits representing that character. This is in addition to placing an equals sign (=) between entry names and values, and an ampersand (&) between entries. For instance, consider the following FORM and its resultant Web page, which sends data to the `EchoServer` developed in Chapter 15 "Client-Server Programming in Java."

```
<FORM ACTION="http://www.apl.jhu.edu:5555/foo/bar">
  <INPUT TYPE="SUBMIT" NAME="Button1">
  <INPUT TYPE="TEXT" NAME="TextField1">
</FORM>
```

Now, when the data in the textfield of Figure 17–6 is sent to the server, the "~" and "/" get encoded as "%7E" (decimal 126 in ASCII and ISO Latin-1) and "%2F" (decimal 47 in ASCII and ISO Latin-1) respectively, as shown in Figure 17–7.

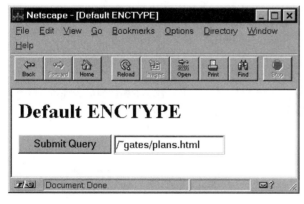

Figure 17–6   Sending data using `application/x-www-form-urlencoded`.

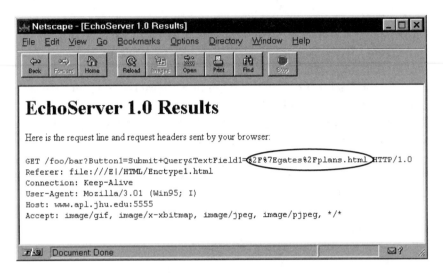

Figure 17–7   Receiving data that was encoded with
`application/x-www-form-urlencoded`.

Some browsers (e.g., Netscape, but not Internet Explorer) support an
additional `ENCTYPE` of `multipart/form-data`. This encoding
places each of the fields as separate parts of a MIME-compatible document, and automatically uses `POST` to submit them. For instance, consider the following `FORM` and its result (Figure 17–8), which is identical
to the previous one except for the addition of the `ENCTYPE`.

```
<FORM ACTION="http://www.apl.jhu.edu:5555/foo/bar"
      ENCTYPE="multipart/form-data">
  <INPUT TYPE="SUBMIT" NAME="Button1">
  <INPUT TYPE="TEXT" NAME="TextField1">
</FORM>
```

Now, when the submission button of Figure 17–8 is clicked, the data is
sent via `POST`, is enclosed in MIME declarations, and the individual
characters are unencoded. This result is shown in Figure 17–9.

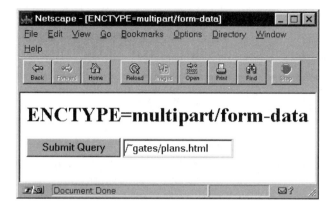

Figure 17–8   Sending data using `multipart/form-data`.

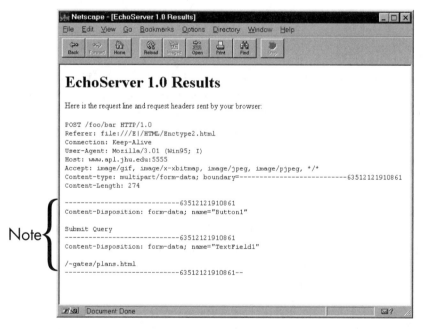

Figure 17–9   Receiving data that was encoded with `multipart/form-data`.

The `multipart/form-data` encoding is most commonly used with `FILE` input forms.

TARGET

The TARGET attribute is used by frame-capable browsers to determine which frame should be used to display the results of the CGI program. The default is to display the results in whatever frame contains the form being submitted. See Chapter 19 for more details on JavaScript.

NAME

The nonstandard NAME attribute is used by JavaScript as a named reference to the form. This is generally more convenient than using an index into the document.forms array. See Chapter 19 for more details.

ONSUBMIT, ONRESET

These attributes are used by JavaScript to attach code that should be executed when the form is submitted or reset.

17.3 FORM Input Elements

The following covers the three types of data input elements that can go inside the FORM element: INPUT, TEXTAREA, and SELECT. The INPUT element can result in a variety of different GUI controls (widgets); each of these is covered separately. Note that although these input elements can only appear inside a FORM element, most standard HTML constructs are also permitted inside a form. Nested forms, however, are forbidden.

Submit Buttons

HTML Element: `<INPUT TYPE="SUBMIT" ...>` (No End Tag)
Attributes: NAME, VALUE, ONCLICK (nonstandard),
ONDBLCLICK (nonstandard), ONFOCUS (nonstandard),
ONBLUR (nonstandard)

When a submit button is clicked, the form is sent to the CGI program designated by the ACTION parameter of the FORM. Although the action can be triggered other ways, such as by clicking on an image map, most forms have at least one submit button. Submit buttons, like other input elements, adopt the look and feel of the client operating system, so will look different on different platforms. Figure 17–10 shows a button on Windows 95, created via

```
<INPUT TYPE="SUBMIT">
```

Submit Query

Figure 17-10 A SUBMIT button with the default label.

NAME, VALUE

Most input elements have a name and an associated value. When the form is submitted, the names and values of active elements are concatenated to form the data string. If a submit button is used simply to initiate the submission of the form, its name can be omitted and then it does not contribute to the data string that is sent. If a name *is* supplied, then only the name and value of the button that was actually clicked is sent. The label is used as the value that is transmitted; supplying an explicit value will change the default label. For instance, the following code snippet creates a textfield and two submit buttons, shown in Figure 17–11. If, for example, the first button is selected, the data string sent to the server would be
"Item=256MB+SIMM&Add=Add+Item+to+Account".

```
<CENTER>
Item:
<INPUT TYPE="TEXT" NAME="Item" VALUE="256MB SIMM"><BR>
<INPUT TYPE="SUBMIT" NAME="Add"
       VALUE="Add Item to Account">
<INPUT TYPE="SUBMIT" NAME="Delete"
       VALUE="Delete Item from Account">
</CENTER>
```

Figure 17-11 SUBMIT buttons with user-defined labels.

ONCLICK, ONDBLCLICK, ONFOCUS, ONBLUR

These nonstandard attributes are used by JavaScript-capable browsers to associate JavaScript code with the button. The ONCLICK and ONDBLCLICK code is executed when the button is pressed, the ONFOCUS code when it gets the input focus, and the ONBLUR code when it loses the focus. Attributes are not case sensitive, and these attributes are traditionally called onClick, onDblClick, onFocus, and onBlur by JavaScript programmers. See Chapter 19 for more information on JavaScript.

Reset Buttons

HTML Element: <INPUT TYPE="RESET" ...> (No End Tag)
Attributes: VALUE, NAME (nonstandard), ONCLICK (nonstandard),
ONDBLCLICK (nonstandard), ONFOCUS (nonstandard),
ONBLUR (nonstandard)

Reset buttons serve to reset the values of all items in the FORM to that specified in the original VALUE parameters. They are never transmitted as part of the form's contents.

VALUE
The VALUE attribute specifies the button label; "Reset" is the default. For instance, the following example creates the button shown in Figure 17–12.

```
<INPUT TYPE="RESET" VALUE="Clear all Purchases">
```

Clear all Purchases

Figure 17-12   A RESET button's label is specified with VALUE.

NAME
Because reset buttons do not contribute to the data string transmitted when the form is submitted, they are not named in standard HTML. However, JavaScript permits a NAME attribute to be used to simplify reference to the element. See Chapter 19 for more information on JavaScript.

ONCLICK, ONDBLCLICK, ONFOCUS, ONBLUR
These nonstandard attributes are used by JavaScript-capable browsers to associate JavaScript code with the button. The ONCLICK and ONDBLCLICK code is executed when the button is pressed, the ONFOCUS code when it gets the input focus, and the ONBLUR code when it loses the focus. Attributes are not case sensitive, and these

attributes are traditionally called `onClick`, `onDblClick`, `onFocus`, and `onBlur` by JavaScript programmers. See Chapter 19 for details.

JavaScript Buttons

HTML Element: `<INPUT TYPE="BUTTON" ...>` (No End Tag)
Attributes: NAME, VALUE, ONCLICK, ONDBLCLICK, ONFOCUS, ONBLUR

The BUTTON input type is an extension to HTML 3.2 recognized only by browsers that support JavaScript. It creates a button with the same visual appearance as a SUBMIT or RESET button and allows the author to attach JavaScript code to the ONCLICK, ONDBLCLICK, ONFOCUS, or ONBLUR attributes. The name/value pair associated with a JavaScript button is not transmitted as part of the data when the form is submitted, even if the button explicitly calls `theForm.submit()`. Arbitrary code can be associated with the button, but one of the most common uses is to verify that all input elements are in the proper format before the form is submitted to the server. For instance, the following would create a button where the `validate-Form` method would be called whenever it is activated. The result is shown in Figure 17–13. See Chapter 19 for more information on JavaScript.

```
<INPUT TYPE="BUTTON" VALUE="Check Values"
onClick="validateForm()">
```

Figure 17–13   A JavaScript button that verifies input elements are in the proper format.

VALUE
The VALUE attribute specifies the label of the button.

NAME
The NAME attribute is used to supply the button a reference that can be used in JavaScript code.

ONCLICK, ONDBLCLICK, ONFOCUS, ONBLUR
These attributes can be used to supply code to be executed when the button is clicked, receives the input focus, and loses the focus, respectively.

Checkboxes

HTML Element: <INPUT TYPE="CHECKBOX" NAME="..." ...>
(No End Tag)
Attributes: NAME (required), VALUE, CHECKED, ONCLICK (nonstandard),
ONFOCUS (nonstandard), ONBLUR (nonstandard)

This input element creates a checkbox whose name/value pair is transmitted
if the checkbox is checked when the form is submitted. For instance, the following code results in the checkbox shown in Figure 17–14.

```
<P>
<INPUT TYPE="CHECKBOX" NAME="GeekBox" CHECKED>
Geeks check here
```

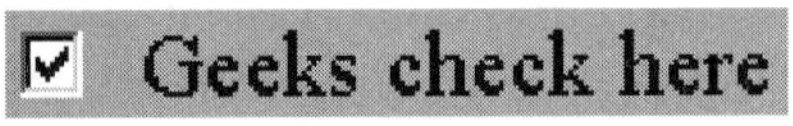

☑ **Geeks check here**

Figure 17-14   A CHECKBOX that transmits the
associated name/value pair when activated.

Note that the descriptive text associated with the checkbox is normal
HTML, and care should be taken to guarantee that it appears next to the
checkbox. Thus, the <P> in the preceding example ensures that the checkbox
isn't part of the previous paragraph.

Core Alert

*Paragraphs inside a FORM are filled and wrapped just like regular
paragraphs. So be sure to insert explicit HTML markup to keep input
elements with the text that describes them.*

NAME

This supplies the name that is sent to the server. It is required for standard HTML checkboxes but optional when used with JavaScript.

VALUE

The VALUE attribute is optional, and defaults to "on". Recall that the
name and value is only sent to the server if the checkbox is checked
when the form is submitted. For instance, in the preceding example

"Geekbox=on" would be added to the data string since the box is checked, but nothing would be added if the box was unchecked.

CHECKED

If the CHECKED attribute is supplied, then the checkbox is initially checked when the associated Web page is loaded. Otherwise, it is initially unchecked.

ONCLICK, ONFOCUS, ONBLUR

These attributes can be used to supply code to be executed when the button is clicked, receives the input focus, and loses the focus, respectively.

Radio Buttons

HTML Element: <INPUT TYPE="RADIO" NAME="..." VALUE="..." ...> (No End Tag)

Attributes: NAME (required), VALUE (required), CHECKED, ONCLICK (nonstandard), ONFOCUS (nonstandard), ONBLUR (nonstandard)

You indicate a group of radio buttons by providing all of them with the same NAME. Only one button in a group can be depressed at a time; selecting a new button when one is already selected results in the previous choice becoming deselected. The value of the one selected is sent when the form is submitted. Note that radio buttons, like Checkbox's in a CheckboxGroup in Java, technically need not appear next to each other, although this is almost always recommended.

NAME

Unlike the NAME attribute of most input elements, this NAME is shared by multiple elements. All radio buttons associated with the same name are grouped logically so that no more than one can be selected at any given time. Note that attribute values are case sensitive, so the following would result in two radio buttons that are *not* logically connected.

```
<INPUT TYPE="RADIO" NAME="Foo" VALUE="Value1">
<INPUT TYPE="RADIO" NAME="FOO" VALUE="Value2">
```

Core Warning

Be sure the NAME *of each radio button in a logical group matches exactly.*

VALUE

The VALUE attribute supplies the value that gets transmitted with the NAME when the form is submitted. It doesn't affect the appearance of the radio button. Instead, normal text and HTML markup is placed around the radio button, just as with checkboxes.

CHECKED

If the CHECKED attribute is supplied, then the checkbox is initially checked when the associated Web page is loaded. Otherwise it is initially unchecked.

ONCLICK, ONFOCUS, ONBLUR

These attributes can be used to supply JavaScript code to be executed when the button is clicked, receives the input focus, and loses the focus, respectively.

An example of a radio button group follows. Because input elements are wrapped as part of normal paragraphs, a DL list is used to make sure that the buttons appear under each other in the resultant page. Figure 17–15 shows the result. In this case, "Type=Nerd" would get sent as part of the FORM data when it is submitted.

```
<DL>
  <DT>Your Type:
  <DD><INPUT TYPE="RADIO" NAME="Type" VALUE="Geek">
      Geek (Good)
  <DD><INPUT TYPE="RADIO" NAME="Type"
             VALUE="Nerd" CHECKED>
      Nerd (Better)
  <DD><INPUT TYPE="RADIO" NAME="Type"
             VALUE="Hacker">
      Hacker (Best)
</DL>
```

Your Type:
○ Geek (Good)
⊙ Nerd (Better)
○ Hacker (Best)

Figure 17-15 RADIO buttons can only be depressed one at a time.

Textfields

HTML Element: `<INPUT TYPE="TEXT" NAME="..." ...>`
(No End Tag)
Attributes: NAME (required), VALUE, SIZE, MAXLENGTH,
ONCHANGE (nonstandard), ONSELECT (nonstandard),
ONFOCUS (nonstandard), ONBLUR (nonstandard),
ONKEYDOWN (nonstandard), ONKEYPRESS (nonstandard),
ONKEYUP (nonstandard)

This creates a single-line input field where the user can enter text. See
TEXTAREA for multi-line fields. TEXT is the default TYPE in INPUT forms,
although it is recommended that TEXT be supplied explicitly. As usual, you
should remember that the normal browser word wrapping applies inside
FORM elements, so care should be taken to avoid having the descriptive text
separated from the associated texfield. Some browsers submit the form when
the user hits ENTER when the cursor is in a textfield, but you should avoid
depending on this behavior because it is not standard. For instance, Netscape
Navigator submits the form when the user types a carriage return only if the
current form has a single textfield, regardless of the number of forms on the
page. Internet Explorer submits the form on ENTER only when there is a
single form on the page, regardless of the number of textfields in the form.
Mosaic submits the form on ENTER only when the cursor is in the last textfield on the entire page.

Core Warning

*Don't rely on the browser submitting the form when the user hits ENTER
when in a textfield. Always include a button or image map that submits the
form explicitly.*

NAME

The NAME attribute identifies the textfield when the form is submitted. In standard HTML it is required; with JavaScript it is recommended but not required.

VALUE

A VALUE attribute, if supplied, specifies the *initial* contents of the text-field. When the form is submitted, the *current* contents are sent. In the following example (see Figure 17–16), "TypeString=Geek" will be transmitted with the FORM data. With textfields, the name/value pair is sent even if the textfield is empty. So, for instance, if the field shown in the example of Figure 17–16 contains no text, "TypeString=" will be transmitted.

SIZE

This specifies the width of the textfield, based on the average character width of the font being used. If text beyond this size is entered, the textfield scrolls to accommodate it.

MAXLENGTH

MAXLENGTH gives the maximum number of *allowable* characters. This is in contrast to the number of *visible* characters, which is specified via SIZE.

ONCHANGE, ONSELECT, ONFOCUS, ONBLUR, ONDBLDOWN, ONKEYPRES, ONKEYUP

These attributes are used only by browsers that support JavaScript. They specify the action to take when the mouse leaves the textfield after a change has occurred, when the user selects text in the textfield, when the textfield gets the input focus, when it loses the input focus, and when individual keys are pressed.

The following code creates the textfield shown in Figure 17–16.

```
<P>
Your Type: <INPUT TYPE="TEXT" NAME="TypeString"
           SIZE=10 VALUE="Geek">
```

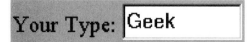

Figure 17–16   A 10-character TEXT field.

Password Fields

HTML Element: `<INPUT TYPE="PASSWORD" NAME="..." ...>`
(No End Tag)

Attributes: NAME (required), VALUE, SIZE, MAXLENGTH,
ONCHANGE (nonstandard), ONSELECT (nonstandard),
ONFOCUS (nonstandard), ONBLUR (nonstandard),
ONKEYDOWN (nonstandard), ONKEYPRESS (nonstandard),
ONKEYUP (nonstandard)

Password fields are created and used just like textfields, except that when the user enters text, the input is not echoed but instead some obscuring character (usually an asterisk) is displayed. The regular, unobscured text is transmitted as the value of the field when the form is submitted. As a result, you will want to use the POST method when using a password field so that a bystander cannot read the unobscured password off the URL display at the top of the browser.

Core Security

To protect the user's privacy, always use POST *when creating forms with password fields.*

NAME, VALUE, SIZE, MAXLENGTH, ONCHANGE, ONSELECT, ONFOCUS, ONBLUR, ONKEYDOWN, ONKEYPRESS, ONKEYUP

Attributes for password fields are used in exactly the same manner as with textfields.

The following example creates a password field. The result after entering "FooBar" is shown in Figure 17–17. In such a case, "Secret-Word=FooBar" would be added to the data being sent to the server.

```
<FORM ACTION="URL" METHOD="POST">
...
<P>
Enter Secret Word: <INPUT TYPE="PASSWORD"
                          NAME="SecretWord" SIZE=10>
...
</FORM>
```

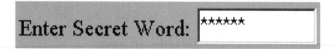

Figure 17-17   A PASSWORD field with obscured characters protects the user's privacy.

Server-Side Image Maps

HTML Element: `<INPUT TYPE="IMAGE" ...>` (No End Tag)
Attributes: NAME (required), SRC, ALIGN

This displays an image that, when clicked, sends the form to the CGI program specified via the enclosing form's ACTION. The name itself is not sent; instead *name*.x and *name*.y are sent with the coordinates (relative to the upper-left corner of the image) of the mouse click.

NAME
The NAME attribute identifies the textfield when the form is submitted.

SRC
SRC designates the URL of the associated image.

ALIGN
The ALIGN attribute has the same options (TOP, MIDDLE, BOTTOM, LEFT, RIGHT) and default (BOTTOM) as the ALIGN attribute of the IMG tag, and is used in the same way. See Section 3.4 (Embedded Images) for details.

Listing 17.3 shows a simple example, where the form's ACTION specifies the EchoServer developed in Section 15.7. Figures 17–18 and 17–19 show the results before and after the image is clicked.

Listing 17.3 `Image.html`

```
<!DOCTYPE HTML PUBLIC "-//W3C//DTD HTML 3.2//EN">
<HTML>
<HEAD>
  <TITLE>The IMAGE Input Element</TITLE>
</HEAD>

<BODY>
<H1 ALIGN="CENTER">
The <CODE>IMAGE</CODE> Input Element</H1>
Which island is Java? Click and see if you are correct.

<FORM ACTION="http://www.apl.jhu.edu:5555/java-test">
  <INPUT TYPE="IMAGE" NAME="Map" SRC="indonesia.gif">
</FORM>

Of course, image maps can be implemented <B>in</B>
Java as well. :-)

</BODY>
</HTML>
```

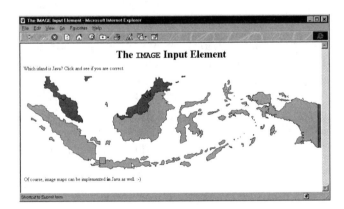

Figure 17–18   An `IMAGE` input element with `NAME="Map"`.

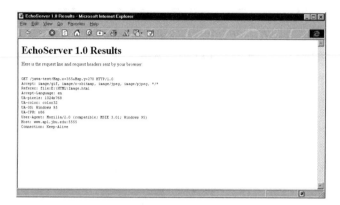

Figure 17–19   Selecting the image at (355,270) adds
`Map.x=355&Map.y=270` to the form's data.

Attached Files

HTML Element: `<INPUT TYPE="FILE" ...>` (No End Tag)

Attributes: NAME (required), VALUE, SIZE, MAXLENGTH, ACCEPT,
ONCHANGE (nonstandard), ONSELECT (nonstandard),
ONFOCUS (nonstandard), ONBLUR (nonstandard)

This lets the user enter a filename. On some systems (such as Internet
Explorer), it is little different than a textfield. However, other systems (such
as Netscape) insert a "Browse" button that, when clicked, brings up a file
selection dialog to select the name. Then, when the form is submitted, the
contents of the file are included as long as an ENCTYPE of `multipart/`
`form-data` was specified in the initial FORM declaration. This provides a
convenient way to make user-supported CGI pages, where the user enters
symptoms of a problem then submits the symptom description along with
associated data or configuration files.

Core Tip

*If you want to let Netscape users include the contents of a file with their
form submission, be sure to specify* `ENCTYPE="multipart/`
`form-data"` *in the* FORM *tag.*

NAME

The NAME attribute identifies the textfield when the form is submitted.

VALUE

The VALUE attribute places an initial filename in the textfield. For this to be meaningful, you will probably have to make some assumptions about what operating system the client will be using.

SIZE, MAXLENGTH

The SIZE and MAXLENGTH attributes are used the same way as in text-fields, specifying the number of visible and maximum allowable characters, respectively.

ACCEPT

The ACCEPT attribute is intended to be a comma-separated list of MIME types used to restrict the available file names. However, very few browsers support this attribute.

ONCHANGE, ONSELECT, ONFOCUS, ONBLUR

These attributes are used only by browsers that support JavaScript, but because FILE input elements are most commonly used with Netscape, it is quite likely that if the user's browser supports attached files it also supports JavaScript. The attributes specify the action to take when the mouse leaves the textfield after a change has occurred, when the user selects text in the textfield, when the textfield gets the input focus, and when it loses the input focus, respectively.

For instance, the following code creates a file input form. Figure 17–20 shows the initial result in Netscape, while Figure 17–21 shows a typical pop-up window that results when the "Browse" button is activated.

```
<P>
Enter data file below:<BR>
<INPUT TYPE="FILE" NAME="Filename">
```

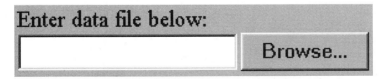

Figure 17–20 A FILE input element as shown in Netscape.

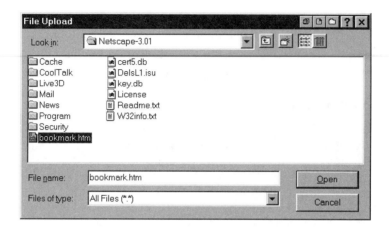

Figure 17–21   Results of clicking "Browse" in `FILE` element.

Hidden Fields

HTML Element: `<INPUT TYPE="HIDDEN" NAME="..."` `VALUE="...">` (No End Tag)

Attributes: NAME (required), VALUE

HTTP connections do not maintain a history of previous connections, so it is difficult to carry on a "conversation" where context matters. Because a CGI program can generate an HTML page (which may contain a FORM to reconnect), the program can embed contextual information in these hidden fields. Hidden fields can also be used to embed version or configuration information that affects how the CGI program processes the data but that doesn't affect what the user sees. The name/value pairs are sent to the server, but no graphical element is created in the browser. For instance, with the following example, "LastOperation=delete" will always get sent with the FORM data.

```
<INPUT TYPE="HIDDEN" NAME="LastOperation"
        VALUE="delete">
```

Because there is no reliable way to "hide" the HTML that generates a page, authors are cautioned not to use hidden fields to embed passwords or other validation information.

Text Areas

HTML Element: `<TEXTAREA NAME="..." ROWS=xxx`
                    `COLS=yyy> ...`
               `</TEXTAREA>`

Attributes: `NAME` (required), `ROWS` (required), `COLS` (required), `WRAP`
(nonstandard), `ONCHANGE` (nonstandard), `ONSELECT`
(nonstandard), `ONFOCUS` (nonstandard), `ONBLUR`
(nonstandard), `ONKEYDOWN` (nonstandard), `ONKEYPRESS`
(nonstandard), `ONKEYUP` (nonstandard)

This creates a multiline text field. There is no `VALUE` attribute; instead, text between the start and end tags is used as the initial contents of the text area. The initial text between `<TEXTAREA ...>` and `</TEXTAREA>` is treated similarly to text inside the `XMP` element (Section 2.2). That is, whitespace in this initial text is maintained and HTML markup between the start and end tags is taken literally, except for character entities such as "`&lt;`," "`&copy;`," and so forth., which are interpreted normally. All characters including those generated from character entities are URL encoded before being transmitted.

NAME

This specifies the name that will be sent to the CGI program.

ROWS

`ROWS` specifies the number of visible lines of text. If more lines of text than can fit are entered, scrollbars will be added.

COLS

`COLS` specifies the visible width of the text area, based on the average width of characters in the font being used.

WRAP

The nonstandard `WRAP` attribute specifies what to do with lines that are longer than the size specified by `COLS`. It is supported by Netscape in version 2.0 and later. A value of `OFF` disables word wrap, and is the default. The user can still enter explicit line breaks in such a case. A value of `HARD` causes words to wrap on screen *and* the associated line breaks to be transmitted when the form is submitted. Finally, a value of `SOFT` causes the words to wrap on screen, but no extra line breaks to be transmitted when the form is submitted.

ONCHANGE, ONSELECT, ONFOCUS, ONBLUR, ONKEY-DOWN, ONKEYPRESS and ONKEYUP

These attributes apply only to browsers that support JavaScript, and specify code to be executed when certain conditions arise. ONCHANGE handles the situation when the user leaves the text area after it has changed, ONSELECT describes what to do when text in the text area is selected by the user, ONFOCUS and ONBLUR specify what to do when the text area acquires or loses the input focus, and the remaining attributes determine what to do when individual keys are typed.

The following example creates a text area with 5 visible rows that can hold about 30 characters per row. The result is shown in Figure 17–22.

```
<P>
Enter some HTML:<BR>
<TEXTAREA NAME="HTML" ROWS=5 COLS=30>
Delete this text and replace
with some HTML to validate.
</TEXTAREA>
```

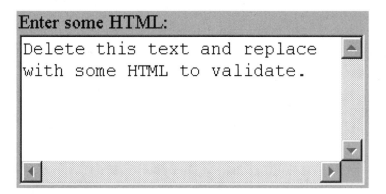

Figure 17–22   A textarea 5 lines high and 30 characters wide.

Combo Boxes and List Boxes

A SELECT element is used to present a set of options to the user. If only a single entry can be selected and no visible size has been specified, the options are typically presented in a combo box (drop-down menu), while list boxes are usually used when multiple selections are permitted or a specific visible size has been specified. The choices themselves are specified via OPTION entries embedded inside the SELECT element. The typical format is as follows:

```
<SELECT NAME="Name" ...>
  <OPTION VALUE="Value1">Choice 1 Text
  <OPTION VALUE="Value2">Choice 2 Text
  ...
  <OPTION VALUE="ValueN">Choice N Text
</SELECT>
```

HTML Element: `<SELECT NAME="..." ...> ... </SELECT>`

Attributes: NAME (required), SIZE, MULTIPLE, ONCLICK (nonstandard),
ONFOCUS (nonstandard), ONBLUR (nonstandard), ONCHANGE
(nonstandard)

SELECT creates a combo box or list box for selecting among choices. You
specify each choice via an OPTION element between <SELECT ...> and
</SELECT>.

NAME

NAME identifies the form to the target CGI program.

SIZE

SIZE gives the number of visible rows. If it is used, the SELECT menu
is usually represented as a list box instead of a combo box, which is the
normal representation when neither SIZE nor MULTIPLE is supplied.

MULTIPLE

The MULTIPLE attribute specifies that multiple entries can be selected
simultaneously. If MULTIPLE is omitted, only a single selection is permitted.

ONCLICK, ONFOCUS, ONBLUR, ONCHANGE

These nonstandard attributes are supported by browsers that understand JavaScript, and indicate code to be executed when the entry is
clicked on, gains the input focus, loses the input focus, and loses the
focus after having been changed, respectively.

HTML Element: `<OPTION ...>` (No End Tag)

Attributes: SELECTED, VALUE

Only valid inside a SELECT element, this element specifies the menu
choices.

SELECTED

If present, SELECTED specifies that the particular menu item shown is selected when the page is first loaded.

VALUE

VALUE gives the value to be associated with the NAME of the SELECT menu if the current option is selected. This is *not* the text that is displayed to the user; that is specified by separate text listed after the OPTION tag.

The following example creates a menu of standard personality types. Because only a single selection is allowed and because no visible SIZE is specified, it is displayed as a combo box, shown in Figures 17–23 and 17–24. If the entry "Hacker (Best)" is active when the form is submitted, then "Type2=Hacker" is sent to the CGI program. Notice that it is the VALUE field, not the descriptive text, that is transmitted.

```
<P>
Choose Your Type
<SELECT NAME="Type2">
  <OPTION VALUE="Geek" SELECTED>Geek (Good)
  <OPTION VALUE="Nerd">Nerd (Better)
  <OPTION VALUE="Hacker">Hacker (Best)
</SELECT>
```

Figure 17-23   A SELECT element displayed as a combo box.

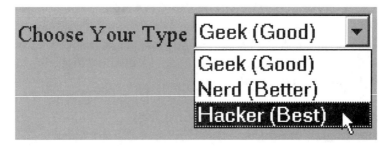

Figure 17-24   Choosing options from a SELECT menu.

The second example shows a SELECT element rendered as a list box. If more than one entry is active when the form is submitted, then more than one value is sent, listed as separate entries (repeating the NAME). For instance, in the example shown in Figure 17–25, "Language=CPP&Language=Java" gets added to the data being sent to the server.

```
<P>
Choose the languages you know:<BR>
<SELECT NAME="Language" MULTIPLE SIZE=5>
  <OPTION VALUE="C">C
  <OPTION VALUE="CPP">C++
  <OPTION VALUE="Lisp">Lisp
  <OPTION VALUE="Smalltalk">Smalltalk
  <OPTION VALUE="Java" SELECTED>Java
</SELECT>
```

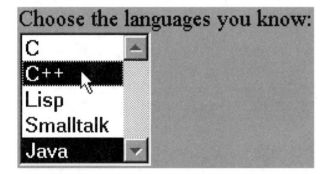

Figure 17–25 A SELECT element with MULTIPLE or SIZE specified results in a list box.

17.4 ISINDEX

ISINDEX is not a FORM element, but can be used to make simple textual input fields for CGI programming. Due to its limited flexibility, it is not recommended for most CGI applications. It can appear in either the HEAD or the BODY of the document.

HTML Element: <ISINDEX ...> (No End Tag)
Attributes: PROMPT, ACTION (nonstandard)

This element produces a simple textfield for user input.

PROMPT

PROMPT specifies the advisory text to be displayed before the textfield. If it is left unspecified, then the browser chooses some default like "This is a searchable index. Enter search keywords:".

ACTION

Unless the non-standard ACTION attribute is supplied (Internet Explorer only), when the user hits a carriage return in the textfield, *the data in the textfield is sent to the same URL from which the original page was loaded*. This means that in the absence of ACTION, the page containing the ISINDEX must itself be the output of a CGI program. The typical scenario involves the CGI program first checking if it received any data, then either generating the request page (no data received) or the results page (data received). In general, ISINDEX is a poor choice compared to HTML forms. However, the data it transmits does not contain an equals sign (=), and thus is easier to process (see Chapter 18 on the server side of CGI programming). So it is still occasionally used for simple interfaces. For instance, http://hoo-hoo.ncsa.uiuc.edu/cgi-bin/finger is a CGI program that provides an interface to the "finger" user-identification service. If a connection is made with no attached data, a data input page is created. Listing 17.4 shows the HTML generated for this page, with the result shown in Figure 17–26.

Listing 17.4 NCSA's input page for the "finger" service

```
<TITLE>Finger Gateway</TITLE>
<H1>Finger Gateway</H1>

<ISINDEX>

This is a gateway to "finger". Type a user@host combination in
your browser's search dialog.<P>
```

However, when the same URL is requested with accompanying data, either directly or by entering data in the textfield as above, the result page is returned instead, as shown in Figure 17–27.

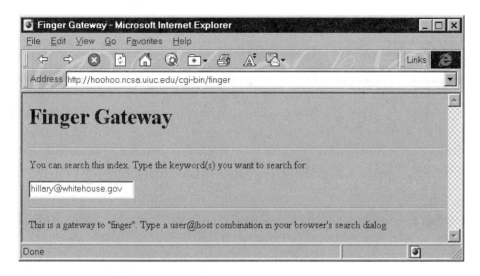

Figure 17–26 Accessing the finger program with no attached data generates an input page that uses `ISINDEX`.

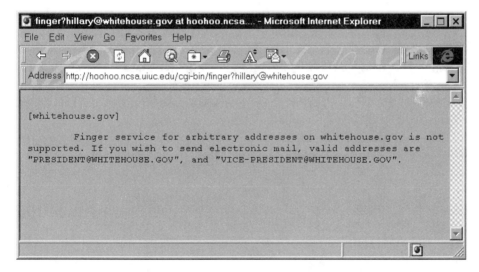

Figure 17–27 Accessing the finger program with attached data generates the results page.

17.5 ISMAP—Alternative Server-Side Image Maps

ISMAP is an optional attribute of the IMG element, and can be used in a similar manner to the <IMAGE TYPE="IMAGE" ...> FORM entry. ISMAP, like ISINDEX, is not actually a FORM element at all, but can still be used for simple connections to CGI programs. If an image with ISMAP is inside a hypertext link, then clicking on the image results in the coordinates of the click being sent to the specified URL. Coordinates are separated by commas and are specified in pixels relative to the top left corner of the image. For instance, Listing 17.5 embeds an image that uses the ISMAP attribute inside a hypertext link to http://www.apl.jhu.edu:5555/foo, which is answered by the mini HTTP server developed in Section 15.7. Figure 17–28 shows the result, which is identical to what would have been shown had the ISMAP attribute been omitted. However, when the mouse button is pressed 64 pixels to the right and 137 pixels below the top left corner of the image, the browser requests the URL http://www.apl.jhu.edu:5555/foo?64,137, as is shown in Figure 17–29. Note that if a server-side image map is used simply to select among a static set of destination URLs, the client-side MAP element is a much better option because the server doesn't have to be contacted just to decide which URL applies. See Section 3.5 for details on MAP. If the image map is intended to be mixed with other input elements, then the IMAGE input type is preferred instead. However, for a stand-alone image map where the URL associated with a region changes frequently or requires calculation, an image with ISMAP is a reasonable choice.

Listing 17.5 `IsMap.html`

```html
<!DOCTYPE HTML PUBLIC "-//W3C//DTD HTML 3.2//EN">
<HTML>
<HEAD>
  <TITLE>The ISMAP Attribute</TITLE>
</HEAD>

<BODY>
<H1 ALIGN="CENTER">The <CODE>ISMAP</CODE> Attribute</H1>
<H2>Select a pin:</H2>
<A HREF="http://www.apl.jhu.edu:5555/cgi-bin/foo">
<IMG SRC="chip.gif" BORDER=0 ISMAP></A>

</BODY>
</HTML>
```

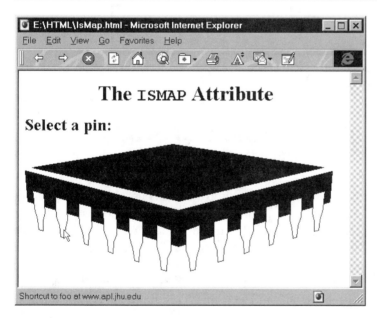

Figure 17–28 Setting the ISMAP attribute changes the action that results when the image is selected.

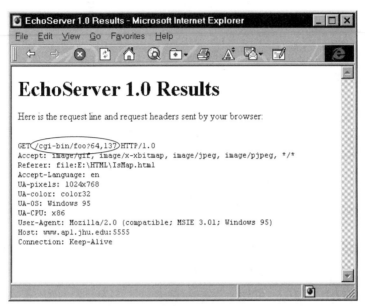

Figure 17-29   When an `ISMAP` image is selected, the coordinates of the selection are transmitted with the URL.

17.6 Using Java Applets to Send GET Data to CGI Programs

HTML forms provide a simple but limited way of collecting user input and transmitting it to CGI programs. Sometimes, however, a more sophisticated user interface is required. Java gives you much more control over the size, color, and font of the GUI controls; provides more built-in capability (sliders, line drawing, pop-up windows, and the like); lets you track mouse and keyboard events; and supports the development of custom input forms (dials, thermometers, draggable icons, and so forth). This, however, comes at a cost, as it tends to be more effort to design an interface in Java than using HTML forms, particularly if the interface contains lots of formatted text. The following sections will not focus on developing the interface itself, as this was covered in Chapter 13 (Graphical User Interface Controls). Instead, we will focus on the process of transmitting the data to the CGI program. With

HTML forms, GET and POST requests are handled almost exactly the same way. All the input elements are identical; only the METHOD attribute of the FORM element needs to change. In Java, however, the process is quite a bit different depending on whether GET or POST is being used. This section covers two ways of using GET. The first method imitates an HTML form, with data being transmitted and the resultant page being displayed by the browser. The second method shows how to send data to a CGI program and read the results so that they can be used directly by the sending applet. Section 17.7 discusses using POST from applets, and Section 17.8 explains how an applet can bypass the HTTP server altogether and talk directly to a server program running on the applet's home machine.

Sending Data via GET and Displaying the Resultant Page

The showDocument method can be used to request the browser to display a particular URL. Because data can be transmitted to a CGI program by appending it to the program's URL after a "?," you simply need to append the data to the string from which the URL is built, then create the URL object and call showDocument in the normal manner as discussed in Chapter 9 (Applets, Graphical Applications, and Basic Drawing). A basic template for doing this in Java follows, assuming that baseURL is a string representing the URL of the core CGI program, and that someData is the information to be sent with the request.

```
try {
  URL cgiURL = new URL(baseURL + "?" + someData);
  getAppletContext().showDocument(cgiURL);
} catch(MalformedURLException mue) { ... }
```

However, when data is sent by a browser, it is "URL encoded," which means spaces are converted to plus signs (+) and nonalphanumeric characters into a percent sign (%) followed by the two hex digits representing that character. The preceding example assumes that someData has already been encoded properly. Java has a URLEncoder class with a static encode method that can be used to perform this process. So, if a Java applet is contacting a CGI program that normally receives GET data from HTML forms, it would need to encode the value of each entry name, but not the equals sign (=) between the form entry name and its value or the ampersand (&)

between entries. So you can't necessarily simply call `URLEn-coder.encode(someData)`, but need to selectively encode the value parts of each name/value pair. This could be accomplished as follows:

```
String someData =
  name1 + "=" + URLEncoder.encode(val1) + "&" +
  name2 + "=" + URLEncoder.encode(val2) + "&" +
  ...
  nameN + "=" + URLEncoder.encode(valN);
try {
  URL cgiURL = new URL(baseURL + "?" + someData);
  getAppletContext().showDocument(cgiURL);
} catch(MalformedURLException mue) { ... }
```

Example: Using Search Services from Java

As an illustration, let's create a generic interface to a Web search service. It will take a string specifying a base URL and a search service name as input, then create a textfield for data entry and a button for submitting the data. When the button is activated or a carriage return is entered in the textfield, the data in the textfield is URL encoded, appended to the base URL after a question mark, transmitted, and the result displayed in a different frame.

Listing 17.6 SearchService.java

```java
import java.applet.Applet;
import java.awt.*;
import java.net.*;

public class SearchService extends Applet {
  private TextField searchField;
  protected String baseURL, serviceName, frame="Results";
  protected int textFieldSize = 30;

  public void setup() {
    Panel inputPanel = new Panel();
    inputPanel.add(new Label("Search String: "));
    searchField = new TextField(textFieldSize);
    inputPanel.add(searchField);
    add(inputPanel);
    add(new Button("Submit to " + serviceName));
  }

  public boolean action(Event event, Object object) {
    String searchString
      = URLEncoder.encode(searchField.getText());
    showSearch(searchString);
    return(true);
  }

  public void showSearch(String searchString) {
    try {
      URL url = new URL(baseURL + searchString);
      getAppletContext().showDocument(url, frame);
    } catch(MalformedURLException mue) {
      System.out.println("Illegal URL: " + baseURL
                            + searchString);
    }
  }
}
```

Listings 17.7 (Java source) and 17.8 (HTML that loads applet) show an instantiation that supports searches of the Yahoo! database. with the resulting Web page shown in Figure–14-30.

Listing 17.7 `SearchYahoo.java`

```
public class SearchYahoo extends SearchService {
  public void init() {
    baseURL = "http://search.yahoo.com/bin/search?p=";
    serviceName = "Yahoo";
    setup();
  }
}
```

Listing 17.8 `SearchYahoo.html`

```
<HTML>
<HEAD>
  <TITLE>SearchYahoo</TITLE>
</HEAD>

<FRAMESET ROWS="100,*">
  <FRAME SRC="YahooFrame.html" SCROLLING="NO">
  <FRAME SRC="Results.html" NAME="Results">

  <NOFRAMES>
    <BODY>
    Your browser doesn't support Frames. See
    <A HREF="YahooFrame.html">non-Frames version.</A>
    </BODY>
  </NOFRAMES>
</FRAMESET>

</HTML>
```

Listing 17.9 gives a variation that searches Excite instead (see Figure 14–31). This illustrates another advantage of Java interfaces over HTML forms:

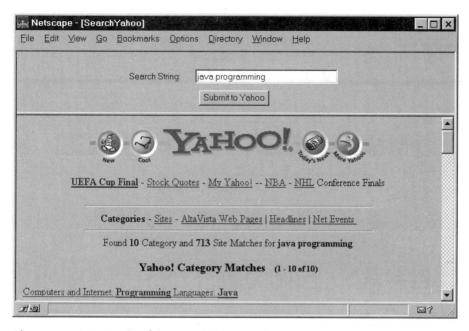

Figure 17–30   Results of the SearchYahoo applet.

reuse. With HTML, an interface developed for one application has to be completely copied if used for another application. If you then decide to make a change to the interfaces, you have to make the change both places. With Java, you can build up a complicated interface class, then reuse the class multiple places, or, as in this example, make a subclass that modifies its behavior while making use of much of the previous layout.

Listing 17.9 `SearchExcite.java`

```
public class SearchExcite extends SearchService {
  public void init() {
    baseURL = "http://www.excite.com/search.gw?search=";
    serviceName = "Excite";
    setup();
  }
}
```

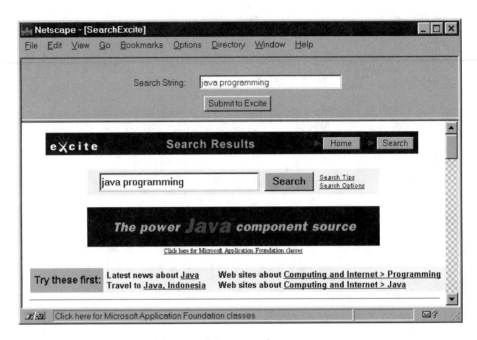

Figure 17–31   Results of the SearchExcite applet.

Sending Data via GET and Processing the Results

In the previous example, a Java applet requested that the output of a CGI program be sent to a particular frame. This is a reasonable approach when working with existing CGI services, since most CGI programs are already set up to return HTML documents. However, if you are developing both the client and the server ends of the process, it sometimes seems a bit wasteful to send back an entire HTML document, and it would be nice to simply return some data to an applet that is already running. This applet could then present the data in a graph or some other custom format. This can be done in Java by using the URL object, as was discussed in Chapter 15 (Client-Server Programming in Java) in Section 15.5. However, the security manager associated with most browsers only permits this when connecting back to the system from which the applet was originally loaded. In general, this is a good precaution, as it prevents applets from browsing behind corporate firewalls and reporting the results to the applet's author. In this case, however, it prevents some types of useful CGI clients. For instance, it would not be possible to write an applet that connected to multiple search engines, merged the results, and displayed a composite list of pages matching the query. Nevertheless, this is a useful capability in some applications, and the approach described in Chapter 15 is briefly reiterated below.

Create a URL Object

```
try {
  URL url = new URL("http://...");
} catch(MalformedURLException mue) { ... }
```

The URL created must be on the same machine as the applet itself.

Create an Input Stream

```
BufferedInputStream buffer =
  new BufferedInputStream(url.openStream());
DataInputStream in =
  new DataInputStream(buffer);
```

Read Each Line of the HTML Document

```
String line;
while ((line = in.readLine()) != null)
  doSomethingWith(line);
```

Close the Input Stream

```
in.close();
```

As an example of this process, Listing 17.10 shows a Java applet that can be used to retrieve and display HTML documents contained in the directory holding the current document. A `TextField` gathers the user's input, requests the document, and puts the results in a `TextArea`. If the user leaves the textfield blank, the current document's HTML source is displayed, as shown in Figure 17–32. If a specific filename is specified, then that file is retrieved, as shown in Figure 17–33. Now, these files don't result from CGI programs at all. But the whole point is that the process is the same either way; you simply read the contents of some URL. In fact, in general you can't even tell if a particular URL is simply a static file or is generated by a CGI program. Nevertheless, the weather report page given in Section 17.7 (Using Java Applets to Send POST Data to CGI Programs) could be implemented using GET just as easily as POST. See Listing 17.11 for details.

Listing 17.10 `ShowFile.java`

```java
import java.applet.Applet;
import java.awt.*;
import java.net.*;
import java.io.*;

public class ShowFile extends Applet {
  private TextArea fileArea;
  private TextField filename;

  public void init() {
    Panel topPanel = new Panel();
    topPanel.setLayout(new BorderLayout());
    topPanel.add("North",
                 new Label("Enter a URL relative to " +
                           "the current document's " +
                           "home directory",
                           Label.CENTER));
    Panel inputPanel = new Panel();
    inputPanel.add(new Label("File:"));
    filename = new TextField(20);
    inputPanel.add(filename);
    inputPanel.add(new Button("Show It"));
    topPanel.add("Center", inputPanel);
    setLayout(new BorderLayout());
    add("North", topPanel);
    fileArea = new TextArea();
    fileArea.setFont(new Font("Courier", Font.BOLD, 12));
    add("Center", fileArea);
  }

  public boolean action(Event e, Object o) {
    try {
      URL file = new URL(getDocumentBase(),
                         filename.getText());
      BufferedInputStream buffer =
        new BufferedInputStream(file.openStream());
      DataInputStream in =
        new DataInputStream(buffer);
      fileArea.setText("");
      String line;
      while ((line = in.readLine()) != null) {
        fileArea.appendText(line);
        fileArea.appendText("\n");
      }
      in.close();
    } catch(MalformedURLException mue) {
      System.out.println("Bad URL: " + mue);
    } catch(IOException ioe) {
      System.out.println("IOException: " + ioe);
    }
    return(true);
  }
}
```

Figure 17–32 The ShowFile class retrieving the current document.

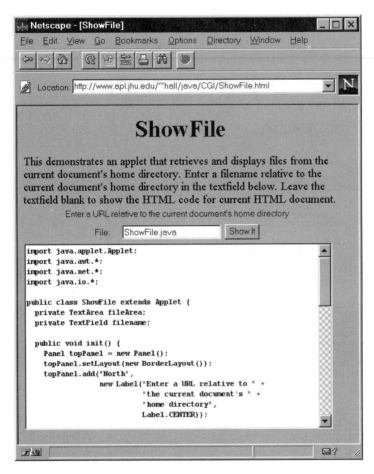

Figure 17–33   The `ShowFile` class retrieving the Java file that defined the class.

17.7 Using Java Applets to Send POST Data to CGI Programs

Unfortunately, Java does not have a mechanism for specifying that POST be used when creating a URL that will be requested with showDocument. Thus, due to security restrictions, most browsers only permit POST requests to be made to CGI programs running on the server from which the applet was loaded, and there is no portable way to tell the browser to display the results. You should note, however, that in Netscape version 3.0 and later, there is a standard way for Java to call JavaScript, and JavaScript can be used to display arbitrary HTML. See Chapter 19 for details on Java-Script. In general applications, however, Java applets are effective for communicating with CGI programs that use POST *only* if these programs are on the applet's home machine and if the applet is going to process the results itself. The process is similar to that followed when processing the results of a GET request, except that you use a URLConnection object and open an output stream to send data before reading the result. If you do this, Java knows to use the POST method when contacting the HTTP server. The following section gives more details on this process, and is followed by an example that uses this process to request and display on-line weather information for various cities.

Template for Reading POST Data

Create a URL Object

```
try {
  URL url = new URL("http://...");
} catch(MalformedURLException mue) { ... }
```

Create a URLConnection Object from the URL

```
URLConnection connection =
  weatherInfo.openConnection();
```

Specify that the URLConnection Allows Output

```
connection.setDoOutput(true);
```

Some browsers (such as Internet Explorer) don't require this, but other browsers (such as Netscape Navigator) do, and it can't hurt even when not required.

Open an Output Stream and Send the POST Data

```
PrintStream out =
   new PrintStream(connection.getOutputStream());
out.println(name + URLEncoder.encode(value));
```

Close the Output Stream

```
out.close();
```

Open an Input Stream

If a large amount of data is being sent, you probably want to use buffering to speed up the reading process, as follows:

```
BufferedInputStream buffer =
   newBufferedInputStream(connection.getInputStream())
DataInputStream in =
   new DataInputStream(buffer);
```

However, because POST can only be used by applets to process data (not to display a resultant HTML file), the response will not typically be an HTML file at all, and might be quite short. In that case, omitting the buffering might be simpler. This approach follows:

```
DataInputStream in =
   new DataInputStream(connection.getInputStream());
```

Read from the Input Stream

```
String line;
while ((line = in.readLine()) != null)
  doSomethingWith(line);
```

Close the Input Stream

```
in.close();
```

Using POST to Implement a Weather Report Page

Although the use of POST is somewhat limited in Java applets, it is still quite useful for situations where you are the author of both the applet and the associated CGI program. For instance, Listing 17.11 shows an applet used to create a Web page that lets the user get weather forecasts for various cities. Once the user has selected a city, the applet uses the getWeather method to send the city via POST to a CGI program on its home machine (written in Java, of course) that responds with a single-line plain-text file containing one of the words rainy, cloudy, partly-cloudy, or sunny. Based on this response, the applet chooses an appropriate image file to display, as shown in Figures 17–34, 17–35, and 17–36. Listings 17.12 and 17.13 show the CityChooser and WeatherPanel objects used by the applet to select the city and display the icon, respectively. This process is faster than it would be with traditional CGI, because the server is sending a very small amount of data rather than a regular HTML document and an image file.

Listing 17.11 `Weather.java`

```java
import java.applet.Applet;
import java.awt.*;
import java.net.*;
import java.io.*;

public class Weather extends Applet {
  protected String initialCity = "Los Angeles";
  private CityChooser cityChooser;
  private Button forecastButton;
  private WeatherPanel weatherPanel;

  public void init() {
    Panel topPanel = new Panel();
    topPanel.add(new Label("City:"));
    cityChooser = new CityChooser(initialCity);
    topPanel.add(cityChooser);
    forecastButton = new Button("Get Forecast");
    topPanel.add(forecastButton);
    setLayout(new BorderLayout());
    add("North", topPanel);
    weatherPanel =
      new WeatherPanel(initialCity,
                       getWeather(initialCity),
                       this);
    add("Center", weatherPanel);
  }


  public boolean action(Event e, Object o) {
    if (e.target == forecastButton) {
      String city = cityChooser.getCity();
      weatherPanel.setCity(city);
      weatherPanel.setWeather(getWeather(city));
      weatherPanel.repaint();
      return(true);
    } else
      return(false);
  }
```

Listing 17.11 `Weather.java` **(continued)**

```java
public String getWeather(String city) {
  String weather = "partly-cloudy";
  try {
    URL weatherInfo =
      new URL("http://www.apl.jhu.edu/" +
              "cgi-instruct/hall/WeatherInfo");
    URLConnection connection =
      weatherInfo.openConnection();
    connection.setDoOutput(true);
    PrintStream out =
      new PrintStream(connection.getOutputStream());
    out.println("city=" + URLEncoder.encode(city));
    out.close();
    DataInputStream in =
      new DataInputStream(connection.getInputStream());
    weather = in.readLine();
    in.close();
  } catch(MalformedURLException mue) {
    showStatus("Illegal URL: " + mue);
  } catch(IOException ioe) {
    showStatus("IOException: " + ioe);
  } catch(Exception e) {
    showStatus("Error: " + e);
  }
  return(weather);
}
}
```

Figure 17–34   Weather report for Los Angeles.

Figure 17–35 Weather report for Chicago.

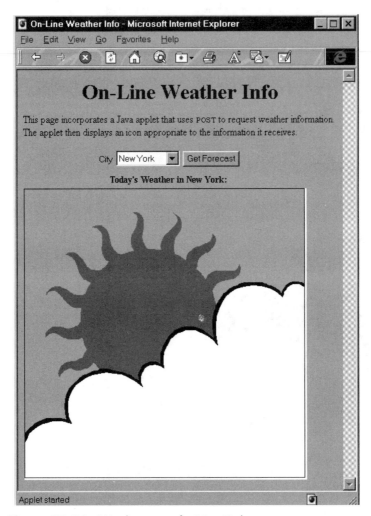

Figure 17–36   Weather report for New York.

Listing 17.12 `CityChooser.java`

```java
import java.awt.*;

public class CityChooser extends Choice {
  public CityChooser(String city) {
    String[] cities = {"Chicago", "Dallas",
                       "Los Angeles", "Miami",
                       "New York", "Seattle" };
    for(int i=0; i<cities.length; i++)
      addItem(cities[i]);
    select(city);
  }

  public String getCity() {
    return(getSelectedItem());
  }
}
```

Listing 17.13 `WeatherPanel.java`

```java
import java.applet.Applet;
import java.awt.*;

public class WeatherPanel extends Panel {
  protected String city, weather;
  protected String[] weathers =
    {"rainy", "cloudy", "partly-cloudy", "sunny"};
  protected int iconWidth = 456, iconHeight=456;
  private Applet app;
  private Image[] icons = new Image[weathers.length];
  private Label cityLabel = new Label();
```

continued

Listing 17.13 `WeatherPanel.java` (continued)

```java
public WeatherPanel(String city, String weather, Applet app) {
    setCity(city);
    setWeather(weather);
    setApplet(app);
    for(int i=0; i<icons.length; i++)
      icons[i] = getImage(weathers[i] + ".gif");
    setLayout(new BorderLayout());
    cityLabel = new Label("Today's Weather in " +
                          city + ":",
                          Label.CENTER);
    cityLabel.setFont(new Font("TimesRoman",
                              Font.BOLD, 14));
    add("North", cityLabel);
}

public void paint(Graphics g) {
    g.drawImage(getIcon(), size().width-iconWidth,
                size().height-iconHeight, this);
}

private Image getIcon() {
    for(int i=0; i<weathers.length; i++)
      if (weathers[i].equals(weather))
        return(icons[i]);
    app.showStatus("Error: unrecognized weather '" +
                   weather + "'.");
    return(null);
}

private Image getImage(String file) {
    return(app.getImage(app.getDocumentBase(), file));
}
```

continued

Listing 17.13 `WeatherPanel.java` (continued)

```java
public void setCity(String city) {
    this.city = city;
    cityLabel.setText("Today's Weather in " +
                      city + ":");
    invalidate();
    validate();
}

public void setWeather(String weather) {
    this.weather = weather;
}

private void setApplet(Applet app) {
    this.app = app;
}

}
```

17.8 Bypassing the HTTP Server and Using Sockets Directly

The CGI process is a bit cumbersome, but was the only alternative before Java was developed. However, with Java applets, there is no requirement to communicate via an intermediate HTTP server at all! Instead, the applet can talk directly to a server program specific to its application. For instance, the weather report applet shown in the previous section could have been implemented by the applet talking directly to a program that returns forecasts given a city. This would be faster, because the CGI process starts the program every time, but with a direct socket connection it would already be running. Also, it simplifies the work of the program on the server, because it can concentrate on sending data, not formatting it as HTML. This is not really "CGI Programming," but is listed here because it accomplishes the same purpose: connecting a Web page to an external program. It allows much more flexible and efficient communications, but has three drawbacks:

- An additional server must be running,
- Most browsers restrict the applet to talking to programs on the applet's host, and
- The applet has to format the result itself.

The client process was discussed in the client section of Chapter 15 (Client-Server Programming in Java). The basic approach doesn't change when this is done from applets; the only modification is that the host must be the one from which the applet was loaded. The client communication process is reiterated briefly here; see Chapter 15 for details and examples.

Create a Socket object

```
Socket client =
    new Socket("hostname", portNumber);
```

Create an output stream that can be used to send info to the Socket

The most common one is `PrintStream`.

```
PrintStream out =
    new PrintStream(client.getOutputStream());
```

Create an input stream to read the response from the server

The most common one is `DataInputStream`.

```
DataInputStream in =
    new DataInputStream(client.getInputStream());
```

Alternatively, a buffered version can be used:

```
BufferedInputStream buffered =
    new BufferedInputStream(client.getInputStream());
DataInputStream in = new DataInputStream(buffered);
```

Do I/O with Input and Output Streams

Close the socket when done

```
client.close();
```

This closes the associated input and output streams as well.

A similar option is to use JDBC to talk directly to database servers. This also was direct socket connections, but the socket details are hidden from you. For more information on JDBC, see Section 15.9.

17.9 Summary

The Common Gateway Interface (CGI) provides a link between Web pages and programs running on an external server. When you create a Web-based interface to a CGI program, you have two main choices: do it in HTML or do it in Java.

Although there are a couple of rarely used options that don't involve forms (ISINDEX and images with ISMAP), in most cases HTML interfaces are created using the FORM element. This element provides a placeholder for input elements and specifies the CGI program and communication method (GET or POST) associated with the interface. The actual input elements are contained inside this FORM element and consist of various GUI controls created with INPUT, TEXTAREA, and SELECT. When the data has been collected, it is sent to a CGI program, which returns an HTML document showing the results.

Building an interface in Java requires a bit more work, but gives you more flexibility in the size, color, and variety of input elements. Once data has been collected, it can be transmitted to a CGI program using either the HTTP GET or the HTTP POST method. When using GET, an applet can follow the traditional CGI process where the output of the CGI program is an HTML program that is simply displayed by the browser. Alternatively, if the CGI program is on the applet's home system, the applet can process the results directly. An applet that wants to use POST *must* use this latter approach, contacting programs only on its home host and processing the results directly. Finally, you should remember that applets, unlike HTML interfaces, don't have to use CGI at all, but can open a direct socket connection to a specialized server on their home host and exchange data directly.

But all this is only half of the story. You can collect and transmit data from a Web page on the client machine. Great. But how do you process this information back on the server? Read on; that's the topic of the next chapter.

CGI PROGRAMMING AND BEYOND— THE SERVER SIDE

Topics in this Chapter

- The process CGI programs use to handle requests
- Reading GET data via the QUERY_STRING variable
- Other useful environment variables
- Reading GET data via command-line arguments
- Handling ISINDEX requests
- Reading POST data
- Java classes to parse the request data
- Using cookies to store data on the client system
- Server-Side Java and the Servlet API
- Server APIs, server-side JavaScript, and other alternatives to CGI

Chapter 18

The Common Gateway Interface lets Web pages communicate with databases or other programs on a system running an HTTP server. In CGI programming, the HTTP server is configured to treat URLs in certain locations specially. When the user requests a URL in such a reserved location, instead of treating it as a *file* whose *contents* should be returned, the HTTP server treats it as a *program* whose *output* should be returned. In Chapter 17 we discussed the client side of this process: how to collect input from HTML forms or via Java applets, and how to transmit that data to CGI programs. This chapter describes the server side of the process: how to write the programs that process data from CGI clients and return the results. Technically, "CGI" refers to the situation when the HTTP server starts an external program to process the data and generate results. However, the approach is very similar when the server is directly linked with databases or shared libraries, or when the server has an embedded interpreter or compiler for server-side programs in languages such as Java and JavaScript. These latter approaches are discussed at the end of this chapter.

18.1 The CGI Interaction Process

A CGI program should perform four basic steps, outlined as follows.

Read the data
Data can be sent by GET or by POST; the CGI program reads it differently in each case.

Output HTTP Headers

The CGI program's job is to mimic the HTTP server, either partially or completely. The most common approach is to do so only partially, generating an incomplete set of HTTP headers and letting the HTTP server fill in the rest. In this case, `Content-Type` is the only header that the CGI program *must* generate, but it is free to specify others. Alternatively, the program can generate a complete HTTP header, including status line, `Date`, `Content-Type`, and possibly `Server`, `Content-Length`, and so forth.

Send a Blank Line

A blank line separates the headers from the main document.

Generate a Document

Finally, the CGI program should send a document consistent with the `Content-Type` header it specified. In most cases, this is an HTML document, but this is not required.

For example, Listing 18.1 gives a very simple CGI program to be hosted on a Unix system, written using the Unix Bourne shell scripting language. Figure 18–1 shows the result.

Listing 18.1   The CgiHello Executable Script

```
#!/bin/sh
echo "Content-Type: text/plain"
echo ""
echo "Hello, world."
```

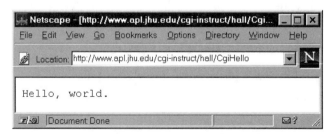

Figure 18–1   Result of the `CgiHello` Program.

Before going further, we recommend that you get a simple program of this type working to be sure that you are using the proper directory, understand the interaction process, and have execute permissions set properly. If you get a "Server Error" (status 500, generally), this probably means that you are sending incorrect headers, perhaps by a spelling error in "Content-Type" or by generating whitespace such as a space character instead of a completely blank line. If you get a "Forbidden" (403) message, this may mean that your program does not have execute permissions set (use "chmod a+x *program*" on Unix to make a script executable). A "Not Found" (404) error often means that you have supplied the wrong name for the CGI program or misunderstood which directory your server uses for CGI programs.

18.2 Reading GET Data: The QUERY_STRING Variable

When the client requests a CGI URL of the form `http://server/cgi-bin/program?data`, the HTTP server calls "program" after first setting the `QUERY_STRING` environment variable to "data". The program is responsible for reading the data out of the environment variable, parsing it to find the pieces of interest, then generating output that mimics an HTTP server. For instance, Listing 18.2 presents a simple Unix shell script that accepts a `GET` request and generates a plain-text page that describes the input it received.

Listing 18.2   The Executable ShowData Script

```
#!/bin/sh

echo "Content-Type: text/plain"
echo ""
echo "QUERY STRING is '$QUERY_STRING'"
```

If installed as an executable file named `ShowData` in `http://www.apl.jhu.edu/cgi-instruct/hall`, then `GET` requests get answered as illustrated in Figure 18–2.

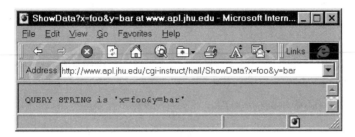

Figure 18–2   Supplying data via GET to ShowData CGI program.

The examples in these sections assume that the HTTP server is running on Unix, a popular choice for large Web sites. The exact details of getting data to the CGI program may vary on other platforms. For instance, some Windows-based servers use temporary files for input and output, rather than environment variables and standard input/output as in the original CGI standard. In general, however, the target program needs to be in a format that the host operating system considers to be executable. Popular languages for CGI programs include Perl, the Unix Bourne or Korn shells, Windows batch files, C, C++, Visual Basic, AppleScript, and, increasingly, Java. To do something interesting with the data in Java, the shell script can pass the data to a Java program to process it, as illustrated in Listing 18.3. This intermediate shell script (or .bat file if on Windows) is necessary to pass along the value of the QUERY_STRING variable even if your Java compiler generates stand-alone executables. This is because Java has no method to directly read environment variables due to the fact that this concept is foreign to some operating systems supported by Java. Note the use of the full path to the Java executable in this example, because the process owning the HTTP server may not have the same search path as the user writing the program.

Listing 18.3   The CgiGet executable script

```
#!/bin/sh

/usr/local/JDK/bin/java CgiGet "$QUERY_STRING"
```

Once the shell script passes the data to CgiGet.java (Listing 18.4), the Java program can then generate an HTML page describing the results.

Listing 18.4   CgiGet.java

```java
public class CgiGet {
  public static void main(String[] args) {
    CgiGet app = new CgiGet("CgiGet", args);
    app.printFile();
  }

  private String name;
  private String[] args;
  protected String type = "GET";

  public CgiGet(String name, String[] args) {
    this.name = name;
    this.args = args;
  }

  public void printFile() {
    printHeader(name);
    printBody(args);
    printTrailer();
  }

  protected void printHeader(String name) {
    System.out.println
      ("Content-Type: text/html\n" +
       "\n" +
       "<!DOCTYPE HTML PUBLIC " +
         "\"-//W3C//DTD HTML 3.2//EN\">\n" +
       "<HTML>\n" +
       "<HEAD>\n" +
       "<TITLE>The " + name + " Program</TITLE>\n" +
       "</HEAD>\n" +
       "\n" +
       "<BODY>\n" +
       "<H1>The " + name + " Program</H1>\n" +
       "This program illustrates CGI programs\n" +
       "in Java that receive <TT>" + type +
         "</TT> requests.\n" +
       "<P>");
  }

  protected void printBody(String[] data) {
    System.out.println("Data was '" + data[0] + "'.");
  }

  protected void printTrailer() {
    System.out.println("</BODY>\n</HTML>");
  }
}
```

Now, if the shell script is installed as CgiGet on the same server as in the previous example, GET requests would result in an HTML document being returned instead of plain text, as illustrated in Figure 18–3.

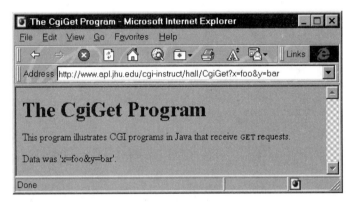

Figure 18–3   Results of the CgiGet program.

18.3 The Standard CGI Environment Variables

In addition to the QUERY_STRING environment variable that stores the data that was appended to the URL, HTTP servers set several other variables containing information such as the host making the request, the port number used, and so forth. These variables can be accessed from the CGI programs written in Perl, C, C++, or scripting languages, or, with a one-line intermediate script, from Java.

Passing Variables as Named Parameters

In the CgiGet example in the previous section, we passed the query string data to the CgiGet program as a command-line argument. When supplying multiple variables, however, listing them all as command-line arguments makes maintenance difficult. This is because changes to the number or order of variables supplied requires changes to both the shell script (or .bat file, depending on the OS) *and* the Java program. A more convenient alternative is to supply the variables as properties, allowing the Java program to look them up by name. Entries that are passed to the Java interpreter or JIT compiler via "-D*name*=*value*" can be accessed from within the program via `System.getProperty("name")`, returning *value* as a `String`. Listing 18.5 gives a simple example, with results shown in Listing 18.6.

Listing 18.5   PropertyTest.java

```
public class PropertyTest {
  public static void main(String[] args) {
    System.out.println
      ("Java: " + System.getProperty("java") + "\n" +
       "CGI: " + System.getProperty("cgi") + "\n" +
       "C++: " + System.getProperty("cpp"));
  }
}
```

Listing 18.6   Results of the PropertyTest program

```
> java PropertyTest
Java: null
CGI: null
C++: null
> java -Djava=cool -Dcgi=hot -Dcpp=stale PropertyTest
Java: cool
CGI: hot
C++: stale
```

An interface to a Java-based CGI program would then invoke the program via

```
java -DVAR1="$VAR1" -DVAR2="$VAR2" ... CgiProgram
```

Summary of CGI Variables

The following list summarizes the standard variables available to CGI programs.

AUTH_TYPE
The `AUTH_TYPE` variable gives authentication method used by the server to validate a user. It is taken from the `Auth-Scheme` header.

CONTENT_LENGTH
This variable specifies the number of characters (bytes) contained in `QUERY_STRING`. It is *always* supplied for `POST` requests, but it is usually not supplied for requests that use the `GET` method.

CONTENT_TYPE

If supplied, this specifies the MIME type of the attached data. It is usually left unspecified.

DOCUMENT_ROOT

When a user accesses `http://some.host/some.file`, the HTTP server looks for `some.file` in a designated directory. The `DOCUMENT_ROOT` variable gives the pathname of that directory. This variable is omitted by some servers.

GATEWAY_INTERFACE

This gives the server's CGI version, e.g. "`CGI/1.1`".

HTTP_XXX

This set of variables gives the contents of standard HTTP headers. The name of the environment variable is derived from the header name, with dashes changed to underscores and "`HTTP_`" attached. For instance, the contents of the `Cookie` header would be stored in the variable `HTTP_COOKIE`, `Referer` in `HTTP_REFERER`, `User-Agent` in `HTTP_USER_AGENT`, and so forth. See Section 16.3 (HTTP Request Headers) for an explanation of the standard headers. Note, however, that the server might not set variables for all headers, and some variables (e.g., `HTTP_AUTHORIZATION` from the `Authorization` header) *should* not be made available to CGI programs.

PATH_INFO

This gives a virtual pathname to be used by the CGI program. `PATH_TRANSLATED` gives the actual path this represents. It is supplied by the client by appending it to the URL, but without a leading "?". The data for `QUERY_STRING` can be supplied after this. For example, the value of `PATH_INFO` would be `/virtual/path` in both `http://host.com/cgi-bin/program.cgi/virtual/path` and `http://host.com/cgi-bin/program.cgi/virtual/path?query_data`. `QUERY_STRING` would be empty in the first case and be "`query_data`" in the second case.

PATH_TRANSLATED

This variable specifies the actual path of the file given in `PATH_INFO`. Note, however, that for security reasons many servers do not support this variable.

QUERY_STRING

This variable contains the data sent by the user by appending it to the URL after a "?". It will arrive URL-encoded if sent via HTML forms unless a nonstandard encoding type was used. See Section 17.2 (The HTML FORM Element) for details on changing the encoding type via the `ENCTYPE` attribute of `FORM`.

REMOTE_ADDR, REMOTE_HOST

These variables specify the IP address and fully qualified name of the requesting host. They can be used to restrict access to CGI resources to users from certain sites. However, this is not absolutely foolproof due to the risk of IP-spoofing by sophisticated attackers.

REMOTE_IDENT

This variable gives the name of the user on the remote system. It is supplied only if identification is supported by the client, which is rare.

REMOTE_USER

`REMOTE_USER` gives the user name supplied for authentication purposes. It is available only if authentication is supported and the CGI program requires authorization for access.

REQUEST_METHOD

The method by which the HTTP request was made, usually `GET` or `POST`.

SCRIPT_NAME

This is the URI of the CGI program (that is, the part of the URL after the protocol and hostname). For example, for the URL `http://www.somewhere.com/cgi-bin/program.cgi`, the value would be `/cgi-bin/program.cgi`.

SERVER_NAME

This is the hostname or IP address of the server.

SERVER_PORT

The gives the port on which the server is listening.

SERVER_PROTOCOL

This gives the name and version of the protocol used for the request (e.g., "HTTP/1.0").

SERVER_SOFTWARE

This gives the name and version of the HTTP server (e.g., "NCSA/1.5.2").

18.4 CGI Command-Line Arguments

With GET requests in general, the data appended to the URL gets placed in the QUERY_STRING variable, and the application is responsible for reading this variable and parsing the data. However, there is a special case when the data supplied does not contain an equals sign (=). In such a case, in addition to be stored in QUERY_STRING, the data is separated at the plus signs (+) and then passed as command-line arguments to the CGI program. Note that this situation will never occur when using HTML forms to generate the CGI request, because forms that send *any* data always transmit at least one equals sign. So this only happens when using ISINDEX, Java applets, or generating the request by hand.

Core Note

HTML forms never generate CGI command-line arguments. You must use the QUERY_STRING *variable to process form data.*

For instance, suppose that the URL http://www.some-isp.com/cgi-bin/test?foo+bar+baz is requested. In such a case, the program test is called with foo, bar, and baz as arguments, and its results returned to the client in the normal manner.

To use a Java program to process such a request, the executable shell script or batch file would pass the normal arguments to the Java program instead of the QUERY_STRING variable, as illustrated in Listing 18.7. In fact, on Java systems that generate stand-alone executables (e.g., Asymetrix' SuperCede or the MicroSoft SDK), the shell script or .bat file can be omitted altogether, and the URL can refer directly to the executable Java program. This cannot be done in the general case because Java applications do not have a portable way to retrieve the value of environment variables.

Listing 18.7   The CgiCommandLine executable script

```
#!/bin/sh

/usr/local/JDK/bin/java CgiCommandLine "$@"
```

The Java program would then read its arguments in the normal way, and generate output describing the results in the same manner as in the CgiGet example. For example, in Listing 18.8, the CgiCommandLine program places each of the arguments in a separate entry in a bulleted (UL) list. Figure 18–4 shows the results.

Listing 18.8   CgiCommandLine.java

```java
public class CgiCommandLine extends CgiGet {
  public static void main(String[] args) {
    CgiCommandLine app
      = new CgiCommandLine("CgiCommandLine", args);
    app.printFile();
  }

  public CgiCommandLine(String name, String[] args) {
    super(name, args);
  }

  protected void printBody(String[] data) {
    System.out.println("Data supplied:\n<UL>");
    for(int i=0; i<data.length; i++)
      System.out.println("  <LI>" + data[i]);
    System.out.println("</UL>");
  }
}
```

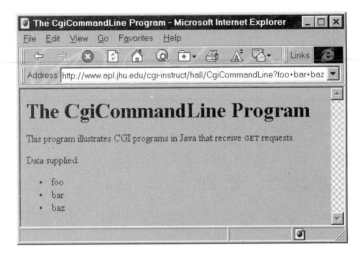

Figure 18-4   Results of the `CgiCommandLine` program.

18.5 Handling **ISINDEX**

When working with HTML forms, a common mode of interaction is to have one URL be an HTML document that gathers the input and have another URL be the CGI program specified by the `ACTION` attribute of the form. For instance, the Web search service at `http://www.lycos.com/` gathers the search strings, then contacts the search engine at `http://www.lycos.com/cgi-bin/pursuit`. The `ISINDEX` element is quite unusual in that the URL that is contacted when the user hits return in the textfield is always the current document's own URL. This means that

- `ISINDEX` forms are only useful in pages that are generated by CGI programs, and
- The CGI program needs to check the command-line arguments to determine whether to generate the original data-input page or the secondary-results page.

Furthermore, the data is not sent in the *name1=value1&name2=value2...* format of HTML forms, and thus can be delivered as command-line arguments to the destination program. This is even safe if the user enters an equals sign (=) explicitly, as it will be URLencoded to %3D before being transmitted.

For instance, Listings 18.9 and 18.10 contain a variation of the CgiCommandLine program that checks the number of command-line arguments before taking action. It generates a page with <ISINDEX ...> if there are zero arguments and creates a page with a list of the arguments if one or more arguments are supplied.

Listing 18.9   The IsIndex executable script

```
#!/bin/sh

/usr/local/JDK/bin/java IsIndex "$@"
```

Listing 18.10   IsIndex.java

```java
public class IsIndex extends CgiCommandLine {
  public static void main(String[] args) {
    IsIndex app = new IsIndex("IsIndex", args);
    app.printFile();
  }

  public IsIndex(String name, String[] args) {
    super(name, args);
  }

  protected void printBody(String[] args) {
    if (args.length > 0)
      super.printBody(args);
    else
      System.out.println
        ("Input is collected via the\n" +
        "<TT>ISINDEX</TT> element. Enter some data\n" +
        "and then hit RETURN.\n" +
        "<ISINDEX PROMPT=\"Data: \">");
  }
}
```

When the URL corresponding to IsIndex is requested with no attached data, the resultant page contains a textfield that allows the user to enter data, as shown in Figure 18–5.

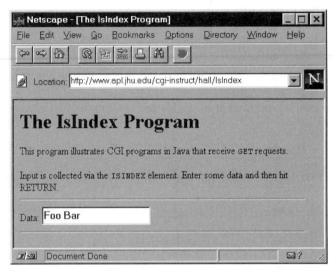

Figure 18–5   Results of the IsIndex program when no data is supplied.

However, if the same URL is requested with attached data (e.g., after hitting RETURN in the textfield of Figure 18–5), the results page (Figure 18–6) is shown instead.

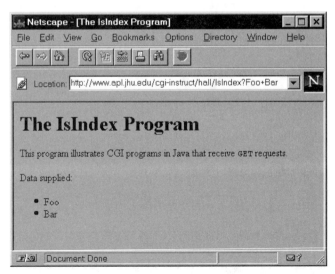

Figure 18–6   Results of the IsIndex program when data is supplied.

18.6 Reading POST Data

When using the GET method to talk to CGI programs, the client data is appended to the URL of the server program, after a question mark (?). With POST, however, no information is attached to the URL itself. Instead, the client program sends a POST line, a Content-Length line, additional optional HTTP headers, a blank line, and then some data. This data (after the blank line) is available to the specified program as standard input. In principle, the client could send multiple lines of data in a variety of formats. In practice, however, HTML forms that have a METHOD of POST send a single line of data that is one big long string of the same form as the data that is supplied in QUERY_STRING for GET requests (*name1=value1&name2=value2...*).

The POST method has several disadvantages. A Java applet cannot display a page (using getAppletContext().showDocument) generated by a CGI program that uses POST, nor can it read data from a POST program on a host other than the applet's home machine. Secondly, a POST request cannot be generated by the user simply by opening a particular URL in a WWW browser. On the other hand, POST has several advantages. First of all, because the data is being transmitted separately from the URL, there is no danger of having the data truncated due to a particular browser's limit on URL length, nor, for ISINDEX data or applet data not containing an equals sign (=), of exceeding the command-line argument limit of the language implementing the CGI program. Secondly, POST can be used to send private information because the information sent does not show up in the URL, which is often displayed at the top of the browser. Thirdly, because Java programs can read from standard input but not access environment variables, the intermediate shell script or batch file can be omitted for CGI programs developed in Java with compilers that generate stand-alone executables. For instance, .class files are automatically passed to Java on recent versions of Linux, the Microsoft SDK can wrap class files inside executable files, and Asymetrix' SuperCede compiler can generate executables that can run completely independent of a separate Java run-time system.

For example, Listings 18.11 and 18.12 show a POST program that reads one line of standard input and returns a page showing that data.

Listing 18.11   The CgiPost executable script

```
#!/bin/sh

/usr/local/JDK/bin/java CgiPost
```

Listing 18.12 `CgiPost.java`

```java
import java.io.*;

public class CgiPost extends CgiGet {
  public static void main(String[] args) {
    try {
      DataInputStream in
        = new DataInputStream(System.in);
      String[] data = { in.readLine() };
      CgiPost app = new CgiPost("CgiPost", data);
      app.printFile();
    } catch(IOException ioe) {
      System.out.println
        ("IOException reading POST data: " + ioe);
    }
  }

  public CgiPost(String name, String[] args) {
    super(name, args);
    type = "POST";
  }
}
```

Now, Listing 18.13 shows a simple HTML form that collects some data and sends it by POST to the CgiPost program. This input screen appears in Figure 18–7.

Listing 18.13   CgiPost.html

```
<!DOCTYPE HTML PUBLIC "-//W3C//DTD HTML 3.2//EN">
<HTML>
<HEAD>
  <TITLE>Sending POST Data to a CGI Program</TITLE>
</HEAD>

<BODY>
<H1>Sending POST Data to a CGI Program</H1>

<FORM
  ACTION=
       "http://www.apl.jhu.edu/cgi-instruct/hall/CgiPost"
  METHOD="POST">
  Enter some data:
  <INPUT TYPE="TEXT" NAME="TextField1"><BR>
  Enter some more:
  <INPUT TYPE="TEXT" NAME="TextField2"><BR>
  <INPUT TYPE="SUBMIT" VALUE="Send It">
</FORM>

</BODY>
</HTML>
```

Figure 18–7   The input page for the CgiPost program

Now, when the data is submitted, `CgiPost` can read it from its standard input and generate results using it, as shown in Figure 18–8.

Figure 18–8   Results of the `CgiPost` program after submitting the data shown in Figure 18–7.

18.7 Parsing the Query Data

Whether you read the data from the `QUERY_STRING` variable (`GET`) or from the standard input (`POST`), you need to process it to find the names and associated values, then decode and use the URL-encoded values. This process involves three basic steps, summarized as follows. Many packages to do this in Perl and C or C++ exist already, but such packages are not yet widely available in Java. So I give a Java implementation of each of the three steps in the three following sections (18.8–18.10), with a usage example in Section 18.11.

Break up the input string, first at "&", then at "=".
Given "`a=hello+there&b=%7Ehall&c=&a=bye+bye,`" you want to extract the tokens shown in Table 18.1. You would probably use a `StringTokenizer` for this. See Section 15.2 (Parsing Strings Using StringTokenizer) for details on the `StringTokenizer` class.

Table 18.1 "Raw" Tokens	
Name	*Value*
a	hello+there bye+bye
b	%7Ehall
c	*none*

Decode each of the values.

Convert each "+" to a space and each occurrence of "%XX" to the ASCII/ISO Latin-1 character represented by the hex value "XX." Table 18.2 shows sample results for the same input as in Table 18.1.

Table 18.2 Decoded Tokens	
Name	*Value*
a	hello there bye bye
b	~hall
c	*none*

Store the result in a look-up table.

You will need to provide a convenient method to retrieve the value or values given the associated name, and to get a separate listing of all available names and values. This will involve building a data structure for a table (associative array).

Once you've decoded the data, be careful what you do with it. CGI programs are notorious as trapdoors that let external crackers do mischief on your system. For instance, suppose that you have a textfield for the user to enter an X11 color name (supported by Netscape and Internet Explorer, even on non-X platforms), and you pass the decoded value to a shell script that returns the RGB values used in that name. This might generate the equivalent of the following shell command:

```
Unix> get-rgb-value color-name
```

This is no problem if the color name is something like "blanchedal-mond" or "navy." But what happens if the user enters "white; cd / ; rm -r *"? If substituted in directly, this would generate a shell command of

```
Unix> get-rgb-value white; cd /; rm -r *
```

This generates three consecutive commands, the second two of which instruct the system to go to the root directory and to recursively delete all files there and in every subdirectory. In this particular case, that probably wouldn't do much harm because HTTP servers are normally configured to run as unprivileged users who thus own no files. But there are plenty of other nasty commands people can send. The problem here isn't calling external programs per se, it is calling programs that can be used as interpreters for embedded commands hidden with characters like semicolons and back-quotes, or where the author doesn't realize the program can execute danger-ous commands at all (e.g., MS Word, some PostScript previewers). Note that the C system call and the Perl exec command invoke a command shell, while Java's Runtime.getRuntime().exec method does not.

Core Security

Never trust data supplied by visitors to your CGI page. Check for characters that have special meaning and for hidden instructions before passing it to external programs that could potentially execute commands.

Good sources for additional information on CGI security include the fol-lowing:

The WWW Security FAQ from Lincoln Stein

```
http://www.genome.wi.mit.edu/WWW/faqs/www-security-
faq.html
```

Yahoo's CGI Security Links

```
http://www.yahoo.com/Computers_and_Internet/Internet/
World_Wide_Web/Security/CGI/
```

NCSA's Guide to Secure CGI Scripts

```
http://hoohoo.ncsa.uiuc.edu/cgi/security.html
```

18.8 Breaking Up the Query String

Before values can be decoded, the names and values have to be identified. This has to be done before decoding, so that encoded equals signs or ampersands don't fool you into breaking the string at the wrong places. Listings 18.14 and 18.15 give code for a `QueryStringParser` class that takes a string and returns a look-up table containing the results. Taking a string and breaking it at two predefined characters using `StringTokenizer` is a simple process, but there are two small wrinkles that need to be ironed out. First, we don't know how many unique names are contained in the input string; `countTokens` won't give us this information because the same name may appear multiple times. So rather than allocating a fixed-size array for the names, a `Vector` is used. To simplify things further, we build a `StringVector` (Listing 18.16), which works just like a `Vector` except that items inserted into the table must be strings, and return values are converted to strings automatically. The second issue is that the value itself may not be a single string, but rather an indeterminate number of strings. For instance, multiple-valued `SELECT` lists can send more than one name/value pair for the same name. So we use a `Vector` of `StringVector`'s to hold the values. Once the data is processed, the vectors are converted to arrays for easier handling. Note also that the characters used to separate the tokens ("&" and "=") are not hard coded into the class, but rather supplied as parameters. This will come in handy later on when the underlying `CgiParser` can be reused in the `CookieParser` class given in Listing 18.23 (see Section 18.12, "Using Cookies").

Listing 18.14 `CgiParser.java`

```java
import java.util.*;

public class CgiParser {
  private String data, delims1, delims2;
  private String[] nameArray, valueArray;
  private String[][] fullValueArray;


  public CgiParser(String data,
                   String delims1,
                   String delims2) {
    this.data = data;
    this.delims1 = delims1;
    this.delims2 = delims2;
  }
```

continued

Listing 18.14 `CgiParser.java` **(continued)**

```java
public LookupTable parse() {
  StringVector nameVector = new StringVector();
  Vector valueVector = new Vector();
  if (data == null)
    return(buildTable(nameVector, valueVector, 0));
  StringTokenizer tok =
    new StringTokenizer(data, delims1);
  String nameValuePair, name, value;
  StringTokenizer tempTok;
  int index, numNames=0;
  StringVector values;
  while(tok.hasMoreTokens()) {
    nameValuePair = tok.nextToken();
    tempTok = new StringTokenizer(nameValuePair,
                                  delims2);
    name = URLDecoder.decode(tempTok.nextToken());
    if (tempTok.hasMoreTokens())
      value = URLDecoder.decode(tempTok.nextToken());
    else
      value = "";
    index = nameVector.indexOf(name);
    if (index == -1) {
      nameVector.addElement(name);
      values = new StringVector();
      values.addElement(value);
      valueVector.addElement(values);
      numNames++;
    } else {
      values =
        (StringVector)valueVector.elementAt(index);
      values.addElement(value);
    }
  }
  return(buildTable(nameVector,
                    valueVector,
                    numNames));
}
```

continued

Listing 18.14 `CgiParser.java` (continued)

```java
  private LookupTable buildTable(StringVector nameVector,
                                 Vector valueVector,
                                 int numNames) {
    nameArray = new String[numNames];
    valueArray = new String[numNames];
    fullValueArray = new String[numNames][];
    LookupTable table = new LookupTable(nameArray,
                                        valueArray,
                                        fullValueArray);
    String[] fullValues;
    StringVector values;
    for(int i=0; i<nameVector.size(); i++) {
      nameArray[i] = nameVector.elementAt(i);
      values = (StringVector)valueVector.elementAt(i);
      valueArray[i] = values.firstElement();
      fullValues = new String[values.size()];
      values.copyInto(fullValues);
      fullValueArray[i] = fullValues;
    }
    return(table);
  }
}
```

Listing 18.15 `QueryStringParser.java`

```java
public class QueryStringParser extends CgiParser {
  public QueryStringParser(String queryString) {
    super(queryString, "&", "=");
  }
}
```

Listing 18.16   StringVector.java

```java
import java.util.*;

public class StringVector implements Cloneable {
  protected Vector vector;

  protected StringVector(Vector v) {
    vector = v;
  }

  public StringVector() {
    vector = new Vector();
  }

  public StringVector(int initialCapacity) {
    vector = new Vector(initialCapacity);
  }

  public StringVector(int initialCapacity,
                      int capacityIncrement) {
    vector = new Vector(initialCapacity,
                        capacityIncrement);
  }

  public void addElement(String string) {
    vector.addElement(string);
  }

  public int capacity() {
    return(vector.capacity());
  }

  public Object clone() {
    System.out.println("Orig capacity: " +
                       vector.capacity());
    Vector newVector = (Vector)vector.clone();
    System.out.println("New capacity: " +
                       newVector.capacity());
    StringVector newStringVector = new StringVector();
    newStringVector.vector = newVector;
    return(newStringVector);
  }
```

Listing 18.16 `StringVector.java` (continued)

```java
  public boolean contains(String string) {
    return(vector.contains(string));
  }

  public void copyInto(String[] strings) {
    vector.copyInto(strings);
  }

  public String elementAt(int index) {
    return((String)vector.elementAt(index));
  }

  public Enumeration elements() {
    return(vector.elements());
  }

  public void ensureCapacity(int minCapacity) {
    vector.ensureCapacity(minCapacity);
  }

  public String firstElement() {
    return((String)vector.firstElement());
  }

  public int indexOf(String string) {
    return(vector.indexOf(string));
  }

  public int indexOf(String string, int startIndex) {
    return(vector.indexOf(string, startIndex));
  }

  public void insertElementAt(String string, int index) {
    vector.insertElementAt(string, index);
  }

  public boolean isEmpty() {
    return(vector.isEmpty());
  }

  public String lastElement() {
    return((String)vector.lastElement());
  }
```

continued

Listing 18.16 `StringVector.java` **(continued)**

```java
  public int lastIndexOf(String string) {
    return(vector.lastIndexOf(string));
  }

  public int lastIndexOf(String string, int endIndex) {
    return(vector.lastIndexOf(string, endIndex));
  }


  public void removeAllElements() {
    vector.removeAllElements();
  }

  public boolean removeElement(String string) {
    return(vector.removeElement(string));
  }

  public void removeElementAt(int index) {
    vector.removeElementAt(index);
  }

  public void setElementAt(String string, int index) {
    vector.setElementAt(string, index);
  }

  public void setSize(int size) {
    vector.setSize(size);
  }

  public int size() {
    return(vector.size());
  }

  public String toString() {
    return(vector.toString());
  }

  public void trimToSize() {
    vector.trimToSize();
  }
}
```

18.9 Decoding URL-Encoded Values

Surprisingly, Java includes a URLEncoder class with an encode method, but no corresponding URLDecoder class with a decode method. But this situation is easily remedied by creating a URLDecoder class (Listing 18.17) that processes a string one character at a time. If the character is a plus sign (+), a space is generated instead. If the character is a percent sign (%), it is discarded and the following two characters are used as the hex value of a character to generate. The static parseInt method of Integer comes in handy here; we supply a base of 16 to convert from hex instead of from decimal. Otherwise, the character is passed through unchanged. For instance:

```
> java URLDecoder %63%67%69+programming

cgi programming
```

Listing 18.17   URLDecoder.java

```java
public class URLDecoder {
  public static void main(String[] args) {
    System.out.println(decode(args[0]));
  }

  public static String decode(String encoded) {
    System.out.println("encoded=" + encoded);
    StringBuffer decoded = new StringBuffer();
    int i=0;
    String charCode;
    char currentChar, decodedChar;
    while(i < encoded.length()) {
      currentChar = encoded.charAt(i);
      if (currentChar == '+') {
        decoded.append(" ");
        i = i + 1;
      } else if (currentChar == '%') {
        charCode = encoded.substring(i+1, i+3);
        decodedChar
          = (char)Integer.parseInt(charCode, 16);
        decoded.append(String.valueOf(decodedChar));
        i = i + 3;
      } else {
        decoded.append(String.valueOf(currentChar));
        i = i + 1;
      }
    }
    return(decoded.toString());
  }
}
```

Note the use of the `StringBuffer` class in Listing 18.17 to avoid the wasted copying that would result if a `String` were used throughout. `String` objects are *immutable*; once created they cannot change. A new `String` can be assigned to an existing *variable*, but the `String` *object* itself cannot change. This means that in the following code `s2` doesn't care what happens to `s1` and doesn't have to know anything about what happens in the `doSomethingWith` method; its value remains `"Some String"` regardless.

```
String s1 = "Some String";
String s2 = s1;
s1 = s1 + "Some Extra Stuff"
doSomethingWith(s2);
```

For Java to be able to provide this behavior, it has to copy the lefthand string in operations like `s1 + "Some Extra Stuff."` This means that repeated concatenation is very expensive. For instance, the following method of building a string of N consecutive letters is extremely inefficient.

```
public String buildString(String letter, int n) {
   String result = "";
   for(int i=0; i<n; i++)
     result = result + letter;
}
```

In fact, it takes time proportional to N^2. It first copies a string of length 0, then of length 1, then of length 2, and so forth up to length $N-1$. As all good computer scientists know,

$$\sum_{i=0}^{N-1} i = \frac{(N-1)N}{2}$$

This sum grows as the square of N. A `StringBuffer`, on the other hand, is a mutable data structure; more like a `char*` array in C or C++. So for an input string of length N, it takes approximately N operations to build the decoded `StringBuffer`, and another N to copy the result into a regular `String`. This gives a total process whose time grows linearly with N, a dramatic improvement over the pure-`String` approach. The moral of the story is that you need to know the underlying data structure being used in order to know how efficient your algorithms are, and the copying nature of the data structure used to implement `String` catches a lot of people off guard.

18.10 Building a Look-Up Table for Query Data

The `CgiParser` class took an input `String`, chopped it up into names and associated values, decoded the individual pieces, then passed the resulting array of names and values to the `LookupTable` constructor. But how can we conveniently implement such a look up table that will give us the value or values associated with a name? Listing 18.18 gives an implementation that simply scans the array of N names until it finds a match, then returns the value at the corresponding location in the value array. The user can either ask for a single value associated with a name (giving the first value if there are more than one), or get an array of all associated values. After the lecture on data structures and efficiency given in Section 18.9, you might be tempted to try to find something faster than this, since this approach takes time proportional to N, while data structures like heaps or hash tables provide lower growth rates. In fact, Java provides a very nice `HashTable` class which can be used to implement look-up tables where, under many reasonable conditions, the time required to insert or retrieve an element from the table is *independent* of the number of entries in the table. Although this is a very useful class in general, the overhead required to implement hashing doesn't pay for itself when N is small, and N is typically not more than one or two hundred in CGI applications, usually much less.

Listing 18.18 `Look-UpTable.java`

```java
public class LookupTable {
  private String[] nameArray, valueArray;
  private String[][] fullValueArray;

  public LookupTable(String[] nameArray,
                     String[] valueArray,
                     String[][] fullValueArray) {
    this.nameArray = nameArray;
    this.valueArray = valueArray;
    this.fullValueArray = fullValueArray;
  }
```

continued

Listing 18.18 `Look-UpTable.java` (continued)

```java
public String[] getNames() {
    return(nameArray);
}

public String[] getValues() {
    return(valueArray);
}

public String[][] getFullValues() {
    return(fullValueArray);
}

public String getValue(String name) {
    for(int i=0; i<nameArray.length; i++)
        if (nameArray[i].equals(name))
            return(valueArray[i]);
    return(null);
}

public String[] getFullValue(String name) {
    for(int i=0; i<nameArray.length; i++)
        if (nameArray[i].equals(name))
            return(fullValueArray[i]);
    return(null);
}

public int numValues(String name) {
    String[] values = getFullValue(name);
    if (values == null)
        return(0);
    else
        return(values.length);
}
}
```

18.11 Parsing Query Data: An Example

Now that we have all three pieces of the parser in place (splitting the string, decoding the pieces, and putting the results in a look-up table), let's build a CGI program that uses it. The ShowParse script (Listing 18.19) takes the request method and query string and passes it to the ShowParse Java class (Listing 18.20). This class first uses the REQUEST_METHOD variable to determine if it should use the supplied data (GET) or read the query string from standard input (POST). It then builds an HTML table of all supplied names and associated values.

Listing 18.19   The ShowParse Executable Script

```
#!/bin/sh

/usr/local/JDK/bin/java \
-DREQUEST_METHOD=$REQUEST_METHOD \
-DQUERY_STRING=$QUERY_STRING \
ShowParse
```

Listing 18.20   ShowParse.java

```java
public class ShowParse extends CgiShow {
  public static void main(String[] args) {
    String method = System.getProperty("REQUEST_METHOD");
    String[] data = new String[1];
    if ("GET".equalsIgnoreCase(method))
      data[0] = System.getProperty("QUERY_STRING");
    else {
      try {
        DataInputStream in =
          new DataInputStream(System.in);
        data[0] = in.readLine();
      } catch(IOException ioe) {
        System.out.println("IOException: " + ioe);
        System.exit(-1);
      }
    }
    ShowParse app = new ShowParse("ShowParse", data,
                                  method);
    app.printFile();
  }

  public ShowParse(String name, String[] queryData,
                   String requestMethod) {
    super(name, queryData, requestMethod);
  }
```

continued

Listing 18.20   `ShowParse.java`   (continued)

```java
protected void printBody(String[] queryData) {
  CgiParser parser = new CgiParser(queryData[0]);
  LookupTable table = parser.parse();
  String[] names = table.getNames();
  String[] values = table.getValues();
  System.out.println("Request method:  <CODE>" +
                     type + "</CODE>.<BR>");
  if (names.length > 0)
    System.out.println("Data supplied:\n" +
                       "<CENTER>\n" +
                       "<TABLE BORDER=1>\n" +
                       "  <TR><TH>Name<TH>Value(s)");
  else
    System.out.println("<H2>No data supplied.</H2>");
  String name, value;
  String[] fullValue;
  for(int i=0; i<names.length; i++) {
    name = names[i];
    System.out.println("  <TR><TD>" + name);
    if (table.numValues(name) > 1) {
      fullValue = table.getFullValue(name);
      System.out.println
        ("      <TD>Multiple values supplied:\n" +
         "            <UL>");
      for(int j=0; j<fullValue.length; j++)
        System.out.println("              <LI>" +
                           fullValue[j]);
      System.out.println("            </UL>");
    } else {
      value = values[i];
      if (value.equals(""))
        System.out.println
          ("      <TD><I>No Value Supplied</I>");
      else
        System.out.println
          ("      <TD>" + value);
    }
  }
  System.out.println("</TABLE>\n</CENTER>");
}
```

Listing 18.20   ShowParse.java   (continued)

```java
  protected void printStyleRules() {
    super.printStyleRules();
    System.out.println
      ("TH { background: black;\n" +
       "     color: white }\n" +
       "UL { margin-top: -10pt }");
  }
}
```

To see the ShowParse class in action, consider Listing 18.21, which shows the HTML page generated for

http://.../ShowParse?a=1&b=2&c=&a=3 .

Figure 18–9 shows the result in Netscape Communicator.

**Listing 18.21   ShowParse Output For Data of
                    "a=1&b=2&c=&a=3"**

```html
<!DOCTYPE HTML PUBLIC "-//W3C//DTD HTML 3.2//EN">
<HTML>
<HEAD>
<TITLE>The ShowParse Program</TITLE>
<STYLE>
<!--
H1 { text-align: center;
     font-family: Arial, sans-serif }
TH { background: black;
     color: white }
UL { margin-top: -10pt }
-->
</STYLE>
</HEAD>

<BODY>
<H1>The <CODE>ShowParse</CODE> Program</H1>
Request method:   <CODE>GET</CODE>.<BR>
Data supplied:
```

continued

Listing 18.21   ShowParse Output For Data of "a=1&b=2&c=&a=3" (continued)

```
<CENTER>
<TABLE BORDER=1>
  <TR><TH>Name<TH>Value(s)
  <TR><TD>a
      <TD>Multiple values supplied:
          <UL>
            <LI>1
            <LI>3
          </UL>
  <TR><TD>b
      <TD>2
  <TR><TD>c
      <TD><I>No Value Supplied</I>
</TABLE>
</CENTER>
</BODY>

</HTML>
```

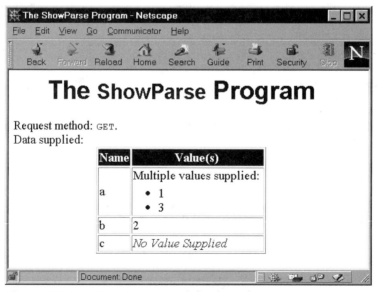

Figure 18-9   ShowParse result for data of "a=1&b=2&c=&a=3"

Finally, for a slightly more complete example, consider the forms-based data input page given in Listing 18.22 and shown in Figure 18–10. When the "Start Toward Success" button is clicked to submit the form, the data is sent via POST to ShowParse. ShowParse uses the Lookup-Table generated by the QueryStringParser to build the result shown in Figure 18–11.

Listing 18.22 `AdBuilder.html`

```
<!DOCTYPE HTML PUBLIC "-//W3C//DTD HTML 3.2//EN">
<HTML>
<HEAD>
  <TITLE>Ad Builder</TITLE>
  <BASE HREF="http://www.apl.jhu.edu/">
</HEAD>


<BODY>
<H1>Ad Builder</H1>
Introducing a dynamic paradigm shift in the creation
of advertisement campaigns! Ad Builder, Inc. lets
you choose the outline of your ad on-line, submit
the results to us, and then we will custom-fit a
top-quality total advertising solution to your needs.
<P>
Following is a <B>free</B> sample that helps you
create an ad for a CASE tool or integrated development
environment. Note that most major vendors used this
system to create their current ads!

<FORM ACTION="cgi-instruct/hall/ShowParse"
      METHOD="POST">
  Your company name:
  <INPUT TYPE="TEXT" NAME="victim"><BR>
  Password (for later access):
  <INPUT TYPE="PASSWORD" NAME="security blanket">
```

continued

Listing 18.22   `AdBuilder.html` (continued)

```
<TABLE BORDER=1>
    <TR><TH>Usefulness<BR>(Choose One or More)
        <TH>Architecture<BR>(Choose One or More)
        <TH>Application<BR>(Choose One)
        <TH>Product<BR>(Choose One)
    <TR><TD><SELECT NAME="adjective 1" MULTIPLE>
            <OPTION VALUE="standard">Revolutionary
            <OPTION VALUE="buggy">Flexible
            <OPTION VALUE="same old">Integrated
            <OPTION VALUE="beta">Robust
        </SELECT>
        <TD><SELECT NAME="adjective 2" MULTIPLE>
            <OPTION VALUE="not VB">Object Oriented
            <OPTION VALUE="buzzword compliant">Modern
            <OPTION VALUE="anti-MS">Open
            <OPTION VALUE="old">Standards-Based
        </SELECT>
        <TD><SELECT NAME="application">
            <OPTION VALUE="obvious">Software
            <OPTION VALUE="more obvious">Computer
            <OPTION VALUE="CASE">Production
            <OPTION VALUE="IDE">Development
        </SELECT>
        <TD><SELECT NAME="target-audience">
            <OPTION VALUE="managers">Paradigm
            <OPTION VALUE="MBAs">Methodology
            <OPTION VALUE="CEOs">Strategy
            <OPTION VALUE="naive-hackers">Tool
        </SELECT>
    </TABLE>
    <P ALIGN="CENTER">
    <INPUT TYPE="SUBMIT" VALUE="Start Toward Success">
</FORM>
</BODY>
</HTML>
```

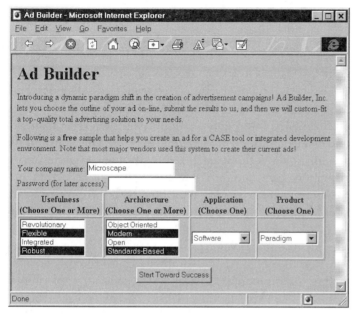

Figure 18-10   A page that sends data to `ShowParse`

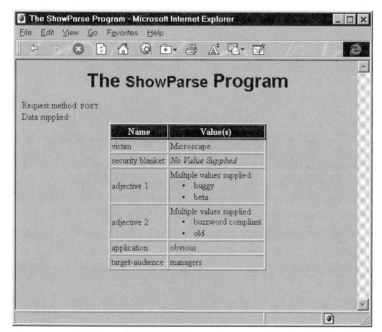

Figure 18-11   Output of `ShowParse`

18.12 Using Cookies

Hidden fields in HTML input forms can maintain data between connections in a single session, but this data is lost in later sessions or if the user directly loads a page without also including query data. However, as discussed in Section 16.6, "Cookies: Storing Persistent Data on the Client," "cookies" can be used in Netscape, Internet Explorer, and a few other browsers to maintain persistent data on client machines, even between sessions. This is useful for CGI programs that want to allow the user to select permanent preferences, provide access information, or maintain contextual information across sessions. To instruct the client to store cookies associated with the current URL, the CGI program should include `Set-Cookie` response headers in its output. It can read the `Cookie` request line via the `HTTP_COOKIE` variable, yielding a string of the form "name1=value1; name2=value2; ... ; nameN=valueN." Fortunately, parsing the cookie data is simple because the process is so similar to that of parsing the query data. Listing 18.23 gives an implementation that uses the `CgiParser` class (Listing 18.14) to break cookie strings at the semicolon and then at the equals sign, building a look-up table of the result.

Listing 18.23 `CookieParser.java`

```
public class CookieParser extends CgiParser {
  public CookieParser(String cookies) {
    super(cookies, "; ", "=");
  }
}
```

Given this tool, we will build a CGI program that lets people experiment with style sheets (discussed in Chapter 5, "Cascading Style Sheets"). The CGI program enables users to interactively select various font, color, and indentation values, then reconfigures the current page using the selected values. Furthermore, the values selected are stored in cookies. Then, when the user revisits the page in the same or future sessions, the previous settings are used both in the style sheets and as the defaults in the combo boxes that gather user input.

Listing 18.24 gives a Unix script that is used as the target of the URL. It simply passes the query data and cookie values to the `CssTest` Java class, given in Listing 18.25 (see Figure 15–12). To simplify software maintenance, the options for the various pull-down menus and other data that can be changed without altering the basic CssTest structure are placed in a separate class (CssChoices.java, Listing 18.26 and Figure 15–13). Although the CssTest code is a bit long because it builds a medium-sized HTML document, the approach is pretty straightforward. First, the various settings are initialized to their default values. This is done via a call to processData with a default-settings string that is in cookie format. The processData method is then called on the actual cookie string, replacing the default values for any entries that are contained in the cookies. Finally, processData is called on the query string data, again overriding any previous values. The final values are then used in two places. First, in printHttpHeaders, the Set-Cookie fields are generated using the values just obtained. Second, in printDocument, the values are placed in the style rules and then options for the various SELECT menus are listed as SELECTED if they match the value associated with the name of the SELECT form.

Listing 18.24   The CssTest Executable Script

```
#!/bin/sh

/usr/local/JDK/bin/java \
  -DQUERY_STRING="$QUERY_STRING" \
  -DHTTP_COOKIE="$HTTP_COOKIE" \
  CssTest
```

Listing 18.25   CssTest.java

```java
public class CssTest {
  public static void main(String[] args) {
    new CssTest(System.getProperty("QUERY_STRING"),
                System.getProperty("HTTP_COOKIE"));
  }


  protected final boolean COOKIES = true;
  protected final boolean QUERY_STRING = false;
  protected  String[] names = CssChoices.names;
  protected String[] values = new String[names.length];
  protected LookupTable lookupTable;
```

continued

Listing 18.25   `CssTest.java` (continued)

```java
public CssTest(String data, String cookies) {
  processData(CssChoices.defaults, COOKIES);
  processData(cookies, COOKIES);
  processData(data, QUERY_STRING);
  lookupTable = new LookupTable(names, values, null);
  printBody();
}


protected void printBody() {
  printHttpHeaders();
  printDocument();
}


protected void processData(String data,
                           boolean cookieFlag) {
  LookupTable table;
  if (cookieFlag) {
    CookieParser parser = new CookieParser(data);
    table = parser.parse();
  } else {
    QueryStringParser parser =
      new QueryStringParser(data);
    table = parser.parse();
  }
  String value;
  for(int i=0; i<names.length; i++) {
    value = table.getValue(names[i]);
    if (value != null && !value.equals(""))
      values[i] = value;
  }
}
```

Listing 18.25 CssTest.java (continued)

```java
protected void printHttpHeaders() {
  String expires = CssChoices.expires;
  System.out.println
    ("Content-Type: text/html\n" +
     "Set-Cookie: repeatVisitor=true" + expires);
  for (int i=1; i<names.length; i++)
    System.out.println
      ("Set-Cookie: " +
       names[i] + "=" + values[i] + expires);
  System.out.println();
}

protected void printDocument() {
  System.out.println
    ("<!DOCTYPE HTML PUBLIC " +
       "\"-//W3C//DTD HTML 3.2//EN\">\n" +
     "<HTML>\n<HEAD>\n" +
     "<TITLE>CSS1 Test</TITLE>\n" +
     "<STYLE>\n<!--");
  printStyleRules();
  System.out.println
    ("-->\n</STYLE>\n</HEAD>\n\n" +
     "<BODY>\n" +
     "<H1>CSS1 Test</H1>\n" +
     welcomeMessage() +
     "This page demonstrates a few of the\n" +
     "capabilities of cascading style sheets\n" +
     "by letting you select options interactively.\n" +
     "If your browser supports cookies, values\n" +
     "you select in this session will be used\n" +
     "as initial settings in future sessions.\n" +
     "<FORM ACTION=\"" + CssChoices.url + "\">\n" +
     "  <H2>Background</H2>");
  printSelect("  Color Name:", "bgColor",
              CssChoices.bgColor);
```

continued

Listing 18.25 `CssTest.java` (continued)

```
System.out.println
  ("  <H2>Main Headings:</H2>");
printSelect("  Size:", "headingSize",
            CssChoices.headingSize);
printSelect("  Font:", "headingFont",
            CssChoices.headingFont);
printSelect("Alignment", "headingAlignment",
            CssChoices.headingAlignment);

System.out.println
  ("  <H2>Indentation</H2>\n" +
   "  CSS1 allows you to define margins\n" +
   "  for built-in and custom paragraph classes.\n" +
   "  <P CLASS=\"indent1\">\n" +
   "  These lines are indented<BR>\n" +
   "  according to the first-level<BR>\n" +
   "  margin setting below (in inches).<BR>\n" +
   "  <P CLASS=\"indent2\">\n" +
   "  These lines are indented<BR>\n" +
   "  according to the second-level<BR>\n" +
   "  margin setting below (in inches).\n" +
   "  </P>");
printSelect("  First-Level:", "indent1",
            CssChoices.indent);
printSelect("  Second-Level:", "indent2",
            CssChoices.indent);
System.out.println
  ("  <P>\n" +
   "  <CENTER>\n" +
   "    <INPUT TYPE=\"SUBMIT\" VALUE=\"Try It\">\n" +
   "  </CENTER>\n" +
   "</FORM>\n</BODY>\n</HTML>");
}
```

Listing 18.25 `CssTest.java` (continued)

```
protected void printStyleRules() {
  System.out.println
    ("BODY { background: " + val("bgColor") + " }\n" +
    "H1 { text-align: " + val("headingAlignment") +
    ";\n" +
    "      font-size: " + val("headingSize") +
    "pt;\n" +
    "      font-family: " + val("headingFont") +
    " }\n" +
    "P.indent1 { margin-left: " + val("indent1") +
    "in }\n" +
    "P.indent2 { margin-left: " + val("indent2") +
    "in }");
}


protected String val(String name) {
  return(lookupTable.getValue(name));
}


protected void printOption(String value, String name) {
  System.out.print
    ("    <OPTION VALUE=\"" + value + "\"");
  if (value.equals(val(name)))
    System.out.print(" SELECTED>");
  else
    System.out.print(">");
  System.out.println(value);
}
```

continued

Listing 18.25 `CssTest.java` (continued)

```java
protected void printSelect(String intro,
                           String name,
                           String[] options) {
  System.out.println
    (intro + "\n" +
     "  <SELECT NAME=\"" + name + "\">");
  for (int i=0; i<options.length; i++)
    printOption(options[i], name);
  System.out.println
    ("  </SELECT>");
}


protected String welcomeMessage() {
  if(val("repeatVisitor") != null)
    return("Welcome back!\n");
  else
    return("Welcome, first time visitor!\n");
}
}
```

Listing 18.26 `CssChoices.java`

```java
public class CssChoices {
  public static  String[] names =
    { "repeatVisitor", "headingFont", "headingSize",
      "headingAlignment", "bgColor",
      "indent1", "indent2" };
  public static String defaults =
    "headingFont=Times+New+Roman; " +
    "headingSize=30; " +
    "headingAlignment=left; " +
    "bgColor=white; " +
    "indent1=0.25; " +
    "indent2=0.50";
  public static String[] bgColor =
    { "white", "gray", "ivory",
      "whitesmoke", "blanchedalmond" };
  public static String[] headingSize =
    { "20", "30", "40", "50", "60", "70", "80" };
  public static String[] headingFont =
    { "Impact", "Arial", "Times New Roman",
      "Brush Script MT", "Braggadocio" };
  public static String[] headingAlignment =
    { "left", "center", "right" };
  public static String[] indent =
    { "0.0", "0.25", "0.50", "0.75",
      "1.0", "1.25", "1.50", "1.75", "2.0" };
  public static String url =
    "http://www.apl.jhu.edu/cgi-instruct/hall/CssTest";
  public static String  expires =
    "; expires=Friday, 31-Dec-99 23:59:59 GMT";
}
```

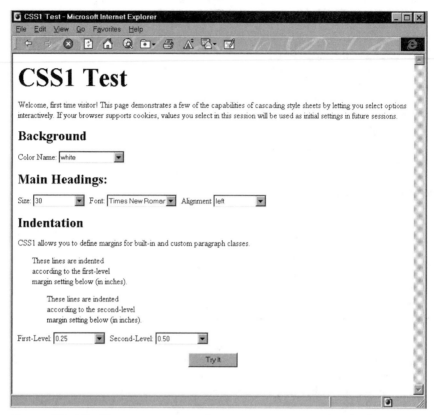

Figure 18-12   The `CssTest` page lets users experiment with style sheets.

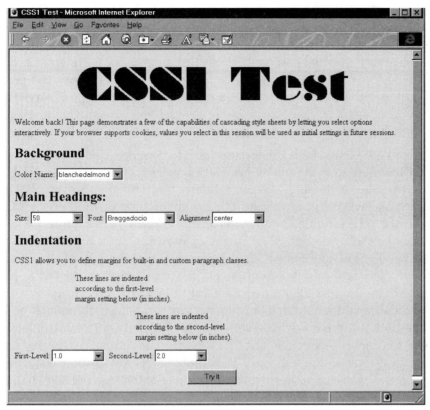

Figure 18–13   Cookies allow `CssTest` to use the most recent settings as defaults, even if they were set in a previous session.

18.13 Server-Side Java

One of the major problems with CGI is that the HTTP server starts an entirely new program every time a request is made. The overhead that this requires tends to make CGI applications inefficient, especially for small tasks where this delay can be a significant percentage of the total processing time. Consequently, many HTTP servers have ways of associating programs with the HTTP server itself, running in the same address space and staying loaded between requests. Section 18.14 (Other CGI Alternatives) surveys several of them, but this section concentrates on one important new alternative: server-side Java. With this approach, a Java VM is associated with the HTTP server, and there is a standard way of associating Java programs with various URLs.

In addition, there are Java classes for parsing the data string and extracting the values of all the standard CGI environment variables. Aside from the added efficiency and convenience, there are security advantages to this approach as well. Normal Java applications that are run as CGI programs can perform any operation that the process that owns the HTTP server can perform, just as with CGI programs in other language. However, Java "servlets" are run by a `SecurityManager` and in Java 1.1 can have varying levels of access privileges based on digital signatures associated with the class.

Several Web servers built similar interfaces to do server-side Java, but now most of them are unifying under JavaSoft's Servlet API. Most major HTTP servers (Apache, Netscape, Microsoft Internet Information Server, W3C's Jigsaw, Sun's Java Web Server, and others) either support the Servlet API directly, or can be extended to do so via an embeddable package freely available from JavaSoft. See `http://jserv.javasoft.com` for information on the Servlet API, the Servlet Developer's Kit, and the Java Web Server (formerly "Jeeves"), a server written in Java that supports this API. Jef Poskanzer has also provided a free mini-HTTP server written in Java (with source code!) that does nothing but support server-side Java. Running it on a separate port is a great way of testing things out until your main server is updated to support servlets. See `http://www.acme.com/java/soft-ware/` to download the software. It is probably easiest to download the entire "Acme" package rather than to separately obtain each of the classes needed for the server system.

Using Servlets

Complete coverage of the servlet API is beyond the scope of this book, but we will give a quick summary of the most common usage. There are three basic steps involved:

- Build an `HttpServlet`
- Implement the `service` method
- Register the servlet with the server

Building an HttpServlet

The `HttpServlet` is the most common type of servlet used in response to HTTP `GET`, `POST`, and `HEAD` requests. Other types of servlets can be used to generate custom HTML via server-side includes.

```
import java.servlet.*;
import java.servlet.http.*;
import java.io.*;

public class MyServlet extends HttpServlet {
...
}
```

Implementing the service method

All servlets have stubs for `init`, `destroy`, and `getServletInfo` methods to initialize, destroy/clean up after, and print author and version information about servlets. The most important method, however, is `service`, which is the method that performs the real processing. The body of the `service` method will behave similarly to standard CGI programs implemented in Java, except that several utility classes have been provided to simplify things.

```
import java.servlet.*;
import java.servlet.http.*;
import java.io.*;

public class MyServlet extends HttpServlet {
  public void service(HttpServletRequest request,
                      HttpServletResponse response)
      throws ServletException, IOException {
  ...
  }
}
```

A summary of `HttpServletRequest` and `HttpServletResponse`, the classes of the arguments supplied to `service`, is given after the `ColorTester` example.

Registering the servlet with the server

This part of the process is not standardized. The Java Web Server from JavaSoft has a Web-based interface that lets you interactively associate servlets with various types of URLs. The mini-HTTP server from Jef Poskanzer has an `addServlet` method that takes a URL pattern and an associated servlet object. Other servers have their own approach.

A Servlet to Help Select Colors

Listing 18.27 gives a simple servlet in the "mrh" subdirectory that uses the values of `Background` and `Foreground` to build a page that displays text in this color. Note the use of Acme.Serve.xxx package names instead of java.xxx because this is executed using the Poskanzer server. To associate this servlet with the URL http://*host*:*port*/ColorTester, we use the following.

```
server.addServlet("/ColorTester", new ColorTester());
```

Note that although the servlet API is consistent across servers and platforms, the particulars of associating a URL with the servlet is implementation dependent.

Listing 18.27 `ColorTester.java`

```java
package Acme.Serve.mrh;

import Acme.Serve.servlet.*;
import Acme.Serve.servlet.http.*;
import java.io.*;

public class ColorTester extends HttpServlet {
  public void service(HttpServletRequest request,
                      HttpServletResponse response)
      throws ServletException, IOException {
    response.setStatus(HttpServletResponse.SC_OK);
    response.setContentType("text/html");
    ServletOutputStream out = response.getOutputStream();
    String bgColor = request.getParameter("Background");
    if (bgColor == null || bgColor.equals(""))
      bgColor = "white";
    String fgColor = request.getParameter("Foreground");
    if (fgColor == null || fgColor.equals(""))
      fgColor = "black";
    out.println
      ("<!DOCTYPE HTML PUBLIC " +
          "\"-//W3C//DTD HTML 3.2//EN\">\n" +
        "<HTML>\n" +
        "<HEAD>\n" +
        "<TITLE>ColorTester</TITLE>\n" +
        "</HEAD>\n" +
        "\n" +
        "<BODY BGCOLOR=\"" + bgColor + "\"\n" +
        "      TEXT=\"" + fgColor + "\">\n" +
        "<H1>ColorTester</H1>\n" +
        "Based on your input, this page is being\n" +
        "displayed with a background color of\n" +
        "'" + bgColor + "' and a foreground color of\n" +
        "'" + fgColor + "'.\n" +
        "</BODY>\n" +
        "</HTML>");
  }
}
```

A simple forms-based interface to this servlet is given in Listing 18.28, with Figures 18–14 and 18–15 showing the input and results page, respectively.

Listing 18.28 `ColorTester.html`

```
<!DOCTYPE HTML PUBLIC "-//W3C//DTD HTML 3.2//EN">
<HTML>
<HEAD>
  <TITLE>ColorTester</TITLE>
</HEAD>

<BODY>
<H1>ColorTester</H1>
This page lets you test out foreground and background
colors interactively. Enter standard HTML 3.2 color
names, or, if you are on Netscape or Internet Explorer,
use X11 color names also.
<CENTER>
<FORM ACTION="http://www.apl.jhu.edu:8080/ColorTester">
  Background: <INPUT TYPE="TEXT" NAME="Background"><BR>
  Foreground: <INPUT TYPE="TEXT" NAME="Foreground"><BR>
  <INPUT TYPE="SUBMIT" VALUE="Show a Sample Page">
</CENTER>
</FORM>

</BODY>
</HTML>
```

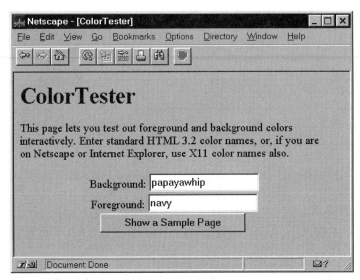

Figure 18–14 Interface to the `ColorTester` servlet.

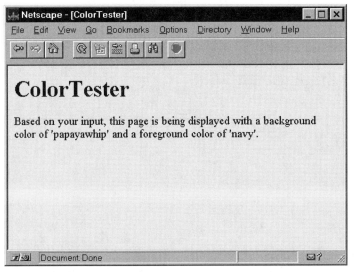

Figure 18–15 Results of the `ColorTester` servlet.

The HttpServletRequest Class

The first argument to the HttpServlet's service method was of type HttpServletRequest. We used its getParameter method to extract the value of Background and Foreground from the name/value pairs contained in the data string. In addition to getParameter, it contains a variety of other useful methods as well. Following is a quick summary.

public String getAuthType()

This returns the authorization method used, if any.

public int getContentLength()

This returns the number of bytes in the request or –1 if not known. Generally only POST requests have this information.

public String getContentType()

This returns the MIME type of the data, or null if unspecified.

public long getDateHeader(String name)

This returns the value of the header specified by name, interpreted as a date. –1 is returned if the header is not found. Header names are not case sensitive.

public String getHeader(String name)

This method provides access to headers that don't already have a getXxx helper method. For instance, because there is no getCookie method, getHeader("Cookie") could be used instead. Header names are not case sensitive.

public Enumeration getHeaderNames()

This returns an Enumeration of all available HTTP request header names.

public ServletInputStream getInputStream()

This provides an input stream that can be used to read the request.

public int getIntHeader(String name)

This gives the value of the integer-valued field specified by the given name, or –1 if the name is not found. Header names are not case sensitive.

public String getMethod()

This method returns "POST", "GET", or "HEAD", depending on the request method that was used.

public String getParameter(String name)

This provides the URL-encoded value of the specified query string parameter name. Parameter names are case sensitive.

public Enumeration getParameterNames()

This method returns an Enumeration of all parameter names contained in the query string.

public String getPathInfo()

This returns any extra path information after the servlet name but before the query string. It returns null if no path info was supplied.

public String getPathTranslated()

This is similar to getPathInfo, but translates the path to a real path.

public String getProtocol()

This returns the protocol used in the request, and is most often "HTTP/1.0".

public String getQueryString()

This returns the original query string, which usually consists of name/value pairs.

public String getRealPath(String path)

The getRealPath method applies alias rules to the specified path to return a real path.

public String getRemoteAddr()

This returns the IP address of the system making the request.

public String getRemoteHost()

This returns the fully qualified host name of the system making the request.

public String getRemoteUser()
This gives the name of the remote user, or `null` in the majority of cases when this is not known.

public String getRequestURI()
This returns the URI requested.

public String getServerName()
This gives the host name of the server that received the request.

public int getServerPort()
This returns the port being used by the server.

public String getServletPath()
This returns the part of the request URI that refers to the servlet being invoked.

The HttpServletResponse Class

The second argument to the `HttpServlet`'s `service` method was of type `HttpServletResponse`. We used its `setStatus` and `setContent-Type` methods to specify that the response would be a normal HTML document, and `getOutPutStream` method to obtain a stream that could be used to write the HTML that was generated. `HttpServletResponse` contains a variety of other useful methods and variables as well. Following is a quick summary.

public ServletOutputStream getOutputStream()
This provides an output stream that can be used to write the document being generated.

public void sendError(int status)
This sends the specified status code to the client, along with the default message for that code.

public void sendError(int status, String message)
This sends the specified status code and error message to the client.

public void sendRedirect(String newLocation)
This forwards the client to a new URL.

public void setContentLength(int length)
This sets the `Content-Length` header in the response.

public void setContentType(String mimeType)
This sets the `Content-Type` header in the response. The most common value is `"text/html"`.

public void setDateHeader(String name, long date)
This sets the specified header to a date given by `date`.

public void setHeader(String name, String value)
The `setHeader` method can be used to supply values for response headers that do not already have a `setXxx` helper method. For instance, because there is no `setCookie` method, `setHeader("Set-Cookie", cookieData)` could be used instead. Header names are not case sensitive.

public void setIntHeader(String name, int value)
This sets the value of the specified integer-valued header.

public void setStatus(int status)
This sets the status of the response, using the default message associated with the status code.

public void setStatus(int status, String message)
This sets the status code and message given in the response.

Constants
The integer variables `SC_ACCEPTED`, `SC_BAD_GATEWAY`, `SC_BAD_REQUEST`, `SC_CREATED`, `SC_FORBIDDEN`, `SC_INTERNAL_SERVER_ERROR`, `SC_MOVED_PERMANENTLY`,

`SC_MOVED_TEMPORARILY`, `SC_NO_CONTENT`, `SC_NOT_FOUND`, `SC_NOT_IMPLEMENTED`, `SC_NOT_MODIFIED`, `SC_OK`, `SC_SERVICE_UNAVAILABLE`, and `SC_UNAUTHORIZED` provide access to the common error codes described in Section 16.4 (The HTTP Response Status Line).

Filtering URLs Using Servlets

The `ColorTester` example showed how to use servlets to provide a more efficient variation of a standard CGI program. However, because the association between the URL and the servlet is determined within the server in a configurable manner, servlets can also be used for logging and filtering of URLs. For instance, Listing 18.29 gives a servlet that returns a rude response to people trying to obtain the Unix system password file through improperly configured CGI links. To associate this servlet with every URL ending in `/etc/passwd`, we use the following.

```
server.addServlet("*/etc/passwd",
                  new CrackerServlet());
```

Figures 18–16 and 18–17 show the results.

Although the passwords in `/etc/passwd` are encrypted using a non-reversible algorithm, "dictionary" attacks where very large sets of common words are pre-encrypted and compared to the encrypted passwords often break 5–10% of passwords on Unix systems that do not enforce hard-to-guess passwords. So logging of sites that search for password files can alert administrators of potential problems. In real life, of course, webmasters who discover such problems should be a bit more circumspect than the confrontational approach given in this example. By the way, note the difference between the term "hacker," which despite confusion in the press, means "an expert programmer" to people in the software community, and the term "cracker" which means "a person who tries to break into or damage computer systems." Fortunately for all of us, the intersection between the two sets is relatively small.

Listing 18.29   CrackerServlet.java

```java
package Acme.Serve.mrh;

import Acme.Serve.servlet.*;
import Acme.Serve.servlet.http.*;
import java.io.*;

public class CrackerServlet extends HttpServlet {
  public void service(HttpServletRequest request,
                      HttpServletResponse response)
     throws ServletException, IOException {
    response.setStatus(HttpServletResponse.SC_OK);
    response.setContentType("text/html");
    ServletOutputStream out = response.getOutputStream();
    String[] imageFiles = {"Cannon.gif", "Club.gif",
                           "Punch.gif", "Skull.gif",
                           "Yell.gif"};
    int index =
       (int)Math.round(Math.floor(Math.random()*5.0));
    String imageFile = imageFiles[index];
    String imageBase =
       "http://www.apl.jhu.edu/~hall/images/";
    String host = request.getRemoteHost();
    out.println
       ("<!DOCTYPE HTML PUBLIC " +
          "\"-//W3C//DTD HTML 3.2//EN\">\n" +
       "<HTML>\n" +
       "<HEAD>\n" +
       "<TITLE>Depart, Vile Cracker!</TITLE>\n" +
       "</HEAD>\n" +
       "\n" +
       "<BODY BGCOLOR=\"WHITE\">\n" +
       "<CENTER>\n" +
       "<H1>Depart, Vile Cracker!</H1>\n" +
       "<IMG SRC=\"" + imageBase + imageFile + "\">\n" +
       "</CENTER>\n" +
       "<P>\n" +
       "Naturally, we use shadow passwords, so\n" +
       "the password file wouldn't have done you\n" +
       "any good anyhow. But as punishment, we have\n" +
       "notified postmaster@" +
       host + " of your scurrilous activity.\n" +
       "<P>\n" +
       "I hope you get");
    if (host.toUpperCase().endsWith("EDU"))
      out.println("kicked out of school.");
    else
      out.println("fired.");
  }
}
```

Figure 18-16   The `CrackerServlet` response to requests ending with `/etc/passwd`.

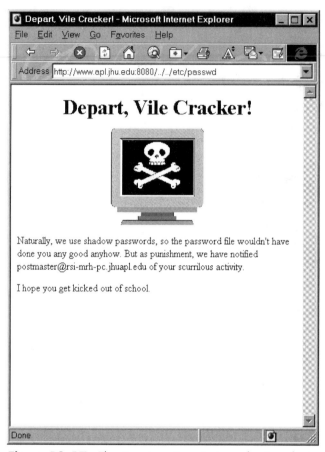

Figure 18-17   The `CrackerServlet` randomizes the image shown.

18.14 Other CGI Alternatives

CGI provides a flexible but inefficient method to connect Web pages to databases and other external programs. The primary efficiency problem is that the HTTP server has to start a new program or open a new database connection for each request. An additional problem is that each author has to write or obtain a package for parsing the query string, accessing environment variables, and generating results. The Java servlet API provided one solution, giving a common way to run programs in the same address space as the HTTP server using a common interface. However, there are many other solutions to this problem. These include Application Programming Interfaces specific to a server or set of servers, server-side includes, server-side JavaScript, direct socket connections from applets to custom servers (including JDBC drivers), and database interfaces especially designed for Web access.

Server APIs

Many HTTP servers provide APIs that simplify the integration of shared libraries, DLLs, and databases. Most of these approaches were originally specific to a particular server, but some such as ISAPI and NSAPI are now supported by servers from third-party vendors.

ISAPI

ISAPI, the Information Server API, was originally developed by Microsoft for its Internet Information Server. It allows Dynamic Linked Libraries (DLLs) to be associated with the server and accessed at predefined entry points when certain requests are made. Several Windows 95 and Windows NT servers now support ISAPI. ISAPI can be used to tell the server what to do when certain requests are made. However, Internet Information Server also supports Active Server Pages (ASP), which let the server generate the *original* page dynamically. Details on ISAPI and ASP can be found at the following URLs.

```
http://www.microsoft.com/win32dev/apiext/isalegal.htm
http://www.microsoft.com/iis/usingiis/resources/aspdocs/
```

NSAPI

NSAPI is Netscape's server-customization API, and allows shared libraries (Unix) or DLLs to be integrated with the server. Documentation can be found at the `http://home.netscape.com/news-ref/std/server_api.html`.

Apache API

The free Apache server is still one of the most widely used HTTP servers on the market. *The* most popular option by a large margin if the Netcraft survey (`http://www.netcraft.com/Survey/`) is accurate. Apache has its own API that lets developers drop a database or other module into the server, then automatically route certain requests to that module. Documentation can be found at `http://www.apache.org/docs/misc/API.html`.

WSAPI

The WebSite API is touted as a more flexible alternative to ISAPI and is supported by O'Reilly's WebSite server. For details, see `http://website.ora.com/wspro/wsapi/html/`.

Server-Side Includes

Many HTTP servers support "server-side includes," a facility originally from the NCSA server that lets you substitute external files, file and time information, environment variables, or the output of external programs for parts of otherwise static HTML documents. Because server-side includes can invoke arbitrary programs, be careful not to enable them for documents submitted in whole or in part (e.g., via a "guestbook") by visitors to your site. For details, see

```
http://hoohoo.ncsa.uiuc.edu/docs/tutorials/
includes.html.
```

LiveWire: Server-Side JavaScript

Netscape provides a facility called "LiveWire" that does two things. Firstly, it lets you run JavaScript on the server, just as JavaSoft's servlet API lets you run Java on the server. However, LiveWire runs only on Netscape servers, unlike server-side Java, which can run on a variety of different HTTP servers. The JavaScript used by LiveWire is enhanced with methods to parse requests and access databases and other external programs, and has a graphical interface for setting up the association between URLs and JavaScript applications. Secondly, LiveWire lets the server generate dynamic documents for the *original* Web page. These two capabilities are similar in functionality to the combination of ISAPI and ASP. Complete documentation on LiveWire can be found at

```
http://developer.netscape.com/library/documentation/
livewire/.
```

JDBC and Direct Socket Connections for Applets

Web pages built using HTML forms must talk to a server that understands HTTP, because the browser automatically generates GET or POST requests when the form is submitted. However, as discussed in Chapter 17, "CGI Programming and Beyond—The Client Side," applets can open direct socket connections to the machine from which they are loaded. This lets them exchange data with arbitrary network servers, including database servers and custom applications. However, because database protocols tend to be relatively complex, building an applet from scratch to communicate using an existing protocol involves a lot of work. JavaSoft has supplied a standard API to do this, the Java DataBase Connectivity (JDBC) package. Almost every major database vendor supports JDBC, either directly or via a JDBC-ODBC bridge. Although the applet's SecurityManager normally restricts applets from making network connections of any sort (JDBC or otherwise) to machines other than the one from which they are loaded, most JDBC drivers can act as a proxy so that the actual database server and the HTTP server need not be on the same system. JDBC is standard with version 1.1 of Java, but a separate JDBC-support package for 1.02 is available free of charge from JavaSoft. JavaSoft and Intersolv also distribute a free test applet that lets users interactively connect to databases, enter SQL queries on screen, and get the results presented in formatted tables. JDBC is covered in Section 15.9.

The WebObjects Adaptor

NeXT (now Apple) was one of the pioneers in the integration of databases and the Web with their WebObjects system. Although several database and 4GL vendors now supply integration tools, WebObjects is still a popular choice. Using this approach, a small program called "The WebObjects Adaptor" is placed on the server machine and integrated with the HTTP server by ISAPI, NSAPI, or traditional CGI. This adaptor serves as the communications bridge between the HTTP server and the database, generating HTML based on the data retrieved and configurable script files. For more information, see `http://www.next.com/WebObjects/`.

18.15 Summary

The Common Gateway Interface (CGI) lets you connect Web pages to databases or other programs running on an external server. Data can be sent using either the HTTP `GET` or `POST` method. Data sent via the `GET` method is normally read from the `QUERY_STRING` environment variable, but if it does not contain an equals sign, it can also be read from the command-line arguments to the CGI program. Data sent via `POST` can be read from the CGI program's standard input. In either case, the CGI program normally builds an HTML document describing the results, then imitates an HTTP server to return it, printing HTTP headers (at least `Content-Type`), a blank line, and then the document. Cookies provide a convenient mechanism for storing user preferences, access codes, or other data on the client computer during or between sessions. This process is typically the same whether the data was generated from HTML forms, from a Java applet, or simply by the user adding some data to the end of the URL when making a request from their browser. However, if the data was generated by an applet, it is sometimes useful to return "raw" data to be processed by the applet.

The traditional CGI process is relatively expensive, because it takes quite a bit of overhead to start a new program for every request. There are a variety of CGI-like approaches that avoid this problem. These approaches include server-side Java or JavaScript; APIs for talking to shared libraries, DLLs, or databases that are running with the HTTP server; and server-side includes. Even so, however, contacting the server can take a long time. For applications that use HTML to gather input and let the user enter strings in text-fields, it requires a round trip to the server simply to determine that the user entered a word where they should have entered a number, or that they forgot to include their ID number when requesting data that requires it. The following chapters discuss JavaScript, an interpreted language that runs in the browser. JavaScript can be applied in a variety of ways to make Web pages more flexible and dynamic, but one of the major applications is to check the format of CGI data *before* it is submitted.

Part 4

JAVASCRIPT

JAVASCRIPT: ADDING DYNAMIC CONTENT TO WEB PAGES

Topics in This Chapter

- Building HTML as the page is loaded
- Monitoring user events
- Building cross-platform scripts
- Basic JavaScript syntax
- Using JavaScript to customize Web pages
- Using JavaScript to make pages more dynamic
- Using JavaScript to validate CGI forms
- Using JavaScript to manipulate HTTP cookies
- Using JavaScript to interact with and control frames
- Controlling applets and calling Java from JavaScript
- Accessing JavaScript from Java

Chapter 19

Despite the similarity in name, JavaScript is very different from Java. JavaScript is a scripting language that is embedded in Web pages and interpreted as the page is loaded. Java is a general-purpose programming language that can be used for applets that execute after the page loads. JavaScript can discover a lot of information about the HTML document it is in, and manipulate a variety of HTML elements. Java, if used in a Web page at all, is relatively isolated from the Web page in which it is embedded. JavaScript has no graphics library, explicit threads, or networking. Java has the AWT, an extensive threading library, and networking options that include sockets, RMI, and JDBC.

There are currently four major browsers that support JavaScript, and, unfortunately, four different versions of JavaScript. JavaScript 1.0 is supported by Netscape 2, JavaScript 1.1 by Netscape 3, and JavaScript 1.2 by Netscape 4. Internet Explorer supports JScript, a version of JavaScript that is about halfway between JavaScript 1.0 and 1.1. I'll discuss all four versions in this chapter and the next, but will give the most attention to the Netscape versions.

A topic *not* covered here is server-side JavaScript. Netscape servers have a package called LiveWire that lets you use JavaScript for CGI-like server applications. This is not yet in widespread use, however. For more information on this and on alternatives, see Chapter 18, "CGI Programming and Beyond—The Server Side."

There are two basic ways that JavaScript can be used in your Web pages. The first is to build HTML dynamically as the Web page is loaded. The second is to monitor various user events and to take action when these events occur. These two syntactic styles are described in the first two sections, with the following section summarizing some other important syntax. These two styles can be combined in a variety of ways, and are used for seven general classes of applications: customizing Web pages, making pages more dynamic, validating CGI forms, manipulating cookies, interacting with frames, calling Java from JavaScript, and accessing JavaScript from Java. The remaining sections of this chapter describe each of these application areas, providing two or three examples of each. The following chapter gives details of the built-in JavaScript objects.

19.1 Generating HTML Dynamically

JavaScript code contained inside a SCRIPT element will be executed as the page is loaded, with any output the code generates being inserted into the document at the place the SCRIPT occurred. Listing 19.1 outlines the basic format. Don't worry about all the syntactic details for now; they will be explained at the end of this section. For now, just note the standard form.

Listing 19.1   Template for Generating HTML with JavaScript

```
...
<BODY>
Regular HTML

<SCRIPT LANGUAGE="JavaScript">
<!--
Build HTML Here
// -->
</SCRIPT>

More Regular HTML
</BODY>
```

In Netscape 3 and 4 and recent copies of Internet Explorer 3, you can use the SRC attribute of SCRIPT to load remote JavaScript code. However, this will not work in Netscape 2, and requires the server to tag JavaScript code with the application/x-JavaScript MIME type, something most HTTP servers do not yet do automatically. For more information, see Section 16.5 (HTTP Response Headers), especially Table 16.1 (Common MIME Types).

The simplest way to build HTML is to use document.write, which places a single string in the current document. Listing 19.2 gives an example, with the result shown in Figure 19–1.

Listing 19.2 FirstScript.html

```
<!DOCTYPE HTML PUBLIC "-//W3C//DTD HTML 3.2//EN">
<HTML>
<HEAD>
  <TITLE>First JavaScript Page</TITLE>
</HEAD>

<BODY>
<H1>First JavaScript Page</H1>

<SCRIPT LANGUAGE="JavaScript">
<!--
document.write("<HR>");
document.write("Hello World Wide Web");
document.write("<HR>");
// -->
</SCRIPT>

</BODY>
</HTML>
```

Figure 19-1   The HR elements and the text in between them were generated by JavaScript.

Now, this script is not particularly useful because the JavaScript did not contribute anything that couldn't have been done with static HTML. It is more common to use the JavaScript to build different HTML in different circumstances. Listing 19.3 gives an example, with Figures 19–2 and 19–3 showing the results in Netscape Navigator and Microsoft Internet Explorer, respectively. Note the use of the `referringPage` helper function and the "+" string concatenation operator. Building one large string for each chunk of HTML often yields code that is easier to read than it would be with a separate `document.write` for each line of HTML. Also note that this script outputs a linefeed after each line of HTML, using `document.writeln` instead of `document.write`, and adding `"\n"` to each line of text. This has no effect whatsoever on the resultant Web page. However, some browser versions (e.g., Netscape on Unix) show the script results when viewing the "source" of a page, and adding the extra newlines makes the result much easier to read. See Figure 19–4 for an example. This is a very useful debugging tool. If your browser shows you the source like this, you can cut and paste the results into a file, then check the syntax of this result using a standard HTML validator (see Section 1.3, "Publishing Your Document on the Web"). Highly recommended!

Core Approach

If your browser shows you the text and markup resulting from your scripts, verify the syntax using a standard HTML validator.

Listing 19.3 `ShowInfo.html`

```
<!DOCTYPE HTML PUBLIC "-//W3C//DTD HTML 3.2//EN">
<HTML>
<HEAD>
  <TITLE>Extracting Document Info with JavaScript</TITLE>
</HEAD>

<BODY BGCOLOR="WHITE">
<H1>Extracting Document Info with JavaScript</H1>
<HR>

<SCRIPT LANGUAGE="JavaScript">
<!--

function referringPage() {
  if (document.referrer.length == 0)
    return("<I>none</I>");
  else
    return(document.referrer);
}

document.writeln
  ("Document Info:\n" +
  "<UL>\n" +
  "  <LI><B>URL:</B> " + document.location + "\n" +
  "  <LI><B>Modification Date:</B> " + "\n" +
        document.lastModified + "\n" +
  "  <LI><B>Title:</B> " + document.title + "\n" +
  "  <LI><B>Referring page:</B> " +
        referringPage() + "\n" +
  "</UL>");
document.writeln
  ("Browser Info:" + "\n" +
  "<UL>" + "\n" +
  "  <LI><B>Name:</B> " + navigator.appName + "\n" +
  "  <LI><B>Version:</B> " + navigator.appVersion +
        "\n" +
  "</UL>");

// -->
</SCRIPT>

<HR>


</BODY>
</HTML>
```

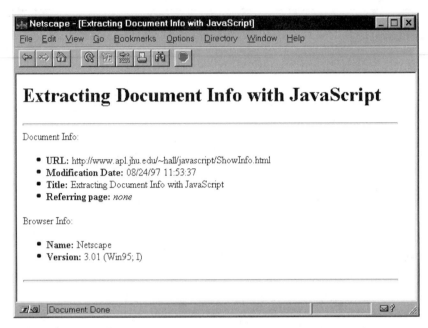

Figure 19–2   `ShowInfo` result in Netscape 3.01 on Windows 95.

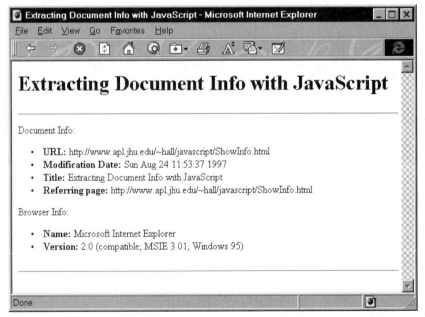

Figure 19–3   `ShowInfo` result in Internet Explorer 3.01 on Windows 95.

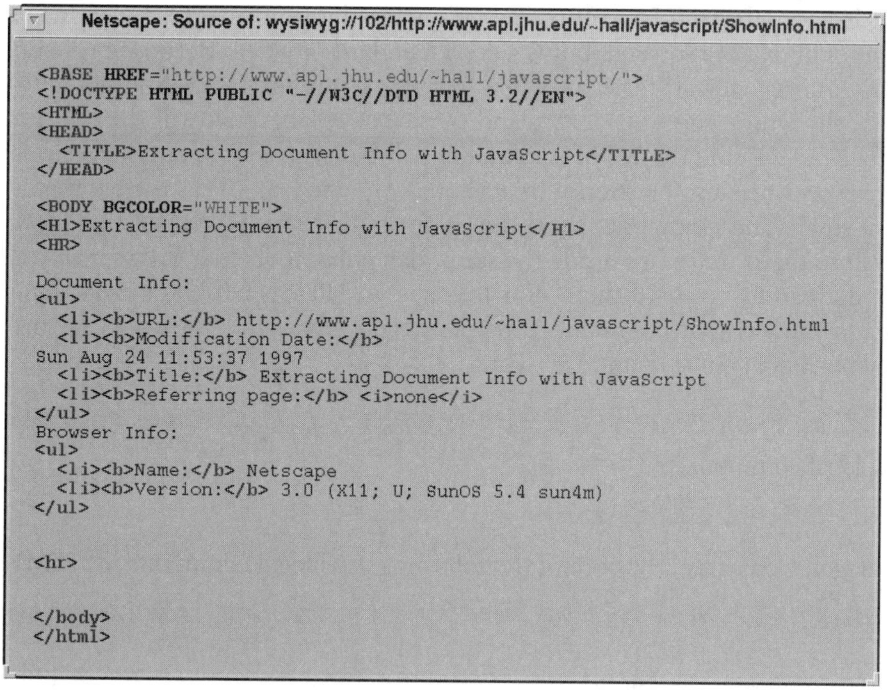

```
┌──────────────────────────────────────────────────────────────────────┐
│  ▽    Netscape: Source of: wysiwyg://102/http://www.apl.jhu.edu/~hall/javascript/ShowInfo.html │
├──────────────────────────────────────────────────────────────────────┤
│  <BASE HREF="http://www.apl.jhu.edu/~hall/javascript/">                │
│  <!DOCTYPE HTML PUBLIC "-//W3C//DTD HTML 3.2//EN">                      │
│  <HTML>                                                                 │
│  <HEAD>                                                                 │
│     <TITLE>Extracting Document Info with JavaScript</TITLE>             │
│  </HEAD>                                                                │
│                                                                         │
│  <BODY BGCOLOR="WHITE">                                                 │
│  <H1>Extracting Document Info with JavaScript</H1>                      │
│  <HR>                                                                   │
│                                                                         │
│  Document Info:                                                         │
│  <ul>                                                                   │
│     <li><b>URL:</b> http://www.apl.jhu.edu/~hall/javascript/ShowInfo.html │
│     <li><b>Modification Date:</b>                                       │
│  Sun Aug 24 11:53:37 1997                                               │
│     <li><b>Title:</b> Extracting Document Info with JavaScript          │
│     <li><b>Referring page:</b> <i>none</i>                              │
│  </ul>                                                                  │
│  Browser Info:                                                          │
│  <ul>                                                                   │
│     <li><b>Name:</b> Netscape                                           │
│     <li><b>Version:</b> 3.0 (X11; U; SunOS 5.4 sun4m)                   │
│  </ul>                                                                  │
│                                                                         │
│                                                                         │
│  <hr>                                                                   │
│                                                                         │
│                                                                         │
│  </body>                                                                │
│  </html>                                                                │
└──────────────────────────────────────────────────────────────────────┘
```

Figure 19–4   Some browser versions will show script *results* when viewing document source.

Compatibility with Multiple Browsers

Note the use of the LANGUAGE attribute in Listings 19.1, 19.2, and 19.3. Although it is not strictly required, it is useful for differentiating among various JavaScript versions. Netscape 2.0 will load scripts indicated via LANGUAGE="JavaScript" but ignore those tagged with "JavaScript1.1" or "JavaScript1.2". Netscape 3 will load scripts tagged with "JavaScript1.1" but ignore those tagged with "JavaScript1.2". Netscape 4 will load scripts tagged any of the three ways. Internet Explorer 3 always honors scripts tagged with "JavaScript", always ignores those tagged with "JavaScript1.2", and is inconsistent with scripts tagged via "JavaScript1.1". On Windows 95/NT, Internet Explorer 3.01 loads "JavaScript1.1" scripts, while Internet Explorer 3.02 doesn't. On the other hand, Internet Explorer 3.02 for the Mac *does* honor such scripts. So it is often better to check the browser vendor and/or version than to rely on the LANGUAGE attribute.

Also note that the JavaScript code is enclosed inside an HTML comment. Again, this is not required, but is a good standard practice. Because browsers ignore unrecognized tags, browsers that don't support JavaScript will automatically ignore the `<SCRIPT>` and `</SCRIPT>` tags, but will still see text in between. Using the HTML comment will hide the script contents as well. This works because JavaScript treats both "`//`" and "`<!--`" as the beginning of a single-line comment. Now, this script-hiding strategy is not foolproof, because there are things inside the script that could fool older browsers if you are not careful to avoid them. For instance, in HTML 2.0, the official comment syntax is that comments must be inside pairs of "`--`", which in turn must be between "`<!`" and "`>`". Thus,

```
<!-- Foo -- -- Bar -->
```

is a legal comment, but

```
<!-- Foo -- Bar -->
```

is illegal. Consequently, both of the following are illegal comments in HTML 2.0.

```
<!--
var x = 3;
if (x-->2) // Illegal
  doOneThing();
else
  doAnotherThing();
// -->
```

```
<!--
var x = 3;
var y = x--; // Illegal
// -->
```

Similarly, if the script itself contains a string of the form `"</SCRIPT>"`, it will prematurely terminate the script, even in HTML 3.2. So be careful to avoid such traps.

Okay, the combination of HTML and JavaScript comments lets you hide the scripts from non-JavaScript browsers. But how do you insert meaningful alternate text in such a case? JavaScript 1.1 introduced the `NOSCRIPT` tag, whose contents are to be ignored by non-JavaScript browsers. But because Netscape 2.0 doesn't understand this tag, it is not particularly useful. The alternative depends on whether or not you want to go to the effort of maintaining Java-Script and non-JavaScript versions of your pages. If you do, you can have users start with a non-JavaScript alternate page, but have it forward JavaScript users to the JavaScript version at the very beginning, as in Listing 19.4.

Listing 19.4 `NonJavaScriptVersion.html`

```
<!DOCTYPE HTML PUBLIC "-//W3C//DTD HTML 3.2//EN">
<HTML>
<HEAD>
  <TITLE>Some Topic</TITLE>

<SCRIPT LANGUAGE="JavaScript">
<!--

// Send "real" browsers to the JavaScript version of
// Some Topic
location = "JavaScriptVersion.html";

// -->
</SCRIPT>
</HEAD>

<BODY>
<H1>Some Topic (Non JavaScript Version)</H1>

Blah, blah, blah.

</BODY>
</HTML>
```

If you don't plan on maintaining entirely separate pages, a better alternative is to include short comments at the end of lines starting with "`<!--  -->`". JavaScript will treat the entire line as a comment, while non-JavaScript browsers will treat anything on the rest of the line as regular HTML. Here is an example.

```
<SCRIPT LANGUAGE="JavaScript">
<!-- --> Sorry, this example requires JavaScript.
<!--

// Real script here

// -->
</SCRIPT>
```

19.2 Monitoring User Events

In addition to being used to build HTML on the fly, JavaScript expressions can be attached to various HTML elements to be triggered when certain user actions are performed. You can monitor events such as clicking on a button or hypertext link, loading or unloading (exiting) a page, moving the mouse on or off a link, giving or taking away the input focus from a FORM element, submitting a CGI form, and getting an error when an image is loaded. Listing 19.5 gives an example where the dontClick method is attached to a button using the OnClick attribute. Figures 19–5 and 19–6 show the result. The BUTTON input element was added to HTML just for JavaScript, but this type of event handler can be attached to a variety of standard HTML elements. Note that dontClick was defined in the HEAD instead of the BODY. This is common practice for functions that don't directly generate HTML.

Listing 19.5   DontClick.html

```
<!DOCTYPE HTML PUBLIC "-//W3C//DTD HTML 3.2//EN">
<HTML>
<HEAD>
  <TITLE>Simple JavaScript Button</TITLE>

<SCRIPT LANGUAGE="JavaScript">
<!--
function dontClick() {
  alert("I told you not to click!");
}
// -->
</SCRIPT>
</HEAD>

<BODY BGCOLOR="WHITE">
<H1>Simple JavaScript Button</H1>

<FORM>
  <INPUT TYPE="BUTTON"
         VALUE="Don't Click Me"
         onClick="dontClick()">
</FORM>

</BODY>
</HTML>
```

Figure 19–5 The `DontClick` page before the button is pressed.

Figure 19–6 The result of clicking the button in the `DontClick` page.

19.3 Basic JavaScript Syntax

The fundamental syntax of JavaScript looks a lot like Java or C. Most simple constructs will look familiar: `if`, "? :", `while`, `for`, `break` and `continue` are used just as in Java. JavaScript 1.2 added a `switch` statement that looks very similar to Java's `switch`, with the exception that the `case` values need not be integers. The operators + (addition and string concatenation), `-`, `*`, `/`, `++`, `--`, `&&`, `||`, and so forth are virtually identical. Trailing semicolons are optional, but I will use them throughout for the sake of familiarity. I want to outline several important features here; details are given in the next chapter "JavaScript Quick Reference." For even more information, including updated features and new additions to the language, see the following URLs.

JavaScript (Netscape)

```
http://developer.netscape.com/library/
documentation/javascript.html
```

JScript (Internet Explorer)

```
http://www.microsoft.com/JScript/us/techinfo/
jsdocs.htm
```

Also note that Netscape provides a convenient interactive JavaScript input window (see Figure 19–7). To use it, simply open a URL of "javascript:" (nothing after the colon).

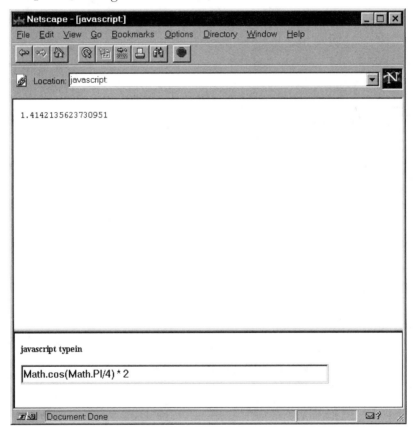

Figure 19–7   Netscape provides an interactive JavaScript "listener."

Dynamic Typing

The most striking difference between Java and JavaScript is the lack of declared types in JavaScript. You don't declare types for local variables, instance variables (called "properties" in JavaScript lingo), or even return types for functions. A variable can even change type during its lifetime. So, for example, the following is perfectly legal.

```
var x = 5;  // int
x = 5.5;  // float
x = "five point five";  // String
```

Function Declarations

Functions are declared using the function reserved word. The return value is not declared, nor are the types of the arguments. Here are some examples.

```
function square(x) {
  return(x * x);
}

function factorial(n) {
  if (n <= 0)
    return(1);
  else
    return(n * factorial(n - 1));
}

function printHeading(message) {
  document.writeln("<H1>" + message + "</H1>");
}
```

Functions can be passed around and assigned to variables, as follows:

```
var fun = Math.sin;
alert("sin(pi/2)=" + fun(Math.PI/2));
```

Figure 19–8 shows the result.

Figure 19–8   JavaScript lets you assign a function to a new name.

You can also reassign existing functions. In fact, you can even override system functions, as in the following example, although you almost always want to avoid this in real applications.

```
Math.sin = Math.cos;  // Don't do this at home
alert("Yikes! sin(pi/2)=" + Math.sin(Math.PI/2));
```

Figure 19–9 shows the result.

Figure 19–9   JavaScript even lets you reassign existing functions.

Objects and Classes

JavaScript's approach to object-oriented programming seems a bit haphazard compared to the strict and consistent approach of Java. Following are a few of the most unusual features.

Fields Can Be Added On-the-Fly

Adding a new property (field) is a simple matter of assigning a value to one. If the field doesn't already exist when you try to assign to it, JavaScript will create it automatically. For instance:

```
var test = new Object();
test.field1 = "Value 1"; // Create field1 property
test.field2 = 7; // Create field2 property
```

Although this simplifies the addition of new properties, it also makes it difficult to catch typos, because misspelled property names will be happily accepted. Also, if you try to look up a property that doesn't exist, you will get the special undefined value. This value compares == to null.

You Can Use Literal Notation in JavaScript 1.2

In JavaScript 1.2, you can create objects using a shorthand "literal" notation of the form

```
{ field1:val1, field2:val2, ... , fieldN:valN }
```

For example, the following gives equivalent values to object1 and object2 in JavaScript 1.2. It results in an error in JavaScript 1.0 or 1.1.

```
var object1 = new Object();
object1.x = 3;
object1.y = 4;
object1.z = 5;

object2 = { x:3, y:4, z:5 };
```

The "for/in" Statement Iterates Over Properties

JavaScript, unlike Java or C++, has a construct that lets you easily retrieve all of the fields of an object. The basic format is as follows:

```
for(fieldName in object)
   doSomethingWith(fieldName);
```

Given a field name, you can access the field via `object["field"]` as well as via `object.field`. This is useful when iterating over fields in an object, as in Listing 19.6, which defines a general-purpose `makeObject-Table` function that will create an HTML table for a given object. Figure 19–10 gives the result in Internet Explorer 3.01.

Listing 19.6   ForIn.html

```
<!DOCTYPE HTML PUBLIC "-//W3C//DTD HTML 3.2//EN">
<HTML>
<HEAD>
  <TITLE>For/In Loops</TITLE>

<SCRIPT LANGUAGE="JavaScript">
<!--

function makeObjectTable(name, object) {
  document.writeln
    ("<H2>" + name + "</H2>");
  document.writeln
    ("<TABLE BORDER=1>\n" +
    "  <TR><TH>Field<TH>Value");
  for(field in object)
    document.writeln
      ("  <TR><TD>" + field + "<TD>" + object[field]);
  document.writeln
    ("</TABLE>");
}

// -->
</SCRIPT>
</HEAD>

<BODY BGCOLOR="#C0C0C0">
<H1>For/In Loops</H1>
```

continued

Listing 19.6   ForIn.html   (continued)

```
<SCRIPT LANGUAGE="JavaScript">
<!--

var test = new Object();
test.field1 = "Field One";
test.field2 = "Field Two";
test.field3 = "Field Three";
makeObjectTable("test", test);

// -->
</SCRIPT>

</BODY>
</HTML>
```

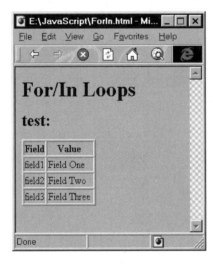

Figure 19-10 The for/in statement iterates over the properties of an object.

A "Constructor" is Just a Function that Assigns to "this"

JavaScript does not have an exact equivalent to Java's class definition. The closest you get is when you define a function that assigns values to properties in the `this` reference. Calling this function using `new` binds `this` to a new `Object`. For example, following is a simple constructor for a `Ship` class.

```
function Ship(x, y, speed, direction) {
   this.x = x;
   this.y = y;
   this.speed = speed;
   this.direction = direction;
}
```

Given the previous definition of `makeObjectTable`, putting the following in a script in the BODY of a document yields the result shown in Figure 19–11.

```
var ship1 = new Ship(0, 0, 1, 90);
makeObjectTable("ship1", ship1);
```

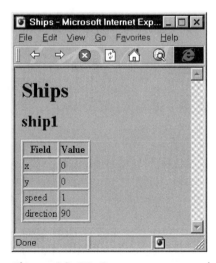

Figure 19–11 Constructors are simply a shorthand way to define objects and assign properties.

Methods Are Function-Valued Properties

There is no special syntax for defining methods of objects. Instead, you simply assign a function to a property. For instance, here is a version of the Ship class that includes a move method.

```
function degreesToRadians(degrees) {
  return(degrees * Math.PI / 180.0);
}

function move() {
  var angle = degreesToRadians(this.direction);
  this.x = this.x + this.speed * Math.cos(angle);
  this.y = this.y + this.speed * Math.sin(angle);
}

function Ship(x, y, speed, direction) {
  this.x = x;
  this.y = y;
  this.speed = speed;
  this.direction = direction;
  this.move = move;
}
```

Here is an example of its use, with the result shown in Figure 19–12.

```
var ship1 = new Ship(0, 0, 1, 90);
makeObjectTable("ship1 (originally)", ship1);
ship1.move();
makeObjectTable("ship1 (after move)", ship1);
```

The "prototype" Property

In JavaScript 1.1, you can simplify the creation of methods and constant properties by use of the special prototype property. This is available in Netscape 3 and 4 and Internet Explorer, but not in Netscape 2. Once at least one object of a given class exists, assigning values to a field in the object stored in the prototype property of the class object (really the function object named for the class) gives a shared reference to this value to all members of the class that do not override it. For instance, here is a definition of Ship that adds a shared maxSpeed property intended to specify the highest speed *any* Ship can go:

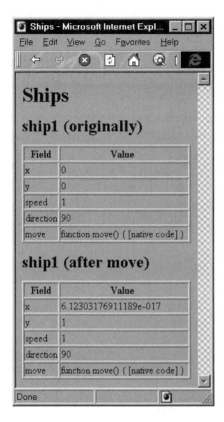

Figure 19–12 Methods are really a special type of property.

```
function Ship(x, y, speed, direction) {
  this.x = x;
  this.y = y;
  this.speed = speed;
  this.direction = direction;
}
// JavaScript 1.1 only
new Ship(0, 0, 0, 0);
Ship.prototype.move = move;
Ship.prototype.maxSpeed = 50;
```

Arrays

For the most part, you can use arrays in JavaScript a lot like Java arrays. Java-Script 1.1 introduced the `Array` constructor to simplify building arrays. Here are a few examples.

```
var squares = new Array(5);
for(var i=0; i<squares.length; i++)
  vals[i] = i * i;
// Or, in one fell swoop:
var squares = new Array(0, 1, 4, 9, 16);
```

Using arrays this way is probably the simplest. Behind the scenes, however, JavaScript simply represents arrays as objects with numbered fields. You can access named fields using either `object.field` or `object["field"]`, but numbered fields only via `object[fieldNumber]`. Here is an example, with Figure 19–13 showing the result.

```
var arrayObj = new Object();
arrayObj[0] = "Index zero";
arrayObj[10] = "Index ten";
arrayObj.field1 = "Field One";
arrayObj["field2"] = "Field Two";

makeObjectTable("arrayObj", arrayObj);
```

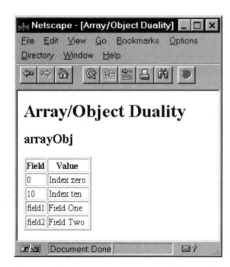

Figure 19–13 Arrays are really just objects with numbered fields.

In general, it is a good idea to avoid mixing array and object notation, and to treat them as two separate varieties of object. Occasionally, however, it is convenient to mix the notations, because the array notation is required when an existing string is to be used as a property name. For instance, the `make-ObjectTable` (Listing 19.6) function relied upon this capability.

Literal Array Notation in JavaScript 1.2

In JavaScript 1.2, you can create arrays by supplying comma-separated values inside square brackets. For example, the following assigns equivalent values to `array1` and `array2` in JavaScript 1.2. It results in an error in JavaScript 1.0 and 1.1.

```
var array1 = new Array("fee", "fie", "fo", "fum");
var array2 = [ "fee", "fie", "fo", "fum" ];
```

19.4 Using JavaScript to Customize Web Pages

Because JavaScript can determine several characteristics of the current browser and document, you can use it to build different Web pages in different circumstances. For instance, you might want to use certain Microsoft-specific features on Internet Explorer and Netscape-specific features on Netscape Navigator. Or omit certain background information if users came to your page from another one of your pages, as opposed to an outside page. Or use smaller images if the user has a small screen. Or use embedded objects only if the browser has a plug in that supports them. Integration with Java (Section 19.9) will allow additional applications such as printing only a "Sorry, no Web page for you buddy!" page to users who visit from spam-tolerant ISP's, or removing the prominent link to your resumé when people access your Web page from your company domain. Following are three examples. The first shows how to customize the page based on whether the browser supports the BGCOLOR attribute of tables. The second shows how to customize the page based on the browser window size. The third illustrates how to tell if certain plug ins are available.

Avoiding Incompatibility When Using Extensions

In Section 2.4 (Tables), I pointed out that although applying the BGCOLOR attribute to table rows or cells can improve the appearance of some tables, careless use can cause catastrophic results in browsers that don't support it, because your text might be invisible. Listing 19.7 shows a page that checks the browser release version, only using white on black headings if this version is three or higher. Figures 19–14 and 19–15 show the results in Netscape 3.01 and 2.02, respectively.

Note the use of "var" before the `headingCellColor` and `heading-FontColor` variables. This is JavaScript's indication of a local variable. If you forget it, JavaScript won't complain, but it will treat the variable as a property of the current window, so like-named variables in different functions could conflict with each other. This can lead to very-hard-to-diagnose problems, so it is a good standard practice even when not using functions.

Core Approach

Introduce all local variables with "`var`".

This use of JavaScript exchanges one type of incompatibility for another. Non-JavaScript browsers (e.g., Mosaic, Lynx) won't see the table at all, but users of Netscape 2 will get a better result than if the same white-on-black colors were used everywhere as in the example of Section 2.4. Although Java-Script can be used to tack on event handlers that can safely be ignored in incompatible browsers, it is difficult to use JavaScript to build HTML dynamically and still maintain compatibility with non-JavaScript browsers. In a corporate environment, you may well know which browsers will be using your page. For general Web applications, however, if you build HTML with JavaScript you will have to evaluate the benefit against the fact that you will lose some viewers.

Listing 19.7 `DynamicTable.html`

```
<!DOCTYPE HTML PUBLIC "-//W3C//DTD HTML 3.2//EN">
<HTML>
<HEAD>
  <TITLE>Some Strawberry Varieties</TITLE>
</HEAD>

<BODY BGCOLOR="WHITE">
<H1>Some Strawberry Varieties</H1>

The following table summarizes a few
strawberry varieties, giving their resistance to
leafspot, size, relative ripening day (day 0 is
about June 1 in zone 7), and fresh/frozen quality.
<P>

<SCRIPT LANGUAGE="JavaScript">
```

Listing 19.7 `DynamicTable.html` (continued)

```
<!--
if (navigator.appVersion.substring(0,1) >= 3) {
  var headingCellColor = "BLACK";
  var headingFontColor = "WHITE";
} else {
  var headingCellColor = "WHITE";
  var headingFontColor = "BLACK";
}

document.writeln
  ("<TABLE BORDER=1>\n" +
  "  <TR BGCOLOR=" + headingCellColor + ">\n" +
  "    <TH><FONT COLOR=" + headingFontColor + ">\n" +
  "        Variety</FONT>\n" +
  "    <TH><FONT COLOR=" + headingFontColor + ">\n" +
  "        Leafspot Resistance</FONT>\n" +
  "    <TH><FONT COLOR=" + headingFontColor + ">\n" +
  "        Size</FONT>\n" +
  "    <TH><FONT COLOR=" + headingFontColor + ">\n" +
  "        Ripening Day</FONT>\n" +
  "    <TH><FONT COLOR=" + headingFontColor + ">\n" +
  "        Quality Fresh</FONT>\n" +
  "    <TH><FONT COLOR=" + headingFontColor + ">\n" +
  "        Quality Frozen</FONT>\n" +
  "  <TR><TD>Blakemore\n" +
  "      <TD>medium\n" +
  "      <TD>small\n" +
  "      <TD>0\n" +
  "      <TD>fair\n" +
  "      <TD>good\n" +
  "  <TR><TD>Cardinal\n" +
  "      <TD>high\n" +
  "      <TD>medium\n" +
  "      <TD>5\n" +
  "      <TD>good\n" +
  "      <TD>good\n" +
  "  <TR><TD>Sparkle\n" +
  "      <TD>low\n" +
  "      <TD>small\n" +
  "      <TD>9\n" +
  "      <TD>good\n" +
  "      <TD>good\n" +
```

continued

Listing 19.7   `DynamicTable.html` (continued)

```
"   <TR><TD>Surecrop\n" +
"        <TD>high\n" +
"        <TD>large\n" +
"        <TD>3\n" +
"        <TD>good\n" +
"        <TD>fair\n" +
"   <TR><TD>Tenn. Beauty\n" +
"        <TD>medium\n" +
"        <TD>medium\n" +
"        <TD>9\n" +
"        <TD>good\n" +
"        <TD>good\n" +
"</TABLE>");

// -->
</SCRIPT>

</BODY>
</HTML>
```

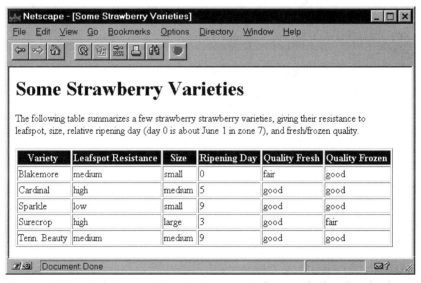

Figure 19–14 In Netscape 3 or 4 or Internet Explorer 3, the heading background is black and the heading foreground is white.

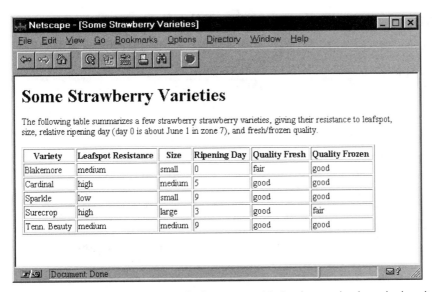

Figure 19–15 In Netscape 2, which ignores table background colors, the heading foreground is black.

Setting Attribute Values with JavaScript

If you are building HTML elements where only a few attributes change, you have a shorthand alternative in Netscape 3.0 and later. You can have the browser evaluate attribute values dynamically using the following syntax.

```
<ELEMENT ATTRIBUTE="&{ JavaScript-Expression };">
```

For instance, the previous example could be simplified in Netscape 3 and 4 by setting the colors in the HEAD, omitting the SCRIPT in the BODY, and using

```
<TABLE BORDER=1>
  <TR BGCOLOR="&{ headingCellColor };">
  . . .
</TABLE>
```

Of course, this would accomplish little in this particular example, because the whole goal is to support Netscape 2.0, but this is a useful capability for applications that only need to support more recent browsers.

Adjusting to the Browser Window Size

Netscape 4.0 introduced the `window.innerWidth` and `window.inner-Height` properties, which let you determine the usable size of the current browser window. Listing 19.8 uses this to shrink/stretch images to a fixed percent of the window width and to adjust the size of a heading font accordingly. Figures 19–16 through 19–18 show the results in a large, medium, and small browser window. To avoid incompatibility with earlier browsers, a fixed image and font size is used in browser versions 3 and earlier.

There are a couple of other stylistic notes to make about this example. First of all, notice that the function definitions are placed in the HEAD, even though they are used in the BODY. This is a standard practice that has three benefits. Number one: It can make the actual script easier to read. Number two: It allows a single function to be used multiple places. And number three: Because the HEAD is parsed before the BODY, it means that JavaScript routines defined in the HEAD will be available even if the user interrupts the loading or clicks on an image or cross reference before the page is done loading. This is particularly valuable for event-handling functions.

Core Approach

Define JavaScript functions in the HEAD, *especially if they will be used in event handlers.*

Also note the use of single quotes instead of double quotes for strings in this example. JavaScript allows either, so using single quotes for `document.writeln` makes it easier to embed double quotes inside the string, which are needed in this case for the "better berry" quotation.

Core Note

Either single or double quotes can be used for JavaScript strings. Double quotes can be embedded inside strings created with single quotes; single quotes can be used inside strings made with double quotes.

Listing 19.8   `Strawberries.html`

```
<!DOCTYPE HTML PUBLIC "-//W3C//DTD HTML 3.2//EN">
<HTML>
<HEAD>
  <TITLE>Strawberries</TITLE>

<SCRIPT LANGUAGE="JavaScript">
<!--
function image(url, width, height) {
 return('<IMG SRC="' + url + '"' +
          ' WIDTH=' + width +
          ' HEIGHT=' + height + '>');
}

function strawberry1(width) {
  return(image("Strawberry1.gif", width,
            Math.round(width*1.323)));
}

function strawberry2(width) {
  return(image("Strawberry2.gif", width,
            Math.round(width*1.155)));
}
// -->
</SCRIPT>
</HEAD>

<BODY BGCOLOR="WHITE">

<HR>
<SCRIPT LANGUAGE="JavaScript">
<!--
if (navigator.appVersion.substring(0,1) >= 4) {
  var imageWidth = window.innerWidth/4;
  var fontSize =
    Math.min(7, Math.round(window.innerWidth/100));
} else {
  var imageWidth = 200;
  var fontSize = 5;
}
```

continued

Listing 19.8 `Strawberries.html` (continued)

```
document.writeln
  ('<TABLE>\n' +
  '  <TR><TD>' + strawberry1(imageWidth) + '\n' +
  '      <TH><FONT SIZE=' + fontSize + '>\n' +
  '          "Doubtless God <I>could</I> have made\n' +
  '          a better berry, but doubtless He\n' +
  '          never did."</FONT>\n' +
  '      <TD>'  + strawberry2(imageWidth) + '\n' +
  '</TABLE>');
// -->
</SCRIPT>
<HR>

Strawberries are my favorite garden crop; a fresh
strawberry picked five minutes ago makes the dry and
woody grocery store variety seem like a <B>totally</B>
different fruit. My favorite varieties are Surecrop
and Cardinal.

</BODY>
</HTML>
```

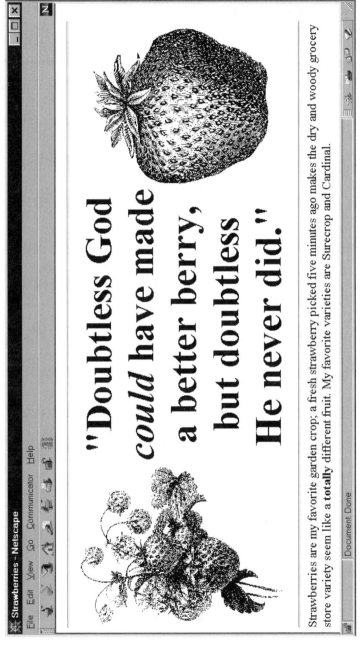

Figure 19–16 In a large browser, large images and fonts are used.

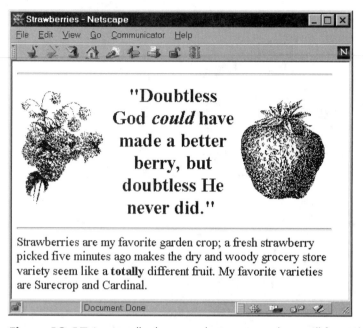

Figure 19–17 In a smaller browser, the images and text still fit nicely.

Figure 19–18 Even in a tiny browser window, the heading is still legible.

Determining if Plug Ins are Available

In Netscape 3 and 4 (but not Internet Explorer), the `navigator.plu-gins` array contains information about the available browser plug ins. Each element in this array is a `Plugin` object that has `name`, `description`, `filename`, and `length` properties, and contains an array of `MimeType` objects. These properties give a short name to the plug in, a textual description, the filename containing the plug in, and the number of supported MIME types, respectively. Each `MimeType` object has properties `type` (MIME datatype such as "text/html"), `description` (descriptive text), `enabledPlugin` (the `Plugin` object supporting this type), and `suffixes` (a comma-separated list of file extensions associated with this type). An interesting aspect of JavaScript arrays is that you can reference them using a string "index" instead of an integer. In fact, as explained in Section 19.3 (Basic JavaScript Syntax) arrays in JavaScript are really just objects with numbered fields. Anyhow, you can use this shortcut to determine if a plug in is installed, as in the following snippet.

```
if (navigator.plugins["Cosmo Player 1.0"])
    document.write('<EMBED SRC="coolWorld.vrml" ...>"');
else
    document.write('This example requires VRML.');
```

Note that this tells you if a *particular* plug in is available. If you are more concerned about whether a certain MIME type is supported *somehow* (directly, through a plug in, or via an external application), you can check the `navigator.mimeTypes` property. For example,

```
if (navigator.mimeTypes["application/postscript"])
    addPostScriptLink();
```

For more information, see Section 20.19 (The MimeType Object).

Compatibility Across Browser Versions

The `navigator.plugins` property is not available in Netscape 2. In many cases, rather than checking the browser name it is easier to use `"JavaScript1.1"` (no spaces, capitalized "J" and "S") as the value of the `LANGUAGE` attribute, as follows:

```
<SCRIPT LANGUAGE="JavaScript1.1">
```

Scripts tagged this way will be ignored in Netscape 2 but honored in Netscape 3 and 4. If your script is specific to Netscape 4, use

```
<SCRIPT LANGUAGE="JavaScript1.2">
```

Now, this brings up the issue of Internet Explorer (version 3). The variation of JavaScript it supports (JScript) is partway between JavaScript 1.0 and 1.1, and support for the `JavaScript1.1` value is inconsistent. For instance, on Windows 95 and NT, Internet Explorer 3.01 honors scripts tagged that way, while Internet Explorer 3.02 ignores them! Internet Explorer 3.02 on the Mac honors them. Consequently, code that depends on 1.1 features not available in Internet Explorer should designate `"JavaScript1.1"` *and* test the browser vendor, as follows:

```
<SCRIPT LANGUAGE="JavaScript1.1">
<!--
if (navigator.appName == "Netscape") {
  // script actions here
}
// -->
</SCRIPT>
```

Core Approach

When using capabilities specific to Netscape 3 or 4, use `LANGUAGE="JavaScript1.1"` *and check* `navigator.appName`. *Alternatively, use* `LANGUAGE="JavaScript"` *and check* `navigator.appVersion`.

Listing 19.9 uses this approach to build a table of available plug ins and their supported MIME types. Figures 19–19 and 19–20 show results in Netscape 3 and 4, respectively.

Listing 19.9 Plugins.html

```html
<!DOCTYPE HTML PUBLIC "-//W3C//DTD HTML 3.2//EN">
<HTML>
<HEAD>
  <TITLE>Plugins Supported</TITLE>

<SCRIPT LANGUAGE="JavaScript1.1">
<!--

function printRow(plugin) {
  document.write
    ("  <TR><TD>" + plugin.name + "\n" +
     "      <TD>" + plugin.description + "\n" +
     "      <TD>");
  document.write(plugin[0].type);
  for(var i=1; i<plugin.length; i++)
    document.writeln("<BR>" + plugin[i].type);
}

// -->
</SCRIPT>
</HEAD>

<BODY>
<H1>Plugins Supported</H1>

<SCRIPT LANGUAGE="JavaScript1.1">
<!--

if (navigator.appName == "Netscape") {
  document.writeln
    ("<TABLE BORDER=1>\n" +
     "  <TR><TH>Plugin\n" +
     "      <TH>Description\n" +
     "      <TH>MIME Types Supported");
  for(var i=0; i<navigator.plugins.length; i++)
    printRow(navigator.plugins[i]);
  document.writeln
    ("\n</TABLE>");
}

// -->
</SCRIPT>

</BODY>
</HTML>
```

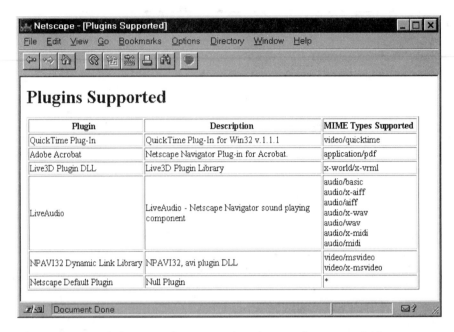

Figure 19–19 This version of Netscape 3.01 has six plug ins available.

19.5 Using JavaScript to Make Pages Dynamic

In most of the previous examples, parts of the document were built dynamically (when the page was loaded), but the resultant document was normal HTML. JavaScript can also be used to create elements that are dynamic. For instance, one common application is to create images that change when the user moves the mouse over them. This can be used to implement toolbars with regions that "light up" to indicate hypertext links or custom buttons that show a grayed-out image when you press them. Alternatively, by using timers, JavaScript can animate images even without being triggered by user events. In Netscape 4, the possibilities are even greater. JavaScript can manipulate layers, scroll the document, and even move the browser window around on the screen. This opens up myriad possibilities for abuse; if you think users hate <BLINK>, wait until they try your page with bouncing regions. Run for cover! On the other hand, if used with restraint, these new features can add value to certain types of pages.

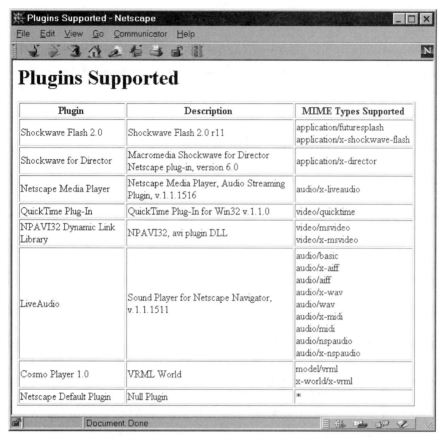

Figure 19–20 This version of Netscape 4.01 has eight plug ins available.

Modifying Images Dynamically

In JavaScript 1.1 (Netscape 3 and 4 but *not* Internet Explorer), the docu-
ment.images property contains an array of Image objects corresponding
to each IMG element in the current document. To display a new image, simply set the SRC property of an existing image to a string representing a different image file. For instance, the following function changes the first image in
a document.

```
function changeImage() {
   document.images[0].src = "images/new-image.gif";
}
```

This function could be invoked from an event handler (e.g. when the user clicks a button) or even executed automatically after a certain amount of time. Now, referring to images by number is not very flexible, because the addition of a new image in the middle of the document would require changing the references to all later images. Fortunately, JavaScript lets you name images using a new NAME attribute of the IMG element as follows:

```
<IMG SRC="cool-image.jpg" NAME="cool"
     WIDTH=75 HEIGHT=25>
```

Because JavaScript lets you refer to array elements by name instead of number, you could then do the following:

```
function improveImage() {
  document.images["cool"].src = "way-cool.jpg";
}
```

However, be careful with this; images embedded in table cells appear *twice* in the images array in Netscape 3. This bug is fixed in Netscape 4.

A Clickable Image Button

This idea can be used to create images that change when you click on them. For example, following is a clickButton function that temporarily changes an image, switching it back to the original version after 1/10 of a second. To do this, it uses the setImage and setTimeout function. The first of these is defined as follows, while setTimeout is a built-in routine which takes a string designating a JavaScript expression and a time in milliseconds. It returns immediately, but starts a background process that waits for the specified time then executes the code specified by the string.

```
function setImage(name, image) {
  document.images[name].src = image;
}

function clickButton(name, grayImage) {
  var origImage = document.images[name].src;
  setImage(name, grayImage);
  var resetString =
    "setImage('" + name + "', '" + origImage + "')";
  setTimeout(resetString, 100);
}
```

To use this for a clickable image button, we need to do two more things: (1) attach the routine to a button or buttons, and (2) make sure that the images needed are already cached by the browser. The first step is straightforward: simply use the `onClick` attribute of the `<A HREF...>` element, as shown below. Remember to put the `</A>` on the same line as the `IMG` element to prevent the Netscape bug that would otherwise display an underscore after the image. See Section 3.3 (Specifying Hypertext Links) for more information on this problem.

```
<A HREF="location1.html"
   onClick="clickButton('Button1',
                        'images/Button1-Down.gif')">
<IMG SRC="images/Button1-Up.gif" NAME="Button1"
     WIDTH=150 HEIGHT=25></A>

<A HREF="location2.html"
   onClick="clickButton('Button2',
                        'images/Button2-Down.gif')">
<IMG SRC="images/Button2-Up.gif" NAME="Button2"
     WIDTH=150 HEIGHT=25></A>
```

Finally, before trying to display an image, you should make sure it is already loaded. This will prevent long pauses when the button is pressed. You can do this by creating an `Image` object (Section 20.12), then setting its `SRC` property. Oddly, this `Image` object never actually gets used; its only purpose is to force the browser to load (and cache) the image. Here is an example.

```
imageFiles = new Array("images/Button1-Up.gif",
                       "images/Button1-Down.gif",
                       "images/Button2-Up.gif",
                       "images/Button2-Down.gif");
imageObjects = new Array(imageFiles.length);

for(var i=0; i<imageFiles.length; i++) {
  imageObjects[i] = new Image(150, 25);
  imageObjects[i].src = imageFiles[i];
}
```

If you are handling a lot of images, you can simplify the process by having a consistent naming scheme for the images; I'll give an example later in this section.

Now, this process is sufficient for browsers that support image manipulation. However, if the browser understands `onClick` but not the `Image` object, the code will result in an error. This is a serious problem, since both Netscape 2 and Internet Explorer 3 (on Windows 95/NT) are in this category. Surprisingly, Internet Explorer 3.02 supports image manipulation on the Macintosh, but not on Windows 95/NT. So checking the JavaScript version or browser vendor is not a sufficient test. A better approach is to explicitly test if images are supported by checking for the `document.images` property, as below:

```
var imagesSupported = (document["images"] != null);
```

Then, you can wrap the image manipulation code inside

```
if (imagesSupported) {
    ...
}
```

This will prevent errors on incompatible browsers, while still allowing the image highlighting on as many browsers as possible. If this seems like an awful lot of work to go through to maintain portability, you are absolutely right! It takes quite a bit of effort to create JavaScript documents that support as many browsers as possible while still working reasonably on less-capable systems. Listing 19.10 shows the whole process put together.

Core Approach

Make image manipulation code portable by checking for the existence of `document.images`.

Listing 19.10 `ImageButton.html`

```html
<!DOCTYPE HTML PUBLIC "-//W3C//DTD HTML 3.2//EN">
<HTML>
<HEAD>
  <TITLE>JavaScript Image Buttons</TITLE>

<SCRIPT LANGUAGE="JavaScript">
<!--

// Netscape 2.0 and Windows versions of Internet
// Explorer understand onMouseOver but not
// the Image stuff, so we need to have an empty
// placeholder for the clickButton method.

function clickButton(name, grayImage) {}

// -->
</SCRIPT>
```

Listing 19.10 `ImageButton.html` (continued)

```
<SCRIPT LANGUAGE="JavaScript1.1">
<!--

var imagesSupported = (document["images"] != null);

if (imagesSupported) {
  imageFiles = new Array("images/Button1-Up.gif",
                         "images/Button1-Down.gif",
                         "images/Button2-Up.gif",
                         "images/Button2-Down.gif");
  imageObjects = new Array(imageFiles.length);

  for(var i=0; i<imageFiles.length; i++) {
    imageObjects[i] = new Image(150, 25);
    imageObjects[i].src = imageFiles[i];
  }
}

function setImage(name, image) {
  document.images[name].src = image;
}

function clickButton(name, grayImage) {
  if (imagesSupported) {
    var origImage = document.images[name].src;
    setImage(name, grayImage);
    var resetString =
      "setImage('" + name + "', '" + origImage + "')";
    setTimeout(resetString, 100);
  }
}

// -->
</SCRIPT>
</HEAD>

<BODY>
<H1>JavaScript Image Buttons</H1>

<A HREF="location1.html"
   onClick="clickButton('Button1',
                        'images/Button1-Down.gif')">
```

continued

Listing 19.10 `ImageButton.html` (continued)

```
<IMG SRC="images/Button1-Up.gif" NAME="Button1"
     WIDTH=150 HEIGHT=25></A>

<A HREF="location2.html"
   onClick="clickButton('Button2',
                         'images/Button2-Down.gif')">
<IMG SRC="images/Button2-Up.gif" NAME="Button2"
     WIDTH=150 HEIGHT=25></A>

</BODY>
</HTML>
```

Highlighting Images Under the Mouse

An even more common application of the image modification process is to
create a series of images that change as the user moves the mouse over them,
using the hypertext link's `onMouseOver` to display the highlighted image
and `onMouseOut` to change the image back. This can make toolbars more
appealing by providing visual cues as to which regions are clickable. However, when dealing with a large number of images, listing each explicitly
when preloading them can be tedious. Listing 19.11 shows an approach that
simplifies this process considerably: using consistent names. The normal
image and highlighted image are both derived from the NAME of the IMG element (see `regularImageFile` and `negativeImageFile`), negating
the need to list the full filenames in the array listing the images to be preloaded, or to pass the highlighted image name in the `onMouseOver` call.
Toolbars of this type are most commonly used with frames; Listing 19.12 and
Listing 19.13 show the rest of the frame structure, while Figures 19–21 and
19–22 show the results.

If you can't remember how to use frames, this would be a good time to
review them (Chapter 4), because they are used quite frequently with Java-
Script.

Listing 19.11 `HighPeaksNavBar.html`

```html
<!DOCTYPE HTML PUBLIC "-//W3C//DTD HTML 3.2//EN">
<HTML>
<HEAD>
  <TITLE>High Peaks Navigation Bar</TITLE>

<SCRIPT LANGUAGE="JavaScript">
<!--

// Netscape 2.0 and Windows versions of Internet
// Explorer understand onMouseOver but not
// the Image stuff, so we need to have empty
// placeholders for highlight and unHighlight.

function highlight(imageName) {}
function unHighlight(imageName) {}

// -->
</SCRIPT>

<SCRIPT LANGUAGE="JavaScript1.1">
<!--

var imagesSupported = (document["images"] != null);

// Given "Foo", returns "images/Foo.gif"

function regularImageFile(imageName) {
  return("images/" + imageName + ".gif");
}

// Given "Bar", returns "images/Bar-Negative.gif"

function negativeImageFile(imageName) {
  return("images/" + imageName + "-Negative.gif");
}

// Cache image at specified index. E.g., given
// index 0, take imageNames[0] to get "Home".
// Then preload images/Home.gif and
// images/Home-Negative.gif
```

continued

Listing 19.11 `HighPeaksNavBar.html` (continued)

```
function cacheImages(index) {
  regularImageObjects[index] = new Image(150, 25);
  regularImageObjects[index].src =
    regularImageFile(imageNames[index]);
  negativeImageObjects[index] = new Image(150, 25);
  negativeImageObjects[index].src =
    negativeImageFile(imageNames[index]);
}

if (imagesSupported) {
  imageNames = new Array("Home", "Tibet", "Nepal",
                         "Austria", "Switzerland");
  regularImageObjects = new Array(imageNames.length);
  negativeImageObjects = new Array(imageNames.length);

  // Put images in cache for fast highlighting
  for(var i=0; i<imageNames.length; i++)
    cacheImages(i);
}

// This is attached to onMouseOver -- change image
// under the mouse to negative (reverse video) version.

function highlight(imageName) {
  if (imagesSupported)
    document.images[imageName].src =
      negativeImageFile(imageName);
}

// This is attached to onMouseOut -- return image to
// normal.

function unHighlight(imageName) {
  if (imagesSupported)
    document.images[imageName].src =
      regularImageFile(imageName);
}

// -->
</SCRIPT>
</HEAD>

<BODY BGCOLOR="WHITE">
```

Listing 19.11 `HighPeaksNavBar.html` (continued)

```
<TABLE BORDER=0 WIDTH=150 BGCOLOR="WHITE"
        CELLPADDING=0 CELLSPACING=0>
  <TR><TD><A HREF="Home.html"
            TARGET="Main"
            onMouseOver="highlight('Home')"
            onMouseOut="unHighlight('Home')">
         <IMG SRC="images/Home.gif"
             NAME="Home"
             WIDTH=150 HEIGHT=25 BORDER=0>
         </A>
  <TR><TD><A HREF="Tibet.html"
            TARGET="Main"
            onMouseOver="highlight('Tibet')"
            onMouseOut="unHighlight('Tibet')">
         <IMG SRC="images/Tibet.gif"
             NAME="Tibet"
             WIDTH=150 HEIGHT=25 BORDER=0>
         </A>
  <TR><TD><A HREF="Nepal.html"
            TARGET="Main"
            onMouseOver="highlight('Nepal')"
            onMouseOut="unHighlight('Nepal')">
         <IMG SRC="images/Nepal.gif"
             NAME="Nepal"
             WIDTH=150 HEIGHT=25 BORDER=0></A>
  <TR><TD><A HREF="Austria.html"
            TARGET="Main"
            onMouseOver="highlight('Austria')"
            onMouseOut="unHighlight('Austria')">
         <IMG SRC="images/Austria.gif"
             NAME="Austria"
             WIDTH=150 HEIGHT=25 BORDER=0></A>
  <TR><TD><A HREF="Switzerland.html"
            TARGET="Main"
            onMouseOver="highlight('Switzerland')"
            onMouseOut="unHighlight('Switzerland')">
         <IMG SRC="images/Switzerland.gif"
             NAME="Switzerland"
             WIDTH=150 HEIGHT=25 BORDER=0></A>
</TABLE>


</BODY>
</HTML>
```

Listing 19.12 `HighPeaks.html`

```html
<!DOCTYPE HTML PUBLIC "-//W3C//DTD HTML 3.2//EN">
<HTML>
<HEAD>
  <TITLE>High Peaks Travel Inc.</TITLE>
</HEAD>

<FRAMESET COLS="160,*" FRAMEBORDER=0 BORDER=0>
  <FRAME SRC="HighPeaksNavBar.html" SCROLLING="NO">
  <FRAME SRC="HighPeaksIntro.html" NAME="Main">

  <NOFRAMES>
    If you can't hack frames, how do you expect
    to handle the Himalayas? Get a real browser.
  </NOFRAMES>
</FRAMESET>

</HTML>
```

Listing 19.13 `HighPeaksIntro.html`

```html
<!DOCTYPE HTML PUBLIC "-//W3C//DTD HTML 3.2//EN">
<HTML>
<HEAD>
  <TITLE>High Peaks Travel Inc.</TITLE>
</HEAD>

<BODY BGCOLOR="WHITE">
<CENTER>
  <IMG SRC="images/peak2.gif" WIDTH=511 HEIGHT=128>
</CENTER>
<H1 ALIGN="CENTER">High Peaks Travel Inc.</H1>
<HR>

<IMG SRC="images/peak1.gif" WIDTH=170 HEIGHT=121
     ALIGN="RIGHT">
Tired of the same old vacations in Cleveland?
Tour the high peaks with <B>High Peaks Travel</B>!
<P>
```

Listing 19.13 `HighPeaksIntro.html` (continued)

```
We have package deals for beginner, experienced, and
expert climbers, discount priced (*) for the
budget-conscious traveller.
<BR CLEAR="ALL">
<IMG SRC="images/peak.jpg" WIDTH=320 HEIGHT=240
    ALIGN="LEFT">
HPT is currently arranging trips to the following
exciting locations:
<UL>
  <LI><A HREF="Tibet.html">Tibet</A>
  <LI><A HREF="Nepal.html">Nepal</A>
  <LI><A HREF="Austria.html">Austria</A>
  <LI><A HREF="Switzerland.html">Switzerland</A>
</UL>
Sign up today!

<BR CLEAR="ALL">
<CENTER>
<FONT SIZE="-2">(*) No ropes or safety equipment provided
on discount tours. </FONT>
</CENTER>

</BODY>
</HTML>
```

Figure 19–21 The toolbar in the top-left corner is in a separate frame and remains up when the "main" page changes from the introduction to one of the country-specific pages.

Figure 19–22 Toolbar entries light up when you move the mouse over them.

Moving Layers

Netscape 4.0 introduced "layers." These are HTML regions that can overlap and be positioned arbitrarily, and are discussed at length in Sections 5.13 (Specifying Layers Using the LAYER and ILAYER Elements) and 5.14 (Specifying Layers Using Style Sheets). JavaScript 1.2 lets you access layers via the document.layers array, each element of which is a Layer object with properties corresponding to the attributes of the LAYER element. A named layer can be accessed via document.layers["layer name"] rather than by using an index, or simply by using document.layerName. Layers can be accessed this way no matter how they are defined in the HTML: by the LAYER element, by the ILAYER element, or via style sheets.

Listing 19.14 presents an example with two layers that are initially hidden (Figure 19–23). When a certain button is pressed, the first layer is made visible near the upper left corner, then moves down over the top of the regular page to its final location, where it annotates an image (Figure 19–24). Clicking a second button hides the first layer and displays a second, which also drifts to its final location (Figure 19–25). The properties and methods of the Layer object are described in Section 20.15, but for this example the properties of interest are visibility ("show" or "hidden") and pageX (absolute location in window). The methods used are moveToAbsolute (position layer at absolute location) and moveBy (move layer relative to its previous position).

Listing 19.14 Camps.html

```
<!DOCTYPE HTML PUBLIC "-//W3C//DTD HTML 3.2//EN">
<HTML>
<HEAD>
  <TITLE>Camps on K-3</TITLE>

<SCRIPT LANGUAGE="JavaScript1.2">
<!--

function hideCamps() {
  // Or document.baseCamp.visibility = "hidden";
  document.layers["baseCamp"].visibility = "hidden";
  document.layers["highCamp"].visibility = "hidden";
}

function moveBaseCamp() {
  baseCamp.moveBy(1, 3);
  if (baseCamp.pageX < 130)
    setTimeout("moveBaseCamp()", 10);
}

// Hide camps, position base camp near top-left
// corner, make it visible, then have it slowly
// drift down to final position.
```

Listing 19.14 `Camps.html` (continued)

```
function showBaseCamp() {
  hideCamps();
  baseCamp =  document.layers["baseCamp"];
  baseCamp.moveToAbsolute(0, 20);
  baseCamp.visibility = "show";
  moveBaseCamp();
}

function moveHighCamp() {
  highCamp.moveBy(2, 1);
  if (highCamp.pageX < 110)
    setTimeout("moveHighCamp()", 10);
}

// Hide camps, position high camp near top-left
// corner, make it visible, then have it slowly
// drift down to final position.

function showHighCamp() {
  hideCamps();
  highCamp =  document.layers["highCamp"];
  highCamp.moveToAbsolute(0, 65);
  highCamp.visibility = "show";
  moveHighCamp();
}

// -->
</SCRIPT>
</HEAD>

<BODY>

<IMG SRC="images/peak4.gif" WIDTH=511 HEIGHT=600
     ALIGN="LEFT">
<H1>Camps on K-3</H1>
The High Peaks Tours trip to the summit:
<UL>
  <LI>Day 1: Travel to Base Camp
  <LI>Day 2: Climb to High Camp
  <LI>Day 3: Ascend summit, return to High Camp
  <LI>Day 4: Descend to Base Camp
  <LI>Day 5: Return Home
</UL>
<BR CLEAR="ALL">
```

continued

Listing 19.14 `Camps.html` (continued)

```
<LAYER ID="highCamp" PAGEX=50 PAGEY=100
       VISIBILITY="hidden">
  <TABLE>
    <TR><TH BGCOLOR="WHITE" WIDTH=50>
        <FONT SIZE="+2">High Camp</FONT>
        <TD><IMG SRC="images/Arrow-Right.gif">
  </TABLE>
</LAYER>

<LAYER ID="baseCamp" PAGEX=50 PAGEY=100
       VISIBILITY="hidden">
  <TABLE>
    <TR><TH BGCOLOR="WHITE" WIDTH=50>
        <FONT SIZE="+3">Base Camp</FONT>
        <TD><IMG SRC="images/Arrow-Right.gif">
  </TABLE>
</LAYER>

<FORM>
  <INPUT TYPE="Button" VALUE="Show Base Camp"
         onClick="showBaseCamp()">
  <INPUT TYPE="Button" VALUE="Show High Camp"
         onClick="showHighCamp()">
  <INPUT TYPE="Button" VALUE="Hide Camps"
         onClick="hideCamps()">
</FORM>


</BODY>
</HTML>
```

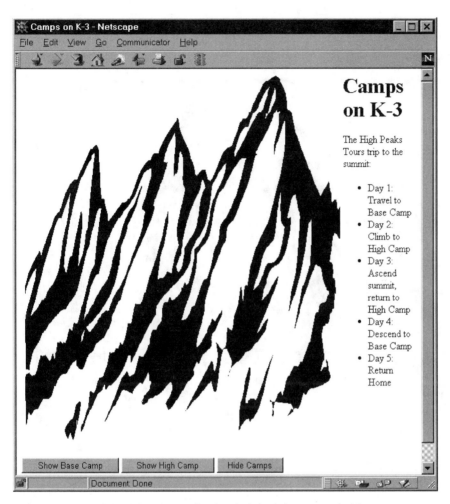

Figure 19–23 When the page is first loaded, both layers are hidden.

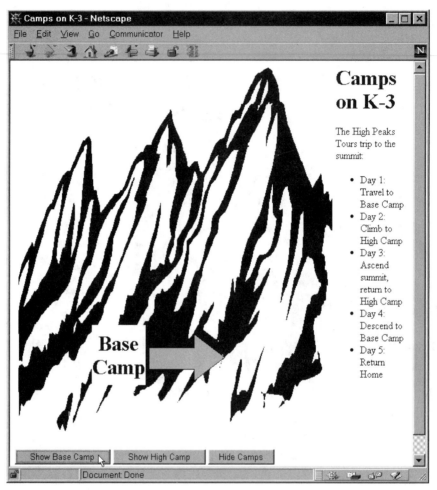

Figure 19–24 Clicking "Show Base Camp" turns on the base camp layer near the top-left corner of the page. It then drifts down to its final position.

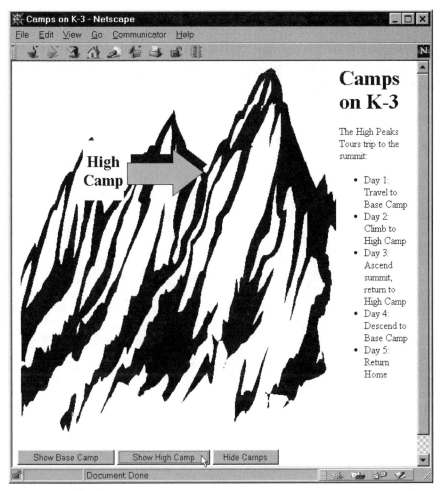

Figure 19–25 Clicking "Show High Camp" hides the previous layer, then displays and moves the high camp layer.

19.6 Using JavaScript to Validate CGI Forms

Another important application of JavaScript is to check the format of CGI forms before the form is submitted to the server. Contacting the server can be expensive, especially over a slow connection, and simple tasks like checking that all required fields are filled out or making sure textfields that should contain numbers don't have strings should be performed on the client if at all possible. The `document.forms` property contains an array of `Form` entries contained in the document. As usual in JavaScript, named entries can be accessed via name instead of by number, plus named forms are automatically inserted as properties in the `document` object, so any of the following formats would be legal to access forms.

```
var firstForm = document.forms[0];
// Assumes <FORM NAME="orders" ...>
var orderForm = document.forms["orders"];
// Assumes <FORM NAME="register" ...>
var registrationForm = document.register;
```

The `Form` object contains an elements property that holds an array of `Element` objects. You can retrieve form elements by number, by name from the array, or via the property name:

```
var firstElement = firstForm.elements[0];
// Assumes <INPUT ... NAME="quantity">
var quantityField = orderForm.elements["quantity"];
// Assumes <INPUT ... NAME="submitSchedule">
var submitButton = register.submitSchedule;
```

Different elements can be manipulated different ways. Some generally important capabilities include the ability to execute code before a form is submitted (via the `onSubmit` attribute of `FORM`), look up and change form values (via the element's value property), to recognize when keyboard focus is gained or lost (via `onFocus` and `onBlur`), and to notice changed values automatically (via `onChange`). The following examples illustrate two major ways form entries are checked: individually (each time one changes) and en masse (only when the form is submitted). For more details, see the `Form` and `Element` objects (Sections 20.6 and 20.8).

Checking Values Individually

Listing 19.15 gives a very simple input form containing a single textfield and a `SUBMIT` button. JavaScript is used in two ways. First, when the textfield gets the input focus, text describing the expected value is printed in the status line. The status line is reset when the textfield loses the focus. Secondly, if the user changes the textfield value to something illegal, a warning is issued when they leave the textfield. Then the textfield value is reset (changing the value via JavaScript does *not* trigger `onChange`) and it is given the input focus for the user to enter a correction. Figures 19–26 and 19–27 show the results.

Listing 19.15 CheckText.html

```
<!DOCTYPE HTML PUBLIC "-//W3C//DTD HTML 3.2//EN">
<HTML>
<HEAD>
  <TITLE>On-Line Training</TITLE>

<SCRIPT LANGUAGE="JavaScript">
<!--

// Print a description of the legal text in the
// status line

function describeLanguage() {
  status = "Enter an important Web language";
}

// Clear status line

function clearStatus() {
  status = "";
}

// When the user changes and leaves textfield, check
// that a valid choice was entered. If not, alert
// user, clear field, and set focus back there.

function checkLanguage() {
  // or document.forms["langForm"].elements["langField"]
  var field = document.langForm.langField;
  var lang = field.value;
  var prefix = lang.substring(0, 4).toUpperCase();
  if (prefix != "JAVA") {
    alert("Sorry, '" + lang + "' is not valid.\n" +
          "Please try again.");
    field.value = "";   // Erase old value
    field.focus();      // Give keyboard focus
  }
}

// -->
</SCRIPT>
</HEAD>

<BODY BGCOLOR="WHITE">
<H1>On-Line Training</H1>
```

continued

Listing 19.15 `CheckText.html` **(continued)**

```
<FORM ACTION="cgi-bin/registerLanguage" NAME="langForm">
To see an introduction to any of our on-line training
courses, please enter the name of an important Web
programming language below.
<P>
<B>Language:</B>
<INPUT TYPE="TEXT" NAME="langField"
       onFocus="describeLanguage()"
       onBlur="clearStatus()"
       onChange="checkLanguage()">
<P>
<INPUT TYPE="SUBMIT" VALUE="Show It To Me">
</FORM>

</BODY>
</HTML>
```

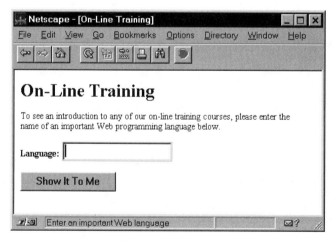

Figure 19–26 When the textfield gets the input focus, a descriptive prompt is displayed in the status line.

Figure 19–27 If the user enters an illegal value, a warning is printed when the textfield is left.

Checking Values When Form Is Submitted

Sometimes it is more convenient to check the entire form in one fell swoop. Some people feel that correcting the user after every mistake is too intrusive, since they may enter values temporarily but correct them before submission. Other times it is simply easier to check a bunch of values than to create a separate function for each of several dozen input elements. The key idea is that the function invoked by the FORM onSubmit attribute prevents submission of the form if it returns false.

Checking numeric values is one of the most common validation tasks, but the value property of textfields and text areas is a string, not a number. Fortunately, JavaScript provides two built-in functions to assist in this: parseInt and parseFloat. These take a string as input and return either an integer or a floating point number. In JavaScript 1.1, if no prefix of the string is a valid number, they return the special value NaN which can be recognized with the built-in isNaN function (not by ==, because NaNs return false for all comparisons). Unfortunately, in JavaScript 1.0 these functions return 0 for illegal numbers, and the isNaN function is not defined, making it difficult to recognize incorrect numeric values in scripts that must run on both platforms. Surprisingly, JavaScript does not have a property corresponding to "the current language version," so you have to create your own as in the following example.

```
<SCRIPT LANGUAGE="JavaScript">
<!--
languageVersion = 1.0;
// -->
</SCRIPT>
<SCRIPT LANGUAGE="JavaScript1.1">
<!--
languageVersion = 1.1;
// -->
</SCRIPT>
<SCRIPT LANGUAGE="JavaScript1.2">
<!--
languageVersion = 1.2;
// -->
</SCRIPT>
```

This idea is used to make the following portable version of isInt, except that Internet Explorer is classified as JavaScript 1.0, since its treatment of parseInt is like Netscape 2, not Netscape 3.

```
function isInt(numString) {
  if (languageVersion == 1.0) {
    var val = parseInt(numString);
    return((numString.substring(0,1) == "0") ||
          (val != 0));
  } else {
    return(!isNaN(parseInt(numString)));
  }
}
```

Listing 19.16 illustrates this function, with the results in Netscape 2.02, Netscape 3.01, Netscape 4.01, and Internet Explorer 3.02 shown in Figures 19–28 through 19–31.

Listing 19.16 `Numbers.html`

```html
<!DOCTYPE HTML PUBLIC "-//W3C//DTD HTML 3.2//EN">
<HTML>
<HEAD>
  <TITLE>Testing Numbers</TITLE>

<SCRIPT LANGUAGE="JavaScript">
<!--
languageVersion = 1.0;
// -->
</SCRIPT>

<SCRIPT LANGUAGE="JavaScript1.1">
<!--
if (navigator.appName == "Netscape")
  languageVersion = 1.1;
else
  languageVersion = 1.0;
// -->
</SCRIPT>

<SCRIPT LANGUAGE="JavaScript1.2">
<!--
languageVersion = 1.2;
// -->
</SCRIPT>

<SCRIPT LANGUAGE="JavaScript">
<!--
```

Listing 19.16 `Numbers.html` **(continued)**

```
function isInt(numString) {
  if (languageVersion == 1.0) {
    // It's an int if parseInt is non-zero *and*
    // input is not really "0" or "0xxxxx"
    var val = parseInt(numString);
    return((numString.substring(0,1) == "0") ||
           (val != 0));
  } else {        // 1.1 or 1.2
    // It's an int if parseInt doesn't return NaN
    return(!isNaN(parseInt(numString)));
  }
}

// -->
</SCRIPT>
</HEAD>

<BODY BGCOLOR="WHITE">

<SCRIPT LANGUAGE="JavaScript">
<!--

function testInt(numString) {
  return("<TR><TD>" + numString +
         "<TD>" + parseInt(numString) +
         "<TD>" + isInt(numString) + "\n");
}

document.writeln
  ("<H1>Testing for Numbers in JavaScript " +
     languageVersion + "</H1>\n" +
   "<TABLE BORDER=5 CELLSPACING=5>\n" +
   "<TR><TH>Input<TH>Parsed Value<TH>" +
     "Legal Integer?\n" +
   testInt("0") +
   testInt("10") +
   testInt("-10") +
   testInt("FF") +
   testInt("#FF") +
   testInt("123abc") +
   testInt("abc123") +
   "</TABLE>");

// -->
</SCRIPT>

</BODY>
</HTML>
```

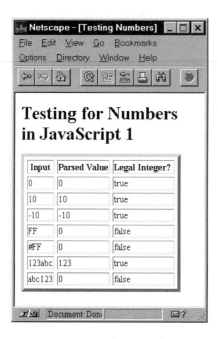

Figure 19-28 The `parseInt` method returns 0 for illegal numbers in Netscape 2.02.

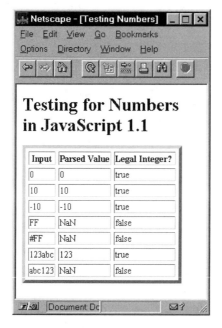

Figure 19-29 The `parseInt` method returns `NaN` for illegal numbers in Netscape 3.01.

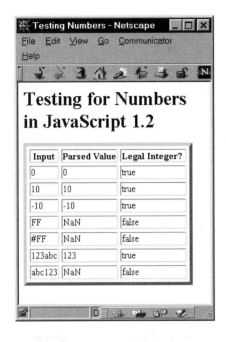

Figure 19-30 The `parseInt` method returns NaN for illegal numbers in Netscape 4.01.

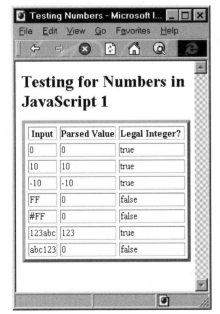

Figure 19-31 The `parseInt` method returns 0 for illegal numbers in Internet Explorer 3.01.

If a textfield value is supposed to be greater than zero, you can simplify the test considerably by relying on the fact that NaN returns false when compared to any other number. Here is a variation of isInt that uses this idea. It works in Internet Explorer as well as all versions of Netscape.

```
function isInt(string) {
  var val = parseInt(string);
  return(val > 0);
}
```

Listing 19.17 uses this to create a simple input form with three textfields. The first and third should contain numbers and the second should contain a string. Rather than correcting values as they are entered, the only action taken during data entry is to print a descriptive message whenever a textfield has the input focus. However, when the form is submitted, the checkRegistration function is invoked. This function verifies that the first and third entries are integers and that the second is neither an integer nor is missing. Results are shown in Figures 19–32 and 19–33.

Listing 19.17 CheckSeveral.html

```
<!DOCTYPE HTML PUBLIC "-//W3C//DTD HTML 3.2//EN">
<HTML>
<HEAD>
  <TITLE>Camp Registration</TITLE>

<SCRIPT LANGUAGE="JavaScript">
<!--

function clearStatus() { status = ""; }

function promptAge() { status = "Age (no fractions)"; }

function promptRank() { status = "Rank Name"; }

function promptSerial() { status = "Serial Number"; }

// In JavaScript 1.1, parseInt returns NaN (recognizable
// via isNaN() for nonintegers. But JavaScript 1.0
// returns 0 and doesn't have an isNaN routine.
// Since comparisons to NaN always fail, the > 0
// test works on either version.
```

Listing 19.17 `CheckSeveral.html` **(continued)**

```
function isInt(string) {
  var val = parseInt(string);
  return(val > 0);
}

// Four tests:
// 1) Age is an integer.
// 2) Rank is not an integer.
// 3) Rank is not missing.
// 4) Serial number is an integer.
// If any of the tests pass, submission is canceled.

function checkRegistration() {
  var ageField = document.registerForm.ageField;
  if (!isInt(ageField.value)) {
    alert("Age must be an integer.");
    return(false);
  }
  var rankField = document.registerForm.rankField;
  if (isInt(rankField.value)) {
    alert("Use rank name, not rank number.");
    return(false);
  }
  if (rankField.value == "") {
    alert("Missing rank.");
    return(false);
  }
  var serialField = document.registerForm.serialField;
  if (!isInt(serialField.value)) {
    alert("Serial number must be an integer.");
    return(false);
  }
  // Format looks OK. Submit form.
  return(true);
}

// -->
</SCRIPT>
</HEAD>

<BODY BGCOLOR="WHITE">
<H1>Camp Registration</H1>
```

continued

Listing 19.17 `CheckSeveral.html` (continued)

```
<FORM ACTION="cgi-bin/register"
      NAME="registerForm"
      onSubmit="return(checkRegistration())">
Age: <INPUT TYPE="TEXT" NAME="ageField"
            onFocus="promptAge()"
            onBlur="clearStatus()">
<BR>
Rank: <INPUT TYPE="TEXT" NAME="rankField"
             onFocus="promptRank()"
             onBlur="clearStatus()">
<BR>
Serial Number: <INPUT TYPE="TEXT" NAME="serialField"
                      onFocus="promptSerial()"
                      onBlur="clearStatus()">
<P>
<INPUT TYPE="SUBMIT" VALUE="Submit Registration">
</FORM>

</BODY>
</HTML>
```

Figure 19–32 No checking is done as values are entered.

Figure 19–33 Wait! That *is* an integer! Sorry, Charlie, the page designer wasn't planning on hex input.

19.7 Using JavaScript to Store and Examine Cookies

A "cookie" is a small amount of textual information about a page that is stored by the browser on the client system. The structure and syntax of cookies are explained in Section 16.6, and Section 18.12 gives examples of server-side CGI programs manipulating them. They can also be manipulated entirely on the client through the use of the document.cookie property. This property behaves in a very unusual fashion. If you look up the value of document.cookie, you will get a *single* big string containing all the cookie values, as sent by the browser via the Cookie HTTP request header. For example, if the current page has three cookies name1, name2, and name3, the value of document.cookie would be something like.

```
"name1=val1; name2=val2; name3=val3"
```

However, you do not assign values to document.cookie using a single large string like this. Instead, you specify a single cookie at a time using the same format as would be used in the Set-Cookie HTTP response header. See Section 16.6 (Cookies: Storing Persistent Data on the Client) for a complete description of the syntax, but here are a couple of examples.

```
document.cookie = "name1=val1";
document.cookie = "name2=val2; expires=" + someDate;
document.cookie = "name3=val3; path=/;
    domain=test.com";
```

Each time document.cookie is set, the cookie is stored by the browser. The cookies persist as long as the browser remains open, and if an expiration date is specified, the cookie is reloaded in a later session. This works in Java-Script 1.0, 1.1, and 1.2, but it only works in Internet Explorer when the page is loaded from the network. Local files cannot set cookies, making page development and testing somewhat more cumbersome on Internet Explorer than on Netscape.

Core Warning

Cookies are ignored by Internet Explorer when the page comes from a local file.

To illustrate the use of cookies, Listing 19.18 creates a simplified order form for "Widgets R Us" corporation. When the form is submitted, the first and last name and account number are stored in cookies. The name and number can be stored without submitting an order by clicking the "Register Account" button. When the page is visited later in the same or a different session, the cookie values are used to fill in the first three textfields automatically as a time-saving feature for the user.

There are two particular things you should pay attention to in this example. The first is that the function that fills the textfield values is invoked from the onLoad attribute of BODY. This guarantees that the page is done loading before the function is invoked, so there is no risk of trying to access textfields that do not yet exist. The second thing to note is the cookieVal function, which takes a cookie name (e.g., "name2") and a cookie string (e.g., "name1=val1; name2=val2; name3=val3") and returns the value associated with the name (e.g., "val2").

```
function cookieVal(cookieName, cookieString) {
  var startLoc = cookieString.indexOf(cookieName);
  if (startLoc == -1)
    return("");   // No such cookie
  var sepLoc = cookieString.indexOf("=", startLoc);
  var endLoc = cookieString.indexOf(";", startLoc);
  if (endLoc == -1)   // Last one has no ";"
    endLoc = cookieString.length;
  return(cookieString.substring(sepLoc+1, endLoc));
}
```

This function uses two important methods of the String class: indexOf and substring. The first of these takes two strings as arguments and, if the first appears in the second, returns the location in the second string corresponding to the left-most occurrence of the first string. There is also a lastIndexOf method that returns the starting index of the right-most occurrence. In either case, –1 is returned if the second string does not contain the first. The substring method takes a start index and an end index and returns the string starting at the start index (inclusive) and going up to the end index (exclusive). The `cookieVal` function might have been a little simpler if the `split` method had been used; this takes a string and returns an array derived from breaking the string at whitespace or at a user-specified delimiter. However, `split` is available only in JavaScript 1.1. See Section 20.31 for a complete description of the `String` object.

This version of `cookieVal` does not distinguish between an empty value (e.g., the value corresponding to `"bar"` in `"foo=a; bar=; baz=c"`) and a missing cookie (e.g., the value corresponding to `"quux"` in `"foo=a; bar=;  baz=c"`). If you wanted to differentiate these two cases, simply return `null` instead of the empty string from the line containing the "No such cookie" comment. In this case, however, returning an empty string either way simplifies the processing considerably.

Figures 19–34 through 19–37 show the before and after results in Netscape 3.01 and Internet Explorer 3.01. If you're interested, the names shown in the figures are the chief developers of JavaScript for Netscape and Microsoft.

Listing 19.18 `Widgets.html`

```
<!DOCTYPE HTML PUBLIC "-//W3C//DTD HTML 3.2//EN">
<HTML>
<HEAD>
  <TITLE>Widgets "R" Us</TITLE>

<SCRIPT LANGUAGE="JavaScript">
<!--

// Read last name, first name, and account number
// from textfields and store as cookies

function storeCookies() {
  var expires =
    "; expires=Friday, 31-Dec-99 23:59:59 GMT";
  var first = document.widgetForm.firstField.value;
  var last = document.widgetForm.lastField.value;
  var account = document.widgetForm.accountField.value;
  document.cookie = "first=" + first + expires;
  document.cookie = "last=" + last + expires;
  document.cookie = "account=" + account + expires;
}

// Store cookies and give user confirmation
```

continued

Listing 19.18 `Widgets.html` **(continued)**

```
function registerAccount() {
  storeCookies();
  alert("Registration Successful.");
}

// This does not distinguish an empty cookie
// from no cookie at all, since it doesn't matter here.

function cookieVal(cookieName, cookieString) {
  var startLoc = cookieString.indexOf(cookieName);
  if (startLoc == -1)
    return("");  // No such cookie
  var sepLoc = cookieString.indexOf("=", startLoc);
  var endLoc = cookieString.indexOf(";", startLoc);
  if (endLoc == -1)  // Last one has no ";"
    endLoc = cookieString.length;
  return(cookieString.substring(sepLoc+1, endLoc));
}

// If cookie values for name or account exist,
// fill in textfields with them.

function presetValues() {
  var firstField = document.widgetForm.firstField;
  var lastField = document.widgetForm.lastField;
  var accountField = document.widgetForm.accountField;
  var cookies = document.cookie;
  firstField.value = cookieVal("first", cookies);
  lastField.value = cookieVal("last", cookies);
  accountField.value = cookieVal("account", cookies);
}

// -->
</SCRIPT>
</HEAD>

<BODY BGCOLOR="WHITE" onLoad="presetValues()">

<H1>Widgets "R" Us</H1>

<FORM ACTION="cgi-bin/widgets"
      NAME="widgetForm"
      onSubmit="storeCookies()">
```

Listing 19.18 `Widgets.html` (continued)

```
First Name: <INPUT TYPE="TEXT" NAME="firstField">
<BR>
Last Name: <INPUT TYPE="TEXT" NAME="lastField">
<BR>
Account Number: <INPUT TYPE="TEXT" NAME="accountField">
<BR>
Widget Name: <INPUT TYPE="TEXT" NAME="widgetField">
<BR>
<INPUT TYPE="BUTTON" VALUE="Register Account"
       onClick="registerAccount()">
<INPUT TYPE="SUBMIT" VALUE="Submit Order">

</FORM>

</BODY>
</HTML>
```

Figure 19–34 The initial page lets the user order widgets. The name and account number are stored when the order is submitted or if "Register Account" is pressed.

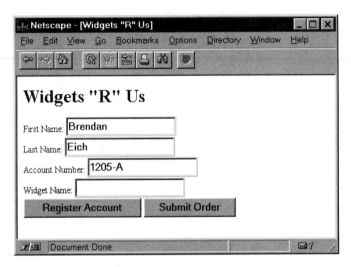

Figure 19–35 Even after quitting Netscape and restarting at a later time, the previous name and account number are automatically filled in.

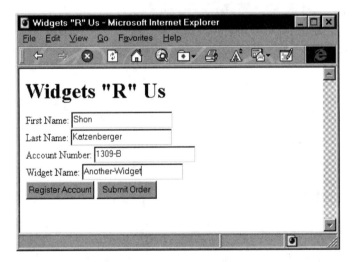

Figure 19–36 You can use cookies from JavaScript in Netscape 2, 3, and 4 as well as in Internet Explorer 3.

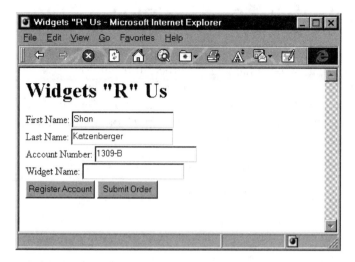

Figure 19–37 The Widgets page in a later session. This page and the previous one (Figure 19–36) were loaded via HTTP. Cookies are ignored in Internet Explorer when local files are used.

19.8 Using JavaScript to Interact with Frames

JavaScript gives you a variety of tools for accessing and manipulating frames. The default `Window` object contains a `frames` property holding an array of frames (other `Window` objects) contained by the current window or frame. It also has `parent` and `top` properties referring to the directly enclosing frame or window and the top-level window, respectively. All of the properties of `Window` can be applied to any of these entries; see Section 20.35 (The Window Object) for details on the available properties. I'll show two examples here: having one frame direct another to display a particular URL, and transferring the input focus to a frame when its contents change. Two additional examples were given in Chapter 4, "Frames." The first showed how you could update the contents of two frames at once, and the second showed how to use JavaScript to prevent your document from appearing as a frame in someone else's Web page. For details, see Section 4.6 (Solving Common Frame Problems).

Directing a Particular Frame to Display a URL

Because each of the frames specified by `frames`, `top`, and `bottom` has a `location` property that, when changed, redirects the window to a new URL, it is quite straightforward for JavaScript code in one frame to force other frames to show a particular URL. Once you have a reference to the parent frame of the one you want to change, you simply look up the frame in the `frames` array and set `location`. Here is an example.

```
someFrame.frames["frameName"].location = "url";
```

Alternatively, because Java automatically creates a property for each frame in a window, you could do.

```
someFrame.frames.frameName.location = "url";
```

The key point to doing this is that you have to know enough about the frame structure to follow the `parent`, `top`, and `frames` links to the frame of interest. Alternatively, you can create new windows at run-time and direct documents to be displayed there. Section 20.35 (The Window Object) gives several examples of this process.

Listing 19.19 creates a page that initially displays two frames: `GetURL.html` (Listing 19.20) and `DisplayURL.html` (Listing 19.21). The top frame contains a textfield for collecting a URL of interest. Entering a value and pressing the "Show URL" button instructs the other frame to display the specified URL. The process is amazingly simple. First a function to display the URL is created, as follows:

```
function showURL() {
  var url = document.urlForm.urlField.value;
  parent.displayFrame.location = url;
}
```

Next, this function is attached to a button using the `onClick` attribute, as in the following snippet.

```
<INPUT TYPE="BUTTON" VALUE="Show URL"
       onClick="showURL()">
```

That's all there is to it, and the process works in JavaScript 1.0, 1.1, and 1.2. Figures 19–38 and 19–39 show the results in Internet Explorer. Figures 19–40 and 19–41 show Netscape results.

Listing 19.19 `ShowURL.html`

```html
<HTML>
<HEAD>
  <TITLE>Show a URL</TITLE>
</HEAD>

<FRAMESET ROWS="150, *">
  <FRAME SRC="GetURL.html" NAME="inputFrame">
  <FRAME SRC="DisplayURL.html" NAME="displayFrame">
</FRAMESET>

</HTML>
```

Listing 19.20 `GetURL.html`

```html
<!DOCTYPE HTML PUBLIC "-//W3C//DTD HTML 3.2//EN">
<HTML>
<HEAD>
  <TITLE>Choose a URL</TITLE>

<SCRIPT LANGUAGE="JavaScript">
<!--

function showURL() {
  var url = document.urlForm.urlField.value;
  // or parent.frames["displayFrame"].location = url;
  parent.displayFrame.location = url;
}

function preloadUrl() {
  if (navigator.appName == "Netscape")
    document.urlForm.urlField.value =
      "http://home.netscape.com/";
  else
    document.urlForm.urlField.value =
      "http://www.microsoft.com/";
}

// -->
</SCRIPT>

</HEAD>
```
continued

Listing 19.20 `GetURL.html` (continued)

```
<BODY BGCOLOR="WHITE" onLoad="preloadUrl()">
<H1 ALIGN="CENTER">Choose a URL</H1>

<CENTER>
<FORM NAME="urlForm">
URL: <INPUT TYPE="TEXT" NAME="urlField" SIZE=35>
<INPUT TYPE="BUTTON" VALUE="Show URL"
       onClick="showURL()">
</FORM>
</CENTER>

</BODY>
</HTML>
```

Listing 19.21 `DisplayURL.html`

```
<!DOCTYPE HTML PUBLIC "-//W3C//DTD HTML 3.2//EN">
<HTML>
<HEAD>
  <TITLE>Display URL</TITLE>
</HEAD>

<BODY BGCOLOR="WHITE">
<H2>Enter a URL in the textfield above. Press
"Show URL" to display it in this frame.</H2>

</BODY>
</HTML>
```

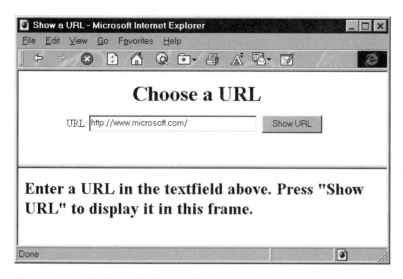

Figure 19–38 The textfield's initial value is set for Internet Explorer, but arbitrary values can be entered.

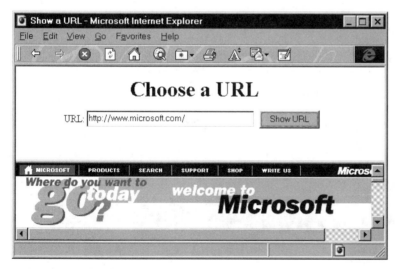

Figure 19–39 Pressing "Show URL" instructs the bottom frame to show the URL entered in the textfield of the top frame.

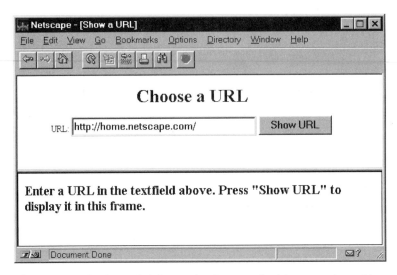

Figure 19–40 The textfield's initial value is set for Netscape, but arbitrary values can be entered.

Figure 19–41 Pressing "Show URL" instructs the bottom frame to show the URL entered in the textfield of the top frame.

Giving a Frame the Input Focus

One of the surprising features of frames is that when you click on a hypertext link that directs the result to a particular frame, that frame does not automatically get the input focus. This can be annoying for a couple of reasons. First of all, it can give unintuitive results when printing. Suppose that a page is using a small borderless frame to act as a navigation bar. Now you click in that toolbar to display a page of interest, then select "Print." What do you get? A nice printout of the toolbar, that's what! Hardly what you were expecting. Secondly, it can decrease the value of keyboard shortcuts. Some users commonly use keyboard shortcuts to scroll in large documents. For instance, the up and down arrows will cause scrolling on most systems, but only if the window has the input focus. So if you use a hypertext link that sends a document to a frame, you have to click in that frame before using the keyboard shortcuts.

When JavaScript code is being used to display frames, the fix is trivial: just include a call to focus. For instance, here is an improved version of showURL that can be used in GetURL.html to give the bottom frame the input focus when a URL is sent there.

```
function showURL() {
  var url = document.urlForm.urlField.value;
  parent.displayFrame.location = url;
  // Give frame the input focus
  parent.displayFrame.focus();
}
```

Fixing the problem in regular HTML documents is a bit more tedious. It requires adding onClick handlers that call focus to each and every occurrence of A and AREA that includes a TARGET, and a similar onSubmit handler to each FORM that uses TARGET.

19.9 Accessing Java from JavaScript

Netscape 3.0 introduced a package called LiveConnect that allows JavaScript to talk to Java and vice versa. This is a very important capability because prior to the introduction of LiveConnect, applets were self-contained programs that had little knowledge of or interaction with the rest of the Web page that contained them. Now applets can manipulate frames and windows, control images loaded from HTML, read and set values of form elements, read and store cookies, and all the other things that were previously restricted to JavaScript. This section discusses ways to use Java routines and control Java applets from within JavaScript. Section 19.10 explains the other side of the process: using JavaScript capabilities from within a Java applet. Here, I'll discuss three classes of applications.

- *Calling Java methods directly.* In particular, this section shows how to print debugging messages to the Java console.

- *Using applets to perform operations for JavaScript.* In particular, this section shows how a hidden applet can be used to obtain the client hostname, information not otherwise available to JavaScript.

- *Controlling applets from JavaScript.* In particular, this section shows how LiveConnect allows user actions in the HTML part of the page to trigger actions in the applet.

Calling Java Methods Directly

JavaScript can access Java variables and methods simply by using the fully qualified name. For instance, using

```
java.lang.System.out.println("Hello Console");
```

will send the string `"Hello Console"` to the Java console. This is a useful debugging tool when developing JavaScript-enabled Web pages. You can also use new from within JavaScript to construct Java classes. For example, Listing 19.22 creates a simple page using the `getProperty` method `java.lang.System` and an instance of the `java.awt.Point` class. Figure 19–42 shows the result.

Use of Java from JavaScript has several limitations. First of all, you cannot perform any operation that would not be permitted in an applet. So you cannot use Java to open local files, call local programs, discover the user's login name, or execute any other such restricted operation. Secondly, because JavaScript has no `try/catch`, you cannot call Java methods that throw exceptions (other than `RuntimeException`, which need not be caught). Thirdly, and most significantly, JavaScript provides no mechanism for writing Java methods or creating subclasses. As a result, you will want to create an applet for all but the simplest uses of `java.lang.System.out.println` or a data structure like `java.util.StringTokenizer`.

Listing 19.22 `CallJava.html`

```html
<!DOCTYPE HTML PUBLIC "-//W3C//DTD HTML 3.2//EN">
<HTML>
<HEAD>
  <TITLE>Calling Java</TITLE>
</HEAD>

<BODY>
<H1>Calling Java</H1>

<SCRIPT LANGUAGE="JavaScript">
<!--

document.writeln
  ("This browser uses a virtual machine from " +
   java.lang.System.getProperty("java.vendor") + ".");
var pt = new java.awt.Point(3, 5);
pt.translate(7, 5);
document.writeln("<P>");
document.writeln
  ("Translating (3,5) by (7,5) yields (" +
   pt.x + "," + pt.y + ").");

// -->
</SCRIPT>

</BODY>
</HTML>
```

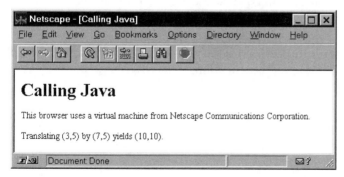

Figure 19–42 JavaScript can utilize Java even if the current page does not contain an applet.

Using Applets to Perform Operations for JavaScript

With its strong object-oriented framework and (on most platforms) Just In Time compiler, Java is better suited to writing complex data structures and performing long computations than is JavaScript. If JavaScript needs such things, a good alternative is to write them in Java, include them in a "hidden" applet, then call them from JavaScript. JavaScript can access applets either via the document.applets array, or, if the applet is named, via document.appletName. Any public method of the applet can be called by JavaScript. For example, suppose that the applet Acoustics has a simple model for computing sound propagation through water, and you want to create a Web page to demonstrate the model. You could include the applet in your page via

```
<APPLET CODE="Acoustics" WIDTH=10 HEIGHT=10
        NAME="acoustics">
</APPLET>
```

You could then call the public getSignalExcess method as follows:

```
function signalExcess(...) {
   return(document.acoustics.signalExcess(...));
}
```

To illustrate this, Listing 19.23 creates a Web page with a hypertext link that takes visitors to one of two different resumés, depending on the domain of the client system. Since JavaScript doesn't have a way of determining the client hostname, the page uses a simple hidden applet (Figure 19–43, Listing 19.24) that uses InetAddress.getLocalHost to determine this information. If the hostname is inside the author's own company network, the author displays a corporately-politically-correct resumé (Figure 19–44, Listing 19.25), while outside readers get a very different result (Figure 19–45, Listing 19.26) when clicking on the same link.

Listing 19.23 Wonder-Widget.html

```html
<!DOCTYPE HTML PUBLIC "-//W3C//DTD HTML 3.2//EN">
<HTML>
<HEAD>
  <TITLE>WonderWidget</TITLE>

<SCRIPT LANGUAGE="JavaScript">
<!--

function contains(string, substring) {
  return(string.indexOf(substring) != -1);
}

function showResume() {
  if (contains(document.gethost.getHost(),
               "widgets-r-us.com"))
    location = "ResumeLoyal.html";
  else
    location = "ResumeReal.html";
  return(false);
}

// -->
</SCRIPT>
</HEAD>

<BODY BGCOLOR="WHITE">
<H1>WonderWidget</H1>

<APPLET CODE="GetHost" WIDTH=10 HEIGHT=10 NAME="gethost">
</APPLET>

Description:
<UL>
  <LI>Name: Wonder Widget
  <LI>Serial Number: 1544X
  <LI>Cost: $7.95 (plus 22.50 shipping and handling)
  <LI>Designer:
      <A HREF="ResumeLoyal.html"
      onClick="return(showResume())">
      J. Random Hacker</A>

</BODY>
</HTML>
```

Listing 19.24 `GetHost.java`

```java
import java.applet.Applet;
import java.awt.*;
import java.net.*;

public class GetHost extends Applet {
  private String host;

  public void init() {
    setBackground(Color.white);
    try {
      host = InetAddress.getLocalHost().toString();
    } catch(UnknownHostException uhe) {
      host = "Unknown Host";
    }
  }

  public String getHost() {
    return(host);
  }
}
```

Figure 19–43 This page contains an applet, even though the applet doesn't contribute to the appearance of the page.

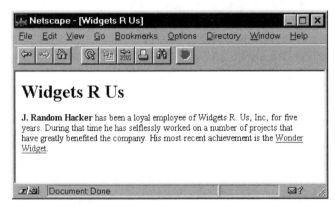

Figure 19–44 If the "J. Random Hacker" link is selected from within the widgets-r-us domain or from a non-JavaScript browser, this first resumé is displayed.

Figure 19–45 If Java reports a "safe" hostname, a different resumé is displayed.

Listing 19.25 `ResumeLoyal.html`

```
<!DOCTYPE HTML PUBLIC "-//W3C//DTD HTML 3.2//EN">
<HTML>
<HEAD>
  <TITLE>Widgets R Us</TITLE>
</HEAD>

<BODY BGCOLOR="WHITE">
<H1>Widgets R Us</H1>

<B>J. Random Hacker</B> has been a loyal employee of
Widgets R. Us, Inc, for five years. During that time
he has selflessly worked on a number of projects that
have greatly benefited the company. His most recent
achievement is the <A HREF="Wonder-Widget.html">
Wonder Widget</A>.

</BODY>
</HTML>
```

Listing 19.26 `ResumeReal.html`

```
<!DOCTYPE HTML PUBLIC "-//W3C//DTD HTML 3.2//EN">
<HTML>
<HEAD>
  <TITLE>J. Random Hacker</TITLE>
</HEAD>

<BODY>
<H1>J. Random Hacker</H1>

<H2>I'm looking for a job!</H2>

For the last five years, I've been underpaid and
underappreciated by Widgets R Us, Inc. Now I'm ready
to take my immense talents elsewhere. Who will open
the bidding?

</BODY>
</HTML>
```

Controlling Applets from JavaScript

If an applet is designed with public methods to start it, stop it, customize its appearance, and control its behavior, the applet can be completely controlled from JavaScript. There are several reasons why you might want to do this in JavaScript instead of using GUI controls in Java. First of all, you might want to mix the controls with formatted text, something HTML excels at. For example, you might want to put controls into a table, and it is far easier to make nicely formatted tables in HTML than in Java. Secondly, you might want the applet actions to correspond to user events such as submitting a form, something Java could not detect by itself. Thirdly, embedding controls in JavaScript lets you perform a consistent set of actions for *all* applets in a page. For example, Listing 19.27 gives a Web page that lets you control any number of "simulations" showing mold growth. You can insert any number of applets; the "Start" and "Stop" buttons apply to every applet on the page. The results are shown in Figures 19–46 and 19–47.

Listing 19.27 `MoldSimulation.html`

```
<!DOCTYPE HTML PUBLIC "-//W3C//DTD HTML 3.2//EN">
<HTML>
<HEAD>
  <TITLE>Mold Propagation Simulation</TITLE>

<SCRIPT LANGUAGE="JavaScript">
<!--

// Start simulation for all applets in document

function startCircles() {
  for(var i=0; i<document.applets.length; i++)
    document.applets[i].startCircles();
}

// Stop simulation for all applets in document

function stopCircles() {
  for(var i=0; i<document.applets.length; i++)
    document.applets[i].stopCircles();
}
```
continued

Listing 19.27 `MoldSimulation.html` (continued)

```
// -->
</SCRIPT>
</HEAD>

<BODY BGCOLOR="C0C0C0">
<H1>Mold Propagation Simulation</H1>

<APPLET CODE="RandomCircles.class" WIDTH=100 HEIGHT=100>
</APPLET>
<P>
<APPLET CODE="RandomCircles.class" WIDTH=300 HEIGHT=100>
</APPLET>
<P>
<APPLET CODE="RandomCircles.class" WIDTH=500 HEIGHT=100>
</APPLET>

<FORM>
<INPUT TYPE="BUTTON" VALUE="Start Simulations"
       onClick="startCircles()">
<INPUT TYPE="BUTTON" VALUE="Stop Simulations"
       onClick="stopCircles()">
</FORM>

</BODY>
</HTML>
```

Listing 19.28 `RandomCircles.java`

```java
import java.applet.Applet;
import java.awt.*;

/** Draw random circles in a background thread.
 *  Needs an external event to start/stop drawing.
 */

public class RandomCircles extends Applet
                           implements Runnable {
  private boolean drawCircles = false;

  public void init() {
    setBackground(Color.white);
  }

  public void startCircles() {
    Thread t = new Thread(this);
    t.start();
  }

  public void run() {
    drawCircles = true;
    Color[] colors = { Color.lightGray, Color.gray,
                       Color.darkGray, Color.black };
    int colorIndex = 0;
    Graphics g = getGraphics();
    while(drawCircles) {
      int x =
        (int)Math.round(size().width * Math.random());
      int y =
        (int)Math.round(size().height * Math.random());
      g.setColor(colors[colorIndex]);
      colorIndex = (colorIndex + 1) % colors.length;
      g.fillOval(x, y, 10, 10);
      pause(0.1);
    }
  }

  public void stopCircles() {
    drawCircles = false;
  }

  private void pause(double seconds) {
    try {
      Thread.sleep((int)(Math.round(seconds * 1000.0)));
    } catch(InterruptedException ie) {}
  }
}
```

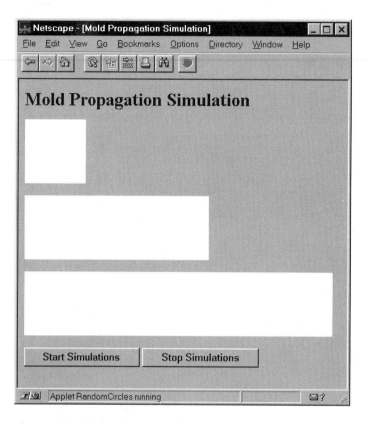

Figure 19–46 Initially, none of the simulations are running.

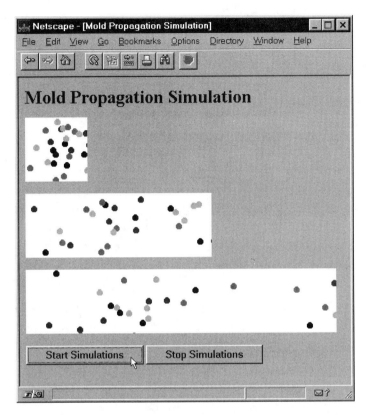

Figure 19–47 All three applet simulations can be controlled from a single HTML button. Adding additional applets does not require any changes to the Java or JavaScript code.

19.10 Accessing JavaScript from Java

Not only does LiveConnect let you call Java methods and control applets from JavaScript, but it also lets applets access JavaScript. This can be done in two ways. The simplest but least flexible approach is to create URLs that use the "javascript:" protocol. The following first section illustrates this process by creating an applet that lets you enter arbitrary HTML, displaying the result in a frame of the user's choice. A more powerful approach is to use the `netscape.javascript.JSObject` class provided by Netscape. The following second section illustrates this with an applet that allows user interaction to store values in HTML text input forms contained in the Web page that holds the applet.

Using the "javascript:" URL

Java permits you to designate "javascript:" as the protocol for URL objects that you create. If the applet is running on Netscape 3, using `getApplet-Context().showDocument` on a URL of the form

```
"javascript:'<HTML> ... </HTML>'"
```

will show the specified HTML document in the browser. There are some restrictions, however. First of all, the HTML code contained between the single quotes cannot itself contain single quotes or carriage returns. This means that routines that read in an HTML document from a socket would need to modify the document before feeding it to such a URL. Secondly, although `showDocument` lets you specify a particular frame for the result, it does not give you control over creating new browser windows, as does the `open` method of the JavaScript `Window` object. Both of these restrictions can be overcome through use of the `JSObject` class, but using the simpler approach does not require you to install this class on your development system. I don't recommend it for most serious applications, but it is useful for quick tests and small applet enhancements. For serious applications, use `JSObject` to do the equivalent of the following standard JavaScript technique for building HTML on-the-fly:

```
var win = window.open("", frameName); // Eg "_self"
win.document.writeln("<HEAD>...</HEAD>");
win.document.writeln(<BODY>...</BODY>);
win.document.close();
```

To illustrate this, Listing 19.29 creates a static `showPage` method that can be used by an applet to display an HTML string in the entire window or a particular frame. Listing 19.30 uses this method to create the applet shown in Figure 19–48, which lets you enter some HTML for the `BODY` part of a document, builds an HTML page, inserts your text in it, then displays the result in the frame of your choice. Note that `TestHTML.java` (Listing 19.30) makes use of the `LabeledTextField` class. This class was first used in an example illustrating Java DataBase Connectivity; the source code is given there (Section 15.9). Finally, Listings 19.31 through 19.33 give the HTML documents used to create the frames and to hold the applet.

Listing 19.29 ShowHTML.java

```java
/** A Netscape3-specific way to generate an HTML page
 *  on-the-fly and pass it to the browser. Simply
 *  generate a URL of the form
 *    "javascript:'[Entire HTML Page]'"
 *  and call showDocument on it. Note that there should
 *  not be any carriage returns or single quotes in
 *  the string. Using netscape.javascript.JSObject is
 *  a much more robust approach.
 */

import java.applet.Applet;
import java.net.*;

public class ShowHTML {

  /** Show in full page. */

  public static void showPage(Applet app, String html) {
    URL page = makeJavascriptURL(html);
    app.getAppletContext().showDocument(page);
  }

  /** Show in particular frame. */

  public static void showPage(Applet app, String html,
                              String frameName) {
    URL page = makeJavascriptURL(html);
    app.getAppletContext().showDocument(page, frameName);
  }

  /** No \n's or single quotes in the String! */

  public static URL makeJavascriptURL(String html) {
    try {
      URL page = new URL("javascript:'" + html + "'");
      return(page);
    } catch(MalformedURLException mue) {
      System.out.println("Illegal URL: " + mue);
      return(null);
    }
  }
}
```

Listing 19.30 `TestHTML.java`

```java
/** Illustrates use of the showPage method of ShowHTML.
 *  Generates HTML on-the-fly and sends it to the
 *  browser via the "javascript:" URL. Using JSObject
 *  is much more flexible, but this approach doesn't
 *  require any special Java classes.
 *  <B>Only works in Netscape 3.0 and later.</B>
 */

import java.applet.Applet;
import java.awt.*;

public class TestHTML extends Applet {
  private LabeledTextField sampleLine, frameName;

  public void init() {
    setBackground(Color.white);
    sampleLine =
      new LabeledTextField("Sample HTML:", 80);
    frameName =
      new LabeledTextField("Frame Name:", 15);
    add(sampleLine);
    add(frameName);
    add(new Button("Generate HTML"));
  }

  public boolean action(Event e, Object o) {
    String text = sampleLine.getTextField().getText();
    String frame = frameName.getTextField().getText();
    String html = "<HEAD>" +
                  "<TITLE>Generated HTML</TITLE>" +
                  "</HEAD>" +
                  "<BODY BGCOLOR=WHITE>" +
                  "<H1>Generated HTML</H1>" +
                  "<H2>Your input:</H2>" +
                  "<XMP>" + text + "</XMP>" +
                  "<H2>Result:</H2>" +
                  text +
                  "</BODY>";
    if (frame.length() == 0)
      ShowHTML.showPage(this, html);
    else
      ShowHTML.showPage(this, html, frame);
    return(true);
  }
}
```

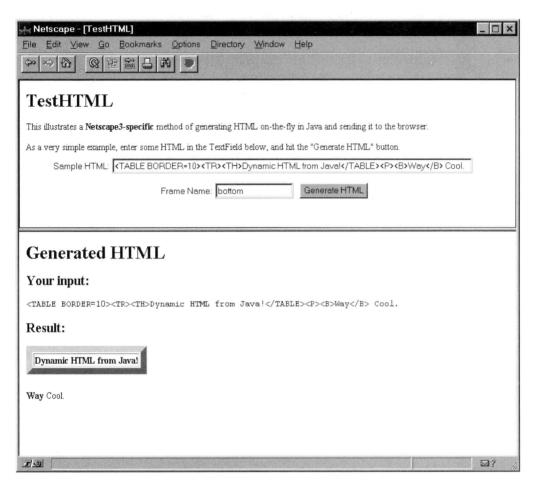

Figure 19–48 Using `showDocument` on a URL of the form `"javascript:'html document'"` lets you display dynamically generated HTML from Java in Netscape 3 and 4.

Listing 19.31 TestHTML.html

```
<HTML>
<HEAD>
  <TITLE>TestHTML</TITLE>
</HEAD>

<FRAMESET ROWS="2*,3*">
  <FRAME SRC="TestHTMLTop.html" NAME="top">
  <FRAME SRC="TestHTMLBottom.html" NAME="bottom">
</FRAMESET>

</HTML>
```

Listing 19.32 TestHTMLTop.html

```
<!DOCTYPE HTML PUBLIC "-//W3C//DTD HTML 3.2//EN">
<HTML>
<HEAD>
  <TITLE>TestHTML</TITLE>
</HEAD>

<BODY BGCOLOR="WHITE">
<H1>TestHTML</H1>
This illustrates a <B>Netscape3-specific</B> method of
generating HTML on-the-fly in Java and sending it to the
browser.
<P>
As a very simple example, enter some HTML in
the TextField below, and hit the "Generate HTML" button.

<APPLET CODE="TestHTML.class" WIDTH=800 HEIGHT=100>
  <B>Error! You must use a Java enabled browser.</B>
</APPLET>

</BODY>
</HTML>
```

Listing 19.33 `TestHTMLBottom.html`

```html
<!DOCTYPE HTML PUBLIC "-//W3C//DTD HTML 3.2//EN">
<HTML>
<HEAD>
  <TITLE>TestHTML</TITLE>
</HEAD>

<BODY BGCOLOR="WHITE">
<H1>TestHTML</H1>

This frame is named "bottom". If you want results to
appear here, use this name in the textfield above.

</BODY>
</HTML>
```

Using JSObject

For more flexible access to JavaScript from Java applets, use the `netscape.javascript.JSObject` class. This lets you use Java syntax to access all JavaScript objects, read and set all available properties, and call any legal method. Furthermore, you can use the `eval` method to invoke arbitrary JavaScript code when that is easier than using Java syntax. This process involves seven steps, as follows:

1. Obtain and install the `JSObject` class.
2. Import it in your applet.
3. From the applet, obtain a JavaScript reference to the current window.
4. Read the JavaScript properties of interest.
5. Set the JavaScript properties of interest.
6. Call the JavaScript methods of interest.
7. Give the applet permission to access its Web page.

Following are some details on these steps.

Obtain and install the JSObject class

This class is provided by Netscape along with Netscape Navigator. In Netscape 3.0, it is embedded inside an uncompressed zip file entitled `java_30` or `java_301`, depending on your browser version. The location of this file will vary among operating systems. On Windows 95, it should be in

```
NetscapeInstallPath\Program\Java\Classes\
```

Use "find" from your Start menu if you have trouble finding it. On Unix, this file will generally be in the Netscape installation directory. If you cannot find it, try the following

```
Unix> cd /usr/local
Unix> find . -name java_30 -print
```

Once you have this file, you simply need to add it to the end of your CLASSPATH; the Java compiler knows how to look inside zip files already. If you do this, be sure to unset CLASSPATH before trying to use appletviewer; it will not function properly otherwise. In fact, since both Netscape and Internet Explorer grant special privileges to classes that appear in the CLASSPATH, it is best to unset the CLASSPATH before starting any browser. If you prefer, you can copy the zip file, unzip the copy, extract the JSObject.class file, and install it separately. You will *need* to do this if you develop and compile your code on a system that does not have Netscape installed. Of course, Netscape is required to run the applets you create, but that might not be on the same machine as the development system. In Netscape 4, the file is called java40.jar.

Import it in your applet
At the top of your applet code, add the line:

```
import netscape.javascript.JSObject;
```

From the applet, obtain a JavaScript reference to the current window
Use the static getWindow method of JSObject to obtain a reference to the window containing the applet.

```
JSObject window =
    JSObject.getWindow(this); // this=applet
```

A complete list of the available methods in the JSObject class is given at the end of this section.

Read the JavaScript properties of interest
Use the getMember method to read properties of the main JavaScript window. Then use getMember on the results to access properties of other JavaScript objects. For example,

```
JSObject document =
  (JSObject)window.getMember("document");
String cookies =
  (String)document.cookie;
JSObject someForm =
  (JSObject)document.getMember("someFormName");
JSObject someElement =
  (JSObject)someForm.getMember("someElementName");
```

You can also use `getSlot` with an index to access elements of an array.

Set the JavaScript properties of interest
Use the `setMember` method for this. E.g.,

```
document.setMember("bgColor", "red");
someElement.setMember("value", "textfield value");
```

Note that the second argument to `setMember` must be a Java `Object`, so primitive objects must be converted to their corresponding wrapper type before being passed. Thus, an `int` named `intValue` must be turned into an `Integer` via `new Integer(intValue)` before being assigned to a property expecting an integer. An alternative is to construct a string corresponding to the assignment in JavaScript, then pass that string to `eval` (see below).

Call the JavaScript methods of interest
JavaScript methods are called using either the `call` method or by constructing a JavaScript expression containing the method calls and passing it to `eval`. The `call` method takes the method name and an array of arguments; `eval` takes a single string. For instance,

```
String[] message = { "An alert message" };
window.call("alert", message);
window.eval("alert('An alert message')");
```

Give the applet permission to access its Web page
To prevent Web page authors from accidentally using applets that read or modify their pages (perhaps reporting results over the network), the Web page author must explicitly give the applet permission to access the page. This is done via the `MAYSCRIPT` attribute of the `APPLET` element. For example,

```
<APPLET CODE=... WIDTH=... HEIGHT=... MAYSCRIPT>
  ...
</APPLET>
```

Example: Matching Applet Background with Web Page

One of the problems with writing general-purpose applets is that they don't have access to the background color of the Web page that contains them, so they can't adapt their color to match. A common solution is to supply the background color as a PARAM entry, but this has the drawback that the color has to be repeated (once in the BODY tag, and again in the PARAM), risking inconsistency if one is updated without the other. With LiveConnect, the applet can read the background color from the Document object and set its color automatically. Listings 19.34 and 19.35 give an example.

Listing 19.34 `MatchColor.java`

```
import java.applet.Applet;
import java.awt.*;
import netscape.javascript.JSObject;

public class MatchColor extends Applet {
  public void init() {
    JSObject window =
      JSObject.getWindow(this); // this=applet
    JSObject document =
      (JSObject)window.getMember("document");
    // E.g. "#ff0000" for red
    String pageColor =
      (String)document.getMember("bgColor");
    // E.g. parseInt("ff0000", 16) --> 16711680
    int bgColor =
      Integer.parseInt(pageColor.substring(1, 7), 16);
    setBackground(new Color(bgColor));
  }
}
```

Listing 19.35 `MatchColor.html`

```
<!DOCTYPE HTML PUBLIC "-//W3C//DTD HTML 3.2//EN">
<HTML>
<HEAD>
  <TITLE>MatchColor</TITLE>
</HEAD>

<BODY BGCOLOR="RED">
<H1>MatchColor</H1>

<APPLET CODE="MatchColor.class" WIDTH=300 HEIGHT=300
        MAYSCRIPT>
</APPLET>

</BODY>
</HTML>
```

Example: An Applet that Controls HTML Form Values

For a more extensive example, Listing 19.36 creates a page that lets users select mountain climbing trips based upon two criteria: the altitude they want to attain and the budget they want to stay within. On any platform, users can enter these two values directly in the HTML form and submit them to get information on available options. On Netscape 3 and 4, however, a notification is inserted that the attached applet (Listing 19.37) can be used to control the form values. Moving the cost slider changes the value displayed in the HTML form, while moving the mouse up and down the mountain changes the value displayed in the altitude form. Figure 19–49 shows the result after dragging the slider and moving the mouse partway up the mountain.

Listing 19.36 `Everest.html`

```
<!DOCTYPE HTML PUBLIC "-//W3C//DTD HTML 3.2//EN">
<HTML>
<HEAD>
  <TITLE>Design Your Trek!</TITLE>
</HEAD>

<BODY>

<APPLET CODE="Everest.class" WIDTH=400 HEIGHT=600
        MAYSCRIPT ALIGN="LEFT">
</APPLET>

<H1 ALIGN="CENTER">Design Your Trek!</H1>
To see a listing of the treks that interest you,
enter the desired altitude (up to 29,000 feet)
and the maximum cost you think your budget can afford.
Then choose "Show Treks" below. We'll show a list
of all planned High Peaks Travel expeditions that
are under that price and reach the desired altitude
or higher.
<P>

<SCRIPT LANGUAGE="JavaScript1.1">
<!--

if (navigator.appName == "Netscape")
  document.writeln
    ("You can enter values directly in the\n" +
     "textfields. Alternatively, select a cost\n" +
     "with the slider. Also, clicking the mouse on\n" +
     "the mountain peak will set the altitude.");

// -->
</SCRIPT>

<CENTER>
<FORM ACTION="cgi-bin/trekOptions"
      NAME="highPeaksForm">
<B>Desired Altitude:</B>
<INPUT TYPE="TEXT" NAME="altitudeField">
<BR>
<B>Maximum Cost:</B>
<INPUT TYPE="TEXT" NAME="costField">
<BR>
<INPUT TYPE="SUBMIT" VALUE="Show Treks">
</FORM>
</CENTER>

</BODY>
</HTML>
```

Listing 19.37 `Everest.java`

```java
import java.applet.Applet;
import java.awt.*;
import netscape.javascript.JSObject;

/** An applet that draws a mountain image and displays
 *  a slider. Dragging the slider changes a textfield
 *  in the HTML file containing the applet. Moving the
 *  mouse over the image changes another textfield in the
 *  containing HTML file, using an altitude value
 *  where the bottom of the applet corresponds to 0
 *  and the top to 29000 feet. This requires
 *  an HTML file with a form named "highPeaksForm"
 *  containing two text fields: one named "costField"
 *  and one named "altitudeField". It also requires use
 *  of the MAYSCRIPT tag in the <APPLET ...> declaration.
 *  <B>Works only in Netscape, in version 3.0
 *  or later.</B>.
 */

public class Everest extends Applet {
  private Image mountain;
  private JSObject window, document, highPeaksForm,
          costField, altitudeField;
  private int width, height;

  public void init() {
    setBackground(Color.lightGray);
    mountain = getImage(getCodeBase(),
                      "images/peak5.gif");
    width = size().width;
    height = size().height;
    // Start image loading immediately
    prepareImage(mountain, width, height, this);
    setLayout(new BorderLayout());
    Font sliderFont =
      new Font("Helvetica", Font.BOLD, 18);
    LabeledCostSlider costSlider =
      new LabeledCostSlider("Specify a maximum cost:",
                            sliderFont,
                            2000, 20000, 5000,
                            this);
    add("South", costSlider);
```

continued

Listing 19.37 `Everest.java` (continued)

```java
      // Get references to HTML textfields via JavaScript
      window = JSObject.getWindow(this); // this=applet
      document =
        (JSObject)window.getMember("document");
      highPeaksForm =
        (JSObject)document.getMember("highPeaksForm");
      costField =
        (JSObject)highPeaksForm.getMember("costField");
      altitudeField =
        (JSObject)highPeaksForm.getMember("altitudeField");
      setCostField(5000);
      setAltitudeField(15000);
  }

  public void paint(Graphics g) {
    g.drawImage(mountain, 0, 0, width, height, this);
  }

  /** When user moves the mouse, scale the y value
   *   from 29000 (top) to 0 (bottom) and send it
   *   to external textfield through JavaScript.
   */

  public boolean mouseMove(Event event, int x, int y) {
    setAltitudeField((height - y) * 29000 / height);
    return(true);
  }

  /** Change textfield via JavaScript. */

  public void setCostField(int val) {
    costField.setMember("value",
                        String.valueOf(val));
  }

  /** Change textfield via JavaScript. */

  private void setAltitudeField(int val) {
    altitudeField.setMember("value",
                            String.valueOf(val));
  }
}
```

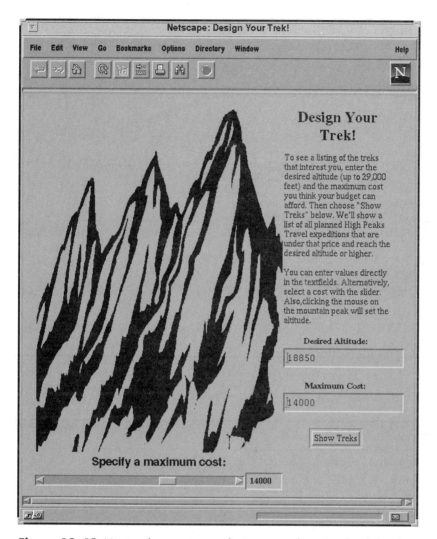

Figure 19–49 Moving the mouse over the image or dragging the slider changes the values in the HTML textfields.

The "Everest" applet makes use of a `LabeledCostSlider` (shown in the bottom left region of Figure 19–49). Source for this extension to `Slider` is given in Listings 19.38 and 19.39.

Listing 19.38 `LabeledCostSlider.java`

```java
import java.awt.*;

/** A CostSlider with a label centered above it. */

public class LabeledCostSlider extends Panel {
  public LabeledCostSlider(String labelString,
                           Font labelFont,
                           int minValue, int maxValue,
                           int initialValue,
                           Everest app) {
    setLayout(new BorderLayout());
    Label label = new Label(labelString, Label.CENTER);
    if (labelFont != null)
      label.setFont(labelFont);
    add("North", label);
    CostSlider slider =
      new CostSlider(minValue, maxValue, initialValue,
                     app);
    add("Center", slider);
  }
}
```

`CostSlider` is a simple variation of the `Slider` class developed in Section 13.12.

Listing 19.39 `CostSlider.java`

```java
/** A Slider that takes an Everest applet as an
 *  argument, calling back to its setCostField when
 *  the slider value changes.
 */

public class CostSlider extends Slider {
  private Everest app;

  public CostSlider(int minValue, int maxValue,
                    int initialValue, Everest app) {
    super(minValue, maxValue, initialValue);
    this.app = app;
  }

  public void doAction(int value) {
    app.setCostField(value);
  }
}
```

Methods in the JSObject Class

The following summarizes the methods available as part of JSObject. JSObject is final, so cannot be subclassed.

public Object call(String methodName, Object[ ] args)
This lets you call the JavaScript method of the specified name.

public Object eval(String javaScriptCode)
This lets you evaluate an arbitrary JavaScript expression.

public Object getMember(String propertyName)
This returns a property value. Cast the result to the appropriate type.

public Object getSlot(int arrayIndex)
This returns an array value. Cast the result to the appropriate type.

public static JSObject getWindow(Applet applet)
This *static* method retrieves the JavaScript Window corresponding to the one holding the applet.

public void removeMember(String propertyName)
This deletes a property.

public void setMember(String propertyName, Object value)
This assigns a value to the specified property.

public void setSlot(int arrayIndex, Object value)
This places a value in the specified location in the array.

19.11 Summary

This chapter introduced JavaScript and gave examples of the main ways in which JavaScript can be applied to

- Customize Web pages based on the situation
- Make pages more dynamic
- Validate CGI forms
- Manipulate cookies
- Control frames
- Integrate Java and JavaScript

This chapter did not, however, give a complete description of Window, Document, Navigator and other standard classes. The Quick Reference given in the next chapter provides this.

JAVASCRIPT QUICK REFERENCE

Topics in This Chapter

- Objects corresponding to the browser and its environment: Navigator, Plug in, Screen, and similar high-level objects.

- Objects corresponding to HTML elements: Window, Document, Layer, Image, and similar objects directly associated with specific markup elements.

- Objects corresponding to HTML forms and input elements: Form, Text, Button, Select, and similar objects used in CGI input forms.

- Internal data structures: String, Array, Function, Math, Date, and similar utility libraries.

- Regular expressions: RegExp.

Chapter 20

The previous chapter introduced JavaScript and gave examples of its use. This chapter gives a quick description of all of the constructors, properties, methods, and event handlers in each of the major JavaScript 1.0, 1.1, and 1.2 objects. Each entry is tagged by the version of JavaScript in which it first became available.

20.1 The Array Object

This object was added to JavaScript in Netscape 3.0. It is available in Netscape 3 and 4 and Internet Explorer 3.

Constructors

new Array() [JavaScript 1.1]
This builds a new zero-length array. Adding an element to a specified index will change the length automatically. For example,

```
var a = new Array(); // a.length = 0
a[12] = "foo";       // a.length = 13
```

new Array(length) [JavaScript 1.1]

This builds an array with indices from 0 to `length-1`. All the values will initially be `null`.

new Array(entry0, entry1, ... , entryN) [JavaScript 1.1]

This creates an array of length *N* containing the specified elements.

[entry0, entry1, ... , entryN] [JavaScript1.2]

JavaScript 1.2 lets you create arrays using "literal" notation. For example, the following two statements create equivalent arrays.

```
var a1 = new Array("foo", "bar", "baz"); // JS 1.1
var a2 = [ "foo", "bar", "baz" ];        // JS 1.2
```

Properties

length [JavaScript 1.1]

This gives the number of elements in the array. It is one greater than the index of the last element, and is read/write. If you set `length` smaller, array elements beyond that point are lost. If you set `length` bigger, array elements beyond the old length have the special `undefined` value (which compares == to `null`).

Methods

concat(secondArray) [JavaScript 1.2]

This returns a new array formed by concatenating the current array with the specified array.

join() [JavaScript 1.1]

This returns a single large string made up of converting all the array elements to strings then concatenating the results.

join(delimiterString) [JavaScript 1.1]

This is similar to `join()` except that it inserts the delimiter string between each element (but not at the beginning or end).

reverse() [JavaScript 1.1]

This changes the existing array so that the elements now appear in the opposite order. It does *not* create a new array.

slice(startIndex) [JavaScript 1.2]
slice(startIndex, endIndex) [JavaScript 1.2]

This returns a new array formed by extracting the elements from `startIndex` (inclusive) to `endIndex` (exclusive).

sort() [JavaScript 1.1]

This puts the array in alphabetical order. It does not create a new array.

sort(comparisonFunction) [JavaScript 1.1]

This puts the array in the order specified by the comparison function. This function should take two array elements as arguments, returning a negative number if the arguments are in order (the first is "less" than the second), zero if they are in order but would also be if swapped (the first is "equal to" the second in sorting value), and a positive number if they are out of order (the second is "less" than the first). For example, here is a comparison function that takes two `Car` objects and compares their `maxSpeed` properties.

```
function slower(car1, car2) {
  return(car1.maxSpeed - car2.maxSpeed);
}
```

Listing 20.1 uses this to create an array of `Car` objects and then sort it based on their `maxSpeed` property. Figure 20–1 shows the result.

Listing 20.1 `Sort.html`

```
<!DOCTYPE HTML PUBLIC "-//W3C//DTD HTML 3.2//EN">
<HTML>
<HEAD>
  <TITLE>Sorting</TITLE>

<SCRIPT LANGUAGE="JavaScript">
<!--

function makeObjectTable(name, object) {
  document.writeln
    ("<H2>" + name + "</H2>");
  document.writeln
    ("<TABLE BORDER=1>\n" +
    "  <TR><TH>Field<TH>Value");
  for(field in object)
```
continued

Listing 20.1 `Sort.html` (continued)

```
    document.writeln
       ("   <TR><TD>" + field + "<TD>" + object[field]);
  document.writeln
     ("</TABLE>");
}

// -->
</SCRIPT>
</HEAD>

<BODY>
<H1>Sorting</H1>

<SCRIPT LANGUAGE="JavaScript">
<!--

function carString() {
  return("Car{" + this.maxSpeed + "}");
}

function Car(maxSpeed) {
  this.maxSpeed = maxSpeed;
  this.toString = carString;
}

function slower(car1, car2) {
  return(car1.maxSpeed - car2.maxSpeed);
}

var cars = new Array(new Car(10), new Car(20),
                     new Car(30), new Car(25),
                     new Car(15), new Car(5));

makeObjectTable("Original Car Array", cars);

cars.sort(slower);

makeObjectTable("Sorted Array (slow to fast)", cars);

// -->
</SCRIPT>

</BODY>
</HTML>
```

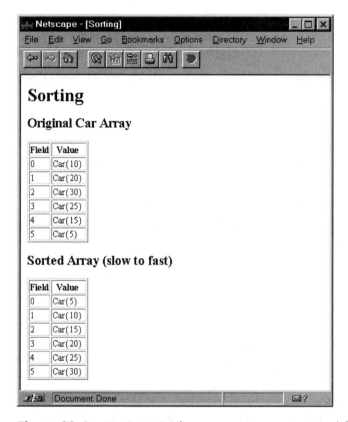

Figure 20–1 JavaScript 1.1 lets you sort arrays using user-defined ordering functions.

Event Handlers

None.

20.2 The Button Object

The Button object corresponds to form elements created via

```
<INPUT TYPE="BUTTON" ...>
```

Most of its characteristics are shared by elements created via

```
<INPUT TYPE="SUBMIT" ...>
<INPUT TYPE="RESET" ...>
```

However, SUBMIT and RESET buttons have more specific types; Submit and Reset respectively. A Button is typically accessed either through the elements array of the corresponding Form, or, if both the form and the button are named, via document.formName.buttonName.

Properties

form [JavaScript 1.0]
This gives the Form object containing the button. It is read only.

name [JavaScript 1.0]
If the button used the NAME attribute, this property retrieves it. It is read only.

type [JavaScript 1.1]
For pure Button objects, this property is always equal to "button". For SUBMIT and RESET buttons, the type will be "submit" and "reset", respectively. In JavaScript 1.1 and later, all Element objects contain the type property, so it can be used to distinguish among the element types. It is read only.

value [JavaScript 1.0]
This gives the label of the button and, for SUBMIT buttons, is transmitted with the button name when the button is used to trigger form submission. It is read/write.

Methods

blur() [JavaScript 1.1]
This removes the keyboard focus from the button.

click() [JavaScript 1.0]
This acts as though the button was clicked, but without triggering the onClick handler. For SUBMIT and RESET buttons, you can use the form's submit and reset methods instead of this.

focus() [JavaScript 1.1]

This gives the keyboard focus to the button.

Event Handlers

onblur() [JavaScript 1.1]

This method is called when the button loses the input focus. It is normally set via the `onBlur` attribute, as below.

```
<INPUT TYPE="BUTTON" ...
       onBlur="doSomeAction()">
```

onclick() [JavaScript 1.0]

This method is called when the user clicks on the button, but not when the `click` method is called programmatically. It is normally set via the `onClick` attribute.

```
<INPUT TYPE="BUTTON" ...
       onClick="doSomeAction()">
```

If you return `false` from this method, then any additional action the button would trigger (i.e. submitting or resetting the form) is suppressed. For example,

```
<INPUT TYPE="RESET" ...
       onClick="return(maybeReset())">
```

The same effect can be achieved by the `onSubmit` and `onReset` handlers on the form containing the button.

ondblclick() [JavaScript 1.2]

This Netscape 4 method is called on the second click of a double click. The `onclick` handler, if any, will be called first. It is set by the `onDblClick` attribute and is not supported on the Macintosh.

onfocus() [JavaScript 1.1]

This method is called when the button gains the input focus. It is normally set via the `onFocus` attribute.

20.3 The Checkbox Object

The Checkbox object corresponds to form elements created via

```
<INPUT TYPE="CHECKBOX" ...>
```

A Checkbox is typically accessed either through the elements array of the corresponding Form, or, if both the form and the checkbox are named, via document.formName.checkboxName.

Properties

checked [JavaScript 1.0]
This is a Boolean specifying whether or not the box is currently checked. It is read/write.

defaultChecked [JavaScript 1.0]
This is a Boolean specifying whether or not the box should be initially set. It is set via the CHECKED attribute, and is read only.

form [JavaScript 1.0]
This refers to the Form object containing the checkbox. It is read only.

name [JavaScript 1.0]
This gives the name of the checkbox as given in the NAME attribute. It is read only.

type [JavaScript 1.1]
This property contains the string "checkbox". Since all Element objects have this property, it can be used to differentiate among them when looking at the form.elements array. It is read only.

value [JavaScript 1.0]
This gives the value that will be sent with the name to the CGI program if the form is submitted when the box is checked. It is read/write.

Methods

blur() [JavaScript 1.1]
This removes the keyboard focus from the checkbox.

click() [JavaScript 1.0]

This acts as though the checkbox was clicked, but without triggering the `onClick` handler.

focus() [JavaScript 1.1]

This gives the keyboard focus to the checkbox.

Event Handlers

onblur() [JavaScript 1.1]

This method is called when the checkbox loses the input focus. It is normally set via the `onBlur` attribute, as below.

```
<INPUT TYPE="CHECKBOX" ...
        onBlur="doSomeAction()">
```

onclick() [JavaScript 1.0]

This method is called when the user clicks on the checkbox, but not when the `click` method is called programmatically. It is usually specified via the `onClick` attribute of the input element.

onfocus() [JavaScript 1.1]

This method is called when the checkbox gains the input focus. It is normally set via the `onFocus` attribute.

20.4 The Date Object

This object is used to create and manipulate dates and times. It is very unreliable in Netscape 2.0. Internet Explorer 3 cannot represent dates prior to 1970.

Constructors

new Date() [JavaScript 1.0]

This creates a `Date` object for the current time.

new Date(year, month, day, hrs, mins, secs) [JavaScript 1.0]

This creates a `Date` object for the specified time.

new Date(year, month, day) [JavaScript 1.0]
This creates a `Date` object for midnight on the morning of the specified day.

new Date("month day, year hrs:mins:secs") [JavaScript 1.0]
This creates a `Date` object from the given string. The month should be the full name, not a number. For example,

```
var bDay =
  new Date("January 30, 1962 00:00:00");
```

new Date(millisecondsSinceEpoch) [JavaScript 1.0]
This creates a `Date` object for the time corresponding to the specified number of milliseconds after midnight (GMT) on January 1, 1970.

Properties

None.

Methods

Note that `parseDate` and `UTC` are not really methods of `Date` objects, but instead act like static methods of the `Date` "class" (really constructor). They *must* be invoked as `Date.parseDate` and `Date.UTC`, respectively, never through an individual `Date` object. The other methods should be invoked via `someDateObject.method(args)`.

getDate() [JavaScript 1.0]
This returns the day of the month as an integer from 1 to 31.

getDay() [JavaScript 1.0]
This returns the day of the week as an integer from 0 (Sunday) to 6 (Saturday).

getHours() [JavaScript 1.0]
This returns the hour of the day as an integer from 0 to 23.

getMinutes() [JavaScript 1.0]
This returns the number of minutes past the hour given in `getHours`, specified as an integer from 0 to 59.

getMonth() [JavaScript 1.0]

This returns the month of the year as an integer from 0 (January) to 11 (December).

getSeconds() [JavaScript 1.0]

This returns the number of seconds past the minute given by get-Minutes. It is an integer from 0 to 59.

getTime() [JavaScript 1.0]

This returns the number of milliseconds after midnight January 1, 1970, GMT.

getTimezoneOffset() [JavaScript 1.0]

This gives the difference in *minutes* between GMT and the local time.

getYear() [JavaScript 1.0]

This returns the year. Netscape 2, 3, and 4 return only the last two digits for years in the 20th century, but the full year for dates in the 21st century. So they would return 97 for a Date in 1997 and 2001 for a Date in 2001. Internet Explorer returns 1900 minus the current year in all cases, so it would return 97 for a Date in 1997 and 101 for a Date in 2001.

parse(dateString) [JavaScript 1.0]

This is not really a method of Date objects, but rather a method named Date.parse. It *must* be invoked that way, not on a Date object. It takes a string in any of a variety of formats as input and returns the corresponding number of milliseconds after midnight, January 1, 1970. It understands the standard IETF date formats used on the Internet (and generated by toGMTString), so, for instance, the following generates "Wed Sep 03 11:30:00 1997" on systems on the U.S. east coast, which is in EDT (minus 4 hours offset from GMT).

```
// US Pacific Time
var dateString = "Wed, 3 Sep 1997 08:30:00 -0700";
var d1 = new Date(Date.parse(dateString));
// US Eastern Time
document.writeln(d1.toLocaleString());
```

It can also understand strings of the form "Month Day, Year", where the month is spelled out completely or the first three letters are used (upper or lower case). In the IETF format, you can also use U.S. time zone abbreviations (e.g., "EDT") instead of numeric offsets.

setDate(dayOfMonth) [JavaScript 1.0]
This changes the day of the month; see `getDate`.

setHours(hours) [JavaScript 1.0]
This changes the hours entry; see `getHours`.

setMinutes(minutes) [JavaScript 1.0]
This changes the minutes entry; see `getMinutes`.

setMonth(monthIndex) [JavaScript 1.0]
This changes the month entry; see `getMonth`.

setSeconds(seconds) [JavaScript 1.0]
This changes the seconds entry; see `getSeconds`.

setTime(millisecondsSinceEpoch) [JavaScript 1.0]
This completely changes the date; see `getTime`.

setYear(year) [JavaScript 1.0]
This changes the year entry. You can always use four-digit dates, even though `getYear` in Netscape returns two-digit dates for dates in the 1900s.

toGMTString() [JavaScript 1.0]
This generates a string representing the date in GMT. It is formatted using IETF conventions; see `parse`.

toLocaleString() [JavaScript 1.0]
This generates a string representing the date in the local time zone. It is formatted using local conventions.

UTC(year, month, day) [JavaScript 1.0]
UTC(year, month, day, hrs) [JavaScript 1.0]
UTC(year, month, day, hrs, mins) [JavaScript 1.0]
UTC(year, month, day, hrs, mins, secs) [JavaScript 1.0]
This is not really a method of `Date` objects, but rather a method named `Date.UTC`. It *must* be invoked that way, not on a `Date` object. It assumes that the input parameters are in GMT (also called UTC—Universal Coordinated Time) and returns the number of milliseconds since midnight, Jan 1, 1970, GMT.

Event Handlers

None. `Date` does not correspond to an HTML element.

20.5 The Document Object

Each `Window` object contains a `document` property referring to the document contained in the window. The top-level document is obtained via `window.document`, or, more commonly, simply by `document`.

Properties

alinkColor [JavaScript 1.0]

This string specifies the color of activated links. It is initially set by the `ALINK` attribute of `BODY`, and can only be modified by scripts that run in the `HEAD` of the document (which are parsed before the `BODY`). After that it is read only.

anchors [JavaScript 1.0]

This is intended to be an array of `Anchor` objects, one for each occurrence of `<A NAME=...>` in the document. However, in current browsers all array entries contain `null`.

applets [JavaScript 1.1]

This is an array of `Applet` objects, one for each occurrence of `<APPLET ...>` in the document. If the `APPLET` tag includes a `MAYSCRIPT` attribute, you can call the applet's methods directly from JavaScript. See Section 19.9 (Accessing Java from JavaScript) for an example.

bgColor [JavaScript 1.0]

This string specifies the background color of the document. It is initially set by the `BGCOLOR` attribute of `BODY`, but is read/write (anytime, not just in the `HEAD` as with other colors). For example,

```
document.bgColor = "red";
document.bgColor = "#00FF00"; // green
```

cookie [JavaScript 1.0]

This string is the value of the cookie associated with the document. It is read/write; setting the value has the side effect of changing the cookie stored by the browser. For more details, see Section 19.7 (Using Java-Script to Store and Examine Cookies).

domain [JavaScript 1.1]

This string specifies the Internet domain that the document came from. It is read only. JavaScript provides no standard way to find the domain or hostname of the *client* system (the one currently viewing the page), but you can do this in Netscape 3 and 4 with a little help from Java. See Section 19.9 (Accessing Java from JavaScript).

embeds [JavaScript 1.1]

This is an array of JavaObject corresponding to plug-in entries inside EMBED elements in the document. If the embedded object is not a Java-enabled plug in, you cannot do anything with it, but if it is, you can call its public methods. Synonymous with the plugins array.

fgColor [JavaScript 1.0]

This string specifies the foreground color of the document. It is initially set by the TEXT attribute of BODY, and can only be modified by scripts that run in the HEAD of the document. After that it is read only.

forms [JavaScript 1.0]

This is an array of Form objects, one for each occurrence of <FORM . . .> in the document. See Section 20.8 for more on Form.

images [JavaScript 1.1]

This is an array of Image objects, one for each occurrence of <IMG . . .> in the document. See Section 19.5 (Using JavaScript to Make Pages Dynamic) for examples.

lastModified [JavaScript 1.0]

This gives the date of the most recent change to the document. Inserting this information near the top of the document is useful for readers who visit a page repeatedly looking for new information. It is read only.

linkColor [JavaScript 1.0]

This string specifies the color of unvisited links. It is initially set via the LINK attribute of BODY, and can only be modified by scripts that run in the HEAD of the document. After that it is read only.

links [JavaScript 1.0]

This is an array of Link objects, one for each occurrence of <A HREF...> in the document.

location [JavaScript 1.0]

In JavaScript 1.0, this is a string giving the *actual* URL of the current document. This differs from the window.location property, which contains the *requested* URL, which might have been redirected. In JavaScript 1.1 and 1.2, this refers to the same Location object as window.location, and document.URL gives the actual URL. It is read only.

plugins [JavaScript 1.1]

This is a synonym for the embeds array. Note that the array contains objects of type JavaObject, not Plugin, and describes embedded plug ins in the current document, not plugins available to the browser. Use navigator.plugins to get an array describing the available plug ins.

referrer [JavaScript 1.0]

This string, possibly empty, gives the URL of the document that contained the link to the current one. It is read only.

title [JavaScript 1.0]

This gives the string specified via <TITLE>. It is read only.

URL [JavaScript 1.1]

This string gives the actual URL of the current document. It is read only.

vlinkColor [JavaScript 1.0]

This string specifies the color of visited hypertext links. It is initially set via the VLINK attribute of BODY, and can only be modified by scripts that run in the HEAD of the document. After that it is read only.

Methods

clear() [JavaScript 1.0]

In JavaScript 1.0, this erased the specified document. It should no longer be used; instead, `close` the current document and `open` a new one.

close() [JavaScript 1.0]

This closes the output stream to the specified document, displaying any results that haven't already been displayed. It is used when building new documents with `open`.

getSelection() [JavaScript 1.2]

This string gives the text contained in the selected area, if any.

open() [JavaScript 1.0]
open(mimeType) [JavaScript 1.0]
open(mimeType, "replace") [JavaScript 1.1]

This method is used to create a new document in the current window. The most common usage is simply to call `open()`, then use `write` and `writeln` to add the content. However, you can optionally specify a MIME type, as follows:

- `text/html`—for regular HTML; the default
- `text/plain`—for ASCII text with newline characters to delimit lines
- `image/gif`—for encoded bytes representing a GIF file
- `image/jpg`—for encoded bytes representing a JPEG file
- `image/x-bitmap`—for encoded bytes representing an X-bitmap
- *pluginName*—for loading into plug ins. For instance, specify `"x-world/vrml"`. Future `write/writeln` calls go to the plug in.

If `"replace"` is specified, the new document replaces the previous one in the history list. Otherwise a new history entry is created.

write(arg1, arg2, ... , argN) [JavaScript 1.0]
writeln(arg1, arg2, ... , argN) [JavaScript 1.0]
These methods send output to the document, with or without a trailing newline character.

Event Handlers

Technically, `Document` has none; the `onLoad` and `onUnload` attributes of `BODY` set the `onload` and `onunload` event handlers of the `Window` object, not the `Document`.

20.6 The Element Object

This object corresponds to a form element, and is contained in the `elements` array of the `Form` object. The form objects are accessible via the `document.forms` array or, if named, by `document.formName`. Rather than treating elements of the elements array as `Element` objects, it is usually better to treat them as `Button` objects, `Checkbox` objects, and so forth, based on their more specific types. In general, you should name objects and access them via their name, but in JavaScript 1.1 you can take an arbitrary `Element` and determine its more specific type by looking at the `type` property.

Properties

The following only lists the more specific type of `Element` that uses these properties. See the sections describing those objects for details on the properties.

checked [JavaScript 1.0]
This property is used by `Checkbox` and `Radio` objects.

defaultChecked [JavaScript 1.0]
This property is used by `Checkbox` and `Radio` objects.

defaultValue [JavaScript 1.0]
This is used by `FileUpload`, `Password`, `Text`, and `Textarea` objects.

form [JavaScript 1.0]

This property is used by all Element objects, and refers to the HTML form containing the element.

length [JavaScript 1.0]

This is used only by Select objects.

name [JavaScript 1.0]

This property is used by all Element objects and gives the value of the HTML NAME attribute.

options [JavaScript 1.0]

This is used only by Select objects.

selectedIndex [JavaScript 1.0]

This is used only by Select objects.

type [JavaScript 1.1]

In JavaScript 1.1, this is used by all Element objects and can be used to differentiate among element types. The value of this property will be one of "button", "checkbox", "file", "hidden", "password", "radio", "reset", "select-one", "select-multiple", "submit", "text", or "textarea".

value [JavaScript 1.0]

This property is used by all Element objects and gives the value that will be associated with the element's name when the form is submitted.

Methods

Again, the following only lists the more specific type of Element that uses these methods. See the sections describing those objects for more information on the methods.

blur() [JavaScript 1.1]

In JavaScript 1.1, this method is used by all Element types except Hidden.

click() [JavaScript 1.0]

This is used by Button, Checkbox, Radio, Reset, and Submit objects.

focus() [JavaScript 1.1]

In JavaScript 1.1, this method is used by all `Element` types except `Hidden`.

select() [JavaScript 1.0]

This is used by all elements that have textual values, namely `FileUpload`, `Password`, `Text`, and `Textarea`.

Event Handlers

Again, the following only lists the more specific type of `Element` that uses these methods.

onblur() [JavaScript 1.1]

This is used by all `Element` types except `Hidden`.

onchange() [JavaScript 1.0]

This is used by `FileUpload`, `Password`, `Text`, `Textarea`, and `Select` objects.

onclick() [JavaScript 1.0]

This is used by `Button`, `Checkbox`, `Radio`, `Reset`, and `Submit` objects.

ondblclick [JavaScript 1.2]

This is used by `Button`, `Reset`, and `Submit`.

onfocus() [JavaScript 1.1]

This is used by all `Element` types except `Hidden`.

20.7 The FileUpload Object

This object corresponds to form elements declared via

```
<INPUT TYPE="FILE" ...>
```

Objects of this type are generally accessed via the `elements` array of the `Form` object.

Properties

form [JavaScript 1.0]
This gives the Form object containing the element. It is read only.

name [JavaScript 1.0]
If the element used the NAME attribute, this property retrieves it. It is read only.

type [JavaScript 1.1]
This property is always equal to "file". In JavaScript1.1, all Element objects contain this property, so it can be used to distinguish among the various types. It is read only.

value [JavaScript 1.1]
This gives the string set in the VALUE attribute. It is read only.

Methods

blur() [JavaScript 1.1]
This removes the keyboard focus from the element.

focus() [JavaScript 1.1]
This gives the keyboard focus to the element.

select() [JavaScript 1.0]
This selects the text in the element. Any user entry will replace the existing text.

Event Handlers

None of these handlers is available in JavaScript 1.0.

onblur() [JavaScript 1.1]
This method is called when the element loses the input focus. It is normally set via the onBlur attribute, as follows:

```
<INPUT TYPE="FILE" ...
        onBlur="doSomeAction()">
```

onchange() [JavaScript 1.1]

This method is called when the element loses the focus after its value has been changed. It is normally set via the onChange attribute.

onfocus() [JavaScript 1.1]

This method is called when the element gains the input focus. It is normally set via the onFocus attribute.

20.8 The Form Object

Form objects correspond to elements created with the HTML FORM element. They are normally accessed from the document.forms array, or, if named, via document.formName.

Properties

action [JavaScript 1.0]

This string specifies the URL to which the form should be submitted. It is read/write.

elements [JavaScript 1.0]

This is an array of Element objects corresponding to the input elements contained in the HTML form. See Section 20.6 for information on Element.

encoding [JavaScript 1.0]

This string specifies the form's encoding method, as initially set by the ENCTYPE attribute. It is read/write.

method [JavaScript 1.0]

This string is either "get" or "post". It is initially set via the METHOD attribute, but is read/write.

target [JavaScript 1.0]

This string specifies the frame in which the form results should be displayed. It is initially set via the TARGET attribute, but is read/write.

Methods

reset() [JavaScript 1.1]

This calls `onreset`, then, if the return value is not `false`, restores all input elements to the values originally specified in the document. The result is the same as if a RESET button was pressed.

submit() [JavaScript 1.0]

This submits the form *without* first calling `onsubmit`.

Event Handlers

onreset() [JavaScript 1.1]

This method is called when the user presses a RESET button or the `reset` method is called. If the method returns `false`, the form is not reset. It is normally specified via the `onReset` attribute, as follows:

```
<FORM ACTION="..." ...
      onReset="return(maybeReset())">
```

onsubmit() [JavaScript 1.0]

This method is called when the user presses a SUBMIT button. It is *not* automatically called by `submit`. If the method returns `false`, the form is not submitted. It is normally specified via the `onSubmit` attribute, as follows:

```
<FORM ACTION="..." ...
      onSubmit="return(validateEntries())">
```

For an example, see Section 19.6 (Using JavaScript to Validate CGI Forms).

20.9 The Function Object

This object corresponds to a JavaScript function, not to any HTML element.

Constructor

new Function(arg0Name, ... , argNName, bodyString) [JavaScript 1.1]

This builds a new function. For instance, the following two forms have the same effect, but the second can be performed inside another routine at run-time.

```
function square(x) { return(x * x); }
square = new Function("x", "return(x * x)");
```

Properties

arguments [JavaScript 1.0]

From within the body of a function, this gives an array of arguments used to call the function. This can be used to create variable-argument functions. For example, the following function adds any number of values together.

```
function sum() {
  var total = 0;
  for(var i=0; i<arguments.length; i++)
    total = total + arguments[i];
  return(total);
}
```

arity [JavaScript 1.2]

This gives the number of arguments a function expects. This may be different than the number it is actually called with, which is given from within the body by the `length` property. It is read only.

caller [JavaScript 1.0]

From within the body of a function, this gives the `Function` that called this one. The value is `null` if the function was called at the top level. It is read only.

prototype [JavaScript 1.0]
For constructors, this defines properties that are shared by all objects of the specified type. For an example, see Section 19.3 (Basic JavaScript Syntax).

Methods

None other than those defined for every `Object`.

Event Handlers

None. `Function` does not correspond to an HTML element.

20.10 The Hidden Object

This object corresponds to elements created via

```
<INPUT TYPE="HIDDEN" ...>
```

Objects of this type are usually accessed via the `elements` property of `Form`, or, if both the form and the hidden element are named, via `document.formName.elementName`.

Properties

form [JavaScript 1.0]
This refers to the `Form` object that holds this element. It is read only.

name [JavaScript 1.0]
This gives the name of the element, as specified by the `NAME` attribute. It is read only.

type [JavaScript 1.1]
This property contains the value `"hidden"`. It is read only.

value [JavaScript 1.0]
This gives the string that will be sent along with the name when the form is submitted. It is read/write.

Methods

None.

Event Handlers

None.

20.11 The History Object

This object corresponds to the current window or frame's list of previously visited URLs. It is accessible through the `history` property of `Window`, which can be accessed via `window.history` or just `history`.

Properties

current [JavaScript 1.1]
This property is a string specifying the URL of the current document. It is available only when "data tainting" has been enabled. Data tainting means that you have explicitly allowed access to your page by setting the `NS_ENABLE_TAINT` environment variable. It is read only.

length [JavaScript 1.0]
This gives the number of URLs contained in the history list. It is read only.

next [JavaScript 1.1]
This string specifies the URL of the next document in the history list. It is available only when "data tainting" has been enabled. It is read only.

previous [JavaScript 1.1]
This string specifies the URL of the next document in the history list. It is available only when "data tainting" has been enabled. It is read only.

Methods

back() [JavaScript 1.0]
This instructs the browser to go back one entry in the history list.

forward() [JavaScript 1.0]
This instructs the browser to go forward one entry in the history list.

go(n) [JavaScript 1.0]
This instructs the browser to go *n* entries forward (if *n* is positive) or backward (if *n* is negative) in the history list. Unfortunately, this is not implemented reliably. In Internet Explorer, *n* must be –1, 0, or 1, so provides no advantage over back and forward. In Netscape 3, go works incorrectly with frames, although it works properly for the top-level window.

toString() [JavaScript 1.1]
In Netscape 3, this returns an HTML table describing the history list, but *only* if data tainting is enabled.

Event Handlers

None. History does not correspond directly to an HTML element on the page.

20.12 The Image Object

This object corresponds to HTML elements inserted via <IMG SRC="..." ...>. An Image object is accessed via the document.images array, or, if the image is named, via document.imageName. Manipulating images via JavaScript is an important capability; see Section 19.5 (Using JavaScript to Make Pages Dynamic) for examples. However, support for this object is inconsistent across platforms. It is fully supported by Netscape 3 and 4. It is unsupported in Netscape 2. Internet Explorer 3.02 supports it on Macintosh systems, but not on Windows. If you want to write portable code that manipulates images on platforms that support it and does nothing (but without error messages) on other platforms, you should insert something akin to the following in a script in the HEAD of your document.

```
imagesSupported = (document["images"] != null);
```

Then, you can wrap all of your image-manipulation code inside a test like the following:

```
if (imagesSupported) { ... }
```

Constructor

new Image(width, height) [JavaScript 1.1]

This allocates a new `Image` object of the specified size. The main purpose for this is to then set its `src` property in order to preload images that will be used later. In such an application, the `Image` object is never actually used after its `src` is set; the purpose is to get the *browser* to cache the image. See Section 19.5 (Using JavaScript to Make Pages Dynamic) for an example of this.

Properties

border [JavaScript 1.1]

This gives the size of the border around images that appear inside hypertext links. It is specified via the `BORDER` attribute of the `IMG` element. It is read only.

complete [JavaScript 1.1]

This is a boolean that determines if the image has finished loading. It is read only.

height [JavaScript 1.1]

This gives the height of the image either as specified via the `HEIGHT` attribute (if present) or as it is in the actual image file. It is read only.

hspace [JavaScript 1.1]

This gives the number of empty pixels on the left and right of the image as given in the `HSPACE` attribute. It is read only.

lowsrc [JavaScript 1.1]

Netscape (but not Internet Explorer) supports the nonstandard `LOWSRC` attribute in the `IMG` element. This gives an alternate image to show on low-resolution displays. This property gives that value (as a string). It is read/write.

name [JavaScript 1.1]

This gives the name of the image as given by the `NAME` attribute. It is read only.

src [JavaScript 1.1]

This property gives a string representing the URL of the image file. It is read/write.

vspace [JavaScript 1.1]

This gives the number of empty pixels on the top and bottom of the image as given in the VSPACE attribute. It is read only.

width [JavaScript 1.1]

This gives the width of the image either as specified via the HEIGHT attribute (if present) or as it is in the actual image file. It is read only.

Methods

None.

Event Handlers

onabort() [JavaScript 1.1]

This method is called when the user halts image loading by pressing the "Stop" button or clicking on a hypertext link to go to another page. It is normally specified via the onAbort attribute, as below.

```
<IMG SRC="..." ...
      onAbort="takeSomeAction()">
```

onerror() [JavaScript 1.1]

This method is called when the image file cannot be found or is in illegal format. It is normally specified by the onError attribute, as follows:

```
<IMG SRC="..." ...
      onAbort="alert('Error loading image')">
```

Supplying a value of null will suppress error messages, as in this example.

```
<IMG SRC="..." ...
      onAbort="null">
```

onload() [JavaScript 1.1]

This method is called when the browser *finishes* loading the image. Every time the src is changed, this method is called again. It is normally set via the onLoad attribute, as follows:

```
<IMG SRC="..." ...
      onLoad="startImageAnimation()">
```

In an example like this, the startImageAnimation would change the src to a new image (perhaps after a fixed pause), which, when done, would trigger startImageAnimation all over again.

20.13 The JavaObject Object

A JavaObject is a JavaScript representation of either a real Java object (an applet) or a plug in from the document.embeds array that is treated as a Java object. There are no predefined properties or methods, but you can use for/in to look at the specific properties of any particular JavaObject. This is an interesting capability, given that you cannot do that directly in Java prior to Java 1.1.

20.14 The JavaPackage Object

Objects of this type are accessed through the java, netscape, sun, and Packages properties of Window. They can be used to access Java objects; for instance you can call java.lang.System.getProperty. For an example, see Section 19.9 (Accessing Java from JavaScript).

20.15 The Layer Object

Netscape 4.0 supports layered HTML; HTML in separate, possibly overlapping regions. They can be defined using the LAYER or ILAYER element (Section 5.13) or via cascading style sheets (Section 5.14). JavaScript 1.2 can access and manipulate layers; see Section 19.5 (Using JavaScript to Make Pages Dynamic) for examples.

Constructors

new Layer(width) [JavaScript 1.2]
This creates a new Layer object. You can specify its contents by setting the src property or by using the load method.

new Layer(width, parentLayer) [JavaScript 1.2]
This builds a layer that is a child of the one specified.

Properties

above [JavaScript 1.2]
This specifies the layer above the current one. It is read only.

background [JavaScript 1.2]
This specifies the image to use for the layer of the background. It is read/write. For example,

```
someLayer.background.src = "bricks.gif";
```

below [JavaScript 1.2]
This specifies the layer below the current one. It is read only.

bgColor [JavaScript 1.2]
Layers are normally transparent, but the bgColor property can make them opaque. It is read/write. For instance,

```
someLayer.bgColor = "blue";
anotherLayer.bgColor = "#FF00FF";
thirdLayer.bgColor = null; // transparent
```

clip [JavaScript 1.2]
This defines the clipping rectangle, and is composed of clip.top, clip.bottom, clip.left, clip.right, clip.width, and clip.height. It is read/write.

document [JavaScript 1.2]
Each layer contains its own Document object. This property references it. It is read only.

name [JavaScript 1.2]
This gives the layer name as specified via the ID or NAME attributes. It is read only.

left [JavaScript 1.2]
This is the horizontal position of the layer with respect to the parent layer or, for floating layers, with respect to the natural document flow position. It is read/write.

pageX [JavaScript 1.2]

This is the absolute horizontal position of the layer in the page. It is read/write.

pageY [JavaScript 1.2]

This is the absolute vertical position of the layer in the page. It is read/write.

parentLayer [JavaScript 1.2]

This yields the enclosing layer, if there is one. Otherwise it returns the enclosing `Window` object. It is read only.

siblingAbove [JavaScript 1.2]

Of the layers that share the same parent as the current one, this is the one directly above the current one. It is read only.

siblingBelow [JavaScript 1.2]

Of the layers that share the same parent as the current one, this is the one directly below the current one. It is read only.

src [JavaScript 1.2]

This gives a URL specifying the content of the layer. It is read/write.

top [JavaScript 1.2]

This is the vertical position of the layer with respect to the parent layer or, for floating layers, with respect to the natural document flow position. It is read/write.

visibility [JavaScript 1.2]

This determines the layer's visibility. Legal values are `"show"` (layer is visible), `"hide"` or `"hidden"` (layer is invisible), or `"inherit"` (use parent's visibility). It is read/write.

zIndex [JavaScript 1.2]

This specifies the stacking order relative to sibling layers. Lower numbers are underneath; higher numbers on top. It is read/write.

Methods

load(sourceString, width) [JavaScript 1.2]
This changes the source of the layer while simultaneously changing its width. See the `src` property.

moveAbove(layer) [JavaScript 1.2]
This stacks the current layer above the one specified.

moveBelow(layer) [JavaScript 1.2]
This stacks the current layer below the one specified.

moveBy(dx, dy) [JavaScript 1.2]
This changes the layer's location by the specified number of pixels.

moveTo(x, y) [JavaScript 1.2]
This moves the layer so that its top-left corner is at the specified location in the containing layer or document. See the `left` and `top` properties.

moveToAbsolute(x, y) [JavaScript 1.2]
This moves the layer so that its top-left corner is at the specified location in the window. See the `pageX` and `pageY` properties.

resizeBy(dWidth, dHeight) [JavaScript 1.2]
This changes the layer's width and height by the specified number of pixels. See the `clip.width` and `clip.height` properties.

resizeTo(width, height) [JavaScript 1.2]
This changes the layer's width and height to the specified size in pixels. See the `clip.width` and `clip.height` properties.

Event Handlers

onblur() [JavaScript 1.2]
This is called when the layer loses the keyboard focus. It is specified via the `onBlur` attribute of `LAYER` or `ILAYER`. If the layer is created with style sheets, you have to set this by directly assigning a function, as below.

```
function blurHandler() { ... }
someLayer.onblur = blurHandler;
```

onfocus() [JavaScript 1.2]
This is called when the layer gets the keyboard focus. It is normally specified by the onFocus attribute.

onload() [JavaScript 1.2]
This is called when the layer is loaded (which may be before it is displayed). It is normally specified by the onLoad attribute.

onmouseout() [JavaScript 1.2]
This is called when the mouse moves off of the layer. It is normally specified through the use of the onMouseOut attribute.

onmouseover() [JavaScript 1.2]
This is called when the mouse moves onto the layer. It is normally specified through the use of the onMouseOver attribute.

20.16 The Link Object

This object corresponds to a hypertext link created via <A HREF=...>. In JavaScript 1.2, or in JavaScript 1.1 on non-Windows platforms, the AREA client-side image map element also results in Link objects. Links are normally accessed via the document.links array. You cannot name links via the NAME attribute, since using NAME inside an A element creates an anchor for internal hypertext links.

Properties

hash [JavaScript 1.0]
This gives the "section" part of the hypertext reference, and includes the leading "#" (hash mark). It is read/write.

host [JavaScript 1.0]
This returns a string of the form "hostname:port". It is read/write.

hostname [JavaScript 1.0]
This returns the hostname. It is read/write.

href [JavaScript 1.0]
This gives the complete URL. It is read/write.

pathname [JavaScript 1.0]

This gives the part of the URL that came after the host and port. It is read/write.

port [JavaScript 1.0]

This is a *string* (not integer) specifying the port. It is read/write.

protocol [JavaScript 1.0]

This specifies the protocol. The colon is included as part of this property. It is read/write.

search [JavaScript 1.0]

This gives the search part (i.e. `"?x,y"` from an `ISMAP` entry) or query part (i.e. `"?x=1&y=2"` from a form submission) of the URL. It is read/write.

target [JavaScript 1.0]

This gives the name given as the value of the `TARGET` attribute. It is read/write. For instance, to redirect all hypertext links to a frame named `frame1`, you could do the following:

```
for(var i=0; i<document.links.length; i++)
  document.links[i].target = "frame1";
```

Methods

None (other than the event handlers).

Event Handlers

onclick() [JavaScript 1.0]

This method is called when the user clicks on the hypertext link. In JavaScript 1.1 and later, returning `false` prevents the browser from following the link. It is normally specified via the `onClick` attribute, as follows:

```
<A HREF="..." ...
  onClick="return(maybeCancel())">
```

ondblclick() [JavaScript 1.2]

This Netscape 4 method is called on the second click of a double click. The `onclick` handler, if any, will be called first. It is set by the `onDblClick` attribute and is not supported on the Macintosh.

onmouseout() [JavaScript 1.1]

This is called when the user moves the mouse off the link. Combined with `onmouseover`, this provides a good method to highlight images under the mouse. For an example, see Section 19.5 (Using JavaScript to Make Pages Dynamic). It is normally specified by using the `onMouseOut` attribute.

onmouseover() [JavaScript 1.0]

This is called when the user moves the mouse over a link. It is normally specified by using the `onMouseOver` attribute. If the method returns `true`, the browser does not display the associated URL in the status line. This lets you use this method to display custom status-line messages. However, this is less useful in JavaScript 1.0, given the lack of `onmouseout` to reset the status line when the mouse leaves.

20.17 The Location Object

This object corresponds to a window's current URL, as given in the `window.location` property.

Properties

hash [JavaScript 1.0]

This gives the "section" part of the hypertext reference, and includes the leading "#" (hash mark). It is read/write.

host [JavaScript 1.0]

This returns a string of the form `"hostname:port"`. It is read/write.

hostname [JavaScript 1.0]

This returns the hostname. It is read/write.

href [JavaScript 1.0]

This gives the complete URL. It is read/write.

pathname [JavaScript 1.0]

This gives the part of the URL that came after the host and port. It is read/write.

port [JavaScript 1.0]

This is a *string* (not integer) specifying the port. It is read/write.

protocol [JavaScript 1.0]

This specifies the protocol. The colon is included as part of this property. It is read/write.

search [JavaScript 1.0]

This gives the search part (i.e. "?x,y" from an ISMAP entry) or query part (i.e. "?x=1&y=2" from a form submission) of the URL. It is read/write. You can use this property to implement self-processing "server"-side image maps or CGI forms by specifying the current document as the target URL, then checking location.search at the top of the document. See the unescape function, described in Section 20.31 (The String Object), for URL-decoding strings.

Methods

reload() [JavaScript 1.1]

This reloads the document if the server reports it as having changed since last loaded.

reload(true) [JavaScript 1.1]

This reloads the document.

replace(newURL) [JavaScript 1.1]

This replaces the current document with a new one (just like setting location to a new value), but without adding a new entry in the history list.

Event Handlers

None.

20.18 The Math Object

The Math object does not correspond to an HTML element, but is used for basic arithmetic operations. It supports substantially the same methods as does the `java.lang.Math` class in Java. You never make a new Math object, but instead access the properties and methods via `Math.proper-tyName` or `Math.methodName(...)`.

Properties

Using these constants saves time over recalculating them each time.

E [JavaScript 1.0]
This is e, the base used for natural logarithms.

LN10 [JavaScript 1.0]
This is $\ln(10)$, i.e. $\log_e(10)$.

LN2 [JavaScript 1.0]
This is $\ln(2)$, i.e. $\log_e(2)$.

LOG10E [JavaScript 1.0]
This is $\log_{10}(e)$.

LOG2E [JavaScript 1.0]
This is $\lg(e)$, i.e. $\log_2(e)$.

PI [JavaScript 1.0]
This is π.

SQRT1_2 [JavaScript 1.0]
This is $\sqrt{1/2}$, i.e. $1/\sqrt{2}$.

SQRT2 [JavaScript 1.0]
This is $\sqrt{2}$.

Methods

General-Purpose Methods

abs(num) [JavaScript 1.0]

This returns the absolute value of the specified number.

ceil(num) [JavaScript 1.0]

The `ceil` method returns the smallest integer greater than or equal to the specified number.

exp(num) [JavaScript 1.0]

This returns e^{num}.

floor(num) [JavaScript 1.0]

This returns the greatest integer less than or equal to num.

log(num) [JavaScript 1.0]

This returns the natural logarithm of the specified number. JavaScript does not provide a method to calculate logarithms using other common bases (e.g. 10 or 2), but following is a method that does this using the relationship

$$\log_{b1}(n) = \frac{\log_{b2}(n)}{\log_{b2}(b1)}$$

```
function log(num, base) {
   return(Math.log(num) / Math.log(base));
}
```

max(num1, num2) [JavaScript 1.0]

This returns the larger of the two numbers.

min(num1, num2) [JavaScript 1.0]

This returns the smaller of the two numbers.

pow(base, exponent) [JavaScript 1.0]

This returns $base^{exponent}$.

random() [JavaScript 1.0]

This returns a random number from 0.0 (inclusive) to 1.0 (exclusive). It is only reliable in Netscape versions 3 and 4. In Netscape 2, `random` is only implemented on Unix platforms. In Internet Explorer, it is not randomly seeded, so produces the same sequence of numbers each time the browser is restarted.

round(num) [JavaScript 1.0]

This rounds toward the nearest number, rounding up if `num` is of the form `xxx.5`.

sqrt(num) [JavaScript 1.0]

This returns $\sqrt{num}$. Taking the square root of a negative number returns NaN.

Trigonometric Methods

All of these methods deal in radians, not degrees. Convert degrees to radians using

```
function degreesToRadians(degrees) {
  return(degrees * Math.PI / 180);
}
```

acos(num) [JavaScript 1.0]

This returns the arc cosine of the specified value. The result is expressed *in radians*.

asin(num) [JavaScript 1.0]

This returns the arc sine of the specified number.

atan(num) [JavaScript 1.0]

This returns the arc tangent of the specified number.

atan2(x, y) [JavaScript 1.0]

This returns the θ part of the polar coordinate (r, θ) that corresponds to the cartesian coordinate (x, y). This is the arc tangent of y/x that is in the range $-\pi$ to π.

cos(radians) [JavaScript 1.0]

This returns the cosine of the specified number, interpreted as a number in radians.

sin(radians) [JavaScript 1.0]

This returns the sine of the specified number.

tan(radians) [JavaScript 1.0]

This returns the tangent of the specified number.

Event Handlers

None. Math does not correspond to an HTML element.

20.19 The MimeType Object

This object describes a MIME type. The navigator.mimeTypes array lists all types supported by the browser, either directly by plug ins, or through external "helper" applications. For example, you could use code like the following to insert a link to an Adobe Acrobat file only if the current browser supports Acrobat, using a plain text document otherwise:

```
document.writeln('For more information, see');
if (navigator.mimeTypes["application/pdf"] != null)
  document.writeln
    ('<A HREF="manual.pdf">the widget manual</A>.');
else
  document.writeln
    ('<A HREF="manual.text">the widget manual</
A>.');
```

For a list of common MIME types, see Table 16.1.

Properties

description [JavaScript 1.1]

This gives a textual description of the type. It is read only.

enabledPlugin [JavaScript 1.1]
This refers to the `Plugin` object that supports this MIME type, if it is enabled. It is `null` if no installed and enabled plug in supports this type. It is read only.

suffixes [JavaScript 1.1]
This gives a comma-separated list of the filename extensions that are assumed to be of this type. It is read only.

type [JavaScript 1.1]
This string is the type itself, e.g. `"application/postscript"`.

Methods

None.

Event Handlers

None. `MimeType` does not correspond directly to any HTML element.

20.20 The Navigator Object

The `Navigator` object provides information about the browser. It is available through the `navigator` property of `Window`; i.e., via `window.navigator` or simply `navigator`.

Properties

Following the property descriptions, Listing 20.2 shows a page that makes a table of several properties. Results are shown in Figures 20–2 and 20–3.

appCodeName [JavaScript 1.0]
This is intended to give the code name of the browser, but Internet Explorer uses `"Mozilla"` for this property, just like Netscape. It is read only.

appName [JavaScript 1.0]
This is the browser name, either `"Netscape"` or `"Microsoft Internet Explorer"`. It is read only.

appVersion [JavaScript 1.0]
This gives operating system and release number information. It is read only.

language [JavaScript 1.2]
This gives the browser translation. For English versions, this will be the string `"en"`. It is read only.

mimeTypes [JavaScript 1.1]
This is an array of `MimeType` objects supported by the browser either via plug ins or through helper applications. See Section 20.19 (The MimeType Object).

platform [JavaScript 1.2]
This gives the machine type for which the browser was compiled. For instance, on Windows 95 and NT, this is `"Win32"`. It is read only.

plugins [JavaScript 1.1]
This is an array of `Plugin` objects supported by the browser. See Section 19.4 (Using JavaScript to Customize Web Pages) for an example of its use.

userAgent [JavaScript 1.0]
This is the string sent by the browser to the server in the `User-Agent` HTTP request header. It is read only.

Figures 20–2 and 20–3 show examples of some of these properties, based on a page generated from Listing 20.2.

Listing 20.2 `Navigator.html`

```
<!DOCTYPE HTML PUBLIC "-//W3C//DTD HTML 3.2//EN">
<HTML>
<HEAD>
  <TITLE>The Navigator Object</TITLE>

<SCRIPT LANGUAGE="JavaScript1.1">
<!--

function makePropertyTable(name, object, propertyList) {
  document.writeln
    ("<H2>" + name + "</H2>");
  document.writeln
    ("<TABLE BORDER=1>\n" +
    "  <TR><TH>Property<TH>Value");
  var propertyName;
  for(var i=0; i<propertyList.length; i++) {
    propertyName = propertyList[i];
    document.writeln
      ("  <TR><TD>" + propertyName +
        "<TD>" + object[propertyName]);
  }
  document.writeln
    ("</TABLE>");
}

// -->
</SCRIPT>
</HEAD>

<BODY BGCOLOR="WHITE">

<SCRIPT LANGUAGE="JavaScript1.1">
<!--

var propNames = new Array("appCodeName", "appName",
                          "appVersion", "userAgent");
makePropertyTable("The Navigator Object", navigator,
                  propNames);

// -->
</SCRIPT>

</BODY>
</HTML>
```

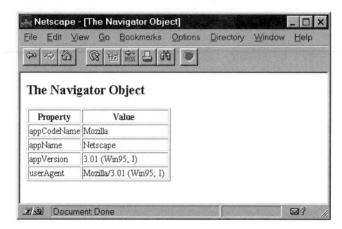

Figure 20-2   Navigator properties in Netscape 3.01 on WIndows 95.

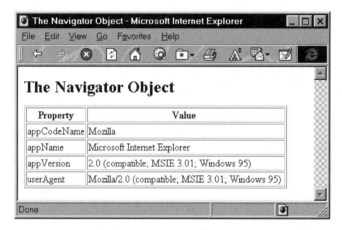

Figure 20-3   Navigator properties in Internet Explorer 3.01 on WIndows 95.

Methods

javaEnabled() [JavaScript 1.1]
This returns `true` if the browser supports Java *and* currently has it enabled. It returns `false` otherwise.

taintEnabled() [JavaScript 1.1]
This returns `true` if the browser has data tainting enabled. This will be the case if the user has set the `NS_ENABLE_TAINT` environment variable to allow JavaScript on one page to discover privileged information about other pages.

Event Handlers

None. `Navigator` does not correspond to an HTML element.

20.21 The Number Object

This object is used to access information about numbers. You do not need to create an object of this type to access the properties, but rather access `Number.propertyName`. The main reason for making a `Number` object is to call `toString()`, which lets you specify a radix. This object is in JavaScript 1.1, but is not supported by Internet Explorer 3.

Constructor

new Number(value) [JavaScript 1.1]
This constructs a `Number` object for the specified primitive value.

Properties

MAX_VALUE [JavaScript 1.1]
This specifies the largest number representable in JavaScript.

MIN_VALUE [JavaScript 1.1]
This specifies the smallest number representable in JavaScript.

NaN [JavaScript 1.1]
This is the special not-a-number value. Use the global `isNaN` function to compare to it, since all comparisons with `NaN` return `false`, including testing (`Number.NaN == Number.NaN`).

NEGATIVE_INFINITY [JavaScript 1.1]
This represents negative overflow values. For instance, `Number.MAX_VALUE` times –2 returns this value. This value times any number is this value. Any number divided by this value is 0, except that an infinite value divided by another infinite value is `NaN`. This is supposed to be part of JavaScript 1.1, but its value is `null` in Netscape 3.01 on Windows 95. It works properly in Netscape 3 on Unix and in Netscape 4 on Windows 95. Internet Explorer 3 does not support any of the `Number` properties.

POSITIVE_INFINITY [JavaScript 1.1]
This represents positive overflow values. This is supposed to be part of JavaScript 1.1, but its value is `null` in Netscape 3.01 on Windows 95. It works properly in Netscape 3 on Unix and in Netscape 4 on Windows 95.

Methods

toString(radix) [JavaScript 1.1]
This converts a number to a string in the specified radix. Strangely, on most platforms Netscape 3 uses ":" instead of "a" for 10 in hexadecimal notation. Netscape 4 uses "a" as expected. For example, Listing 20.3 creates a table of numbers in various radixes. Figure 20–4 shows the result in Netscape 3.01 on Windows 95.

Listing 20.3   `NumberToString.html`

```
<!DOCTYPE HTML PUBLIC "-//W3C//DTD HTML 3.2//EN">
<HTML>
<HEAD>
  <TITLE>Converting Numbers to Strings</TITLE>

<SCRIPT LANGUAGE="JavaScript1.1">
<!--

function makeNumberTable(numberList, radixList) {
  document.write("<TABLE BORDER=1>\n<TR>");
  for(var i=0; i<radixList.length; i++)
    document.write("<TH>Base " + radixList[i]);
  var num;
  for(var i=0; i<numberList.length; i++) {
    document.write("\n<TR>");
    num = new Number(numberList[i]);
    for(var j=0; j<radixList; j++) {
      document.write("<TD>" +
                     num.toString(radixList[j]));
    }
  }
  document.writeln("\n</TABLE>");
}

// -->
</SCRIPT>
</HEAD>

<BODY BGCOLOR="WHITE">
<H1>Converting Numbers to Strings</H1>

<SCRIPT LANGUAGE="JavaScript">
<!--

var nums = new Array(0, 1, 2, 4, 5, 6, 7, 8, 9, 10,
                     11, 12, 13, 14, 15, 16,
                     100, 512, 1000);
var radixes = new Array(10, 2, 8, 16);

makeNumberTable(nums, radixes);

// -->
</SCRIPT>

</BODY>

</HTML>
```

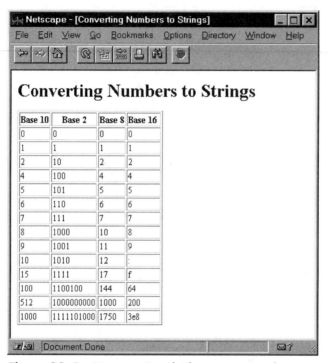

Figure 20–4   Netscape 3 and 4 let you print numbers in any radix, but with an inconsistency for "a" in Netscape 3.

toString() [JavaScript 1.1]
This is the same as calling `toString(10)`.

valueOf() [JavaScript 1.1]
This returns the primitive number value associated with the Number.

Event Handlers

None. Number does not correspond to an HTML element.

20.22 The Object Object

This is the object upon which all others are built. Properties and methods here are shared by *all* JavaScript objects.

Constructors

new Object() [JavaScript 1.0]
This builds a generic Object.

new Object(primitiveValue) [JavaScript 1.1]
Depending on the argument type, this creates a Number, String, Boolean, or Function "wrapper" object.

{prop1:val1, prop2:val2, ... , propN:valN} [JavaScript 1.2]
In Netscape 4, you can create objects using "literal" notation.

Properties

constructor [JavaScript 1.1]
This refers to the JavaScript function that created the object instance. It is read only.

prototype [JavaScript 1.1]
This is not actually a property of Object, but rather of all constructor functions. It is mentioned here since it is used in a general purpose way for all user-defined objects. See Section 19.3 (Basic JavaScript Syntax) for more details.

Methods

assign(value) [JavaScript 1.1]
This method is called when an object of the type you define appears on the left side of an assignment operation. In most cases the version of assign that you build calls new and fills in fields appropriately.

eval(javaScriptCode) [JavaScript 1.0]
This takes an arbitrary string and evaluates it.

toString() [JavaScript 1.0]

This generates a string for the object. You define this in your classes to get custom string representations.

valueOf() [JavaScript 1.1]

This returns the primitive value this Object represents, if there is one. See the Number object (Section 20.21).

Event Handlers

None.

20.23 The Option Object

This object represents OPTION entries in a SELECT element. It is normally accessed via the options array of a Select object, which in turn is accessed through the elements array of a Form object.

Constructors

new Option() [JavaScript 1.0]
new Option(text) [JavaScript 1.0]
new Option(text, value) [JavaScript 1.0]
new Option(text, value, defaultSelected) [JavaScript 1.0]
new Option(text, value, defaultSelected, selected) [JavaScript 1.0]

This creates a new Option object, which can be dynamically inserted into a Select object by placing it on the end of the options array.

Properties

defaultSelected [JavaScript 1.0]

This Boolean property determines if the Option is selected by default. It is specified via the SELECTED attribute and is read only.

index [JavaScript 1.0]

This gives the position of this Option within its Select object's options array. It is read only.

selected [JavaScript 1.0]

This is a `Boolean` specifying whether or not the option is currently selected. It is read/write.

text [JavaScript 1.0]

This gives the text following the option in the `SELECT` element. It is read only in JavaScript 1.0, read/write in JavaScript 1.1 and 1.2.

value [JavaScript 1.0]

This designates the value that will be transmitted along with the `Select` object's name when the form is submitted. It is initially specified via the `VALUE` attribute, and is read/write.

Methods

None.

Event Handlers

None. The `onblur`, `onfocus`, and `onchange` handlers are associated with the enclosing `Select` object, not with the `Option` object itself.

20.24 The Password Object

This object corresponds to HTML elements created via `<INPUT TYPE="PASSWORD"  ...>`. Password objects are normally accessed through the `elements` array of the enclosing `Form` object, or, if both it and the form are named, via `document.formName.passwordName`.

Properties

defaultValue [JavaScript 1.0]

This is the initial value as given in the `VALUE` attribute. It is read only.

form [JavaScript 1.0]

This is the `Form` object containing the password field. It is read only.

name [JavaScript 1.0]
This is the value of the NAME attribute. It is read only.

type [JavaScript 1.1]
This contains the value "password". It is read only.

value [JavaScript 1.0]
This gives the plain-text value of the password field. In Netscape 2.0, it is always empty. In Netscape 3 and 4, you are not *supposed* to be able to read the value unless data tainting is enabled, but in practice you can on Windows platforms. On Unix, you get a string of asterisks that show you the number of characters the user entered, but not the actual value. Internet Explorer has no prohibition against reading this property.

Methods

blur() [JavaScript 1.0]
This method removes the keyboard focus from the element.

focus() [JavaScript 1.0]
This gives the keyboard focus to the element.

select() [JavaScript 1.0]
This highlights the text in the element. If the user types, the input replaces the existing text.

Event Handlers

onblur() [JavaScript 1.0]
This method is called when the password field loses the input focus. It is normally specified by means of the onBlur attribute.

onchange() [JavaScript 1.0]
This method is called when the password field loses the input focus after its value has changed. It is normally specified by means of the onChange attribute.

onfocus() [JavaScript 1.0]
This method is called when the password field gets the input focus. It is normally specified by means of the onFocus attribute.

onkeydown() [JavaScript1.2]

This is called when the user first presses any key in the password field. Returning `false` cancels the input of the character.

onkeypress() [JavaScript1.2]

When the user first presses a key, this method is called after `onkeydown`. It is also called repeatedly when the key is held down, while `onkeydown` is not. Returning `false` cancels the input of the character.

onkeyup() [JavaScript1.2]

This is called when the user releases a key.

20.25 The Plug In Object

This describes an installed plug in, accessible through the `navigator.plugins` array. This array gives the plug ins installed in the browser, not the objects in the current document that require plug ins; for that, see the `embeds` array of Document. This is an unusual object in that it has normal properties, plus you can index it as an array (remember that JavaScript arrays are really just objects with number-valued property names). Each element of this array is a `MimeType` object. See Section 19.4 (Using JavaScript to Customize Web Pages) for an example of using `Plugin` and its associate `MimeType` objects.

Properties

description [JavaScript 1.1]

This is a textual description of the plugi n, provided by the plug-in vendor. It is read only.

filename [JavaScript 1.1]

This gives the name of the file containing the code for the plug-in. It is read only.

length [JavaScript 1.1]

This specifies the number of `MimeType` objects in the array.

name [JavaScript 1.1]
This gives a short name for the plug in. You can use the name as an index into the `document.plugins` array.

Methods

None.

Event Handlers

None. A `Plugin` does not correspond to any HTML element.

20.26 The Radio Object

This object corresponds to HTML input elements created inside a form via `<INPUT TYPE="RADIO" ...>`. Radio objects are normally accessed through the elements array of the enclosing `Form` object. If both the `Radio` object and the surrounding `Form` are named, you can access the `Radio` object via `document.formName.radioName`.

Properties

checked [JavaScript 1.0]
This is a `Boolean` specifying whether or not the radio button is currently checked. It is read/write.

defaultChecked [JavaScript 1.0]
This is a `Boolean` specifying whether or not the radio button should be initially set. It is set via the `CHECKED` attribute, and is read only in JavaScript.

form [JavaScript 1.0]
This refers to the `Form` object containing the radio button. It is read only.

name [JavaScript 1.0]
This gives the name of the radio button as given in the `NAME` attribute. Remember that the whole point of radio buttons is that multiple entries

share the same name, but only one can be checked at any one time. It is read only.

type [JavaScript 1.1]

This property contains the string `"radio"`. Since all `Element` objects have this property, it can be used to differentiate among them when looking at the `form.elements` array. It is read only.

value [JavaScript 1.0]

This gives the value that will be sent with the name to the CGI program if the form is submitted when the radio button is checked. It is read/write.

Methods

blur() [JavaScript 1.1]

This removes the keyboard focus from the radio button.

click() [JavaScript 1.0]

This acts as though the radio button was clicked, but without triggering the `onClick` handler. Thus, calling this is just like setting the `checked` property.

focus() [JavaScript 1.1]

This gives the keyboard focus to the radio button.

Event Handlers

onblur() [JavaScript 1.1]

This method is called when the radio button loses the input focus. It is normally set via the `onBlur` attribute, as below.

```
<INPUT TYPE="RADIO" ...
        onBlur="doSomeAction()">
```

onclick() [JavaScript 1.0]

This method is called when the user clicks on the radio button, but not when the `click` method is called programmatically. It is usually specified via the `onClick` attribute of the input element.

onfocus() [JavaScript 1.1]

This method is called when the radio button gains the input focus. It is normally set via the `onFocus` attribute.

20.27 The RegExp Object

Netscape 4.0 introduced the `RegExp` object for representing regular expressions, and added support for it in the `String` object via the `match`, `replace`, `search`, and `split` methods.

Constructors

new RegExp("pattern") [JavaScript 1.2]

This builds a regular expression. A regular expression is a string containing some special characters that Java uses to check for occurrences of certain patterns in strings. These characters are listed in Table 20.1, but the most important three are "+", which means "match one or more occurrences of the previous character"; "*", which means "match zero or more occurrences of the previous character"; and "?", which means "match zero or one occurrence of the previous character." In the absence of these special characters, characters in the regular expression are matched exactly against some comparison string. For example, the following regular expression means "a 'z', followed by one or more 'a's, followed by a 'b', followed by zero or more 'c's, followed by zero or one 'd', followed by an 'e'."

```
var re = new RegExp("za+bc*d?e");
```

`RegExp` has a `test` method that takes a string and returns `true` if and only if it contains the regular expression. Given the above definition of `re`, all of the following would return `true`:

```
re.test("zabcde");
re.test("xxxxxzabcdexxxxx");
re.test("zaaaabcde");
re.test("zaaaabde");
re.test("zaaaabe");
re.test("XXzaabcccccdeYY");
```

new RegExp("pattern", "g") [JavaScript 1.2]

This builds a regular expression for global matches in a string. `String` has a `match` method that returns an array describing the matches against a particular string. If g is not specified, the first match will be returned. With g, all matches will be returned. For example, the first call to `exec` below returns an array containing `"abc"`, while the second returns an array containing `"abc"` and `"abbbbc"`.

```
var str = "abcabbbbcABCABBBBC";
var re1 = new RegExp("ab+c");
var re2 = new RegExp("ab+c", "g");
var result1 = str.match(re1);
var result2 = str.match(re2);
```

new RegExp("pattern", "i") [JavaScript 1.2]

This builds a regular expression for case insensitive matches.

new RegExp("pattern", "gi") [JavaScript 1.2]

This builds a regular expression for global, case insensitive matches. For example, the following builds an array containing `"abc"`, `"abbbbc"`, `"ABC"`, and `"ABBBBC"`.

```
var str = "abcabbbbcABCABBBBC";
var re = new RegExp("ab+c", "gi");
var result = str.match(re);
```

/pattern/ [JavaScript 1.2]

This is a shorthand for `new RegExp("pattern")`. For example, the following two statements create equivalent regular expressions.

```
var re1 = /ab+c/;
var re2 = new RegExp("ab+c");
```

See further examples in Section 20.31 (The String Object).

/pattern/g [JavaScript 1.2]

This is shorthand for `new RegExp("pattern", "g")`.

/pattern/i [JavaScript 1.2]

This is shorthand for `new RegExp("pattern", "i")`.

/pattern/gi [JavaScript 1.2]

This is shorthand for `new RegExp("pattern", "gi")`.

Properties

These are properties of the global `RegExp` object, not of individual regular expressions. Thus, they are always accessed via `RegExp.propertyName`. The short version of the property names (`$_`, `$*`, etc.) are taken from the Perl language.

input [JavaScript 1.2]
$_ [JavaScript 1.2]
If a regular expression's `exec` or `test` methods are called with no associated string, it uses the value of this global property. When an event handler for a `Text`, `TextArea`, `Select`, or `Link` object is invoked, this property is automatically filled in with the associated text. This property is read/write.

lastMatch [JavaScript 1.2]
$& [JavaScript 1.2]
This gives the last matched substring. It is filled in after `exec` is called, and is read only.

lastParen [JavaScript 1.2]
$+ [JavaScript 1.2]
This gives the value of the last parenthesized match. It is filled in after `exec` is called, and is read only.

leftContext [JavaScript 1.2]
$' [JavaScript 1.2]
This gives the left part of the string, up to but not including the most recent match. It is filled in after `exec` is called, and is read only.

multiline [JavaScript 1.2]
$* [JavaScript 1.2]
This is a `Boolean` determining if matching should occur across line breaks. Set this before calling `exec`; the `Textarea` event handler automatically sets this to `true`. It is read/write.

rightcontext [JavaScript 1.2]
$' [JavaScript 1.2]
This gives the right part of the string, starting after the most recent match. It is filled in after `exec` is called, and is read only.

$1 [JavaScript 1.2]
$2 [JavaScript 1.2]

...
$9 [JavaScript 1.2]
These give the values of the first nine parenthesized matches. They are
filled in after exec is called, and are read only.

Methods

These methods belong to individual regular expression objects, not to the
global RegExp object.

compile(pattern, flags) [JavaScript 1.2]
This takes a regular expression and compiles it for faster execution.

exec(string) [JavaScript 1.2]
This searches the string for the regular expression, filling in the
fields of the RegExp object as described under Properties. As a
shorthand, you can use someRegExp(string) instead of
someRegExp.exec(string).

exec() [JavaScript 1.2]
This is the same as exec(RegExp.input).

test(string) [JavaScript 1.2]
This simply determines if the string contains at least one occurrence of
the regular expression, returning true or false. Using some-
RegExp.test(string) is equivalent to string.search(some-
RegExp).

Event Handlers

None. RegExp does not correspond to an HTML element.

Special Patterns in Regular Expressions

The discussion of the RegExp constructors explained the purpose of the
"+", "*", and "?" characters. Table 20.1 gives a complete list of special characters and patterns. For clarity in the examples, I will typically say something like "/ab+c/ matches "abbbc"", but note that /ab+c/ also

matches `"XXabbbc"` and `"XXabbbcYYYY"`; i.e. the string only has to *contain* a match, not *be* a match.

Table 20.1   Special Regular Expression Patterns

Pattern	*Interpretation*
+	Match one or more occurrences of the previous character. For instance, `/ab+c/` will match `"abc"` and `"abbbbbc"`, but not `"ac"`.
*	Match zero or more occurrences of the previous character. For instance, `/ab*c/` will match `"ac"`, `"abc"` and `"abbbbbc"`.
?	Match zero or one occurrence of the previous character. For instance, `/ab?c/` will match `"ac"` and `"abc"`, but not `"abbbbbc"`.
.	Match exactly one character. For instance, `/a.c/` matches `"abc"` or `"aqc"`, but not `"ac"` or `"abbc"`. A newline does *not* match ".".
\	Treat the next character literally if it is a special character; treat it specially otherwise. For instance, `/a\**b/` matches `"ab"`, `"a*b"`, and `"a*****b"`.
(pattern)	Match *pattern*, but also "remembers" the match for access via the $*N* properties of `RegExp`.
p1|*p2*	Match either *p1* or *p2*. For instance `/foo|bar/` matches `"football"` and `"barstool"`.
{*n*}	Match exactly *n* occurrences of the previous character. For instance, `/ab{3}c/` matches `"abbbc"` but not `"abbc"` or `"abbbbc"`.
{*n*,}	Match at least n occurrences of the previous character. For instance, `/ab{3,}c/` matches `"abbbc"` and `"abbbbc"` but not `"abbc"`.

Table 20.1	Special Regular Expression Patterns (continued)

Pattern	Interpretation
{n1,n2}	Match at least *n1* but no more than *n2* occurrences of the previous character.
[$c_1c_2...c_n$]	Match any one of the enclosed characters. For instance, `/a[pl]*e/` matches `"ae"`, `"apple"`, and `"allpe"`. You can use dashes to represent series: e.g. `[a-z]` for any lower-case character, `[0-7]` for any digit from 0 to 7, and so forth.
[^$c_1c_2...c_n$]	Match any one character that is not part of the designated set. For instance, `/a[^pl]*e/` matches `"ae"` and `"aqqxxe"`, but not `"apple"` or `"allpe"`.
\b, \B	Match a word boundary (`\b`) or any one nonword-boundary character (`\B`). For example, `/a\bc/` matches `"a c"` but not `"abc"`, while `/a\Bc/` matches `"abc"` but not `"a c"`.
\w, \W	Matches any word (`\w`) or nonword (`\W`) character. `\w` is equivalent to `[A-Za-z0-9_]` while `\W` is like `[^A-Za-z0-9_]`.
\d, \D	Match any digit (`\d`) or nondigit (`\D`). Equivalent to `[0-9]` or `[^0-9]`, respectively.
\f, \n, \r, \t, \v	Match form-feed, line feed, carriage return, tab, and vertical tab, respectively.
\s, \S	Match any whitespace (`\s`) or nonwhitespace character (`\S`). `\s` is equivalent to `[\f\n\r\t\v]` while `\S` is the same as `[^\f\n\r\t\v]`.
/xxx/	Match the character represented by the ASCII code *xxx*.

20.28 The Reset Object

This object corresponds to buttons created via `<INPUT TYPE="RESET" ...>` in an HTML form. `Reset` objects are normally accessed through the elements array of the enclosing `Form` object. If both the button and the form are named, they can also be accessed via `document.formName.reset-ButtonName`.

Properties

form [JavaScript 1.0]
This gives the `Form` object containing the button. It is read only.

name [JavaScript 1.0]
If the button used the `NAME` attribute, this property retrieves it. It is read only.

type [JavaScript 1.1]
This property is always equal to `"reset"`. All `Element` objects contain this property, so it can be used to distinguish among the various types. It is read only.

value [JavaScript 1.0]
This gives the label of the button. It is read/write.

Methods

blur() [JavaScript 1.1]
This removes the keyboard focus from the button.

click() [JavaScript 1.0]
This acts as though the button was clicked, but without triggering the `onClick` handler. You can use the form's `reset` method instead of this.

focus() [JavaScript 1.1]
This gives the keyboard focus to the button.

Event Handlers

onblur() [JavaScript 1.1]

This method is called when the button loses the input focus. It is normally set via the `onBlur` attribute, as below.

```
<INPUT TYPE="RESET" ...
        onBlur="doSomeAction()">
```

onclick() [JavaScript 1.0]

This method is called when the user clicks on the button, but not when the `click` method is called programmatically. It is normally set via the `onClick` attribute:

```
<INPUT TYPE="RESET" ...
        onClick="doSomeAction()">
```

In Netscape 3 and later, if you return `false` from this method, then the form is not actually reset. For example,

```
<INPUT TYPE="RESET" ...
        onClick="return(maybeReset())">
```

The same effect can be achieved by `onReset` handler on the form containing the button.

ondblclick() [JavaScript 1.2]

This Netscape 4 method is called on the second click of a double click. The `onclick` handler, if any, will be called first. It is set by the `onDblClick` attribute. It is not supported on the Macintosh.

onfocus() [JavaScript 1.1]

This method is called when the button gains the input focus. It is normally set via the `onFocus` attribute.

20.29 The Screen Object

This object, accessible through the global `screen` variable, contains information about the current screen's resolution and color. It is new in Netscape 4.

Properties

availHeight [JavaScript 1.2]

This gives the height of the screen (in pixels), minus space occupied by semi-permanent user interface elements such as the Windows 95 taskbar. It is read only.

availWidth [JavaScript 1.2]

This gives the width of the screen (in pixels), minus space occupied by semi-permanent user interface elements. It is read only.

height [JavaScript 1.2]

This gives the height of the screen in pixels. It is read only.

width [JavaScript 1.2]

This gives the width of the screen in pixels. It is read only.

pixelDepth [JavaScript 1.2]

This specifies the number of bits per pixel being used for color. It is read only.

colorDepth [JavaScript 1.2]

This specifies the number of simultaneous colors it is possible to display. It is read only.

Methods

None.

Event Handlers

None. It does not correspond to an HTML element.

20.30 The Select Object

A Select object corresponds to an HTML element created via <SELECT ...>. It is normally accessed through the elements array of the enclosing

Form. If the Form and Select objects both have names, you can also use document.formName.selectName.

Listing 20.4 shows a page that presents a pull-down menu of color choices. Choosing an entry changes the page's background color.

Listing 20.4 SelectColor.html

```
<!DOCTYPE HTML PUBLIC "-//W3C//DTD HTML 3.2//EN">
<HTML>
<HEAD>
  <TITLE>Changing the Background Color</TITLE>
<SCRIPT LANGUAGE="JavaScript">
<!--

function setBackgroundColor() {
  var selection = document.colorForm.colorSelection;
  document.bgColor =
    selection.options[selection.selectedIndex].value;
}

// -->
</SCRIPT>
</HEAD>

<BODY BGCOLOR="WHITE">
<H1>Changing the Background Color</H1>

<FORM NAME="colorForm">
<SELECT NAME="colorSelection"
        onChange="setBackgroundColor()">
  <OPTION VALUE="#FFFFFF" SELECTED>White
  <OPTION VALUE="#C0C0C0">Gray
  <OPTION VALUE="#FF0000">Red
  <OPTION VALUE="#00FF00">Green
  <OPTION VALUE="#0000FF">Blue
</SELECT>

</FORM>

</BODY>
</HTML>
```

Properties

form [JavaScript 1.0]

This refers to the Form object containing the selection element. It is read only.

length [JavaScript 1.0]

This specifies the number of Option elements contained in the selection. It is the same as options.length, and is read only.

name [JavaScript 1.0]

This gives the name as specified via the NAME attribute. It is read only.

options [JavaScript 1.0]

This is an array of Option objects contained in the selection. You are permitted to add Option objects to the end of this array.

selectedIndex [JavaScript 1.0]

This gives the index of the currently-selected option. It will be –1 if none is selected, and will give the first selected index for Select elements that were created via <SELECT ... MULTIPLE>. In JavaScript 1.0, this is read only; it is read/write in JavaScript 1.1 and 1.2.

type [JavaScript 1.0]

This property contains either "select-one" or "select-multiple", depending on whether the MULTIPLE attribute was included. It is read only.

Methods

blur() [JavaScript 1.1]

This removes the keyboard focus from the selection.

focus() [JavaScript 1.1]

This gives the keyboard focus to the selection.

Event Handlers

onblur() [JavaScript 1.1]
This method is called when the selection loses the input focus. It is normally set via the `onBlur` attribute, as below.

```
<SELECT ... onBlur="doSomeAction()">
```

onchange() [JavaScript 1.0]
This method is called when the selection loses the input focus after the selected option has changed. See Listing 20.4 for an example of its use.

onfocus() [JavaScript 1.1]
This method is called when the selection gains the input focus. It is normally set via the `onFocus` attribute.

20.31 The String Object

`String` is an important datatype in JavaScript. It does not correspond directly to any particular HTML elements, but is widely used.

Constructor

new String(value) [JavaScript 1.1]
This builds a new `String`.

Properties

length [JavaScript 1.0]
This gives the number of characters in the string. It is read only.

Methods

anchor(name) [JavaScript 1.0]
This returns a copy of the current string, embedded between `<A NAME="name">` and `</A>`. For example,

```
"Chapter One".anchor("Ch1")
```

evaluates to

```
'<A NAME="Ch1">Chapter One</A>'
```

big() [JavaScript 1.0]
This returns a copy of the string, embedded between `<BIG>` and `</BIG>`.

blink() [JavaScript 1.0]
This returns a copy of the string, embedded between `<BLINK>` and `</BLINK>`.

bold() [JavaScript 1.0]
This returns a copy of the string, embedded between `<B>` and `</B>`. For example,

```
"Wow".italics().bold()
```

evaluates to

```
"<B><I>Wow</I></B>"
```

charAt(index) [JavaScript 1.0]
This returns a 1-character string taken from the character at the specified location. Strings, like most datatypes in JavaScript, are zero indexed.

charCodeAt(index) [JavaScript 1.2]
This returns the ISO Latin-1 number for the character at the designated location. The first 127 values correspond to ASCII values.

charCodeAt() [JavaScript 1.2]
This returns `charCodeAt(0)`.

concat(suffixString) [JavaScript 1.2]
This method concatenates two strings. The following two forms are equivalent in Netscape 4.

```
var newString = string1.concat(string2);
var newString = string1 + string2;
```

escape(string)[JavaScript 1.0]
The `escape` method is actually not a method of `String`, but rather is a standard top-level function. However, because it is used for string

manipulation, it is described here. It URL-encodes a string so that it can be attached to the query portion (`search` property) of a `Location` object. Note that this replaces spaces with "%20", not with "+". For example, the following results in Figure 20–5.

```
alert(escape("Hello, world!"));
```

Figure 20–5 The `escape` method is used to URL-encode

See unescape for URL decoding.

fixed() [JavaScript 1.0]
This returns a copy of the string, embedded between `<TT>` and `</TT>`.

fontcolor(colorName)
This returns a copy of the string, embedded between `<FONT COLOR="colorName">` and `</FONT>`.

fontsize(size) [JavaScript 1.0]
This returns a copy of the string, embedded between `<FONT SIZE=size>` and `</FONT>`.

fromCharCode(code0, code1, ... , codeN) [JavaScript 1.2]
This creates a string composed of the designated ISO Latin-1 characters. It is not actually a method of individual string objects, but rather of the `String` constructor function itself. Thus, it is always called via `String.fromCharCode(...)`. For example, the following assigns the string "HELLO" to `helloString`.

```
var helloString =
    String.fromCharCode(72, 69, 76, 76, 79);
```

indexOf(substring) [JavaScript 1.0]
If the specified substring is contained in the string, this returns the beginning index of the first match. Otherwise –1 is returned. For example, here is a `contains` predicate that returns `true` if and only if the second string is contained somewhere in the first.

```
function contains(string, possibleSubstring) {
  return(string.substring(possibleSubstring) != -1);
}
```

indexOf(substring, startIndex) [JavaScript 1.0]

If the specified substring is contained somewhere starting at or to the right of the specified starting point, this returns the beginning index (relative to the whole string, not with respect to the starting point) of the first match. In Netscape, this returns the empty string if startIndex is greater than the string's length. Internet Explorer returns –1 in such a case.

italics() [JavaScript 1.0]

This returns a copy of the string, embedded between <I> and </I>.

lastIndexOf(substring) [JavaScript 1.0]

If the specified substring is contained in the string, this returns the beginning index of the last match. Otherwise –1 is returned.

lastIndexOf(substring, startIndex) [JavaScript 1.0]

If the specified substring is contained somewhere starting at or to the right of the specified starting point, this returns the beginning index of the last match.

link(url) [JavaScript 1.0]

This returns a copy of the string, embedded between
<A HREF="url"> and </A>.

match(regExp) [JavaScript 1.2]

This returns an array showing the matches of the RegExp argument in the string. For example, the following builds an array result containing the strings "abc", "abbbbc", "ABC", and "ABBBBC".

```
var str = "abcabbbbcABCABBBBC";
var re = /ab+c/gi;
var result = str.match(re);
```

Since the g in re means "find all" and the i means "case insensitive match", this is interpreted as saying "find all occurrences of an 'a' or 'A' followed by one or more 'b's and/or 'B's followed by a 'c' or 'C'." See the RegExp object (Section 20.27) for more details.

replace(regExp, replacementString) [JavaScript 1.2]

This returns a new string formed by replacing the regular expression by the designated replacement string. All occurrences will be replaced if the regular expression includes the g (global) designation. For example, the following generates a result of "We will use Java, Java, and Java".

```
var str = "We will use C, C++, and Java.";
var re = /C\+*/g;
var result = str.replace(re, "Java");
```

search(regExp) [JavaScript 1.2]

This is invoked just like the match method, but simply returns true or false depending on whether there was at least one match. If all you care about is whether the string appears, this is faster than match.

slice(startIndex, endIndex) [JavaScript 1.2]

With a positive ending index, slice is just like substring. However, you can also supply a negative ending index, which is interpreted as an offset from the end of the string. Here are some examples.

```
var str = "0123456789";
var str2 = str.slice(1, 5);      //  "1234"
var str3 = str.substring(1, 5); //  "1234"
var str4 = str.slice(1, -2);     //  "1234567"
```

small() [JavaScript 1.0]

This returns a copy of the string, embedded between <SMALL> and </SMALL>.

split() [JavaScript 1.1]

This returns an array containing the string. Using split with a delimiter is much more useful.

split(delimChar) [JavaScript 1.1]

This returns an array formed by breaking the string at each occurrence of the delimiter character. For instance, the following creates a three-element array containing the strings "foo", "bar", and "baz" (in that order).

```
var test = "foo,bar,baz".split(",");
```

If you use LANGUAGE="JavaScript1.2" in the SCRIPT tag, someString.split(" ") returns an array of the strings that were separated by *any* number of whitespace characters (spaces, tabs, new-lines). This method is the inverse of the `join` method of `Array`.

split(regExp) [JavaScript 1.2]
This Netscape 4.0 variation splits on a regular expression. For example, the following creates a a three-element array containing the strings `"foo"`, `"bar"`, and `"baz"` (in that order).

```
var str = "foo,bar,,,,,,baz";
var re = /,+/;
var result = str.split(re);
```

split(separator, limit) [JavaScript 1.2]
This extracts at most `limit` entries from the string. The separator can be a delimiter character or a `RegExp` object.

strike() [JavaScript 1.0]
This returns a copy of the string, embedded between `<STRIKE>` and `</STRIKE>`.

sub() [JavaScript 1.0]
This returns a copy of the string, embedded between `<SUB>` and `</SUB>`.

substr(startIndex, numChars) [JavaScript 1.2]
This returns the substring of the current string that starts at `start-Index` and is `numChars` long.

substring(startIndex, endIndex) [JavaScript 1.0]
This returns a new string taken from the characters from `startIndex` (inclusive) to `endIndex` (exclusive). For example, the following assigns `"is"` to the variable `test`.

```
var test = "this is a test".substring(5, 7);
```

sup() [JavaScript 1.0]
This returns a copy of the string, embedded between `<SUP>` and `</SUP>`.

toLowerCase() [JavaScript 1.0]
This returns a copy of the original string, converted to lower case.

toUpperCase() [JavaScript 1.0]

This returns a copy of the original string, converted to upper case.

unescape(string) [JavaScript 1.0]

The unescape method is actually not a method of String, but rather is a standard top-level function. However, since it is used for string manipulation, it is described here. It URL decodes a string with the unfortunate shortcoming that it does not map "+" to a space character.

Event Handlers

None. String does not correspond to an HTML element.

20.32 The Submit Object

This object corresponds to buttons created via <INPUT TYPE="SUBMIT" ...> in an HTML form. Submit objects are normally accessed through the elements array of the enclosing Form object. If both the button and the form are named, they can also be accessed via document.formName.submitButtonName.

Properties

form [JavaScript 1.0]

This gives the Form object containing the button. It is read only.

name [JavaScript 1.0]

If the button used the NAME attribute, this property retrieves it. It is read only.

type [JavaScript 1.1]

This property is always equal to "submit". All Element objects contain this property, so it can be used to distinguish among the various types. It is read only.

value [JavaScript 1.0]

This gives the label of the button. It is read/write.

Methods

blur() [JavaScript 1.1]

This removes the keyboard focus from the button.

click() [JavaScript 1.0]

This acts as though the button was clicked, but without triggering the onClick handler. You can use the form's submit method instead of this.

focus() [JavaScript 1.1]

This gives the keyboard focus to the button.

Event Handlers

onblur() [JavaScript 1.1]

This method is called when the button loses the input focus. It is normally set via the onBlur attribute, as below.

```
<INPUT TYPE="SUBMIT" ...
      onBlur="doSomeAction()">
```

onclick() [JavaScript 1.0]

This method is called when the user clicks on the button, but not when the click method is called programmatically. It is normally set via the onClick attribute.

```
<INPUT TYPE="SUBMIT" ...
      onClick="doSomeAction()">
```

In JavaScript 1.1 and 1.2, if you return false from this method, then the form is not actually submitted. For example,

```
<INPUT TYPE="SUBMIT" ...
      onClick="return(maybeSubmit())">
```

The same effect can be achieved by onSubmit handler on the form containing the button.

ondblclick() [JavaScript 1.2]

This Netscape 4 method is called on the second click of a double click. The onclick handler, if any, will be called first. It is set by the onDblClick attribute. It is not supported on the Macintosh.

onfocus() [JavaScript 1.1]

This method is called when the button gains the input focus. It is normally set via the onFocus attribute.

20.33 The Text Object

This object corresponds to HTML elements created via <INPUT TYPE="TEXT" ...>. Text objects are normally accessed through the elements array of the enclosing Form object, or, if both it and the form are named, via document.formName.textfieldName.

Properties

defaultValue [JavaScript 1.0]

This is the initial value as given in the VALUE attribute. It is read only.

form [JavaScript 1.0]

This is the Form object containing the password field. It is read only.

name [JavaScript 1.0]

This is the value of the NAME attribute. It is read only.

type [JavaScript 1.1]

This contains the value "text". It is read only.

value [JavaScript 1.0]

This gives the current text contained in the textfield. It is read/write.

Methods

blur() [JavaScript 1.0]

This method removes the keyboard focus from the textfield.

focus() [JavaScript 1.0]

This gives the keyboard focus to the textfield.

select() [JavaScript 1.0]
This highlights the text in the element. If the user types, the input replaces the existing text.

Event Handlers

onblur() [JavaScript 1.0]
This method is called when the textfield loses the input focus. It is normally specified by means of the onBlur attribute.

onchange() [JavaScript 1.0]
This method is called when the textfield loses the input focus after its value has been changed by the user. It is *not* called each time the user hits a key; that cannot be detected prior to JavaScript 1.2. It is normally specified by means of the onChange attribute.

onfocus() [JavaScript 1.0]
This method is called when the textfield gets the input focus. It is normally specified by means of the onFocus attribute.

onkeydown() [JavaScript 1.2]
This is called when the user first presses any key in the textfield. Returning false cancels the input of the character, so it can be used to restrict the type of text that can be placed in the field.

onkeypress() [JavaScript 1.2]
When the user first presses a key, this method is called after onkey-down. It is also called repeatedly when the key is held down, while onkeydown is not. Returning false cancels the input of the character.

onkeyup() [JavaScript 1.2]
This is called when the user releases a key.

20.34 The Textarea Object

This object corresponds to HTML elements created via <TEXTAREA ...> and </TEXTAREA>. Textarea objects are normally accessed through the elements array of the enclosing Form object, or, if both it and the form are named, via document.formName.textareaName.

Properties

defaultValue [JavaScript 1.0]
This is the initial value as given by the text that appears between
<TEXTAREA> and</TEXTAREA>. It is read only.

form [JavaScript 1.0]
This is the Form object containing the text area. It is read only.

name [JavaScript 1.0]
This is the value of the NAME attribute. It is read only.

type [JavaScript 1.1]
This contains the value "textarea". It is read only.

value [JavaScript 1.0]
This gives the current text contained in the text area. It is read/write,
however, there is no way to determine the number of rows or columns
used by the textfield, so it may be difficult to insert properly formatted
text.

Methods

blur() [JavaScript 1.0]
This method removes the keyboard focus from the text area.

focus() [JavaScript 1.0]
This gives the keyboard focus to the text area.

select() [JavaScript 1.0]
This highlights the text in the element. If the user types, the input
replaces the existing text.

Event Handlers

onblur() [JavaScript 1.0]
This method is called when the text area loses the input focus. It is normally specified by means of the onBlur attribute.

onchange() [JavaScript 1.0]

This method is called when the text area loses the input focus after its value has been changed by the user. It is normally specified by means of the onChange attribute.

onfocus() [JavaScript 1.0]

This method is called when the text area gets the input focus. It is normally specified by means of the onFocus attribute.

onkeydown() [JavaScript1.2]

This is called when the user first presses any key in the text area. Returning false cancels the input of the character, so it can be used to restrict the type of text that can be placed in the field.

onkeypress() [JavaScript1.2]

When the user first presses a key, this method is called after onkeydown. It is also called repeatedly when the key is held down, while onkeydown is not. Returning false cancels the input of the character.

onkeyup() [JavaScript1.2]

This is called when the user releases a key.

20.35 The Window Object

The Window object is used to describe a browser window or frame. The current window is available through the window reference, but you can omit that prefix when accessing its properties and methods. So, for instance, you can refer to the Document associated with the current window via window.document or simply by document. Similarly, to transfer the current window to a new page, you can set the window.location property, or simply set location.

Properties

closed [JavaScript 1.1]

This Boolean specifies whether the window has been closed. It is read only.

defaultStatus [JavaScript 1.0]

This string specifies the default string that should appear in the status line. It is read/write.

document [JavaScript 1.0]

This refers to the Document object contained in the window. See Section 20.5 for details on Document. It is read only.

frames [JavaScript 1.0]

This array of Window objects refers to the entries contained in the frames of the current document.

history [JavaScript 1.0]

This gives the History object associated with the window. It is read only.

innerHeight [JavaScript 1.2]

This property gives the inner size of the browser window. It is read/write; changing it resizes the window.

innerWidth [JavaScript 1.2]

This property gives the inner width of the browser window. See Section 19.4 (Using JavaScript to Customize Web Pages) for an example of its use. It is read/write; changing it resizes the window.

java [JavaScript 1.1]

This is a reference to the JavaPackage object that is the top of the java.* package hierarchy. For example, you can call java.lang.Math.random() to use Java's random number generator instead of JavaScript's, or use java.lang.System.out.println to send output to Netscape's Java Console. It is read only.

length [JavaScript 1.0]

This is the same as frames.length. It is read only.

location [JavaScript 1.0]

This refers to the Location object for this window, which is the *requested* URL. Due to redirection, this may be different than the *actual* URL. For that, see document.URL. This is a read/write variable; setting it changes the window to display a new document.

locationbar [JavaScript 1.2]
Signed scripts in JavaScript 1.2 can set the visible property of locationbar to hide or show the Netscape 4.0 location bar. Legal values are true (or 1) and false (or 0).

Math [JavaScript 1.0]
This is a reference to the Math object.

menubar [JavaScript 1.2]
Signed scripts in JavaScript 1.2 can set the visible property of menubar to hide or show the Netscape 4.0 menu bar. Legal values are true (or 1) and false (or 0).

name [JavaScript 1.0]
When a window is created, you can specify a name. This property retrieves it. It is read only in JavaScript 1.0; read/write in JavaScript 1.1 and 1.2.

navigator [JavaScript 1.0]
This is a reference to the Navigator object. It is read only.

netscape [JavaScript 1.1]
This is a reference to the JavaPackage object corresponding to the netscape.* package. It is read only.

opener [JavaScript 1.1]
This is a reference to the Window object that created this one, if any. It is read/write.

outerHeight [JavaScript 1.2]
This property gives the outside height of the browser window. It is read/write; changing it resizes the window. Windows smaller than 100x100 pixels can only be created from secure (signed) scripts.

outerWidth [JavaScript 1.2]
This property gives the outside width of the browser window. It is read/write.

Packages [JavaScript 1.1]

This is a reference to the `JavaPackage` object that represents the top of the package hierarchy. It is read only.

pageXOffset [JavaScript 1.2]

This JavaScript 1.2 property gives the x offset of the page with respect to the window's content area. It is useful when deciding how much to scroll. It is read only; use `scrollTo` or `scrollBy` to change it.

pageYOffset [JavaScript 1.2]

This JavaScript 1.2 property gives the y offset of the page with respect to the window's content area. It is useful when deciding how much to scroll. It is read only; use `scrollTo` or `scrollBy` to change it.

parent [JavaScript 1.0]

This gives the parent window or frame. For a top-level window `win`, `win.parent` is simply `win`. It is read only.

personalbar [JavaScript 1.2]

Signed scripts in JavaScript 1.2 can set the `visible` property of `personalbar` to hide or show the Netscape 4.0 personal (directories) bar. Legal values are `true` (or 1) and `false` (or 0).

screen [JavaScript 1.2]

This is actually a global variable, not a property of `Window`. However, it is mentioned here since most seemingly global variables (`document`, `Math`, etc.) are really properties of the current window. See Section 20.29.

scrollbars [JavaScript 1.2]

Signed scripts in JavaScript 1.2 can set the `visible` property of `scrollbars` to hide or show scrollbars. Legal values are `true` (or 1) and `false` (or 0).

self [JavaScript 1.0]

This is a reference to the window itself and is synonymous with `window`. It is read only.

status [JavaScript 1.0]

This string represents the contents of the status bar. It is read/write. An ill-advised fad in the early JavaScript days was to put scrolling messages in the status bar via this property.

statusbar [JavaScript 1.2]

Signed scripts in JavaScript 1.2 can set the `visible` property of `personalbar` to hide or show the status bar. Legal values are `true` (or 1) and `false` (or 0).

sun [JavaScript 1.1]

This is a reference to the `JavaPackage` object that is the top of the `sun.*` package hierarchy. It is read only.

tags [JavaScript 1.2]

This can be used by JavaScript style sheets to set style sheet properties. See Section 5.2 (Using Local and External Style Sheets) for an example.

toolbar [JavaScript 1.2]

Signed scripts in JavaScript 1.2 can set the `visible` property of `toolbar` to hide or show the Netscape 4.0 tool bar. Legal values are `true` (or 1) and `false` (or 0).

top [JavaScript 1.0]

This refers to the top-level window containing the current one. It is the same as the current one if frames are not being used. It is read only.

window [JavaScript 1.0]

This is a reference to the window itself and is synonymous with `self`. It is read only.

Methods

alert(message) [JavaScript 1.0]

This displays a message in a pop-up dialog box.

back() [JavaScript 1.2]

This method switches the window to the previous entry in the history list, as if the user clicked on the "Back" button.

blur() [JavaScript 1.0]

This removes the keyboard focus from the current window, usually by putting window in the background.

captureEvents(eventType) [JavaScript 1.2]

This sets the window to capture all events of the specified type.

clearInterval(intervalID) [JavaScript 1.2]

The `setInterval` method returns an ID. Supplying it to `clearInterval` kill the interval routine.

clearTimeout(timeoutID) [JavaScript 1.0]

The `setTimeout` method returns an ID. Supplying it to `clearTimeout` kills the timeout routine.

close() [JavaScript 1.0]

This closes a window. You aren't supposed to be able to close windows that you didn't create, but there are some bugs that let you do this anyhow.

confirm(questionString) [JavaScript 1.0]

This methods pops up a dialog box displaying your question. If the user presses "OK", `true` is returned. "Cancel" results in `false` being returned. You can embed `\n` (newline) characters in the string to split the question across multiple lines.

disableExternalCapture() [JavaScript 1.2]

In JavaScript 1.2, signed scripts can capture events in external pages. This disables it.

enableExternalCapture() [JavaScript 1.2]

In JavaScript 1.2, signed scripts can capture events in external pages. This enables it.

find() [JavaScript 1.2]
find(searchString) [JavaScript 1.2]
find(searchString, caseSensitivityFlag, backwardFlag)
   [JavaScript 1.2]

The `find` method searches for strings in the current document. If you omit the search string, the "Find" dialog box pops up to let the user

enter a string. Alternatively, you can supply a search string and optionally two boolean flags. These flags determine if a case sensitive match
should be used (`true` for the second parameter) or if the file should be
searched from the end going backwards (`true` for the third parameter). The methods return `true` if the string was found, `false` otherwise.

focus() [JavaScript 1.0]

This gives the specified window the keyboard focus. On most platforms,
this brings it to the front.

forward() [JavaScript 1.2]

In Netscape 4.0, this moves the window forward in the history list.

handleEvent(event) [JavaScript 1.2]

If `captureEvents` has been set, then events of the specified type get
passed to `handleEvent`.

home() [JavaScript 1.2]

In Netscape 4.0, this switches the window to the home document, as if
the user clicked on the "Home" button.

moveBy(x, y) [JavaScript 1.2]

This moves the Netscape 4.0 window on the screen by the specified
number of pixels. Moving it off-screen requires a signed script, but even
so, this method can easily be abused.

moveTo(x, y) [JavaScript 1.2]

This moves the Netscape 4.0 window to an absolute location on the
screen. Moving it off-screen requires a signed script, but even so, this
method can easily be abused.

open(url, name) [JavaScript 1.0]
open(url, name, features) [JavaScript 1.0]
open(url, name, features, replaceFlag) [JavaScript 1.1]

This method can be used to find an existing window or to open a new
one. To avoid confusion with `document.open`, it is common practice
to use `window.open(...)` instead of simply `open(...)`. Specifying an empty string for the URL opens a blank window. You can then
write into it using that window's `document` property. The name can be

used for other JavaScript methods or as the TARGET attribute in A, BASE, AREA, and FORM elements. The replaceFlag specifies whether the new window replaces the old entry in the history list (true) or if a new entry should be created (false). The features string gives comma-separated *feature=value* entries (with *no* spaces!) and determines what browser features the window should include (all if features is omitted). Using *feature* is shorthand for *feature=yes*. If the features entry is omitted, *all* standard features are used, regardless of what the user has set in the preferences. Legal feature names are summarized in Table 20.2. Listing 20.5 (at the end of this section) gives a couple examples of using window.open, with results shown in Figures 20–6 through 20–9.

Core Warning

Feature lists should not have any blank spaces, or they will not be parsed properly.

Table 20.2   Features available in the open method

Feature	Legal Values	Meaning
alwaysLowered	yes/no	Should window always be below others? Available only with signed JavaScript 1.2 scripts.
alwaysRaised	yes/no	Should window always be below others? Available only with signed JavaScript 1.2 scripts.
dependent	yes/no	Is window a child of creating window? That is, should it close when parent window closes and be omitted from Windows taskbar? JavaScript 1.2 only.
directories	yes/no	Show the directory buttons ("What's Cool?", etc.)?
height	pixels	The window's height. Use innerHeight in JavaScript 1.2. Unix users should note that .Xdefaults entries can override this.

continued

| Table 20.2   Features available in the open method   (continued) |

Feature	Legal Values	Meaning
hotkeys	yes/no	Disable most hotkeys? JavaScript 1.2 only.
innerHeight	pixels	Sets the content area height in JavaScript 1.2.
innerWidth	pixels	Sets the content area width in JavaScript 1.2.
location	yes/no	Show the current location textfield?
menubar	yes/no	Show the menubar?
outerHeight	pixels	Sets the outside window height in JavaScript 1.2.
outerWidth	pixels	Sets the outside window width in JavaScript 1.2.
resizable	yes/no	Let the user stretch the window?
screenX	pixels	Sets the location of the left side of the window in JavaScript 1.2.
screenY	pixels	Sets the location of the top side of the window in JavaScript 1.2.
scrollbars	yes/no	Use scrollbars if necessary?
status	yes/no	Show the status line at the bottom?
titlebar	yes/no	Include title bar? Disabling it requires a signed JavaScript 1.2 script.
toolbar	yes/no	Show the toolbar that contains back/forward/home/stop buttons?
width	pixels	Gives the window size. Use innerWidth in JavaScript 1.2. Unix users should note that .Xdefaults entries can override this.
z-lock	yes/no	Prevent window from being raised/lowered? Available only in JavaScript 1.2 signed scripts.

Note that Netscape 2.0 has a bug that prevents the URL from being recognized if the window doesn't already exist. A common workaround is to repeat the open call twice in a row.

Core Approach

If your code needs to be compatible with Netscape Navigator 2.0, use two consecutive identical calls to open *when creating a new window.*

print() [JavaScript 1.2]

This prints the document as though by the "Print" button. Note that this brings up a dialog box; there is (fortunately) no way to print documents without user confirmation.

prompt(message) [JavaScript 1.0]
prompt(message, defaultText) [JavaScript 1.0]

This pops up a dialog box with a simple textfield, returning the value entered when it is closed. You can supply the initial string as the second argument if desired.

releaseEvents(eventType) [JavaScript 1.2]

This tells JavaScript to stop capturing the specified event type.

resizeBy(x, y) [JavaScript 1.2]

This lets you change the size of the browser window by the specified amount.

resizeTo(x, y) [JavaScript 1.2]

This changes the *outer* width and height to the specified size.

routeEvent(event) [JavaScript 1.2]

This method is used by handleEvent to send the event along the normal event-handling path.

scroll(x, y) [JavaScript 1.1]

This scrolls the document so that the upper left corner of the window shows the specified location of the document. Use scrollTo in JavaScript 1.2.

scrollBy(x, y) [JavaScript 1.2]

This scrolls by the specified number of pixels.

scrollTo(x, y) [JavaScript 1.2]

This is the JavaScript 1.2 replacement for `scroll` (which is still available for backward compatibility).

setInterval(code, delay) [JavaScript 1.2]

This new JavaScript 1.2 capability takes a string representing code and executes it *repeatedly* until the window is destroyed or `clearInterval` is called. See `setTimeout`.

setTimeout(code, delay) [JavaScript 1.0]

This takes a string specifying JavaScript code and a delay time in milliseconds. The code is executed after the specified delay unless `clearTimeout` is called with the `setTimeout` return value in the meantime. Note that `setTimeout` *returns* immediately, it just doesn't *execute* the code until later.

stop() [JavaScript 1.2]

This stops the current document download, as if via the "Stop" button.

Event Handlers

JavaScript 1.2 added significant new event-handling capability. For details, see `http://developer.netscape.com/library/documentation/communicator/jsguide/eventmod.htm` and `.../events.htm`. The following describes the standard approach.

onblur() [JavaScript 1.1]

This is the method called when the window loses the keyboard focus. It is normally set via the `onBlur` attribute of BODY or FRAMESET, as in the following example.

```
<BODY onBlur="alert('We will miss you')">
...
</BLUR>
```

A more useful application might be to halt certain processing when the user leaves the window, restarting it via `onfocus`.

ondragdrop() [JavaScript 1.2]

This method is called in Netscape 4 when a file or shortcut is dragged onto the Navigator window and released. If the method returns `false`, the normal action of loading the file is canceled. It is set by the `onDragDrop` attribute.

onerror() [JavaScript 1.1]

This method is called when a JavaScript error occurs. This error handler has no associated HTML attribute, so you have to set it directly as in the example below.

```
function reportError() {
  return(!confirm("An error occurred.\n" +
                  "Please report it to\n" +
                  "gates@microsoft.com.\n\n" +
                  "See more details?"));
}


onerror = reportError;
```

Returning `true` prevents the browser from also reporting it, so in the preceding example the user will only see the standard error report if they click "OK" in the confirmation dialog box. Setting the value of `onerror` to `null` suppresses error reporting altogether.

onfocus() [JavaScript 1.1]

This is the method that is called when the window gets the keyboard focus. It is normally set via the `onFocus` attribute of BODY or FRAMESET, as in the following example.

```
<FRAMESET ROWS=...
          onFocus="alert('Welcome back')">
...
</FRAMESET>
```

onload() [JavaScript 1.0]

This method is called when the browser finishes loading the page. It is normally set via the `onLoad` attribute of BODY or FRAMESET. It is useful for recording that the document finished loading so that functions that depend on various pieces of the document will operate correctly.

onmove() [JavaScript 1.2]

This method is called *after* the window is moved (either by the user or programmatically). It is set via the onMove attribute, as follows:

```
<BODY onMove="alert('Hey, move me back!')" ...>
...
</BODY>
```

onresize() [JavaScript 1.2]

This method is called when the user or JavaScript code stretches or shrinks the window. It is normally set by using the onResize attribute.

onunload() [JavaScript 1.0]

This method is called when the user leaves the page. It is normally set via the onUnload attribute of BODY or FRAMESET.

An Example of the "open" Method

Listing 20.5 gives examples of several different features used in the window.open method. Figures 20–6 through 20–9 show the results.

Listing 20.5   `OpenWindows.html`

```
<!DOCTYPE HTML PUBLIC "-//W3C//DTD HTML 3.2//EN">
<HTML>
<HEAD>
  <TITLE>Opening Windows with JavaScript</TITLE>

<SCRIPT LANGUAGE="JavaScript">
<!--

function openSmallWindow() {
  window.open("http://home.netscape.com/",
              "smallWindow",
              "width=275,height=100");
}
```

Listing 20.5   `OpenWindows.html`   (continued)

```
function openMediumWindow() {
  window.open
    ("http://home.netscape.com/",
     "mediumWindow",
     "width=525,height=225," +
     "menubar,scrollbars,status,toolbar");
}

function openBigWindow() {
  window.open
    ("http://home.netscape.com/",
     "bigWindow",
     "width=900,height=450," +
     "directories,location,menubar," +
     "scrollbars,status,toolbar");
}

// -->
</SCRIPT>
</HEAD>

<BODY>
<H1>Opening Windows with JavaScript</H1>

<FORM>
  <INPUT TYPE="BUTTON" VALUE="Open Small Window"
         onClick="openSmallWindow()">
  <INPUT TYPE="BUTTON" VALUE="Open Medium Window"
         onClick="openMediumWindow()">
  <INPUT TYPE="BUTTON" VALUE="Open Big Window"
         onClick="openBigWindow()">
</FORM>

</BODY>
</HTML>
```

Figure 20–6   `OpenWindows.html` before any buttons are clicked.

Figure 20–7   Using `window.open` with a width and height but no other features results in a bare-bones, undecorated browser window.

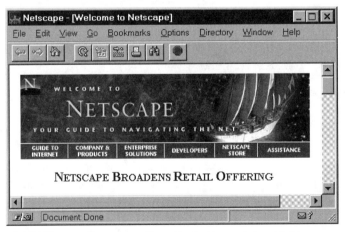

Figure 20–8   This version creates a moderately decorated browser window.

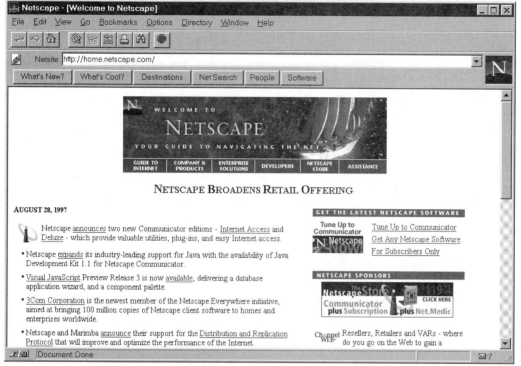

Figure 20–9   By specifying enough features, you can make a fully-loaded browser window.

20.36 Summary

Whew! You finished the book. Congratulations. Hopefully you are now comfortable with the basics of HTML, Java, CGI Programming, and JavaScript, so you can develop Web applications from beginning to end. Now you can go back and focus on specific areas that you skimmed earlier. You're familiar with standard HTML; maybe now you should go back and look at style sheets or layers. You have a handle on Java; maybe this is the time to try out threading, RMI, or JDBC. Perhaps you've used CGI, but haven't seen what servlets can buy you. Or maybe you've limited yourself to JavaScript 1.1, and now want to see how JavaScript regular expressions can help you. But don't worry, you don't have to be an expert in everything; few people are. No matter where you choose to concentrate, a solid base will serve you well.

But before you move on, relax and take a day off. Oh, and tell your boss that I said you deserve a raise. Hmm, 20% ought to do it, don't you think?

Have fun!

Index

LICENSE AGREEMENT AND LIMITED WARRANTY

READ THE FOLLOWING TERMS AND CONDITIONS CAREFULLY BEFORE OPENING THIS CD PACKAGE, *CORE WEB PROGRAMMING*. THIS LEGAL DOCUMENT IS AN AGREEMENT BETWEEN YOU AND PRENTICE-HALL, INC. (THE "COMPANY"). BY OPENING THIS SEALED CD PACKAGE, YOU ARE AGREEING TO BE BOUND BY THESE TERMS AND CONDITIONS. IF YOU DO NOT AGREE WITH THESE TERMS AND CONDITIONS, DO NOT OPEN THE CD PACKAGE. PROMPTLY RETURN THE UNOPENED CD PACKAGE AND ALL ACCOMPANYING ITEMS TO THE PLACE YOU OBTAINED THEM FOR A FULL REFUND OF ANY SUMS YOU HAVE PAID.

1. **GRANT OF LICENSE:** In consideration of your purchase of this book, and your agreement to abide by the terms and conditions of this Agreement, the Company grants to you a nonexclusive right to use and display the copy of the enclosed software program (hereinafter the "SOFTWARE") on a single computer (i.e., with a single CPU) at a single location so long as you comply with the terms of this Agreement. The Company reserves all rights not expressly granted to you under this Agreement.

2. **OWNERSHIP OF SOFTWARE:** You own only the magnetic or physical media (the enclosed CD) on which the SOFTWARE is recorded or fixed, but the Company and the software developers retain all the rights, title, and ownership to the SOFTWARE recorded on the original CD copy(ies) and all subsequent copies of the SOFTWARE, regardless of the form or media on which the original or other copies may exist. This license is not a sale of the original SOFTWARE or any copy to you.

3. **COPY RESTRICTIONS:** This SOFTWARE and the accompanying printed materials and user manual (the "Documentation") are the subject of copyright. The individual programs on the CD are copyrighted by the authors of each program. Some of the programs on the CD include separate licensing agreements. If you intend to use one of these programs, you must read and follow its accompanying license agreement. You may <u>not</u> copy the Documentation or the SOFTWARE, except that you may make a single copy of the SOFTWARE for backup or archival purposes only. You may be held legally responsible for any copying or copyright infringement which is caused or encouraged by your failure to abide by the terms of this restriction.

4. **USE RESTRICTIONS:** You may <u>not</u> network the SOFTWARE or otherwise use it on more than one computer or computer terminal at the same time. You may physically transfer the SOFTWARE from one computer to another provided that the SOFTWARE is used on only one computer at a time. You may <u>not</u> distribute copies of the SOFTWARE or Documentation to others. You may <u>not</u> reverse engineer, disassemble, decompile, modify, adapt, translate, or create derivative works based on the SOFTWARE or the Documentation without the prior written consent of the Company.

5. **TRANSFER RESTRICTIONS:** The enclosed SOFTWARE is licensed only to you and may <u>not</u> be transferred to any one else without the prior written consent of the Company. Any unauthorized transfer of the SOFTWARE shall result in the immediate termination of this Agreement.

6. **TERMINATION:** This license is effective until terminated. This license will terminate automatically without notice from the Company and become null and void if you fail to comply with any provisions or limitations of this license. Upon termination, you shall destroy the Documentation and all copies of the SOFTWARE. All provisions of this Agreement as to warranties, limitation of liability, remedies or damages, and our ownership rights shall survive termination.

7. **MISCELLANEOUS:** This Agreement shall be construed in accordance with the laws of the United States of America and the State of New York and shall benefit the Company, its affiliates, and assignees.

8. **LIMITED WARRANTY AND DISCLAIMER OF WARRANTY:** The Company warrants that the SOFTWARE, when properly used in accordance with the Documentation, will operate in substantial conformity with the description of the SOFTWARE set forth in the Documentation. The

Company does not warrant that the SOFTWARE will meet your requirements or that the operation of the SOFTWARE will be uninterrupted or error-free. The Company warrants that the media on which the SOFTWARE is delivered shall be free from defects in materials and workmanship under normal use for a period of thirty (30) days from the date of your purchase. Your only remedy and the Company's only obligation under these limited warranties is, at the Company's option, return of the warranted item for a refund of any amounts paid by you or replacement of the item. Any replacement of SOFTWARE or media under the warranties shall not extend the original warranty period. The limited warranty set forth above shall not apply to any SOFTWARE which the Company determines in good faith has been subject to misuse, neglect, improper installation, repair, alteration, or damage by you. EXCEPT FOR THE EXPRESSED WARRANTIES SET FORTH ABOVE, THE COMPANY DISCLAIMS ALL WARRANTIES, EXPRESS OR IMPLIED, INCLUDING WITHOUT LIMITATION, THE IMPLIED WARRANTIES OF MERCHANTABILITY AND FITNESS FOR A PARTICULAR PURPOSE. EXCEPT FOR THE EXPRESS WARRANTY SET FORTH ABOVE, THE COMPANY DOES NOT WARRANT, GUARANTEE, OR MAKE ANY REPRESENTATION REGARDING THE USE OR THE RESULTS OF THE USE OF THE SOFTWARE IN TERMS OF ITS CORRECTNESS, ACCURACY, RELIABILITY, CURRENTNESS, OR OTHERWISE.

IN NO EVENT, SHALL THE COMPANY OR ITS EMPLOYEES, AGENTS, SUPPLIERS, OR CONTRACTORS BE LIABLE FOR ANY INCIDENTAL, INDIRECT, SPECIAL, OR CONSEQUENTIAL DAMAGES ARISING OUT OF OR IN CONNECTION WITH THE LICENSE GRANTED UNDER THIS AGREEMENT, OR FOR LOSS OF USE, LOSS OF DATA, LOSS OF INCOME OR PROFIT, OR OTHER LOSSES, SUSTAINED AS A RESULT OF INJURY TO ANY PERSON, OR LOSS OF OR DAMAGE TO PROPERTY, OR CLAIMS OF THIRD PARTIES, EVEN IF THE COMPANY OR AN AUTHORIZED REPRESENTATIVE OF THE COMPANY HAS BEEN ADVISED OF THE POSSIBILITY OF SUCH DAMAGES. IN NO EVENT SHALL LIABILITY OF THE COMPANY FOR DAMAGES WITH RESPECT TO THE SOFTWARE EXCEED THE AMOUNTS ACTUALLY PAID BY YOU, IF ANY, FOR THE SOFTWARE.

SOME JURISDICTIONS DO NOT ALLOW THE LIMITATION OF IMPLIED WARRANTIES OR LIABILITY FOR INCIDENTAL, INDIRECT, SPECIAL, OR CONSEQUENTIAL DAMAGES, SO THE ABOVE LIMITATIONS MAY NOT ALWAYS APPLY. THE WARRANTIES IN THIS AGREEMENT GIVE YOU SPECIFIC LEGAL RIGHTS AND YOU MAY ALSO HAVE OTHER RIGHTS WHICH VARY IN ACCORDANCE WITH LOCAL LAW.

ACKNOWLEDGMENT

YOU ACKNOWLEDGE THAT YOU HAVE READ THIS AGREEMENT, UNDERSTAND IT, AND AGREE TO BE BOUND BY ITS TERMS AND CONDITIONS. YOU ALSO AGREE THAT THIS AGREEMENT IS THE COMPLETE AND EXCLUSIVE STATEMENT OF THE AGREEMENT BETWEEN YOU AND THE COMPANY AND SUPERSEDES ALL PROPOSALS OR PRIOR AGREEMENTS, ORAL, OR WRITTEN, AND ANY OTHER COMMUNICATIONS BETWEEN YOU AND THE COMPANY OR ANY REPRESENTATIVE OF THE COMPANY RELATING TO THE SUBJECT MATTER OF THIS AGREEMENT.

Should you have any questions concerning this Agreement or if you wish to contact the Company for any reason, please contact in writing at the address below.

Robin Short

Prentice Hall PTR

One Lake Street

Upper Saddle River, New Jersey 07458

Java™ Development Kit
Version 1.1.x
Binary Code License
This binary code license ("License") contains rights and restrictions associated with use of the accompanying software and documentation ("Software"). Read the License carefully before installing the Software. By installing the Software you agree to the terms and conditions of this License.

1. Limited License Grant. Sun grants to you ("Licensee") a non-exclusive, non-transferable limited license to use the Software without fee for evaluation of the Software and for development of Java™ compatible applets and applications. Licensee may make one archival copy of the Software. Licensee may not re-distribute the Software in whole or in part, either separately or included with a product. Refer to the Java Runtime Environment Version 1.1 binary code license (http://www.java-soft.com/products/JDK/1.1/index.html) for the availability of runtime code which may be distributed with Java compatible applets and applications.

2. Java Platform Interface. Licensee may not modify the Java Platform Interface ("JPI", identified as classes contained within the "java" package or any subpackages of the "java" package), by creating additional classes within the JPI or otherwise causing the addition to or modification of the classes in the JPI. In the event that Licensee creates any Java-related API and distributes such API to others for applet or application development, Licensee must promptly publish an accurate specification for such API for free use by all developers of Java-based software.

3. Restrictions. Software is confidential copyrighted information of Sun and title to all copies is retained by Sun and/or its licensors. Licensee shall not modify, decompile, disassemble, decrypt, extract, or otherwise reverse engineer Software. Software may not be leased, assigned, or sublicensed, in whole or in part. Software is not designed or intended for use in on-line control of aircraft, air traffic, aircraft navigation or aircraft communications; or in the design, construction, operation or maintenance of any nuclear facility. Licensee warrants that it will not use or redistribute the Software for such purposes.

4. Trademarks and Logos. This License does not authorize Licensee to use any Sun name, trademark or logo. Licensee acknowledges that Sun owns the Java trademark and all Java-related trademarks, logos and icons including the Coffee Cup and Duke ("Java Marks") and agrees to: (i) to comply with the Java Trademark Guidelines at http://java.com/trademarks.html; (ii) not do anything harmful to or inconsistent with Sun's rights in the Java Marks; and (iii) assist Sun in protecting those rights, including assigning to Sun any rights acquired by Licensee in any Java Mark.

5. Disclaimer of Warranty. Software is provided "AS IS," without a warranty of any kind. ALL EXPRESS OR IMPLIED REPRESENTATIONS AND WARRANTIES, INCLUDING ANY IMPLIED WARRANTY OF MERCHANTABILITY, FITNESS FOR A PARTICULAR PURPOSE OR NON-INFRINGEMENT, ARE HEREBY EXCLUDED.

6. Limitation of Liability. SUN AND ITS LICENSORS SHALL NOT BE LIABLE FOR ANY DAMAGES SUFFERED BY LICENSEE OR ANY THIRD PARTY AS A RESULT OF USING OR DISTRIBUTING SOFTWARE. IN NO EVENT WILL SUN OR ITS LICENSORS BE LIABLE FOR ANY LOST REVENUE, PROFIT OR DATA, OR FOR DIRECT, INDIRECT, SPECIAL, CONSEQUENTIAL, INCIDENTAL OR PUNITIVE DAMAGES, HOWEVER CAUSED

AND REGARDLESS OF THE THEORY OF LIABILITY, ARISING OUT OF THE USE OF OR INABILITY TO USE SOFTWARE, EVEN IF SUN HAS BEEN ADVISED OF THE POSSIBILITY OF SUCH DAMAGES.

7. Termination. Licensee may terminate this License at any time by destroying all copies of Software. This License will terminate immediately without notice from Sun if Licensee fails to comply with any provision of this License. Upon such termination, Licensee must destroy all copies of Software.

8. Export Regulations. Software, including technical data, is subject to U.S. export control laws, including the U.S. Export Administration Act and its associated regulations, and may be subject to export or import regulations in other countries. Licensee agrees to comply strictly with all such regulations and acknowledges that it has the responsibility to obtain licenses to export, re-export, or import Software. Software may not be downloaded, or otherwise exported or re-exported (i) into, or to a national or resident of, Cuba, Iraq, Iran, North Korea, Libya, Sudan, Syria or any country to which the U.S. has embargoed goods; or (ii) to anyone on the U.S. Treasury Department's list of Specially Designated Nations or the U.S. Commerce Department's Table of Denial Orders.

9. Restricted Rights. Use, duplication or disclosure by the United States government is subject to the restrictions as set forth in the Rights in Technical Data and Computer Software Clauses in DFARS 252.227-7013(c) (1) (ii) and FAR 52.227-19(c) (2) as applicable.

10. Governing Law. Any action related to this License will be governed by California law and controlling U.S. federal law. No choice of law rules of any jurisdiction will apply.

11. Severability. If any of the above provisions are held to be in violation of applicable law, void, or unenforceable in any jurisdiction, then such provisions are herewith waived to the extent necessary for the License to be otherwise enforceable in such jurisdiction. However, if in Sun's opinion deletion of any provisions of the License by operation of this paragraph unreasonably compromises the rights or increase the liabilities of Sun or its licensors, Sun reserves the right to terminate the License and refund the fee paid by Licensee, if any, as Licensee's sole and exclusive remedy.

About the CD-ROM

The CD-ROM contains the following tools for Windows 95, Windows NT, and Macintosh platforms. For other operating systems, please see the on-line source code archive at http://www.apl.jhu.edu/~hall/CWP-Sources/.

- An HTML guide to all resources given in this book, organized by chapter. This includes
  - More than 200 HTML and JavaScript documents used throughout the text. You can view them on-line, examine their source code, and adapt them for your projects.
  - Complete source code for more than 250 Java classes illustrated or used in various chapters. Permission is granted to freely use or adapt these classes for any application.
  - On-line versions of all Java applets.
  - Hypertext links to all URLs listed in this book.
- The Java Development Kit, version 1.02. This includes `javac`, the Java source to bytecode compiler; `java`, the Java run-time system; and `javadoc`, the hypertext documentation generator.
- The Java Development Kit, version 1.1. This includes `javac`, `java`, `javadoc`, and `rmic`.(Windows 95/NT only).
- The WinEdit text editor, customized for Java programming (Windows 95/NT only).
- Microsoft Internet Explorer version 3.

System Requirements

Windows 95/NT

Java requires Windows 95 or Windows NT, at least 4MB RAM, and at least 10 MB of hard disk space. Internet Explorer requires Windows 95 or Windows NT 4.0, at least 8MB RAM, and at least 50MB of hard disk space.

MacOS

Java requires MacOS 7.5 or later on a Power Macintosh or a 68030 25MHz or faster processor, at least 4MB RAM, and at least 10MB of hard disk space. Internet Explorer requires MacOS 7.1 or later on a Power Macintosh or 68030, at least 8MB RAM, and at least 25MB of hard disk space.

Technical Support

Prentice Hall does not offer technical support for this software. However, if there is a problem with the media, you may obtain a replacement copy by emailing us with your problem at:

discexchange@phptr.com